COLLINS

ENGLISH
DICTIONARY

COLLINS

ENGLISH
DICTIONARY

HarperCollins Publishers
Westerhill Road
Bishopbriggs
Glasgow
G64 2QT
Great Britain

First edition 2007

Reprint 10 9 8 7 6 5 4 3 2 1 0

© HarperCollins Publishers 2006

ISBN 978-0-00-779332-7

Collins® is a registered trademark of
HarperCollins Publishers Limited

www.collins.co.uk

A catalogue record for this book is
available from the British Library

Designed by Mark Thomson

Typeset by Wordcraft Ltd, Glasgow

Printed in Great Britain by
Clays Ltd, St Ives plc

Acknowledgements
We would like to thank those authors and
publishers who kindly gave permission for
copyright material to be used in the Collins
Word Web. We would also like to thank
Times Newspapers Ltd for providing
valuable data.

CONTENTS

EDITORIAL STAFF

EDITORS
Cormac McKeown
Elspeth Summers

FOR THE PUBLISHERS
Morven Dooner
Elaine Higgleton
Lorna Knight

FOREWORD

This dictionary is easy to use and understand. Its layout is refreshingly clear and clutter-free, taking you straight to the information you want with a minimum of fuss. Every definition is presented in straightforward English. Where a word has more than one sense, the one given first is the most common meaning in today's language. Other senses of a word – for example, historical and technical senses – are explained after the main present-day meaning.

As you would expect, entries show the spelling and meaning of each word. Other features which make this dictionary particularly helpful include simple pronunciations for words that may be unfamiliar or confusing. Over 100 spelling tips are also included, with useful advice on how to avoid common errors.

In compiling this dictionary our lexicographers have been able to consult an unparalleled 2.5-billion-word database of written and spoken English from a huge variety of sources around the globe. By analysing this data, lexicographers have ensured that you, as a dictionary user, are given the most up-to-date information about how English is really used today. Examples have been taken from real English to help illustrate meaning within the definitions.

New words and senses have been gathered through close analysis of our database, as well an extensive reading, listening, and viewing programme, taking in all kinds of broadcasts and publications. There is also specialist vocabulary from subjects such as science, technology, and computing.

USING THIS DICTIONARY

Main Entry Words printed in large bold type, eg

abbey

All main entry words, including abbreviations and combining forms, in one alphabetical sequence, eg

abbot
abbreviate
ABC
abdicate

Variant spellings shown in full, eg

adrenalin, adrenaline

Note: where the spellings **–ize** and **–ization** are used at the end of a word, the alternative forms **-ise** and **-isation** are equally acceptable.

Pronunciations given in square brackets for words that are difficult or confusing; the word is respelt as it is pronounced, with the stressed syllable in bold type, eg

antipodes [an-**tip**-pod-deez]

Parts of Speech   shown in italics as an abbreviation, eg

ablaze *adj*

When a word can be used as more than one part of speech, the change of part of speech is shown after an arrow, eg

mock *v* make fun of; mimic ▷ *adj* sham or imitation

Parts of speech may be combined for some words, eg

alone *adj, adv* without anyone or anything else

Cross References   shown in bold type, eg

doner kebab *n* see **kebab**

Irregular Parts   or confusing forms of verb,
                      nouns, adjectives, and
                      adverbs shown in bold
                      type, eg

                      begin *v* **–ginning, -gan, -gun**
                      regret *v* **–gretting, -gretted**
                      anniversary *n, pl* **–ries**
                      angry *adj* **–grier, -griest**
                      well *adv* **better, best**

Meanings   separated by semicolons, eg

                      casual *adj* careless,
                      nonchalant; (of work or
                      workers) occasional; for
                      informal wear; happening
                      by chance.

Phrases and Idioms included immediately
                      after the meanings of the
                      main entry word, eg

                      hand *n* ... *v* ... **have a hand**
                      in be involved **lend a hand**
                      help ...

Related Words

shown in the same paragraph as the main entry word, eg

absurd *adj* incongruous or ridiculous **absurdly** *adv* **absurdity** *n*

Note: where the meaning of a related word is not given, it may be understood from the main entry word, or from another related word.

Compounds

shown in alphabetical order at the end of the paragraph, eg

ash *n* ... **ashtray** *n* receptacle for tobacco ash and cigarette butts
Ash Wednesday first day of Lent

ABBREVIATIONS USED IN THIS DICTIONARY

AD	anno Domini
adj	adjective
adv	adverb
anat	anatomy
archit	architecture
astrol	astrology
Aust	Australia(n)
BC	before Christ
biol	biology
Brit	British
chem	chemistry
C of E	Church of England
conj	conjunction
E	East
eg	for example
esp	especially
etc	et cetera
fem	feminine
foll	followed
geom	geometry
hist	history
interj	interjection
lit	literary
masc	masculine
med	medicine

ABBREVIATIONS USED IN THIS DICTIONARY

meteorol	meteorology
mil	military
n	noun
N	North
naut	nautical
NZ	New Zealand
obs	obsolete
offens	offensive
orig	originally
photog	photography
pl	plural
prep	preposition
pron	pronoun
psychol	psychology
®	trademark
RC	Roman Catholic
S	South
S Afr	South Africa(n)
Scot	Scottish
sing	singular
US	United States
usu	usually
v	verb
W	West
zool	zoology

a *indefinite article* (before a vowel sound *an*) used before a noun being mentioned for the first time: *a tractor; an apple*

a- *prefix* **1** (before a vowel *an-*) meaning not, without or opposite to: *amoral* **2** meaning towards or in a state of: *aback; asleep*

aardvark *noun* S African anteater with long ears and snout

aback *adverb* **taken aback** startled or very surprised

abacus abacuses *noun* beads on a wire frame, used for doing calculations

abalone *noun* edible sea creature with a shell lined with mother of pearl

abandon *verb* **1** to desert or leave (someone or something) **2** to give up (something) completely ▷ *noun* **3** lack of inhibition: *He began to laugh with abandon* > **abandoned** *adjective* **1** deserted **2** uninhibited > **abandonment** *noun*

abase abases abasing abased *verb formal* to humiliate or degrade (yourself)

abashed *adjective* embarrassed and ashamed

abate abates abating abated *verb* to make or become less strong

abattoir *noun* place where animals are killed for meat

abbey abbeys *noun* church with buildings attached to it in which monks or nuns live or lived

abbot *noun* head of an abbey of monks

abbreviate abbreviates abbreviating abbreviated *verb* to shorten (a word) by leaving out some letters

abbreviation *noun* shortened form of a word or words

abdicate abdicates abdicating abdicated *verb* to give up (the throne or a responsibility) > **abdication** *noun*

abdomen *noun* part of the body containing the stomach and intestines > **abdominal** *adjective* relating to the stomach and intestines

abduct *verb* to take (someone) away by force > **abduction** *noun*: *the abduction of a boy* > **abductor** *noun*

aberration *noun* **1** sudden change from what is normal, accurate or correct **2** brief lapse in control of your thoughts or feelings

abet abets abetting abetted *verb* to help (someone) do something criminal or wrong

abhor abhors abhorring abhorred *verb formal* to hate (something) > **abhorrence** *noun*: *their abhorrence of racism* > **abhorrent** *adjective* hateful, loathsome

abide abides abiding abided *verb* **1** to bear or stand: *I can't abide that song* **2** **abide by** to act in accordance with (a rule or decision) > **abiding** *adjective* lasting

ability abilities *noun* intelligence

or skill needed to do something

abject *adjective* **1** very bad: *abject failure* **2** lacking all self-respect > **abjectly** *adverb*

ablaze *adjective* burning fiercely

able abler ablest *adjective* capable or competent

-able *suffix* meaning **1** capable of or susceptible to: *enjoyable; breakable* **2** causing: *comfortable*

able-bodied *adjective* strong and healthy

ably *adverb* skilfully and successfully

abnormal *adjective* not normal or usual > **abnormality** *noun* something that is not normal or usual > **abnormally** *adverb*

aboard *adverb, preposition* on, in, onto or into (a ship, train or plane)

abode *noun* old-fashioned home

abolish abolishes abolishing abolished *verb* to do away with > **abolition** *noun*: *the abolition of slavery*

abominable *adjective* detestable or very bad > **abominably** *adverb*

abominable snowman *noun* see **yeti**

abomination *noun* thing, person or action that is shockingly unpleasant

Aborigine *noun* someone descended from the people who ⬡ed in Australia before Europeans ⬡arrived > **Aboriginal** *adjective*

abort *verb* **1** to cause (a fetus) to be deliberately expelled from the womb ending the pregnancy prematurely so that the baby does not survive **2** to end (a plan or process) before completion

abortion *noun* operation or medical procedure to end a pregnancy

abortive *adjective* unsuccessful

abound *verb* to exist in large numbers

about *preposition* **1** concerning or on the subject of **2** in or near (a place) ▷ *adverb* **3** nearly, approximately **4** nearby **5** **about to** shortly going to **6** **not about to** determined not to

about-turn *noun* complete change of attitude

above *adverb, preposition* **1** over or higher (than) **2** greater (than) **3** superior (to)

above board *adjective* completely open and legal

abrasion *noun* scraped area on the skin

abrasive *adjective* **1** unpleasant and rude **2** rough and able to be used to clean or polish hard surfaces

abreast *adjective* **1** alongside and facing in the same direction **2** **abreast of** up to date with: *He will be keeping abreast of the news*

abridge abridges abridging abridged *verb* to shorten (a piece of writing) by using fewer words

abroad *adverb* to or in a foreign country

abrupt *adjective* **1** sudden and unexpected **2** not friendly or polite > **abruptly** *adverb* > **abruptness** *noun*

abscess abscesses *noun* painful swelling containing pus

abscond *verb formal* to run away suddenly and secretly

abseil *verb* to go down a steep drop by sliding down a rope fastened at the top and tied around your body

abseiling *noun* sport of going down a cliff or a tall building by sliding down ropes

absent *adjective* **1** not present **2** lacking **3** inattentive ▷ *verb* **4** **absent yourself** *formal* to stay away > **absence** *noun*

absentee *noun* person who should

be present but is not

absently *adverb* inattentively: *He nodded absently*

absent-minded *adjective* inattentive or forgetful > **absent-mindedly** *adverb* > **absent-mindedness** *noun* forgetfulness

absolute *adjective* **1** complete or perfect: *absolute honesty* **2** not limited, unconditional: *the absolute ruler* **3** pure: *absolute alcohol* > **absolutely** *adverb* **1** completely ▷ *interjection* **2** certainly, yes

absolution *noun formal* (in Christianity) formal forgiveness for sins

absolve absolves absolving absolved *verb* to declare (someone) to be free from blame or sin

absorb *verb* **1** to soak up (a liquid) **2** to deal with or cope with (a shock, change or effect)

absorbed *adjective* very interested in or by something or someone

absorbent *adjective* able to absorb liquid

absorption *noun* **1** soaking up of a liquid **2** great interest in something

abstain *verb* **1** to choose not to do or have (something) **2** to choose not to vote > **abstainer** *noun* **1** person who does not drink alcohol **2** person who chooses not to vote > **abstention** *noun* abstaining, especially from voting

abstemious *adjective* taking very little alcohol or food

abstinence *noun* state or practice of choosing not to take or do something, especially not to drink alcohol

abstract *adjective* **1** existing as a quality or idea rather than objects or events **2** *Art* using patterns of shapes and colours rather than realistic likenesses **3** (of nouns) referring to qualities or ideas rather than to physical objects, *eg happiness, a question* ▷ *noun* **4** summary **5** abstract work of art ▷ *verb* **6** to summarize **7** to remove or extract

abstruse *adjective formal* not easy to understand

absurd *adjective* **1** ridiculous and stupid **2** obviously senseless and illogical > **absurdity** *noun*: *the absurdity of the situation* > **absurdly** *adverb*

abundance *noun* great amount or large number > **abundant** *adjective* present in great amounts or large numbers > **abundantly** *adverb*

abuse abuses abusing abused *verb* **1** to use (something) wrongly **2** to ill-treat (someone) violently **3** to speak harshly and rudely to (someone) ▷ *noun* **4** prolonged ill-treatment **5** harsh and vulgar comments **6** wrong use of something > **abuser** *noun*: *a convicted child abuser*

abusive *adjective* **1** cruel and violent **2** (of language) very rude and insulting > **abusively** *adverb*

abysmal *adjective* very bad indeed > **abysmally** *adverb*

abyss abysses *noun* very deep hole or chasm

acacia *noun* type of thorny shrub with small yellow or white flowers

academic *adjective* **1** of an academy or university **2** of theoretical interest only ▷ *noun* **3** lecturer or researcher at a university > **academically** *adverb*

academy academies *noun* **1** organization of scientists, artists, writers or musicians **2** institution for training in a particular skill: *a*

military academy **3** Scot secondary
school

**accelerate accelerates
accelerating accelerated** verb
to move or cause to move more
quickly

acceleration noun rate at
which the speed of something is
increasing

accelerator noun pedal in a
motor vehicle, which is pressed to
increase speed

accent noun **1** distinctive style of
pronunciation of a local, national
or social group: She had an Australian
accent **2** mark over a letter to
show how it is pronounced **3** an
emphasis on something: The accent
is on action and special effects

accentuate verb to stress or
emphasize (something)

accept verb **1** to receive (something)
willingly **2** to tolerate (a situation)
3 to consider (something) to be
true **4** to receive (someone) into a
community or group > **acceptable**
adjective **1** tolerable **2** satisfactory
> **acceptably** adverb > **acceptance**
noun **1** act of accepting something
2 favourable reception **3** belief or
agreement

**access accesses accessing
accessed** noun **1** right or
opportunity to enter a place or to
use something ▷ verb **2** to obtain
(data) from a computer

accessible adjective **1** easy to
reach **2** easily understood or used
> **accessibility** noun

accession noun taking up of an
office or position: her accession to
the throne

accessory accessories noun
1 extra part **2** person involved in a
crime although not present when it
is committed

accident noun **1** mishap, often
causing injury or death **2** event
that happens by chance

accidental adjective happening
by chance or unintentionally
> **accidentally** adverb

acclaim verb formal **1** to praise
(someone or something) ▷ noun
2 enthusiastic approval

**acclimatize acclimatizes
acclimatizing acclimatized**; also
spelt **acclimatise** verb to adapt
to a new climate or environment
> **acclimatization** noun: a period of
acclimatization

accolade noun formal great praise
or an award given to someone

**accommodate accommodates
accommodating
accommodated** verb **1** to provide
(someone) with lodgings **2** to
have room for **3** to oblige or do a
favour for

accommodating adjective willing
to help and to adjust to new
situations

accommodation noun house or
room for living in

accompaniment noun
1 something that accompanies:
Melon is a good accompaniment to cold
meats **2** Music supporting part that
goes with a solo

accompanist noun pianist who
accompanies a singer or musician

**accompany accompanies
accompanying accompanied**
verb **1** to go with **2** to occur at the
same time as or as a result of **3** to
provide a musical accompaniment
for

accomplice noun person who helps
another to commit a crime

**accomplish accomplishes
accomplishing accomplished**
verb to succeed in doing

(something)

accomplished *adjective* very talented at something

accomplishment *noun* 1 completion of something 2 personal ability or skill

accord *noun* 1 agreement or harmony 2 **of your own accord** willingly ▷ *verb* 3 to grant (something to someone) 4 **accord with** *formal* to fit in with or be consistent with

accordance *noun* **in accordance with** conforming to or according to

according to *preposition* 1 as stated by 2 in conformity with > **accordingly** *adverb* 1 in an appropriate manner 2 consequently

accordion *noun* portable musical instrument played by moving the two sides apart and together and pressing a keyboard or buttons to produce the notes

accost *verb* to approach, stop and speak to (someone)

account *noun* 1 report or description 2 business arrangement making credit available 3 record of money received and paid out with the resulting balance 4 person's money held in a bank 5 **on account of** because of 6 **of no account** of no importance or value > **account for** *verb* 1 to give reasons for; explain 2 to be a particular amount or proportion of (something): *The brain accounts for 3% of body weight*

accountable *adjective* responsible to someone or for something: *The committee is accountable to Parliament* > **accountability** *noun* > **accountably** *adverb*

accountancy *noun* job of keeping or inspecting financial accounts

accountant *noun* person whose job is to keep or inspect financial accounts

accounting *noun* keeping and checking of financial accounts

accredited *adjective* officially appointed or recognized

accrue accrues accruing accrued *verb* (of money or interest) to increase gradually

accumulate accumulates accumulating accumulated *verb* to gather together in increasing quantity > **accumulation** *noun* something that has been collected

accuracy *noun* quality of being true or correct

accurate *adjective* completely correct or precise > **accurately** *adverb*

accusation *noun* allegation that a person is guilty of doing something wrong

accusative *noun* grammatical case indicating the direct object

accuse accuses accusing accused *verb* to charge (someone) with wrongdoing > **accused** *noun* defendant appearing on a criminal charge > **accuser** *noun*

accustom *verb* **accustom yourself to** to become familiar with or used to (something) from habit or experience > **accustomed** *adjective* 1 usual 2 **accustomed to a** used to (something) **b** in the habit of (doing something)

ace *noun* 1 playing card with one symbol on it 2 *informal* expert ▷ *adjective* 3 *informal* good or skilful

acerbic *adjective formal* harsh or bitter

acetic acid *noun* colourless liquid used to make vinegar

ache aches aching ached *noun* 1 dull continuous pain ▷ *verb* 2 to be in or cause continuous dull pain

achieve achieves achieving achieved *verb* to gain by hard work or ability

achievement *noun* something accomplished

Achilles heel *noun* small but fatal weakness or weakest point in someone's character

Achilles tendon *noun* cord connecting the calf muscle to the heel bone

acid *noun* **1** *Chemistry* one of a class of compounds, corrosive and sour when dissolved in water, that combine with a base to form a salt **2** *informal* the drug LSD ▷ *adjective* **3** containing acid **4** sour-tasting > **acidic** *adjective* > **acidity** *noun*

acid rain *noun* rain polluted by acid in the atmosphere which has come from factories

acid test *noun* conclusive test of value

acknowledge acknowledges acknowledging acknowledged *verb* **1** to recognize or admit the truth or reality of **2** to show recognition of a person by a greeting or glance **3** to let someone know that you have received (their letter or message) > **acknowledgment** or **acknowledgement** *noun* **1** act of acknowledging something or someone **2** something done or given as an expression of gratitude

acne *noun* lumpy spots that cover someone's face

acorn *noun* fruit of the oak tree, consisting of a pale oval nut in a cup-shaped base

acoustic *adjective* **1** relating to sound and hearing **2** (of a musical instrument) not electronically amplified

acoustics *noun* **1** science of sounds ▷ *plural* **2** features of a room or building determining how sound is heard within it

acquaint *verb* **acquaint with** to make (someone) familiar with

acquaintance *noun* person known slightly but not well

acquiesce acquiesces acquiescing acquiesced *verb* *formal* to agree to what someone wants

acquire acquires acquiring acquired *verb* to obtain (something), usually permanently

acquired taste *noun* thing you learn to like

acquisition *noun* **1** thing acquired **2** act of getting

acquisitive *adjective* eager to gain material possessions

acquit acquits acquitting acquitted *verb* **1** to pronounce (someone) innocent **2** **acquit yourself** to behave or perform in a particular way: *The French team acquitted themselves well*

acquittal *noun* formal declaration of someone's innocence

acre *noun* unit for measuring areas of land. One acre equals 4840 square yards (4046.86 square metres)

acrid *adjective* sharp and bitter: *the acrid smell of burning*

acrimony *noun* *formal* bitterness and anger > **acrimonious** *adjective* (of a dispute or argument) bitter and angry

acrobat *noun* person skilled in gymnastic feats requiring agility and balance > **acrobatic** *adjective* involving agility and balance > **acrobatics** *plural noun* acrobatic feats

acronym *noun* word formed from

the initial letters of other words, such as 'NASA' and 'NATO'

across *adverb, preposition* **1** from side to side (of) **2** on or to the other side (of)

across-the-board *adjective* affecting everyone equally: *across-the-board tax cuts*

acrostic *noun* lines of writing in which the first or last letters of each line spell a word or saying

acrylic *noun* **1** type of man-made cloth **2** kind of artists' paint which can be used like oil paint or thinned down with water

act *noun* **1** single thing done: *It was an act of disloyalty to the King* **2** law or decree **3** section of a play or opera **4** one of several short performances in a show **5** pretended attitude ▷ *verb* **6** to do something: *It would be irresponsible not to act swiftly* **7** to behave in a particular way **8** to perform in a play, film, etc

acting *noun* **1** art of an actor ▷ *adjective* **2** temporarily performing the duties of: *the acting manager*

action *noun* **1** process of doing something **2** thing done **3** legal proceeding: *a libel action* **4** operating mechanism **5** fighting in a war or battle: *255 men killed in action*

activate activates activating activated *verb* to make active or capable of working > **activation** *noun*: *A computer controls the activation of the air bag*

active *adjective* **1** moving or working **2** busy and energetic **3** *Grammar* (of a verb) in a form indicating that the subject is performing the action, *eg* threw in *Kim threw the ball* > **actively** *adverb*

activist *noun* person who works energetically to achieve political or social goals

activity activities *noun* **1** situation in which a lot of things are happening or being done **2** something you spend time doing

Act of God Acts of God *noun* unpredictable natural event

actor *noun* person who acts in a play, film, etc

actress actresses *noun* woman who acts in a play, film, etc

actual *adjective* real, rather than imaginary or guessed at > **actually** *adverb* really, indeed

actuate actuates actuating actuated *verb* to start up (a device)

acumen *noun* ability to make good judgments: *business acumen*

acupuncture *noun* treatment of illness or pain involving the insertion of needles at various points on the body

acupuncturist *noun* person who performs acupuncture

acute *adjective* **1** severe or intense: *an acute shortage of beds* **2** very intelligent **3** sensitive or keen **4** (of an angle) less than 90° ▷ *noun* **5** accent (´) over a letter to indicate the quality or length of its sound, as in café > **acutely** *adverb*

ad *noun informal* advertisement

AD *abbreviation* (*Latin: anno Domini*) used in dates to indicate the number of years after the birth of Jesus Christ: *70 AD*

ad- *prefix meaning* near or next to: *adjoining*

adage *noun* wise saying

adamant *adjective* unshakable in determination or purpose > **adamantly** *adverb*

Adam's apple Adam's apples *noun* a lump at the front of the neck which is more obvious in men than in women or young boys

adapt *verb* **1** to adjust (something or yourself) to new conditions **2** to change (something) to suit a new purpose > **adaptability** *noun* > **adaptable** *adjective* able to adjust to new conditions

adaptation *noun* **1** thing produced by adapting something: *a TV adaptation of a Victorian novel* **2** act of adapting

adaptor or **adapter** *noun* device for connecting several electrical appliances to a single socket

add *verb* **1** to combine (numbers or quantities) **2** to join (something to something else) **3** to say or write (something more)

adder *noun* small poisonous snake

addict *noun* **1** person who is unable to stop taking drugs **2** *informal* person devoted to something > **addicted** *adjective* **1** dependent on a drug **2** devoted to something > **addiction** *noun*

addictive *adjective* causing addiction

addition *noun* **1** process of adding numbers together **2** thing added **3 in addition** besides, as well

additional *adjective* extra or more: *the decision to take on additional staff* > **additionally** *adverb*

additive *noun* something added, especially to a foodstuff, to improve it or prevent deterioration

address addresses addressing addressed *noun* **1** place where a person lives **2** destination or sender's location written on a letter, etc **3** location **4** formal public speech ▷ *verb* **5** to mark the destination on (an envelope, parcel, etc) **6** to attend to (a problem, task, etc) **7** to talk to (someone)

adenoids *plural noun* soft lumpy tissue at the back of the throat

adept *adjective* very skilful at doing something: *adept at motivating others*

adequacy *noun* sufficiency of something

adequate *adjective* enough in amount or good enough for a purpose > **adequately** *adverb*

adhere adheres adhering adhered *verb* **1** to stick (to) **2** to act according (to a rule or agreement) **3** to continue to support or hold (an opinion or belief) > **adherence** *noun*: *strict adherence to the rules*

adhesion *noun* quality or condition of sticking together

adhesive *noun* **1** substance used to stick things together ▷ *adjective* **2** able to stick to things

ad hoc *adjective, adverb* Latin for a particular purpose only: *an ad hoc ceasefire*

adjacent *adjective* **1** near or next (to): *a hotel adjacent to the beach* **2** *Maths* (of angles) sharing one side and having the same point opposite their bases

adjective *noun* word that adds information about a noun or pronoun > **adjectival** *adjective*

adjoining *adjective* next to and joined onto: *adjoining rooms*

adjourn *verb* **1** to stop (a trial or meeting) temporarily; suspend **2** (of a court, parliament, meeting) to come to a stop with a temporary suspension of activities **3** to go (to another place): *We adjourned to the lounge*

adjournment *noun* temporary stopping of a trial or meeting

adjudicate adjudicates adjudicating adjudicated *verb* *formal* **1** to give a formal decision on a dispute **2** to serve as a judge, for example in a competition > **adjudication** noun: *unbiased adjudication of cases*

adjudicator noun judge in a competition or dispute

adjust verb **1** to adapt to new conditions **2** to alter (something) slightly to improve its suitability or effectiveness > **adjustable** adjective able to be adapted or altered: *adjustable seats* > **adjustment** noun slight alteration

ad-lib ad-libs ad-libbing ad-libbed verb **1** to improvise a speech etc without preparation: *I ad-lib on radio but use a script on TV* ▷ noun **2** comment that has not been prepared beforehand

administer verb **1** to manage (business affairs) **2** to organize and put into practice **3** to give (medicine or treatment)

administrate administrates administrating administrated verb to manage (an organization or system) > **administrator** noun person who manages an organization or system

administration noun **1** management of an organization **2** people who manage an organization **3** government

administrative adjective of the management of an organization

admirable adjective very good and deserving to be admired > **admirably** adverb

admiral noun highest naval rank

admire admires admiring admired verb to respect and approve of (a person or thing) > **admiration** noun respect and approval > **admirer** noun > **admiring** adjective: *an admiring glance* > **admiringly** adverb

admissible adjective allowed to be brought in as evidence in court

admission noun **1** permission to enter **2** entrance fee **3** confession: *an admission of guilt*

admit admits admitting admitted verb **1** to confess or acknowledge (a crime or mistake) **2** to concede (the truth of something) **3** to allow (someone) to enter **4** to make (someone) an in-patient in a hospital: *He was admitted to hospital with chest pains*

admittance noun permission to enter

admittedly adverb it must be said

admonish admonishes admonishing admonished verb formal to tell (someone) off firmly but not harshly > **admonition** noun warning or criticism

ado noun fuss or trouble: *without further ado*

adolescent noun person between puberty and adulthood > **adolescence** noun period between puberty and adulthood

adopt verb **1** to take (someone else's child) as your own **2** to take up (a plan or principle) > **adoption** noun **1** taking up of a plan or principle **2** process of adopting a child

adorable adjective sweet and attractive

adoration noun great admiration and love for someone or something

adore adores adoring adored verb **1** to love intensely or deeply **2** informal to like very much

adorn verb to decorate or embellish > **adornment** noun decoration

adrenal adjective near the kidneys

adrenal glands plural noun glands covering the top of the kidneys

adrenalin or **adrenaline** noun hormone produced by the body when a person is angry, nervous or excited, making the heart beat faster and giving the body more energy

adrift *adjective, adverb* **1** drifting **2** without a clear purpose

adroit *adjective* quick and skilful in actions and behaviour > **adroitly** *adverb*

adulation *noun* uncritical admiration > **adulatory** *adjective*: *adulatory reviews*

adult *adjective* **1** fully grown; mature ▷ *noun* **2** adult person or animal

adulterate adulterates adulterating adulterated *verb* to spoil (something) by adding something inferior to it > **adulteration** *noun*: *adulteration of food*

adultery *noun* sexual intercourse between a married person and someone he or she is not married to > **adulterer** *noun* person who commits adultery > **adulterous** *adjective* of or relating to adultery

adulthood *noun* time when a person is an adult

advance advances advancing advanced *verb* **1** to go or bring forward **2** to further (a cause) **3** to propose (an idea) **4** to lend (a sum of money) ▷ *noun* **5** forward movement **6** improvement: *scientific advance* **7** loan **8 in advance** ahead ▷ *adjective* **9** done or happening before an event

advanced *adjective* **1** at a late stage in development **2** not elementary

advancement *noun* **1** promotion **2** progress, improvement or furthering

advances *plural noun* approaches to a person with the hope of starting a romantic or sexual relationship

advantage *noun* **1** more favourable position or state **2** benefit or profit **3** *Tennis* point scored after deuce **4 take advantage of a** to use (a person) unfairly **b** to use (an opportunity)

advantageous *adjective* likely to bring benefits > **advantageously** *adverb*

advent *noun* **1** arrival or coming into existence **2 Advent** season of four weeks before Christmas in the Christian calendar

adventure *noun* exciting and risky undertaking or exploit

adventurer *noun* **1** person who enjoys doing dangerous and exciting things **2** person who unscrupulously seeks money or power

adventurous *adjective* willing to take risks and do new and exciting things > **adventurously** *adverb*

adverb *noun* word that adds information about a verb, adjective or other adverb > **adverbial** *adjective*

adversary adversaries *noun* opponent or enemy

adverse *adjective* unfavourable to your interests > **adversely** *adverb*

adversity adversities *noun* time of danger or difficulty

advert *noun informal* advertisement

advertise advertises advertising advertised *verb* **1** to present or praise (goods or services) to the public in order to encourage sales **2** to make (a vacancy, event, etc) known publicly > **advertiser** *noun* person or company that pays for something to be advertised > **advertising** *noun*

advertisement *noun* public announcement to sell goods or publicize an event

advice *noun* recommendation as to

what to do

▌ The noun *advice* is spelt with a *c* and the verb *advise* with an *s*

advisable *adjective* prudent, sensible > **advisability** *noun*: *doubts about the advisability of surgery*

advise advises advising advised *verb* **1** to offer advice to **2** *formal* to inform or notify: *We advised them of our decision*

▌ The verb *advise* is spelt with an *s* and the noun *advice* is spelt with a *c*

advised *adjective* **1 well advised** wise **2 ill-advised** unwise

advisedly *adverb* deliberately

adviser or **advisor** *noun* person who offers advice, for example on careers

advisory *adjective* giving advice

advocate advocates advocating advocated *verb* **1** to propose or recommend ▷ *noun* **2** person who publicly supports a cause **3** *Scot*, *S Afr* barrister > **advocacy** *noun* public support of a cause

aerate aerates aerating aerated *verb* to put gas into (a liquid), as when making a fizzy drink

aerial *adjective* **1** in, from or operating in the air: *aerial combat* ▷ *noun* **2** metal pole, wire, etc, for receiving or transmitting radio or TV signals

aerial top dressing *noun* spreading of fertilizer from an aeroplane onto remote areas

aero- *prefix meaning* involving the air, the atmosphere or aircraft: *aerobatics*

aerobics *noun* exercises designed to increase the amount of oxygen in the blood > **aerobic** *adjective* designed for or relating to aerobics

aerodynamic *adjective* having a streamlined shape that moves

easily through the air

aerodynamics *noun* study of how air flows around moving solid objects

aeronautics *noun* study or practice of aircraft flight > **aeronautical** *adjective*: *aeronautical engineering*

aeroplane *noun* powered flying vehicle with fixed wings

aerosol *noun* pressurized can from which a substance can be dispensed as a fine spray

aerospace *noun* **1** earth's atmosphere and space beyond ▷ *adjective* **2** involved in making and designing aeroplanes and spacecraft

aesthete *noun formal* person who has or who pretends to have a highly developed appreciation of beauty

aesthetic *adjective formal* relating to the appreciation of art and beauty > **aesthetically** *adverb*

aesthetics *noun* study of art, beauty and good taste

afar *adverb literary* **from afar** from or at a great distance

affable *adjective* friendly and easy to talk to > **affability** *noun* > **affably** *adverb*

affair *noun* **1** event or happening **2** sexual relationship outside marriage **3** thing to be done or attended to: *My wife's career is her own affair* **4 affairs a** personal or business interests **b** matters of public interest

affect *verb* **1** to influence (someone or something): *The difficult conditions continued to affect our performance* **2** to move (someone) emotionally **3** to put on a show of: *He affects ignorance*

▌ Do not confuse the spelling of the verb *affect* with the noun *effect.* Something that *affects* you has an *effect* on you

affectation *noun* attitude or manner put on to impress

affected *adjective* 1 rather artificial and not genuine 2 pretended: *an affected indifference*

affecting *adjective* very moving

affection *noun* 1 fondness or love 2 **affections** feelings of love for someone

affectionate *adjective* full of fondness for someone; loving > **affectionately** *adverb*

affidavit *noun* formal written statement, made under oath, which may be used as evidence in a court of law

affiliate affiliates affiliating affiliated *verb* 1 (of a group) to link up with a larger group > *noun* 2 organization which has a close link with another, larger group > **affiliation** *noun*: *The group has no affiliation to any political party*

affinity affinities *noun* close similarity or understanding between two things or people

affirm *verb* 1 to declare to be true 2 to indicate support or confirmation of (an idea or belief) > **affirmation** *noun*: *His work is an affirmation of life*

affirmative *adjective* meaning or indicating yes

affix affixes affixing affixed *verb* 1 *formal* to attach or fasten > *noun* 2 word or syllable added to a word to change its meaning

afflict *verb* to cause someone unhappiness or suffering > **affliction** *noun* 1 something that causes unhappiness or suffering 2 condition of great distress or suffering

affluent *adjective* having plenty of money > **affluence** *noun* wealth

afford *verb* 1 to have enough money to buy 2 to be able to spare (the time etc) 3 to give or supply > **affordable** *adjective*

afforestation *noun* planting of large numbers of trees to form forests

affray affrays *noun Brit, Aust, NZ law* noisy fight; brawl

affront *verb* 1 to offend the pride or dignity of > *noun* 2 insult

Afghan *adjective* 1 of Afghanistan or its language > *noun* 2 someone from Afghanistan

afield *adverb* **far afield** far away

afloat *adverb, adjective* 1 floating on water 2 at sea or aboard ship 3 successful and making enough money: *Companies are struggling hard to stay afloat*

afoot *adverb, adjective* happening; in operation: *Plans are afoot to build a new museum*

afraid *adjective* 1 frightened 2 regretful: *I'm afraid I lost my temper*

afresh *adverb* again and in a new way

Africa *noun* second largest continent, which is surrounded by sea, with the Atlantic on its west side, the Mediterranean to the north and the Indian Ocean and the Red Sea to the east

African *adjective* 1 belonging or relating to Africa > *noun* 2 someone, especially a Black person, from Africa

African-American *noun* American whose ancestors came from Africa

Afrikaans *noun* language used in South Africa, descended from Dutch

Afrikaner *noun* Afrikaans-speaking South African of usually Dutch, German or French Huguenot ancestry

afro afros *noun* hairstyle in which hair is a great mass of very small curls

Afro- *prefix meaning* African: *Afro-Caribbean*

aft *adverb* at or towards the rear of a ship or aircraft

after *preposition* **1** following in time or place **2** in pursuit of: *He was after my mother's jewellery* **3** concerning: *He asked after Laura* **4** considering: *You seem all right after what happened last night* **5** next in excellence or importance to: *After India, Italy is our most important customer* **6** with the same name as: *The building is named after the architect* ▷ *conjunction* **7** at a later time than the time when: *She arrived after the reading had begun* ▷ *adverb* **8** at a later time

aftereffect *noun* result occurring some time after its cause

afterlife *noun* life after death

aftermath *noun* results of an event considered together

afternoon *noun* time between noon and evening

afters *plural noun* Brit informal dessert

aftershave *noun* pleasant-smelling liquid men put on their faces after shaving

afterthought *noun* **1** idea occurring later **2** something added later

afterwards or **afterward** *adverb* later

again *adverb* **1** happening one more time: *He's done it again* **2** returning to the same state or place as before: *there and back again* **3** in addition to an amount that has already been mentioned: *I could eat twice as much again*

against *preposition* **1** in opposition or contrast to: *the Test match against England* **2** touching and leaning

on: *He leaned against the wall* **3** as a protection from: *precautions against fire* **4** in comparison with: *The euro is now at its highest rate against the dollar*

agate *noun* semiprecious form of quartz with striped colouring

age ages ageing or **aging aged** *noun* **1** length of time a person or thing has existed: *What age was he when he died?* **2** time of life: *He should know better at his age* **3** state of being old or the process of becoming older: *The fabric was showing signs of age* **4** period of history: *the Iron Age* **5** **ages** informal long time: *He's been talking for ages* **6** **come of age** to become legally responsible for your actions (usually at 18) ▷ *verb* **7** to make or grow old

aged *adjective* **1** old **2** being at the age of: *people aged 16 to 24*

ageless *adjective* **1** apparently never growing old **2** seeming to have existed for ever

agency agencies *noun* organization providing a particular service

agenda *noun* list of things to be dealt with, especially at a meeting

agent *noun* **1** person acting on behalf of another **2** person who works for a country's secret service **3** person or thing producing an effect: *bleaching agents*

age of consent *noun* age at which a person can legally marry or have sex

age-old *adjective* having existed for a very long time

aggravate aggravates aggravating aggravated *verb* **1** to make (a disease, situation or problem) worse **2** informal to annoy > **aggravating** *adjective* > **aggravation** *noun*

Some people think that using *aggravate* to mean 'annoy' is wrong

aggregate *noun* **1** total made up of several smaller amounts **2** rock consisting of a mixture of minerals **3** sand or gravel used to make concrete ▷ *adjective* **4** gathered into a mass **5** total or final

aggression *noun* violent and hostile behaviour

aggressive *adjective* **1** full of hostility and violence **2** determined and eager to succeed: *aggressive sales techniques* > **aggressively** *adverb* > **aggressiveness** *noun*

aggressor *noun* person or country that starts a fight or a war

aggrieved *adjective* upset and angry

aghast *adjective* overcome with amazement or horror

agile *adjective* **1** able to move quickly and easily **2** mentally quick > **agilely** *adverb* > **agility** *noun* ability to move or think quickly

agitate agitates agitating agitated *verb* **1** to disturb or excite **2** to stir or shake (a liquid) **3** to stir up public opinion for or against something > **agitation** *noun* **1** state of disturbance or excitement **2** act of stirring or shaking something **3** stirring up of public opinion for or against something > **agitator** *noun: a political agitator*

AGM AGMs *abbreviation* annual general meeting: meeting held once a year by an organization for all its members

agnostic *noun* **1** person who believes that it is impossible to know whether God exists or not ▷ *adjective* **2** of agnostics > **agnosticism** *noun* belief that it is impossible to know whether God exists or not

ago *adverb* in the past

agog *adjective* excited and eager to know more about something

agonize agonizes agonizing agonized; also spelt **agonise** *verb* to worry greatly: *He agonized over the decision for days*

agonizing or **agonising** *adjective* extremely painful, either physically or mentally

agony agonies *noun* extreme physical or mental pain

agoraphobia *noun* fear of open spaces > **agoraphobic** *adjective* suffering from agoraphobia

agrarian *adjective formal* of land or agriculture: *agrarian economies*

agree agrees agreeing agreed *verb* **1** to be of the same opinion **2** to consent: *She agreed to go* **3** to reach a joint decision **4** to be similar or consistent **5** **agree with** to be good for (someone)

agreeable *adjective* **1** pleasant and enjoyable **2** prepared to consent to something > **agreeably** *adverb*

agreement *noun* **1** decision that has been reached by two or more people **2** legal contract

agriculture *noun* raising of crops and livestock > **agricultural** *adjective* of or relating to agriculture

aground *adverb* onto the bottom of shallow water

ahead *adverb* **1** in front: *He looked ahead* **2** more advanced than someone or something else: *We are five years ahead of the competition* **3** in the future

ahoy *interjection* shout used at sea to attract attention

aid *noun* **1** money, equipment or services provided for people in need **2** help or support **3** something that makes a task easier ▷ *verb* **4** to help or assist

aide *noun* assistant to an important person, especially in the government or the army

AIDS *abbreviation* acquired immunodeficiency syndrome: a viral disease that destroys the body's ability to fight infection

ailing *adjective* **1** sick or ill, and not getting better **2** getting into difficulties, especially with money: *an ailing company*

ailment *noun* minor illness

aim *verb* **1** to point (a weapon or missile) or direct (a blow or remark) at someone or something **2** to propose or intend ▷ *noun* **3** intention or purpose; goal **4** aiming

aimless *adjective* having no purpose > **aimlessly** *adverb* > **aimlessness** *noun*

air *noun* **1** mixture of gases forming the earth's atmosphere **2** space above the ground or sky **3** breeze **4** quality or manner: *an air of defiance* **5** simple tune **6 on the air** in the act of broadcasting on radio or television **7 airs** manners put on to impress people: *We never put on airs* ▷ *verb* **8** to make known publicly **9** to expose to air to dry or ventilate

air bag *noun* vehicle safety device which inflates automatically in a crash to protect the driver or passenger when they are thrown forward

airborne *adjective* **1** carried by air **2** (of aircraft) flying

air-conditioning *noun* system that controls the temperature and humidity of the air in a building > **air-conditioned** *adjective*

aircraft *noun* any machine that flies, such as an aeroplane

▍ The plural of *aircraft* is *aircraft*

aircraft carrier *noun* warship for the launching and landing of aircraft

aircrew *noun* aircraft's pilot, navigator and other people needed to operate it

airfield *noun* place where aircraft can land and take off

air force *noun* branch of the armed forces responsible for air warfare

air gun *noun* gun fired by compressed air

air hostess air hostesses *noun* female flight attendant

airing *noun* **1** exposure to air for drying or ventilation **2** exposure to public debate: *Both these ideas got an airing during the campaign*

airing cupboard *noun* warm dry cupboard, usually containing a hot-water tank, in which washed clothes may be aired

airless *adjective* stuffy

airlift *noun* **1** transport of troops or cargo by aircraft when other routes are blocked ▷ *verb* **2** to transport by airlift

airline *noun* company which provides air travel

airliner *noun* large passenger aircraft

airlock *noun* **1** air bubble blocking the flow of liquid in a pipe **2** compartment between places that do not have the same pressure, for example in a spacecraft or a submarine

airmail *noun* **1** system of sending mail by aircraft **2** mail sent in this way

airman airmen *noun* man who serves in his country's air force

air miles *plural noun* miles of free air travel that can be earned by buying airline tickets and various other products

airport *noun* airfield for civilian aircraft, with facilities for aircraft maintenance and passengers

air raid *noun* attack by aircraft, in which bombs are dropped

airship *noun* large aircraft, consisting of a rigid balloon filled with gas and powered by an engine, with a passenger compartment underneath

airspace *noun* atmosphere above a country, regarded as its territory

airstrip *noun* cleared area where aircraft can take off and land

airtight *adjective* sealed so that air cannot enter

air-traffic control *noun* organization that gives instructions to pilots by radio about the course and height of their aircraft > **air-traffic controller** *noun* person whose job is to give pilots instructions about the course and height of their aircraft

airworthy *adjective* (of aircraft) fit to fly

airy airier airiest *adjective* **1** full of fresh air and light **2** light-hearted and casual: *an airy wave of his hand* > **airily** *adverb*

aisle *noun* passageway separating the seating areas in a church, theatre, etc, or the rows of shelves in a supermarket

ajar *adjective, adverb* (of a door) partly open

akimbo *adverb* **with arms akimbo** with hands on hips and elbows outwards

akin *adjective* **akin to** similar, related: *The taste is akin to veal*

alabaster *noun* type of smooth white stone used for making ornaments

à la carte *adjective, adverb French* with individually-priced dishes

alacrity *noun* **with alacrity** quickly and eagerly

alarm *noun* **1** sudden fear caused by awareness of danger **2** warning sound **3** device that gives this **4** alarm clock ▷ *verb* **5** to fill with fear > **alarming** *adjective*

alarm clock *noun* clock which sounds at a set time to wake someone up

alas *adverb* unfortunately, regrettably

Albanian *adjective* **1** belonging or relating to Albania ▷ *noun* **2** someone from Albania **3** main language spoken in Albania

albatross albatrosses *noun* **1** large white sea bird with very long wings **2** a commitment that causes a great deal of difficulty

albeit *conjunction formal* even though: *He was making progress, albeit slowly*

albino albinos *noun* person or animal with white skin and hair and pink eyes

album *noun* **1** CD, cassette or record with a number of songs on it **2** book with blank pages for keeping photographs or stamps in

alchemy *noun* medieval form of chemistry concerned with trying to turn base metals into gold and to find the elixir of life > **alchemist** *noun* medieval scientist who tried to turn base metals into gold

alcheringa *noun* same as **Dreamtime**

alcohol *noun* **1** colourless flammable liquid present in intoxicating drinks **2** intoxicating drinks generally

alcoholic *adjective* **1** of alcohol: *alcoholic drinks* ▷ *noun* **2** person addicted to alcohol > **alcoholism** *noun* addiction to alcohol

alcopop *noun Brit, Aust, S Afr informal* alcoholic drink that tastes like a soft drink

alcove *noun* recess in the wall of a room

ale *noun* kind of beer

alert *adjective* **1** paying full attention to what is happening ▷ *noun* **2** warning of danger **3 on the alert** watchful ▷ *verb* **4** to warn of danger > **alertness** *noun*

algae *plural noun* plants which live in or near water and have no true stems, leaves or roots

algebra *noun* branch of mathematics in which symbols and letters are used instead of numbers to express relationships between quantities > **algebraic** *adjective*

Algerian *adjective* **1** belonging or relating to Algeria ▷ *noun* **2** someone from Algeria

algorithm *noun* logical arithmetical or computational procedure for solving a problem

alias aliases *adverb* **1** also known as ▷ *noun* **2** false name

alibi alibis *noun* **1** plea of being somewhere else when a crime was committed **2** *informal* excuse

alien *adjective* **1** foreign **2** strange and outside your normal experience; different **3** from another world ▷ *noun* **4** foreigner **5** being from another world

alienate alienates alienating alienated *verb* to cause (someone) to become hostile

alienation *noun* state of being an outsider or the feeling of being isolated

alight *verb* **1** *formal* to step out (of a vehicle): *We alighted at Lenzie station* **2** to land: *thirty finches alighting on a*

ledge ▷ *adjective* **3** on fire

align *verb* **1** to bring (a person or group) into agreement with the policy of another **2** to place (two objects) in a straight line > **alignment** *noun*

alike *adjective* **1** like or similar ▷ *adverb* **2** in the same way

alimentary canal *noun* passage in the body through which food passes from the mouth to the anus

alimony *noun* allowance paid under a court order to a separated or divorced spouse

alive *adjective* **1** living; not dead **2** lively and active

alkali alkalis *noun* substance with a pH value of more than 7 > **alkaline** *adjective*: *Some soils are too alkaline for certain plant life* > **alkalinity** *noun*

all *adjective, pronoun* **1** whole quantity or number (of): *90% of all households; all our belongings; That was all I had* ▷ *adverb* **2** wholly, entirely **3** (in the score of games) each: *The final score was six points all* ▷ *noun* **4 give your all** to make the greatest possible effort

Allah *noun* name of God in Islam

allay allays allaying allayed *verb* to reduce (someone's fears or doubts)

allegation *noun* unproved accusation

allege alleges alleging alleged *verb* to state without proof > **alleged** *adjective*: *an alleged beating* > **allegedly** *adverb*

allegiance *noun* loyalty to a person, country or cause

allegory allegories *noun* story with an underlying meaning as well as the literal one. For example, George Orwell's novel *Animal Farm* is an allegory in that the animals who revolt in the farmyard are symbols of the political leaders in the Russian Revolution > **allegorical** *adjective*: *an allegorical novel*

alleluia *interjection* same as **hallelujah**

allergy allergies *noun* extreme sensitivity to a substance, which causes the body to react to it > **allergic** *adjective* having or caused by an allergy

alleviate alleviates alleviating alleviated *verb* to lessen (pain or suffering): *measures to alleviate poverty* > **alleviation** *noun*

alley alleys *noun* **1** narrow street or path **2** long narrow enclosure in which tenpin bowling or skittles is played

alliance *noun* **1** state of being allied **2** formal relationship between countries or groups for a shared purpose

allied *adjective* **1** united by political or military agreements: *the Allied forces* **2** similar or related to something else: *steel and allied industries*

alligator *noun* reptile of the crocodile family, found in the southern US and China

alliteration *noun literary* use of the same sound at the start of words occurring together, *eg moody music* > **alliterative** *adjective* relating to or connected with alliteration

allocate allocates allocating allocated *verb* to assign (something) to someone or for a particular purpose > **allocation** *noun*: *the allocation of funding*

allot allots allotting allotted *verb* to assign as a share or for a particular purpose: *Space was allotted for visitors' cars*

allotment *noun* **1** *Brit* small piece of public land rented to grow

vegetables on **2** share of something

allow *verb* **1** to permit (someone to do something) **2** to set aside **3 allow for** to take into account > **allowable** *adjective* able to be accepted or admitted

allowance *noun* **1** amount of money given at regular intervals **2** amount permitted **3 make allowances for a** to treat or judge (someone) less severely because he or she has special problems **b** to take (something) into account

alloy alloys *noun* mixture of two or more metals

all right *adjective* **1** adequate or satisfactory **2** unharmed ▷ *interjection* **3** expression of approval or agreement

all-rounder *noun* person who is good at lots of different things, especially in sport

allude alludes alluding alluded *verb* **allude to** to refer indirectly to

> You *allude to* something. Do not confuse *allude* with *elude*

allure *noun* attractiveness: *the allure of foreign travel* > **alluring** *adjective*

allusion *noun* indirect reference: *English literature is full of classical allusions*

ally allies allying allied *noun* **1** country, person or group with an agreement to support another ▷ *verb* **2 ally yourself with** to join as an ally

almanac *noun* **1** yearly calendar with detailed information on anniversaries, phases of the moon, etc **2** book published every year giving information about a particular subject

almighty *adjective* **1** having absolute power **2** *informal* very great ▷ *noun* **3 the Almighty** God

almond *noun* edible brown oval-

shaped nut which grows on a
small tree

almost *adverb* very nearly

alms *plural noun old-fashioned* gifts
of money, food or clothing to poor
people

aloft *adverb* up in the air or in a high
position

alone *adjective, adverb* without
anyone or anything else; on your
own

along *preposition* **1** over part or all
the length of ▷ *adverb* **2** moving
forward: *We marched along, singing as
we went* **3** in company with others:
Why not take her along? **4** **all along**
from the beginning of a period of
time right up to now: *You've known
that all along*

alongside *preposition, adverb* beside
(something)

aloof *adjective* distant or haughty
in manner

aloud *adverb* spoken in a voice that
can be heard

alpha *noun* first letter in the Greek
alphabet

alphabet *noun* set of letters used in
writing a language > **alphabetical**
adjective in the conventional
order of the letters of an alphabet
> **alphabetically** *adverb*

alpha male *noun* dominant male
animal or person in a group

alpine *adjective* existing in or
relating to high mountains

already *adverb* **1** before the present
time **2** sooner than expected

alright *adjective, interjection* all right
Some people think that *all right*
is the only correct spelling and
that *alright* is wrong

Alsatian *noun* large wolflike dog

also *adverb* in addition, too

also-ran *noun* loser in a race,
competition or election

altar *noun* **1** table used for
Communion in Christian churches
2 raised structure on which
sacrifices are offered and religious
rites are performed

alter *verb* to make or become
different > **alteration** *noun: simple
alterations to your diet*

altercation *noun formal* heated
argument

**alternate alternates
alternating alternated** *verb*
1 to occur or to cause (something)
to occur by turns ▷ *adjective*
2 occurring by turns **3** every second
(one) of a series **4** (of two angles) on
opposite sides of a line that crosses
two other lines > **alternately**
adverb > **alternation** *noun: The
alternation of sun and snow continued*

alternating current *noun* electric
current that reverses direction at
frequent regular intervals

alternative *noun* **1** something
you can do or have instead of
something else ▷ *adjective* **2** able
to be done or used instead of
something else **3** (of medicine,
lifestyle, etc) not conventional
> **alternatively** *adverb*

alternator *noun* electric generator
for producing alternating current

although *conjunction* despite the
fact that

altitude *noun* height above sea
level: *an altitude of 1330 metres*

alto altos *noun Music* **1** short
for **contralto** **2** (singer with)
the highest adult male voice
3 instrument with the second-
highest pitch in its group

altogether *adverb* **1** entirely **2** on
the whole **3** in total

altruism *noun formal* unselfish
concern for the welfare of others
> **altruist** *noun* person unselfishly

concerned for the welfare of others
> **altruistic** adjective: altruistic
behaviour > **altruistically** adverb

aluminium noun light silvery-white metal that does not rust

always adverb **1** at all times **2** for ever

am verb see **be**

a.m. abbreviation (Latin: ante meridiem) before noon: We got up at 6 a.m.

amalgam noun **1** blend or combination **2** alloy of mercury and another metal, used in dental fillings

amalgamate amalgamates amalgamating amalgamated verb to combine or unite
> **amalgamation** noun: an amalgamation of two organizations

amandla noun S Afr political slogan calling for power to the Black population

amass amasses amassing amassed verb to collect or accumulate: He amassed a huge fortune

amateur noun **1** person who engages in a sport or activity as a pastime rather than as a profession **2** person unskilled in something ▷ adjective **3** not professional

amateurish adjective lacking skill
> **amateurishly** adverb

amaze amazes amazing amazed verb to surprise greatly; astound > **amazed** adjective: You'd be amazed at the mess people leave
> **amazement** noun: I stared at her in amazement > **amazing** adjective very surprising or remarkable
> **amazingly** adverb

ambassador noun senior diplomat who represents his or her country in another country

amber noun **1** clear yellowish fossil

resin ▷ adjective **2** brownish-yellow

ambi- prefix meaning both: ambidextrous

ambidextrous adjective able to use both hands with equal ease

ambience noun formal atmosphere of a place

ambient adjective surrounding: low ambient temperatures

ambiguous adjective having more than one possible meaning
> **ambiguity** noun: considerable ambiguity about the meaning of the agreement > **ambiguously** adverb

ambition noun **1** desire for success: He's talented and full of ambition **2** something so desired; goal: His ambition is to be an actor

ambitious adjective **1** having a strong desire for success **2** requiring great effort or ability: an ambitious rebuilding schedule
> **ambitiously** adverb

ambivalent adjective having or showing two conflicting attitudes or emotions > **ambivalence** noun: her ambivalence about getting married again

amble ambles ambling ambled verb **1** to walk at a leisurely pace ▷ noun **2** leisurely walk or pace

ambulance noun motor vehicle designed to carry sick or injured people

ambush ambushes ambushing ambushed noun **1** act of waiting in a concealed position to make a surprise attack **2** attack from a concealed position ▷ verb **3** to attack suddenly from a concealed position

ameliorate ameliorates ameliorating ameliorated verb formal to make (something) better > **amelioration** noun: the amelioration of conditions

amen *interjection* so be it: used at the end of a prayer

amenable *adjective* likely or willing to cooperate: *Both brothers were amenable to the arrangement*

amend *verb* to make small changes to correct or improve (something) > **amendment** *noun* improvement or correction

amends *plural noun* **make amends for** to compensate for

amenity amenities *noun* useful or enjoyable feature available for the public to use

America *noun* **1** the whole of North, South and Central America **2** the United States

American *adjective* **1** of the United States of America or the American continent ▷ *noun* **2** someone from America or the American continent

amethyst *noun* bluish-violet variety of quartz used as a gemstone

amiable *adjective* friendly, pleasant-natured: *The hotel staff were very amiable* > **amiability** *noun*: *I found his amiability charming* > **amiably** *adverb*

amicable *adjective* fairly friendly: *an amicable divorce* > **amicably** *adverb*

amid or **amidst** *preposition formal* in the middle of; among

amino acid *noun* organic compound found in protein

amiss *adverb* **1** wrongly, badly **2 take something amiss** to be offended by something ▷ *adjective* **3** wrong or faulty

ammonia *noun* strong-smelling alkaline gas containing hydrogen and nitrogen, used in household cleaning materials, explosives and fertilizers

ammunition *noun* **1** bullets, bombs and shells that can be fired from or as a weapon **2** facts that can be used in an argument

amnesia *noun* loss of memory

amnesty amnesties *noun* general pardon for offences against a government

amoeba amoebae or **amobas** *noun* smallest kind of living creature, consisting of one cell. Amoebas reproduce by dividing into two

amok *adverb* **run amok** to run about in a violent frenzy

among or **amongst** *preposition* **1** surrounded by **2** in the company of **3** to each of: *Divide it among yourselves*

amoral *adjective* without moral standards

Do not confuse *amoral* and *immoral*. You use *amoral* to talk about people with no moral standards, but *immoral* for people who are aware of moral standards but go against them

amorous *adjective* feeling, showing or relating to sexual love: *an amorous relationship* > **amorously** *adverb* > **amorousness** *noun*

amorphous *adjective formal* having no definite shape or structure

amount *noun* **1** extent or quantity ▷ *verb* **2 amount to** to be equal or add up to

amp *noun* **1** ampere **2** *informal* amplifier

ampere *noun* basic unit of electric current

ampersand *noun* the character (&), meaning *and*

amphetamine *noun* drug used as a stimulant

amphibian *noun* animal that lives on land but breeds in water

amphibious *adjective* **1** (of an animal) living partly on land and partly in the water **2** (of a military operation) using boats to land soldiers on an enemy shore **3** (of a vehicle) able to move on both land and water

amphitheatre *noun* large semicircular open area with sloping sides covered with rows of seats

ample *adjective* **1** more than sufficient **2** large > **amply** *adverb*

amplifier *noun* piece of equipment in a radio or stereo system which causes sounds or signals to become louder

amplify amplifies amplifying amplified *verb* **1** to increase the strength of (a current or sound signal) **2** to explain in more detail **3** to increase the size or effect of > **amplification** *noun*

amplitude *noun* Physics the amplitude of a wave is how far its curve moves away from its normal position

amputate amputates amputating amputated *verb* to cut off (a limb or part of a limb) for medical reasons > **amputation** *noun*: *the amputation of his left leg*

Amrit *noun* **1** in the Sikh religion, a special mixture of sugar and water used in rituals **2** ceremony that takes place when someone is accepted as a full member of the Sikh community and drinks Amrit as part of the ceremony

amulet *noun* small charm or other object worn for good luck or to ward off bad luck

amuse amuses amusing amused *verb* **1** to cause to laugh or smile **2** to entertain or keep interested > **amused** *adjective*: *an amused look on her face* > **amusing** *adjective* funny or entertaining

amusement *noun* **1** state of being amused **2** something that amuses or entertains someone

an *adjective* form of **a** used before vowel sounds

-an *suffix* forming nouns and adjectives which show where or what someone or something comes from or belongs to: *American; Victorian; Christian*

anachronism *noun* person or thing placed in the wrong historical period or seeming to belong to another time: *The President regarded the Church as an anachronism* > **anachronistic** *adjective*: *Many of its practices seem anachronistic*

anaemia *noun* deficiency in the number of red blood cells, resulting in tiredness and a pale complexion > **anaemic** *adjective*

anaesthesia *noun* loss of bodily feeling

anaesthetic *noun* **1** substance causing loss of bodily feeling ▷ *adjective* **2** causing loss of bodily feeling

anaesthetist *noun* doctor trained to administer anaesthetics

anaesthetize anaesthetizes anaesthetizing anaesthetized; also spelt **anaesthetise** *verb* to cause to feel no pain by administering an anaesthetic

anagram *noun* word or phrase made by rearranging the letters of another word or phrase

anal *adjective* relating to the anus

analgesic *adjective* **1** pain-relieving ▷ *noun* **2** substance that relieves pain

analogue *noun* **1** something that is similar in some respects to something else ▷ *adjective* **2** displaying information by means of a dial

analogy analogies *noun*
comparison made to show a
similarity > **analogous** *adjective*
similar in some respects

**analyse analyses analysing
analysed** *verb* **1** to examine
(something) in detail in order to
discover its meaning or essential
features **2** to break (something)
down into its components **3** to
psychoanalyse (someone)

analysis analyses *noun* separation
of a whole into its parts for study
and interpretation

analyst *noun* person skilled in
analysis

analytical or **analytic**
adjective using logical reasoning
> **analytically** *adverb*

anarchism *noun* political belief
that all governments should be
abolished

anarchist *noun* **1** person who
advocates the abolition of
government **2** person who causes
disorder

anarchy *noun* lawlessness and
disorder > **anarchic** *adjective*:
*anarchic attitudes and complete
disrespect for authority*

anathema *noun formal* detested
person or thing: *The very colour was
anathema to him*

anatomy anatomies *noun*
1 science of the structure of
the body **2** physical structure
3 person's body > **anatomical**
adjective: *anatomical details*
> **anatomically** *adverb*

ANC *abbreviation* African National
Congress

ancestor *noun* **1** person from whom
you are descended **2** forerunner
> **ancestral** *adjective*: *the family's
ancestral home*

ancestry ancestries *noun* **1** family

descent: *of Japanese ancestry*
2 origin or roots

anchor *noun* **1** heavy hooked device
attached to a boat by a cable and
dropped overboard to fasten the
ship to the sea bottom ▷ *verb* **2** to
fasten with or as if with an anchor

anchorage *noun* place where boats
can be anchored

anchovy anchovies *noun* small
strong-tasting fish

ancient *adjective* **1** dating from very
long ago: *ancient Greece* **2** very old or
having a long history

ancillary *adjective* **1** supporting
the main work of an organization:
hospital ancillary workers **2** used as
an extra or supplement

and *conjunction* **1** in addition to **2** as
a consequence **3** then or afterwards

androgynous *adjective formal*
having both male and female
characteristics

android *noun* robot resembling
a human

anecdote *noun* short amusing
account of an incident > **anecdotal**
adjective based on individual
accounts rather than on reliable
research and statistics: *anecdotal
evidence*

anemone *noun* plant with white,
purple or red flowers

anew *adverb* **1** once more **2** in a
different way

angel *noun* **1** spiritual being
believed to be an attendant or
messenger of God **2** person who is
kind, pure or beautiful > **angelic**
adjective **1** of or relating to angels
2 very kind, pure or beautiful
> **angelically** *adverb*

angelica *noun* **1** aromatic plant
2 its candied stalks, used in cookery

anger *noun* **1** fierce displeasure or
extreme annoyance ▷ *verb* **2** to

make (someone) angry

angina *noun* (also **angina pectoris**) heart disorder causing sudden severe chest pains

angle angles angling angled *noun* **1** space between or shape formed by two lines or surfaces that meet **2** distance between two lines or surfaces at the point where they meet, measured in degrees **3** corner **4** point of view ▷ *verb* **5** to bend or place (something) at an angle **6** to fish with a hook and line > **angle for** *verb* to try to get (something) by hinting

angler *noun* person who fishes with a hook and line > **angling** *noun* sport of fishing with a hook and line

Anglican *noun* **1** member of the Church of England ▷ *adjective* **2** of the Church of England

Anglo- *prefix meaning* **1** English: *Anglo-Scottish* **2** British: *Anglo-American*

Anglo-Saxon *noun* **1** member of any of the West Germanic tribes that settled in England from the fifth century AD **2** language of the Anglo-Saxons ▷ *adjective* **3** of the Anglo-Saxons or their language

Angolan *adjective* **1** belonging or relating to Angola ▷ *noun* **2** someone from Angola

angora *noun* **1** variety of goat, cat or rabbit with long silky hair **2** hair of the angora goat or rabbit **3** cloth made from this hair

angry angrier angriest *adjective* **1** full of anger **2** inflamed > **angrily** *adverb*

anguish *noun* great mental pain > **anguished** *adjective*: *an anguished cry*

angular *adjective* **1** (of a person) lean and bony **2** having straight lines

and sharp points

animal *noun* **1** living being except a plant or any mammal except a human being ▷ *adjective* **2** of animals **3** of physical needs or desires

animate animates animating animated *verb* **1** to give life to **2** to make lively **3** to produce (a story) as an animated cartoon ▷ *adjective* **4** having life

animated *adjective* **1** lively and interesting: *an animated conversation* **2** (of a film) made using animation: *an animated cartoon* > **animatedly** *adverb*

animation *noun* **1** technique of making cartoon films **2** liveliness and enthusiasm > **animator** *noun* person who makes animated cartoons

animosity animosities *noun* feeling of strong dislike and anger towards someone

aniseed *noun* liquorice-flavoured seeds of the anise plant

ankle *noun* joint between the foot and leg > **anklet** *noun* ornamental chain worn round the ankle

annals *plural noun* yearly records of events: *the annals of military history*

annex annexes annexing annexed *verb* **1** to seize (territory) **2** to take (something) without permission **3** to join or add (something) to something larger > **annexation** *noun*

annexe *noun* **1** extension to a building **2** nearby building used as an extension

annihilate annihilates annihilating annihilated *verb* to destroy (a place or a group of people) completely > **annihilation** *noun*

anniversary anniversaries

noun **1** date on which something occurred in a previous year **2** celebration of this

annotate annotates annotating annotated *verb* to add notes to (a written work)

announce announces announcing announced *verb* to make known publicly > **announcement** *noun* public statement

announcer *noun* person who introduces radio or television programmes

annoy annoys annoying annoyed *verb* to irritate or displease > **annoyance** *noun* > **annoyed** *adjective* > **annoying** *adjective*

annual *adjective* **1** happening once a year: *their annual conference* **2** lasting for a year: *the United States' annual budget for national defence* ▷ *noun* **3** plant that completes its life cycle in a year **4** book published once every year > **annually** *adverb*

annuity annuities *noun* fixed sum paid every year

annul annuls annulling annulled *verb* to declare (something, especially a marriage) officially invalid > **annulment** *noun*

anoint *verb* to smear with oil as a sign of consecration > **anointment** *noun* act of anointing someone

anomaly anomalies *noun* something that deviates from the normal: *a statistical anomaly* > **anomalous** *adjective*: *This anomalous behaviour has baffled scientists*

anon *adverb* old-fashioned in a short time; soon: *Well, see you anon*

anon. *abbreviation* anonymous

anonymous *adjective* by someone whose name is unknown or withheld > **anonymity** *noun*: *the anonymity of the voting booth* > **anonymously** *adverb*

anorak *noun* light waterproof hooded jacket

anorexia *noun* (also **anorexia nervosa**) psychological disorder characterized by fear of becoming fat and refusal to eat > **anorexic** *adjective* **1** suffering from anorexia ▷ *noun* **2** person suffering from anorexia

another *adjective, pronoun* **1** one more **2** different (one)

answer *noun* **1** reply to a question, request, letter, etc **2** solution to a problem **3** reaction or response ▷ *verb* **4** to give an answer (to) **5** to be responsible to (a person) **6** to respond or react: *a dog that answers to the name of Pugg*

answerable *adjective* **answerable for** *or* **to** responsible for or accountable to

answering machine *noun* device for answering a telephone automatically and recording messages

ant *noun* small insect living in large colonies

-ant *suffix* forming adjectives and nouns: *important; deodorant*

antagonism *noun* open opposition or hostility

antagonist *noun* opponent or adversary

antagonistic *adjective* in active opposition > **antagonistically** *adverb*

antagonize antagonizes antagonizing antagonized; also spelt **antagonise** *verb* to arouse hostility in

Antarctic *noun* **1 the Antarctic** area around the South Pole ▷ *adjective* **2** of this region

Antarctic Circle *noun* imaginary circle around the southernmost part of the earth

ante- *prefix meaning* before in time or position: *antenatal; antechamber*

anteater *noun* mammal which feeds on ants by means of a long snout

antecedent *noun* **1** event or circumstance happening or existing before another ▷ *adjective* **2** preceding, prior

antechamber *noun* small room leading to a bigger room

antediluvian *adjective* extremely old-fashioned: *antediluvian ideas*

antelope *noun* deerlike mammal with long legs and horns

antenatal *adjective* concerned with the care of pregnant women and their unborn children

antenna antennae antennas *noun* **1** long thin feeler, of which there are two, attached to an insect's head **2** *Aust, NZ, US* radio or television aerial

> Note that the plural of sense 1 is *antennae* and the plural of sense 2 is *antennas*

anthem *noun* **1** song of loyalty, especially to a country **2** piece of choral music, usually set to words from the Bible

anther *noun* part of a flower's stamen containing pollen

anthology anthologies *noun* collection of poems or other literary pieces by various authors

anthrax *noun* highly infectious disease of cattle and sheep, causing fever, a swollen throat and painful boils. It can also be caught by humans

anthropo- *prefix meaning* involving or to do with human beings: *anthropology*

anthropoid *adjective* **1** like a human: *an anthropoid ape* ▷ *noun* **2** ape, such as a chimpanzee, that resembles a human

anthropology *noun* study of human origins, institutions and beliefs > **anthropological** *adjective*: *anthropological theories* > **anthropologist** *noun* person who studies or is an expert in anthropology

anthropomorphic *adjective formal* relating to or involving the giving of human form or personality to a god, animal or object: *He always talked about his pets in anthropomorphic terms* > **anthropomorphism** *noun* giving human form or personality to a god, animal or object

anti- *prefix meaning* **1** against or opposed to: *anti-war* **2** opposite to: *anticlimax* **3** counteracting: *antifreeze*

anti-aircraft *adjective* for defence against aircraft attack

antibiotic *noun* **1** chemical substance capable of destroying bacteria ▷ *adjective* **2** of antibiotics

antibody antibodies *noun* protein produced in the blood, which destroys bacteria

anticipate anticipates anticipating anticipated *verb* to foresee and act in advance of > **anticipation** *noun*: *smiling in happy anticipation*

anticlimax anticlimaxes *noun* something that does not live up to expectations or is disappointing, especially in contrast to what has gone before

anticlockwise *adverb, adjective* in the opposite direction to the rotation of the hands of a clock

antics *plural noun* funny or silly ways of behaving

anticyclone *noun* area of high air pressure which causes settled weather

antidote *noun* substance that acts against the effect of a poison

antifreeze *noun* liquid added to water to lower its freezing point, used in car radiators

antigen *noun* substance, usually a toxin, causing the blood to produce antibodies

anti-globalization *noun* opposition to globalization

antihero antiheroes *noun* central character in a book, film, etc, who lacks the traditional heroic virtues

antihistamine *noun* drug used to treat allergies

antipathy *noun* strong feeling of dislike or hostility towards something or someone

antiperspirant *noun* substance used to reduce or prevent sweating

antipodes *plural noun* **1** any two places diametrically opposite one another on the earth's surface **2 the Antipodes** *Brit* Australia and New Zealand > **antipodean** *adjective*: *our antipodean visitors*

antiquarian *adjective* of or relating to antiquities or rare books: *antiquarian books*

antiquated *adjective* out-of-date

antique *noun* **1** object of an earlier period, valued for its beauty, workmanship or age > *adjective* **2** from or concerning the past **3** old-fashioned

antiquity antiquities *noun* **1** great age **2** distant past, especially the time of the ancient Egyptians, Greeks and Romans **3 antiquities** objects dating from ancient times

antiracism *noun* policy of challenging racism and promoting racial tolerance

anti-Semitism *noun* hatred of or discrimination against Jews > **anti-Semite** *noun* person who hates or discriminates against Jews > **anti-Semitic** *adjective*: *anti-Semitic literature*

antiseptic *adjective* **1** preventing infection by killing germs ▷ *noun* **2** antiseptic substance

antisocial *adjective* **1** avoiding the company of other people **2** (of behaviour) harmful to society

antithesis antitheses *noun formal* **1** exact opposite: *Work is the antithesis of leisure* **2** *literary* placing together of contrasting ideas or words to produce an effect of balance

antitoxin *noun* substance produced by the body to reduce the effect of a poison

antivenene *noun* substance which reduces the effect of a venom, especially a snake venom

antler *noun* branched horn of a male deer

antonym *noun* word that means the opposite of another

anus anuses *noun* hole between the buttocks through which bodily wastes are excreted

anvil *noun* heavy iron block on which metals are hammered into particular shapes

anxiety anxieties *noun* nervousness or worry

anxious *adjective* **1** worried and tense **2** intensely desiring: *She was anxious to have children* > **anxiously** *adverb*

any *adjective, pronoun* **1** one, some or no matter which ▷ *adverb* **2** at all: *it isn't any worse*

anybody *pronoun* any person

anyhow *adverb* **1** in any case **2** in a careless way

anyone *pronoun* **1** any person **2** person of any importance

anything *pronoun* any object, event, situation or action

anyway *adverb* **1** at any rate, nevertheless **2** in any manner

anywhere *adverb* in, at or to any place

Anzac *noun* **1** (in World War 1) a soldier serving with the Australian and New Zealand Army Corps **2** Australian or New Zealand soldier

Anzac Day *noun* 25th April, a public holiday in Australia and New Zealand commemorating the Anzac landing at Gallipoli in 1915

aorta *noun* main artery of the body, carrying oxygen-rich blood from the heart

apart *adverb* **1** to or in pieces ▷ *adverb, adjective* **2** to or at a distance

apartheid *noun* (in South Africa until its abolition in 1994) former official government policy of keeping people of different races apart

apartment *noun* **1** room in a building **2** flat

apathetic *adjective* not interested in anything

apathy *noun* lack of interest or enthusiasm

ape apes aping aped *noun* **1** tailless monkey such as the chimpanzee or gorilla **2** stupid, clumsy or ugly man ▷ *verb* **3** to imitate

aperture *noun* narrow opening or hole

apex apexes or **apices** *noun* **1** highest point of something: *At the apex of the party was its central committee* **2** pointed top or end of something: *the apex of the pyramid*

aphid *noun* small insect which sucks the sap from plants

aphorism *noun* short clever saying expressing a general truth

aphrodisiac *noun* **1** substance that arouses sexual desire ▷ *adjective* **2** arousing sexual desire

apiece *adverb* each

aplomb *noun* relaxed confidence

apocalypse *noun* **1** end of the world **2** event of great destruction **3 the Apocalypse** book of Revelation, the last book of the New Testament > **apocalyptic** *adjective*: *an apocalyptic vision*

apocryphal *adjective* (of a story) generally believed not to have really happened

apolitical *adjective* not interested in politics

apologetic *adjective* showing or expressing regret > **apologetically** *adverb*

apologist *noun* person who formally defends a cause

apologize apologizes apologizing apologized; also spelt **apologise** *verb* to make an apology

apology apologies *noun* **1** expression of regret for wrongdoing **2 apology for** poor example (of)

apostle *noun* **1** ardent supporter of a cause or movement **2 Apostle** one of the twelve disciples chosen by Christ to preach his gospel

apostrophe *noun* punctuation mark (') showing the omission of a letter or letters in a word, *eg don't*, or forming the possessive, *eg Jill's car*

appal appals appalling appalled *verb* to fill with horror

appalling *adjective* so bad as to be shocking

apparatus *noun* equipment for a particular purpose

apparent *adjective* **1** readily seen; obvious **2** seeming as opposed to real > **apparently** *adverb*

apparition *noun* figure, especially a ghostlike one

appeal *verb* **1** to make an earnest request **2** to attract, please or interest **3** *Law* to apply to a higher court to review (a case or issue decided by a lower court) ▷ *noun* **4** earnest request: *an appeal for peace* **5** attractiveness **6** *Law* request for a review of a lower court's decision by a higher court > **appealing** *adjective*

appear *verb* **1** to become visible or present **2** to seem: *He appeared to be searching for something* **3** to be seen in public

appearance *noun* **1** sudden or unexpected arrival of someone or something at a place **2** an act or instance of appearing **3** introduction or invention of something **4** way a person or thing looks

appease **appeases** **appeasing** **appeased** *verb* **1** to pacify (a person) by yielding to his or her demands **2** to satisfy or relieve (a feeling) > **appeasement** *noun* pacification of a person by yielding to his or her demands

append *verb* to add (something) as a supplement, especially at the end of something

appendage *noun* less important part attached to a main part

appendicitis *noun* painful illness in which a person's appendix becomes infected

appendix **appendices** or **appendixes** *noun* **1** separate additional material at the end of a book **2** *Anatomy* short closed tube attached to the large intestine

The plural of the extra section in a book is *appendices*. The plural of the body part is *appendixes*.

appetite *noun* **1** desire for food or drink **2** liking or willingness

appetizer *noun* thing eaten or drunk before a meal in order to stimulate the appetite

appetizing or **appetising** *adjective* (of food) looking and smelling delicious and stimulating the appetite

applaud *verb* **1** to show approval of (something) by clapping your hands **2** to approve strongly of

applause *noun* approval shown by clapping your hands

apple *noun* round firm fleshy fruit that grows on trees

appliance *noun* device with a specific function: *kitchen appliances*

applicable *adjective* relevant or appropriate

applicant *noun* person who applies for something

application *noun* **1** formal request **2** act of applying something to a particular use **3** diligent effort **4** act of putting something, such as a lotion or paint, onto a surface

applied *adjective* (of a skill, science, etc) put to practical use: *applied mathematics*

appliqué *noun* kind of decoration in which one material is cut out and attached to another

apply **applies** **applying** **applied** *verb* **1** to make a formal request **2** to put to practical use: *He applied his mind to the problem* **3** to put onto a surface: *She applied lipstick to her mouth* **4** to be relevant or appropriate: *The legislation applies only to people living in England and Wales* **5** **apply yourself** to concentrate on doing something or thinking about it

appoint *verb* **1** to assign (someone) to a job or position **2** to fix or decide (a time or place for something)

appointment *noun* **1** arrangement to meet a person **2** act of placing someone in a job **3** the job itself; position **4** **appointments** fixtures or fittings

apportion *verb* to divide out in shares

apposite *adjective* appropriate and relevant: *This year her theme was particularly apposite*

apposition *noun* grammatical construction in which two nouns or phrases referring to the same thing are placed one after another without a conjunction: *my son the doctor*

appraisal *noun* an assessment of the worth or quality of a person or thing

appraise appraises appraising appraised *verb* to estimate the value or quality of

appreciable *adjective* large enough to be noticed: *an appreciable difference* > **appreciably** *adverb*

appreciate appreciates appreciating appreciated *verb* **1** to value highly **2** to be aware of and understand **3** to be grateful for **4** to rise in value

appreciation *noun* **1** gratitude **2** awareness and understanding **3** sensitive appreciation of good qualities **4** increase in value

appreciative *adjective* **1** understanding and enthusiastic **2** thankful and grateful > **appreciatively** *adverb*

apprehend *verb formal* **1** to arrest and take into custody **2** to understand (something) fully

apprehensive *adjective* fearful

or anxious about a future event > **apprehension** *noun* **1** dread, anxiety **2** arrest **3** understanding > **apprehensively** *adverb*

apprentice *noun* **1** someone working for a skilled person for a fixed period in order to learn his or her trade ▷ *verb* **2** to take or place (someone) as an apprentice > **apprenticeship** *noun* period of learning a trade from a skilled worker

approach *verb* **1** to come near or nearer (to): *As autumn approached, the trees began to change colour* **2** to make a proposal or suggestion to **3** to begin to deal with (a matter) ▷ *noun* **4** act of coming close or closer: *the approach of spring* **5** suggestion or proposal made to someone **6** road or path that leads to a place **7** approximation

approachable *adjective* friendly and easy to talk to

appropriate appropriates appropriating appropriated *adjective* **1** suitable or fitting *He didn't think jeans were appropriate for a vice-president* ▷ *verb* **2** *formal* to take (something) for yourself **3** *formal* to put (money) aside for a particular purpose: *The cash has already been appropriated for the youth club* > **appropriately** *adverb* > **appropriation** *noun*

approval *noun* **1** agreement given to a plan or request **2** favourable opinion **3** **on approval** (of goods) with an option to be returned without payment if unsatisfactory

approve approves approving approved *verb* **1** to consider good or right **2** to authorize; agree to > **approved** *adjective*: *an approved method* > **approving** *adjective*: *an approving look*

approximate approximates approximating approximated *adjective* **1** almost but not quite exact ▷ *verb* **2 approximate to a** to come close to **b** to be almost the same as > **approximately** *adverb*

approximation *noun* rough or imprecise version, description or estimate

apricot *noun* **1** yellowish-orange juicy fruit like a small peach ▷ *adjective* **2** yellowish-orange

April *noun* **1** fourth month of the year **2 April fool** victim of a practical joke played on April 1 (**April Fools' Day**)

apron *noun* **1** garment worn over the front of the body to protect the clothes **2** area at an airport or hangar for manoeuvring and loading aircraft **3** part of a stage in front of the curtain

apropos *adjective* **1** appropriate ▷ *adverb* **2** by the way **3 apropos of** with regard to

apse *noun* arched or domed recess, especially in a church

apt *adjective* **1** having a specified tendency: *They are apt to jump to the wrong conclusions* **2** suitable: *a very apt description* **3** quick to learn: *an apt pupil* > **aptly** *adverb*

aptitude *noun* natural ability

aqua- *prefix meaning* of or relating to water: *aquatic*

aquamarine *noun* **1** greenish-blue gemstone ▷ *adjective* **2** greenish-blue

aquarium aquariums or **aquaria** *noun* **1** tank in which fish and other underwater creatures are kept **2** building containing such tanks

Aquarius *noun* eleventh sign of the zodiac, represented by a person carrying water

aquatic *adjective* **1** living in or near water **2** done in or on water: *aquatic sports*

aqueduct *noun* long bridge with many arches carrying a water supply over a valley

aquiline *adjective* (of a nose) curved like an eagle's beak

Arab *noun* **1** member of a group of people who used to live in Arabia but who now live throughout the Middle East and North Africa ▷ *adjective* **2** of the Arabs

Arabic *noun* **1** language of the Arabs ▷ *adjective* **2** of Arabic, Arabs or Arabia

arable *adjective* suitable for growing crops on

arbiter *noun* person empowered to judge in a dispute

arbitrary *adjective* based on personal choice or chance, rather than reason > **arbitrarily** *adverb*

arbitrate arbitrates arbitrating arbitrated *verb* to settle a dispute by acting as an impartial referee > **arbitrator** *noun* impartial referee chosen to settle a dispute

arbitration *noun* hearing and settling of a dispute by an impartial referee chosen by both sides

arc *noun* **1** part of a circle or other curve ▷ *verb* **2** to form an arc

▌ Do not confuse the spellings of *arc* and *ark*

arcade *noun* **1** covered passageway lined with shops **2** set of arches and their supporting columns

arcane *adjective* mysterious and secret

arch arches arching arched *noun* **1** curved structure supporting a bridge or roof **2** something curved **3** curved lower part of the foot ▷ *verb* **4** to (cause to) form an arch ▷ *adjective* **5** superior or knowing

6 coyly playful: *an arch smile*

arch- *prefix meaning* chief or principal: *archenemy*

archaeology or **archeology** *noun* study of ancient cultures from their physical remains > **archaeological** *adjective*: *an archaeological dig* > **archaeologist** *noun* person who studies the physical remains of ancient cultures

archaic *adjective* **1** ancient **2** out-of-date

archangel *noun* chief angel

archbishop *noun* chief bishop

archdeacon *noun* Anglican priest ranking just below a bishop

archer *noun* person who shoots with a bow and arrow

archery *noun* sport in which people shoot at a target with a bow and arrow

archetype *noun* **1** perfect specimen: *He is the archetype of a first-class athlete* **2** original model

archipelago archipelagos *noun* group of islands

architect *noun* person qualified to design and supervise the construction of buildings

architecture *noun* **1** style in which a building is designed and built **2** designing and construction of buildings > **architectural** *adjective*: *a unique architectural style*

archive archives archiving archived *noun* (*often plural*) **1** collection of records or documents **2** place where these are kept ▷ *verb* **3** to store (something) in an archive

archway archways *noun* passageway under an arch

Arctic *noun* **1** **the Arctic** area around the North Pole ▷ *adjective* **2** of this region **3** **arctic** *informal* very cold

Arctic Circle *noun* imaginary circle around the northernmost part of the world

ardent *adjective* full of enthusiasm and passion > **ardently** *adverb*

ardour *noun* strong and passionate feeling of love or enthusiasm

arduous *adjective* hard to accomplish and requiring much effort

are *verb* see **be**

area *noun* **1** particular part of a place, country or the world **2** size of a two-dimensional surface **3** subject field

arena *noun* **1** seated enclosure for sports events **2** area of a Roman amphitheatre where gladiators fought **3** sphere of activity: *the political arena*

aren't are not

Argentinian *adjective* **1** belonging or relating to Argentina ▷ *noun* **2** someone from Argentina

arguable *adjective* (of an idea or point) not necessarily true or correct and therefore worth questioning > **arguably** *adverb*

argue argues arguing argued *verb* **1** to try to prove by giving reasons: *She argued that her client had been wrongly accused* **2** to debate **3** to quarrel

argument *noun* **1** quarrel **2** discussion **3** point presented for or against something

argumentative *adjective* always disagreeing with other people

aria *noun* elaborate song for solo voice, especially one from an opera

arid *adjective* **1** parched, dry **2** uninteresting

Aries *noun* first sign of the zodiac, represented by a ram

arise arises arising arose arisen

verb **1** to come about **2** to come into notice **3** *formal* to get up from a sitting, kneeling or lying position

aristocracy aristocracies *noun* highest social class

aristocrat *noun* member of the aristocracy ▷ **aristocratic** *adjective*: *a wealthy, aristocratic family*

arithmetic *noun* **1** calculation by or of numbers ▷ *adjective* **2** of arithmetic > **arithmetical** *adjective* of arithmetic > **arithmetically** *adverb*

ark *noun* Old Testament boat built by Noah, which survived the Flood

Do not confuse the spellings of *arc* and *ark*

arm *noun* **1** either of the upper limbs from the shoulder to the wrist **2** sleeve of a garment **3** side of a chair **4** section of an organization: *the political arm of the organization* **5 arms a** weapons used in a war **b** heraldic symbols of a family or country ▷ *verb* **6** to supply with weapons **7** to prepare (a bomb etc) for use

armada *noun* large number of warships

armadillo armadillos *noun* small South American mammal covered in strong bony plates

Armageddon *noun* **1** *New Testament* final battle between good and evil at the end of the world **2** catastrophic conflict

armament *noun* **1** military weapons **2** preparation for war

armchair *noun* upholstered chair with side supports for the arms

armed *adjective* **1** carrying a weapon or weapons **2** (of an explosive device) prepared for use

armful *noun* as much as can be held in the arms

armhole *noun* opening in a garment through which the arm passes

armistice *noun* agreed suspension of fighting

armorial *adjective formal* concerned with heraldry and coats of arms

armour *noun* **1** metal clothing formerly worn to protect the body in battle **2** metal plating of tanks, warships, etc

armoured *adjective* covered with thick steel for protection from gunfire and other missiles: *an armoured car*

armourer *noun* maker, repairer or keeper of arms or armour

armour-plate *noun* heavy, tough steel used for protecting warships and tanks

armoury armouries *noun* place where weapons are stored

armpit *noun* hollow under the arm at the shoulder

army armies *noun* military land forces of a nation

aroma *noun* pleasant smell > **aromatic** *adjective* having a distinctive pleasant smell

aromatherapy *noun* massage with fragrant oils to relieve tension

arose *verb* past tense of **arise**

around *preposition, adverb* **1** on all sides (of) **2** from place to place (in) **3** somewhere in or near **4** (at) approximately

arouse arouses arousing aroused *verb* **1** to stimulate; stir up **2** to awaken > **arousal** *noun*: *Thinking angry thoughts can provoke strong physical arousal*

arrange arranges arranging arranged *verb* **1** to plan **2** to agree **3** to put in order: *He started to arrange the books in piles* **4** to adapt (music) for performance in a certain way > **arrangement**

noun: travel arrangements; flower arrangement

array arrays arraying arrayed noun **1** impressive display or collection ▷ verb **2** to arrange in order

arrears plural noun **1** money owed: mortgage arrears **2 in arrears** late in paying a debt

arrest verb **1** to take (a person) into custody **2** to stop the movement or development of **3** to catch and hold (the attention) ▷ noun **4** act of taking a person into custody **5** slowing or stopping > **arresting** adjective attracting attention, striking

arrival noun **1** the act or time of arriving **2** person or thing that has just arrived

arrive arrives arriving arrived verb **1** to reach a place or destination **2** to happen or come **3** informal to attain success

arrogant adjective proud and overbearing > **arrogance** noun: the arrogance of those in power > **arrogantly** adverb

arrow noun **1** pointed shaft shot from a bow **2** arrow-shaped sign or symbol used to show direction

arsenal noun place where arms and ammunition are made or stored

arsenic noun highly poisonous substance

arson noun crime of intentionally setting property on fire > **arsonist** noun person who sets property on fire intentionally

art noun **1** creation of works of beauty, especially paintings or sculpture **2** works of art collectively **3** skill **4 arts** literature, music, painting and sculpture, considered together

artefact noun something made by

human beings

artery arteries noun **1** one of the tubes carrying blood from the heart **2** major road or means of communication

artesian well noun well bored vertically so that the water is forced to the surface by natural pressure

artful adjective cunning, wily > **artfully** adverb

arthritis noun painful inflammation of a joint or joints > **arthritic** adjective affected by arthritis

artichoke noun flower head of a thistle-like plant, cooked as a vegetable

article noun **1** written piece in a magazine or newspaper **2** item or object: an article of clothing **3** clause in a document **4** Grammar any of the words the a or an

articulate articulates articulating articulated adjective **1** able to express yourself clearly and coherently ▷ verb **2** to speak or express (something) clearly and coherently > **articulately** adverb > **articulation** noun **1** expressing of an idea in words **2** process of articulating a speech sound

articulated adjective **1** jointed **2** (of a lorry) having two sections, a cab part and a trailer, joined together

artificial adjective **1** not occurring naturally; man-made: artificial colouring **2** made in imitation of something natural **3** not sincere: an artificial smile > **artificially** adverb

artillery noun **1** large, powerful guns **2** branch of the army who use these

artisan noun skilled worker, craftsman

artist noun **1** person who produces works of art, especially paintings or sculpture **2** person skilled at something

artiste *noun* professional entertainer such as a singer or dancer

artistic *adjective* **1** able to create good paintings, sculpture or other works of art **2** concerning or involving art or artists > **artistically** *adverb*

artistry *noun* artistic skill: *his artistry as a cellist*

arty artier artiest *adjective informal* interested in painting, sculpture and other works of art

as *conjunction* **1** while or when **2** in the way that **3** that which: *do as you are told* **4** since or seeing that **5** for instance > *adverb, conjunction* **6** used to indicate amount or extent in comparisons: *He is as tall as you (are)* > *preposition* **7** in the role of; being: *As a mother, I am concerned*

asbestos *noun* fibrous mineral which does not burn

ascend *verb formal* to go or move up

ascendancy *noun formal* condition of being dominant

ascendant *adjective* **1** dominant or influential > *noun* **2 in the ascendant** increasing in power or influence

ascent *noun* upward journey

ascertain *verb formal* to find (something) out definitely

ascetic *adjective* **1** abstaining from worldly pleasures and comforts > *noun* **2** person abstaining from worldly pleasures and comforts

ascribe ascribes ascribing ascribed *verb* **1** to attribute or put (something) down (to): *His stomach pains were ascribed to his intake of pork* **2** to attribute (a particular quality to someone or something)

asexual *adjective* **1** having no sex or sexual organs **2** involving no sexual activity or processes

ash ashes *noun* **1** powdery substance left when something is burnt **2** tree with grey bark **3 ashes** remains after burning, especially of a human body after cremation

ashamed *adjective* feeling shame

ashen *adjective* grey or pale

ashore *adverb* towards or on land

ashtray ashtrays *noun* receptacle for tobacco ash and cigarette butts

Asia *noun* largest continent, with Europe on its western side, the Arctic to the north, the Pacific to the east, and the Indian Ocean to the south. Asia includes several island groups, including Japan, Indonesia and the Philippines

Asian *adjective* **1** of the continent of Asia or any of its peoples or languages > *noun* **2** someone from Asia or a descendant of one

aside *adverb* **1** to one side **2** out of other people's hearing > *noun* **3** remark not meant to be heard by everyone present

ask *verb* **1** to say or write (something) in a form that requires an answer **2** to make a request or demand **3** to invite **4 asking for trouble** doing something that will cause problems

askance *adverb* **look askance at 1** to look at with an oblique glance **2** to regard with suspicion

askew *adverb, adjective* to one side; crooked

asleep *adjective* **1** not awake; sleeping **2** (of limbs) numb

asp *noun* small poisonous snake

asparagus *noun* plant whose shoots are cooked as a vegetable

aspect *noun* **1** feature or element **2** position facing a particular direction: *The southern aspect of the* *cottage faces over fields* **3** appearance or look

aspersion *noun* **cast aspersions on** to make derogatory remarks about

asphalt *noun* black hard tarlike substance used for road surfaces etc

asphyxiate asphyxiates asphyxiating asphyxiated *verb* to suffocate > **asphyxiation** *noun* suffocation

aspirate aspirates aspirating aspirated *Phonetics verb* **1** to pronounce with an *h* sound ▷ *noun* **2** *h* sound

aspiration *noun* strong desire or aim

aspire aspires aspiring aspired *verb* **aspire to** to yearn for: *He aspires to public office* > **aspiring** *adjective*: *an aspiring actor*

aspirin *noun* **1** drug used to relieve pain and fever **2** tablet of this

ass asses *noun* **1** donkey **2** *informal* stupid person

assagai *noun* same as **assegai**

assail *verb formal* to attack violently

assailant *noun* someone who attacks another person

assassin *noun* person who murders a prominent person

assassinate assassinates assassinating assassinated *verb* to murder (a political or religious leader) > **assassination** *noun*: *the assassination of Martin Luther King*

assault *noun* **1** violent attack ▷ *verb* **2** to attack violently

assegai or **assagai** *noun* slender spear used in South Africa

assemble assembles assembling assembled *verb* **1** to collect or congregate **2** to put together the parts of (a machine)

assembly assemblies *noun* **1** assembled group **2** assembling

assent *noun* **1** agreement or consent ▷ *verb* **2** to agree

assert *verb* **1** to declare forcefully **2** to insist upon (your rights etc) **3** **assert yourself** to put yourself forward forcefully

assertion *noun* firm statement, usually made without evidence

assertive *adjective* confident and direct in dealing with others > **assertively** *adverb* > **assertiveness** *noun*: *his lack of assertiveness*

assess assesses assessing assessed *verb* **1** to judge the worth or importance of **2** to estimate the value of (income or property) for taxation purposes > **assessment** *noun* evaluation of someone or something

assessor *noun* person whose job is to assess the value of something

asset *noun* **1** valuable or useful person or thing **2** **assets** property that a person or firm can sell, especially to pay debts

assiduous *adjective* working very hard and paying great attention to detail > **assiduously** *adverb*

assign *verb* **1** to appoint (someone) to a job or task **2** to give a task or duty (to someone) **3** to set apart (a place or time) for a particular event

assignation *noun literary* secret meeting with someone, especially a lover

assignment *noun* **1** job someone is given to do **2** act of assigning

assimilate assimilates assimilating assimilated *verb* **1** to learn and understand (information) **2** to absorb or be absorbed > **assimilation** *noun*: *assimilation of knowledge; assimilation of minority ethnic groups*

assist *verb* to give help or support
> **assistance** *noun* help or support

assistant *noun* 1 helper ▷ *adjective*
2 junior or deputy: *an assistant
teacher*

**associate associates
associating associated** *verb*
1 to connect in the mind 2 to
mix socially ▷ *noun* 3 partner in
business 4 friend or companion
▷ *adjective* 5 having partial rights
or subordinate status: *associate
member*

association *noun* 1 society or club
2 act of associating 3 friendship:
*Their association had to remain a
secret* 4 mental connection of ideas
or feelings

assonance *noun* rhyming of vowel
sounds but not consonants, as in
time and *light*

assorted *adjective* consisting of
various types mixed together:
assorted swimsuits

assortment *noun* group of similar
things that are different sizes and
colours

**assume assumes assuming
assumed** *verb* 1 to take to be true
without proof: *I assumed that he
would turn up* 2 to take (something)
upon yourself: *He assumed command*
3 to pretend: *I assumed indifference*

assumption *noun* 1 belief that
something is true, without
thinking about it 2 taking of power
or responsibility: *their assumption of
power in 1997*

assurance *noun* 1 something
said which is intended to make
people less worried 2 confidence
3 insurance that provides for
events that are certain to happen,
such as death

assure assures assuring assured
verb 1 to promise or guarantee 2 to

convince 3 to make (something)
certain 4 to insure against loss
of life

assuredly *adverb* definitely

asterisk *noun* 1 star-shaped symbol
(*) used in printing or writing to
indicate a footnote etc ▷ *verb* 2 to
mark with an asterisk

astern *adverb* 1 at or towards the
stern of a ship 2 backwards

asteroid *noun* any of the small
planets that orbit the sun between
Mars and Jupiter

asthma *noun* illness causing
difficulty in breathing > **asthmatic**
adjective suffering from asthma

**astonish astonishes astonishing
astonished** *verb* to surprise
greatly > **astonished** *adjective*
greatly surprised > **astonishing**
adjective > **astonishingly** *adverb*
> **astonishment** *noun*: *We won,
much to our astonishment*

astound *verb* to overwhelm with
amazement > **astounded** *adjective*
> **astounding** *adjective*

astray *adverb* off the right path

astride *adjective* 1 with a leg on
either side 2 with legs far apart
▷ *preposition* 3 with a leg on either
side of

astringent *adjective* 1 causing
contraction of body tissue
2 checking the flow of blood from
a cut 3 severe or harsh ▷ *noun*
4 astringent substance

astro- *prefix meaning* involving
the stars and planets: *astronomy;
astronaut*

astrology *noun* study of the alleged
influence of the stars, planets
and moon on human affairs
> **astrologer** *noun* person who
studies astrology > **astrological**
adjective: *astrological predictions*

astronaut *noun* person trained for

travelling in space

astronomer *noun* person who studies or is an expert in astronomy

astronomical *adjective* **1** involved with or relating to astronomy **2** extremely large in amount > **astronomically** *adverb*

astronomy *noun* scientific study of stars and planets

astute *adjective* perceptive or shrewd: *an astute diplomat* > **astutely** *adverb* > **astuteness** *noun*: *the astuteness of his observations*

asunder *adverb literary* into parts or pieces

asylum *noun* **1** refuge or sanctuary **2** *old-fashioned* mental hospital

asymmetrical or **asymmetric** *adjective* unbalanced or with one half not exactly the same as the other half > **asymmetry** *noun* lack of symmetry

at *preposition* **1** indicating location or position: *She met us at the airport* **2** towards or in the direction of: *She was staring at the wall behind him* **3** indicating position in time: *We arrived at 2.30* **4** engaged in: *children at play* **5** during the passing of: *She works at night as a nurse's aide* **6** for or in exchange for: *Crude oil is selling at its highest price for 14 years* **7** indicating the object of an emotion: *I'm angry at him*

ate *verb* past tense of **eat**

atheist *noun* someone who believes there is no God > **atheism** *noun* belief that there is no God > **atheistic** *adjective*: *atheistic philosophers*

athlete *noun* person trained in or good at athletics

athletic *adjective* **1** physically fit or strong **2** relating to an athlete or athletics > **athletically** *adverb*

athletics *plural noun* track-and-field sports such as running, jumping, throwing, etc

Atlantic *noun* ocean separating North and South America from Europe and Africa

atlas atlases *noun* book of maps

atmosphere *noun* **1** mass of gases surrounding a heavenly body, especially the earth **2** air in a particular place: *a musty atmosphere* **3** prevailing tone or mood (of a place etc): *a relaxed atmosphere* **4** mood created by the writer of a novel or play > **atmospheric** *adjective* **1** relating to the atmosphere of a planet **2** (of a place or a piece of music) having a quality which is interesting or exciting and which evokes an emotion

atoll *noun* ring-shaped coral reef enclosing a lagoon

atom *noun* **1** smallest unit of matter which can take part in a chemical reaction **2** very small amount

atom bomb same as **atomic bomb**

atomic *adjective* **1** relating to or using atomic bombs or atomic energy **2** relating to atoms

atomic bomb *noun* bomb in which the energy is provided by nuclear fission

atone atones atoning atoned *verb formal* to make amends (for sin or wrongdoing) > **atonement** *noun* a gesture of atonement

atrocious *adjective* **1** extremely cruel or wicked **2** horrifying or shocking **3** *informal* very bad > **atrociously** *adverb*

atrocity atrocities *noun* act of cruelty

atrophy atrophies atrophying atrophied *formal noun* **1** wasting away of an organ or part ▷ *verb* **2** to waste away

attach attaches attaching
attached *verb* **1** to join, fasten or
connect **2** to attribute or ascribe:
He attaches particular importance to
the proposed sale

attaché *noun* specialist attached to
a diplomatic mission: *the Russian*
Cultural Attaché

attached *adjective* **1** married,
engaged or in an exclusive sexual
relationship **2 attached to** fond of

attachment *noun* **1** affection or
regard for **2** piece of equipment
attached to a tool or machine to
do a particular job **3** *Computing* file
attached to an e-mail message

attack *verb* **1** to launch a physical
assault (against) **2** to criticize: *He*
attacked the government's economic
policies **3** to set about (a job or
problem) with vigour **4** to affect
adversely: *fungal diseases that attack*
crops **5** to take the initiative in
a game or sport ▷ *noun* **6** act of
attacking **7** sudden bout of illness
> **attacker** *noun* person who
attacks someone

attain *verb formal* to achieve,
accomplish or reach: *He*
eventually attained the rank of
major > **attainable** *adjective*: *an*
attainable goal > **attainment** *noun*
accomplishment

attempt *verb* **1** to try, make an
effort: *They attempted to escape*
▷ *noun* **2** effort or endeavour: *He*
made no attempt to go for the ball

attend *verb* **1** to be present at **2** to
go regularly to a school, college, etc
3 to look after: *They were attended*
by numerous servants **4 attend to**
to apply yourself to (something)
> **attendance** *noun* **1** attending
2 number attending

attendant *noun* **1** person who

assists, guides or provides a service
▷ *adjective* **2** accompanying:
increasing road traffic and its
attendant pollution

attention *noun* **1** concentrated
direction of the mind
2 consideration **3** care **4** alert
position in military drill

attentive *adjective* **1** giving
attention: *an attentive*
audience **2** considerately
helpful > **attentively** *adverb*
> **attentiveness** *noun* **1** alertness
2 thoughtfulness

attest *verb* (often followed by *to*) to
affirm or prove the truth of

attic *noun* space or room within the
roof of a house

attire *noun formal* clothing

attitude *noun* **1** way of thinking
and behaving **2** way of sitting,
standing or lying

attorney attorneys *noun* **1** person
legally appointed to act for another
2 *US, S Afr* lawyer

attract *verb* **1** to arouse the interest
or admiration of **2** (of a magnet)
to draw (something) closer by
exerting a force on it

attraction *noun* **1** act or quality
of attracting **2** object or place
people visit for interest or pleasure
3 quality that attracts someone or
something

attractive *adjective* **1** pleasant to
look at or be with **2** interesting
and possibly advantageous: *an*
attractive proposition > **attractively**
adverb > **attractiveness** *noun*: *his*
attractiveness to women

attribute attributes attributing
attributed *verb* **1** **attribute**
something to to regard
something as belonging to or
produced by: *a play attributed*
to Shakespeare ▷ *noun* **2** quality

or feature representative of a person or thing > **attributable** *adjective*: *deaths attributable to smoking* > **attribution** *noun* act of attributing

attrition *noun* constant wearing down to weaken or destroy

attuned *adjective* accustomed or well adjusted (to something)

aubergine *noun* Brit dark purple tropical fruit, cooked and eaten as a vegetable. It is also called an eggplant

auburn *adjective* (of hair) reddish-brown

auction *noun* **1** public sale in which articles are sold to the highest bidder ▷ *verb* **2** to sell (something) by auction

auctioneer *noun* person who conducts an auction

audacious *adjective* recklessly bold or daring: *an audacious escape from jail* > **audaciously** *adverb* > **audacity** *noun* audacious behaviour

audi- *prefix meaning* involving hearing or sound: *audible*; *auditorium*

audible *adjective* loud enough to be heard > **audibility** *noun* > **audibly** *adverb*

audience *noun* **1** group of spectators or listeners **2** private or formal meeting with an important person: *an audience with the Queen*

audio *adjective* **1** of sound or hearing **2** of or for the transmission or reproduction of sound

audit *noun* **1** official examination of business accounts ▷ *verb* **2** to examine (business accounts) officially > **auditor** *noun* person qualified to audit accounts

audition *noun* **1** test of a performer's ability for a particular role or job ▷ *verb* **2** to test (someone) or be tested in an audition

auditorium auditoriums or **auditoria** *noun* area of a concert hall or theatre where the audience sits

augment *verb formal* to increase or enlarge

augur *verb formal* to be a sign that events will go (well or badly)

August *noun* eighth month of the year

auk *noun* northern sea bird with short wings and black-and-white plumage

aunt *noun* **1** father's or mother's sister **2** uncle's wife

au pair *noun* young foreign person who does housework in return for board and lodging

aura *noun* distinctive air or quality of a person or thing

aural *adjective* relating to or done through the sense of hearing

auspices *plural noun* **under the auspices of** *formal* with the support and approval of

auspicious *adjective formal* showing signs of future success: *It was an auspicious start to the month* > **auspiciously** *adverb*

austere *adjective* **1** stern or severe **2** without luxuries **3** severely simple or plain > **austerely** *adverb*

austerity *noun* **1** state of being austere **2** reduced availability of luxuries and consumer goods: *the years of austerity which followed the war*

Australasia *noun* Australia, New Zealand and neighbouring islands in the Pacific > **Australasian** *adjective*

Australia *noun* smallest continent and the largest island in the world, situated between the Indian Ocean and the Pacific

Australia Day *noun Aust* public holiday on 26th January

Australian *adjective* 1 belonging or relating to Australia ▷ *noun* 2 someone from Australia

Austrian *adjective* 1 belonging or relating to Austria ▷ *noun* 2 someone from Austria

authentic *adjective* known to be real; genuine > **authentically** *adverb* > **authenticity** *noun*: *doubts cast on the painting's authenticity*

authenticate authenticates authenticating authenticated *verb* to establish (something) as genuine > **authentication** *noun* process of checking that something is genuine

author *noun* 1 writer of a book etc 2 originator or creator

Use *author* to talk about both men and women writers, as *authoress* is now felt to be insulting

authoritarian *adjective* insisting on strict obedience to authority: *thirty years of authoritarian government* > **authoritarianism** *noun* 1 state of being authoritarian 2 belief that the state has a right to control its citizens' lives

authoritative *adjective* 1 recognized as being reliable 2 possessing authority > **authoritatively** *adverb*

authority authorities *noun* 1 power to command or control others: *the authority of the state* 2 *Brit* local government department: *local health authorities* 3 expert in a particular field: *the world's leading authority on fashion* 4 **the authorities** people with the power to make decisions: *A*

third escapee turned himself in to the authorities

authorize authorizes authorizing authorized; also spelt **authorise** *verb* 1 to give authority to 2 to give permission for > **authorization** *noun*: *authorization to use military force*

autism *noun* disorder characterized by lack of response to people and limited ability to communicate > **autistic** *adjective* suffering from autism

auto- *prefix meaning* self-: *autobiography*

autobiography autobiographies *noun* account of a person's life written by that person > **autobiographical** *adjective* (of a piece of writing) relating to events in the life of the author

autocrat *noun* 1 ruler with absolute authority 2 dictatorial person > **autocratic** *adjective* of rule by an autocrat

Autocue® *noun* electronic television prompting device displaying a speaker's script, unseen by the audience

autograph *noun* 1 handwritten signature of a (famous) person ▷ *verb* 2 to write your signature on or in

automate automates automating automated *verb* to make (a manufacturing process) automatic > **automation** *noun* use of automatic methods to control industrial processes

automatic *adjective* 1 (of a device) operating mechanically by itself 2 (of a process) performed by automatic equipment 3 done without conscious thought 4 (of a firearm) self-loading 5 occurring as a necessary consequence: *The penalty for murder is an automatic life sentence* ▷ *noun* **6** self-loading firearm **7** vehicle in which the gears change automatically as the vehicle's speed changes > **automatically** *adverb*

automaton automatons or **automata** *noun* **1** robot **2** person who acts mechanically

automobile *noun US* motor car

autonomous *adjective* **1** having self-government **2** independent of others > **autonomy** *noun* self-government

autopsy autopsies *noun* examination of a corpse to determine the cause of death

autumn *noun* season between summer and winter > **autumnal** *adjective*: *the autumnal colour of the trees*

auxiliary auxiliaries *adjective* **1** secondary or supplementary: *auxiliary fuel tanks* **2** supporting ▷ *noun* **3** person or thing that supplements or supports: *nursing auxiliaries*

auxiliary verb *noun* verb used to form the tense, voice or mood of another, such as *will* in *I will go*

avail *verb* **1** to be of use or advantage (to) **2** **avail yourself of** to make use of ▷ *noun* **3** use or advantage: *to no avail*

available *adjective* **1** obtainable or accessible **2** ready for work or free for people to talk to > **availability** *noun*: *the easy availability of guns*

avalanche *noun* **1** mass of snow or ice falling down a mountain **2** sudden overwhelming quantity of anything

avant-garde *noun* **1** group of innovators, especially in the arts ▷ *adjective* **2** innovative and progressive

avarice *noun formal* greed for wealth and possessions > **avaricious** *adjective* greedy for wealth and possessions

avenge avenges avenging avenged *verb* to take revenge in retaliation for (harm done) or on behalf of (a person harmed) > **avenger** *noun*

avenue *noun* **1** wide street **2** road between two rows of trees **3** means of doing something: *We are exploring a number of avenues*

average averages averaging averaged *noun* **1** typical or normal amount or quality **2** result obtained by adding quantities together and dividing the total by the number of quantities **3** **on average** usually or typically: *Men are, on average, taller than women* ▷ *adjective* **4** usual or typical: *the average American teenager* **5** calculated as an average ▷ *verb* **6** to calculate the average of **7** to amount to as an average: *Monthly sales averaged more than 110,000*

averse *adjective* **averse to** opposed to or against: *He's not averse to publicity*

aversion *noun* **1** strong dislike **2** person or thing disliked

avert *verb* **1** to turn away: *He had to avert his eyes* **2** to ward off: *a final attempt to avert war*

aviary aviaries *noun* large cage or enclosure for birds

aviation *noun* art or science of flying aircraft

aviator *noun old-fashioned* pilot of an aircraft

avid *adjective* **1** keen or enthusiastic **2** greedy (for) > **avidly** *adverb*

avocado avocados *noun* pear-shaped tropical fruit with a leathery green skin and yellowish-green flesh

avoid *verb* **1** to prevent from happening **2** to refrain from doing **3** to keep away from > **avoidable** *adjective*: *This accident was avoidable* > **avoidance** *noun*: *the avoidance of stress*

avowed *adjective formal* **1** openly declared: *an avowed supporter of vegetarianism* **2** (of a belief or aim) strongly held: *the council's avowed intention to stamp on racism* > **avowedly** *adverb*

avuncular *adjective* friendly and helpful in manner towards younger people, rather like an uncle

await *verb* **1** to wait for **2** to be in store for

awake awakes awaking awoke awoken *verb* **1** to emerge or rouse from sleep **2** to become or cause to become alert ▷ *adjective* **3** not sleeping **4** alert

awaken *verb* **1** to awake **2** to cause (someone) to be aware of

award *verb* **1** to give (something, such as a prize) formally ▷ *noun* **2** something awarded, such as a prize

aware *adjective* having knowledge; informed > **awareness** *noun*: *an awareness of green issues*

awash *adverb, adjective* washed over by water

away *adverb* **1** from a place: *go away* **2** to another place: *put that gun away* **3** out of existence: *fade away* **4** continuously: *laughing away* ▷ *adjective* **5** not present **6** distant: *two miles away* **7** *Sport* played on an opponent's ground

awe *noun formal* wonder and respect mixed with dread

awesome *adjective* **1** inspiring awe **2** *informal* excellent or outstanding

awful *adjective* **1** very bad or unpleasant **2** *informal* very great: *It took an awful lot of courage* > **awfully** *adverb* **1** in an unpleasant way **2** *informal* very

awkward *adjective* **1** clumsy or ungainly **2** embarrassed **3** difficult **4** inconvenient > **awkwardly** *adverb* > **awkwardness** *noun* **1** shyness **2** clumsiness

awning *noun* canvas roof supported by a frame to give protection against the weather

awoke *verb* past tense of **awake**

awoken *verb* past participle of **awake**

awry *adverb, adjective* **1** with a twist to one side; askew **2** wrong or not as planned: *Why had their plans gone so badly awry?*

axe axes axing axed *noun* **1** tool with a sharp blade for felling trees or chopping wood **2** *informal* dismissal from employment etc ▷ *verb* **3** *informal* to dismiss (employees), restrict (expenditure) or terminate (a project)

axiom *noun* **1** generally accepted principle **2** self-evident statement > **axiomatic** *adjective* self-evident

axis axes *noun* **1** (imaginary) line round which a body can rotate or about which an object or geometrical figure is symmetrical **2** one of two fixed lines on a graph, against which quantities or positions are measured

axle *noun* shaft on which a wheel or pair of wheels turns

ayatollah *noun* Islamic religious leader in Iran

aye or **ay** *interjection* **1** yes ▷ *noun* **2** affirmative vote or voter

azure *literary noun* **1** deep blue colour of a clear blue sky ▷ *adjective* **2** deep blue

BA BAs *abbreviation* Bachelor of Arts

babble babbles babbling babbled
verb to talk excitedly or foolishly

baboon *noun* large monkey with a
pointed face and a long tail

baby babies *noun* **1** very young
child; infant **2** *informal* sweetheart
▷ *adjective* **3** comparatively small of
its type > **babyhood** *noun* period
of being a baby > **babyish** *adjective*
immature

**baby-sit baby-sits baby-sitting
baby-sat** *verb* to take care of a child
while the parents are out > **baby-
sitter** *noun* person who baby-sits
> **baby-sitting** *noun*

bach baches baching bached
noun **1** NZ small holiday cottage
▷ *verb* **2** *Aust, NZ informal* to live and
keep house on your own, especially
when unused to it

bachelor *noun* unmarried man

back *noun* **1** rear part of the human
body, from the neck to the pelvis;
also the corresponding part of an
animal's body **2** part or side of an
object opposite the front **3** *Ball
games* defensive player or position
▷ *verb* **4** to move (a car) backwards
5 to provide money for (a person
or organization) **6** to bet on the
success of (a competitor) **7 back
onto** to have the back facing
towards (something) ▷ *adjective*
8 at, to or towards the rear ▷ *adverb*
9 at, to or towards the rear **10** to
or towards the original starting
point or condition > **back down**
verb (often followed by *on*, *over*) to
withdraw an earlier claim, demand
or committment > **back out** *verb* to
pull out (of an arrangement) > **back
up** *verb* to support (someone)

backbone *noun* **1** spinal column
2 strength of character

**backdate backdates backdating
backdated** *verb* to make (a
document or arrangement) valid
from an earlier date than the one on
which it is completed

backdrop *noun* the background to a
situation or event

backer *noun* person who provides
financial support

**backfire backfires backfiring
backfired** *verb* **1** (of a plan) to have
the opposite result to the one
intended; fail **2** (of an engine) to
make a loud noise like an explosion

background *noun* **1** events or
circumstances that help to explain
something **2** person's social
circumstances, education and
experience **3** part of a scene or
picture furthest from the viewer

backing *noun* **1** support or help
2 music that accompanies a pop
song

backlash *noun* sudden and hostile
reaction

backlog *noun* accumulation of
things still to be done

backpack *noun* large bag carried
on the back

backside *noun informal* buttocks

backward *adjective* **1** directed

towards the back **2** (of a country
or society) not having modern
industries or technology **3** (of a
child) unable to learn as quickly as
other children ▷ *adverb* **4** the same
as **backwards** > **backwardness**
noun being backward

backwards *adverb* **1** in reverse **2** in
the reverse direction **3** behind

bacon *noun* salted or smoked
pig meat

bacteria *plural noun* very tiny
organisms which can cause disease
> **bacterial** *adjective: a bacterial
infection*

▌The word *bacteria* is plural. The
singular form is *bacterium*

bad worse worst *adjective* **1** of poor
quality **2** lacking skill or talent
3 harmful **4** immoral or evil **5** rotten
or decayed **6** unpleasant > **badly**
adverb > **badness** *noun*

bade *verb* a past tense of **bid**

badge *noun* piece of metal, plastic
or cloth worn to show membership
of an organization, support for a
cause, etc

badger *noun* **1** burrowing animal
of Europe, Asia and North America
with a black and white head ▷ *verb*
2 to pester or harass

badminton *noun* game played with
rackets and a shuttlecock, which is
hit back and forth over a high net

Bafana bafana *plural noun* S Afr
South African national soccer team

baffle baffles baffling baffled
verb to perplex or puzzle > **baffled**
adjective > **baffling** *adjective*

bag *noun* container for carrying
things in

bagel *noun* hard ring-shaped
bread roll

baggage *noun* suitcases packed
for a journey

baggy baggier baggiest *adjective*

(of clothes) hanging loosely

bagpipes *plural noun* musical wind
instrument with reed pipes and an
inflatable bag

bail *noun Law* money deposited with
a court as security for a person's
reappearance in court > **bail out**
verb **1** to remove (water) from a boat
2 to make an emergency parachute
jump from an aircraft

bailiff *noun* **1** law officer who makes
sure that the decisions of a court
are obeyed **2** landlord's agent

bait *noun* **1** piece of food put on a hook
or in a trap in order to catch fish or
animals ▷ *verb* **2** to put a piece of food
on or in **3** to persecute or tease

baize *noun* woollen fabric, usually
green, used to cover billiard and
card tables

bake bakes baking baked *verb*
1 to cook (food) by dry heat, as in an
oven **2** to heat (earth or clay) until
it hardens

baker *noun* person whose business
is to make or sell bread, cakes, etc
> **bakery** *noun* place where bread,
cakes, etc are baked or sold

bakkie *noun* S Afr small truck

balaclava *noun* close-fitting
woollen hood covering your head
and neck but leaving your face
uncovered

**balance balances balancing
balanced** *noun* **1** state in which
a weight or amount is evenly
distributed **2** amount that
remains: *the balance of what you owe*
3 difference between the credits
and debits of an account ▷ *verb* **4** to
remain steady **5** to equalize the
money going into and coming out
of (an account)

balcony balconies *noun* **1** platform
on the outside of a building with
a rail along the outer edge **2** area

of upstairs seats in a theatre or cinema

bald *adjective* **1** having little or no hair on the scalp **2** plain or blunt > **baldly** *adverb* plainly or bluntly > **baldness** *noun* being bald

bale bales baling baled *noun* large bundle of hay or paper tightly bound together > **bale out** *verb* same as **bail out**

balk or **baulk** *verb* (followed by *at*) to object to and refuse to do (something)

ball *noun* **1** round or nearly round object, especially one used in games **2** large formal social event at which people dance

ballad *noun* **1** long song or poem that tells a story **2** slow romantic pop song

ballast *noun* substance, such as sand, used to stabilize a ship when it is not carrying cargo

ballerina *noun* female ballet dancer

ballet *noun* **1** classical style of expressive dancing based on conventional steps **2** theatrical performance of this

balloon *noun* **1** inflatable rubber bag used as a plaything or decoration **2** large bag inflated with air or gas, that travels through the air with passengers in a basket underneath

ballot *noun* **1** method of voting in which other people do not see how you vote **2** actual vote or paper indicating a person's choice ▷ *verb* **3** to ask for a vote from (people)

ballpoint *noun* pen with a tiny ball bearing as a writing point

ballroom *noun* very large room used for dancing or formal balls

balm *noun* sweet-smelling soothing ointment

balmy balmier balmiest *adjective* (of weather) mild and pleasant

balsa *noun* very light wood from a tropical American tree

balustrade *noun* railing or wall on a balcony or staircase

bamboo *noun* tall tropical plant with hard hollow stems used for making furniture

ban bans banning banned *verb* **1** to prohibit or forbid (something) officially ▷ *noun* **2** official prohibition

banal *adjective* ordinary and unoriginal > **banality** *noun* being ordinary and unoriginal

banana *noun* long curved fruit with a yellow skin

band *noun* **1** group of musicians playing together **2** group of people with a common purpose **3** strip of some material, used to hold objects **4** *Physics* range of frequencies or wavelengths between two limits

bandage bandages bandaging bandaged *noun* **1** piece of material used to cover a wound or wrap an injured limb ▷ *verb* **2** to cover (a wound) with a bandage

bandicoot *noun* small Australian marsupial with a long pointed muzzle and a long tail

bandit *noun* robber, especially a member of an armed gang

bandstand *noun* roofed outdoor platform for a band

bandwagon *noun* **jump on the bandwagon** to become involved in something that seems assured of success

bandy bandies bandying bandied *verb* to use (a name, term, etc) frequently

bane *noun* person or thing that causes misery or distress

bang *noun* **1** short loud explosive noise **2** hard blow or loud knock ▷ *verb* **3** to hit or knock (something), especially with a loud noise **4** to close (a door) noisily

Bangladeshi Bangladeshis *adjective* **1** belonging or relating to Bangladesh ▷ *noun* **2** person from Bangladesh

bangle *noun* decorative ring worn round the arm or the ankle

banish banishes banishing banished *verb* **1** to send (someone) into exile **2** to get rid of (something) > **banishment** *noun*

banisters *plural noun* railing supported by posts on a staircase

banjo banjos or **banjoes** *noun* guitar-like musical instrument with a circular body

bank *noun* **1** business that looks after people's money **2** any supply, store or reserve **3** sloping side of an area of raised ground **4** sloping ground at the side of a river **5** long row or mass of something ▷ *verb* **6** to deposit (cash or cheques) in a bank **7** (of an aircraft) to tip to one side on turning > **banker** *noun* manager or owner of a bank > **banking** *noun* business activity of banks > **bank on** *verb* to rely on

bank holiday bank holidays *noun* public holiday, when banks are officially closed

banknote *noun* piece of paper money

bankrupt *noun* **1** person declared by a court to be unable to pay his or her debts ▷ *adjective* **2** financially ruined ▷ *verb* **3** to make (someone) bankrupt > **bankruptcy** *noun* bankrupt state

banksia *noun* Australian evergreen tree or shrub with yellow flowers

banner *noun* **1** long strip of cloth with a message or slogan on it **2** placard carried in a demonstration or procession

3 advertisement that extends across the top of a web page

bannisters *plural noun* same as **banisters**

banquet *noun* grand formal dinner

banter *noun* teasing or joking conversation

baobab *noun* small fruit tree that grows in Africa and northern Australia

baptism *noun* ceremony in which someone is baptized

Baptist *noun* member of a Protestant church that believes in adult baptism by immersion

baptize baptizes baptizing baptized; also spelt **baptise** *verb* to sprinkle water on (someone) or immerse (someone) in water, as a sign that he or she has become a Christian

bar bars barring barred *noun* **1** counter or room where alcoholic drinks are served **2** long straight piece of metal, wood, etc **3** solid, usually rectangular block, of any material: *a bar of soap* **4** *Music* one of the many very short sections into which any piece of music is divided. Each bar in a piece usually contains the same set number of beats **5** unit of atmospheric pressure **6 the Bar** profession of a barrister ▷ *verb* **7** to secure (a door) with a bar **8** to obstruct (the way) **9** to ban or forbid ▷ *preposition* **10** (also **barring**) except for

barb *noun* point facing in the opposite direction to the main point of a fish-hook etc

barbarian *noun* member of a wild or uncivilized people

barbaric *adjective* cruel or brutal > **barbarity** *noun*

barbecue barbecues barbecuing barbecued *noun* **1** grill on which food is cooked over hot charcoal, usually outdoors **2** outdoor party at which barbecued food is served ▷ *verb* **3** to cook (food) on a barbecue

barbed *adjective* unkind or spiteful remark that appears innocent

barbed wire *noun* strong wire with protruding sharp points

barber *noun* person who cuts men's hair and shaves beards

bar code *noun* arrangement of numbers and lines on a package, which can be electronically scanned at a checkout to give the price of the goods

bard *noun literary* poet

bare bares baring bared *adjective* **1** unclothed or naked **2** without the natural or usual covering **3** empty **4** plain, simple and unadorned **5** just sufficient ▷ *verb* **6** to uncover

barefoot *adjective, adverb* not wearing anything on the feet

barely *adverb* only just

bargain *noun* **1** agreement establishing what each party will give, receive or perform in a matter that involves them both **2** something bought or offered at a low price ▷ *verb* **3** to negotiate the terms of an agreement > **bargain for** *verb* to anticipate (something) or take (something) into account

barge barges barging barged *noun* **1** flat-bottomed boat used to transport freight ▷ *verb* **2** *informal* to push violently

baritone *noun* man with a fairly deep singing voice, lower than a tenor but higher than a base

bark *noun* **1** loud harsh cry of a dog **2** tough outer layer of a tree ▷ *verb* **3** (of a dog) to make its typical cry **4** to shout (something) in an angry tone

barley *noun* tall grasslike plant grown for grain

bar mitzvah bar mitzvahs *noun* ceremony that takes place on a Jewish boy's 13th birthday, after which he is regarded as an adult

barmy barmier barmiest *adjective informal* insane

barn *noun* large building on a farm used for storing grain

barnacle *noun* shellfish that lives attached to rocks, ship bottoms, etc

barometer *noun* instrument that measures air pressure and shows when the weather is changing

baron *noun* member of the lowest rank of nobility > **baronial** *adjective* of or relating to a baron

baroness baronesses *noun* woman who has the rank of baron or who is the wife of a baron

baronet *noun* man holding the lowest hereditary title of honour

baroque *noun* **1** highly ornamental style of art, architecture or music from the late 16th to the early 18th century ▷ *adjective* **2** highly ornamental in style

barracks *plural noun* building where soldiers live

barracuda *noun* large tropical sea fish with sharp teeth

barrage *noun* **1** continuous delivery of questions, complaints, etc **2** continuous artillery fire **3** artificial barrier across a river to control the water level

barrel *noun* **1** cylindrical container with rounded sides and flat ends **2** tube-shaped part of a gun through which bullets are fired

barren *adjective* **1** (of a woman or female animal) incapable of having babies or young; infertile **2** (of land) unable to support the growth of crops, fruit, etc

barricade barricades barricading barricaded noun **1** barrier, especially one put up hastily for defence ▷ verb **2** to put up a barricade across (an entrance)

barrier noun anything that prevents access, progress or agreement

barrister noun Brit, Aust, NZ lawyer qualified to plead in a higher court

barrow noun **1** wheelbarrow **2** movable stall used by street traders

barter verb **1** to trade (goods) in exchange for other goods ▷ noun **2** trade by the exchange of goods

base bases basing based noun **1** bottom or supporting part of anything **2** centre of operations, organization or supply **3** Chemistry compound that reacts with an acid to form a salt ▷ verb **4** **base something on** or **upon** to make up the basic elements of something using **5** (followed by at, in) to position or place (someone) somewhere ▷ adjective **6** dishonourable or immoral **7** of inferior quality or value

baseball noun team game in which runs are scored by hitting a ball with a bat then running round four bases

basement noun partly or wholly underground storey of a building

bases noun the plural of **basis**

bash bashes bashing bashed informal verb **1** to hit (someone) violently or forcefully ▷ noun **2** heavy blow

bashful adjective shy or modest

basic adjective **1** of or forming a base or basis **2** elementary or simple > **basically** adverb: It's basically a vegan diet > **basics** plural noun essential main principles, facts, etc

basil noun herb used for flavouring in cooking

basilica noun rectangular church with a rounded end and two aisles

basin noun **1** round open container **2** sink for washing the hands and face **3** bowl of land from which water runs into the river

basis bases noun essential main principle from which something is started or developed

bask verb to lie in or be exposed to something, especially pleasant warmth

basket noun container made of thin strips of cane woven together

basketball noun team game in which points are scored by throwing the ball through a high horizontal hoop

bass¹ basses noun **1** man with a very deep singing voice **2** musical instrument that provides the rhythm and lowest part in the harmonies

bass² bass or **basses** noun edible sea fish

basset hound noun smooth-haired dog with short legs and long ears

bassoon noun low-pitched woodwind instrument

bastard noun **1** offensive despicable person **2** old-fashioned person whose parents were not married when he or she was born

baste bastes basting basted verb to moisten (meat) during cooking with hot fat

bastion noun something that protects a system or way of life

bat bats batting batted noun **1** any of various types of club used to hit the ball in certain sports **2** mouselike flying animal, active at night ▷ verb **3** to strike (the ball) with or as if with a bat

batch batches *noun* group of people or things dealt with at the same time

bated *adjective* **with bated breath** in suspense or fear

bath *noun* **1** large container in which to wash the body **2** act of washing in such a container **3** **baths** public swimming pool ▷ *verb* **4** to wash in a bath

bathe bathes bathing bathed *verb* **1** to swim in open water for pleasure **2** to apply liquid to (the skin or a wound) in order to cleanse or soothe **3** (followed by *in*) to fill (a place) with something: *bathed in sunlight* > **bather** *noun* person who swims > **bathing** *noun* swimming or washing

bathroom *noun* room with a bath or shower, washbasin and, usually, a toilet

baton *noun* **1** thin stick used by the conductor of an orchestra **2** short stick passed from one runner to another in a relay race **3** police officer's truncheon

batsman batsmen *noun* Cricket person who bats or specializes in batting

battalion *noun* army unit consisting of three or more companies

batten *noun* strip of wood fixed to something, especially to hold it in place > **batten down** *verb* to secure (sonething) with battens

batter *verb* **1** to hit (someone) repeatedly ▷ *noun* **2** mixture of flour, eggs and milk, used in cooking > **battering** *noun*

battery batteries *noun* **1** device that produces electricity in a torch, radio, etc **2** group of heavy guns operating as a single unit ▷ *adjective* **3** (of hens) kept in small cages for the mass production of eggs

battle battles battling battled *noun* **1** fight between large armed forces **2** conflict or struggle ▷ *verb* **3** to struggle

battlefield *noun* place where a battle is fought

battlement *noun* wall with gaps along the top for firing guns or arrows through

battleship *noun* large heavily armoured warship

batty battier battiest *adjective* informal eccentric or crazy

bauble *noun* trinket of little value

bawdy bawdier bawdiest *adjective* (of writing etc) containing humorous references to sex

bawl *verb* to shout or weep noisily

bay bays baying bayed *noun* **1** stretch of coastline that curves inwards; inlet **2** area set aside for a particular purpose: *loading bay* **3** Mediterranean laurel tree **4** reddish-brown horse ▷ *adjective* **5** (of a horse) reddish-brown ▷ *verb* **6** to make a deep howling noise

bayonet *noun* sharp blade that can be fixed to the end of a rifle

bazaar *noun* **1** sale in aid of charity **2** market area, especially in Eastern countries

BC *abbreviation* before Christ

be *verb* **1** to exist or live **2** used to link the subject of a sentence and its complement: *John is a musician* **3** used to form continuous tenses: *The man is running* **4** used to form the passive voice: *He was brought up by his grandparents*

be- *prefix* (forming verbs from nouns) to treat as: *to befriend*

beach beaches *noun* area of sand or pebbles on a shore

beacon *noun* fire or light on a hill or

tower, used as a warning

bead noun **1** small piece of plastic, wood, etc, pierced for threading on a string to form a necklace etc **2** small drop of moisture

beady adjective (of eyes) small, round and glittering

beagle noun small hound with short legs and drooping ears

beak noun **1** projecting horny jaws of a bird **2** informal nose

beaker noun **1** large drinking cup **2** glass container with a lip that is used in laboratories

beam noun **1** broad smile **2** ray of light **3** long thick piece of wood, metal, etc, used in building ▷ verb **4** to smile broadly

bean noun seed or pod of various plants, eaten as a vegetable or used to make coffee etc

bear bears bearing bore borne verb **1** to support (something) or hold (something) up **2** to give birth to (a baby); see also **born 3** to tolerate or endure (someone or something) **4** to hold (something) in the mind ▷ noun **5** large strong wild animal with a shaggy coat > **bearable** adjective able to be tolerated > **bearer** noun person who carries or presents something

beard noun hair growing on the lower parts of a man's face > **bearded** adjective having a beard

bearing noun **1** relevance **2** way in which a person moves or stands

beast noun **1** large wild animal **2** brutal or uncivilized person

beastly beastlier beastliest adjective unpleasant or disagreeable

beat beats beating beat beaten verb **1** to hit (someone or something) hard and repeatedly **2** to move (wings) up and down **3** (of a heart) to pump blood with

a regular rhythm **4** to stir or mix (eggs, cream or butter) vigorously **5** to overcome or defeat ▷ noun **6** regular pumping action of the heart **7** area patrolled by a particular police officer **8** main rhythm of a piece of music > **beater** noun tool for beating eggs, cream or butter > **beating** noun > **beat up** verb to injure (someone) by repeated blows or kicks

beaut Aust, NZ informal noun **1** outstanding person or thing ▷ adjective **2** good, excellent

beautiful adjective very attractive or pleasant > **beautifully** adverb

beauty beauties noun **1** combination of all the qualities of a person or thing that delight the senses and mind **2** very attractive woman **3** informal something outstanding of its kind

beaver noun animal with a big flat tail and webbed hind feet

became verb past tense of **become**

because conjunction **1** on account of the fact that **2 because of** on account of

beck noun **at someone's beck and call** having to be constantly available to do as someone asks

beckon verb (followed by to) to summon (someone) with a gesture

become becomes becoming became become verb **1** to come to be (something) **2** to suit (someone) **3 become of** to happen to

bed noun **1** piece of furniture for sleeping on **2** area of ground in which plants are grown **3** bottom of a river, lake or sea **4** layer of rock

bedclothes plural noun sheets and covers that are used on a bed

bedding noun sheets and covers that are used on a bed

bedlam noun noisy confused

situation

bedpan *noun* container used as a toilet by people too ill to get out of bed

bedraggled *adjective* untidy, wet or dirty

bedridden *adjective* confined to bed because of illness or old age

bedrock *noun* 1 solid rock beneath the surface soil 2 basic facts or principles

bedroom *noun* room used for sleeping in

bedspread *noun* cover put over a bed, on top of the sheets and blankets

bedstead *noun* metal or wooden frame of an old-fashioned bed

bee *noun* winged insect that makes wax and honey

beech beeches *noun* tree with a smooth greyish bark

beef *noun* flesh of a cow, bull or ox

beefy beefier beefiest *adjective* 1 like beef 2 *informal* strong and muscular

beehive *noun* structure in which bees live

beeline *noun* **make a beeline for** *informal* to go to (a place) as quickly and directly as possible

been *verb* past participle of **be**

beer *noun* alcoholic drink brewed from malt and hops

beet *noun* plant with an edible root and leaves, such as *sugar beet* or *beetroot*

beetle *noun* insect with a hard wing cover on its back

beetroot *noun* type of beet plant with a dark red root

befall befalls befalling befell befallen *verb old-fashioned* to happen to (someone)

before *conjunction, preposition, adverb* 1 earlier than or prior to

2 previously: *I'd never been there before* 3 in front of 4 in preference to or rather than: *death before dishonour*

beforehand *adverb* in advance

befriend *verb* to become friends with (someone)

beg begs begging begged *verb* 1 to ask for money or food, especially in the street 2 to ask (someone) anxiously to do something

began *verb* past tense of **begin**

beggar *noun* person who lives by begging

begin begins beginning began begun *verb* to start or commence > **beginner** *noun* person who has just started learning to do something > **beginning** *noun*

begonia *noun* tropical plant with brightly coloured flowers

begrudge begrudges begrudging begrudged *verb* to be envious of and resent (someone) for something that he or she possesses

begun *verb* past participle of **begin**

behalf *noun* **on behalf of** in the interest of or for the benefit of

behave behaves behaving behaved *verb* 1 to act in a particular way 2 to conduct (oneself) properly

behaviour *noun* manner of behaving

behead *verb* to cut off the head of

beheld *verb* past of **behold**

behind *preposition* 1 at the back of: *behind the wall* 2 not as far advanced as: *behind schedule* 3 responsible for or causing: *the reasons behind her departure* 4 supporting: *The whole country was behind him* ▷ *adverb* 5 remaining after other people have gone: *He stayed behind to clear up* 6 not up to date: *He's behind with his rent* ▷ *noun* 7 *informal* buttocks

behold beholds beholding beheld *verb old-fashioned* to look at

> **beholder** *noun*

beige *adjective* pale creamy-brown

being *noun* **1** state or fact of existing **2** something that exists or is thought to exist **3** human being ▷ *verb* **4** present participle of **be**

belated *adjective* late or too late > **belatedly** *adverb*

belch belches belching belched *verb* **1** to expel wind from the stomach noisily through the mouth **2** (of smoke or fire) to come out in large amounts: *smoke belched from the factory* ▷ *noun* **3** act of belching

beleaguered *adjective* **1** struggling against difficulties or criticism **2** besieged by an enemy

belfry belfries *noun* part of a tower where bells are hung

Belgian *adjective* **1** belonging or relating to Belgium ▷ *noun* **2** person from Belgium

belief *noun* **1** faith or confidence **2** opinion **3** principle accepted as true, often without proof

believe believes believing believed *verb* **1** to accept (something) as true or real **2** to think, assume or suppose (something) > **believable** *adjective* > **believe in** *verb* to be convinced of the truth or existence of > **believer** *noun*

belittle belittles belittling belittled *verb* to treat (someone) as having little value or importance

bell *noun* **1** hollow, usually metal, cup-shaped or round instrument with a swinging piece inside that causes a ringing sound when it strikes against the sides as the bell is moved **2** device that rings or buzzes as a signal

bellbird *noun* Australian or New Zealand bird that makes a sound like a bell

belligerent *adjective* aggressive and keen to start a fight > **belligerence** *noun* aggressiveness > **belligerently** *adverb* aggressively

bellow *verb* **1** to make a low deep cry like that of a bull **2** to shout (something) in anger ▷ *noun* **3** loud deep roar

bellows *plural noun* piece of equipment used for blowing air into a fire to make it burn more fiercely

belly bellies *noun* **1** part of the body that contains the intestines **2** stomach **3** front, lower or inner part of something

belong *verb* **1** (followed by *to*) to be the property (of someone) **2** (usually followed by *to*) to be a part or member (of something) **3** to have a rightful place; go: *It belongs in the kitchen* > **belongings** *plural noun* personal possessions

beloved *adjective* dearly loved

below *preposition, adverb* at or to a position lower (than); underneath

belt *noun* **1** band of cloth, leather, etc, usually worn round the waist **2** long narrow area: *a belt of trees* **3** circular strip of rubber that drives moving parts in a machine ▷ *verb* **4** *informal* to hit (someone) very hard **5** *informal* to move very fast

bemused *adjective* puzzled or confused

bench benches *noun* **1** long seat **2** long narrow work table **3** **the bench** judge or magistrate sitting in court, or judges and magistrates collectively

bend bends bending bent *verb* **1** to form a curve or cause (something) to form a curve **2** (often followed by *down, forward etc*) to move the head and shoulders forwards and downwards ▷ *noun* **3** curved part

bene- *prefix meaning* good or well: *beneficial*

beneath *adverb* **1** below ▷ *preposition* **2** below **3** not worthy of

benefactor *noun* person who supports a person or institution by giving money

beneficial *adjective* helpful or advantageous > **beneficially** *adverb* helpfully or advantageously

beneficiary beneficiaries *noun* person who gains or benefits from something

benefit *noun* **1** something that improves or promotes **2** advantage or sake: *I'm doing this for your benefit* **3** money given by the government to people who are unemployed or ill ▷ *verb* **4** (followed by *from*) to gain an advantage or help from

benevolence *noun* kindness and helpfulness > **benevolent** *adjective* kind and helpful > **benevolently** *adverb*: *smiling benevolently*

benign *adjective* **1** showing kindliness **2** (of a tumour) not threatening to life > **benignly** *adverb* kindly

bent *verb* **1** past of **bend** ▷ *adjective* **2** curved **3** *informal* dishonest or corrupt **4** **bent on** determined to do (something)

bequeath *verb* to leave (money or property) to someone in a will

bequest *noun* legal gift of money or property by someone who has died

berate berates berating berated *verb* to scold (someone) harshly

bereaved *adjective* having recently lost a close friend or relative through death > **bereavement** *noun*: *those who have suffered a bereavement*

bereft *adjective* (followed by *of*) deprived (of): *bereft of ideas*

beret *noun* round flat close-fitting brimless cap

berm *noun NZ* narrow grass strip between the road and the footpath in a residential area

berry berries *noun* small soft stoneless fruit

berserk *adjective* **go berserk** to become violent or destructive

berth *noun* **1** bunk in a ship or train **2** space in a harbour where a ship stays when being loaded or unloaded to dock (a ship)

beseech beseeches beseeching beseeched or **besought** *verb* to ask (someone) earnestly for something > **beseeching** *adjective*: *She gave him a beseeching look*

beset besets besetting beset *verb* to trouble or harass (someone) constantly

beside *preposition* **1** at, by or to the side of **2** as compared with **3** **beside yourself** overwhelmed or overwrought

besiege besieges besieging besieged *verb* **1** to surround (a place) with military forces **2** to overwhelm (someone), as with requests

besought *verb* a past of **beseech**

best *adjective* **1** most excellent of a particular group etc ▷ *adverb* **2** in a manner that is better than all others ▷ *noun* **3** most outstanding or excellent person, thing or group in a category

best man *noun* groom's attendant at a wedding

bestow *verb* (followed by *on*) to give (something) to someone

bet bets betting bet *noun* **1** the act of staking a sum of money on the outcome of an event **2** sum of money risked on the outcome of an event ▷ *verb* **3** to make or place a bet

4 *informal* to predict (something)
> **betting** *noun*

betray betrays betraying betrayed *verb* **1** to do something that harms (someone who trusts you), such as helping his or her enemies **2** to reveal (your feelings or thoughts) unintentionally > **betrayal** *noun* act of betraying someone or something > **betrayer** *noun* person who betrays someone

betrothed *adjective old-fashioned* engaged to be married > **betrothal** *noun* engagement to be married

better *adjective* **1** more excellent than others; superior **2** improved or fully recovered in health ▷ *adverb* **3** in a more excellent manner **4** in or to a greater degree

between *preposition, adverb* indicating position in the middle, alternatives, etc

beverage *noun* drink

bevy bevies *noun* flock or group

beware *verb* (usually followed by *of*) to be on your guard (against)

bewilder *verb* to confuse utterly > **bewildered** *adjective* greatly confused > **bewildering** *adjective* very confusing > **bewilderment** *noun* great confusion

bewitch bewitches bewitching bewitched *verb* **1** to attract and fascinate **2** to cast a spell over > **bewitched** *adjective* > **bewitching** *adjective*

beyond *preposition* **1** at or to a point on the other side of **2** outside the limits or scope of ▷ *adverb* **3** at or to the far side of something

bi- *prefix meaning* two or twice: *bicentenary*

bias biases or **biasses biasing** or **biassing biased** or **biassed** *noun* **1** mental tendency, especially prejudice ▷ *verb* **2** to cause

(someone) to have a bias > **biased** or **biassed** *adjective* prejudiced

bib *noun* **1** piece of cloth or plastic worn to protect a very young child's clothes when eating **2** upper front part of dungarees etc

Bible *noun* sacred writings of the Christian religion > **biblical** *adjective* of or relating to the Bible

bicentenary bicentenaries *noun* 200th anniversary

biceps *noun* large muscle in the upper part of your arm
■ The plural of *biceps* is *biceps*

bicker *verb* to argue over petty matters

bicycle *noun* vehicle with two wheels, one behind the other, pedalled by the rider

bid bids bidding bade or **bid bidden** *verb* **1** to offer (a sum) in an attempt to buy something **2** *old-fashioned* to give (a greeting) to (someone) ▷ *noun* **3** offer to buy something for a specified amount **4** attempt to do something
▌ When *bid* is used with sums of money (sense 1), the past tense and past participle are bid. When *bid* is used with greetings (sense 2), the past tense is bade and the past participle is bidden

biddy-biddy biddy-biddies *noun* prickly low-growing plant found in New Zealand

bide bides biding bided *verb* **bide your time** to wait patiently for an opportunity

bidet *noun* low basin for washing the genital area

big bigger biggest *adjective* large or important > **biggish** *adjective* fairly big > **bigness** *noun* largeness

bigamy *noun* crime of marrying a person while still legally married to someone else > **bigamist** *noun* person who commits bigamy

bighead *noun informal* conceited person > **big-headed** *adjective* conceited

bigot *noun* person with strong, unreasonable prejudices, especially regarding religion or race > **bigoted** *adjective* extremely prejudiced in an unreasonable way, especially regarding religion or race > **bigotry** *noun*: *religious bigotry*

bike *noun informal* bicycle or motorcycle

bikini bikinis *noun* woman's brief two-piece swimming costume

bilateral *adjective* (of an agreement) made between two groups or countries

bile *noun* bitter yellow fluid produced by the liver

bilge *noun* the lowest part of a ship, where dirty water collects

bilingual *adjective* involving or using two languages

bill *noun* **1** statement of money owed for goods or services supplied **2** formal statement of a proposed new law **3** poster **4** *Chiefly US & Canadian* piece of paper money **5** list of events, such as a theatre programme **6** bird's beak

billabong *noun Aust* lagoon or pool formed from part of a river

billboard *noun* large board on which advertisements are displayed

billet *verb* **1** to assign a lodging to (a soldier) ▷ *noun* **2** building for housing soldiers

billiards *noun* game played on a table with balls and a cue

billion *adjective, noun* **1** one thousand million (1,000,000,000) **2** formerly, one million million (1,000,000,000,000) **3 billions** large but unspecified number; lots

> **billionth** *adjective, noun*

As the meaning of *billion* has changed from one million million to one thousand million, a writer may mean either of these things when using it, depending on when the book or article was written

billow *noun* **1** large sea wave ▷ *verb* **2** to rise up or swell out

billy billies *noun* (also **billycan**) *Aust, NZ* metal pot for boiling water over a camp fire

bin *noun* container, especially one for rubbish

binary *adjective* **1** composed of two parts **2** *Maths, computers* of or in a counting system with only two digits, 0 and 1

bind binds binding bound *verb* **1** to make (something) secure with or as if with a rope **2** to place (someone) under an obligation **3** to enclose and fasten (the pages of a book) between covers ▷ *noun* **4** *informal* annoying situation

bindi-eye *noun* small Australian plant with prickly fruits

binding *noun* **1** anything that binds or fastens **2** book cover

binge *noun informal* wild bout of drinking or eating too much

bingo *noun* gambling game in which numbers are called out and covered by the players on their individual cards

binoculars *plural noun* instrument with lenses for each eye through which you look in order to see distant objects or people

bio- *prefix meaning* life or living things: *biology*

biochemistry *noun* study of the chemistry of living things > **biochemical** *adjective* relating to chemical processes that happen in living things > **biochemist** *noun*

biodegradable *adjective* capable of being decomposed by natural means

biography biographies *noun* account of a person's life by another person > **biographer** *noun* > **biographical** *adjective*

biology *noun* study of living things > **biological** *adjective* of or relating to biology > **biologically** *adverb* > **biologist** *noun*

biometric *adjective* (of any automated system) using physiological or behavioural traits as a means of identification: *biometric data*

bionic *adjective* having a part of the body that is operated electronically

biopsy biopsies *noun* examination of tissue from a living body

birch birches *noun* tree with thin peeling bark

bird *noun* creature with feathers and wings, most types of which can fly

Biro® **Biros** *noun* ballpoint pen

birth *noun* **1** process of bearing young; childbirth **2** act of being born **3** beginning of something **4** **give birth to** to bear (a baby)

birthday birthdays *noun* anniversary of the day of your birth

birthmark *noun* mark on the skin formed before birth

biscuit *noun* small flat dry sweet or plain cake

bisect *verb* to divide (a line or area) into two equal parts

bisexual *adjective* sexually attracted to both men and women

bishop *noun* **1** high-ranking clergyman in some Christian Churches **2** chessman which is moved diagonally

bison *noun* large hairy animal of the cattle family, native to North America and Europe

bistro bistros *noun* small restaurant

bit *noun* **1** small piece, portion or quantity **2** metal mouthpiece on a horse's bridle **3** cutting or drilling part of a tool **4** *Computers* smallest unit of information held in a computer's memory, either 0 or 1 **5** **a bit** rather, somewhat **6** **bit by bit** gradually ▷ *verb* **7** past tense of **bite**

bitch bitches *noun* **1** female dog, fox or wolf **2** *offensive* spiteful woman > **bitchy** *adjective* spiteful

bite bites biting bit bitten *verb* **1** to cut into (something or someone) with your teeth ▷ *noun* **2** act of biting **3** wound or sting inflicted by biting **4** snack

bitter *adjective* **1** having a sharp unpleasant taste; sour **2** showing or caused by hostility or resentment **3** extremely cold > **bitterly** *adverb* > **bitterness** *noun*

bivouac *noun* temporary camp in the open air

bizarre *adjective* odd or unusual

blab blabs blabbing blabbed *verb* to reveal (secrets) indiscreetly

black *adjective* **1** of the darkest colour, like coal **2** **Black** dark-skinned **3** (of a situation) without hope **4** angry or resentful: *black looks* **5** involving jokes about death or suffering: *black comedy* ▷ *noun* **6** darkest colour **7** **Black** member of a dark-skinned race **8** complete darkness > **blackness** *noun* being very dark > **black out** *verb* to lose consciousness

blackberry blackberries *noun* small blackish edible fruit

blackbird *noun* common European bird, the male of which has black feathers

blackboard *noun* hard black

surface used by teachers for writing on with chalk

black box black boxes noun an electronic device in an aircraft which collects and stores information during flights

blackcurrant noun very small blackish edible fruit that grows in bunches

blacken verb 1 to make (something) black 2 **blacken someone's name** to say bad things about someone

blackhead noun very small black spot on the skin caused by a pore being blocked with dirt

blacklist noun 1 list of people or organizations considered untrustworthy etc ▷ verb 2 to put (someone) on a blacklist

blackmail noun 1 act of attempting to obtain money from someone by threatening to reveal information ▷ verb 2 to attempt to obtain money from (someone) by blackmail > **blackmailer** noun person who blackmails someone

black market noun illegal trade in goods or currencies

blackout noun temporary loss of consciousness

blacksmith noun person who makes things out of iron, such as horseshoes

bladder noun part of the body where urine is held until it leaves the body

blade noun 1 cutting edge of a weapon or tool 2 thin flattish part of a propeller, oar, etc 3 leaf of grass

blame blames blaming blamed verb 1 to consider (someone) responsible for something that is wrong ▷ noun 2 responsibility for something that is wrong

blameless adjective not responsible

for something that is wrong

blanch blanches blanching blanched verb 1 to become white or pale 2 to prepare (vegetables etc) by plunging them in boiling water

bland adjective dull and uninteresting > **blandly** adverb

blank adjective 1 not written on 2 showing no interest or expression

blanket noun 1 large thick cloth used as covering for a bed 2 thick covering of something, such as snow

blare blares blaring blared verb 1 to make a loud harsh noise ▷ noun 2 loud harsh noise

blaspheme blasphemes blaspheming blasphemed verb to speak disrespectfully of God or religion > **blasphemer** noun person who blasphemes > **blasphemous** adjective > **blasphemy** noun

blast noun 1 explosion 2 sudden strong gust of air or wind 3 sudden loud sound, as of a trumpet ▷ verb 4 to blow up (a rock etc) with explosives

blatant adjective extremely obvious

blaze blazes blazing blazed noun 1 strong fire or flame 2 very bright light ▷ verb 3 to burn or shine brightly

blazer noun lightweight jacket, often in the colours of a school etc

bleach bleaches bleaching bleached verb 1 to make (material or hair) white or pale ▷ noun 2 chemical used to make material or hair white or to disinfect

bleak adjective 1 exposed and barren 2 offering little hope

bleary adjective (of eyes) red and watery, through tiredness

bleat verb 1 (of a sheep or goat) to utter its characteristic high-pitched cry ▷ noun 2 cry of sheep and goats

bleed bleeds bleeding bled *verb* to lose blood from a wound

bleep *noun* short high-pitched sound made by an electrical device

blemish blemishes blemishing blemished *noun* **1** mark that spoils the appearance of something ▷ *verb* **2** to spoil (someone's reputation)

blend *verb* **1** to mix (parts or ingredients) **2** to look good together ▷ *noun* **3** mixture

blender *noun* machine for mixing liquids and foods at high speed

bless blesses blessing blessed or **blest** *verb* to ask God to protect (someone or something) > **blessed** *adjective* (followed by *with*) having (a particular quality or talent) > **blessing** *noun* **1** something good that you are thankful for **2 with someone's blessing** with someone's approval

blew *verb* past tense of **blow**

blight *noun* **1** something that damages or spoils other things **2** disease that makes plants wither ▷ *verb* **3** to harm (something) seriously

blind *adjective* **1** unable to see **2** (followed by *to*) unable or unwilling to understand (something) **3** not determined by reason: *blind hatred* ▷ *verb* **4** to deprive (someone) of sight **5** to deprive (someone) of good sense, reason or judgment ▷ *noun* **6** covering for a window > **blindly** *adverb*: *She groped blindly for the glass* > **blindness** *noun* inability to see

blindfold *verb* **1** to prevent (someone) from seeing by covering the eyes ▷ *noun* **2** piece of cloth used to cover the eyes

blinding *adjective* (of a light) so

bright that it hurts your eyes > **blindingly** *adverb* **blindingly obvious** *informal* very obvious indeed

blink *verb* to close and immediately reopen (the eyes)

blinkers *plural noun* leather flaps on a horse's bridle to prevent sideways vision

bliss *noun* perfect happiness > **blissful** *adjective*: *We spent a blissful week together* > **blissfully** *adverb*

blister *noun* **1** small bubble on the skin containing watery liquid, caused by a burn or rubbing ▷ *verb* **2** (of the skin) to develop a blister > **blistering** *adjective* **1** (of weather) very hot **2** (of criticism) extremely harsh

blithe *adjective* casual and indifferent > **blithely** *adverb* casually and indifferently

blitz blitzes blitzing blitzed *noun* **1** bombing attack by enemy aircraft on a city ▷ *verb* **2** to make a bombing attack on (a city)

blizzard *noun* heavy snowstorm with strong winds

bloated *adjective* larger than normal, often because of the liquid or gas inside

blob *noun* **1** soft mass or drop **2** indistinct or shapeless form

bloc *noun* people or countries combined by a common interest

block *noun* **1** large solid piece of wood, stone, etc **2** large building of offices, flats, etc **3** area of land in a town that has streets on all its sides **4** obstruction or hindrance **5** *informal* person's head ▷ *verb* **6** to obstruct (something) by introducing an obstacle

blockade blockades blockading blockaded *noun* **1** action that prevents goods from reaching a place ▷ *verb* **2** to prevent supplies from reaching (a place)

blockage *noun* something that blocks a pipe or tunnel

bloke *noun informal* man

blonde or **blond** *adjective, noun* fair-haired (person)

blood *noun* **1** red fluid that flows around the body **2** race or ancestors **3 in cold blood** deliberately

bloodhound *noun* large dog with very good sense of smell

bloodless *adjective* **1** (of face, skin) very pale **2** (of coup, revolution) without casualties

blood pressure *noun* measure of how forcefully your blood is being pumped round your body

bloodshed *noun* slaughter or killing

bloodshot *adjective* (of an eye) inflamed and red

bloodstream *noun* flow of blood round the body

bloodthirsty *adjective* taking pleasure in violence

blood transfusion *noun* process in which blood is injected into the body of someone who has lost a lot of blood

blood vessel *noun* narrow tube in the body through which the blood flows

bloody bloodier bloodiest *adjective* **1** covered with blood **2** marked by much killing

bloom *noun* **1** blossom on a flowering plant **2** youthful or healthy glow ▷ *verb* **3** to bear flowers **4** to be in a healthy glowing condition

blossom *noun* **1** growth of flowers that appears on a tree before the fruit ▷ *verb* **2** (of a tree) to produce blossom

blot blots blotting blotted *noun* **1** drop of ink spilled on a surface **2** something that spoils something, such as someone's reputation > **blot out** *verb* to be in front of (something) and hide (it) completely

blotch blotches *noun* discoloured area or stain > **blotchy** *adjective* having discoloured areas or stains

blouse *noun* woman's shirt

blow blows blowing blew blown *verb* **1** (of air, the wind, etc) to move **2** to move or be carried as if by the wind **3** to expel (air etc) through the mouth or nose **4** to cause (a musical instrument) to sound by forcing air into it **5** *informal* to spend (money) freely ▷ *noun* **6** hard hit **7** sudden setback > **blow up** *verb* **1** to destroy (something) with an explosion **2** to fill (a balloon or tyre) with air **3** *informal* to enlarge (a photograph)

blow-dry blow-dries blow-drying blow-dried *verb* to style (the hair) with a hand-held dryer

blown *verb* past participle of **blow**

blubber *noun* fat of whales, seals, etc

bludge bludges bludging bludged *Aust, NZ informal verb* **1** to avoid work **2** to scrounge

bludgeon *noun* **1** short thick club ▷ *verb* **2** to hit (someone) with a bludgeon **3** to force or bully (someone) into doing something

blue bluer bluest; blues *noun* **1** colour of a clear unclouded sky **2 out of the blue** unexpectedly **3 the blues a** feeling of depression **b** type of folk music of Black American origin ▷ *adjective* **4** of the colour blue > **bluish** or **blueish** *adjective* slightly blue

bluebell *noun* flower with blue bell-shaped flowers

bluebottle *noun* **1** large fly with a dark-blue body **2** *Aust, NZ* small stinging jellyfish

blue-collar *adjective* denoting manual industrial workers

blueprint *noun* description of how a plan is expected to work

bluff *verb* 1 to pretend to be confident in order to influence (someone) ▷ *noun* 2 act of bluffing 3 steep cliff or bank ▷ *adjective* 4 good-naturedly frank and hearty

blunder *noun* 1 clumsy mistake ▷ *verb* 2 to make a blunder 3 to act clumsily

blunt *adjective* 1 not having a sharp edge or point 2 (of people, speech, etc) straightforward or uncomplicated

blur blurs blurring blurred *verb* 1 to become vague or less distinct or to make (something) vague or less distinct ▷ *noun* 2 something vague, hazy or indistinct > **blurred** *adjective*: blurred vision

blurt out *verb* to say (something) suddenly after trying to keep it a secret

blush blushes blushing blushed *verb* 1 to become red in the face, especially from embarrassment or shame ▷ *noun* 2 reddening of the face

bluster *verb* 1 to speak loudly or in a bullying way ▷ *noun* 2 empty threats or protests > **blustery** *adjective* (of weather) rough and windy

boa *noun* 1 any of various large snakes that kill by crushing 2 long scarf of fur or feathers

boa constrictor *noun* large snake that kills by crushing

boar *noun* 1 male pig used for breeding 2 wild pig

board *noun* 1 long flat piece of sawn timber 2 smaller flat piece of rigid material for a specific purpose:

ironing board; chess board 3 group of people who run a company, trust, etc 4 meals provided for money 5 **on board** on or in a ship, aeroplane, etc ▷ *verb* 6 to go aboard (a train, aeroplane, etc) 7 to cover (something) with boards 8 to receive meals and lodgings in return for money

boarder *noun* Brit pupil who lives at school during the school term

boarding house *noun* private house that provides meals and accommodation for paying guests

boarding school *noun* school where the pupils live during the term

boardroom *noun* room where the board of a company meets

boast *verb* 1 to speak too proudly about your talents, etc; brag 2 to possess (something to be proud of) ▷ *noun* 3 bragging statement > **boastful** *adjective* speaking too proudly about your talents etc

boat *noun* small vehicle for travelling across water

bob bobs bobbing bobbed *verb* 1 to move up and down repeatedly 2 to cut (the hair) in a bob ▷ *noun* 3 short abrupt movement 4 hairstyle in which the hair is cut short evenly all round the head

bobbin *noun* reel on which thread is wound

bode bodes boding boded *verb* to be an omen of (good or ill)

bodice *noun* upper part of a dress

bodily *adjective* 1 relating to the body ▷ *adverb* 2 by taking hold of the body

body bodies *noun* 1 entire physical structure of an animal or human 2 trunk or torso 3 corpse 4 organized group of people 5 main part of anything 6 woman's one-piece undergarment

bodyguard *noun* person or group of people employed to protect someone

bodywork *noun* outer shell of a motor vehicle

boer *noun* (in South Africa) a white farmer, especially one of Dutch descent

boerewors *noun* S Afr spiced sausage

bog *noun* **1** wet spongy ground **2** *informal* toilet

boggle boggles boggling boggled *verb* to be surprised, confused or alarmed

bogus *adjective* not genuine

bohemian *adjective* leading an unconventional life

boil *verb* **1** to change from a liquid to a vapour or cause (a liquid) to change to a vapour so quickly that bubbles are formed **2** to cook (food) by the process of boiling ▷ *noun* **3** painful red swelling on the skin

boiler *noun* piece of equipment that provides hot water

boiling *adjective informal* very hot

boisterous *adjective* noisy and lively

bold *adjective* **1** confident and fearless **2** immodest or impudent **3** clear and noticeable: *bold colours* > **boldly** *adverb* in a bold manner > **boldness** *noun* being bold

bollard *noun* short thick post used to prevent the passage of motor vehicles

bolster *verb* to support or strengthen (something)

bolt *noun* **1** sliding metal bar for fastening a door etc **2** metal pin that screws into a nut **3** flash (of lightning) ▷ *adverb* **4 bolt upright** stiff and rigid ▷ *verb* **5** to run away suddenly **6** to fasten (a door) with a bolt **7** to eat (food) hurriedly

bomb *noun* **1** container fitted with explosive material **2** *informal* large amount of money **3 the bomb** nuclear bomb ▷ *verb* **4** to attack (a place) with bombs **5** to move very quickly > **bomber** *noun* **1** aircraft that drops bombs **2** person who throws or puts a bomb in a particular place

bombard *verb* **1** to attack (a place) with heavy gunfire or bombs **2** to attack (someone) verbally, especially with questions > **bombardment** *noun*

bombshell *noun* shocking or unwelcome surprise

bona fide *adjective* genuine

bond *noun* **1** something that binds, fastens or holds things together **2** something that unites people; link **3** written or spoken agreement **4** *Finance* certificate of debt issued to raise funds **5 bonds** chains or ropes used to restrain or imprison ▷ *verb* **6** to link or attach (things)

bondage *noun* slavery

bone bones boning boned *noun* **1** any of the hard parts in the body that form the skeleton ▷ *verb* **2** to remove the bones from (meat for cooking etc) > **boneless** *adjective*

bonfire *noun* large outdoor fire

bonnet *noun* **1** metal cover over a vehicle's engine **2** hat that ties under the chin

bonny bonnier bonniest *adjective* Scot beautiful

bonus bonuses *noun* something given, paid or received above what is due or expected

bony bonier boniest *adjective* very thin

boo *interjection* **1** shout of disapproval ▷ *verb* **2** to shout 'boo' to show disapproval of (someone or something)

boobook *noun* small brown Australian owl with a spotted back and wings

book *noun* 1 number of pages bound together between covers 2 long written work 3 number of tickets, stamps, etc fastened together ▷ *verb* 4 to reserve (a hotel room, travel, etc) in advance 5 to record the name of (a person who has committed an offence)

bookcase *noun* piece of furniture with shelves for books

bookie *noun informal* bookmaker

booking *noun* arrangement to book something such as a hotel room

book-keeping *noun* recording of the money spent and received by a business

booklet *noun* small book with a paper cover

bookmaker *noun* person whose occupation is taking bets

bookmark *noun* piece of card put between the pages of a book to mark your place

boom *verb* 1 to make a loud deep echoing sound 2 to increase rapidly ▷ *noun* 3 loud deep echoing sound 4 rapid increase in something

boomerang *noun* curved wooden missile that can be made to return to the thrower

boon *noun* something helpful or beneficial

boost *noun* 1 encouragement or help 2 increase ▷ *verb* 3 to cause (something) to improve or increase

booster *noun* 1 something that increases a good quality: *a morale booster* 2 device providing extra power 3 small additional injection of a vaccine

boot *noun* 1 outer covering for the foot that extends above the ankle 2 space in a car for luggage 3 **to**

boot in addition ▷ *verb* 4 *informal* to kick 5 to start up (a computer)

booth *noun* 1 small partly enclosed cubicle 2 stall at a fair or market

booty *noun* valuable articles obtained as plunder

booze boozes boozing boozed *verb, noun informal* (to consume) alcoholic drink > **boozer** *noun informal* 1 person who is fond of drinking alcohol 2 *Brit, Aust, NZ* pub > **boozy boozier booziest** *adjective* fond of drinking alcohol

border *noun* 1 dividing line between political or geographical regions 2 band around or along the edge of something ▷ *verb* 3 to form a border next to 4 (followed by *on*) to be nearly the same as: *resentment that borders on hatred*

borderline *adjective* only just acceptable as a member of a class or group: *a borderline case*

bore bores boring bored *verb* 1 to make (a hole) with a drill etc 2 to make (someone) weary by being dull and uninteresting 3 past tense of **bear** ▷ *noun* 4 dull or repetitious person or thing > **bored** *adjective* tired and impatient; fed up > **boredom** *noun* being bored > **boring** *adjective* dull and uninteresting

> You can say that you are *bored with* or *bored by* someone or something, but not *bored of*

born *verb* 1 **be born** to come out of your mother's womb at birth ▷ *adjective* 2 possessing certain qualities from birth: *a born musician*

borne *verb* a past participle of **bear**

borough *noun* *Chiefly Brit* town or district with its own council

borrow *verb* 1 to obtain (something) temporarily 2 to adopt (ideas etc) from another source > **borrower**

noun person who borrows something

> You *borrow* something *from* a person, not *off* them. Do not confuse *borrow* and *lend*. If you *borrow* something, you get it from another person for a while; if you *lend* something, someone gets it from you for a while

Bosnian *adjective* 1 belonging to or relating to Bosnia ▷ *noun* 2 person from Bosnia

bosom *noun* 1 chest of a person, especially the female breasts ▷ *adjective* 2 very dear: *a bosom friend*

boss bosses bossing bossed *noun* person in charge of or employing others > **boss around** *verb* to keep telling (someone) what to do

bossy bossier bossiest *adjective* enjoying telling other people what to do > **bossiness** *noun*: *They resent what they see as bossiness*

botany *noun* study of plants > **botanic** or **botanical** *adjective* > **botanist** *noun*

botch botches botching botched *verb* to spoil (something) through clumsiness

both *adjective, pronoun* two considered together

bother *verb* 1 to take the time or trouble (to do something) 2 to give annoyance or trouble to (someone) 3 to pester (someone) ▷ *noun* 4 trouble, fuss or difficulty > **bothersome** *adjective* causing annoyance or trouble

bottle bottles bottling bottled *noun* 1 container for holding liquids 2 *Brit informal* courage ▷ *verb* 3 to put (something) in a bottle > **bottle up** *verb* to restrain (strong feelings)

bottleneck *noun* narrow stretch of road where traffic is held up

bottle store *noun Aust, NZ, S Afr*

shop licensed to sell alcohol for drinking elsewhere

bottom *noun* 1 lowest, deepest or farthest removed part of a thing 2 buttocks ▷ *adjective* 3 lowest or last > **bottomless** *adjective* having or seeming to have no bottom

bough *noun* large branch of a tree

bought *verb* past of **buy**

boulder *noun* large rounded rock

boulevard *noun* wide, usually tree-lined, street

bounce bounces bouncing bounced *verb* 1 (of a ball etc) to rebound from an impact 2 *informal* (of a cheque) to be returned uncashed owing to a lack of funds in the account ▷ *noun* 3 act of rebounding 4 springiness 5 *informal* vitality or vigour

bouncy bouncier bounciest *adjective* 1 lively and enthusiastic 2 capable of bouncing

bound *verb* 1 past of **bind** 2 to move forwards by jumps 3 to form a boundary of (something) ▷ *noun* 4 jump upwards or forwards 5 **bounds** limits ▷ *adjective* 6 destined or certain (to do something) 7 compelled or obliged (to do something) 8 going or intending to go towards: *homeward bound*

boundary boundaries *noun* dividing line that indicates the farthest limit

boundless *adjective* without end or limit

bountiful *adjective* freely available in large amounts

bounty *noun* 1 generosity 2 generous gift or reward

bouquet *noun* 1 bunch of flowers 2 aroma of wine

bourgeois *adjective* (used expressing disapproval) typical of fairly rich middle-class people > **bourgeoisie** *noun* fairly rich middle-class people in a society

bout *noun* **1** period of activity or illness **2** boxing or wrestling match

boutique *noun* small clothes shop

bovine *adjective* **1** relating to cattle **2** rather slow and stupid

bow¹ *verb* **1** to lower (your head) or bend (your knee or body) as a sign of respect or shame **2** (followed by *to*) to comply with or accept ▷ *noun* **3** movement made when bowing **4** front end of a ship

bow² *noun* **1** knot with two loops and loose ends **2** weapon for shooting arrows **3** long stick stretched with horsehair for playing stringed instruments

bowel *noun* **1** intestine, especially the large intestine **2** **bowels** innermost part

bowerbird *noun* bird found in Australia, the male of which builds a shelter during courtship

bowl *noun* **1** round container with an open top **2** hollow part of an object **3** large heavy ball ▷ *verb* **4** Cricket to send (a ball) towards the batsman > **bowling** *noun* game in which bowls are rolled at a group of pins

bowler *noun* **1** Cricket player who sends a ball towards the batsman **2** person who plays bowls or bowling **3** stiff felt hat with a rounded crown

bowls *noun* game played on smooth grass with wooden bowls

bow tie *noun* man's tie in the form of a bow, often worn at formal occasions

box boxes boxing boxed *noun* **1** container with a firm flat base and sides **2** separate compartment in a theatre, stable, etc **3** evergreen tree with shiny leaves **4** **the box**

informal television ▷ *verb* **5** to put (something) into a box **6** to fight an opponent in a boxing match

boxer *noun* **1** person who participates in the sport of boxing **2** medium-sized dog with smooth hair and a short nose

boxer shorts or **boxers** *plural noun* men's underpants shaped like shorts but with a front opening

boxing *noun* sport of fighting with the fists, wearing padded gloves

box office *noun* place where tickets are sold in a theatre or cinema

boy boys *noun* male child > **boyhood** *noun* period of being a boy > **boyish** *adjective: a boyish grin*

boycott *verb* **1** to refuse to deal with (an organization or country) ▷ *noun* **2** instance of boycotting

boyfriend *noun* male friend with whom a person is romantically involved

bra *noun* woman's undergarment for supporting the breasts

braaivleis or **braai braaivleises** or **braais** *S Afr noun* **1** grill on which food is cooked over hot charcoal, usually outdoors **2** outdoor party at which food is cooked in this way

brace braces bracing braced *noun* **1** object fastened to something to straighten or support it **2** pair, especially of game birds ▷ *verb* **3** to steady or prepare (yourself) for something unpleasant **4** to strengthen or fit (something) with a brace

bracelet *noun* ornamental chain or band for the wrist

braces *plural noun* straps worn over the shoulders to hold up trousers

bracing *adjective* refreshing and invigorating

bracken *noun* large fern

bracket *noun* **1** pair of characters

used to enclose a section of writing **2** group that falls within certain defined limits **3** support fixed to a wall ▷ *verb* **4** to put (words or letters) in brackets **5** to class (people or things) together

brag brags bragging bragged *verb* to speak arrogantly and boastfully

Brahma *noun* Hindu god, one of the Trimurti

Brahman *noun* in the Hindu religion, the ultimate and impersonal divine reality of the universe

brahmin *noun* member of the highest caste in Hindu society

braid *verb* **1** to plait (hair, thread, etc) ▷ *noun* **2** length of hair etc that has been plaited **3** narrow ornamental tape of woven silk etc

Braille *noun* system of printing for blind people in which letters are represented by raised dots that can be felt

brain *noun* **1** soft mass of nervous tissue in the head that controls the body and enables thinking and feeling **2** intellectual ability

brainchild *noun* idea produced by creative thought

brainwash brainwashes brainwashing brainwashed *verb* to cause (a person) to alter his or her beliefs, especially by methods based on isolation, sleeplessness, etc > **brainwashing** *noun*

brainwave *noun* sudden clever idea

brainy brainier brainiest *adjective informal* clever

braise braises braising braised *verb* to cook (food) slowly in a covered pan with a little liquid

brake brakes braking braked *noun* **1** device for slowing or stopping a vehicle ▷ *verb* **2** to slow down or stop a vehicle by using

a brake

| Do not confuse the spellings of *brake* and *break*

bramble *noun* prickly shrub that produces blackberries

bran *noun* husks of cereal grain

branch branches branching branched *noun* **1** part of a tree that grows out from its trunk **2** one of the offices or shops that are part of an organization **3** one of the areas of study or activity that are part of a subject ▷ *verb* **4** (of stems, roots, etc) to divide, then develop in different directions > **branch out** *verb* to try something different

brand *noun* **1** particular product **2** particular kind or variety **3** identifying mark burnt onto the skin of an animal ▷ *verb* **4** to mark (an animal) with a brand **5** to give (someone) a reputation for being as specified: *I was branded as a rebel*

brandish brandishes brandishing brandished *verb* to wave (a weapon etc) in a threatening way

brand-new *adjective* absolutely new

brandy brandies *noun* alcoholic spirit distilled from wine

brash *adjective* offensively loud, showy or self-confident > **brashness** *noun* being brash

brass *noun* **1** alloy of copper and zinc **2** family of wind instruments made of brass **3** N English *dialect* money

brassiere *noun* bra

brat *noun* unruly child

bravado *noun* showy display of self-confidence

brave braver bravest; braves braving braved *adjective* **1** having or showing courage and daring ▷ *noun* **2** Native American warrior ▷ *verb* **3** to confront (an unpleasant or dangerous situation) with courage > **bravely** adverb > **bravery** noun brave behaviour

bravo interjection well done!

brawl noun 1 noisy fight ▷ verb 2 to fight noisily

brawn noun physical strength > **brawny** adjective strong and muscular

bray brays braying brayed verb 1 (of a donkey) to utter its loud harsh sound ▷ noun 2 donkey's loud harsh sound

brazen adjective shameless and bold > **brazenly** adverb in a shameless and bold manner

brazier noun portable container for burning charcoal or coal

Brazilian adjective 1 belonging or relating to Brazil ▷ noun 2 person from Brazil

breach breaches breaching breached noun 1 breaking of a promise, obligation, etc 2 gap or break ▷ verb 3 to break (a promise, law, etc) 4 to make a gap in (a barrier)

bread noun 1 food made by baking a mixture of flour and water or milk 2 informal money

breadth noun extent of something from side to side

breadwinner noun person whose earnings support a family

break breaks breaking broke broken verb 1 to separate (something) into two or more pieces or become separated into two or more pieces 2 to damage (something) or become damaged so as to be unusable 3 to fail to observe (an agreement etc) 4 to end: The good weather broke at last 5 to weaken or be weakened, as in spirit 6 (of a boy's voice) to become permanently deeper 7 **break even**

to make neither a profit nor a loss ▷ noun 8 act or result of breaking 9 gap or interruption in continuity > **breakable** adjective > **break down** verb 1 to stop working 2 to start crying > **break up** verb 1 to come to an end 2 (of a school) to close for the holidays

Do not confuse the spellings of break and brake

breakage noun act of breaking something or a thing that has been broken

breakaway adjective (of a group) separated from a larger group

breakdown noun 1 act or instance of breaking down 2 nervous breakdown 3 details relating to the separate elements of something

breaker noun large wave

breakfast noun first meal of the day

break-in noun illegal entering of a building, especially by a burglar

breakneck adjective fast and dangerous

breakthrough noun important development or discovery

breakwater noun wall that extends into the sea to protect a coast from the force of the waves

bream noun 1 freshwater fish with silvery scales 2 food fish of European seas

breast noun 1 either of the two soft fleshy milk-secreting glands on a woman's chest 2 chest

breath noun 1 taking in and letting out of air during breathing 2 air taken in and let out during breathing

breathe breathes breathing breathed verb to take air into the lungs and let it out again

breathless adjective breathing fast or with difficulty > **breathlessly** adverb in a breathless manner

> **breathlessness** *noun*

breathtaking *adjective* very beautiful or exciting

bred *verb* past of **breed**

breeches *plural noun* trousers reaching to just below the knee

breed breeds breeding bred *verb* **1** to keep (animals or plants) in order to produce more animals or plants with particular qualities **2** to mate and produce offspring; reproduce ▷ *noun* **3** group of animals or plants within a species that have particular qualities

breeze *noun* gentle wind

brevity *noun* shortness

brew *verb* **1** to make (beer) by boiling and fermenting malt **2** to make (tea or coffee) in a pot by pouring hot water over it **3** to be about to happen ▷ *noun* **4** beverage produced by brewing > **brewer** *noun* person or company that brews beer

brewery breweries *noun* place where beer is brewed

briar *noun* same as **brier**

bribe bribes bribing bribed *verb* **1** to offer or give something to (someone) to gain favour, influence, etc ▷ *noun* **2** something given or offered as a bribe > **bribery** *noun* practice of bribing

bric-a-brac *noun* small ornaments or pieces of furniture of no great value

brick *noun* rectangular block of baked clay used in building

bricklayer *noun* person who builds with bricks

bride *noun* woman who has just been or is about to be married > **bridal** *adjective*: *a bridal gown*

bridegroom *noun* man who has just been or is about to be married

bridesmaid *noun* girl or woman who attends a bride at her wedding

bridge *noun* **1** structure for crossing a river etc **2** platform from which a ship is steered or controlled **3** upper part of the nose **4** piece of wood supporting the strings of a violin etc **5** card game based on whist, played between two pairs

bridle *noun* headgear for controlling a horse

brief *adjective* **1** lasting a short time ▷ *noun* **2** set of instructions ▷ *verb* **3** to give information and instructions to > **briefly** *adverb*

briefcase *noun* small flat case for carrying papers, books, etc

briefing *noun* meeting at which information and instructions are given

brier or **briar** *noun* wild rose with long thorny stems

brigade *noun* army unit smaller than a division

brigadier *noun* high-ranking army officer

brigalow *noun* type of Australian acacia tree

bright *adjective* **1** giving out or reflecting a lot of light; brilliant **2** (of colours) intense or vivid **3** clever > **brightly** *adverb* > **brightness** *noun*

brighten *verb* **1** to become brighter **2** to look suddenly happier > **brighten up** *verb* to make (something) more attractive and cheerful

brilliant *adjective* **1** shining with light **2** splendid **3** extremely clever > **brilliance** *noun* > **brilliantly** *adverb*

brim *noun* **1** upper rim of a cup etc **2** wide part of a hat that sticks outwards at the bottom

brine *noun* salt water

bring brings bringing brought

verb **1** to carry, convey or take (something or someone) to a particular place or person **2** to cause (something) to happen > **bring about** *verb* to cause (something) to happen > **bring off** *verb* to succeed in achieving (something) > **bring out** *verb* to produce (a new product) and offer it for sale > **bring up** *verb* **1** to rear (a child) **2** to mention (a subject) **3** to vomit (food)

brink *noun* edge of a steep place

brisk *adjective* lively and quick > **briskly** *adverb* > **briskness** *noun*

bristle bristles bristling bristled *noun* **1** short stiff hair ▷ *verb* **2** (of hair on an animal's body) to stand up like bristles > **bristly** *adjective* (of hair) thick and rough

British *adjective* **1** belonging or relating to the United Kingdom of Great Britain and Northern Ireland ▷ *plural noun* **2 the British** the people of the United Kingdom

British Isles *plural noun* the group of islands that consists of Great Britain, Ireland, the Isle of Man, Orkney, the Shetland Islands, the Channel Islands and the other islands close to these

Briton *noun* person from the United Kingdom of Great Britain and Northern Ireland

brittle *adjective* hard but easily broken

broach broaches broaching broached *verb* to introduce (a topic) for discussion

broad *adjective* **1** having great breadth or width **2** not detailed **3** having many different aspects or concerning many different people: *broad support* **4** strongly marked: *a broad American accent* > **broadly** *adverb* to a large extent or in most cases

broadband *noun* telecommunication transmission technique using a wide range of frequencies

broad bean *noun* thick flat edible bean

broadcast broadcasts broadcasting broadcast *noun* **1** programme or announcement on radio or television ▷ *verb* **2** to transmit (a programme or announcement) on radio or television **3** to make (information) widely known > **broadcaster** *noun* > **broadcasting** *noun* transmission of radio or television programmes

broaden *verb* **1** to become wider **2** to cause (something) to involve more things or concern more people

broad-minded *adjective* tolerant or open-minded

broadsheet *noun* newspaper with large pages and long news stories

brocade *noun* rich fabric woven with a raised design

broccoli *noun* green vegetable, similar to cauliflower

brochure *noun* booklet that contains information about a product or service

brogue *noun* **1** sturdy walking shoe **2** strong accent, especially Irish

broil *verb Aust, NZ, US, Canadian* to cook by direct heat under a grill

broke *verb* **1** past tense of **break** ▷ *adjective* **2** *informal* having no money

broken *verb* past participle of **break**

broker *noun* person whose job is to buy and sell shares for other people

brolga *noun* large grey Australian crane with a red and green head and a trumpeting call; also called **native companion**

brolly brollies *noun informal*

umbrella

bronchitis *noun* inflammation of the tubes which connect your windpipe to your lungs

brontosaurus brontosauruses *noun* very large plant-eating four-footed dinosaur

bronze *noun* **1** alloy of copper and tin **2** statue, medal, etc made of bronze ▷ *adjective* **3** made of, or coloured like, bronze

brooch brooches *noun* ornament with a pin, worn fastened to clothes

brood *noun* **1** number of birds produced at one hatching ▷ *verb* **2** to think long and unhappily

brook *noun* small stream

broom *noun* **1** long-handled sweeping brush **2** yellow-flowered shrub

broth *noun* soup, usually containing vegetables

brothel *noun* place where men pay to have sex with prositutes

brother *noun* **1** boy or man with the same parents as another person **2** member of a male religious order > **brotherly** *adjective: a brotherly kiss*

brotherhood *noun* **1** affection and loyalty between brothers or close male friends **2** association, such as a trade union

brother-in-law brothers-in-law *noun* **1** brother of your husband or wife **2** husband of your sister

brought *verb* past of **bring**

brow *noun* **1** part of the face from the eyes to the hairline **2** eyebrow **3** top of a hill

brown *noun* **1** colour of earth or wood ▷ *adjective* **2** of the colour brown

Brownie Guide or **Brownie** *noun* junior Guide

browse browses browsing

browsed *verb* **1** to look through (a book or articles for sale) in a casual manner **2** *Computers* to look for information on the Internet

browser *noun* *Computers* software package that lets you look at websites on the Internet

bruise bruises bruising bruised *noun* **1** discoloured area on the skin caused by an injury ▷ *verb* **2** to cause a bruise on (a part of the body)

brumby brumbies *noun* *Aust, NZ* wild horse

brunette *noun* girl or woman with dark brown hair

brunt *noun* main force or shock of a blow, attack, etc

brush brushes brushing brushed *noun* **1** device made of bristles, wires, etc used for cleaning, painting, etc ▷ *verb* **2** to clean or scrub (something) with a brush **3** to touch (something) lightly and briefly > **brush off** *verb informal* to dismiss or ignore (someone) > **brush up** *verb* to refresh your knowledge of (a subject)

brusque *adjective* blunt or curt in manner or speech > **brusquely** *adverb* > **brusqueness** *noun*

Brussels sprout *noun* vegetable like a tiny cabbage

brutal *adjective* cruel and violent > **brutality** *noun* > **brutally** *adverb*

brute *noun* **1** brutal person **2** large animal ▷ *adjective* **3** wholly instinctive or physical, like an animal **4** without reason > **brutish** *adjective* of or like an animal

bubble bubbles bubbling bubbled *noun* **1** ball of air in a liquid or solid ▷ *verb* **2** to form bubbles **3** to move or flow with a gurgling sound > **bubbly bubblier bubbliest** *adjective* **1** excited and lively **2** full of bubbles

buck *noun* **1** male of the goat, hare, kangaroo, rabbit and reindeer **2 pass the buck** *informal* to shift blame or responsibility onto someone else ▷ *verb* **3** (of a horse etc) to jump with legs stiff and back arched > **buck up** *verb* to become more cheerful

bucket *noun* deep open-topped container with a handle; pail

buckle buckles buckling buckled *noun* **1** clasp for fastening a belt or strap ▷ *verb* **2** to fasten (a belt or strap) with a buckle **3** to bend out of shape through pressure or heat

bud buds budding budded *noun* **1** swelling on a tree or plant that develops into a leaf or flower ▷ *verb* **2** to produce buds > **budding** *adjective* just beginning to develop

Buddha *noun* Indian religious teacher and founder of Buddhism

Buddhism *noun* eastern religion founded by Buddha > **Buddhist** *noun* **1** person who believes in Buddhism ▷ *adjective* **2** of or relating to Buddhism

budge budges budging budged *verb* to move slightly

budgerigar *noun* small cage bird bred in many different-coloured varieties

budget *noun* **1** financial plan for a period of time **2** money allocated for a specific purpose ▷ *verb* **3** to plan the spending of money or time ▷ *adjective* **4** cheap > **budgetary** *adjective* of or relating to a financial plan

budgie *noun informal* short for **budgerigar**

buff *adjective* dull yellowish-brown

buffalo buffaloes *noun* **1** wild animal like a large cow with long curved horns **2** *US* bison

buffer *noun* something that lessens shock or protects from damaging impact, circumstances, etc

buffet¹ *noun* **1** café at a station **2** meal at which people serve themselves

buffet² *verb* (of wind or sea) to strike (a place or person) violently and repeatedly

bug bugs bugging bugged *noun* **1** small insect **2** *informal* minor illness **3** small mistake in a computer program **4** concealed microphone ▷ *verb* **5** *informal* to irritate (someone) **6** to conceal a microphone in (a room or telephone)

bugle *noun* instrument like a small trumpet > **bugler** *noun* person who plays a bugle

build builds building built *verb* **1** to make, construct or form (something) by joining parts or materials ▷ *noun* **2** shape of the body

builder *noun* person who builds something

building *noun* structure with walls and a roof

building society building societies *noun* organization where money can be borrowed or invested

built *verb* past of **build**

built-up *adjective* having many buildings

bulb *noun* **1** (also **light bulb**) the glass part of an electric light **2** onion-shaped root which grows into a flower or plant

Bulgarian *adjective* **1** belonging or relating to Bulgaria ▷ *noun* **2** person from Bulgaria **3** language spoken in Bulgaria

bulge bulges bulging bulged *noun* **1** swelling on an otherwise flat or smooth surface ▷ *verb* **2** to swell outwards

bulk *noun* 1 size or volume, especially when great 2 main part 3 **in bulk** in large quantities

bulky bulkier bulkiest *adjective* large and heavy

bull *noun* male of some animals, such as cattle, elephants and whales

bulldog *noun* squat dog with a broad head and a muscular body

bulldozer *noun* powerful tractor for moving earth

bullet *noun* small piece of metal fired from a gun

bulletin *noun* short official report or announcement

bullion *noun* gold or silver in the form of bars

bullock *noun* young castrated bull

bullroarer *noun* wooden slat attached to a string that is whirled round to make a roaring noise, used by Australian Aborigines in religious ceremonies

bully bullies bullying bullied *noun* 1 person who uses strength or power to hurt or frighten other people ▷ *verb* 2 to make (someone) do something by using force or threats

bump *verb* 1 (often followed by *into*) to knock or strike (something or someone) with a jolt ▷ *noun* 2 soft or dull noise made by something knocking into something else 3 raised uneven part; lump > **bump off** *verb informal* to murder > **bumpy** *adjective*

bumper *noun* 1 bar on the front or back of a vehicle to protect against damage ▷ *adjective* 2 unusually large or abundant

bun *noun* 1 small sweet bread roll or cake 2 hair gathered into a ball shape at the back of the head

bunch bunches bunching **bunched** *noun* 1 number of things growing, fastened or grouped together ▷ *verb* 2 to group (things) together or be grouped together in a bunch

bundle bundles bundling **bundled** *noun* 1 number of things gathered loosely together ▷ *verb* 2 to push (someone or something) somewhere quickly and roughly

bung *noun* 1 stopper for a cask etc ▷ *verb* 2 *Brit informal* to throw (something) somewhere in a careless manner > **bung up** *verb informal* to block (a hole)

bungalow *noun* one-storey house

bungle bungles bungling **bungled** *verb* to spoil (something) through incompetence

bunion *noun* painful lump on the big toe

bunk *noun* narrow shelflike bed

bunker *noun* 1 sand-filled hollow forming an obstacle on a golf course 2 underground shelter 3 large storage container for coal etc

bunting *noun* decorative flags

bunyip *noun Aust* legendary monster said to live in swamps and lakes

buoy buoys *noun* floating object anchored in the sea to warn of danger

buoyant *adjective* 1 able to float 2 lively and cheerful > **buoyancy** *noun*

burden *noun* 1 heavy load 2 something difficult to cope with; worry > **burdensome** *adjective*: *a burdensome debt*

bureau bureaux *noun* 1 office that provides a service 2 writing desk with shelves and drawers

bureaucracy *noun* complex system of rules and procedures that operates in government departments > **bureaucratic** *adjective* involving complicated rules and procedures

bureaucrat *noun* person who works in a government department, especially one who follows rules and procedures strictly

burgeoning *adjective* growing or developing rapidly

burglar *noun* thief who breaks into a building > **burglary** *noun*

burgle burgles burgling burgled *verb* to break into (someone's house) and steal things

burial *noun* burying of a dead body

burly burlier burliest *adjective* (of a person) broad and strong

burn burns burning burned or **burnt** *verb* 1 to be on fire or set (something) on fire 2 to destroy (something) by fire or be destroyed by fire 3 to damage, injure or mark (someone or something) by heat 4 to feel strong emotion 5 to record data on (a compact disc) > *noun* 6 injury or mark caused by fire or exposure to heat

You can write either *burned* or *burnt* as the past form of *burn*

burp *informal verb* 1 to belch > *noun* 2 belch

burrow *noun* 1 hole dug in the ground by a rabbit etc > *verb* 2 to dig holes in the ground

bursar *noun* treasurer of a school, college or university

bursary bursaries *noun* sum of money given to someone to help fund their education

burst bursts bursting burst *verb* 1 to break open or apart noisily and suddenly 2 to come or go somewhere suddenly and forcibly 3 to be full to the point of breaking

open > *noun* 4 instance of breaking open suddenly 5 sudden outbreak or occurrence > **burst into** *verb* to be overcome by (tears or an emotion) suddenly

bury buries burying buried *verb* 1 to place (a dead body) in a grave 2 to place (something) in the earth and cover it with soil 3 to conceal or hide (something)

bus buses *noun* large motor vehicle for carrying passengers

bush bushes *noun* 1 dense woody plant, smaller than a tree 2 wild uncultivated part of a country

bushman bushmen *noun* 1 *Aust, NZ* person who lives or travels in the bush 2 *NZ* person whose job is to clear the bush for farming

Bushman Bushmen *noun* member of a group of people in southern Africa who live by hunting and gathering food

bushranger *noun Aust, NZ* in the past, an outlaw living in the bush

bushy bushier bushiest *adjective* (of hair) thick and shaggy

business businesses *noun* 1 purchase and sale of goods and services 2 commercial establishment; company 3 trade or profession 4 proper concern or responsibility 5 affair or matter

businesslike *adjective* efficient and methodical

businessman businessmen *noun* man who works in business

businesswoman businesswomen *noun* woman who works in business

busker *noun* street entertainer

bust busts busting bust or **busted** *noun* 1 woman's bosom 2 sculpture of the head and shoulders > *verb informal* 3 to burst or break 4 (of the police) to raid (a place) or arrest (someone) ▷ *adjective informal* **5** broken **6 go bust** to become bankrupt

bustle bustles bustling bustled *verb* **1** to hurry with a show of activity or energy ▷ *noun* **2** energetic and noisy activity

busy busier busiest; busies busying busied *adjective* **1** occupied doing something **2** crowded or full of activity ▷ *verb* **3** to keep (yourself) busy > **busily** *adverb* very actively

but *conjunction* **1** contrary to expectation **2** in contrast **3** other than **4** without it happening ▷ *preposition* **5** except ▷ *adverb* **6** only **7 but for** if it had not been for

butcher *noun* shopkeeper who sells meat

butler *noun* chief male servant

butt *noun* **1** thicker end of something **2** unused end of a cigar or cigarette **3** person or thing that is the target of ridicule **4** large barrel ▷ *verb* **5** to strike (something or someone) with the head or horns > **butt in** *verb* to interrupt a conversation

butter *noun* **1** soft fatty food made from cream, often eaten spread on bread or used in cooking ▷ *verb* **2** to put butter on (bread, etc)

butter bean *noun* large pale flat edible bean

buttercup *noun* small yellow wild flower

butterfly butterflies *noun* insect with brightly coloured wings

buttock *noun* either half of the human bottom

button *noun* **1** small disc or knob sewn onto clothing, which can be passed through a slit in another piece of fabric to fasten it **2** knob that operates a piece of equipment

when pressed ▷ *verb* **3** to fasten (a garment) with buttons

buttonhole *noun* **1** slit in a garment through which a button is passed **2** flower worn on a lapel

buxom *adjective* (of a woman) large, healthy and attractive

buy buys buying bought *verb* **1** to acquire (something) by paying money for it ▷ *noun* **2** thing acquired through payment > **buyer** *noun* **1** customer **2** person employed to buy merchandise

buzz buzzes buzzing buzzed *noun* **1** rapidly vibrating humming sound **2** *informal* sense of excitement ▷ *verb* **3** to make a humming sound **4** to be filled with an air of excitement

buzzard *noun* bird of prey of the hawk family

buzzer *noun* device that makes a buzzing sound

by *preposition* **1** indicating the doer of an action: *bitten by a dog* **2** indicating the manner or means of something: *travelling by train; He frightened her by hiding in the bushes* **3** beside or next to: *down by the river* **4** past: *driving by the school* **5** at or before: *in bed by midnight* ▷ *adverb* **6** past **7 by and by** eventually **8 by and large** in general

bye or **bye-bye** *interjection informal* goodbye

by-election *noun* election held to choose a new member of parliament after the previous member has resigned or died

bygone *adjective* past or former

bypass bypasses *noun* main road built to avoid a city

bystander *noun* person present but not involved

byte *noun* *Computers* group of bits processed as one unit of data

cab *noun* **1** taxi **2** enclosed driver's compartment on a train, truck, etc

cabaret *noun* dancing and singing show in a nightclub

cabbage *noun* vegetable with a large head of green leaves

cabbage tree *noun* **1** palm-like tree found in New Zealand with a tall bare trunk and big bunches of spiky leaves **2** similar tree found in eastern Australia

cabin *noun* **1** room in a ship or boat where a passenger sleeps **2** area where the passengers or the crew sit in a plane **3** small wooden hut, usually in the country

cabinet *noun* **1** piece of furniture with drawers or shelves **2** **Cabinet** committee of senior government ministers

cable cables cabling cabled *noun* **1** strong thick rope **2** bundle of wires that carries electricity or electronic signals **3** telegram sent abroad ▷ *verb* **4** to send (someone) a message by cable

cable car *noun* vehicle pulled up a steep slope by a moving cable

cable television *noun* television service thaat people can subscribe to and which is received from underground wires which carry the signals

cacao *noun* tropical tree with seed pods from which chocolate and cocoa are made

cache *noun* hidden store of weapons or treasure: *a cache of guns*

cachet *noun formal* status and respect that something has

cackle cackles cackling cackled *verb* **1** to laugh harshly ▷ *noun* **2** harsh laugh

cacophony *noun formal* harsh discordant sound

cactus cacti or **cactuses** *noun* fleshy desert plant with spines but no leaves

cad *noun old-fashioned* man who behaves dishonourably

caddie caddies caddying caddied; also spelt **caddy** *noun* **1** person who carries a golfer's clubs ▷ *verb* **2** to act as a golf caddie

caddy caddies *noun Chiefly Brit* small container in which tea is stored ▷ *noun, verb* **2** same as **caddie**

cadence *noun* rise and fall in the pitch of the voice

cadet *noun* young person training for the armed forces or police

cadge cadges cadging cadged *verb informal* to get (something) by taking advantage of someone's generosity: *I cadged a lift*

Caesarean or **Caesarian** *noun* (also **Caesarean section**) surgical operation in which a pregnant woman's baby is delivered through a cut in its mother's abdomen

café *noun* **1** small or inexpensive restaurant serving light refreshments **2** *S Afr* corner shop or grocer's shop

cafeteria *noun* self-service

restaurant

caffeine *noun* stimulant found in tea and coffee

caftan *noun* same as **kaftan**

cage *noun* **1** enclosure of bars or wires, for keeping animals or birds **2** enclosed platform of a lift in a mine > **caged** *adjective* kept in a cage

cagey cagier cagiest *adjective* *informal* reluctant to go into details

cagoule *noun* *Brit* lightweight hooded waterproof jacket

cahoots *plural noun* **in cahoots** *informal* conspiring together

cairn *noun* mound of stones erected as a memorial or marker

cajole cajoles cajoling cajoled *verb* to persuade by flattery: *He was cajoled into staying on*

cake cakes caking caked *noun* **1** sweet food baked from a mixture of flour, eggs, etc **2** flat compact mass of something, such as soap ▷ *verb* **3** to form into a hardened mass or crust

calamity calamities *noun* event that causes disaster or distress > **calamitous** *adjective* resulting in or from disaster

calcium *noun* *Chemistry* silvery-white metallic element found in bones, teeth, limestone and chalk

calculate calculates calculating calculated *verb* **1** to work out by a mathematical procedure or by reasoning **2** to plan deliberately; intend

calculating *adjective* selfishly scheming: *a calculating man*

calculation *noun* **1** act or result of calculating **2** selfish scheming

calculator *noun* small electronic device for making calculations

calculus *noun* branch of mathematics dealing with

infinitesimal changes to a variable number or quantity

calendar *noun* **1** chart showing a year divided up into months, weeks and days **2** system for determining the beginning, length and division of years: *the Jewish calendar* **3** schedule of events or appointments

calf calves *noun* **1** young cow, bull, elephant, whale or seal **2** leather made from calf skin **3** back of the leg between the ankle and knee

calibre *noun* **1** person's ability or worth: *a player of her calibre* **2** diameter of the bore of a gun or of a shell or bullet

call *verb* **1** to name **2** to shout to attract attention **3** to telephone **4** to summon **5** (often followed by *on*) to visit **6** to arrange (a meeting, strike, etc) ▷ *noun* **7** cry or shout **8** animal's or bird's cry **9** telephone communication **10** short visit **11** summons or invitation **12** need or demand > **call for** *verb* **1** to require **2** to come and fetch > **call off** *verb* to cancel > **call up** *verb* **1** to summon to serve in the armed forces **2** to cause you to remember (something)

call box call boxes *noun* kiosk for a public telephone

call centre *noun* office where staff deal with customers' orders or questions over the telephone

calligraphy *noun* (art of) beautiful handwriting

calling *noun* **1** profession or career, especially a caring one **2** strong urge to follow a particular career or profession, especially a caring one

callisthenics *plural noun* light keep-fit exercises

callous *adjective* showing no concern for other people's feelings

> **callously** *adverb* > **callousness** *noun*: *the callousness of his attacker*

callow *adjective* young and inexperienced

calm *adjective* **1** not agitated or excited **2** (of sea or weather) not affected by the wind ▷ *noun* **3** peaceful state ▷ *verb* **4** to calm down > **calm down** *verb* to make (someone) calm or become calm > **calmly** *adverb* > **calmness** *noun*

calorie *noun* **1** unit of measurement for the energy value of food **2** unit of heat equal to about 4.187 joules > **calorific** *adjective* of calories or heat

calumny calumnies *noun* false or malicious statement

calves the plural of **calf**

calypso calypsos *noun* West Indian song with improvised topical lyrics

calyx calyxes or **calyces** *noun Botany* outer leaves that protect a flower bud

camaraderie *noun* feeling of trust and friendship between a group of people

camber *noun* slight upward curve towards the centre of a road

camcorder *noun* combined portable video camera and recorder

came *verb* past tense of **come**

camel *noun* humped mammal that can survive long periods without food or water in desert regions

cameo cameos *noun* **1** small part in a film or play performed by a well-known actor or actress **2** brooch or ring with a carving on it, typically of a head in profile, in a different coloured stone from the background

camera *noun* **1** apparatus used for taking photographs or pictures for television or cinema **2** **in camera** in private session

camomile or **chamomile** *noun* plant with a strong smell and daisy-like flowers which are used to make herbal tea

camouflage camouflages camouflaging camouflaged *noun* **1** use of natural surroundings or artificial aids to conceal or disguise something ▷ *verb* **2** to conceal by camouflage

camp *noun* **1** (place for) temporary lodgings consisting of tents, huts or cabins **2** group supporting a particular idea or belief: *the pro-government camp* ▷ *verb* **3** to stay in a camp ▷ *adjective informal* **4** effeminate or homosexual **5** consciously artificial or affected > **camper** *noun* person who stays temporarily in a tent, hut or cabin > **camping** *noun* activity of staying in tents, huts or cabins by holidaymakers, travellers, etc

campaign *noun* **1** series of coordinated activities designed to achieve a goal ▷ *verb* **2** to take part in a campaign > **campaigner** *noun* person who campaigns to achieve a goal

camp-drafting *noun Aust* competition in which men on horseback select cattle or sheep from a herd or flock

campus campuses *noun* area of land and the buildings that make up a university or college

can¹ could *verb* **1** to be able to: *I can speak Italian* **2** to be allowed to: *You can go to the cinema*

can² cans canning canned *noun* **1** metal container for food or liquids ▷ *verb* **2** to put (something) into a can

Canadian *adjective* **1** belonging or relating to Canada ▷ *noun* **2** someone from Canada

canal *noun* **1** artificial waterway **2** passage in the body

canapé *noun* small piece of bread or toast with a savoury topping

canary canaries *noun* small yellow songbird often kept as a pet

can-can *noun* lively high-kicking dance performed by a female group

cancel cancels cancelling cancelled *verb* **1** to stop (something that has been arranged) from taking place **2** to mark (a cheque or stamp) with an official stamp to prevent further use **3 cancel out** to make ineffective by having the opposite effect: *Their opening goal was cancelled out just before half-time* > **cancellation** *noun*

cancer *noun* **1** serious disease resulting from a malignant growth or tumour **2** malignant growth or tumour > **cancerous** *adjective* resulting from cancer

Cancer *noun* fourth sign of the zodiac, represented by a crab

candelabra or **candelabrum** *noun* large branched candle holder

candid *adjective* honest and straightforward > **candidly** *adverb*

candidate *noun* **1** person seeking a job or position **2** person taking an examination > **candidacy** or **candidature** *noun* position of being a candidate in an election

candied *adjective* covered or cooked in sugar

candle *noun* stick of wax enclosing a wick, which is burned to produce light

candlestick *noun* holder for a candle

candour *noun* honesty and straightforwardness

candy candies *noun* US sweet or sweets

candyfloss *noun* light fluffy mass of spun sugar on a stick

cane canes caning caned *noun* **1** stem of the bamboo or similar plant **2** flexible rod used to beat someone **3** slender walking stick ▷ *verb* **4** to beat with a cane

canine *adjective* **1** of or like a dog ▷ *noun* **2** sharp pointed tooth between the incisors and the molars

canister *noun* metal container

canker *noun* disease which causes sores around the mouth or ears of animals or people

cannabis *noun* drug obtained from the dried leaves and flowers of the hemp plant

canned *adjective* **1** preserved in a can **2** (of music or laughter on a television or radio show) recorded beforehand

cannibal *noun* **1** person who eats human flesh **2** animal that eats others of its own kind > **cannibalism** *noun* practice of eating the flesh of one's own kind

cannibalize cannibalizes cannibalizing cannibalized; also spelt **cannibalise** *verb* to use parts from (one machine) to repair another

cannon *noun* large wheeled gun formerly used in battles to fire heavy metal balls

cannot *verb* can not: *She cannot come home yet*

canny cannier canniest *adjective* clever and cautious > **cannily** *adverb*

canoe *noun* light narrow open boat propelled by a paddle or paddles > **canoeing** *noun* sport of rowing in a canoe > **canoeist** *noun* person who rows a canoe

canon *noun* **1** priest serving in

a cathedral **2** Church decree regulating morals or religious practices **3** general rule or standard: *the first canon of nursing*

canonize canonizes canonizing canonized; also spelt **canonise** *verb* to declare (a dead person) officially to be a saint

canopy canopies *noun* **1** covering above a bed, door, etc **2** any large or wide covering: *the thick forest canopy*

cant *noun* moral or religious statements made by someone who does not believe what they are saying

can't *verb* can not

cantankerous *adjective* quarrelsome or bad-tempered

canteen *noun* **1** restaurant attached to a workplace or school **2** box containing a set of cutlery

canter *noun* **1** movement of a horse at a speed between a trot and a gallop ▷ *verb* **2** to move at a canter

cantilever *noun* beam or girder fixed at one end only

canton *noun* political and administrative region of a country, especially Switzerland

canvas canvases *noun* **1** heavy coarse cloth used for sails and tents **2** piece of canvas or similar material on which you can paint with oils **3** oil painting on canvas

canvass canvasses canvassing canvassed *verb* **1** to try to get votes or support for a particular person or political party: *a woman who canvassed for the Conservatives* **2** to find out the opinions of (people) by conducting a survey ▷ *noun* **3** activity of canvassing

canyon *noun* deep narrow valley

cap caps capping capped *noun* **1** soft flat hat, often with a peak at the front **2** small lid **3** small

explosive device used in a toy gun **4** upper financial limit ▷ *verb* **5** to cover or top with something **6** to select (a player) for a national team **7** to impose an upper limit on (a tax) **8** to outdo or excel: *capping anecdote with anecdote*

capability capabilities *noun* ability or skill to do something

capable *adjective* **1** **capable of** able to do (something): *a man capable of extreme violence* **2** skilful or talented > **capably** *adverb*

capacity capacities *noun* **1** ability to contain, absorb or hold **2** maximum amount or number that can be contained or produced: *a seating capacity of eleven thousand* **3** physical or mental ability: *people's creative capacities* **4** position or role: *in his capacity as councillor*

cape *noun* **1** short cloak with no sleeves **2** large piece of land that juts out into the sea

caper *noun* **1** a light-hearted practical joke ▷ *verb* **2** to skip about playfully

capers *plural noun* pickled flower buds of a Mediterranean shrub used in sauces

capillary capillaries *noun* very fine blood vessel

capital *noun* **1** chief city of a country **2** amount of money or property owned or used by a business **3** sum of money saved or invested in order to gain interest **4** large letter, as used at the beginning of a name or sentence **5** top part of a stone column, often decorated ▷ *adjective* **6** *law* involving or punishable by death: *a capital offence*

capitalism *noun* economic system based on the private ownership of industry > **capitalist** *adjective* **1** of capitalists or capitalism

2 supporting capitalism ▷ *noun*
3 supporter of capitalism **4** person
who owns a business

capitalize capitalizes
capitalizing capitalized; also
spelt **capitalise** *verb* **1** to write
or print (words) in capitals **2** to
convert into or provide with capital
3 capitalize on to take advantage
of (a situation)

capital punishment *noun* legal
killing used as a punishment for
certain crimes

capitulate capitulates
capitulating capitulated *verb*
to surrender on agreed terms
> **capitulation** *noun* surrender
under agreed conditions

cappuccino cappuccinos *noun*
coffee with steamed milk, sprinkled
with powdered chocolate

capricious *adjective* often changing
unexpectedly

Capricorn *noun* tenth sign of the
zodiac, represented by a goat

capsize capsizes capsizing
capsized *verb* (of a boat) to
overturn accidentally

capsule *noun* **1** soluble gelatine
case containing a dose of medicine
2 plant's seed case **3** detachable
crew compartment of a spacecraft

captain *noun* **1** commander of a ship
or civil aircraft **2** middle-ranking
naval officer **3** junior officer in
the army **4** leader of a team or
group ▷ *verb* **5** to be captain of
> **captaincy** *noun* position of being
captain

caption *noun* **1** title or explanation
accompanying an illustration
▷ *verb* **2** to provide with a caption

captivate captivates
captivating captivated *verb* to
attract and hold the attention of: *I
was captivated by her* > **captivating**

adjective: *her captivating smile*

captive *noun* **1** person kept in
confinement ▷ *adjective* **2** kept in
confinement: *a captive bird* **3** (of
an audience) unable to leave
> **captivity** *noun* state of being
kept in confinement

captor *noun* person who captures a
person or animal

capture captures capturing
captured *verb* **1** to take by force
2 to succeed in representing (a
quality or mood): *Today's newspapers
capture the mood of the nation* ▷ *noun*
3 capturing: *the fifth anniversary of
his capture*

car *noun* **1** motor vehicle designed
to carry a small number of people
2 passenger compartment of a
cable car, lift, etc **3** US railway
carriage

carafe *noun* glass bottle for serving
water or wine

caramel *noun* **1** chewy sweet made
from sugar and milk **2** burnt sugar,
used for colouring and flavouring
food

carat *noun* **1** unit of weight of
precious stones **2** measure of the
purity of gold in an alloy

caravan *noun* **1** large enclosed
vehicle for living in, designed to be
towed by a car **2** group travelling
together in Eastern countries

carbohydrate *noun* any of a
large group of energy-producing
compounds in food, such as sugars
and starches

carbon *noun* non-metallic element
occurring as charcoal, graphite,
and diamond, found in all organic
matter

carbonated *adjective* (of a drink)
containing carbon dioxide

carbon dioxide *noun* colourless
gas breathed out by people

and animals, and used in fire extinguishers and in making fizzy drinks

carbon monoxide *noun* colourless poisonous gas formed when carbon burns in a very small amount of air

carburettor *noun* device which mixes petrol and air in an internal-combustion engine

carcass carcasses; also spelt **carcase** *noun* dead body of an animal

card *noun* **1** piece of thick stiff paper or cardboard used for identification, reference or sending greetings or messages: *a birthday card* **2** one of a set of cards with a printed pattern, used for playing games **3** small rectangle of stiff plastic with identifying numbers for use as a credit card, cheque card or charge card **4 cards** any card game, or card games in general **5 on the cards** very likely to happen

cardboard *noun* thin stiff board made from paper pulp

cardiac *adjective* relating to the heart

cardigan *noun* knitted jacket that fastens up the front

cardinal *noun* **1** any of the high-ranking clergymen of the RC Church who elect the Pope and act as his counsellors ▷ *adjective* **2** fundamentally important

cardinal number *noun* ordinary number, such as one, thirteen and ninety, as opposed to first, thirteenth and ninetieth. Compare **ordinal number**

care cares caring cared *verb* **1** to be concerned **2** to like (to do something) ▷ *noun* **3** careful attention or caution: *Treat with extreme care* **4** protection or charge:

The children are now in the care of an orphanage **5** trouble or worry: *money cares* **6 in care** (of a child) cared for by the state **7 care of** at the address of ▷ **care for** *verb* **1** to like or be fond of **2** to look after

career *noun* **1** series of jobs in a profession or occupation that a person has through his or her life **2** part of a person's life spent in a particular occupation ▷ *verb* **3** to rush in an uncontrolled way

carefree *adjective* having no worries or responsibilities

careful *adjective* **1** acting sensibly and with care: *Be careful what you say to him* **2** complete and well done: *It needs very careful planning* ▷ **carefully** *adverb*

careless *adjective* **1** done badly without enough attention: *careless driving* **2** relaxed and unconcerned: *careless laughter* ▷ **carelessly** *adverb* ▷ **carelessness** *noun*

caress caresses caressing caressed *noun* **1** gentle affectionate touch or embrace ▷ *verb* **2** to touch gently and affectionately

caretaker *noun* **1** person employed to look after a place ▷ *adjective* **2** temporarily in charge until a new leader or government is appointed; acting: *O'Leary was named caretaker manager*

cargo cargoes *noun* goods carried by a ship, aircraft, etc

Caribbean *noun* **1 the Caribbean** Caribbean Sea east of Central America and the islands in it ▷ *adjective* **2** relating to or typical of the Caribbean

caricature caricatures caricaturing caricatured *noun* **1** drawing or description of a person that exaggerates features

for comic effect ▷ *verb* **2** to make a
caricature of

carnage *noun* violent killing of large
numbers of people

carnal *adjective formal* of a sexual or
sensual nature

carnation *noun* cultivated plant
with fragrant white, pink or red
flowers

carnival *noun* festive period with
processions, music and dancing
in the street

carnivore *noun* meat-eating
animal > **carnivorous** *adjective*
meat-eating

carol *noun* joyful religious song sung
at Christmas time

carousel *noun* **1** revolving conveyor
belt for luggage or photographic
slides **2** *US* merry-go-round

carp *noun* **1** large freshwater fish
▷ *verb* **2** to complain or find fault

car park *noun* area or building
reserved for parking cars

carpel *noun* seed-bearing female
part of a flowering plant

carpenter *noun* person who makes
or repairs wooden structures
> **carpentry** *noun* skill or work of
a carpenter

carpet *noun* **1** heavy fabric for
covering floors ▷ *verb* **2** to cover
with a carpet

carriage *noun* **1** one of the sections
of a train for passengers **2** four-
wheeled horse-drawn vehicle
3 moving part of a machine that
supports and shifts another part:
a typewriter carriage **4** charge made
for conveying goods **5** way a person
holds his or her head and body
when he or she moves

carriageway carriageways *noun*
1 *Brit* part of a road along which
traffic passes in one direction **2** *NZ*
part of a road used by vehicles

carrier *noun* **1** person or thing that
carries something: *a troop carrier*
2 person or animal that does
not suffer from a disease but can
transmit it to others

carrier bag *noun* bag made of
plastic or paper, used for carrying
shopping

carrion *noun* dead and rotting flesh

carrot *noun* **1** long tapering orange
root vegetable **2** something offered
as an incentive

carry carries carrying carried
verb **1** to take (something) from
one place to another **2** to have
(something) with you habitually,
in your pocket etc **3** to be capable
of transmitting (a disease) **4** to
have as a factor or result: *The charge
carries a maximum penalty of twenty
years* **5** to secure the adoption of
(a bill or motion) **6** (of sound) to
travel a certain distance > **carry
away** *verb* **be** or **get carried
away** to behave hastily or foolishly
through excitement > **carry on**
verb **1** to continue **2** *informal* to
cause a fuss > **carry out** *verb* **1** to
follow (an order or instruction) **2** to
accomplish (a task)

cart *noun* **1** vehicle with wheels,
used to carry goods and often
pulled by horses, donkeys or oxen
▷ *verb* **2** to carry, usually with
some effort

cartel *noun* association of
competing firms formed to fix
prices

cartilage *noun* strong flexible
tissue forming part of the skeleton

cartography *noun* map making
> **cartographer** *noun* person who
draws maps

carton *noun* container made of
cardboard or waxed paper

cartoon *noun* **1** humorous or

satirical drawing **2** sequence of these telling a story **3** film made by photographing a series of drawings which give the illusion of movement when projected **> cartoonist** *noun* person who draws cartoons

cartridge *noun* **1** casing containing an explosive charge and bullet for a gun **2** part of the pick-up of a record player that converts the movements of the stylus into electrical signals **3** sealed container of film, tape, etc

cartwheel *noun* acrobatic movement in which you turn over sideways in a wheel-like motion with your weight supported in turns by your hands and feet

carve carves carving carved *verb* **1** to cut (something) to form an object **2** to form (an object or design) by cutting **3** to slice (cooked meat)

carving *noun* carved object

cascade cascades cascading cascaded *noun* **1** waterfall or group of waterfalls **2** something flowing or falling like a waterfall ▷ *verb* **3** to flow or fall in a cascade

case *noun* **1** particular situation, event or example: *a case of mistaken identity* **2** condition or state of affairs **3** set of arguments supporting an action or cause **4** person or problem dealt with by a doctor, social worker, solicitor or police officer **5** container or protective covering **6** trial or lawsuit **7** *Grammar* form of a noun, pronoun or adjective showing its relation to other words in the sentence: *the accusative case* **8 in case** allowing for the possibility that: *I didn't shout in case I startled you*

casement *noun* window that is hinged on one side

cash cashes cashing cashed *noun* **1** banknotes and coins ▷ *verb* **2** to obtain cash for **3 cash in on** *informal* to gain profit or advantage from

cashew *noun* edible kidney-shaped nut

cash flow *noun* money that a business makes and spends

cashier *noun* **1** person responsible for handling cash in a bank, shop, etc ▷ *verb* **2** to dismiss (someone) with dishonour from the armed forces

cashmere *noun* fine soft wool obtained from goats

cash register *noun* till that displays and adds the prices of the goods sold

cash-strapped *adjective* short of money

casing *noun* protective case or covering

casino casinos *noun* public building or room where gambling games are played

cask *noun* **1** barrel used to hold alcoholic drink **2** *Aust* cubic carton containing wine, with a tap for dispensing

casket *noun* **1** small box for valuables **2** *US* coffin

casserole *noun* **1** covered dish in which food is cooked slowly, usually in an oven **2** dish cooked in this way

cassette *noun* plastic case containing a reel of film or magnetic tape

cassette recorder *noun* machine used for recording and playing cassettes

cassock *noun* long tunic, usually black, worn by priests

cassowary cassowaries *noun* large flightless bird of Australia and New Guinea

cast casts casting cast *noun* **1** actors in a play or film collectively **2** object shaped by a mould while molten **3** mould used to shape such an object **4** rigid plaster-of-Paris casing for immobilizing broken bones while they heal ▷ *verb* **5** to select (an actor) to play a part in a play or film **6** to give or deposit (a vote) **7** to throw (a fishing line) into the water **8** to shape (an object) by pouring molten material into a mould **9** to throw with force **10** to direct (a glance)

castanets *plural noun* musical instrument, used by Spanish dancers, consisting of curved pieces of wood clicked together in the hand

castaway castaways *noun* shipwrecked person

caste *noun* **1** any of the four hereditary classes into which Hindu society is divided **2** system of social classes decided according to family, wealth and position

caster sugar or **castor sugar** *noun* finely ground white sugar

castigate castigates castigating castigated *verb formal* to reprimand (a person) harshly

cast-iron *adjective* **1** made of a hard but brittle type of iron **2** definite or unchallengeable

castle *noun* **1** large fortified building, often built as a ruler's residence **2** rook in chess

cast-off *noun* discarded person or thing

castor or **caster** *noun* small swivelling wheel fixed to the bottom of a piece of furniture for easy moving

castor oil *noun* oil obtained from an Indian plant, used as a lubricant and laxative

castrate castrates castrating castrated *verb* to remove the testicles of > **castration** *noun* removal of the testicles from a male animal

casual *adjective* **1** careless or without interest: *a casual glance* **2** (of work or workers) occasional or not permanent: *casual labour* **3** for informal wear **4** happening by chance: *a casual remark* > **casually** *adverb*

casualty casualties *noun* **1** person killed or injured in an accident or war **2** person or thing that has suffered as the result of something

casuarina *noun* Australian tree with jointed green branches

cat *noun* **1** small domesticated furry mammal **2** related wild mammal, such as the lion or tiger **3** **let the cat out the bag** to reveal a secret

catacombs *plural noun* underground burial place consisting of tunnels with recesses for tombs

catalogue catalogues cataloguing catalogued *noun* **1** book containing details of items for sale **2** systematic list of items ▷ *verb* **3** to make a systematic list of

catalyst *noun* **1** substance that speeds up a chemical reaction without itself changing **2** something that causes a change to happen: *the catalyst which provoked civil war*

catamaran *noun* boat with two parallel hulls connected to each other

catapult *noun* **1** Y-shaped device with a loop of elastic, used by children for firing stones ▷ *verb*

2 to shoot forwards or upwards violently **3** to cause (someone) suddenly to be in a particular situation: *catapulted to stardom*

cataract *noun* **1** area of the lens of someone's eye that has become opaque instead of clear, preventing them from seeing properly **2** large waterfall

catarrh *noun* condition in which you get a lot of mucus in your nose and throat

catastrophe *noun* great and sudden disaster > **catastrophic** *adjective* disastrous

catch catches catching caught *verb* **1** to seize and hold **2** to capture: *I caught ten fish* **3** to surprise in an act: *two boys were caught stealing* **4** to hit unexpectedly: *His shoe caught me in the belly* **5** to be in time for (a bus, train, etc) **6** to see or hear **7** to become infected with (an illness) **8** to entangle or become entangled: *The fibres caught on the mesh* **9** to understand or make out: *I didn't catch his meaning* **10 catch it** *informal* to be punished ▷ *noun* **11** device for fastening a door, window, etc **12** *informal* concealed or unforeseen drawback > **catch on** *verb informal* **1** to become popular **2** to understand > **catch out** *verb informal* to trap (someone) in an error or lie > **catch up** *verb* **1** (often followed by *with*) to reach the same place or level (as someone): *She ran to catch up with him* **2** (often followed by *on, with*) to do something in order to get up to date (with something): *He had a lot of paperwork to catch up on* **3 be caught up in** to be unwillingly or accidentally involved in

catching *adjective* infectious

catchy catchier catchiest *adjective* (of a tune) pleasant and easily remembered

catechism *noun* instruction on the doctrine of a Christian Church in a series of questions and answers

categorical *adjective* absolutely clear and certain: *a categorical denial* > **categorically** *adverb*

categorize categorizes categorizing categorized; also spelt **categorise** *verb* to put in a category

category categories *noun* set of things with a particular characteristic in common: *Occupations can be divided into four categories*

cater *verb* to provide what is needed or wanted, especially food or services

caterer *noun* person or business that provides food for parties and groups

caterpillar *noun* wormlike larva of a moth or butterfly

catharsis catharses *noun* *formal* relief of strong suppressed emotions, for example through drama or psychoanalysis > **cathartic** *adjective* causing catharsis: *His laughter was cathartic*

cathedral *noun* important church with a bishop in charge of it

cathode *noun* negative electrode, by which electrons leave a circuit

catholic *adjective* **1** (of tastes or interests) covering a wide range ▷ *noun, adjective* **2 Catholic** (member) of the Roman Catholic Church > **Catholicism** *noun* traditions and beliefs of Catholics

> When *Catholic* begins with a capital letter, it refers to the religion. When it begins with a small letter, it means 'covering a wide range'

cattle *plural noun* domesticated cows and bulls

catty cattier cattiest *adjective informal* unpleasant and spiteful > **cattiness** *noun*

catwalk *noun* narrow pathway or platform that people walk along, for example over a stage

Caucasian *adjective* **1** of the race of people with light-coloured skin ▷ *noun* **2** person belonging to this race

caught *verb* past of **catch**

cauldron *noun* large pot used for boiling

cauliflower *noun* vegetable with a large head of white flower buds surrounded by green leaves

causal *adjective* of or being a cause > **causally** *adverb*

cause causes causing caused *noun* **1** something that produces a particular effect **2 cause for** reason or motive for **3** aim or principle supported by a person or group: *dedication to the cause of peace* ▷ *verb* **4** to be the cause of

causeway causeways *noun* raised path or road across water or marshland

caustic *adjective* **1** capable of burning by chemical action **2** bitter and sarcastic

caution *noun* **1** care, especially in the face of danger **2** warning ▷ *verb* **3** to warn or advise: *He cautioned against an abrupt turnaround* > **cautionary** *adjective* warning

cautious *adjective* acting with or involving great care in order to avoid danger or risk > **cautiously** *adverb*

cavalcade *noun* procession of people on horseback or in cars

cavalier *adjective* **1** arrogant and behaving without sensitivity ▷ *noun* **2 Cavalier** supporter of Charles I in the English Civil War

cavalry cavalries *noun* part of the army originally on horseback, but now using fast armoured vehicles

cave caves caving caved *noun* hollow in the side of a hill or cliff > **cave in** *verb* **1** to collapse inwards **2** *informal* to give way under pressure

caveat *noun* warning

caveman cavemen *noun* prehistoric cave dweller

cavern *noun* large cave

cavernous *adjective* large, deep and hollow

caviar or **caviare** *noun* tiny salted eggs of the sturgeon, regarded as a delicacy

cavity cavities *noun* **1** hollow space **2** decayed area on a tooth

cavort *verb* to jump around excitedly

caw *noun* **1** cry of a crow, rook or raven ▷ *verb* **2** to make this cry

CB *abbreviation* Citizens' Band: range of radio waves which the general public can use to send messages to one another

cc *abbreviation* **1** cubic centimetre **2** carbon copy

CD CDs *abbreviation* compact disc

CD-ROM CD-ROMs *abbreviation* compact disc read-only memory

cease ceases ceasing ceased *verb* to bring or come to an end

ceasefire *noun* agreement between groups that are fighting each other to stop for a period and discuss peace

ceaseless *adjective* going on without stopping > **ceaselessly** *adverb*

cedar *noun* **1** evergreen coniferous tree **2** its wood

cede cedes ceding ceded *verb* to

surrender (territory or legal rights): *Haiti was ceded to France in 1697*

ceilidh *noun* informal social gathering for singing and dancing, especially in Scotland

ceiling *noun* **1** inner upper surface of a room **2** upper limit set on something: *a ceiling on prices*

celebrate celebrates celebrating celebrated *verb* **1** to hold festivities to mark (a happy event, anniversary, etc): *a party to celebrate the end of the exams* **2** to perform (a religious ceremony) ▷ **celebration** *noun*: *a celebration of his life* ▷ **celebratory** *adjective*: *a celebratory meal*

celebrated *adjective* well known

celebrity celebrities *noun* **1** famous person **2** state of being famous

celery *noun* vegetable with long green crisp edible stalks

celestial *adjective formal* **1** heavenly or divine **2** of the sky: *stars, planets and other celestial objects*

celibate *adjective* **1** unmarried and abstaining from sex ▷ *noun* **2** celibate person ▷ **celibacy** *noun* state of being celibate

cell *noun* **1** smallest unit of an organism that is able to function independently **2** small room for a prisoner, monk or nun **3** small compartment of a honeycomb etc **4** small group operating as the core of a larger organization **5** device that produces electrical energy by chemical reaction

cellar *noun* **1** underground room for storage **2** stock of wine

cello cellos *noun* large low-pitched instrument of the violin family ▷ **cellist** *noun* person who plays the cello

Cellophane® *noun* thin transparent cellulose sheeting used as wrapping

cellular *adjective* relating to the cells of animals or plants

celluloid *noun* kind of plastic used to make toys and, formerly, photographic film

Celsius *noun* temperature scale in which water freezes at 0° and boils at 100°

Celt *noun* person from Scotland, Ireland, Wales, Cornwall or Brittany

Celtic *noun* **1** group of languages including Gaelic and Welsh ▷ *adjective* **2** of the Celts or the Celtic languages

cement *noun* **1** fine grey powder mixed with water and sand to make mortar or concrete **2** something that unites, binds or joins **3** material used to fill teeth ▷ *verb* **4** to join, bind or cover with cement **5** to make (a relationship) stronger

cemetery cemeteries *noun* place where dead people are buried

cenotaph *noun* monument honouring soldiers who died in a war

censor *noun* **1** person authorized to examine films, books, etc, to ban or cut anything considered obscene or objectionable ▷ *verb* **2** to ban or cut parts of (a film, book, etc) ▷ **censorship** *noun* practice or policy of censoring films, publications, etc

censure censures censuring censured *noun* **1** severe disapproval ▷ *verb* **2** to criticize (someone or something) severely

census censuses *noun* official count of a population

cent *noun* hundredth part of a monetary unit such as the dollar or euro

centaur *noun* Greek mythological

creature with the head, arms and torso of a man, and the lower body and legs of a horse

centenary centenaries noun Chiefly Brit 100th anniversary or its celebration

centi- prefix meaning one hundredth: centimetre

centigrade adjective same as **Celsius**

| Scientists say and write Celsius rather than Centigrade

centilitre noun one hundredth of a litre

centime noun unit of currency used in Switzerland and some other countries, and formerly used in France and Belgium

centimetre noun one hundredth of a metre

centipede noun small wormlike creature with many legs

central adjective 1 of, at or forming the centre 2 main or most important > **centrally** adverb

Central America noun another name for the Isthmus of Panama, the area of land joining North America to South America

central heating noun system of heating a building in which water or air is heated in a tank and travels through pipes and radiators round the building

centralize centralizes centralizing centralized; also spelt **centralise** verb to bring (a country or an organization) under central control > **centralization** noun process of bringing under central control

centre centres centring centred noun 1 middle point or part 2 place for a specified activity: a health centre 3 political party or group favouring moderation 4 Sport player

who plays in the middle of the field ▷ verb 5 to put in the centre of something 6 **centre on** to have as a centre or main theme

centrifugal adjective moving away from a centre

centripetal adjective moving towards a centre

centurion noun (in ancient Rome) officer commanding 100 men

century centuries noun 1 period of 100 years 2 cricket score of 100 runs by a batsman

ceramic noun 1 hard brittle material made by heating clay to a very high temperature 2 object made of this 3 **ceramics** art of producing ceramic objects ▷ adjective 4 made of ceramic

cereal noun 1 grass plant with edible grain, such as oat or wheat 2 this grain 3 breakfast food made from this grain, eaten mixed with milk

cerebral adjective formal 1 of or relating to the brain 2 involving intelligence rather than emotions or instinct

cerebral palsy noun illness caused by damage to a baby's brain, which makes its muscles and limbs very weak

ceremonial adjective of or relating to ceremony or ritual: ceremonial dress > **ceremonially** adverb

ceremony ceremonies noun 1 set of formal actions performed at a special occasion or important public event: his recent coronation ceremony 2 very formal and polite behaviour: He hung up the phone without ceremony 3 **stand on ceremony** to insist on or act with excessive formality

certain adjective 1 sure: He was certain we'd agree 2 definite: It's not certain it exists 3 some but not much:

a certain resemblance

certainly *adverb* **1** without doubt **2** of course

certainty certainties *noun* **1** state of being sure **2** something that is inevitable: *There are no certainties*

certificate *noun* official document stating the details of a birth, academic course, etc

certify certifies certifying certified *verb* **1** to confirm or attest to **2** to guarantee (that certain required standards have been met) **3** to declare legally insane

cervix cervixes or **cervices** *noun technical* entrance to the womb at the top of the vagina > **cervical** *adjective* relating to the cervix

cessation *noun formal* ending or pause: *a swift cessation of hostilities*

cf compare

CFC CFCs *abbreviation* chlorofluorocarbon

chaff *noun* outer parts of grain separated from the seeds by beating

chaffinch chaffinches *noun* small European songbird with black and white wings

chagrin *noun formal* feeling of annoyance or disappointment

chain *noun* **1** flexible length of connected metal links **2** series of connected facts or events **3** group of shops, hotels, etc owned by one firm ▷ *verb* **4** to restrict or fasten with or as if with a chain: *They had chained themselves to railings*

chain saw *noun* large saw with teeth fixed in a chain that is driven round by a motor

chain-smoke chain-smokes chain-smoking chain-smoked *verb* to smoke (cigarettes) continuously

chair *noun* **1** seat with a back, for one person **2** official position of authority **3** person holding this **4** professorship ▷ *verb* **5** to preside over (a meeting)

chair lift *noun* series of chairs suspended from a moving cable for carrying people up a slope

chairman chairmen *noun* person in charge of a company's board of directors or a meeting > **chairmanship** *noun*: *during his chairmanship* > **chairperson** *noun* > **chairwoman** *noun*

Some people don't like to use *chairman* when talking about a woman. You can use *chair* or *chairperson* to talk about a man or a woman

chalet *noun* **1** kind of Swiss wooden house with a steeply sloping roof **2** similar house, used as a holiday home

chalice *noun* gold or silver cup used in churches to hold the Communion wine

chalk *noun* **1** soft white rock consisting of calcium carbonate **2** piece of chalk, often coloured, used for drawing and writing on blackboards ▷ *verb* **3** to draw or mark with chalk > **chalk up** *verb* to score or register (something): *He chalked up his first win* > **chalky** *adjective* containing or covered with chalk

challenge challenges challenging challenged *noun* **1** testing situation: *a new challenge at the right time in my career* **2** call to take part in a contest or fight **3** questioning of the rightness or value of something: *a challenge to authority* **4** demand by a sentry for identification or a password ▷ *verb* **5** to invite or call (someone) to take part in a contest, fight or argument:

She challenged me to a game **6** to call (a decision or action) into question **7** to order (a person) to stop and be identified > **challenger** *noun* competitor who takes on a champion or leader > **challenging** *adjective* requiring great effort and determination

challenged *adjective* disabled as specified: *physically challenged*

chamber *noun* **1** hall used for formal meetings **2** legislative or judicial assembly **3** *old-fashioned* bedroom **4** hollow place or compartment inside something, especially inside an animal's body or inside a gun **5 chambers** judge's room for hearing private cases not taken in open court

chamberlain *noun History* officer who managed the household of a king or nobleman

chambermaid *noun* woman employed to clean bedrooms in a hotel

chamber music *noun* classical music to be performed by a small group of musicians

chameleon *noun* small lizard that changes colour to blend in with its surroundings

chamois leather *noun* soft leather cloth used for polishing

champ *verb* **1** to chew noisily **2 champ at the bit** *informal* to be impatient to do something ▷ *noun* **3** short for **champion**

champagne *noun* sparkling white French wine

champion *noun* **1** overall winner of a competition **2** someone who defends a person or cause ▷ *verb* **3** to support

championship *noun* competition to find the champion of a sport

chance chances chancing

chanced *noun* **1** likelihood or probability **2** opportunity to do something **3** risk or gamble **4** unpredictable element that causes things to happen one way rather than another: *I found out by chance* ▷ *verb* **5** to try (something) in spite of the risk

chancellor *noun* **1** head of government in some European countries **2** honorary head of a university

Chancellor of the Exchequer Chancellors of the Exchequer *noun Brit* cabinet minister responsible for finance and taxes

chandelier *noun* ornamental light with branches and holders for several candles or bulbs

change changes changing

changed *noun* **1** difference or alteration **2** variety or novelty **3** replacement of something by something else: *a change of clothes* **4** money returned to you if you pay for something with a larger sum than needed **5** coins of low value ▷ *verb* **6** to make or become different **7** to exchange (something for something else) **8** to exchange (money) for smaller coins of the same total value or for a foreign currency **9** to put on other clothes **10** to leave one train, bus, etc and board another

changeable *adjective* changing often

changeover *noun* change from one system or activity to another

channel channels channelling channelled *noun* **1 a** wavelength used to receive programmes broadcast by a television or radio station **b** the station itself **2** means of access or communication **3** broad strait connecting two areas of sea **4** bed or course of a river, stream or canal **5** groove ▷ *verb* **6** to direct or convey through a channel or channels: *a system set up to channel funds to poorer countries*

chant *verb* **1** to repeat (a slogan, name, etc) over and over **2** to sing or recite (a psalm) ▷ *noun* **3** group of words repeated over and over again **4** psalm that has a short simple melody with several words sung on one note

Chanukah another spelling of **Hanukkah**

chaos *noun* complete disorder or confusion > **chaotic** *adjective* in a state of disorder or confusion > **chaotically** *adverb*

chap *noun informal* man or boy

chapati chapatis; also spelt **chapatti** *noun* (in Indian cookery) flat thin unleavened bread

chapel *noun* **1** section of a church or cathedral with its own altar **2** type of small church

chaperone chaperones chaperoning chaperoned *noun* **1** older person who accompanies and supervises a young person or young people on a social occasion ▷ *verb* **2** to act as a chaperone to

chaplain *noun* member of the Christian clergy who regularly works in a hospital, school or prison

chapped *adjective* (of the skin) raw and cracked, through exposure to cold

chapter *noun* **1** division of a book **2** period in a life or history **3** branch of a society or club **4** group of Christian clergy who work in a cathedral

char chars charring charred *verb* to blacken by partial burning > **charred** *adjective* burnt

character *noun* **1** combination of

qualities distinguishing a person, group or place **2** reputation, especially good reputation **3** unusual or interesting quality: *a building of great character* **4** person represented in a play, film or story **5** unusual or amusing person **6** letter, numeral or symbol used in writing or printing

characteristic *noun* **1** distinguishing feature or quality ▷ *adjective* **2** typical > **characteristically** *adverb*

characterization or **characterisation** *noun* **1** way people are portrayed in books, plays or films **2** act or instance of characterizing

characterize characterizes characterizing characterized; also spelt **characterise** *verb* **1** to be a characteristic of **2** **characterize as** to describe as

characterless *adjective* dull and uninteresting

charade *noun* ridiculous and unnecessary activity or pretence > **charades** *noun* game in which one team acts out a word or phrase, which the other team has to guess

charcoal *noun* black form of carbon made by burning wood without air, used as a fuel and also for drawing

charge charges charging charged *verb* **1** to ask (an amount of money) as a price **2** to enter a debit against a person's account for (a purchase) **3** (of the police) to accuse (someone) formally of a crime **4** to rush forward, often to attack **5** to fill (a battery) with electricity **6** *formal* to command or assign: *The president has charged his foreign minister with trying to open talks* ▷ *noun* **7** price charged for something **8** *formal* accusation of a crime in a court of law **9** onrush or attack **10** custody or guardianship: *in the charge of the police* **11** person or thing entrusted to someone's care **12** explosive put in a gun or other weapon **13** amount of electricity stored in a battery **14** **in charge of** in control of

chargeable *adjective* **1** liable to be taxed or charged **2** liable to result in a legal charge: *two chargeable offences*

charger *noun* **1** device for charging or recharging batteries **2** (in the Middle Ages) horse ridden into battle by a knight

chariot *noun* two-wheeled horse-drawn vehicle used in ancient times in wars and races

charisma *noun* person's power to attract or influence people **> charismatic** *adjective* having charisma

charity charities *noun* **1** organization that gives help, such as money or food, to those in need **2** giving of help to those in need **3** help given to those in need **4** kindly attitude towards people **> charitable** *adjective* **1** kind or lenient in your attitude towards others **2** of or for charity: *charitable organizations* **> charitably** *adverb*

charlatan *noun* person who claims expertise that he or she does not have

charm *noun* **1** quality of attracting, fascinating or delighting people **2** trinket worn on a bracelet **3** magic spell ▷ *verb* **4** to attract, fascinate or delight **5** to influence by personal charm **6** to protect or influence as if by magic: *a charmed life*

charmer *noun* person who uses his or her charm to influence people

charming *adjective* very pleasant

and attractive **> charmingly** *adverb*

chart *noun* **1** graph, table or diagram showing information **2** map of the sea or stars **3** **the charts** *informal* weekly lists of the best-selling pop records ▷ *verb* **4** to plot the course of **5** to make a chart of

charter *noun* **1** document granting or demanding certain rights **2** fundamental principles of an organization **3** hire of transport for private use ▷ *verb* **4** to hire by charter **5** to grant a charter to **> chartered** *adjective* officially qualified to practise a profession

chase chases chasing chased *verb* **1** to pursue (a person or animal) persistently or quickly ▷ *noun* **2** act or instance of chasing a person or animal

chasm *noun* **1** deep crack in the earth **2** very large difference between two things or groups of people; gulf: *the chasm between rich and poor*

chassis *noun* frame, wheels and mechanical parts of a vehicle

■ The plural of *chassis* is also *chassis*

chaste *adjective* *old-fashioned* not having sex outside marriage or at all **> chastity** *noun* state of not having sex outside marriage or at all

chasten *verb* to subdue (someone) by criticism

chastise chastises chastising chastised *verb* *formal* to scold severely

chat chats chatting chatted *noun* **1** informal conversation ▷ *verb* **2** to have an informal conversation **> chat up** *verb* *informal* to talk flirtatiously to (someone) with a view to starting a romantic or sexual relationship

chateau chateaux *noun* large

country house or castle in France

chatroom *noun* site on the Internet where users have group discussions by e-mail

chatter *verb* **1** to speak quickly and continuously about unimportant things **2** (of the teeth) to rattle with cold or fear ▷ *noun* **3** unimportant talk

chatty chattier chattiest *adjective* talkative and friendly

chauffeur *noun* person employed to drive a car for someone

chauvinism *noun* irrational belief that your particular country, race, group or sex is superior

chauvinist *noun* person who believes that his or her own country, race, group or sex is superior > **chauvinistic** *adjective* characterized by chauvinism

cheap *adjective* **1** costing relatively little **2** of poor quality **3** not valued highly: *cheap promises* **4** mean or despicable > **cheaply** *adverb*

cheapen *verb* **1** to lower the reputation of **2** to reduce the price of

cheat *verb* **1** to act dishonestly to gain profit or advantage ▷ *noun* **2** person who cheats

check *verb* **1** to examine or investigate **2** to slow the growth or progress of ▷ *noun* **3** test to ensure accuracy or progress **4** break in progress **5** *US* cheque **6** pattern of squares or crossed lines **7** *Chess* position of a king under attack > **check in** *verb* **1** to register your arrival at a hotel or airport **2** to register the arrival of (guests or passengers) at a hotel or airport > **check out** *verb* **1** to pay the bill and leave a hotel **2** to examine or investigate (something) **3** *informal* to have a look at

check-in *noun* **1** place where a person's arrival at a hotel or airport is registered **2** formal registration at a hotel or airport

checkmate *noun Chess* winning position in which an opponent's king is under attack and unable to escape

checkout *noun* counter in a supermarket, where customers pay

checkpoint *noun* place where traffic has to stop in order to be checked

checkup *noun* thorough medical examination

cheek *noun* **1** either side of the face below the eye **2** *informal* impudence, boldness or lack of respect ▷ *verb* **3** *Brit, Aust, NZ informal* to speak impudently to

cheeky cheekier cheekiest *adjective* rather rude and disrespectful > **cheekily** *adverb*

cheer *verb* **1** to applaud or encourage with shouts ▷ *noun* **2** shout of applause or encouragement > **cheer up** *verb* to become or make (someone) happy or hopeful

cheerful *adjective* **1** happy and in good spirits **2** bright and pleasant-looking > **cheerfully** *adverb* > **cheerfulness** *noun* happiness

cheerio *interjection informal* goodbye

cheery cheerier cheeriest *adjective* happy and cheerful

cheese *noun* hard or creamy food made from milk

cheesecake *noun* dessert with a biscuit-crumb base covered with a sweet cream-cheese mixture

cheesy cheesier cheesiest *adjective* **1** like cheese **2** *informal* (of a smile) broad but possibly insincere

cheetah *noun* large fast-running spotted African wild cat

chef *noun* cook in a restaurant

chemical *noun* **1** substance used in or resulting from a reaction involving changes to atoms or molecules ▷ *adjective* **2** involved in chemistry or using chemicals > **chemically** *adverb*

chemist *noun* **1** shop selling medicines and cosmetics **2** person who is qualified to make up prescription medicines; pharmacist **3** scientist who does research in chemistry

chemistry *noun* science of the composition, properties and reactions of substances

chemotherapy *noun* treatment of disease, often cancer, using chemicals

cheque *noun* written order asking your bank to pay money out of your account to a person, shop or organization

chequered *adjective* **1** marked by varied fortunes: *a chequered career* **2** having a pattern of squares

cherish cherishes cherishing cherished *verb* **1** to care deeply about (something) and look after it lovingly **2** to care for

cherry cherries *noun* **1** small red or black fruit with a stone **2** tree on which it grows ▷ *adjective* **3** deep red

cherub cherubs or **cherubim** *noun* angel, often represented as a winged child > **cherubic** *adjective* (of a baby or child) attractive

chess *noun* game for two players with 16 pieces each, played on a chequered board of 64 squares

chessboard *noun* board divided into 64 squares of two alternating colours on which chess is played

chest *noun* **1** front of the body, from neck to waist **2** large strong box with a hinged lid

chestnut *noun* **1** reddish-brown edible nut **2** tree on which it grows **3** reddish-brown horse **4** *informal* old joke ▷ *adjective* **5** (of hair or a horse) reddish-brown

chest of drawers chests of drawers *noun* piece of furniture consisting of drawers in a frame

chew *verb* to grind (food) between the teeth > **chewy** *adjective* requiring a lot of chewing

chewing gum *noun* flavoured gum to be chewed but not swallowed

chic *adjective* **1** stylish or elegant ▷ *noun* **2** stylishness or elegance

chick *noun* baby bird

chicken *noun* **1** domestic fowl **2** its flesh, eaten as food: *roast chicken* **3** *informal* coward ▷ *adjective* **4** *informal* cowardly > **chicken out** *verb informal* (often followed by *of*) to fail to do something through cowardice

chickenpox *noun* infectious disease with an itchy rash

chicory *noun* **1** plant whose bitter leaves are used in salads **2** root of this plant, used as a coffee substitute

chide chides chiding chided *verb old-fashioned* to rebuke or scold

chief *noun* **1** head of a group of people ▷ *adjective* **2** most important: *the chief source of oil* > **chiefly** *adverb* **1** especially **2** mainly

chieftain *noun* leader of a tribe or clan

chiffon *noun* very thin lightweight cloth made of silk or nylon

chihuahua *noun* breed of very small dog with pointed ears

chilblain *noun* inflammation of the fingers or toes, caused by exposure to cold

child children *noun* **1** young human

being, boy or girl **2** son or daughter

childbirth *noun* act of giving birth to a child

childhood *noun* time when a person is a child

childish *adjective* immature and foolish > **childishly** *adverb* > **childishness** *noun* immature and foolish behaviour

> If you call someone *childish*, you think they are immature or foolish. If you call them *childlike*, you think they are innocent like a young child

childless *adjective* having no children

childlike *adjective* like a child in appearance or behaviour

childminder *noun* person who is qualified and paid to look after other people's children while they are at work

Chilean *adjective* **1** belonging or relating to Chile ▷ *noun* **2** someone from Chile

chill *noun* **1** feverish cold **2** moderate coldness ▷ *verb* **3** to make (something) cool or cold **4** to cause (someone) to feel cold or frightened **5** *informal* to relax ▷ *adjective* **6** unpleasantly cold

chilli chillies *noun* small red or green hot-tasting pepper, used in cooking

chilly chillier chilliest *adjective* **1** rather cold **2** unfriendly and without enthusiasm

chilly-bin *noun* NZ *informal* portable container for keeping food and drink cool

chime chimes chiming chimed *noun* **1** musical ringing sound of a bell or clock **2 chimes** set of bells or other objects which make ringing sounds ▷ *verb* **3** to make a musical ringing sound **4** to indicate (the time) by chiming

chimney chimneys *noun* hollow vertical structure for carrying away smoke from a fire

chimp *noun informal* short for **chimpanzee**

chimpanzee *noun* small ape with dark fur that lives in forests in Africa

chin *noun* part of the face below the mouth

china *noun* **1** fine earthenware or porcelain **2** dishes or ornaments made of this **3** S Afr *informal* friend

Chinese *adjective* **1** of China ▷ *noun* **2** person from China **3** any of the languages of China

> The plural of *Chinese* is also *Chinese*

chink *noun* **1** small narrow opening **2** short light ringing sound, like one made by glasses touching each other

chintz chintzes *noun* glazed cotton fabric usually decorated with flowery patterns

chip chips chipping chipped *noun* **1** strip of potato, fried in deep fat **2** tiny wafer of semiconductor material forming an integrated circuit **3** counter used to represent money in gambling games **4** small piece removed by chopping, breaking, etc **5** mark left where a small piece has been broken off something ▷ *verb* **6** to break small pieces from > **chip in** *verb informal* **1** to contribute (money) **2** to interrupt with a remark

chipboard *noun* thin board made of compressed wood particles

chipmunk *noun* small squirrel-like North American rodent with a striped back

chiropodist *noun* person who treats minor foot complaints

> **chiropody** *noun* medical treatment of the feet

chirp *verb* **1** (of a bird or insect) to make a short high-pitched sound ▷ *noun* **2** chirping sound

chisel chisels chiselling chiselled *noun* **1** metal tool with a sharp end for shaping wood or stone ▷ *verb* **2** to carve or form with a chisel

chit *noun* short official note, such as a receipt

chivalry *noun* **1** polite and helpful behaviour, especially by men towards women **2** medieval system and principles of knighthood > **chivalrous** *adjective* gallant or courteous

chives *plural noun* herb with a mild onion flavour

chlorine *noun* strong-smelling greenish-yellow gaseous element, used to disinfect water and to make bleach

chloroform *noun* strong-smelling liquid formerly used as an anaesthetic

chlorophyll *noun* green colouring matter of plants, which enables them to convert sunlight into energy

chock-a-block or **chock-full** *adjective* completely full

chocolate *noun* **1** sweet food made from cacao seeds **2** sweet or drink made from this ▷ *adjective* **3** dark brown

choice *noun* **1** act of choosing or selecting **2** opportunity for choice or power of choosing: *parental choice* **3** person or thing chosen or that may be chosen: *You've made a good choice* **4** alternative action or possibility ▷ *adjective* **5** of high quality: *choice food and drink*

choir *noun* **1** organized group of singers, especially in church **2** part of a church occupied by the choir

choke chokes choking choked *verb* **1** to hinder or stop the breathing of (a person) by strangling or smothering **2** to have trouble in breathing **3** to block or clog up

choko chokos *noun* fruit that is shaped like a pear and used as a vegetable in Australia and New Zealand

cholera *noun* serious infectious disease causing severe vomiting and diarrhoea

cholesterol *noun* fatty substance found in animal tissue, an excess of which can cause heart disease

chook *noun Aust, NZ informal* hen or chicken

choose chooses choosing chose chosen *verb* **1** to select from a number of alternatives **2** to decide (to do something) because you want to

choosy choosier choosiest *adjective* fussy and difficult to satisfy

chop chops chopping chopped *verb* **1** to cut (something) with a blow from an axe or knife **2** to cut into pieces **3** *Boxing, karate* to hit (an opponent) with a short sharp blow **4 chop and change** to change your mind repeatedly ▷ *noun* **5** cutting or sharp blow **6** slice of lamb or pork, usually with a rib

chopper *noun* **1** *informal* helicopter **2** small axe

choppy choppier choppiest *adjective* (of the sea) fairly rough

chopsticks *plural noun* pair of thin sticks used to eat Chinese or other East Asian food

choral *adjective* relating to singing by a choir: *choral music*

chord *noun* **1** *Maths* straight line joining two points on a curve **2** *Music* simultaneous sounding of

chore *noun* uninteresting job that has to be done

choreography *noun* art of composing dance steps and movements > **choreographer** *noun* person who composes dance steps and movements

chorister *noun* singer in a choir

chortle chortles chortling chortled *verb* **1** to chuckle in amusement ▷ *noun* **2** amused chuckle

chorus choruses chorusing chorused *noun* **1** large choir **2** part of a song repeated after each verse **3** something expressed by many people at once **4** group of singers or dancers who perform together in a show **5** **in chorus** in unison ▷ *verb* **6** to sing or say together

chose *verb* past tense of **choose**

chosen *verb* past participle of **choose**

Christ *noun* Jesus of Nazareth, regarded by Christians as the Messiah

christen *verb* **1** to give a Christian name to in baptism **2** to give a name to (a person or thing) > **christening** *noun* Christian ceremony in which a child is given a name and made a member of a church

Christian *noun* **1** person who believes in and follows Christ ▷ *adjective* **2** of Christ or Christianity **3** kind, good and considerate > **Christianity** *noun* religion based on the life and teachings of Christ

Christian name *noun* **1** personal name given to Christians at baptism **2** (loosely) a person's first name

Christmas Christmases *noun* **1** annual festival on Dec. 25 commemorating the birth of Christ **2** period around this time

chromatic *adjective* **1** of colour or colours **2** *Music* (of a scale) proceeding by semitones

chrome *noun* grey metallic element used in steel alloys and for electroplating

chromosome *noun* microscopic gene-carrying body in the nucleus of a cell

chronic *adjective* **1** (of an illness) lasting a long time **2** habitual **3** *Brit, Aust, NZ informal* of poor quality > **chronically** *adverb*

chronicle chronicles chronicling chronicled *noun* **1** record of events in order of occurrence ▷ *verb* **2** to record in or as if in a chronicle

chronological *adjective* arranged in the order in which things happened > **chronologically** *adverb*

chronology chronologies *noun* arrangement or list of events in order of occurrence

chrysalis chrysalises *noun* insect in the stage between larva and adult, when it is in a cocoon

chrysanthemum *noun* garden flower with a large head made up of thin petals

chubby chubbier chubbiest *adjective* plump and round: *his chubby cheeks*

chuck *verb informal* **1** to throw **2** to give up or reject

chuckle chuckles chuckling chuckled *verb* **1** to laugh softly ▷ *noun* **2** soft laugh

chug chugs chugging chugged *noun* **1** short dull sound like the noise of an engine ▷ *verb* **2** to operate or move with this sound

chum *noun informal* close friend

chunk *noun* **1** thick solid piece

2 considerable amount

chunky chunkier chunkiest
adjective **1** (of a person) broad
and heavy **2** (of an object) large
and thick

church churches *noun*
1 building for public Christian
worship **2** particular Christian
denomination: *the Catholic Church*
3 Church institutional religion as
a political or social force: *conflict
between Church and State*

Church of England *noun* Anglican
Church in England, where it is
the state church, with the King or
Queen as its head

churchyard *noun* grounds round a
church, used as a graveyard

churn *noun* **1** machine in which
cream is shaken to make butter
▷ *verb* **2** to stir (cream) vigorously to
make butter **3 churn out** *informal*
to produce (things) rapidly in large
numbers

chute *noun* steep slope down which
things may be slid

chutney chutneys *noun* pickle
made from fruit, vinegar, spices
and sugar

cider *noun* alcoholic drink made
from fermented apple juice

cigar *noun* roll of cured tobacco
leaves for smoking

cigarette *noun* thin roll of shredded
tobacco in thin paper, for smoking

cinder *noun* piece of material that
will not burn, left after burning coal

cine camera *noun* camera for
taking moving pictures

cinema *noun* **1** place for showing
films **2** business of making films

cinnamon *noun* spice obtained
from the bark of an Asian tree

cipher or **cypher** *noun* **1** system
of secret writing **2** unimportant
person

circa *preposition formal* about or
approximately; used especially
before dates

circle circles circling circled *noun*
1 perfectly round geometric figure,
line or shape **2** group of people
sharing an interest or activity
3 *Theatre* section of seats above the
main level of the auditorium ▷ *verb*
4 to move in a circle (round)

circuit *noun* **1** complete route or
course, especially a circular one,
for example a motor-racing track
2 complete path through which an
electric current can flow

circuitous *adjective formal* indirect
and lengthy

circular *adjective* **1** in the shape of
a circle **2** moving in a circle ▷ *noun*
3 letter or advert sent to a lot of
people at the same time

**circulate circulates circulating
circulated** *verb* to send, go or
pass from place to place or person
to person

circulation *noun* **1** flow of blood
around the body **2** number of copies
of a newspaper or magazine sold
3 sending or moving round: *traffic
circulation* > **circulatory** *adjective* of
or relating to circulation

**circumcise circumcises
circumcising circumcised** *verb*
to remove the foreskin of (a male)
> **circumcision** *noun*

circumference *noun* **1** boundary of
a specified area or shape, especially
of a circle **2** distance round this

circumspect *adjective formal*
cautious and careful not to take
risks

circumstance *noun* **1** condition,
situation or event affecting or
influencing a person or event
2 unplanned events and situations
which cannot be controlled: *a victim*

of circumstance **3 circumstances** person's position and conditions in life

circus circuses *noun* (performance given by) a travelling company of acrobats, clowns, performing animals, etc

cistern *noun* water tank, especially one that holds water for flushing a toilet

citadel *noun* fortress in or near a city

cite cites citing cited *verb formal* **1** to quote or refer to **2** to bring forward as proof **3** to summon to appear before a court of law

citizen *noun* **1** native or naturalized member of a state or nation **2** inhabitant of a city or town > **citizenship** *noun* **1** condition or status of a citizen, with its rights and duties **2** person's conduct as a citizen

citrus fruit *noun* juicy sharp-tasting fruit such as an orange or lemon

city cities *noun* **1** large or important town **2 the City** *Brit* part of London which contains the main British financial institutions such as the Stock Exchange

civic *adjective* of or relating to a city or citizens

civil *adjective* **1** relating to the citizens of a country **2** relating to people or things that are not connected with the armed forces: *civil aviation* **3** polite or courteous > **civility** *noun* polite or courteous behaviour > **civilly** *adverb*

civil engineering *noun* design and construction of roads, bridges and public buildings

civilian *noun* **1** person not belonging to the armed forces > *adjective* **2** not relating to the armed forces or police

civilization *noun* **1** high level of human cultural and social development **2** particular society which has reached this level

civilized or **civilised** *adjective* **1** (of a society) having a developed social organization and way of life **2** (of a person) polite and reasonable

civil servant *noun* member of the civil service

civil service *noun* government departments responsible for the administration of a country

civil war *noun* war between people of the same country

cl *symbol* centilitre

clad *adjective literary* (often followed by *in*) dressed or clothed (in)

claim *verb* **1** to assert as a fact **2** to demand (something) as a right ▷ *noun* **3** assertion that something is true **4** assertion of a right **5** something claimed as a right

claimant *noun* person who is making a claim, especially for money

clairvoyant *adjective* **1** able to know about things that will happen in the future ▷ *noun* **2** person who is, or claims to be, clairvoyant

clam clams clamming clammed *noun* edible shellfish with a hinged shell > **clam up** *verb informal* to stop talking, especially through nervousness

clamber *verb* to climb awkwardly, using hands and feet

clammy clammier clammiest *adjective* unpleasantly damp and sticky

clamour *noun* **1** loud protest **2** loud persistent noise or outcry ▷ *verb* **3 clamour for** to demand noisily

clamp *noun* **1** tool with movable jaws for holding things together tightly ▷ *verb* **2** to fasten with a clamp > **clamp down** *verb* (often followed by *on*) to become stricter (about something) in order to stop or control it

clan *noun* **1** group of families with a common ancestor, especially among Scottish Highlanders **2** close group

clandestine *adjective* secret and hidden

clang *verb* **1** to make a loud ringing metallic sound ▷ *noun* **2** ringing metallic sound

clank *noun* **1** harsh metallic sound ▷ *verb* **2** to make such a sound

clap claps clapping clapped *verb* **1** to applaud by hitting the palms of your hands sharply together **2** to place or put quickly or forcibly: *He should be clapped in irons* ▷ *noun* **3** act or sound of clapping **4** sudden loud noise: *a clap of thunder*

clapper *noun* piece of metal inside a bell, which causes it to sound when struck against the side

claret *noun* dry red wine from the Bordeaux region of France

clarify clarifies clarifying clarified *verb* to make (something) clear and easy to understand > **clarification** *noun* explanation that makes something easier to understand

clarinet *noun* woodwind instrument with a single reed

clarity *noun* clearness

clash clashes clashing clashed *verb* **1** to come into conflict **2** (of events) to happen at the same time **3** (of colours) to look unattractive together **4** (of objects) to make a loud harsh sound by being hit together ▷ *noun* **5** a fight or argument **6** fact of two events happening at the same time

clasp *noun* **1** device for fastening

things **2** firm grasp or embrace ▷ *verb* **3** to grasp or embrace firmly

class classes classing classed *noun* **1** group of people sharing a similar social position **2** system of dividing society into such groups **3** group of people or things sharing a common characteristic **4** group of pupils or students taught together **5** standard of quality **6** *informal* elegance or excellence: *a touch of class* ▷ *adjective* **7** *informal* excellent, skilful or stylish: *a class act* ▷ *verb* **8** to place in a class; classify: *They are officially classed as visitors*

classic *adjective* **1** being a typical example of something: *a classic symptom of iron deficiency* **2** of lasting interest because of excellence: *a classic film* **3** attractive because of simplicity of form: *the classic dinner suit* ▷ *noun* **4** something of the highest quality **5** **classics** study of ancient Greek and Roman literature and culture

classical *adjective* **1** of or in a restrained conservative style **2** denoting serious art music **3** of or influenced by ancient Greek and Roman culture > **classically** *adverb*

classified *adjective* officially declared secret by the government

classify classifies classifying classified *verb* to arrange into groups with similar characteristics > **classification** *noun* **1** placing things systematically in categories **2** division or category in a classifying system

classroom *noun* a room in a school where pupils have lessons

classy classier classiest *adjective* *informal* stylish and elegant

clatter *verb* **1** to make a loud rattling noise, as when hard objects hit each other ▷ *noun* **2** loud rattling noise

clause *noun* **1** section of a legal document **2** group of words with a subject and a verb, which may be a complete sentence or one of the parts of a sentence

claustrophobia *noun* abnormal fear of confined spaces > **claustrophobic** *adjective* **1** (of a person) uncomfortable in a confined space **2** (of a place) enclosed, overcrowded or restricting movement

claw *noun* **1** sharp hooked nail of a bird or beast **2** similar part, such as a crab's pincer ▷ *verb* **3** to tear with claws or nails

clay *noun* fine-grained earth, soft when moist and hardening when baked, used to make bricks and pottery

clean *adjective* **1** free from dirt or impurities **2** without anything in it or on it: *a clean sheet of paper* **3** morally acceptable or inoffensive: *good clean fun* **4** (of a reputation or record) free from corruption or dishonesty **5** complete: *a clean break* **6** simple and streamlined in design: *the clean lines of the new model* ▷ *verb* **7** to make (something) free from dirt **8 come clean** *informal* to reveal or admit something > **cleaner** *noun* person, device or substance that removes dirt > **cleanly** *adverb*

cleanliness *noun* state or degree of being clean

cleanse cleanses cleansing cleansed *verb* to remove dirt from > **cleanser** *noun*

clear *adjective* **1** free from doubt or confusion: *It was clear that he did not want to talk* **2** easy to see or hear **3** able to be seen through; transparent **4** free of obstruction **5** (of sky) free from clouds **6** (of

skin) without blemish ▷ *adverb* **7** out of the way ▷ *verb* **8** to make or become clear **9** to pass by or over (something) without contact **10** to prove (someone) innocent of a crime or mistake **11** to make as profit > **clearly** *adverb* > **clear out** *verb* **1** to remove and sort the contents of (a room or container) **2** *Brit, Aust, NZ informal* to go away > **clear up** *verb* **1** to put (a place or thing that is disordered) in order **2** to explain or solve (a problem or misunderstanding) **3** (of the weather) to become brighter **4** (of an illness) to become better

clearance *noun* **1** act of clearing: *slum clearance* **2** official permission

clearing *noun* area of bare ground in a forest

cleavage *noun* **1** division between a woman's breasts, as revealed by a low-cut dress **2** division or split

cleaver *noun* butcher's heavy knife with a square blade

clef *noun Music* symbol at the beginning of a stave to show the pitch: *treble clef*

cleft *noun* narrow opening or crack

clemency *noun formal* kind or lenient treatment

clementine *noun* small orange citrus fruit

clench clenches clenching clenched *verb* **1** to close or squeeze (your teeth or fist) tightly **2** to grasp firmly

clergy *plural noun* priests and ministers as a group

clergyman clergymen *noun* male member of the clergy

clerical *adjective* **1** of or relating to clerks or office work **2** of the clergy

clerk *noun* employee in an office, bank or court who keeps records, files and accounts

clever *adjective* **1** intelligent and quick to understand **2** very effective or skilful > **cleverly** *adverb* > **cleverness** *noun*

clianthus clianthuses *noun* plant with clusters of scarlet flowers, found in Australia and New Zealand

cliché *noun* expression or idea that is no longer effective because of overuse > **clichéd** *adjective*: *The dialogue is clichéd and corny*

click *noun* **1** short sharp sound ▷ *verb* **2** to make this sound **3** *informal* (of two people) to get on well together **4** *informal* to become suddenly clear **5** *Computers* to press and release a button on a mouse in order, for example, to select an option on the screen or highlight something **6** *informal* to be a success

client *noun* person who uses the services of a professional person or company

clientele *noun* customers or clients collectively

cliff *noun* steep rock face, especially along the sea shore

climate *noun* **1** typical weather conditions of an area **2** general attitude and opinion of people at a particular time: *the American political climate* > **climatic** *adjective*: *climatic changes*

climax climaxes *noun* **1** most intense point of an experience, series of events, or story **2** same as **orgasm** > **climactic** *adjective*: *the film's climactic scene*

climb *verb* **1** to go up or ascend (stairs, a mountain, etc) **2** to move or go with difficulty **3** to rise to a higher point or intensity ▷ *noun* **4** act or an instance of climbing **5** place or thing to be climbed, especially a route in mountaineering > **climber** *noun*

clinch clinches clinching clinched *verb* to settle (an argument or agreement) decisively: *Peter clinched the deal*

cling clings clinging clung *verb* **1** (usually followed by *to* or *onto*) to hold (onto) tightly or stay closely attached (to) **2** (followed by *to*) to continue to do or believe in: *still clinging to old-fashioned values*

clingfilm *noun* thin polythene material for wrapping food

clinic *noun* **1** building where outpatients receive medical treatment or advice **2** private or specialized hospital

clinical *adjective* **1** of or relating to the medical treatment of patients: *clinical tests* **2** logical and unemotional: *the cold, clinical attitudes of his colleagues* > **clinically** *adverb*

clip clips clipping clipped *verb* **1** to cut with shears or scissors **2** to attach or hold together with a clip ▷ *noun* **3** short extract of a film **4** *informal* sharp blow **5** device for attaching or holding things together

clippers *plural noun* tool for clipping

clipping *noun* something cut out, especially an article from a newspaper

clique *noun* small group of people who stick together and do not mix with other people

clitoris clitorises *noun* small, highly sensitive organ near the opening of a woman's vagina

cloak *noun* **1** loose sleeveless outer garment ▷ *verb* **2** to cover or conceal

cloakroom *noun* room for coats or a room with toilets and washbasins in a public building

clock *noun* **1** instrument for showing

the time **2** device with a dial for recording or measuring ▷ *verb* **3** to record (time) with a stopwatch, especially in the calculation of a speed

clockwise *adverb, adjective* in the direction in which the hands of a clock rotate

clockwork *noun* **1** mechanism similar to that of a clock, used in wind-up toys **2 like clockwork** with complete regularity and precision

clog clogs clogging clogged *verb* **1** to block or obstruct ▷ *noun* **2** wooden or wooden-soled shoe

cloister *noun* covered pillared arcade, usually in a monastery

clone clones cloning cloned *noun* **1** animal or plant produced artificially from the cells of another animal or plant, and identical to the original **2** *informal* person who closely resembles another ▷ *verb* **3** to produce as a clone

close¹ closes closing closed *verb* **1** to shut **2** to prevent access to **3** to finish business or stop operating **4** to end **5** to bring or come nearer together ▷ *noun* **6** end or conclusion > **closed** *adjective* > **close down** *verb* to stop operating or working: *The factory closed down many years ago*

close² closer closest *adjective* **1** near: *a restaurant close to their home* **2** intimate: *close friends* **3** careful or thorough: *close scrutiny* **4** (of weather) oppressive or stifling ▷ *adverb* **5** near: *He walked close behind her* **6** closely or tightly: *She held him close* > **closely** *adverb* > **closeness** *noun*

closed shop *noun* place of work in which all workers must belong to a particular trade union

close shave *noun informal* narrow escape

closet *noun* **1** *US* cupboard **2** small private room ▷ *adjective* **3** private or secret ▷ *verb* **4** to shut (oneself) away in private

close-up *noun* detailed close view of something, especially a photograph taken close to the subject

closure *noun* closing

clot clots clotting clotted *noun* **1** soft thick lump formed from liquid **2** *Brit, Aust, NZ informal* stupid person ▷ *verb* **3** to form soft thick lumps

cloth *noun* **1** woven fabric **2** piece of woven fabric

clothe clothes clothing clothed *verb* **1** to put clothes on **2** to provide with clothes

clothes *plural noun* things people wear to cover them and keep them warm

clothing *noun* clothes collectively

cloud *noun* **1** mass of condensed water vapour floating in the sky **2** floating mass of smoke, dust, etc ▷ *verb* **3 cloud over** to become cloudy **4** to confuse: *His judgment was clouded by alcohol*

cloudy cloudier cloudiest *adjective* **1** having a lot of clouds **2** (of liquid) not clear

clout *informal noun* **1** hard blow **2** power or influence: *I don't have much clout round here* ▷ *verb* **3** to hit hard

clove *noun* **1** dried closed flower bud of a tropical tree, used as a spice **2** segment of a bulb of garlic

cloven hoof cloven hooves *noun* divided hoof of a cow, goat, etc

clover *noun* **1** plant with three-lobed leaves **2 in clover** *informal* in ease or luxury

clown *noun* **1** comic entertainer in a circus **2** amusing person **3** stupid person ▷ *verb* **4** to behave foolishly **5** to perform as a clown

cloying *adjective* unpleasantly sickly, sweet or sentimental

club clubs clubbing clubbed *noun* **1** association of people with common interests **2** building used by such a group **3** thick stick used as a weapon **4** stick with a curved end used to hit the ball in golf **5** playing card with black three-leaved symbols ▷ *verb* **6** to hit with a club **7** **club together** to combine resources for a common purpose

cluck *noun* **1** low clicking noise made by a hen ▷ *verb* **2** to make this noise

clue *noun* **1** something that helps to solve a mystery or puzzle **2** **not have a clue** to be completely baffled

clueless *adjective* *informal* helpless or stupid

clump *noun* **1** small group of things or people **2** dull heavy tread ▷ *verb* **3** **clump about** to walk or tread with heavy footsteps

clumsy clumsier clumsiest *adjective* **1** lacking skill or physical coordination **2** said or done without thought or tact > **clumsily** *adverb* > **clumsiness** *noun*

clung *verb* past of **cling**

cluster *noun* **1** small close group ▷ *verb* **2** to gather or be gathered in clusters

clutch clutches clutching clutched *verb* **1** to grasp tightly **2** **clutch at** to try to get hold of ▷ *noun* **3** foot pedal that the driver of a motor vehicle presses when changing gear **4** **in someone's clutches** in someone's power or at the mercy of someone

clutter *verb* **1** to fill (a room, desk,

etc) with objects that take up space and cause mess ▷ *noun* **2** untidy mess

cm *symbol* centimetre

Co. *abbreviation* Company

co- *prefix meaning* together, joint or jointly: *coproduction*

c/o *abbreviation* **1** care of **2** *Book-keeping* carried over

coach coaches coaching coached *noun* **1** long-distance bus **2** railway carriage **3** large four-wheeled horse-drawn carriage **4** person who coaches a sport or a subject ▷ *verb* **5** to train or teach

coal *noun* **1** black rock consisting mainly of carbon, used as fuel **2** burning piece of coal

coalition *noun* temporary alliance, especially between political parties forming a government

coarse coarser coarsest *adjective* **1** rough in texture **2** rude or offensive > **coarsely** *adverb* > **coarseness** *noun*

coast *noun* **1** place where the land meets the sea ▷ *verb* **2** to move by momentum, without the use of power > **coastal** *adjective* in or near the coast

coastguard *noun* **1** organization that aids ships and swimmers in trouble and prevents smuggling **2** member of this

coastline *noun* outline of a coast: *a rugged coastline*

coat *noun* **1** outer garment with long sleeves **2** animal's fur or hair **3** covering layer: *a coat of paint* ▷ *verb* **4** to cover (something) with a layer > **coating** *noun* covering layer

coax coaxes coaxing coaxed *verb* **1** to persuade (someone) gently **2** to obtain (something) by persistent coaxing

cobalt *noun* *Chemistry* brittle silvery-white metallic element which is used for producing a blue dye

cobber *noun Aust & old-fashioned NZ informal* friend

cobble cobbles cobbling cobbled *noun* **1** cobblestone ▷ *verb* **2 cobble together** to put together clumsily

cobbler *noun* shoe mender

cobblestone *noun* rounded stone used for paving

cobra *noun* venomous hooded snake of Asia and Africa

cobweb *noun* very thin net that a spider spins for catching insects

cocaine *noun* addictive drug used as a narcotic and as an anaesthetic

cock *noun* **1** male bird, especially of domestic fowl **2** stopcock ▷ *verb* **3** to draw back (the hammer of a gun) to firing position **4** to lift and turn (part of the body)

cockatoo cockatoos *noun* crested parrot of Australia or the East Indies

cockerel *noun* young domestic cock

Cockney Cockneys *noun* **1** native of the East End of London **2** London dialect

cockpit *noun* **1** pilot's compartment in an aircraft **2** driver's compartment in a racing car

cockroach cockroaches *noun* large dark-coloured insect often found in dirty rooms

cocktail *noun* alcoholic drink made from several ingredients

cocky cockier cockiest; cockies *informal adjective* **1** cheeky or too self-confident ▷ *noun* **2** *Aust* cockatoo **3** *Aust, NZ* farmer > **cockiness** *noun*

cocoa *noun* **1** powder made from the seed of the cacao tree **2** drink made from this powder

coconut *noun* **1** very large nut with white flesh, milky juice and a hard hairy shell **2** edible flesh of this fruit

cocoon *noun* **1** silky protective covering of a silkworm or other insect larva, in which the pupa develops **2** protective covering ▷ *verb* **3** to wrap up tightly for protection

cod *noun* large food fish of the North Atlantic

■ The plural of *cod* is also *cod*

code codes coding coded *noun* **1** system of letters, symbols or prearranged signals by which messages can be communicated secretly or briefly **2** group of numbers and letters which is used to identify something **3** set of principles or rules: *a code of practice* ▷ *verb* **4** to put into code > **coded** *adjective*

coeducation *noun* education of boys and girls together > **coeducational** *adjective*

coerce coerces coercing coerced *verb* to compel or force > **coercion** *noun* > **coercive** *adjective*

coffee *noun* **1** drink made from the roasted and ground seeds of a tropical shrub **2** beanlike seeds of this shrub ▷ *adjective* **3** medium-brown

coffin *noun* box in which a dead body is buried or cremated

cog *noun* **1** one of the teeth on the rim of a gearwheel **2** unimportant person in a big organization

cogent *adjective* strong and convincing > **cogency** *noun*

cognac *noun* French brandy

coherent *adjective* **1** logical and consistent **2** capable of intelligible speech > **coherence** *noun* logical or natural connection or consistency

cohesion *noun* sticking together

cohesive *adjective* sticking together to form a whole

coil *verb* **1** to wind in loops **2** to move in a winding course ▷ *noun*

3 something coiled **4** single loop of this

coin *noun* **1** piece of metal money **2** metal currency collectively ▷ *verb* **3** to invent (a word or phrase) **4 coin it in** *informal* to earn money quickly

coinage *noun* **1** coins collectively **2** currency of a country **3** newly invented word or phrase **4** act of coining

coincide coincides coinciding coincided *verb* **1** to happen at the same time **2** to agree or correspond exactly

coincidence *noun* **1** chance occurrence of simultaneous or apparently connected events: *By coincidence, we had both lived there* **2** coinciding > **coincidental** *adjective* resulting from coincidence > **coincidentally** *adverb*

coke *noun* solid fuel left after gas has been distilled from coal

colander *noun* bowl-shaped container with holes in it for straining or rinsing food

cold *adjective* **1** lacking heat **2** lacking affection or enthusiasm **3** (of a colour) giving an impression of coldness ▷ *noun* **4** lack of heat **5** mild illness causing a runny nose, sneezing and coughing > **coldly** *adverb* > **coldness** *noun* lack of affection or enthusiasm

cold-blooded *adjective* **1** showing no pity **2** having a body temperature that varies according to the surrounding temperature

cold war *noun* political hostility between countries without actual warfare

coleslaw *noun* salad dish of shredded raw cabbage in a dressing

colic *noun* severe pains in the stomach and bowels

collaborate collaborates collaborating collaborated *verb* **1** to work with another on a project **2** to cooperate with an enemy invader > **collaboration** *noun* **1** act of working with others on a joint project **2** something created by working with others **3** act of helping the enemy occupiers of one's country > **collaborator** *noun*

collage *noun* **1** art form in which various materials or objects are glued onto a surface **2** picture made in this way

collapse collapses collapsing collapsed *verb* **1** to fall down suddenly **2** to fail completely **3** to fold compactly, especially for storage ▷ *noun* **4** collapsing **5** sudden failure or breakdown

collapsible *adjective* able to be folded up for storage

collar *noun* **1** part of a garment round the neck **2** band put round an animal's neck **3** cut of meat from an animal's neck ▷ *verb informal* **4** *Brit, Aust, NZ* to seize or arrest **5** to catch in order to speak to

collarbone *noun* bone joining the shoulder blade to the breastbone

collateral *noun* money or property which is used as a guarantee that someone will repay a loan, and which the lender can take if the loan is not repaid

colleague *noun* fellow worker, especially in a profession

collect *verb* **1** to gather together: *collecting money for charity* **2** to accumulate (stamps, coins, etc) as a hobby **3** to go to a place to fetch (a person or thing); pick up

collected *adjective* calm and self-controlled

collection *noun* **1** things collected: *a collection of paintings* **2** collecting:

tax collection **3** sum of money collected: *a collection for charity*

collective *adjective* **1** of or done by a group: *a collective decision* ▷ *noun* **2** group of people working together on an enterprise and sharing the benefits from it > **collectively** *adverb*

collective noun *noun* noun that refers to a single unit made up of a number of things, *eg flock, swarm*

collector *noun* **1** person employed to collect something such as taxes, debts or rents **2** person who collects objects as a hobby

college *noun* **1** place where students study after they have left school **2** name given to some secondary schools **3** one of the institutions into which some universities are divided **4** *NZ* teacher training college

collide collides colliding collided *verb* to crash together violently

collie *noun* silky-haired dog used for rounding up sheep

colliery collieries *noun* coal mine

collision *noun* violent crash between moving objects

colloquial *adjective* suitable for informal speech or writing > **colloquialism** *noun* colloquial word or phrase > **colloquially** *adverb*

collusion *noun* secret or illegal cooperation

cologne *noun* mild perfume

colon *noun* **1** punctuation mark (:) **2** part of the large intestine connected to the rectum

colonel *noun* senior commissioned army or air-force officer.

colonial *noun* **1** inhabitant of a colony ▷ *adjective* **2** relating to a colony **3** *Aust* of the period of Australian history before the

Federation in 1901 > **colonialism** *noun* policy of acquiring and maintaining colonies

colonist *noun* settler in a colony

colonize colonizes colonizing colonized; also spelt **colonise** *verb* **1** to establish a colony in (an area) **2** (of plants and animals) to become established in (a new environment) > **colonization** *noun*

colony colonies *noun* **1** group of people who settle in a new country but remain under the rule of their homeland **2** territory occupied by a colony **3** group of people or animals of the same kind living together

colossal *adjective* very large

colour *noun* **1** appearance of things as a result of reflecting light **2** substance that gives colour **3** skin complexion of a person **4** quality that makes something interesting or exciting: *bringing more culture and colour to the city* ▷ *verb* **5** to apply colour to **6** to influence (someone's judgment) > **colouring** *noun*

colour-blind *adjective* unable to distinguish between certain colours

coloured *adjective* having a colour or colours other than black or white

Coloured *adjective* **1** *S Afr* of mixed White and non-White parentage ▷ *noun* **2** *S Afr* person of mixed White and non-White parentage **3** *offensive* person who is not White

colourful *adjective* **1** with bright or varied colours **2** vivid or distinctive in character: *a colourful personality* > **colourfully** *adverb*

colourless *adjective* **1** without colour **2** dull and uninteresting

colours *plural noun* **1** flag of a country, regiment or ship **2** *Sport* badge or symbol denoting membership of a team

colt *noun* young male horse

column *noun* **1** pillar **2** vertical division of a newspaper page **3** regular feature in a newspaper **4** vertical arrangement of numbers **5** narrow formation of troops

columnist *noun* journalist who writes a regular feature in a newspaper

coma *noun* state of deep unconsciousness

comb *noun* **1** toothed implement for arranging the hair ▷ *verb* **2** to use a comb on **3** to search (a place) with great care

combat *noun* **1** fighting ▷ *verb* **2** to fight or struggle against

combination *noun* **1** mixture **2** act of combining or state of being combined **3** set of numbers that opens a special lock

combine combines combining combined *verb* **1** to bring or mix (different things) together **2** to come together ▷ *noun* **3** association of people or firms for a common purpose **4** (also **combine harvester**) machine that reaps and threshes grain in one process

combustion *noun* process of burning

come comes coming came come *verb* **1** to move towards a place or arrive there **2** to occur **3** to reach a specified point or condition: *The sea water came up to his waist* **4** to be produced or be available: *It also comes in other colours* **5** **come from** to be or have been a native or resident of: *My mother comes from Norway* **6** to become: *a dream come true* > **come about** *verb* to happen: *The discussion came about because of the proposed changes* > **come across** *verb* **1** to meet or find by accident **2** **come across as** to give the

impression of being > **come off** *verb* **1** to emerge from a situation in a certain position: *The people who have come off worst are the poor* **2** *informal* to have the intended effect: *It was a gamble that didn't come off* > **come on** *verb* **1** to make progress **2** (of power or water) to start running or functioning **3** to begin: *I think I've got a cold coming on* > **come round** *verb* **1** to recover consciousness **2** to change your opinion > **come to** *verb* **1** to recover consciousness **2** to amount to (a total figure) > **come up** *verb* **1** to be mentioned **2** to be about to happen **3** **come up against** to come into conflict with **4** **come up with** to produce or propose: *a knack for coming up with great ideas*

comeback *noun informal* return to a former position or status: *The sixties singing star is making a comeback*

comedian *noun* **1** entertainer who tells jokes **2** person who performs in comedy

comedienne *noun* a female comedian

comedy comedies *noun* **1** humorous play, film or programme **2** such works as a genre

comet *noun* object that travels around the sun leaving a bright trail behind it

comfort *noun* **1** physical ease or wellbeing **2** something or someone that brings relief from worries or unhappiness **3** **comforts** things that make life easier or more pleasant ▷ *verb* **4** to soothe or console

comfortable *adjective* **1** providing comfort **2** physically relaxed **3** *informal* well-off financially > **comfortably** *adverb*

comic *adjective* **1** funny **2** of or

relating to comedy ▷ *noun*
3 comedian **4** magazine containing
strip cartoons
comical *adjective* amusing
comma *noun* punctuation mark (,)
command *verb* **1** to order **2** to have
authority over **3** to deserve and
get: *a public figure who commands
respect* **4** to have (a view over
something) ▷ *noun* **5** authoritative
instruction that something must
be done **6** authority to command
7 knowledge (of language)
8 military or naval unit with a
specific function
commandant *noun* army officer in
charge of a place or group of people
commandeer *verb* to seize
(something) for military use
commander *noun* **1** military
officer in command of a group or
operation **2** middle-ranking naval
officer
commandment *noun* one of ten
rules of behaviour that, according
to the Old Testament, people
should obey
commando commandos or
commandoes *noun* member of a
military unit trained for swift raids
in enemy territory
**commemorate commemorates
commemorating
commemorated** *verb* to honour
or keep alive the memory of
> **commemoration** *noun*
> **commemorative** *adjective*
**commence commences
commencing commenced** *verb*
formal to begin > **commencement**
noun beginning of something
commend *verb* **1** to praise **2** to
recommend > **commendable**
adjective: *a commendable achievement*
> **commendation** *noun*: *a
commendation from the judges*

comment *noun* **1** remark **2** talk or
gossip **3** explanatory note ▷ *verb*
4 to make a comment
commentary commentaries
noun **1** spoken accompaniment to
a broadcast or film **2** explanatory
notes
commentator *noun* someone
who gives a radio or television
commentary
commerce *noun* buying and selling
of goods and services
commercial *adjective* **1** of
commerce **2** (of television or radio)
paid for by advertisers **3** having
profit as the main aim ▷ *noun*
4 television or radio advertisement
> **commercially** *adverb*
**commiserate commiserates
commiserating commiserated**
verb (followed by *with*) to express
sympathy (for) > **commiseration**
noun: *My commiserations go out
to them*
commission *noun* **1** piece of work
that an artist is asked to do **2** duty
or task **3** percentage paid to a
salesperson for each sale made
4 group of people appointed
to perform certain duties
5 committing of a crime **6** *Military*
rank or authority officially given to
an officer **7** **out of commission**
not in working order ▷ *verb* **8** to
place an order for **9** *Military* to
give a commission to **10** to grant
authority to
**commit commits committing
committed** *verb* **1** to perform
(a crime or error) **2** to pledge
(yourself) to a course of action
3 to send (someone) to prison
or hospital > **committal** *noun*
sending someone to prison or
hospital
commitment *noun* **1** dedication

to a cause **2** engagement or obligation: *business commitments*

committed *adjective* having strong beliefs; devout: *a committed feminist*

committee *noun* group of people appointed to perform a specified service or function

commodity commodities *noun formal* something that can be bought or sold

common *adjective* **1** occurring often **2** belonging to two or more people; shared **3** belonging to the whole community: *common property* **4** lacking in taste or manners ▷ *noun* **5** area of grassy land belonging to a community > **commonly** *adverb*

commoner *noun* person who does not belong to the nobility

commonplace *adjective* happening often

common sense *noun* ability to act or react sensibly, using good judgment

commonwealth *noun* **1** country made up of a number of states: *the Commonwealth of Australia* **2 the Commonwealth** association of independent states that used to be ruled by Britain

commotion *noun* noisy disturbance

communal *adjective* shared

commune communes communing communed *noun* **1** group of people who live together and share everything ▷ *verb* **2 commune with** to feel very close to: *communing with nature*

communicate communicates communicating communicated *verb* to make known or share (information, thoughts or feelings)

communication *noun* **1** process by which people or animals

exchange information **2** thing communicated **3** *formal* letter or telephone call **4 communications** means of travelling or sending messages

communicative *adjective* talking freely

communion *noun* **1** sharing of thoughts or feelings **2 Communion** Christian ritual of sharing consecrated bread and wine **3** religious group with shared beliefs and practices

communism *noun* belief that all property and means of production should be shared by the community > **communist** *noun, adjective*

community communities *noun* **1** all the people living in one district **2** group with shared origins or interests

commute commutes commuting commuted *verb* to travel daily to and from work

commuter *noun* person who commutes to and from work

compact *adjective* **1** closely packed **2** taking up very little space **3** concise or brief ▷ *verb* **4** to pack closely together

compact disc *noun* plastic disc on which sound, images and data are or can be stored for use in CD players and computers

companion *noun* person who associates with or accompanies someone > **companionship** *noun* relationship of friends or companions

company companies *noun* **1** business organization; firm **2** group of actors **3** having someone with you: *I enjoyed her company* **4** person or people with you

comparable *adjective* similar in size or quality: *a job that is comparable to* *yours* > **comparably** *adverb*

comparative *adjective* **1** relative **2** involving comparison: *He studied comparative religion* **3** *Grammar* denoting the form of an adjective or adverb indicating *more* ▷ *noun* **4** *Grammar* comparative form of a word, such as *colder, faster, better* > **comparatively** *adverb*

compare compares comparing compared *verb* **1** to examine (things) and point out the resemblances or differences **2** **compare to** to liken (something) to **3** (often followed by *with*) to be worth in comparison: *How do they compare?*

comparison *noun* **1** analysis of the similarities and differences between things **2** comparing

compartment *noun* **1** section of a railway carriage **2** separate section

compass compasses *noun* **1** instrument for showing direction, with a needle that points north **2** **compasses** hinged instrument for drawing circles; also **pair of compasses**

compassion *noun* pity or sympathy > **compassionate** *adjective* showing or having compassion

compatible *adjective* able to exist, work or be used together > **compatibility** *noun*

compatriot *noun* fellow countryman or countrywoman

compel compels compelling compelled *verb* to force (someone to be or do something)

compelling *adjective* **1** extremely interesting: *a compelling novel* **2** convincing: *compelling evidence*

compensate compensates compensating compensated *verb* **1** to make amends to (someone), especially for injury or loss **2** **compensate for** to cancel out the effects of: *The trip more than compensated for the hardship* > **compensation** *noun* payment to make up for loss or injury > **compensatory** *adjective*

compere comperes compering compered *noun* **1** person who presents a stage, radio or television show ▷ *verb* **2** to be the compere of

compete competes competing competed *verb* **1** to try to be more successful or popular than other similar people or organizations **2** to take part in a competition

competence *noun* ability to do something well or effectively

competent *adjective* able to carry out tasks satisfactorily > **competently** *adverb*

competition *noun* **1** act of competing **2** event in which people compete **3** people against whom you compete

competitive *adjective* **1** involving rivalry **2** showing the urge to compete **3** cheap enough to be successful when compared with similar commercial rivals > **competitively** *adverb*

competitor *noun* person, team or firm that competes

compile compiles compiling compiled *verb* to collect and arrange (information), especially to make a book > **compilation** *noun*: *a compilation of his jazz works* > **compiler** *noun*

complacent *adjective* self-satisfied and unconcerned, and therefore not taking necessary action > **complacency** *noun*: *complacency about the risks of flooding* > **complacently** *adverb*

complain *verb* **1** to express resentment or displeasure

2 complain of to say that you are suffering from (an illness) > **complaint** noun **1** complaining **2** mild illness

complement noun **1** thing that completes something **2** complete amount or number **3** Grammar word or words added to a verb to complete the meaning ▷ verb **4** to make complete > **complementary** adjective: two complementary strategies are necessary

▌ Do not confuse complement and compliment. The e spelling is for senses that involve completion

complete completes completing completed adjective **1** thorough or absolute **2** finished **3** having all the necessary parts ▷ verb **4** to finish **5** to make whole or perfect > **completely** adverb > **completion** noun finishing

complex complexes adjective **1** made up of parts **2** complicated ▷ noun **3** whole made up of parts **4** group of unconscious feelings that influences behaviour > **complexity** noun

complexion noun **1** skin of the face **2** character or nature

compliance noun **1** complying **2** tendency to do what others want > **compliant** adjective: a compliant workforce

complicate complicates complicating complicated verb to make or become complex or difficult to deal with

complicated adjective so complex as to be difficult to understand or deal with

complication noun something that makes a situation more difficult to deal with

compliment noun **1** expression of praise **2 compliments** formal

greetings ▷ verb **3** to praise

▌ Do not confuse compliment and complement.

complimentary adjective **1** expressing praise **2** free of charge

comply complies complying complied verb (followed by with) to act in accordance (with)

component noun, adjective (being) part of a whole

compose composes composing composed verb **1** to put together **2** to be the component parts of **3** to create (a piece of music or writing) **4** to calm (yourself) **5** to arrange artistically

composed adjective calm and in control of your feelings

composer noun person who writes music

composition noun **1** way that something is put together or arranged **2** work of art, especially a musical one **3** essay **4** composing

compost noun decayed plants used as a fertilizer

composure noun ability to stay calm

compound noun **1** thing, especially a chemical, made up of two or more combined parts or elements **2** fenced enclosure containing buildings ▷ adjective **3** made up of two or more combined parts or elements ▷ verb **4** to combine or make by combining **5** to intensify or make worse

comprehend verb formal to understand > **comprehension** noun: This was beyond her comprehension

comprehensible adjective able to be understood

comprehensive adjective **1** including everything necessary or relevant ▷ noun

2 *Brit* comprehensive school
> **comprehensively** *adverb*

comprehensive school *noun Brit* secondary school for children of all abilities

compress compresses compressing compressed *verb* **1** to squeeze together **2** to make shorter ▷ *noun* **3** pad applied to stop bleeding or cool inflammation > **compression** *noun*

comprise comprises comprising comprised *verb formal* to be made up of or to make up

compromise compromises compromising compromised *noun* **1** settlement reached by concessions on each side ▷ *verb* **2** to settle a dispute by making concessions **3** to put (yourself or another person) in a dishonourable position > **compromising** *adjective* revealing an embarrassing or guilty secret about someone

compulsion *noun* **1** irresistible urge **2** forcing by threats or violence

compulsive *adjective* **1** resulting from or acting from a compulsion **2** irresistible or absorbing: *compulsive viewing*

compulsory *adjective* required by rules or laws

compute computes computing computed *verb* to calculate, especially using a computer

computer *noun* electronic machine that stores and processes data

computer-aided design *noun* use of computers and computer graphics to help design things

computerize computerizes computerizing computerized; also spelt **computerise** *verb* to adapt (a system or process) so that it can be handled by computer

computing *noun* use of computers and the writing of programs for them

comrade *noun* **1** fellow member of a union or socialist political party **2** fellow soldier > **comradeship** *noun* friendship between a number of people doing the same job or sharing the same difficulties

con cons conning conned *informal noun* short for **confidence trick 2 pros and cons** see **pro** ▷ *verb* **3** to deceive or swindle

concave *adjective* curving inwards

conceal *verb* **1** to cover and hide **2** to keep secret > **concealment** *noun*

concede concedes conceding conceded *verb* **1** to admit (something) as true or correct **2** to acknowledge defeat in (a contest or argument)

conceit *noun* too high an opinion of yourself

conceited *adjective* having an excessively high opinion of yourself

conceivable *adjective* imaginable or possible > **conceivably** *adverb*

conceive conceives conceiving conceived *verb* **1** to imagine or think **2** to form in the mind **3** to become pregnant

concentrate concentrates concentrating concentrated *verb* **1** to fix your attention or efforts on something **2** to bring or come together in large numbers in one place **3** to make (a liquid) stronger by removing water from it ▷ *noun* **4** concentrated liquid > **concentration** *noun* **1** concentrating **2** proportion of a substance in a mixture or solution

concentrated *adjective* (of a liquid) made stronger by having water removed

concentration camp *noun* prison camp for civilian prisoners, especially in Nazi Germany

concentric *adjective* having the same centre

concept *noun* abstract or general idea > **conceptual** *adjective* of or based on concepts > **conceptually** *adverb*

conception *noun* 1 notion, idea or plan 2 process by which a woman becomes pregnant

concern *noun* 1 anxiety or worry 2 something that is of importance to someone 3 business or firm ▷ *verb* 4 to worry (someone) 5 to involve (yourself) 6 to be relevant or important to

concerned *adjective* 1 interested or involved 2 anxious or worried

concerning *preposition* about or regarding

concert *noun* 1 musical entertainment 2 **in concert a** working together **b** (of musicians) performing live

concerted *adjective* done together

concerto concertos or **concerti** *noun* large-scale composition for a solo instrument and orchestra

concession *noun* 1 grant of rights, land or property 2 reduction in price for a specified category of people 3 conceding 4 thing conceded

conch conchs or **conches** *noun* 1 shellfish with a large spiral shell 2 its shell

conciliatory *adjective* intended to end a disagreement

concise *adjective* brief and to the point > **concisely** *adverb*

conclude concludes concluding concluded *verb* 1 to decide by reasoning 2 to come or bring to an end 3 to arrange or settle finally > **concluding** *adjective*

conclusion *noun* 1 decision based on reasoning 2 ending 3 final arrangement or settlement

conclusive *adjective* ending doubt; convincing > **conclusively** *adverb*

concoct *verb* 1 to make up (a story or plan) 2 to make by combining ingredients > **concoction** *noun*: *a concoction of honey, yogurt and fruit*

concourse *noun* 1 large open public place where people can gather 2 large crowd

concrete *noun* 1 mixture of cement, sand, stone and water, used in building ▷ *adjective* 2 made of concrete 3 definite, rather than general or vague 4 real or solid, not abstract

concur concurs concurring concurred *verb formal* to agree

concurrent *adjective* happening at the same time or place > **concurrently** *adverb* at the same time

concussion *noun* sickness or loss of consciousness caused by a blow to the head > **concussed** *adjective* having concussion

condemn *verb* 1 to express disapproval of 2 to sentence: *He was condemned to death* 3 to force into an unpleasant situation 4 to declare (something) unfit for use > **condemnation** *noun*

condensation *noun* coating of tiny drops formed on a surface by steam or vapour

condense condenses condensing condensed *verb* 1 to make shorter 2 to turn from gas into liquid

condescending *adjective* behaving in a way that suggests you feel superior to someone; patronizing

condition *noun* 1 particular state of being 2 necessary requirement for something else to happen

3 restriction or qualification **4** state of health or physical fitness **5** medical problem **6 conditions** circumstances **7 on condition that** only if ▷ *verb* **8** to train or influence to behave in a particular way **9** to treat with conditioner

conditional *adjective* depending on circumstances

conditioner *noun* thick liquid used when washing to make hair or clothes feel softer

condolence *noun* **1** sympathy **2 condolences** expression of sympathy

condom *noun* rubber sheath worn on the penis or in the vagina during sexual intercourse to prevent conception or infection

condone condones condoning condoned *verb* to overlook or forgive (wrongdoing)

conducive *adjective* **conducive to** likely to lead to

conduct *noun* **1** management of an activity **2** behaviour ▷ *verb* **3** to carry out (a task) **4** *formal* to behave (oneself) **5** to direct (musicians) by moving your hands or a baton **6** to lead or guide **7** to transmit (heat or electricity)

conductor *noun* **1** person who conducts musicians **2** official on a bus who collects fares **3** something that conducts heat or electricity

conduit *noun* channel or tube for fluid or cables

cone *noun* **1** object with a circular base, tapering to a point **2** cone-shaped ice-cream wafer **3** *Brit, Aust, NZ* plastic cone used as a traffic marker on the roads **4** scaly fruit of a conifer tree

confectionery *noun* sweets

confederation *noun* organization formed for business or political purposes

confer confers conferring conferred *verb* **1** to discuss together **2** to grant or give

conference *noun* meeting for discussion

confess confesses confessing confessed *verb* **1** to admit (a fault or crime) **2** to admit to be true **3** to declare (your sins) to God or a priest, in the hope of forgiveness

confession *noun* **1** something confessed **2** confessing

confessional *noun* small stall in which a priest hears confessions

confetti *noun* small pieces of coloured paper thrown at weddings

confidant *noun* *formal* person confided in > **confidante** *noun* woman or girl confided in

confide confides confiding confided *verb* **1** to tell someone (a secret) **2** to entrust

confidence *noun* **1** trust **2** self-assurance **3** something confided **4 in confidence** as a secret

confidence trick *noun* swindle involving gaining a person's trust in order to cheat him or her

confident *adjective* sure, especially of yourself > **confidently** *adverb*

confidential *adjective* **1** private or secret **2** entrusted with someone's secret affairs > **confidentially** *adverb* > **confidentiality** *noun*: *the confidentiality of the client-doctor relationship*

confine confines confining confined *verb* **1** to keep within bounds **2** to restrict the free movement of ▷ *noun* **3 confines** boundaries or limits > **confinement** *noun* **1** being confined **2** period of childbirth

confined *adjective* (of a space) small and enclosed

confirm *verb* 1 to prove to be true 2 to reaffirm or strengthen 3 *Christianity* to administer the rite of confirmation to

confirmation *noun* 1 confirming 2 something that confirms 3 *Christianity* rite that admits a baptized person to full church membership

confirmed *adjective* firmly established in a habit or condition

confiscate confiscates confiscating confiscated *verb* to seize (property) by authority

conflict *noun* 1 disagreement 2 struggle or fight ▷ *verb* 3 to be incompatible

conform *verb* 1 to comply with accepted standards or customs 2 **conform to** or **with** to be like or in accordance with > **conformist** *noun, adjective* (person) complying with accepted standards or customs > **conformity** *noun* compliance with accepted standards or customs

confront *verb* 1 to face 2 to come face to face with 3 (often followed by *about, with*) to tackle (someone) about something or presenting something as evidence

confrontation *noun* serious argument

confuse confuses confusing confused *verb* 1 to mix up 2 to perplex or disconcert 3 to make unclear > **confused** *adjective* > **confusing** *adjective* > **confusion** *noun*

congeal *verb* (of a liquid) to become thick and sticky

congenial *adjective* 1 pleasant or agreeable 2 having similar interests and attitudes

congenital *adjective Medicine* (of a condition) existing from birth

congested *adjective* crowded to excess > **congestion** *noun: traffic congestion*

conglomerate *noun* 1 large corporation made up of many companies 2 thing made up of several different elements

congratulate congratulates congratulating congratulated *verb* to express pleasure to (someone) at his or her good fortune or success > **congratulatory** *adjective*

congratulations *plural noun, interjection* expression of pleasure or joy on another's success or good fortune

congregate congregates congregating congregated *verb* to gather together in a crowd

congregation *noun* people who attend a church

congress congresses *noun* 1 formal meeting for discussion 2 **Congress** federal parliament of the US

conical *adjective* cone-shaped

conifer *noun* cone-bearing tree, such as the fir or pine > **coniferous** *adjective*

conjecture *noun* guesswork about something

conjugate conjugates conjugating conjugated *verb* to give the inflections of (a verb)

conjunction *noun* 1 part of speech joining words, phrases or clauses, such as *and, but* or *because* 2 **in conjunction** done or used together

conjurer or **conjuror** *noun* someone who entertains people by doing magic tricks

conker *noun informal* nut of the horse chestnut

connect *verb* 1 to join together 2 to

associate in the mind

connection or **connexion** noun
1 relationship or association **2** link
or bond **3** opportunity to transfer
from one public vehicle to another
4 influential acquaintance

connective noun word or short
phrase that connects clauses,
phrases or words

connoisseur noun person with
special knowledge of the arts, food
or drink

connotation noun associated idea
conveyed by a word

conquer verb **1** to defeat **2** to
overcome (a difficulty) **3** to take (a
place) by force > **conqueror** noun

conquest noun **1** conquering of a
country or group of people **2** lands
captured by conquest

conscience noun sense of right or
wrong as regards thoughts and
actions

conscientious adjective
painstaking > **conscientiously**
adverb

conscious adjective **1** alert and
awake **2** aware **3** deliberate or
intentional > **consciously** adverb
> **consciousness** noun: She hit her
head and lost consciousness

conscript noun **1** person enrolled
for compulsory military service
▷ verb **2** to enrol (someone) for
compulsory military service
> **conscription** noun

consecrated adjective (of a
building or place) officially declared
to be holy

consecutive adjective in unbroken
succession

consensus noun general
agreement

consent noun **1** agreement or
permission ▷ verb **2** (followed by to)
to agree (to something)

consequence noun **1** result or
effect **2** formal importance: We said
little of consequence

consequent adjective resulting
> **consequently** adverb as a result;
therefore

conservation noun **1** protection
of natural resources and the
environment **2** conserving
> **conservationist** noun

conservative adjective
1 opposing change **2** moderate
or cautious **3** conventional in
style **4** **Conservative** of the
Conservative Party, the British
right-wing political party which
believes in private enterprise and
capitalism ▷ noun **5** conservative
person **6** **Conservative** supporter
or member of the Conservative
Party > **conservatism** noun
> **conservatively** adverb

conservatory conservatories
noun room with glass walls and a
glass roof, attached to a house

conserve conserves conserving
conserved verb **1** to protect from
harm, decay or loss **2** to preserve
(fruit) with sugar ▷ noun **3** jam
containing large pieces of fruit

consider verb **1** to regard as **2** to
think about **3** to be considerate of
4 to discuss **5** to look at

considerable adjective large in
amount or degree > **considerably**
adverb

considerate adjective thoughtful
towards others

consideration noun **1** careful
thought **2** fact that should be
considered **3** thoughtfulness
4 payment for a service

considered adjective presented or
thought out with care

considering preposition taking (a
specified fact) into account

consign *verb* **1** to put somewhere **2** to send (goods)

consignment *noun* shipment of goods

consist *verb* **1 consist of** to be made up of **2 consist in** to have as its main or only feature

consistency consistencies *noun* **1** being consistent **2** degree of thickness or smoothness

consistent *adjective* **1** unchanging or constant **2 consistent with** in agreement with or tallying with > **consistently** *adverb*

consolation *noun* **1** consoling **2** person or thing that consoles

console consoles consoling consoled *verb* **1** to comfort (someone) in distress ▷ *noun* **2** panel of controls for electronic equipment

consolidate consolidates consolidating consolidated *verb* **1** to make or become stronger or more stable **2** to combine into a whole > **consolidation** *noun*: *the consolidation of power*

consonant *noun* **1** speech sound made by partially or completely blocking the breath stream, such as *b* or *f* **2** letter representing this

consort *verb* **1 consort with** to keep company (with) ▷ *noun* **2** husband or wife of a monarch

consortium consortia or **consortiums** *noun* association of business firms

conspicuous *adjective* **1** clearly visible **2** noteworthy or striking > **conspicuously** *adverb*

conspiracy conspiracies *noun* **1** conspiring **2** plan made by conspiring

conspirator *noun* someone involved in a conspiracy

conspire conspires conspiring

conspired *verb* **1** to plan a crime together in secret **2** *literary* to act together as if by design

constable *noun* police officer of the lowest rank

constabulary constabularies *noun* police force of an area

constant *adjective* **1** continuous **2** unchanging **3** faithful ▷ *noun* **4** unvarying quantity **5** something that stays the same > **constancy** *noun* > **constantly** *adverb*

constellation *noun* group of stars

consternation *noun* anxiety or dismay

constipated *adjective* unable to empty your bowels > **constipation** *noun* difficulty in emptying your bowels

constituency constituencies *noun* **1** area represented by a Member of Parliament **2** voters in such an area

constituent *noun* **1** member of a constituency **2** component part ▷ *adjective* **3** forming part of a whole

constitute constitutes constituting constituted *verb* to form or make up

constitution *noun* **1** principles on which a state is governed **2** physical condition **3** structure > **constitutional** *adjective* **1** of a constitution **2** in accordance with a political constitution > **constitutionally** *adverb*

constrained *adjective* compelled or forced (to do something)

constraint *noun* something that limits someone's freedom of action

constrict *verb* to make narrower by squeezing > **constriction** *noun*: *severe constriction of the arteries*

construct *verb* to build or put together

construction *noun* **1** constructing

2 thing constructed
3 interpretation **4** *Grammar* way
in which words are arranged in a
sentence, clause or phrase

constructive *adjective* (of advice,
criticism, etc) useful and helpful
> **constructively** *adverb*

consul *noun* official representing
a state in a foreign country
> **consular** *adjective*: *consular
officials*

consulate *noun* workplace or
position of a consul

consult *verb* to ask advice from or
discuss matters with (someone)

consultancy consultancies *noun*
1 organization whose members
give expert advice on a subject
2 work or position of a consultant

consultant *noun* **1** specialist doctor
with a senior position in a hospital
2 specialist who gives professional
advice

consultation *noun* **1** act of
consulting **2** meeting for
discussion or the seeking of advice
> **consultative** *adjective* giving
advice

**consume consumes consuming
consumed** *verb* **1** to eat or drink
2 to use up **3** to destroy **4** to obsess

consumer *noun* person who buys
goods or uses services

consumerism *noun* belief that a
country will have a strong economy
if its people buy a lot of goods and
spend a lot of money

consuming *adjective* (of passion,
interest, etc) most important and
very engrossing

**consummate consummates
consummating consummated**
verb **1** to make (a marriage) legal by
sexual intercourse **2** to complete
or fulfil ▷ *adjective* **3** supremely
skilled: *a consummate politician*

4 complete or extreme: *consummate
skill* > **consummation** *noun*: *the
consummation of marriage*

consumption *noun* **1** amount
consumed **2** consuming **3** *old-
fashioned* tuberculosis

contact *noun* **1** communicating
2 touching **3** useful acquaintance
4 connection between two
electrical conductors in a circuit
▷ *verb* **5** to get in touch with

contact lens contact lenses *noun*
lens placed on the eyeball to correct
defective vision

contagious *adjective* spreading
by contact

contain *verb* **1** to hold or be capable
of holding **2** to consist of **3** to
control or restrain > **containment**
noun prevention of the spread of
something harmful

container *noun* **1** object used to
hold or store things in **2** large
standard-sized box for transporting
cargo by truck or ship

**contaminate contaminates
contaminating contaminated**
verb **1** to make impure or
pollute **2** to make radioactive
> **contamination** *noun*

**contemplate contemplates
contemplating contemplated**
verb **1** to think deeply about **2** to
consider as a possibility **3** to
gaze at > **contemplation** *noun*:
He was deep in contemplation
> **contemplative** *adjective*: *a quiet
contemplative person*

contemporary contemporaries
adjective **1** present-day or modern
2 living or occurring at the same
time ▷ *noun* **3** person or thing living
or occurring at the same time as
another

contempt *noun* **1** dislike and
disregard **2** open disrespect for the

authority of a court

contemptible *adjective* not worthy of any respect

contemptuous *adjective* showing contempt > **contemptuously** *adverb*

contend *verb* 1 **contend with** to deal with 2 *formal* to state or assert 3 to compete

contender *noun* competitor, especially a strong one

content *noun* 1 meaning or substance of a piece of writing 2 amount of a substance in a mixture 3 **contents a** what something contains **b** list of chapters at the front of a book ▷ *adjective* 4 satisfied with things as they are ▷ *verb* 5 to make (someone) content

contented *adjective* happy and satisfied with your life > **contentedly** *adverb* > **contentment** *noun: a strong feeling of contentment*

contention *noun formal* 1 disagreement or dispute 2 point asserted in argument

contest *noun* 1 competition or struggle ▷ *verb* 2 to dispute or object to 3 to fight or compete for

contestant *noun* person who takes part in a contest

context *noun* 1 circumstances of an event or fact 2 words before and after a word or sentence that help make its meaning clear

continent *noun* 1 one of the earth's large masses of land 2 **the Continent** mainland of Europe > **continental** *adjective*

contingency contingencies *noun* something that may happen

contingent *noun* 1 group of people that represents or is part of a larger group ▷ *adjective* 2 **contingent**

on dependent on (something uncertain)

continual *adjective* 1 constant 2 recurring frequently > **continually** *adverb*

continuation *noun* 1 continuing 2 part added

continue continues continuing continued *verb* 1 to (cause to) remain in a condition or place 2 to carry on (doing something) 3 to resume after an interruption

continuity *noun* smooth development or sequence

continuous *adjective* continuing uninterrupted > **continuously** *adverb*

contort *verb* to twist out of shape > **contorted** *adjective*

contour *noun* 1 outline 2 (also **contour line**) line on a map joining places of the same height

contra- *prefix meaning* against or contrasting: *contraflow*

contraception *noun* prevention of pregnancy by artificial means

contraceptive *noun* 1 device used or pill taken to prevent pregnancy ▷ *adjective* 2 preventing pregnancy

contract *noun* 1 (document setting out) a formal agreement ▷ *verb* 2 to make a formal agreement (to do something) 3 to make or become smaller or shorter 4 to catch (an illness) > **contractual** *adjective*: *contractual obligations*

contraction *noun* 1 contracting or being contracted 2 shortening of a word or group of words, often marked by an apostrophe, for example *I've* for *I have*

contractor *noun* firm that supplies materials or labour

contradict *verb* 1 to declare the opposite of (a statement) to be true 2 to be at variance with > **contradiction** *noun*: *a contradiction of all that the Olympics is supposed to be* > **contradictory** *adjective*: *contradictory statements*

contralto contraltos *noun* (singer with) the lowest female voice

contraption *noun* strange-looking device

contrary *noun* **1** complete opposite ▷ *adjective* **2** opposed or completely different **3** perverse or obstinate ▷ *adverb* **4** in opposition

contrast *noun* **1** obvious difference **2** person or thing very different from another ▷ *verb* **3** to compare in order to show differences **4 contrast with** to be very different from

contravene contravenes contravening contravened *verb formal* to break (a rule or law)

contribute contributes contributing contributed *verb* **1** to give for a common purpose or fund **2 contribute to** to be partly responsible (for) > **contribution** *noun* > **contributor** *noun* > **contributory** *adjective*: *contributory factors*

contrite *adjective* sorry and apologetic > **contritely** *adverb* > **contrition** *noun*: *He was full of contrition*

contrive contrives contriving contrived *verb formal* **1** to make happen **2** to devise or construct

contrived *adjective* planned or artificial

control controls controlling controlled *noun* **1** power to direct something **2** curb or check **3 controls** instruments used to operate a machine ▷ *verb* **4** to have power over **5** to limit or restrain **6** to regulate or operate > **controller** *noun*

controversial *adjective* causing controversy

controversy controversies *noun* fierce argument or debate

conundrum *noun formal* puzzling problem

convalesce convalesces convalescing convalesced *verb* to recover after an illness or operation

convection *noun* transmission of heat in liquids or gases by the circulation of currents

convene convenes convening convened *verb formal* **1** to arrange or call (a meeting) **2** to gather for a formal meeting

convenience *noun* **1** quality of being convenient **2** useful object **3** *Brit formal* public toilet

convenient *adjective* **1** suitable or opportune **2** easy to use **3** nearby > **conveniently** *adverb*

convent *noun* **1** building where nuns live or lived **2** school run by nuns

convention *noun* **1** widely accepted view of proper behaviour **2** assembly or meeting **3** formal agreement

conventional *adjective* **1** (unthinkingly) following the accepted customs **2** customary **3** (of weapons or warfare) not nuclear, biological or chemical > **conventionally** *adverb*

converge converges converging converged *verb* to meet or join

conversant *adjective* **conversant with** having knowledge or experience of

conversation *noun* talk or chat > **conversational** *adjective*: *conversational German* > **conversationalist** *noun*: *a witty conversationalist*

converse converses conversing converted verb **1** formal to have a conversation ▷ noun **2** statement or idea that is the opposite of another ▷ adjective **3** reversed or opposite > **conversely** adverb

conversion noun **1** (thing resulting from) converting **2** Rugby score made after a try by kicking the ball over the crossbar

convert verb **1** to change in form, character or function **2** to cause to change in opinion or belief ▷ noun **3** person who has converted to a different belief or religion

convertible adjective **1** capable of being converted ▷ noun **2** car with a folding or removable roof

convex adjective curving outwards

convey conveys conveying conveyed verb **1** to communicate (information) **2** to carry or transport

conveyor belt noun continuous moving belt for transporting things, especially in a factory

convict verb **1** to declare guilty ▷ noun **2** person serving a prison sentence

conviction noun **1** firm belief **2** instance of being convicted

convince convinces convincing convinced verb to persuade by argument or evidence

convincing adjective believable > **convincingly** adverb

convoluted adjective **1** coiled or twisted **2** (of an argument or sentence) complex and hard to understand

convoy convoys noun group of vehicles or ships travelling together

convulsion noun **1** violent muscular spasm **2** **convulsions** uncontrollable laughter

coo coos cooing cooed verb (of a dove or pigeon) to make a soft murmuring sound

cook verb **1** to prepare (food) by heating **2** (of food) to be cooked **3** **cook up** informal to devise (a story or scheme) ▷ noun **4** person who cooks food

cooker noun Chiefly Brit apparatus for cooking heated by gas or electricity

cookery noun art of cooking

cool adjective **1** moderately cold **2** calm and unemotional **3** indifferent or unfriendly **4** informal sophisticated or excellent ▷ verb **5** to make or become cool ▷ noun **6** coolness **7** informal calmness or composure > **coolly** adverb > **coolness** noun

coolabah coolabahs; also spelt **coolibar** noun Australian eucalypt that grows along rivers

coop¹ noun cage or pen for poultry

coop² noun Brit, US, Aust (shop run by) a cooperative society

cooperate cooperates cooperating cooperated verb to work or act together > **cooperation** noun: cooperation between police and the public

cooperative adjective **1** willing to cooperate **2** (of an enterprise) owned and managed collectively ▷ noun **3** cooperative organization

coordinate coordinates coordinating coordinated verb **1** to bring together and cause to work together efficiently ▷ noun **2** **coordinates** Maths pair of numbers or letters which tell you how far along and up or down a point is on a grid > **coordination** noun: a lack of coordination > **coordinator** noun: the party's campaign coordinator

cop cops copping copped informal

noun **1** policeman ▷ *verb* **2** to take
or seize

cope copes coping coped *verb*
(often followed by *with*) to deal
successfully (with something);
manage

copious *adjective formal* abundant
or plentiful

copper *noun* **1** soft reddish-brown
metal **2** copper or bronze coin **3** *Brit
informal* policeman

copse *noun* small group of trees
growing close together

**copulate copulates copulating
copulated** *verb* to have sexual
intercourse > **copulation** *noun*

copy copies copying copied *noun*
1 thing made to look exactly like
another **2** single specimen of a book
etc **3** material for printing ▷ *verb*
4 to make a copy of **5** to act or try to
be like > **copier** *noun*

copyright *noun* **1** exclusive legal
right to reproduce and control a
book, work of art, etc ▷ *verb* **2** to
take out a copyright on ▷ *adjective*
3 protected by copyright

coral *noun* **1** hard substance formed
from the skeletons of very small sea
animals ▷ *adjective* **2** orange-pink

cord *noun* **1** thin rope or thick string
2 cordlike structure in the body
3 corduroy

cordial *adjective* **1** warm and friendly
▷ *noun* **2** drink with a fruit base

cordon *noun* **1** chain of police,
soldiers, etc, guarding an area
▷ *verb* **2** **cordon off** to form a
cordon round

corduroy *noun* cotton fabric with a
velvety ribbed surface

core cores coring cored *noun*
1 central part of certain fruits,
containing the seeds **2** central or
essential part ▷ *verb* **3** to remove
the core from

cork *noun* **1** thick light bark of a
Mediterranean oak **2** piece of this
used as a stopper ▷ *verb* **3** to seal
with a cork

corkscrew *noun* spiral metal tool
for pulling corks from bottles

cormorant *noun* large dark-
coloured long-necked sea bird

corn *noun* **1** cereal plant such as
wheat or oats **2** grain of such plants
3 *US, Canadian, Aust, NZ* maize
4 painful hard skin on the toe

cornea *noun* transparent
membrane covering the eyeball

corner *noun* **1** area or angle where
two converging lines or surfaces
meet **2** place where two streets
meet **3** remote place **4** *Sport* free
kick or shot from the corner of the
field ▷ *verb* **5** to force into a difficult
or inescapable position **6** (of a
vehicle) to turn a corner **7** to obtain
a monopoly of

cornet *noun* **1** brass instrument
similar to the trumpet **2** cone-
shaped ice-cream wafer

cornflour *noun* **1** *Chiefly Brit* fine
maize flour **2** *NZ* fine wheat flour

cornflower *noun* plant with blue
flowers

cornice *noun* decorative moulding
round the top of a wall

corny cornier corniest
adjective informal very obvious or
sentimental and not at all original:
corny old love songs

corollary corollaries *noun* idea,
argument or fact that results from
something else

coronary coronaries *noun* (also
coronary thrombosis) condition
in which the flow of blood to the
heart is blocked by a blood clot

coronation *noun* ceremony of
crowning a monarch

coroner *noun Brit, Aust, NZ* official

responsible for the investigation of violent, sudden or suspicious deaths

coronet *noun* small crown

corporal *noun* **1** noncommissioned officer in an army ▷ *adjective* **2** of the body

corporal punishment *noun* physical punishment, such as caning

corporate *adjective* **1** of business corporations **2** shared by a group

corporation *noun* **1** large business or company **2** city or town council

corps *noun* **1** military unit with a specific function **2** organized body of people

▋ The plural of *corps* is also *corps*

corpse *noun* dead body

corpuscle *noun* red or white blood cell

correa *noun* Australian shrub with large green and white flowers

correct *adjective* **1** free from error or true **2** in accordance with accepted standards ▷ *verb* **3** to put right **4** to indicate the errors in **5** to rebuke or punish > **correctly** *adverb* > **correction** *noun* **1** correcting **2** alteration correcting something > **corrective** *adjective* intended to put right something wrong

correlate correlates correlating correlated *verb* to be closely connected or to have a mutually influential relationship: *Obesity correlates with increased risk of stroke* > **correlation** *noun*: *the correlation between smoking and disease*

correspond *verb* **1** to be consistent or compatible (with) **2** to be the same or similar **3** to communicate by letter

correspondence *noun* **1** communication by letters **2** letters so exchanged

3 relationship or similarity

correspondent *noun* **1** person employed by a newspaper etc to report on a special subject or from a foreign country **2** letter writer

corresponding *adjective* resulting from a change to something else: *the rise in interest rates and corresponding fall in house values* > **correspondingly** *adverb*

corridor *noun* **1** passage in a building or train **2** strip of land or airspace providing access through foreign territory

corroborate corroborates corroborating corroborated *verb* to support (a fact or opinion) by giving proof > **corroboration** *noun* > **corroborative** *adjective*

corroboree *noun* Aust Aboriginal gathering or dance

corrode corrodes corroding corroded *verb* to eat or be eaten away by chemical action or rust > **corrosion** *noun*: *metal corrosion* > **corrosive** *adjective*: *Sodium is highly corrosive*

corrugated *adjective* folded into alternate grooves and ridges

corrupt *adjective* **1** open to or involving bribery **2** morally depraved **3** (of a text or data) unreliable through errors or alterations ▷ *verb* **4** to make corrupt > **corruptible** *adjective*

corruption *noun* dishonesty and illegal behaviour by people in positions of power

corset *noun* women's close-fitting undergarment worn to provide support or make the wearer look slimmer

cosine *noun* (in trigonometry) ratio of the length of the adjacent side to that of the hypotenuse in a right-angled triangle

cosmetic *noun* **1** preparation used to improve the appearance of a person's skin ▷ *adjective* **2** improving the appearance only

cosmic *adjective* of the whole universe

cosmopolitan *adjective* **1** composed of people or elements from many countries **2** having lived and travelled in many countries

cosmos *noun* the universe

cosset *verb* to pamper

cost costs costing cost *noun* **1** amount of money, time, labour, etc, required for something **2 costs** expenses of a lawsuit ▷ *verb* **3** to have as its cost **4** to involve the loss or sacrifice of **5** (past: **costed**) to estimate the cost of

costly costlier costliest *adjective* **1** expensive **2** involving great loss or sacrifice

costume *noun* **1** style of dress of a particular place or time, or for a particular activity **2** clothes worn by an actor or performer

costume jewellery *noun* inexpensive artificial jewellery

cosy cosier cosiest; cosies *adjective* **1** warm and snug **2** intimate or friendly ▷ *noun* **3** cover for keeping things warm: *a tea cosy* > **cosily** *adverb* > **cosiness** *noun*

cot *noun* **1** baby's bed with high sides **2** small portable bed

cottage *noun* small house in the country

cottage cheese *noun* soft mild white cheese

cotton *noun* **1** white downy fibre covering the seeds of a tropical plant **2** cloth or thread made from this ▷ *verb* **3 cotton on (to)** *informal* to understand

cotton wool *noun* fluffy cotton used for surgical dressings etc

couch couches couching couched *noun* **1** piece of upholstered furniture for seating more than one person ▷ *verb* **2** to express in a particular way

cough *verb* **1** to expel air from the lungs abruptly and noisily ▷ *noun* **2** act or sound of coughing **3** illness which causes coughing

could *verb* past tense of **can**[1]

couldn't could not

coulomb *noun* SI unit of electric charge

council *noun* **1** group meeting for discussion or consultation **2** local governing body of a town or region ▷ *adjective* **3** of or by a council

councillor *noun* member of a council

counsel counsels counselling counselled *noun* **1** advice or guidance **2** barrister or barristers ▷ *verb* **3** to give guidance to **4** to urge or recommend > **counselling** *noun* > **counsellor** *noun*

count *verb* **1** to say numbers in order **2** to find the total of **3** to be important **4** to regard as **5** to take into account ▷ *noun* **6** counting **7** number reached by counting **8** *Law* one of a number of charges **9** European nobleman > **counting** *preposition* including > **count on** *verb* to rely or depend on

countdown *noun* counting backwards to zero of the seconds before an event

countenance *noun* *literary* face or facial expression

counter *verb* **1** to oppose or retaliate against ▷ *adverb* **2** in the opposite direction **3** in direct contrast ▷ *noun* **4** opposing or retaliatory action **5** long flat surface in a bank or shop, on which business is transacted **6** small flat disc used in board games

counter- *prefix meaning* **1** opposite or against: *counterattack* **2** complementary or corresponding: *counterpart*

counteract *verb* to act against or neutralize

counterfeit *adjective* **1** fake or forged ▷ *noun* **2** fake or forgery ▷ *verb* **3** to fake or forge

counterpart *noun* person or thing complementary to or corresponding to another

counterterrorism *noun* measures to prevent terrorist attacks or eradicate terrorist groups

countess countesses *noun* **1** woman holding the rank of count or earl **2** wife or widow of a count or earl

countless *adjective* too many to count

country countries *noun* **1** nation **2** nation's territory **3** nation's people **4** part of the land away from cities

countryman countrymen *noun* **1** person from your native land **2** *Brit, Aust, NZ* person who lives in the country > **countrywoman** *noun*

countryside *noun* land away from cities

county counties *noun* (in some countries) division of a country

coup *noun* **1** successful action **2** (also **coup d'état**) sudden violent overthrow of a government

couple couples coupling coupled *noun* **1** two people who are married or romantically involved **2** two partners in a dance or game **3** **a couple of** a pair of ▷ *verb* **4** to connect or associate

couplet *noun* two consecutive lines of verse, usually rhyming and of the same metre

coupon *noun* **1** piece of paper entitling the holder to a discount or gift **2** detachable order form **3** football pools entry form

courage *noun* ability to face danger or pain without fear > **courageous** *adjective*: *a courageous decision* > **courageously** *adverb*

courgette *noun* type of small vegetable marrow

courier *noun* **1** person employed to look after holiday-makers **2** person employed to deliver urgent messages

course courses coursing coursed *noun* **1** series of lessons or medical treatment **2** route or direction taken **3** area where golf is played or a race is run **4** any of the successive parts of a meal **5** mode of conduct or action **6** natural development of events **7** **of course a** (*adverb*) as expected; naturally **b** (*interjection*) certainly or definitely ▷ *verb* **8** (of liquid) to run swiftly

court *noun* **1** body which decides legal cases **2** place where it meets **3** marked area for playing a racket game **4** courtyard **5** residence, household or retinue of a sovereign ▷ *verb* **6** *old-fashioned* to try to gain the love of **7** to try to win the favour of **8** to invite: *to court disaster*

courteous *adjective* polite

courtesy courtesies *noun* **1** politeness or good manners **2** courteous act **3** (**by**) **courtesy of** with the consent of

courtier *noun* attendant at a royal court

court martial court martials or **courts martial** *noun* military trial

court-martial court-martials court-martialling court-martialled *verb* to try by court martial

courtship *noun formal* courting of an intended spouse or mate

courtyard *noun* paved space enclosed by buildings or walls

cousin *noun* child of your uncle or aunt

cove *noun* small bay or inlet

covenant *noun* **1** contract **2** *Chiefly Brit formal* agreement to make an annual (charitable) payment

cover *verb* **1** to place something over (something) to protect or conceal it **2** to extend over or lie on the surface of **3** to travel over **4** to insure against loss or risk **5** to include **6** to report (an event) for a newspaper **7** to be enough to pay for ▷ *noun* **8** anything that covers **9** outside of a book or magazine **10** insurance **11** shelter or protection > **cover up** *verb* **1** to cover completely **2** to conceal (a mistake or crime)

coverage *noun* amount or extent covered

covering *noun* layer of something which protects or conceals something else

covert *adjective* concealed or secret > **covertly** *adverb*

cover-up *noun* concealment or attempted concealment of a mistake or crime

covet *verb* to long to possess (what belongs to someone else)

cow *noun* mature female of cattle and of certain other mammals, such as the elephant or seal

coward *noun* person who lacks courage > **cowardly** *adjective*

cowardice *noun* lack of courage

cowboy cowboys *noun* (in the US) ranch worker who herds and tends cattle, usually on horseback

cower *verb* to cringe in fear

cox coxes coxing coxed *noun* **1** person who steers a boat ▷ *verb* **2** to act as cox of (a boat)

coy *adjective* affectedly shy or modest > **coyly** *adverb*

coyote *noun* prairie wolf of North America

crab *noun* edible shellfish with ten legs, the first pair modified into pincers

crack *verb* **1** to split partially so that damage lines appear on the surface **2** to tell (a joke) **3** to solve (a code or problem) **4** to (cause to) make a sharp noise **5** to break down or yield under strain ▷ *noun* **6** line that appears on a surface caused by damage **7** narrow gap **8** sudden sharp noise **9** *informal* highly addictive form of cocaine ▷ *adjective* **10** *informal* first-rate; excellent: *a crack shot* > **crack down on** *verb* to take severe measures against

cracker *noun* **1** thin dry biscuit **2** decorated cardboard tube, pulled apart with a bang, containing a paper hat and a joke or toy **3** small explosive firework **4** *informal* outstanding thing or person

crackle crackles crackling crackled *verb* **1** to make small sharp popping noises ▷ *noun* **2** crackling sound

cradle cradles cradling cradled *noun* **1** baby's bed on rockers **2** supporting structure ▷ *verb* **3** to hold gently as if in a cradle

craft *noun* **1** activity such as weaving, carving or pottery that requires skill with one's hands **2** skilful occupation **3** boat, plane or spacecraft

> When *craft* means 'a boat, plane or spacecraft' (sense 3), the plural is *craft* rather than *crafts*

craftsman craftsmen *noun* skilled

worker > **craftsmanship** *noun*: *the fine craftsmanship of his furniture* > **craftswoman** *noun*

crafty craftier craftiest *adjective* skilled in deception

crag *noun* steep rugged rock

craggy craggier craggiest *adjective* (of a mountain or cliff) steep and rocky

cram crams cramming crammed *verb* 1 to force into too small a space 2 to fill too full 3 to study hard just before an examination

cramp *noun* 1 painful muscular contraction 2 clamp for holding masonry or timber together ▷ *verb* 3 to confine or restrict

cramped *adjective* (of a room or building) not large enough for the people or things in it

cranberry cranberries *noun* sour edible red berry

crane cranes craning craned *noun* 1 machine for lifting and moving heavy weights 2 large wading bird with a long neck and legs ▷ *verb* 3 to stretch (your neck) to see something

crank *noun* 1 arm projecting at right angles from a shaft, for transmitting or converting motion 2 *informal* eccentric person ▷ *verb* 3 to start (an engine) with a crank

cranky crankier crankiest *adjective informal* 1 eccentric 2 bad-tempered

cranny crannies *noun* narrow opening

crash crashes crashing crashed *noun* 1 collision involving a vehicle or vehicles 2 sudden loud smashing noise 3 financial collapse ▷ *verb* 4 to (cause to) collide violently with a vehicle, a stationary object or the ground 5 to (cause to) make a loud smashing noise 6 to (cause to) fall

with a crash 7 to collapse or fail financially

crash helmet *noun* protective helmet worn by a motorcyclist

crash-land *verb* (of an aircraft) to land in an emergency, causing damage > **crash-landing** *noun*

crate *noun* large wooden container for packing goods

crater *noun* very large hole in the ground or in the surface of a planet or moon

cravat *noun* man's scarf worn like a tie

crave craves craving craved *verb* 1 to desire intensely 2 to beg or plead for > **craving** *noun*: *a craving for chocolate*

crawfish *noun* same as **crayfish**

crawl *verb* 1 to move on your hands and knees 2 to move very slowly 3 *informal* to act in a servile manner ▷ *noun* 4 crawling motion or pace 5 overarm swimming stroke

crawler *noun* 1 person or animal that crawls 2 *informal* person who behaves in a servile manner to someone in order to gain favour

crayfish crayfish or **crayfishes** *noun* edible shellfish like a lobster

crayon *noun* stick or pencil of coloured wax or clay

craze *noun* short-lived fashion or enthusiasm

crazy crazier craziest *adjective* 1 ridiculous 2 **crazy about** very fond of 3 insane > **crazily** *adverb* > **craziness** *noun*

creak *verb* 1 to make a harsh squeaking sound ▷ *noun* 2 harsh squeaking sound > **creaky** *adjective*: *a creaky door*

cream *noun* 1 fatty part of milk 2 food or cosmetic resembling cream in consistency 3 best part (of something) ▷ *adjective* 4 yellowish-white > **creamy** *adjective*

crease creases creasing creased
noun **1** line made by folding or
pressing **2** *Cricket* line marking the
bowler's and batsman's positions
▷ *verb* **3** to make or become
wrinkled or furrowed > **creased**
adjective: creased trousers

create creates creating created
verb **1** to make or cause to exist **2** to
appoint to a new rank or position

creation *noun* **1** creating or being
created **2** something created or
brought into existence

creative *adjective* imaginative
or inventive > **creatively** *adverb*
> **creativity** *noun*

creator *noun* person who creates

creature *noun* animal, person or
other being

crèche *noun* place where small
children are looked after while their
parents are working, shopping, etc

credence *noun* belief in the truth or
accuracy of a statement

credentials *plural noun* document
giving evidence of a person's
identity or qualifications

credible *adjective* **1** believable
2 trustworthy > **credibility** *noun*:
The Minister has lost his credibility
> **credibly** *adverb*

credit *noun* **1** system of allowing
customers to receive goods
and pay later **2** reputation for
trustworthiness in paying debts
3 money at your disposal in a bank
account **4** side of an account book
on which such sums are entered
5 (source or cause of) praise or
approval **6** **credits** list of people
responsible for the production of a
film, programme or record ▷ *verb*
7 to enter as a credit in an account
8 (followed by *with*) to attribute (to)
9 to believe

creditable *adjective* praiseworthy

credit card *noun* card allowing a
person to buy on credit

creditor *noun* person to whom
money is owed

creed *noun* statement or system of
(Christian) beliefs or principles

creek *noun* **1** narrow inlet or bay
2 *Aust, NZ, US, Canadian* small stream

creep creeps creeping crept *verb*
1 to move quietly and cautiously
2 to crawl with the body near to the
ground **3** (of a plant) to grow along
the ground or over rocks ▷ *noun*
4 *informal* obnoxious or servile
person **5** **give someone the
creeps** *informal* to give someone a
feeling of fear or disgust

creepy creepier creepiest
adjective informal causing a feeling of
fear or disgust

**cremate cremates cremating
cremated** *verb* to burn (a corpse) to
ash > **cremation** *noun*

crematorium crematoriums or
crematoria *noun* building where
corpses are cremated

crepe *noun* **1** fabric or rubber with a
crinkled texture **2** very thin pancake

crept *verb* past of **creep**

crescendo crescendos *noun*
gradual increase in loudness,
especially in music

crescent *noun* **1** (curved shape of)
the moon as seen in its first or last
quarter **2** crescent-shaped street

cress *noun* plant with strong-tasting
leaves, used in salads

crest *noun* **1** top of a mountain,
hill or wave **2** tuft or growth on a
bird's or animal's head **3** heraldic
design used on a coat of arms and
elsewhere > **crested** *adjective*

crevice *noun* narrow crack or gap
in rock

crew *noun* **1** people who work on a

ship or aircraft **2** group of people working together **3** *informal* any group of people ▷ *verb* **4** to serve as a crew member (on)

crib cribs cribbing cribbed *noun* **1** baby's cradle ▷ *verb* **2** to copy (someone's work) dishonestly

crib-wall *noun NZ* retaining wall built against an earth bank

crick *noun* **1** muscle spasm or cramp in the back or neck ▷ *verb* **2** to cause a crick in

cricket *noun* **1** outdoor game played with bats, a ball and wickets by two teams of eleven **2** chirping insect like a grasshopper

cricketer *noun* person who plays cricket

crime *noun* **1** unlawful act **2** unlawful acts collectively

criminal *noun* **1** person guilty of a crime ▷ *adjective* **2** of crime **> criminally** *adverb*

criminology *noun* study of crime **> criminologist** *noun*

crimson *adjective* deep purplish-red

cringe cringes cringing cringed *verb* to flinch or back away in fear or embarrassment

crinkle crinkles crinkling crinkled *verb* **1** to wrinkle, crease or fold ▷ *noun* **2** wrinkle, crease or fold

cripple cripples crippling crippled *noun* **1** person who is lame or disabled ▷ *verb* **2** to make lame or disabled **3** to damage (something) **> crippled** *adjective* **> crippling** *adjective*

crisis crises *noun* **1** crucial stage, turning point **2** time of extreme trouble

crisp *adjective* **1** fresh and firm **2** dry and brittle **3** clean and neat **4** (of weather) cold but invigorating **5** lively or brisk ▷ *noun* **6** *Brit* very thin slice of potato fried till crunchy

crispy crispier crispiest *adjective* hard and crunchy

criterion criteria *noun* standard of judgment

> Use the plural form *criteria* only when referring to more than one *criterion*

critic *noun* **1** professional judge of any of the arts **2** person who finds fault

critical *adjective* **1** very important or dangerous **2** fault-finding **3** able to examine and judge carefully **4** of or relating to a critic or criticism **> critically** *adverb*

criticism *noun* **1** fault-finding **2** analysis of a book, work of art, etc

criticize criticizes criticizing criticized; also spelt **criticise** *verb* to find fault with

critique *noun* critical essay

croak *verb* **1** (of a frog or crow) to give a low hoarse cry **2** to utter or speak with a croak ▷ *noun* **3** low hoarse sound

Croatian *adjective* **1** belonging to or relating to Croatia ▷ *noun* **2** person from Croatia **3** form of Serbo-Croat spoken in Croatia

crochet *verb* **1** to make by looping and intertwining yarn with a hooked needle ▷ *noun* **2** work made in this way

crockery *noun* dishes

crocodile *noun* **1** large amphibious tropical reptile **2** *Brit, Aust, NZ* line of people, especially schoolchildren, walking two by two

crocus crocuses *noun* small plant with yellow, white or purple flowers in spring

croft *noun* small farm worked by one family in Scotland **> crofter** *noun*

croissant *noun* rich flaky crescent-shaped roll

crony cronies *noun* old-fashioned

close friend

crook *noun* **1** *informal* criminal **2** bent or curved part **3** hooked pole

crooked *adjective* **1** bent or twisted **2** set at an angle **3** *informal* dishonest

croon *verb* to sing, hum or speak in a soft low tone

crop crops cropping cropped *noun* **1** cultivated plant **2** season's total yield of produce **3** group of things appearing at one time **4** (handle of) a whip ▷ *verb* **5** to cut very short **6** to produce or harvest as a crop **7** (of animals) to feed on (grass) > **crop up** *verb informal* to happen unexpectedly

croquet *noun* game played on a lawn in which balls are hit through hoops

cross crosses crossing crossed; crosser crossest *verb* **1** to move or go across (something) **2** to meet and pass **3** to place (one's arms or legs) crosswise ▷ *noun* **4** structure, symbol or mark of two intersecting lines **5** such a structure of wood as a means of execution **6** representation of the Cross as an emblem of Christianity **7** mixture of two things ▷ *adjective* **8** angry or annoyed > **crossly** *adverb* > **cross out** *verb* to delete with a cross or lines

Cross *noun* **the Cross** Christianity the cross on which Christ was crucified

crossbow *noun* weapon consisting of a bow fixed at the end of a piece of wood

cross-country *adjective, adverb* **1** by way of open country or fields ▷ *noun* **2** long race run over open ground

cross-examine cross-examines cross-examining cross-

examined *verb Law* to question (a witness for the opposing side) to check his or her testimony > **cross-examination** *noun*

cross-eyed *adjective* with eyes looking towards each other

crossfire *noun* gunfire crossing another line of fire

crosshatching *noun* drawing an area of shade in a picture using two or more sets of parallel lines

crossing *noun* **1** place where a street may be crossed safely **2** place where one thing crosses another **3** journey across water

cross-legged *adjective* sitting with your knees pointing outwards and your feet tucked under them

cross section *noun* **1** (diagram of) a surface made by cutting across something **2** representative sample: *a cross section of society*

crossword *noun* (also **crossword puzzle**) puzzle in which you work out clues and write the answers letter by letter in the numbered blank squares that go across or down on a grid of black and white squares

crotch crotches *noun* part of the body between the tops of the legs

crotchet *noun Music* musical note (♩) half the length of a minim

crouch crouches crouching crouched *verb* **1** to bend low with the legs and body close ▷ *noun* **2** this position

crow *noun* **1** large black bird with a harsh call **2** **as the crow flies** in a straight line ▷ *verb* **3** (of a cock) to make a shrill squawking sound **4** to boast or gloat

crowbar *noun* iron bar used as a lever

crowd *noun* **1** large group of people or things **2** particular group of people ▷ *verb* **3** to gather together in large numbers **4** to press together in a confined space **5** to fill or occupy fully

crowded *adjective* full of people

crown *noun* **1** monarch's headdress of gold and jewels **2** wreath for the head, given as an honour **3** top of the head or of a hill **4** artificial cover for a broken or decayed tooth ▷ *verb* **5** to put a crown on the head of (someone) to proclaim him or her monarch **6** to form or cause to form the top of **7** to put the finishing touch to (a series of events)

Crown *noun* **the Crown** power of the monarchy

crucial *adjective* very important > **crucially** *adverb*

crucifix crucifixes *noun* model of Christ on the Cross

crucifixion *noun* **1** method of execution by fastening to a cross, normally by the hands and feet **2 the Crucifixion** *Christianity* crucifying of Christ

crucify crucifies crucifying crucified *verb* to put to death by fastening to a cross

crude cruder crudest *adjective* **1** rough and simple **2** tasteless or vulgar **3** in a natural or unrefined state: *crude oil* > **crudely** *adverb* > **crudity** *noun*

cruel crueller cruellest *adjective* **1** delighting in others' pain **2** causing pain or suffering > **cruelly** *adverb* > **cruelty** *noun*

cruise cruises cruising cruised *noun* **1** sail for pleasure ▷ *verb* **2** to sail from place to place for pleasure **3** (of a vehicle) to travel at a moderate and economical speed

cruiser *noun* **1** large fast warship **2** motorboat with a cabin

crumb *noun* **1** small fragment of

bread or other dry food **2** small amount

crumble crumbles crumbling crumbled *verb* **1** to break into fragments **2** to fall apart or decay ▷ *noun* **3** pudding of stewed fruit with a crumbly topping

crumbly *adjective* easily breaking into small pieces

crumpet *noun* round soft yeast cake, eaten buttered

crumple crumples crumpling crumpled *verb* **1** to crush or crease **2** to collapse, especially from shock

crunch crunches crunching crunched *verb* **1** to bite or chew with a noisy crushing sound **2** to make a crisp or brittle sound ▷ *noun* **3** crunching sound **4** *informal* critical moment

crunchy crunchier crunchiest *adjective* (of food) pleasantly hard or crisp and making a noise when eaten

crusade crusades crusading crusaded *noun* **1** vigorous campaign in favour of a cause ▷ *verb* **2** to take part in a crusade

crusader *noun* person who campaigns vigorously in favour of a cause

crush crushes crushing crushed *verb* **1** to compress so as to injure, break or crumple **2** to break into small pieces **3** to defeat or humiliate utterly ▷ *noun* **4** dense crowd **5** *informal* infatuation: *a teenage crush* **6** drink made by crushing fruit

crust *noun* **1** hard outer part of something, especially bread ▷ *verb* **2** to cover with or form a crust

crusty crustier crustiest *adjective* having a crust

crutch crutches *noun* long sticklike support with a rest for the armpit, used by a lame person

crux cruxes *noun* crucial or decisive point

cry cries crying cried *verb* **1** to shed tears **2** to call or utter loudly ▷ *noun* **3** fit of weeping **4** loud utterance **5** urgent appeal: *a cry for help* > **cry off** *verb informal* to withdraw from an arrangement > **cry out for** *verb* to need urgently

crypt *noun* vault under a church, especially one used as a burial place

cryptic *adjective* obscure in meaning; secret

crystal *noun* **1** (single grain of) a symmetrically shaped solid formed naturally by some substances **2** very clear and brilliant glass, usually with the surface cut in many planes **3** tumblers, vases, etc, made of crystal ▷ *adjective* **4** bright and clear

crystalline *adjective* **1** of or like crystal or crystals **2** clear

crystallize crystallizes crystallizing crystallized; also spelt **crystallise** *verb* **1** to make or become definite **2** to form into crystals

cub *noun* young wild animal such as a bear or fox

Cuban *adjective* **1** belonging or relating to Cuba ▷ *noun* **2** person from Cuba

cube cubes cubing cubed *noun* **1** object with six equal square sides **2** number resulting from multiplying a number by itself twice ▷ *verb* **3** to cut into cubes **4** to find the cube of (a number)

cubic *adjective* **1** having three dimensions **2** cube-shaped

cubicle *noun* enclosed part of a large room, screened for privacy

Cub Scout *noun* member of a junior branch of the Scout Association

cuckoo cuckoos *noun* migratory bird with a characteristic two-note call, which lays its eggs in the nests of other birds

cucumber *noun* long green-skinned fleshy fruit used in salads

cuddle cuddles cuddling cuddled *verb* **1** to hug ▷ *noun* **2** hug

cuddly cuddlier cuddliest *adjective* (of people, animals or toys) soft and pleasing

cue cues cueing cued *noun* **1** signal to an actor or musician to begin speaking or playing **2** signal or reminder **3** long tapering stick used in billiards, snooker or pool ▷ *verb* **4** to give a cue to **5** to hit (a ball) with a cue

cuff *noun* **1** end of a sleeve **2** **off the cuff** *informal* without preparation

cuff link *noun* one of a pair of decorative fastenings for shirt cuffs

cuisine *noun* style of cooking

cul-de-sac *noun* road with one end blocked off

culinary *adjective* of kitchens or cookery

cull *verb* **1** to choose or gather **2** to remove or kill (inferior or surplus animals) from a herd ▷ *noun* **3** culling

culminate culminates culminating culminated *verb* to reach the highest point or climax > **culmination** *noun*: *the culmination of four years of training*

culpable *adjective* deserving blame

culprit *noun* person guilty of an offence or misdeed

cult *noun* **1** specific system of worship **2** devotion to a person, idea or activity **3** popular fashion

cultivate cultivates cultivating cultivated *verb* **1** to prepare (land) to grow crops **2** to grow (plants) **3** to develop (a feeling or attitude) **4** to try to develop a friendship with

> **cultivation** noun

culture noun 1 ideas, customs and art of a particular society 2 particular society 3 developed understanding of the arts 4 growth of bacteria for study > **cultural** adjective

cultured adjective showing good taste or manners

cumulative adjective increasing steadily

cunjevoi cunjevois noun very small Australian sea creature that lives on rocks

cunning adjective 1 clever at deceiving 2 ingenious ▷ noun 3 cleverness at deceiving 4 ingenuity > **cunningly** adverb

cup cups cupping cupped noun 1 small bowl-shaped drinking container with a handle 2 contents of a cup 3 (competition with) a cup-shaped trophy given as a prize ▷ verb 4 to put (your hands) together to form a shape like a cup 5 to hold in cupped hands

cupboard noun piece of furniture or alcove with a door, for storage

curable adjective able to be cured

curate noun clergyman who assists a parish priest

curator noun person in charge of a museum or art gallery

curb noun 1 something that restrains ▷ verb 2 to control or restrain

curd noun coagulated milk, a thick white substance used to make cheese

curdle curdles curdling curdled verb to turn into curd

cure cures curing cured verb 1 to get rid of (an illness or problem) 2 to make (someone) well again 3 to preserve by salting, smoking or drying ▷ noun 4 (treatment causing) curing of an illness or person 5 remedy or solution

curfew noun 1 law ordering people to stay inside their homes after a specific time at night 2 time set as a deadline by such a law

curiosity curiosities noun 1 eagerness to know or find out 2 rare or unusual object

curious adjective 1 eager to learn or know 2 eager to find out private details 3 unusual or peculiar: a curious discovery > **curiously** adverb

curl noun 1 curved piece of hair 2 curved spiral shape ▷ verb 3 to make (hair) into curls or (of hair) grow in curls 4 to make into a curved spiral shape > **curly** adjective: naturally curly hair

curler noun 1 small tube for curling hair 2 person who plays curling

curlew noun long-billed wading bird

curling noun game like bowls, played with heavy stones on ice

currant noun 1 small dried grape 2 small round berry, such as a redcurrant

currawong noun Australian songbird resembling a crow

currency currencies noun 1 money in use in a particular country 2 general acceptance or use

current adjective 1 of the immediate present 2 most recent, up-to-date 3 commonly accepted ▷ noun 4 flow of water or air in one direction 5 flow of electricity 6 general trend > **currently** adverb

current affairs plural noun political and social events discussed in newspapers and on television and radio

curriculum curriculums or **curricula** noun all the courses of study offered by a school or college

curriculum vitae noun outline

of someone's educational and professional history, prepared for job applications; often abbreviated to **CV**

curry curries currying curried noun **1** Indian dish of meat or vegetables in a hot spicy sauce ▷ verb **2** to prepare (food) with curry powder **3 curry favour** to ingratiate yourself with an important person > **curried** adjective flavoured with hot spices

curse curses cursing cursed verb **1** to swear **2** to swear about ▷ noun **3** swearword **4** (result of) a call to a supernatural power to cause harm to someone **5** something causing trouble or harm > **cursed** adjective

cursor noun arrow or box on a computer monitor which indicates where the next letter or symbol is

cursory adjective quick and superficial

curt adjective brief and rather rude > **curtly** adverb

curtail verb formal **1** to cut short **2** to restrict

curtain noun **1** piece of cloth hung at a window or used to form a screen **2** hanging cloth separating the audience and the stage in a theatre **3** opening or closing of the curtain at the theatre

curtsy curtsies curtsying curtsied; also spelt **curtsey** noun **1** woman's gesture of respect made by bending the knees and bowing the head ▷ verb **2** to make a curtsy

curve curves curving curved noun **1** continuously bending line with no straight parts ▷ verb **2** to form or move in a curve > **curved** adjective > **curvy** adjective

cushion noun **1** bag filled with soft material, to make a seat more comfortable **2** something that provides comfort or absorbs shock ▷ verb **3** to lessen the effects of **4** to protect from injury or shock

custard noun sweet yellow sauce made from milk and eggs

custodian noun person in charge of a public building

custody noun **1** protective care **2** imprisonment prior to being tried > **custodial** adjective: a custodial sentence

custom noun **1** long-established activity or action **2** usual habit **3** formal regular use of a shop or business

customary adjective usual > **customarily** adverb

custom-built or **custom-made** adjective made to the specifications of an individual customer

customer noun **1** person who buys goods or services **2** informal person with whom you have to deal: a tough customer

customs noun **1** government department which collects duty on imports and exports **2** area at a port, airport or border where baggage and freight are examined for goods on which duty is payable

cut cuts cutting cut verb **1** to open up, penetrate, wound or divide with a sharp instrument **2** to divide **3** to trim or shape by cutting **4** to shorten or reduce **5** to suppress **6** to pretend not to recognize ▷ noun **7** stroke or incision made by cutting **8** piece cut off **9** reduction **10** deletion in a text, film or play **11** informal share, especially of profits **12** style in which hair or a garment is cut > **cut back** verb **1** to shorten by cutting **2** to make a reduction > **cut down** verb **1** to fell **2** to make a reduction > **cut off** verb **1** to remove or separate by cutting **2** to stop the supply of **3** to interrupt (a person who is speaking), especially during a telephone conversation > **cut out** *verb* **1** to shape by cutting **2** to delete or remove **3** *informal* to stop doing something **4** (of an engine) to cease to operate suddenly

cutback *noun* decrease or reduction

cute cuter cutest *adjective* **1** appealing or attractive **2** *informal* clever or shrewd

cuticle *noun* skin at the base of a fingernail or toenail

cutlass cutlasses *noun* curved one-edged sword formerly used by sailors

cutlery *noun* knives, forks and spoons

cutlet *noun* **1** small piece of meat like a chop **2** flat croquette of chopped meat or fish

cutting *noun* **1** article cut from a newspaper or magazine **2** piece cut from a plant from which to grow a new plant **3** passage cut through high ground for a road or railway ▷ *adjective* **4** (of a remark) hurtful

CV CVs *abbreviation* curriculum vitae

cyanide *noun* extremely poisonous chemical compound

cyber- *prefix relating to* computers: *cyberspace*

cyberpet *noun* electronic toy that imitates the activities of a pet, and needs to be fed and entertained

cyberspace *noun* place said to contain all the data stored in computers

cycle cycles cycling cycled *verb* **1** to ride a bicycle ▷ *noun* **2** *Brit, Aust, NZ* bicycle **3** *US* motorcycle **4** complete series of recurring events **5** time taken for one such series

cyclical or **cyclic** *adjective* occurring in cycles

cyclist *noun* person who rides a bicycle

cyclone *noun* violent wind moving round a central area

cygnet *noun* young swan

cylinder *noun* **1** solid or hollow body with straight sides and circular ends **2** chamber within which the piston moves in an internal-combustion engine > **cylindrical** *adjective*: *a cylindrical container*

cymbal *noun* percussion instrument consisting of a brass plate which is struck against another or hit with a stick

cynic *noun* person who believes that people always act selfishly

cynical *adjective* believing that people always act selfishly > **cynically** *adverb* > **cynicism** *noun*: *He viewed politicians with cynicism*

cypher *noun* same as **cipher**

cypress cypresses *noun* evergreen tree with dark green leaves

cyst *noun* (abnormal) sac in the body containing fluid or soft matter

czar *noun* same as **tsar** > **czarina** *noun* same as **tsarina**

Czech *adjective* **1** belonging or relating to the Czech Republic ▷ *noun* **2** person from the Czech Republic **3** language spoken in the Czech Republic

Czechoslovak Czechoslovaks *adjective* **1** belonging to or relating to the country that used to be Czechoslovakia ▷ *noun* **2** someone who came from the country that used to be Czechoslovakia

dab dabs dabbing dabbed *verb*
1 to pat lightly **2** to apply with short
tapping strokes ▷ *noun* **3** small
amount of something soft or moist
dabble dabbles dabbling
dabbled *verb* **1** to be involved in
something superficially **2** to splash
about
dachshund *noun* dog with a long
body and short legs
dad *noun informal* father
daddy daddies *noun informal* father
daddy-long-legs *noun* **1** *Brit*
crane fly **2** *US, Canadian* small web-
spinning spider with long legs
　The plural of *daddy-long-legs* is
　daddy-long-legs
daffodil *noun* yellow trumpet-
shaped flower that blooms in
spring
daft *adjective informal* foolish or crazy
dagga *noun S Afr informal* cannabis
dagger *noun* **1** short knifelike
weapon with a pointed blade **2 at**
daggers drawn in a state of open
hostility
dahlia *noun* brightly coloured
garden flower
daily dailies *adjective* **1** occurring
every day or every weekday

▷ *adverb* **2** every day ▷ *noun* **3** daily
newspaper **4** *Brit informal* person
who cleans other people's houses
dainty daintier daintiest *adjective*
delicate or elegant **> daintily**
adverb
dairy dairies *noun* **1** place for the
processing or sale of milk and its
products **2** *NZ* small shop selling
groceries and milk often outside
normal trading hours ▷ *adjective*
3 of milk or its products
dais daises *noun* raised platform in
a hall, used by a speaker
daisy daisies *noun* small wild
flower with a yellow centre and
white petals
dale *noun* (esp. in N England) valley
dally dallies dallying dallied *verb*
1 to waste time **2 dally with** to
deal frivolously with
dalmatian *noun* large dog with
a white coat and black or brown
spots
dam dams damming dammed
noun **1** barrier built across a river
to create a lake **2** lake created by
this ▷ *verb* **3** to build a dam across
(a river)
damage damages damaging
damaged *verb* **1** to harm or spoil
▷ *noun* **2** harm to a person or thing
3 damages money awarded as
compensation for injury or loss
> damaging *adjective*
dame *noun* **1** *Chiefly US & Canadian*
informal woman **2 Dame** title of a
woman who has been awarded the
OBE or another order of chivalry
damn *verb* **1** to condemn as bad or
worthless **2** (of God) to condemn
to hell ▷ *interjection* **3** *informal*
exclamation of annoyance ▷ *adverb*,
adjective **4** *informal* extreme(ly)
damnation *noun* eternal
punishment in Hell after death

damp *adjective* **1** slightly wet ▷ *noun* **2** slight wetness; moisture ▷ *verb* **3** to make damp > **damp down** *verb* to reduce the intensity of (feelings or actions) > **damply** *adverb* > **dampness** *noun*

dampen *verb* **1** to reduce the intensity of **2** to make damp

damper *noun* **1** movable plate to regulate the draught in a fire **2** **put a damper on** to have a depressing or inhibiting effect on

damson *noun* small blue-black plumlike fruit

dance **dances dancing danced** *verb* **1** to move the feet and body rhythmically in time to music **2** to perform (a particular dance) **3** to skip or leap **4** to move rhythmically ▷ *noun* **5** series of steps and movements in time to music **6** social meeting arranged for dancing > **dancer** *noun*: *a ballroom dancer* > **dancing** *noun*

dandelion *noun* yellow-flowered wild plant

dandruff *noun* loose scales of dry dead skin shed from the scalp

dandy **dandies; dandier dandiest** *noun* **1** *old-fashioned* man who is too concerned with the elegance of his appearance ▷ *adjective* **2** *informal* very good

Dane *noun* someone from Denmark

danger *noun* **1** possibility of being injured or killed **2** person or thing that may cause injury or harm **3** likelihood that something unpleasant will happen

dangerous *adjective* able to or likely to cause hurt or harm > **dangerously** *adverb*

dangle **dangles dangling dangled** *verb* **1** to hang loosely **2** to display as an enticement

Danish *adjective* **1** belonging or

relating to Denmark ▷ *noun* **2** main language spoken in Denmark

dank *adjective* unpleasantly damp and chilly

dapper *adjective* (of a man) neat in appearance

dappled *adjective* marked with spots of a different colour

dare **dares daring dared** *verb* **1** to be courageous enough to try (to do something) **2** to challenge (someone) to do something risky ▷ *noun* **3** challenge to do something risky

daredevil *noun* recklessly bold person

daring *adjective* **1** willing to take risks ▷ *noun* **2** courage to do dangerous things

dark *adjective* **1** having little or no light **2** (of a colour) reflecting little light **3** (of hair or skin) brown or black **4** gloomy or sad **5** sinister or evil ▷ *noun* **6** absence of light **7** night > **darkly** *adverb* > **darkness** *noun*

darken *verb* to become or make (something) darker

darkroom *noun* darkened room for processing photographic film

darling *noun* **1** much-loved person **2** favourite ▷ *adjective* **3** much-loved

darn *verb* **1** to mend (a garment) with a series of interwoven stitches ▷ *noun* **2** patch of darned work

dart *noun* **1** small narrow pointed missile that is thrown or shot, especially in the game of darts **2** sudden quick movement **3** tapered tuck made in dressmaking **4** **darts** game in which darts are thrown at a circular numbered board ▷ *verb* **5** to move or direct quickly and suddenly

dash **dashes dashing dashed** *verb* **1** to move quickly **2** to hurl

(something against something)
3 to frustrate (someone's hopes)
▷ *noun* **4** sudden quick movement
5 small amount **6** mixture of style
and courage **7** punctuation mark
– indicating a change of subject

dashboard *noun* instrument panel
in a vehicle

dashing *adjective* stylish and
attractive

dassie *noun* S Afr type of hoofed
rodent-like animal; also **hyrax**

dasyure *noun* small marsupial that
lives in Australia and eats meat

data *noun* **1** information consisting
of observations, measurements or
facts **2** numbers, digits, etc, stored
by a computer

> *Data* is really a plural word, but it
is usually used as a singular

database *noun* store of information
that can be easily handled by a
computer

date dates dating dated *noun*
1 specified day of the month
2 particular day or year when
an event happened **3** *informal*
appointment, especially with a
person to whom you are sexually
attracted **4** *informal* person with
whom you have a date **5** dark-
brown sweet-tasting fruit that
grows on a variety of palm tree
▷ *verb* **6** to mark with the date
7 *informal* to go on a date (with) **8** to
find out the age of (something) by
identifying when it began or was
made **9** to become old-fashioned
10 date from to originate from

dated *adjective* old-fashioned

datum *noun* singular form of **data**

daub *verb* to smear or spread quickly
or clumsily

daughter *noun* female child

**daughter-in-law daughters-in-
law** *noun* son's wife

daunt *verb* to make (someone)
feel worried and intimidated
about their prospects of success
> **daunting** *adjective*

dawn *noun* **1** daybreak **2** beginning
(of something) ▷ *verb* **3** to begin to
grow light **4** to begin to develop or
appear > **dawn on** *verb* to become
apparent to (someone)

day days *noun* **1** period of 24 hours
2 period of light between sunrise
and sunset **3** part of a day occupied
with regular activity, especially
work **4** period or point in time
5 time of success **6 call it a day** to
stop work or other activity

daybreak *noun* time in the morning
when light first appears

daydream *noun* **1** pleasant fantasy
indulged in while awake ▷ *verb* **2** to
indulge in idle fantasy

daylight *noun* light from the sun

day-to-day *adjective* routine

day trip *noun* journey for pleasure
to a place and back again on the
same day

daze *noun* **in a daze** confused and
bewildered

dazed *adjective* stunned and unable
to think clearly

dazzle dazzles dazzling dazzled
verb **1** to impress greatly **2** to blind
temporarily by sudden excessive
light ▷ *noun* **3** bright light that
dazzles > **dazzling** *adjective*: *a
dazzling smile*

de- *prefix indicating* **1** removal: *de-ice*
2 reversal: *declassify*

deacon *noun* Christianity
1 ordained minister ranking
immediately below a priest **2** (in
some Protestant churches) lay
official who assists the minister
> **deaconess** *noun*

dead *adjective* **1** no longer alive **2** no
longer in use **3** numb: *My leg has*

gone dead **4** complete or absolute: *dead silence* **5** *informal* very tired **6** (of a place) lacking activity ▷ *noun* **7** period during which coldness or darkness is most intense: *in the dead of night* ▷ *adverb* **8** *informal* extremely **9** suddenly: *I stopped dead*

dead end *noun* **1** road with one end blocked off **2** situation in which further progress is impossible

deadline *noun* time or date before which something must be completed

deadlock *noun* point in a dispute at which no agreement can be reached

deadly deadlier deadliest *adjective* **1** likely to cause death **2** *informal* extremely boring ▷ *adverb* **3** extremely

deadpan *adjective, adverb* showing no emotion or expression

dead weight *noun* heavy weight

deaf *adjective* **1** unable to hear **2 deaf to** refusing to listen to or take notice of > **deafness** *noun* condition of being unable to hear

deafen *verb* to make deaf, especially temporarily

deafening *adjective* very loud

deal deals dealing dealt *noun* **1** agreement or transaction **2 a great deal (of)** a large amount (of) ▷ *verb* **3** to inflict (a blow) on **4** *Cards* to give out (cards) to the players > **deal in** *verb* to buy or sell (goods) > **deal out** *verb* to distribute > **deal with** *verb* **1** to take action on **2** to be concerned with

dealer *noun* person or firm whose business involves buying or selling things

dealings *plural noun* transactions or business relations

dean *noun* **1** chief administrative official of a college or university **2** chief administrator of a cathedral

dear *noun* **1** someone regarded with affection ▷ *adjective* **2** much-loved **3** costly > **dearly** *adverb*

dearth *noun* inadequate amount or scarcity

death *noun* **1** permanent end of life in a person or animal **2** instance of this **3** ending or destruction

debacle *noun formal* disastrous failure

debase debases debasing debased *verb* to lower in value, quality or character

debatable *adjective* not absolutely certain

debate *noun* **1** discussion ▷ *verb* **2** to discuss (something) formally **3** to consider (a course of action)

debilitating *adjective formal* causing weakness: *a debilitating illness*

debit *noun* **1** acknowledgment of a sum owing by entry on the left side of an account ▷ *verb* **2** to charge (an account) with a debt

debrief *verb* to receive a report from (a soldier, diplomat, etc) after an event > **debriefing** *noun*: *The mission was followed by a full debriefing*

debris *noun* fragments of something destroyed

debt *noun* something owed, especially money

debtor *noun* person who owes money

debut *noun* first public appearance of a performer

debutante *noun* young upper-class woman being formally presented to society

dec- or **deca-** *prefix meaning* ten: *decathlon*

decade *noun* period of ten years

decadence *noun* deterioration in morality or culture > **decadent** *adjective*: *a decadent lifestyle*

decaffeinated *adjective* (of coffee, tea or cola) with caffeine removed

decanter *noun* stoppered bottle for wine or spirits

decapitate decapitates decapitating decapitated *verb* to behead

decathlon *noun* athletic contest with ten different events

decay decays decaying decayed *verb* **1** to become weaker or more corrupt **2** to rot ▷ *noun* **3** process of decaying **4** state brought about by this process

deceased *formal adjective* **1** dead ▷ *noun* **2** **the deceased** the dead person

deceit *noun* behaviour intended to deceive > **deceitful** *adjective*: *a very deceitful little girl*

deceive deceives deceiving deceived *verb* to mislead (someone) by lying

decelerate decelerates decelerating decelerated *verb* to slow down > **deceleration** *noun*

December *noun* twelfth and last month of the year

decency *noun* behaviour that is respectable and follows accepted moral standards

decent *adjective* **1** (of a person) polite and morally acceptable **2** fitting or proper **3** *informal* kind > **decently** *adverb*

decentralize decentralizes decentralizing decentralized; also spelt **decentralise** *verb* to reorganize into smaller local units > **decentralization** *noun*

deception *noun* **1** deceiving **2** something that deceives, trick

deceptive *adjective* likely or designed to deceive > **deceptively** *adverb*

deci- *prefix meaning* one tenth: *decimetre*

decibel *noun* unit for measuring the intensity of sound

decide decides deciding decided *verb* **1** to (cause to) reach a decision **2** to settle (a contest or question)

deciduous *adjective* (of a tree) shedding its leaves annually

decimal *noun* **1** fraction written in the form of a dot followed by one or more numbers ▷ *adjective* **2** relating to or using powers of ten **3** expressed as a decimal

decimal currency decimal currencies *noun* system of currency in which the units are parts or powers of ten

decimal point *noun* dot between the unit and the fraction of a number in the decimal system

decimal system *noun* number system with a base of ten, in which numbers are expressed by combinations of the digits 0 to 9

decimate decimates decimating decimated *verb* to destroy or kill a large proportion of

decipher *verb* to work out the meaning of (something illegible or in code)

decision *noun* **1** judgment, conclusion or resolution **2** act of making up your mind

decisive *adjective* **1** having a definite influence **2** having the ability to make quick decisions > **decisively** *adverb* > **decisiveness** *noun*

deck *noun* **1** area of a ship that forms a floor **2** similar area in a bus > **deck out** *verb* to make more attractive by decorating

deck chair *noun* light folding chair, made from canvas and wood and used outdoors

declaration *noun* firm, forceful statement, often an official announcement: *a declaration of war*

declare declares declaring declared *verb* **1** to state firmly and forcefully **2** to announce officially **3** to acknowledge for tax purposes

decline declines declining declined *verb* **1** to become smaller, weaker or less important **2** to refuse politely to accept or do **3** *Grammar* to list the inflections of (a noun, pronoun or adjective) ▷ *noun* **4** gradual weakening or loss

decode decodes decoding decoded *verb* to convert from code into ordinary language

decoder *noun* device used to decode signals sent in code, for example the television signals from a satellite

decommission *verb* to dismantle (a nuclear reactor, weapon, etc) which is no longer needed

decompose decomposes decomposing decomposed *verb* to be broken down through chemical or bacterial action > **decomposition** *noun*: *the decomposition of plant tissue*

decontaminate decontaminates decontaminating decontaminated *verb* to make (something) safe by removing poisons, radioactivity, etc > **decontamination** *noun*

decor *noun* style in which a room or house is decorated

decorate decorates decorating decorated *verb* **1** to make more attractive by adding something ornamental **2** to paint or wallpaper **3** to award a (military) medal to

decoration *noun* **1** addition that makes something more attractive **2** way in which a room or building is decorated **3** official honour or medal awarded to someone

decorative *adjective* intended to look attractive

decorator *noun* person whose job is painting and putting up wallpaper in rooms and buildings

decorum *noun formal* polite and socially correct behaviour

decoy decoys *noun* **1** person or thing used to lure someone into danger **2** dummy bird or animal, used to lure game within shooting range

decrease decreases decreasing decreased *verb* **1** to make or become less ▷ *noun* **2** lessening or reduction **3** amount by which something has decreased > **decreasing** *adjective*: *decreasing investment in training*

decree decrees decreeing decreed *noun* **1** law made by someone in authority **2** court judgment ▷ *verb* **3** to order by decree

dedicate dedicates dedicating dedicated *verb* **1** to commit (yourself or your time) wholly to a special purpose or cause **2** to inscribe or address (a book etc) to someone as a tribute > **dedicated** *adjective* devoted to a particular purpose or cause > **dedication** *noun* **1** wholehearted devotion **2** inscription in a book dedicating it to a person

deduce deduces deducing deduced *verb* to reach (a conclusion) by reasoning from evidence

deduct *verb* to subtract

deduction *noun* **1** deducting **2** something that is deducted

3 deducing **4** conclusion reached by deducing

deed *noun* **1** something that is done **2** legal document

deem *verb* to consider or judge

deep *adjective* **1** extending or situated far down, inwards, backwards or sideways **2** of a specified dimension downwards, inwards or backwards **3** difficult to understand **4** of great intensity **5 deep in** absorbed in (an activity) **6** (of a colour) strong or dark **7** *Music* low in pitch ▷ *noun* **8 the deep** *poetic* the sea ▷ **deeply** *adverb*

deepen *verb* to make or become deeper or more intense

deer *noun* large wild animal, the male of which has antlers

▌ The plural of *deer* is *deer*

deface defaces defacing defaced *verb* to deliberately spoil the appearance of

default *noun* **1** failure to do something **2** *Computers* instruction to a computer to select a particular option unless the user specifies otherwise **3 by default** happening because something else has not happened **4 in default of** in the absence of ▷ *verb* **5** to fail to fulfil an obligation

defeat *verb* **1** to win a victory over **2** to thwart or frustrate ▷ *noun* **3** defeating

defecate defecates defecating defecated *verb* to discharge waste from the body through the anus

defect *noun* **1** imperfection or blemish ▷ *verb* **2** to desert your cause or country to join the opposing forces ▷ **defection** *noun*

defective *adjective* imperfect or faulty

defence *noun* **1** resistance against attack **2** argument in support of

something **3** country's military resources **4** defendant's case in a court of law

defend *verb* **1** to protect from harm or danger **2** to support in the face of criticism **3** to represent (a defendant) in court

defendant *noun* person accused of a crime

defender *noun* **1** person who supports someone or something in the face of criticism **2** *Sport* player whose chief task is to stop the opposition scoring

defensible *adjective* able to be defended against criticism or attack

defensive *adjective* **1** intended for defence **2** overanxious to protect yourself against (threatened) criticism ▷ **defensively** *adverb* ▷ **defensiveness** *noun*: *There was a note of defensiveness in her voice*

defer defers deferring deferred *verb* **1** to delay (something) until a future time **2 defer to** to comply with the wishes of

deference *noun* polite and respectful behaviour ▷ **deferential** *adjective*: *He was always deferential to his elders* ▷ **deferentially** *adverb*

defiance *noun* open resistance to authority or opposition ▷ **defiant** *adjective*: *The players are in defiant mood* ▷ **defiantly** *adverb*

deficiency deficiencies *noun* **1** state of being deficient **2** lack or shortage

deficient *adjective* **1** lacking some essential thing or quality **2** inadequate in quality or quantity

deficit *noun* amount by which a sum of money is too small

defile defiles defiling defiled *verb* to treat (something sacred or important) without respect

define *verb* **1** to state precisely the meaning of **2** to show clearly the outline of

definite *adjective* **1** firm, clear and precise **2** having precise limits **3** known for certain > **definitely** *adverb*

definition *noun* **1** statement of the meaning of a word or phrase **2** quality of being clear and distinct

definitive *adjective* **1** providing an unquestionable conclusion **2** being the best example of something > **definitively** *adverb*

deflate deflates deflating deflated *verb* **1** to cause (a tyre, balloon, etc) to collapse **2** to collapse through lack of air **3** to make (someone) feel or seem less confident or important **4** *Economics* to cause deflation of (an economy)

deflation *noun* **1** *Economics* reduction in economic activity resulting in lower output and investment **2** feeling of sadness following excitement

deflect *verb* to (cause to) turn aside from a course > **deflection** *noun*: *the deflection of light*

deforestation *noun* destruction of all the trees in an area

deformed *adjective* disfigured or abnormally shaped

deformity deformities *noun* **1** distortion of an organ or part **2** state of being deformed

defraud *verb* to cheat out of money, property, etc

defrost *verb* **1** to make or become free of ice **2** to thaw (frozen food) by removing it from a freezer

deft *adjective* quick and skilful in movement > **deftly** *adverb*

defunct *adjective* no longer existing or operative

defuse defuses defusing defused *verb* **1** to remove the fuse of (an explosive device) **2** to remove the tension from (a situation)

defy defies defying defied *verb* **1** to resist openly and boldly **2** to make impossible: *The condition of the refugees defied description*

degenerate degenerates degenerating degenerated *adjective* **1** having deteriorated to a lower mental, moral or physical level ▷ *noun* **2** degenerate person ▷ *verb* **3** to become degenerate > **degeneration** *noun*

degradation *noun* **1** state of poverty and misery **2** state of humiliation or corruption

degrade degrades degrading degraded *verb* **1** to reduce to dishonour or disgrace **2** to reduce in status or quality **3** *Chemistry* to decompose into smaller molecules

degrading *adjective* humiliating

degree *noun* **1** stage in a scale of relative amount or intensity **2** academic award given by a university or college on successful completion of a course **3** unit of measurement for temperature, angles or latitude and longitude

dehydrated *adjective* weak through losing too much water from your body > **dehydration** *noun*: *a runner suffering from dehydration*

deign *verb formal* to agree (to do something), but as if doing someone a favour

deity deities *noun* **1** god or goddess **2** state of being divine

déjà vu *noun* feeling of having experienced before something that is actually happening now

dejected *adjective* miserable and unhappy > **dejectedly** *adverb* > **dejection** *noun*: *feelings of dejection and despair*

delay delays delaying delayed
verb **1** to put off to a later time **2** to slow up or cause to be late ▷ noun **3** act of delaying **4** interval of time between events

delectable adjective delightful, very attractive

delegate delegates delegating delegated noun **1** person chosen to represent others, especially at a meeting ▷ verb **2** to entrust (duties or powers) to someone **3** to appoint as a delegate

delegation noun **1** group chosen to represent others **2** delegating

delete deletes deleting deleted verb to remove (something written or printed) > **deletion** noun: the deletion of superfluous words

deliberate deliberates deliberating deliberated adjective **1** done on purpose or planned in advance; intentional **2** careful and unhurried ▷ verb **3** to think something over > **deliberately** adverb

deliberation noun careful consideration of a subject

delicacy delicacies noun **1** fine, graceful or subtle in character **2** something particularly good to eat

delicate adjective **1** fine or subtle in quality or workmanship **2** having a fragile beauty **3** (of a taste etc) pleasantly subtle **4** easily damaged **5** requiring tact > **delicately** adverb

delicatessen noun shop selling imported or unusual foods, often already cooked or prepared

delicious adjective very appealing to taste or smell > **deliciously** adverb

delight noun **1** (source of) great pleasure ▷ verb **2** to please greatly **3** **delight in** to take great pleasure in > **delighted** adjective: I was delighted at the news

delightful adjective very pleasant and attractive > **delightfully** adverb

delinquent noun **1** someone, especially a young person, who repeatedly breaks the law ▷ adjective **2** repeatedly breaking the law > **delinquency** noun

delirious adjective **1** unable to speak or act in a rational way because of illness or fever **2** wildly excited and happy > **deliriously** adverb

deliver verb **1** to carry (goods etc) to a destination **2** to hand over **3** to aid in the birth of **4** to present (a lecture or speech) **5** to release or rescue **6** to strike (a blow)

delivery deliveries noun **1** delivering **2** something that is delivered **3** act of giving birth to a baby **4** style in public speaking

dell noun literary small wooded valley

delta noun flat area at the mouth of some rivers where the main stream splits up into several branches

delude deludes deluding deluded verb to make someone believe that something is not true

deluge deluges deluging deluged noun **1** great flood **2** torrential rain **3** overwhelming number ▷ verb **4** to flood **5** to overwhelm

delusion noun **1** mistaken idea or belief **2** state of being deluded

de luxe adjective rich or sumptuous; superior in quality

delve delves delving delved verb to research deeply (for information)

demand verb **1** to request forcefully **2** to require as just, urgent, etc **3** to claim as a right ▷ noun **4** forceful request **5** Economics willingness and ability to purchase goods and services **6** something that requires special effort or sacrifice

demanding *adjective* **1** requiring a lot of time or effort **2** difficult to please or satisfy

demean *verb* **demean yourself** to do something unworthy of your status or character > **demeaning** *adjective*: *demeaning sexist comments*

demeanour *noun* way a person behaves

demented *adjective* mad

dementia *noun* state of serious mental deterioration

demi- *prefix meaning* half

demise *noun* **1** eventual failure (of something successful) **2** *formal* death

demo demos *noun informal* demonstration

democracy democracies *noun* **1** government by the people or their elected representatives **2** state governed in this way

democrat *noun* **1** advocate of democracy **2** **Democrat** member or supporter of the Democratic Party in the US

democratic *adjective* **1** of democracy **2** upholding democracy **3** **Democratic** of the Democratic Party, the more liberal of the two main political parties in the US > **democratically** *adverb*

demography *noun* study of population statistics, such as births and deaths > **demographic** *adjective*: *demographic changes since World War II*

demolish demolishes demolishing demolished *verb* **1** to knock down or destroy (a building) **2** to disprove (an argument) > **demolition** *noun*

demon *noun* **1** evil spirit **2** person who does something with great energy or skill > **demonic** *adjective*

demonstrate demonstrates demonstrating demonstrated *verb* **1** to show or prove (something) by reasoning or evidence **2** to display and explain the workings of **3** to reveal the existence of **4** to show support or opposition by public parades or rallies

demonstration *noun* **1** organized expression of public opinion **2** explanation or display of how something works **3** proof

demonstrator *noun* person who takes part in a public demonstration

demoralize demoralizes demoralizing demoralized; also spelt **demoralise** *verb* to undermine the morale of

demote demotes demoting demoted *verb* to reduce (someone) in status or rank > **demotion** *noun*: *The team now faces demotion from the league*

demure *adjective* quiet, reserved and rather shy > **demurely** *adverb*

den *noun* **1** home of a wild animal **2** small secluded room in a home **3** place where people indulge in criminal or immoral activities

denial *noun* **1** statement that something is not true **2** rejection of a request

denigrate denigrates denigrating denigrated *verb formal* to criticize (someone or something) unfairly

denim *noun* **1** hard-wearing cotton fabric, usually blue **2** **denims** jeans made of denim

denomination *noun* **1** group having a distinctive interpretation of a religious faith **2** unit in a system of weights, values or measures

denominator *noun* Maths number

below the line in a fraction

denote denotes denoting denoted *verb* **1** to be a sign of **2** to have as a literal meaning

denounce denounces denouncing denounced *verb* **1** to speak strongly against **2** to give information against

dense denser densest *adjective* **1** closely packed **2** difficult to see through **3** *informal* stupid > **densely** *adverb*

density densities *noun* **1** degree to which something is filled or occupied **2** measure of the compactness of a substance, expressed as its mass per unit volume

dent *noun* **1** hollow in the surface of something, made by hitting it ▷ *verb* **2** to make a dent in

dental *adjective* of teeth or dentistry

dental floss *noun* waxed thread used to remove food particles from between the teeth

dentist *noun* person qualified to practise dentistry

dentistry *noun* branch of medicine concerned with the teeth and gums

dentures *plural noun* false teeth

denunciation *noun* severe public criticism (of someone or something)

deny denies denying denied *verb* **1** to declare (a statement) to be untrue **2** to refuse to give or allow **3** to refuse to acknowledge

deodorant *noun* substance applied to the body to prevent the smell of perspiration

depart *verb* to leave

department *noun* **1** specialized division of a large organization **2** major subdivision of the administration of a government > **departmental** *adjective*

departure *noun* act of leaving

depend *verb* **depend on 1** to put trust in **2** to be influenced or determined by **3** to rely on for income or support

dependable *adjective* reliable and trustworthy > **dependably** *adverb*

dependant *noun* person who depends on another for financial support

dependence *noun* state of being dependent

dependency dependencies *noun* **1** country controlled by another country **2** overreliance on another person or on a drug

dependent *adjective* depending on someone or something

depict *verb* **1** to produce a picture of **2** to describe in words

deplete depletes depleting depleted *verb* **1** to use up (supplies or money) **2** to reduce in number > **depletion** *noun*

deplorable *adjective* very bad or unpleasant

deplore deplores deploring deplored *verb* to express or feel strong disapproval of

deploy deploys deploying deployed *verb* to organize (troops or resources) into a position ready for immediate action > **deployment** *noun*: *the deployment of troops*

deport *verb* to remove (someone) forcibly from a country > **deportation** *noun*

depose deposes deposing deposed *verb* to remove (someone) from an office or position of power

deposit *verb* **1** to put (something) down **2** to entrust (something) for safekeeping, especially to a bank ▷ *noun* **3** sum of money paid into a bank account **4** money given in part payment for goods or services **5** accumulation of sediments, minerals, etc

depot *noun* **1** building where goods or vehicles are kept when not in use **2** *NZ, US* bus or railway station

depraved *adjective* morally bad

depress depresses depressing depressed *verb* **1** to make (someone) sad **2** to lower (prices or wages) ▷ **depressing** *adjective*

depressant *noun* drug able to reduce nervous activity

depressed *adjective* **1** unhappy and gloomy **2** suffering from economic hardship: *depressed industrial areas*

depression *noun* **1** mental state in which a person has feelings of gloom and inadequacy **2** economic condition in which there is high unemployment and low output and investment **3** area of low air pressure **4** sunken place

depressive *adjective* **1** tending to cause depression ▷ *noun* **2** person who suffers from depression

deprive deprives depriving deprived *verb* **deprive of** to prevent (someone) from (having or enjoying something) ▷ **deprivation** *noun*: *sleep deprivation*

deprived *adjective* lacking adequate living conditions, education, etc

depth *noun* **1** distance downwards, backwards or inwards **2** intensity of emotion **3** profundity of character or thought

deputation *noun* body of people appointed to represent others

deputy deputies *noun* person appointed to act on behalf of another

deranged *adjective* insane or uncontrolled

derby derbies *noun* sporting event between teams from the same area

derelict *adjective* **1** unused and falling into ruins ▷ *noun* **2** *formal* social outcast or tramp

deride derides deriding derided *verb* to treat with contempt or ridicule

derision *noun* attitude of contempt or scorn towards something or someone

derivation *noun* the origin of something, such as a word

derivative *noun* **1** word, idea, etc, derived from another ▷ *adjective* **2** not original, but based on or copied from something else

derive derives deriving derived *verb* (followed by *from*) to get (something) from or develop from

derogatory *adjective* intentionally offensive

descant *noun Music* tune played or sung above a basic melody

descend *verb* **1** to move down (a slope etc) **2** to move to a lower level, pitch, etc **3 descend to** to stoop to (unworthy behaviour) **4 descend on** to visit unexpectedly **5 be descended from** to be connected by a blood relationship to

descendant *noun* person or animal descended from an individual, race or species

descent *noun* **1** descending **2** downward slope **3** family origins

describe describes describing described *verb* **1** to give an account of (something or someone) in words **2** to trace the outline of (a circle etc)

description *noun* **1** statement that describes something or someone **2** sort: *flowers of every description* ▷ **descriptive** *adjective*: *descriptive writing* ▷ **descriptively** *adverb*

desert[1] *noun* region with little or no vegetation because of low rainfall

desert² *verb* **1** to abandon (a person or place) without intending to return **2** *Military* to leave (a post or duty) with no intention of returning > **deserter** *noun* person who leaves the armed forces without permission > **desertion** *noun*

deserts *plural noun* **get your just deserts** to get the punishment you deserve

deserve deserves deserving deserved *verb* to be entitled to or worthy of

deserving *adjective* worthy of help, praise or reward

design *verb* **1** to work out the structure or form of (something), by making a sketch or plans **2** to plan and make artistically **3** to intend for a specific purpose ▷ *noun* **4** preliminary drawing **5** arrangement or features of an artistic or decorative work **6** art of designing **7** intention: *by design*

designate designates designating designated *verb* **1** to give a name to **2** to select (someone) for an office or duty

designation *noun* name

designedly *adverb* intentionally

designer *noun* **1** person who draws up original sketches or plans from which things are made ▷ *adjective* **2** designed by a well-known designer

desirable *adjective* **1** worth having **2** arousing sexual desire > **desirability** *noun*

desire desires desiring desired *verb* **1** to want very much ▷ *noun* **2** wish or longing **3** sexual appetite **4** person or thing desired

desist *verb* **desist from** to stop (doing something)

desk *noun* **1** piece of furniture with a writing surface and drawers **2** service counter in a public building

desktop *adjective* of a convenient size to be used on a desk or table

desolate *adjective* **1** uninhabited and bleak **2** very sad > **desolation** *noun*: *a scene of desolation and ruin*

despair *noun* **1** total loss of hope ▷ *verb* **2** to lose hope > **despairing** *adjective*

despatch *verb, noun* same as **dispatch**

desperate *adjective* **1** in despair and reckless **2** (of an action) undertaken as a last resort **3** having a strong need or desire > **desperately** *adverb* > **desperation** *noun*

despicable *adjective* deserving contempt > **despicably** *adverb*

despise despises despising despised *verb* to feel scorn for

despite *preposition* in spite of

despondent *adjective* unhappy > **despondency** *noun*

dessert *noun* sweet course served at the end of a meal

destination *noun* place to which someone or something is going

destined *adjective* certain to be or to do something

destiny destinies *noun* **1** future marked out for a person or thing **2** the power that predetermines the course of events

destitute *adjective* having no money or possessions > **destitution** *noun*: *She ended her life in destitution*

destroy destroys destroying destroyed *verb* **1** to ruin or demolish **2** to put an end to **3** to kill (an animal)

destroyer *noun* **1** small fast armed warship **2** person or thing that destroys

destruction *noun* **1** destroying **2** cause of ruin

destructive *adjective* (capable of) causing destruction > **destructiveness** *noun*

desultory *adjective* **1** jumping from one thing to another; disconnected **2** random > **desultorily** *adverb*

detach detaches detaching detached *verb* to disengage and separate > **detachable** *adjective*

detached *adjective* **1** *Brit, Aust, S Afr* (of a house) not joined to another house **2** showing no emotional involvement

detachment *noun* **1** lack of emotional involvement **2** small group of soldiers

detail *noun* **1** individual piece of information **2** unimportant item **3** small individual features of something, considered collectively **4** *Chiefly military* (personnel assigned) a specific duty ▷ *verb* **5** to list fully > **detailed** *adjective*

detain *verb* **1** to delay (someone) **2** to hold (someone) in custody

detainee *noun* person confined in prison, particularly because of political activities

detect *verb* **1** to notice **2** to discover or find > **detectable** *adjective*

detection *noun* **1** act of noticing, discovering or sensing something **2** work of investigating crime

detective *noun* policeman or private agent who investigates crime

detector *noun* instrument used to find something

detention *noun* **1** imprisonment **2** form of punishment in which a pupil is detained after school

deter deters deterring deterred *verb* to discourage (someone) from doing something by instilling fear or doubt

detergent *noun* chemical substance for washing clothes or dishes

deteriorate *verb* to become worse > **deterioration** *noun*

determination *noun* condition of being determined or resolute

determine determines determining determined *verb* **1** to settle (an argument or a question) conclusively **2** to find out (facts about something)

determined *adjective* firmly decided and unable to be dissuaded > **determinedly** *adverb*

determiner *noun Grammar* word that goes before a noun group and shows to which thing or to how many things you are referring, *eg: this; all; some*

deterrent *noun* **1** something that deters **2** weapon, especially nuclear, intended to deter attack > **deterrence** *noun: nuclear deterrence*

detest *verb* to dislike (someone or something) intensely

detonate detonates detonating detonated *verb* to make (an explosive device) explode or (of an explosive device) to explode

detonator *noun* small amount of explosive, or a device, used to set off an explosion

detour *noun* route that is not the most direct one

detract *verb* **detract from** to make (something) seem less good

detriment *noun* disadvantage or damage > **detrimental** *adjective: foods suspected of being detrimental to health*

deuce *noun* **1** *Tennis* score of forty all **2** playing card with two symbols or dice with two spots

**devalue devalues devaluing
devalued** verb 1 to reduce the
exchange value of (a currency) 2 to
reduce the value of (something or
someone) > **devaluation** noun:
devaluation of a number of currencies

**devastate devastates
devastating devastated** verb
to damage (a place) severely or
destroy it > **devastation** noun

devastated adjective shocked and
extremely upset

devastating adjective 1 very
destructive 2 overwhelming or
shocking

develop verb 1 to grow or bring to
a later, more elaborate or more
advanced stage 2 to come or bring
into existence 3 to build houses or
factories on (an area of land) 4 to
produce (photographs) by making
negatives or prints from a film

developer noun 1 person who
develops property 2 chemical used
to develop photographs or films

development noun 1 process of
growing or developing 2 product
of developing 3 event that changes
a situation 4 area of land that has
been developed > **developmental**
adjective: the developmental needs
of a child

deviant adjective 1 deviating from
what is considered acceptable
behaviour ▷ noun 2 deviant person

**deviate deviates deviating
deviated** verb 1 to differ from
others in belief or thought 2 to
depart from your previous course
> **deviation** noun

device noun 1 machine or tool used
for a specific task 2 scheme or plan
3 **leave someone to his** or **her
own devices** to leave someone
alone to do as he or she wishes

devil noun 1 **the Devil** (in

Christianity and Islam) chief spirit
of evil and enemy of God 2 evil spirit
3 evil person 4 person: poor devil
5 daring person: be a devil!

devious adjective 1 insincere
and dishonest 2 indirect
> **deviousness** noun

devise devises devising devised
verb to work out (a plan, system
or object)

devoid adjective **devoid of**
completely lacking (in)

devolution noun transfer
of authority from a central
government to regional
governments

**devote devotes devoting
devoted** verb to apply or dedicate
(your time, money or efforts) to a
particular purpose

devoted adjective showing loyalty
or devotion

devotee noun 1 person who is very
enthusiastic about something
2 zealous follower of a religion

devotion noun 1 strong affection for
or loyalty to someone or something
2 religious zeal

devour verb 1 to eat (something)
greedily 2 (of an emotion) to engulf
and destroy (someone) 3 to read (a
book or magazine) eagerly

devout adjective deeply religious
> **devoutly** adverb

dew noun drops of water that form
on the ground at night from vapour
in the air

dexterity noun 1 skill in using
your hands 2 mental quickness
> **dexterous** adjective: as people
grow older they become less dexterous

dharma noun (in the Buddhist
religion) ideal truth as set out in the
teaching of the Buddha

diabetes noun disorder in which
an abnormal amount of urine

containing an excess of sugar is excreted > **diabetic** *adjective, noun*: *diabetic patients; suitable for diabetics*

diabolical *adjective informal* extremely bad

diaeresis diaereses *noun* mark (¨) placed over a vowel to show that it is pronounced separately from the preceding one, for example in *Noël*

diagnose diagnoses diagnosing diagnosed *verb* to determine by diagnosis > **diagnostic** *adjective*: *X-rays and other diagnostic tools*

diagnosis diagnoses *noun* discovery and identification of diseases from the examination of symptoms

diagonal *adjective* **1** from corner to corner **2** slanting ▷ *noun* **3** diagonal line > **diagonally** *adverb*

diagram *noun* sketch showing the form or workings of something

dial dials dialling dialled *noun* **1** face of a clock or watch **2** graduated disc on a measuring instrument **3** control on a radio or television set used to change the station **4** numbered disc on the front of some telephones ▷ *verb* **5** to operate the dial or buttons on a telephone in order to contact (a number)

dialect *noun* form of a language spoken in a particular area

dialogue *noun* **1** conversation between two people, especially in a book, film or play **2** discussion between representatives of two nations or groups

dialogue box dialogue boxes *noun* small window that may open on a computer screen to prompt the user to enter information or select an option

dialysis *noun Medicine* filtering of a person's blood using a special machine to remove waste products

diameter *noun Maths* (length of) a straight line through the centre of a circle or sphere

diametrically *adverb* completely (opposed, opposite or different)

diamond *noun* **1** exceptionally hard, usually colourless, precious stone **2** *Geometry* figure with four sides of equal length forming two acute and two obtuse angles **3** playing card marked with red diamond-shaped symbols ▷ *adjective* **4** (of an anniversary) sixtieth

diaphragm *noun* **1** muscular partition that separates the abdominal cavity and chest cavity **2** contraceptive device placed over the neck of the womb

diarist *noun* person who keeps a diary

diarrhoea *noun* condition in which the faeces are more liquid and frequently produced than usual

diary diaries *noun* (book for) a record of daily events, appointments or observations

dice dice; dices dicing diced *noun* **1** small cube each of whose sides has a different number of spots (1 to 6), used in games of chance ▷ *verb* **2** to cut (food) into small cubes > **diced** *adjective*: *diced carrots*
◼ The plural of *dice* is *dice*

dictate dictates dictating dictated *verb* **1** to say or read (something) aloud for someone else to write down **2 dictate to** to seek to impose your will on (other people) ▷ *noun* **3** authoritative command **4** guiding principle

dictation *noun* **1** act of dictating words to be taken down in writing **2** words dictated

dictator *noun* **1** ruler who has complete power **2** person in

power who acts unfairly or cruelly
> **dictatorship** noun: *a military dictatorship*

dictatorial adjective like a dictator

diction noun manner of pronouncing words and sounds

dictionary dictionaries noun
1 book consisting of an alphabetical list of words with their meanings or translations into another language 2 alphabetically ordered reference book of terms relating to a particular subject

did verb past tense of **do**

didgeridoo noun Australian wind instrument made from a long hollow piece of wood

die dies dying died verb 1 (of a person, animal or plant) to stop living 2 (of something inanimate) to cease to exist or function 3 **be dying for** *or* **to do something** *informal* to be eager for or to do something ▷ noun 4 dice 5 specially shaped or patterned block of metal used to cut or mould other metal
The plural of *die* in sense 4 is *dice*

diesel noun 1 (also **diesel oil**) heavy fuel obtained from petroleum distillation 2 vehicle driven by a diesel engine

diesel engine noun internal-combustion engine in which oil is ignited by compression

diet diets dieting dieted noun 1 food that a person or animal regularly eats 2 specific range of foods, to control weight or for health reasons 3 parliament of some countries ▷ verb 4 to follow a special diet so as to lose weight ▷ adjective 5 (of food) suitable for a weight-reduction diet > **dietary** adjective: *dietary habits*

dietician noun person trained to advise people about healthy eating

differ verb 1 to be unlike 2 to disagree

difference noun 1 the way in which something is unlike something else 2 disagreement 3 remainder left after subtraction

different adjective 1 unlike 2 unusual > **differently** adverb
Use *different from* rather than *different to*

differentiate differentiates differentiating differentiated verb 1 to perceive or show the difference (between) 2 to make (one thing) distinct from other such things > **differentiation** noun

difficult adjective 1 requiring effort or skill to do or understand 2 not easily pleased

difficulty difficulties noun 1 problem 2 fact or quality of being difficult

diffident adjective lacking self-confidence > **diffidence** noun > **diffidently** adverb

diffract verb Physics (of rays of light or sound waves) to break up or change direction after hitting an obstacle > **diffraction** noun: *the diffraction of light*

diffuse diffuses diffusing diffused verb 1 to spread (something) over a wide area ▷ adjective 2 widely spread 3 lacking concision > **diffusion** noun

dig digs digging dug verb 1 to cut into, break up and turn over or remove (earth), especially with a spade 2 **dig up** *or* **out** to find by effort or searching 3 **dig in** *or* **into** to thrust or jab ▷ noun 4 digging 5 archaeological excavation 6 thrust or poke 7 spiteful remark

digest verb 1 to subject (food) to a process of digestion 2 to absorb (something) mentally ▷ noun

3 shortened version of a book, report or article > **digestible** *adjective*: *easily digestible*

digestion *noun* (body's system for) breaking down food into easily absorbed substances

digestive *adjective* relating to digestion

digger *noun* **1** machine used for digging **2** *Aust* friendly name to call a man

digit *noun* **1** finger or toe **2** *Maths* numeral from 0 to 9

digital *adjective* **1** displaying information as numbers rather than with hands and a dial: *a digital clock* **2** transmitting or receiving information in the form of thousands of very small signals: *digital radio* > **digitally** *adverb*

dignified *adjective* full of dignity

dignitary dignitaries *noun* person of high official position

dignity *noun* **1** serious, calm and controlled behaviour or manner **2** quality of being worthy of respect **3** sense of self-importance

digression *noun* departure from the main subject in speech or writing

digs *plural noun Brit, Aust, S Afr informal* lodgings

dike *noun* same as **dyke**

dilapidated *adjective* (of a building) having fallen into ruin

dilate dilates dilating dilated *verb* to make or become wider or larger > **dilated** *adjective*: *dilated pupils* > **dilation** *noun*: *dilation of the blood vessels*

dilemma *noun* situation offering a choice between two equally undesirable alternatives

diligent *adjective* **1** careful and persevering in carrying out duties **2** carried out with care and

perseverance > **diligence** *noun*: *They are pursuing the matter with great diligence* > **diligently** *adverb*

dill *noun* sweet-smelling herb

dilly bag *noun Aust* small bag used to carry food

dilute dilutes diluting diluted *verb* **1** to make (a liquid) less concentrated, especially by adding water **2** to make (a quality etc) weaker in force > **dilution** *noun*

dim dimmer dimmest; dims dimming dimmed *adjective* **1** badly lit **2** not clearly seen **3** unintelligent **4 take a dim view of** to disapprove of ▷ *verb* **5** to become or make (something) dim > **dimly** *adverb* > **dimness** *noun*

dimension *noun* **1** measurement of the size of something in a particular direction **2** aspect or factor

diminish diminishes diminishing diminished *verb* to become or make smaller, fewer or less

diminutive *adjective* **1** very small ▷ *noun* **2** word or affix which implies smallness or lack of importance

dimmer *noun* device for dimming an electric light

dimple *noun* small natural dent, especially in the cheeks or chin

din *noun* loud unpleasant confused noise

dinar *noun* monetary unit of various Balkan, Middle Eastern and North African countries

dine dines dining dined *verb formal* to eat dinner

diner *noun* **1** person eating a meal **2** *Chiefly US* small cheap restaurant

dinghy dinghies *noun* small boat, powered by sails, oars or a motor

dingo dingoes *noun* Australian wild dog

dingy dingier dingiest *adjective* dull and drab

dinkum *adjective Aust, NZ informal* genuine or right

dinner *noun* main meal of the day, eaten either in the evening or at midday

dinner jacket *noun* man's formal black evening jacket

dinosaur *noun* type of extinct prehistoric reptile, many of which were of gigantic size

dint *noun* **by dint of** by means of

diocese *noun* district over which a bishop has control > **diocesan** *adjective: the diocesan synod*

dip dips dipping dipped *verb* **1** to plunge (something) quickly or briefly into a liquid **2** to slope downwards **3** to switch (car headlights) from the main to the lower beam **4** to lower briefly ▷ *noun* **5** dipping **6** brief swim **7** liquid chemical in which farm animals are dipped to rid them of insects **8** hollow or depression in the landscape **9** creamy mixture into which pieces of food are dipped before being eaten > **dip into** *verb* to read passages at random from (a book or journal)

diploma *noun* qualification awarded by a college on successful completion of a course

diplomacy *noun* **1** managing of the relations between nations by peaceful means **2** tact or skill in dealing with people

diplomat *noun* official engaged in diplomacy

diplomatic *adjective* **1** of diplomacy **2** tactful in dealing with people > **diplomatically** *adverb*

dire direr direst *adjective* disastrous, urgent or terrible

direct *adjective* **1** (of a route) shortest or straight **2** without anyone or anything intervening **3** likely to have an immediate effect **4** honest or frank ▷ *adverb* **5** in a direct manner ▷ *verb* **6** to lead and organize **7** to tell (someone to do something) **8** to tell (someone) the way to a place **9** to address (a letter, package, remark, etc) **10** to provide guidance to (actors, cameramen, etc) in (a play or film)

direct current *noun* electric current that flows in one direction only

direction *noun* **1** course or line along which a person or thing moves, points or lies **2** management or guidance **3** **directions** instructions for doing something or for reaching a place

directive *noun* instruction that must be obeyed

directly *adverb* **1** in a direct manner **2** at once ▷ *conjunction* **3** as soon as

director *noun* **1** person or thing that directs or controls **2** member of the governing board of a business etc **3** person responsible for the artistic and technical aspects of the making of a film etc > **directorial** *adjective: her directorial debut*

directorate *noun* board of directors

directory directories *noun* **1** book listing names, addresses and telephone numbers **2** *Computers* area of a disk containing the names and locations of the files it currently holds

direct speech *noun* the reporting of what someone has said by quoting the exact words

dirge *noun* slow sad song of mourning

dirt *noun* **1** unclean substance; filth **2** earth or soil **3** obscene speech or writing **4** *informal* harmful gossip

dirty dirtier dirtiest *adjective*

1 covered or marked with dirt **2** unfair or dishonest **3** obscene **4** displaying dislike or anger: *a dirty look* ▷ *verb* **5** to make (something) dirty

dis- *prefix indicating* **1** reversal: *disconnect* **2** negation or lack: *dissimilar; disgrace* **3** removal or release: *disembowel*

disability disabilities *noun* **1** condition of being disabled **2** something that disables someone

disable disables disabling disabled *verb* to make ineffective, unfit or incapable > **disablement** *noun*: *permanent total disablement*

disabled *adjective* lacking a physical power, such as the ability to walk

disadvantage *noun* unfavourable or harmful circumstance

disadvantaged *adjective* socially or economically deprived

disaffected *adjective* having lost loyalty to or affection for someone or something

disagree disagrees disagreeing disagreed *verb* **1** to argue or have different opinions **2** to be different or conflict **3** **disagree with** to cause physical discomfort to: *Curry disagrees with me* > **disagreement** *noun*: *a minor disagreement*

disagreeable *adjective* **1** unpleasant **2** (of a person) unfriendly or unhelpful

disappear disappears disappearing disappeared *verb* **1** to cease to be visible **2** to cease to exist > **disappearance** *noun*

disappoint *verb* to fail to meet the expectations or hopes of > **disappointed** *adjective*: *I was disappointed that she was not there* > **disappointing** *adjective*

disappointment *noun* **1** feeling of being disappointed **2** person or

thing that disappoints

disapprove disapproves disapproving disapproved *verb* **disapprove of** to consider wrong or bad > **disapproval** *noun*: *It was greeted with universal disapproval* > **disapproving** *adjective*

disarm *verb* **1** to deprive (someone) of weapons **2** to win the confidence or affection of **3** (of a country) to decrease the size of its armed forces

disarmament *noun* reducing or getting rid of military forces and weapons

disarming *adjective* removing hostility or suspicion

disarray *noun* **1** confusion and lack of discipline **2** extreme untidiness

disassemble disassembles disassembling disassembled *verb* to take (something) to pieces

disaster *noun* **1** occurrence that causes great distress or destruction **2** something, such as a project, that fails > **disastrous** *adjective* > **disastrously** *adverb*

disband *verb* to (cause to) cease to function as a group

disc *noun* **1** flat circular object **2** *Anatomy* circular flat structure in the body, especially between the bones in your spine **3** *Computers* same as **disk**

discard *verb* to get rid of (something or someone) as useless or undesirable

discern *verb formal* to see or be aware of (something) clearly

discernible *adjective* able to be seen or recognized

discerning *adjective* having good judgment > **discernment** *noun*

discharge discharges discharging discharged *verb* **1** to allow (a patient) to go **2** to dismiss (someone) from duty or employment **3** to fire (a gun) **4** to release or pour out (a substance or liquid) **5** *formal* to meet the demands of (a duty or responsibility) ▷ *noun* **6** substance that comes out from a place **7** discharging

disciple *noun* follower of the doctrines of a teacher, especially Jesus Christ

discipline disciplines disciplining disciplined *noun* **1** practice of imposing strict rules of behaviour **2** *formal* area of academic study ▷ *verb* **3** to attempt to improve the behaviour of (yourself or someone else) by training or rules **4** to punish > **disciplinary** *adjective*: *They took disciplinary action against him* > **disciplined** *adjective* able to behave and work in a controlled way

disc jockey disc jockeys *noun* person who introduces and plays pop records on a radio programme or at a disco

disclose discloses disclosing disclosed *verb* to make (information) known > **disclosure** *noun*: *disclosure of information*

disco discos *noun* **1** nightclub where people dance to amplified pop records **2** occasion at which people dance to amplified pop records

discomfort *noun* inconvenience, distress or mild pain

disconcert *verb* to embarrass or upset > **disconcerting** *adjective*

disconnect *verb* **1** to undo or break the connection between (two things) **2** to stop the supply of electricity or gas of

disconnected *adjective* (of speech or ideas) not logically connected

disconsolate *adjective* sad beyond comfort > **disconsolately** *adverb*

discontent *noun* lack of contentment > **discontented** *adjective*: *discontented workers*

discontinue discontinues discontinuing discontinued *verb* to bring (something) to an end or come to an end

discord *noun* **1** lack of agreement or harmony between people **2** harsh confused sounds

discount *verb* **1** to take no account of (something) because it is considered to be unreliable, prejudiced or irrelevant **2** to deduct (an amount) from the price of something ▷ *noun* **3** deduction from the full price of something

discourage discourages discouraging discouraged *verb* **1** to deprive (someone) of the will to persist in something **2** to oppose (something) by expressing disapproval > **discouragement** *noun*: *His shoulders drooped with exhaustion and discouragement* > **discouraging** *adjective*

discourse discourses discoursing discoursed *noun* *formal* **1** conversation **2** formal treatment of a subject in speech or writing ▷ *verb* **3** **discourse on** to speak or write about (something) at length

discover *verb* **1** to be the first to find or to find out about **2** to learn about for the first time **3** to find after study or search > **discoverer** *noun*

discovery discoveries *noun* **1** discovering **2** person, place or thing that has been discovered

discredit *verb* **1** to damage the reputation of **2** to cause (an idea) to be disbelieved or distrusted ▷ *noun* **3** damage to someone's reputation

discreet *adjective* **1** careful to avoid embarrassment, especially

by keeping confidences secret
2 unobtrusive > **discreetly** adverb

discrepancy discrepancies noun
conflict or variation between facts,
figures or claims

discrete adjective formal separate
and distinct

discretion noun **1** quality of
behaving in a discreet way
2 freedom or authority to make
judgments and decide what to do
> **discretionary** adjective

**discriminate discriminates
discriminating discriminated**
verb **1** **discriminate against**
or **in favour of** to single out (a
particular person or group) for
worse or better treatment than
others **2** **discriminate between**
to recognize or understand the
difference between

discrimination noun **1** unfair
treatment of a person or group
2 subtle appreciation in matters
of taste

discriminatory adjective based on
prejudice

discus discuses noun heavy disc-
shaped object thrown in sports
competitions

**discuss discusses discussing
discussed** verb **1** to consider
(something) by talking it over **2** to
treat (a subject) in speech or writing

discussion noun conversation or
piece of writing in which a subject
is considered in detail

disdain noun feeling of superiority
and dislike > **disdainful** adjective

disease noun unhealthy condition
in people, animals or plants
> **diseased** adjective: diseased lungs

disembark verb to get off a ship,
aircraft or bus

disembodied adjective **1** lacking a
body **2** seeming not to be attached

to or coming from anyone

disenchanted adjective
disappointed and disillusioned
> **disenchantment** noun

**disentangle disentangles
disentangling disentangled** verb
to release from entanglement or
confusion

**disfigure disfigures disfiguring
disfigured** verb to spoil the
appearance of

**disgrace disgraces disgracing
disgraced** noun **1** condition of
shame, loss of reputation or
dishonour **2** shameful person or
thing ▷ verb **3** to bring shame upon
(yourself or others)

disgraceful adjective shameful or
scandalous > **disgracefully** adverb

disgruntled adjective sulky or
discontented

**disguise disguises disguising
disguised** verb **1** to change the
appearance or manner in order to
conceal the identity of (someone
or something) **2** to misrepresent
(something) in order to obscure its
actual nature or meaning ▷ noun
3 mask, costume or manner that
disguises **4** state of being disguised

disgust noun **1** great loathing
or distaste ▷ verb **2** to sicken or
fill with loathing > **disgusted**
adjective: I'm disgusted with the way he
was treated > **disgusting** adjective

dish dishes noun **1** shallow container
used for holding or serving food
2 particular kind of food > **dish out**
verb informal to distribute > **dish up**
verb informal to serve (food)

dishearten verb to weaken or
destroy the hope, courage or
enthusiasm of > **disheartened**
adjective: She was disheartened by their
hostile reaction > **disheartening**
adjective: a frustrating and

disheartening experience

dishevelled *adjective* (of a person's hair, clothes or general appearance) disordered and untidy

dishonest *adjective* not honest or fair > **dishonestly** *adverb*

dishonesty *noun* behaviour which is meant to deceive people, either by not telling the truth or by cheating

disillusion *verb* 1 to destroy the illusions or false ideas of ▷ *noun* 2 (also **disillusionment**) state of being disillusioned > **disillusioned** *adjective*: *disillusioned with politics*

disinfect *verb* to rid (something) of harmful germs chemically > **disinfection** *noun*

disinfectant *noun* substance that destroys harmful germs

disingenuous *adjective* not sincere > **disingenuously** *adverb*

disinherit *verb* Law to deprive (an heir) of inheritance

disintegrate disintegrates disintegrating disintegrated *verb* (of an object) to break into fragments > **disintegration** *noun*

disinterest *noun* lack of personal involvement in a situation

disinterested *adjective* free from bias or involvement

People sometimes use *disinterested* when they mean *uninterested*. If you want to say that someone shows a lack of interest, use *uninterested*. *Disinterested* would be used in a sentence such as *We asked him to decide because he was a disinterested observer*

disjointed *adjective* having no coherence; disconnected

disk *noun* Computers a circular storage device

dislike dislikes disliking disliked *verb* 1 to consider (something or someone) unpleasant or disagreeable ▷ *noun* 2 feeling of not liking something or someone

dislocate dislocates dislocating dislocated *verb* to displace (a bone or joint) from its normal position

dislodge dislodges dislodging dislodged *verb* to remove (something or someone) from a previously fixed position

dismal *adjective* 1 gloomy and depressing 2 *informal* of poor quality > **dismally** *adverb*

dismantle dismantles dismantling dismantled *verb* to take (something) apart piece by piece

dismay dismays dismaying dismayed *verb* 1 to fill (someone) with alarm or depression ▷ *noun* 2 alarm mixed with sadness

dismember *verb formal* 1 to remove the limbs of 2 to cut to pieces > **dismemberment** *noun*

dismiss dismisses dismissing dismissed *verb* 1 to remove (an employee) from a job 2 to allow (someone) to leave 3 to put (something) out of your mind 4 (of a judge) to state that (a case) will not be brought to trial > **dismissal** *noun*: *Mr Low's dismissal from his post*

dismissive *adjective* scornful or contemptuous

dismount *verb* to get off a horse or bicycle

disobedient *adjective* refusing to obey > **disobedience** *noun*

disobey disobeys disobeying disobeyed *verb* to neglect or refuse to obey

disorder *noun* 1 state of untidiness and disorganization 2 public violence or rioting 3 illness

disorderly *adjective* 1 untidy and

disorganized **2** uncontrolled or unruly

disorganized or **disorganised** *adjective* **1** confused and badly arranged **2** not good at planning work and activities efficiently

disown *verb* to deny any connection with (someone)

disparaging *adjective* critical and scornful: *disparaging remarks*

disparate *adjective* **1** completely different **2** diverse > **disparity** *noun*: *economic disparities between North and South*

dispassionate *adjective* not influenced by emotion > **dispassionately** *adverb*

dispatch dispatches dispatching dispatched *verb* **1** to send off to a destination or to perform a task **2** to carry out (a duty or a task) with speed **3** *old-fashioned* to kill ▷ *noun* **4** official communication or report, sent in haste **5** report sent to a newspaper by a correspondent

dispel dispels dispelling dispelled *verb* to destroy or remove

dispensary dispensaries *noun* place where medicine is dispensed

dispense dispenses dispensing dispensed *verb* **1** to give out **2** to prepare and distribute (medicine) ▷ *verb* **3** **dispense with** to do away with or manage without

dispenser *noun* machine or container from which something is given out: *a cash dispenser*

disperse disperses dispersing dispersed *verb* **1** to scatter over a wide area **2** to (cause to) leave a gathering > **dispersion** or **dispersal** *noun*

dispirited *adjective* depressed and having no enthusiasm for anything

dispiriting *adjective* causing loss of enthusiasm: *a dispiriting defeat*

displace displaces displacing displaced *verb* **1** to move (something) from the usual location **2** to remove (someone) from office

displacement *noun* **1** removal of something from its usual or correct place or position **2** *Physics* weight or volume of liquid displaced by an object submerged or floating in it

display displays displaying displayed *verb* **1** to make visible or noticeable ▷ *noun* **2** displaying **3** something displayed **4** exhibition

displease displeases displeasing displeased *verb* to annoy or upset (someone) > **displeasure** *noun*

disposable *adjective* **1** designed to be thrown away after use **2** available for use: *disposable income*

disposal *noun* **1** getting rid of something **2** **at your disposal** available for your use

dispose disposes disposing disposed *verb* **1** to place in a certain order **2** **dispose of a** to throw away **b** to give, sell or transfer to another **c** to deal with or settle **d** to kill

disposed *adjective* **1** willing or eager **2** having an attitude as specified: *He felt well disposed towards her*

disposition *noun* **1** nature or temperament **2** willingness

dispossess dispossesses dispossessing dispossessed *verb* (followed by *of*) to deprive (someone) of (a possession)

disproportionate *adjective* out of proportion > **disproportionately** *adverb*

disprove disproves disproving disproved *verb* to show (an assertion or claim) to be incorrect

dispute disputes disputing disputed *noun* **1** disagreement, argument ▷ *verb* **2** to argue about (something) **3** to doubt the validity of **4** to fight over possession of

disqualify disqualifies disqualifying disqualified *verb* to stop (someone) officially from taking part in something for wrongdoing > **disqualification** *noun*: *disqualification from the race*

disquiet *noun* **1** feeling of anxiety ▷ *verb* **2** to make (someone) anxious > **disquieting** *adjective*

disregard *verb* **1** to give little or no attention to ▷ *noun* **2** lack of attention or respect

disrepair *noun* condition of being worn out or in poor working order

disreputable *adjective* having or causing a bad reputation

disrespect *noun* lack of respect > **disrespectful** *adjective*

disrupt *verb* to interrupt the progress of > **disruption** *noun*: *disruption to flights* > **disruptive** *adjective*

dissatisfied *adjective* not pleased or contented > **dissatisfaction** *noun*

dissect *verb* **1** to cut open (a corpse) to examine it **2** to examine critically and minutely > **dissection** *noun*

dissent *verb* **1** to disagree ▷ *noun* **2** disagreement > **dissenting** *adjective*: *dissenting voices*

dissertation *noun* written thesis, usually required for a higher university degree

disservice *noun* harmful action

dissident *noun* **1** person who disagrees with and criticizes the government ▷ *adjective* **2** disagreeing with the government

dissimilar *adjective* not alike; different

dissipate dissipates dissipating dissipated *verb* **1** to waste or squander **2** to scatter or disappear

dissipated *adjective* showing signs of overindulgence in alcohol and other physical pleasures

dissolute *adjective* leading an immoral life

dissolution *noun* **1** official breaking up of an organization or institution, such as Parliament **2** official ending of a formal agreement, such as a marriage

dissolve dissolves dissolving dissolved *verb* **1** to (cause to) become liquid **2** to break up or end officially **3** to break down emotionally: *She dissolved into tears*

dissuade dissuades dissuading dissuaded *verb* to deter (someone) from doing something by persuasion

distance distances distancing distanced *noun* **1** space between two points **2** state of being apart **3** remoteness in manner **4** **the distance** most distant part of the visible scene ▷ *verb* **5** **distance yourself** *or* **be distanced from** to separate yourself or be separated mentally from

distant *adjective* **1** far apart **2** separated by a specified distance **3** remote in manner > **distantly** *adverb*

distaste *noun* dislike or disgust

distasteful *adjective* unpleasant or offensive

distil distils distilling distilled *verb* **1** to subject to or obtain by distillation **2** to give off (a substance) in drops **3** to extract the essence of > **distillation** *noun* process of evaporating a liquid and condensing its vapour

distillery distilleries *noun* place where spirit drinks are made

distinct *adjective* **1** not the same **2** easily sensed or understood

3 clear and definite > **distinctly** *adverb*

distinction *noun* **1** act of distinguishing **2** distinguishing feature **3** state of being different **4** special honour, recognition or fame

distinctive *adjective* easily recognizable > **distinctively** *adverb*

distinguish distinguishes distinguishing distinguished *verb* **1** **distinguish between** to make, show or recognize a difference between **2** to be a distinctive feature of **3** to make out by hearing, seeing, etc > **distinguishable** *adjective*: *The brothers are not easily distinguishable* > **distinguished** *adjective* **1** dignified in appearance **2** highly respected > **distinguishing** *adjective*: *distinguishing features*

distort *verb* **1** to misrepresent (the truth or facts) **2** to twist out of shape > **distorted** *adjective*: *a distorted voice* > **distortion** *noun*

distract *verb* **1** to draw the attention of (a person) away from something **2** to entertain > **distracted** *adjective* unable to concentrate, preoccupied > **distractedly** *adverb* > **distracting** *adjective*

distraction *noun* **1** something that diverts the attention **2** something that serves as an entertainment

distraught *adjective* extremely anxious or agitated

distress distresses distressing distressed *noun* **1** extreme unhappiness **2** great physical pain **3** poverty ▷ *verb* **4** to upset badly > **distressed** *adjective* **1** extremely upset **2** in financial difficulties > **distressing** *adjective* very worrying or upsetting

distribute distributes distributing distributed *verb* **1** to hand out or deliver (leaflets, mail, etc) **2** to share (something) among the members of a particular group

distribution *noun* **1** distributing **2** arrangement or spread

distributor *noun* **1** wholesaler who distributes goods to retailers in a specific area **2** device in a petrol engine that sends the electric current to the spark plugs

district *noun* area of land regarded as an administrative or geographical unit

district nurse *noun* nurse who visits and treats people in their own homes

distrust *verb* **1** to regard as untrustworthy ▷ *noun* **2** feeling of suspicion or doubt > **distrustful** *adjective*: *I'm distrustful of all politicians*

disturb *verb* **1** to intrude on **2** to worry or make anxious **3** to change the position or shape of > **disturbing** *adjective*: *I found what she said about him disturbing*

disturbance *noun* **1** interruption or intrusion **2** unruly outburst in public

disuse *noun* state of being no longer used > **disused** *adjective*

ditch ditches ditching ditched *noun* **1** narrow channel dug in the earth for drainage or irrigation ▷ *verb* **2** *informal* to abandon or discard

dither *verb* **1** to be uncertain or indecisive ▷ *noun* **2** state of indecision or agitation

ditto *noun* **1** the same ▷ *adverb* **2** in the same way

ditty ditties *noun* old-fashioned short simple poem or song

diva *noun* distinguished female

singer

dive dives diving dived *verb* **1** to plunge headfirst into water **2** (of a submarine or diver) to submerge under water **3** (of a bird or aircraft) to fly in a steep nose-down descending path **4** to move quickly in a specified direction **5 dive in** *or* **into** to start doing (something) enthusiastically ▷ *noun* **6** diving **7** steep nose-down descent **8** *informal* disreputable bar or club

diver *noun* **1** person who works or explores underwater **2** person who dives for sport

diverge diverges diverging diverged *verb* **1** to separate and go in different directions **2** to deviate (from a prescribed course) **> divergence** *noun*: *a divergence of opinion* **> divergent** *adjective*

diverse *adjective* **1** having variety, assorted **2** different in kind

diversify diversifies diversifying diversified *verb* **1** (of an enterprise) to vary (products or operations) in order to expand or reduce the risk of loss **2** to create different forms of **> diversification** *noun*

diversion *noun* **1** official detour used by traffic when a main route is closed **2** something that distracts someone's attention **3** diverting **4** amusing pastime

diversity diversities *noun* **1** quality of being different or varied **2** range of difference

divert *verb* **1** to change the direction of **2** to distract the attention of **3** to entertain or amuse

divide divides dividing divided *verb* **1** to separate into parts **2** to share or be shared out in parts **3** to (cause to) disagree **4** to keep apart or be a boundary between **5** to calculate how many times

(one number) can be contained in (another) ▷ *noun* **6** division or split

dividend *noun* **1** sum of money representing part of the profit made, paid by a company to its shareholders **2** extra benefit

divination *noun* art of discovering future events, as though by supernatural powers

divine divines divining divined *adjective* **1** of God or a god **2** godlike **3** *informal* splendid ▷ *verb* **4** to discover (something) by intuition or guessing **> divinely** *adverb*

diving *noun* sport or activity of swimming underwater using special breathing equipment

divinity divinities *noun* **1** study of religion **2** god or goddess **3** state of being divine

division *noun* **1** dividing, sharing out **2** one of the parts into which something is divided **3** *Maths* process of dividing one number by another **4** difference of opinion

divisional *adjective* of a division in an organization

divisive *adjective* tending to cause disagreement

divisor *noun* number to be divided into another number

divorce divorces divorcing divorced *noun* **1** legal ending of a marriage **2** any separation, especially a permanent one ▷ *verb* **3** to legally end one's marriage (to) **4** to remove or separate **> divorced** *adjective*: *He is divorced, with a young son*

divorcé *noun* man who is divorced

divorcée *noun* person, especially a woman, who is divorced

divulge divulges divulging divulged *verb* to make (something) known

DIY *abbreviation Brit, Aust, NZ* do-it-yourself

dizzy dizzier dizziest *adjective*
1 having or causing a whirling
sensation **2** mentally confused
▷ *verb* **3** to cause to feel giddy or
confused > **dizziness** *noun*

DJ DJs *abbreviation* **1** disc jockey **2** *Brit*
dinner jacket

DNA *abbreviation* deoxyribonucleic
acid: main constituent of the
chromosomes of all living things

do does doing did done; dos *verb*
1 to perform or complete (a deed
or action) **2** to be adequate: *That
one will do* **3** to suit or improve: *That
style does nothing for you* **4** to find the
answer to (a problem or puzzle) **5** to
cause or produce: *It does no harm
to think ahead* **6** to give or grant: *Do
me a favour* **7** to work at, as a course
of study or a job **8** used to form
questions: *How do you know?* **9** used
to intensify positive statements
and commands: *I do like port; Do
go on* **10** used to form negative
statements and commands: *I do not
know her well; Do not get up* **11** used
to replace an earlier verb: *He gets
paid more than I do* ▷ *noun* **12** informal
party or celebration > **do away
with** *verb* to get rid of > **do up**
verb **1** to fasten **2** to decorate and
repair > **do with** *verb* to find useful
or benefit from: *I could do with a
rest* > **do without** *verb* to manage
without

docile *adjective* (of a person or
animal) easily controlled

dock *noun* **1** enclosed area of water
where ships are loaded, unloaded
or repaired **2** enclosed space in a
court of law where the accused
person sits or stands **3** weed with
broad leaves ▷ *verb* **4** to bring or be
brought into dock **5** to link (two
spacecraft) or (of two spacecraft)

to be linked together in space **6** to
deduct money from (a person's
wages) **7** to remove part of (an
animal's tail) by cutting through
the bone

docker *noun Brit* person employed
to load and unload ships

dockyard *noun* place where ships
are built or repaired

doctor *noun* **1** person licensed to
practise medicine **2** person who
has been awarded a doctorate
▷ *verb* **3** to alter in order to deceive
4 to poison or drug (food or drink)

doctorate *noun* highest academic
degree in any field of knowledge
> **doctoral** *adjective*: *a doctoral thesis*

doctrine *noun* **1** body of teachings
of a religious, political or
philosophical group **2** principle or
body of principles that is taught or
advocated > **doctrinal** *adjective*:
*doctrinal differences among religious
leaders*

document *noun* **1** piece of paper
providing an official record of
something **2** piece of text or
graphics stored in a computer
as a file that can be amended or
altered by document-processing
software ▷ *verb* **3** to record or report
(something) in detail **4** to support
(a claim) with evidence

documentary documentaries
noun **1** film or television programme
presenting the facts about a
particular subject ▷ *adjective* **2** (of
evidence) based on documents

documentation *noun* documents
providing proof or evidence of
something

dodge dodges dodging dodged
verb **1** to avoid (a blow, being seen,
etc) by moving suddenly **2** to
evade by cleverness or trickery
▷ *noun* **3** cunning or deceitful trick

> **dodger** *noun* person who evades a responsibility or duty

dodgy dodgier dodgiest *adjective informal* **1** dangerous or risky **2** untrustworthy

dodo dodos *noun* large flightless extinct bird

doe *noun* female deer, hare or rabbit

does *verb* third person singular of the present tense of **do**

dog dogs dogging dogged *noun* **1** domesticated four-legged mammal of many different breeds **2** related wild mammal, such as the dingo or coyote **3** male animal of the dog family **4** *informal* person: *You lucky dog!* **5 the dogs** *informal* greyhound racing **6 go to the dogs** *informal* to go to ruin physically or morally **7 let sleeping dogs lie** to leave things undisturbed ▷ *verb* **8** to follow (someone) closely **9** to trouble or plague

dog collar *noun* **1** collar for a dog **2** *informal* white collar fastened at the back, worn by members of the clergy

dog-eared *adjective* **1** (of a book) having pages folded down at the corner **2** shabby or worn

dogged *adjective* obstinately determined > **doggedly** *adverb*

dogma *noun* doctrine or system of doctrines proclaimed by authority as true

dogmatic *adjective* habitually stating your opinions forcefully or arrogantly > **dogmatism** *noun*

do-it-yourself *noun* constructing and repairing things yourself

doldrums *plural noun* **1** depressed state of mind **2** state of inactivity

dole doles doling doled *noun Brit, Aust, NZ informal* money received from the state while unemployed

> **dole out** *verb* to distribute in small quantities

doll *noun* **1** small model of a human being, used as a toy **2** *informal* pretty girl or young woman

dollar *noun* standard monetary unit of the USA, Australia, New Zealand, Canada and some other countries

dollop *noun informal* lump (of food)

dolphin *noun* sea mammal of the whale family, with a beaklike snout

domain *noun* **1** field of knowledge or activity **2** land under one ruler or government **3** *Computers* group of computers with the same name on the Internet **4** *NZ* public park

dome *noun* **1** rounded roof built on a circular base **2** something shaped like this > **domed** *adjective*

domestic *adjective* **1** of one's own country or a specific country **2** of or relating to the home or family **3** (of an animal) kept as a pet or to produce food ▷ *noun* **4** person whose job is to do housework in someone else's house > **domestically** *adverb*

domesticate domesticates domesticating domesticated *verb* **1** to bring or keep (a wild animal or plant) under control or cultivation **2** to accustom (someone) to home life > **domesticated** *adjective*

domesticity *noun formal* home life

dominance *noun* power or control

dominant *adjective* **1** having authority or influence **2** main; chief

dominate dominates dominating dominated *verb* **1** to control or govern **2** to tower above (surroundings) **3** to be very significant in > **dominating** *adjective*: *dominating personalities* > **domination** *noun*: *centuries of domination by the Romans*

domineering *adjective* forceful and arrogant

dominion *noun* **1** control or authority **2** land governed by one ruler or government **3** (formerly) self-governing division of the British Empire

domino dominoes *noun* **1** small rectangular block marked with dots, used in dominoes **2 dominoes** game in which dominoes with matching halves are laid together

don dons donning donned *verb* **1** to put on (clothing) ▷ *noun* **2** *Brit* member of the teaching staff at a university or college

donate donates donating donated *verb* to give, especially to a charity or organization

donation *noun* **1** donating **2** thing donated

done *verb* past participle of **do**

donkey donkeys *noun* **1** long-eared member of the horse family **2 donkey's years** *informal* long time

donor *noun* **1** *Medicine* person who provides blood or organs for use in the treatment of another person **2** person who makes a donation

don't do not

doodle doodles doodling doodled *verb* **1** to scribble or draw aimlessly ▷ *noun* **2** shape or picture drawn aimlessly

doom *noun* **1** death or a terrible fate ▷ *verb* **2** to destine or condemn to death or a terrible fate

doomed *adjective* certain to suffer an unpleasant or unhappy experience

doomsday *noun* the end of the world

door *noun* **1** hinged or sliding panel for closing the entrance to a building, room, etc **2** entrance

doorway doorways *noun* opening into a building or room

dope dopes doping doped *noun* **1** *informal* illegal drug, usually cannabis **2** medicine or drug **3** *informal* stupid person ▷ *verb* **4** to give a drug to (a person or animal), especially in order to affect the outcome of a race

dormant *adjective* temporarily quiet, inactive or not being used

dormitory dormitories *noun* large room, especially at a school, containing several beds

dormouse dormice *noun* small mouselike rodent with a furry tail

dosage *noun* size of a dose

dose doses dosing dosed *noun* **1** specific quantity of a medicine taken at one time **2** *informal* something unpleasant to experience ▷ *verb* **3** to give a dose to (someone)

dossier *noun* collection of documents about a subject or person

dot dots dotting dotted *noun* **1** small round mark **2 on the dot** (referring to time) precisely or exactly ▷ *verb* **3** to mark with a dot **4** to scatter or spread around

dotage *noun* weakness as a result of old age

dotcom or **dot.com** *noun* company that does most of its business on the Internet

dote dotes doting doted *verb* **dote on** to love (someone) to an excessive degree > **doting** *adjective*

double doubles doubling doubled *adjective* **1** as much again in number, amount, size, etc **2** composed of two equal or similar parts **3** designed for two users: *double room* **4** folded in two ▷ *adverb*

5 twice over ▷ *noun* **6** twice the number, amount, size, etc **7** person who looks almost exactly like another **8 doubles** game between two pairs of players **9 at** or **on the double** quickly or immediately ▷ *verb* **10** to make or become twice as much or as many **11** to bend or fold (material etc) **12 double as** to have a second role as **13** to turn sharply > **doubly** *adverb*

double bass double basses *noun* stringed instrument, largest and lowest member of the violin family

double-cross double-crosses double-crossing double-crossed *verb* **1** to cheat or betray ▷ *noun* **2** instance of double-crossing

double-decker *noun* **1** bus with two passenger decks one on top of the other ▷ *adjective* **2** *informal* having two layers

double glazing *noun* two panes of glass in a window, fitted to reduce heat loss

doubt *noun* **1** uncertainty about the truth, facts or existence of something **2** unresolved difficulty or point ▷ *verb* **3** to question the truth of **4** to distrust or be suspicious of

doubtful *adjective* **1** unlikely **2** feeling doubt

dough *noun* **1** thick mixture of flour and water or milk, used for making bread etc **2** *informal* money

doughnut *noun* small cake of sweetened dough fried in deep fat

dour *adjective* sullen and unfriendly

douse douses dousing doused *verb* **1** to drench with water or other liquid **2** to put out (a light)

dove *noun* bird with a heavy body, small head and short legs

dovetail *noun* **1** type of joint used in woodwork ▷ *verb* **2** to fit together neatly

dowager *noun* widow possessing property or a title obtained from her husband

dowdy dowdier dowdiest *adjective* dull and old-fashioned

down *preposition, adverb* **1** indicating movement to or position in a lower place ▷ *adverb* **2** indicating completion of an action, lessening of intensity, etc: *Calm down* ▷ *adjective* **3** depressed or unhappy ▷ *verb* **4** *informal* to drink (something) quickly ▷ *noun* **5** soft fine feathers

downcast *adjective* **1** sad and dejected **2** (of the eyes) directed downwards

downfall *noun* (cause of) a sudden loss of position or reputation

downgrade downgrades downgrading downgraded *verb* to reduce (something or someone) in importance, status or value

downhill *adjective* **1** going or sloping down ▷ *adverb* **2** towards the bottom of a hill

download *verb* **1** to transfer (data, files, etc) from the memory of one computer to that of another ▷ *noun* **2** file transferred in such a way

downpour *noun* heavy fall of rain

downright *adjective, adverb* extreme(ly)

downstairs *adverb* **1** to or on a lower floor ▷ *noun* **2** lower or ground floor

downstream *adjective, adverb* in or towards the lower part of a stream

down-to-earth *adjective* sensible and practical

downtrodden *adjective* oppressed and lacking the will to resist

downturn *noun* decline in the economy or in the success of a company or industry

downward *adjective* descending from a higher to a lower level, condition or position ▷ *adverb* 2 same as **downwards**

downwards or **downward** *adverb* 1 from a higher to a lower level, condition or position 2 from an earlier time or source to a later one

downwind *adverb, adjective* in the direction in which the wind is blowing

dowry dowries *noun* property brought by a woman to her husband at marriage

doze dozes dozing dozed *verb* 1 to sleep lightly or briefly 2 **doze off** to fall into a light sleep ▷ *noun* 3 short sleep

dozen *adjective, noun* twelve

Dr *abbreviation* 1 Doctor 2 Drive

drab drabber drabbest *adjective* dull and dreary > **drabness** *noun*: *the drabness of his office*

draconian *adjective* severe or harsh

draft *noun* 1 plan, sketch or drawing of something 2 preliminary outline of a book, speech, etc 3 written order for payment of money by a bank 4 *US, Aust* selection for compulsory military service ▷ *verb* 5 to draw up an outline or plan of 6 to send (people) from one place to another to do a specific job 7 *US, Aust* to select for compulsory military service 8 *Aust, NZ* to select (cattle or sheep) from a herd or flock

drag drags dragging dragged *verb* 1 to pull with force, especially along the ground 2 to trail on the ground 3 to persuade or force (yourself or someone else) to go somewhere 4 *drag on or* out) to last or be prolonged tediously 5 to search (a river) with a dragnet

or hook 6 *Computers* to move (an image) on the screen using the mouse ▷ *noun* 7 person or thing that slows up progress 8 *informal* tedious thing or person 9 *informal* women's clothes worn by a man

dragnet *noun* net used to scour the bottom of a pond or river to search for something

dragon *noun* mythical fire-breathing monster like a huge lizard

dragonfly dragonflies *noun* brightly coloured insect with a long slender body and two pairs of wings

dragoon *noun* 1 heavily armed cavalryman ▷ *verb* 2 to coerce or force

drain *noun* 1 pipe or channel that carries off water or sewage 2 cause of a continuous reduction in energy or resources ▷ *verb* 3 to draw off or remove liquid from 4 to flow away or filter off 5 to drink the entire contents of (a glass or cup) 6 to make constant demands on (energy or resources), exhaust

drainage *noun* 1 system of drains 2 process or method of draining

drake *noun* male duck

drama *noun* 1 serious play for theatre, television or radio 2 writing, producing or acting in plays 3 situation that is exciting or highly emotional

dramatic *adjective* 1 of or like drama 2 behaving flamboyantly > **dramatically** *adverb*

dramatist *noun* person who writes plays

drank *verb* past tense of **drink**

drape drapes draping draped *verb* 1 to cover with material, usually in folds 2 to place casually

drapes *plural noun Aust, NZ, US, Canadian* material hung at an opening or window to shut out light or to provide privacy

drastic *adjective* strong and severe > **drastically** *adverb*

draught *noun* **1** current of cold air, especially in an enclosed space **2** portion of liquid to be drunk, especially medicine **3** gulp or swallow **4** one of the flat discs used in the game of draughts **5 draughts** game for two players using a chessboard and twelve draughts each ▷ *adjective* **6** (of an animal) used for pulling heavy loads **7** (of beer) served straight from barrels rather than in bottles

draughtsman draughtsmen *noun* person employed to prepare detailed scale drawings of machinery, buildings, etc

draughty draughtier draughtiest *adjective* exposed to draughts of air

draw draws drawing drew drawn *verb* **1** to sketch (a figure, picture, etc) with a pencil or pen **2** to pull (a person or thing) closer to or further away from a place **3** to move in a specified direction: *The car drew near* **4** to take from a source: *draw money from bank accounts* **5** to attract or interest **6** to formulate or decide: *to draw conclusions* **7** (of two teams or contestants) to finish a game with an equal number of points ▷ *noun* **8** raffle or lottery **9** contest or game ending in a tie **10** event, act, etc, that attracts a large audience > **draw out** *verb* **1** to encourage (someone) to talk freely **2** to make (something) longer **3** (of a train) to leave a station > **draw up** *verb* **1** to prepare and write out (a contract) **2** (of a vehicle) to come to a stop

drawback *noun* disadvantage

drawbridge *noun* bridge that can be raised or lowered preventing or giving access to a building such as a castle

drawer *noun* sliding box-shaped part of a piece of furniture, used for storage

drawing *noun* **1** picture or plan made by means of lines on a surface **2** art of making drawings

drawing room *noun* old-fashioned room where visitors are received and entertained

drawl *verb* **1** to speak slowly, with long vowel sounds ▷ *noun* **2** drawling manner of speech

drawn *verb* past participle of **draw** ▷ *adjective* **2** haggard, tired or tense in appearance

dread *verb* **1** to anticipate with apprehension or fear ▷ *noun* **2** great fear > **dreaded** *adjective*

dreadful *adjective* **1** very disagreeable or shocking **2** extreme > **dreadfully** *adverb*

dreadlocks *plural noun* hair worn in the Rastafarian style of tightly twisted strands

dream dreams dreaming dreamed or **dreamt** *noun* **1** imagined series of events experienced in the mind while asleep **2** cherished hope **3** *informal* wonderful person or thing ▷ *verb* **4** to see imaginary pictures in the mind while asleep **5 dream of** or **about** to have an image of or fantasy about **6 dream of** to consider the possibility of (something) ▷ *adjective* **7** ideal: *a dream house*

dreamer *noun* person who lives in a world of fantasy

Dreamtime *noun* (in Australian Aboriginal legends) the time when the world was being made and the first people were created

dreamy dreamier dreamiest
adjective **1** vague or impractical
2 *informal* wonderful > **dreamily**
adverb

dreary drearier dreariest *adjective*
dull or boring

dregs *plural noun* **1** solid particles
that settle at the bottom of some
liquids **2** most despised elements

drenched *adjective* soaking wet

dress dresses dressing dressed
noun **1** one-piece garment for a
woman or girl, consisting of a skirt
part and a top part and sometimes
sleeves **2** complete style of clothing
▷ *verb* **3** to put your clothes on
4 to put formal clothes on **5** to put
clothes on (a child, invalid, etc)
6 to apply a protective covering to
(a wound) **7** to arrange or prepare
(salad, meat, etc)

dresser *noun* **1** piece of furniture
with shelves and with cupboards,
for storing or displaying dishes
2 *Theatre* person employed to assist
actors with their costumes

dressing *noun* **1** sauce for salad
2 covering for a wound

dressing gown *noun* coat-shaped
garment worn over pyjamas or a
nightdress

dressing room *noun* room used
for changing clothes, especially
backstage in a theatre

dress rehearsal *noun* last
rehearsal of a play or show, using
costumes, lighting, etc

drew *verb* past tense of **draw**

**dribble dribbles dribbling
dribbled** *verb* **1** to (allow to) flow
in drops **2** to allow saliva to trickle
from the mouth **3** *Sport* to propel (a
ball) by repeatedly tapping it with
the foot, hand or a stick ▷ *noun*
4 small quantity of liquid falling

in drops

dried *verb* past of **dry**

drier *adjective* **1** a comparative of **dry**
▷ *noun* **2** same as **dryer**

driest *adjective* a superlative of **dry**

drift *verb* **1** to be carried along by
currents of air or water **2** to move
aimlessly from one place or activity
to another ▷ *noun* **3** something
piled up by the wind or current,
such as a snowdrift **4** general
movement or development **5** point
or meaning: *Catch my drift?*

drifter *noun* person who moves
aimlessly from place to place or
job to job

drill *noun* **1** tool or machine for
boring holes **2** strict and often
repetitious training **3** *informal*
correct procedure **4** machine for
sowing seed in rows **5** small furrow
for seed ▷ *verb* **6** to bore a hole in
(something) with or as if with a
drill **7** to teach by rigorous exercises
or training

drily *adverb* see **dry**

**drink drinks drinking drank
drunk** *verb* **1** to swallow (a liquid)
2 to consume alcohol, especially to
excess ▷ *noun* **3** (portion of) a liquid
suitable for drinking **4** alcohol,
or its habitual or excessive
consumption > **drink in** *verb* to pay
close attention to > **drink to** *verb* to
drink a toast to > **drinker** *noun*

drip drips dripping dripped *verb*
1 to (let) fall in drops ▷ *noun* **2** falling
of drops of liquid **3** sound made by
falling drops **4** *informal* weak dull
person **5** *Medicine* device by which
a solution is passed in small drops
through a tube into a vein

drive drives driving drove driven
verb **1** to guide the movement
of (a vehicle) **2** to transport in a
vehicle **3** to force (someone) into a

specified state **4** to push or propel **5** *Sport* to hit (a ball) very hard and straight ▷ *noun* **6** journey by car, van, etc **7** (also **driveway**) path for vehicles connecting a building to a public road **8** united effort towards a common goal **9** energy and ambition *Psychology* **10** means by which power is transmitted in a mechanism > **drive at** *verb informal* to intend or mean: *What was he driving at?* > **driver** *noun* person who drives a vehicle > **driving** *noun*

drive-in *adjective, noun* (denoting) a cinema, restaurant, etc, used by people in their cars

drivel *noun* foolish talk

drizzle drizzles drizzling drizzled *noun* **1** very light rain ▷ *verb* **2** to rain lightly > **drizzly** *adjective*

dromedary dromedaries *noun* camel with a single hump

drone drones droning droned *verb* **1** to make a monotonous low dull sound ▷ *noun* **2** monotonous low dull sound **3** male bee > **drone on** *verb* to talk for a long time in a monotonous tone

drool *verb* to allow saliva to flow from the mouth

droop *verb* to hang downwards loosely

drop drops dropping dropped *verb* **1** to (allow to) fall vertically **2** to decrease in amount, strength or value **3** to mention (a hint or name) casually **4** to discontinue **5** **drop in** or **by** to pay someone a casual visit ▷ *noun* **6** small quantity of liquid forming a round shape **7** any small quantity of liquid **8** decrease in amount, strength or value **9** vertical distance that something may fall **10** **drops** liquid medication applied in small drops > **drop off** *verb* **1** *informal*

to fall asleep **2** to grow smaller or less > **drop out** *verb* to abandon or withdraw from a school, job, etc

droplet *noun* small drop

dropout *noun* **1** person who rejects conventional society **2** person who does not complete a course of study

droppings *plural noun* faeces of certain animals, such as rabbits or birds

dross *noun* anything worthless

drought *noun* prolonged shortage of rainfall

drove droves droving droved *verb* **1** past tense of **drive 2** to drive (sheep or cattle) over a long distance ▷ *noun* **3** herd of livestock being driven together

drown *verb* **1** to die or kill by immersion in liquid **2** to forget (your sorrows) temporarily by drinking alcohol **3** to drench thoroughly **4** to make (a sound) inaudible by being louder

drowsy drowsier drowsiest *adjective* feeling sleepy > **drowsiness**

drudgery *noun* hard boring work

drug drugs drugging drugged *noun* **1** substance used in the treatment or prevention of disease **2** chemical substance, especially a narcotic, taken for the effects it produces ▷ *verb* **3** to give a drug to (a person or animal) to cause sleepiness or unconsciousness **4** to mix a drug with (food or drink)

Druid *noun* member of an ancient order of Celtic priests

drum drums drumming drummed *noun* **1** percussion instrument sounded by striking a membrane stretched across the opening of a hollow cylinder **2** cylindrical object or container **3** **the drum** *Aust* information or advice ▷ *verb* **4** to play (music) on a drum **5** to tap rhythmically or regularly > **drummer** *noun* person who plays a drum or drums

drumstick *noun* **1** stick used for playing a drum **2** lower joint of the leg of a cooked chicken etc

drunk *verb* **1** past participle of **drink** ▷ *adjective* **2** intoxicated with alcohol to the extent of losing control over normal functions **3** overwhelmed by a strong influence or emotion ▷ *noun* **4** person who is drunk or who frequently gets drunk

drunken *adjective* **1** drunk or frequently drunk **2** caused by or relating to alcoholic intoxication > **drunkenly** *adverb* > **drunkenness** *noun*

dry drier or **dryer driest; dries drying dried** *adjective* **1** lacking moisture **2** having little or no rainfall **3** *informal* thirsty **4** (of wine) not sweet **5** uninteresting **6** (of humour) subtle and sarcastic **7** prohibiting the sale of alcohol: *a dry town* ▷ *verb* **8** to make or become dry **9** to preserve (food) by removing the moisture > **drily** or **dryly** *adverb*: '*How kind*,' *he said drily* > **dryness** *noun* > **dry up** *verb* **1** to become completely dry **2** *informal* to forget what you were going to say or find that you have nothing left to say

dry-clean *verb* to clean (clothes etc) with chemicals rather than water

dryer or **drier** *noun* apparatus for removing moisture **2** comparative of **dry**

dry stock *noun* NZ cattle raised for meat

dual *adjective* having two parts, functions or aspects

dub dubs dubbing dubbed *verb* **1** to give (a person or place) a name or nickname **2** to provide (a film) with a new soundtrack, especially in a different language **3** to provide (a film or tape) with a soundtrack

dubious *adjective* feeling or causing doubt > **dubiously** *adverb*

duchess duchesses *noun* **1** woman who holds the rank of duke **2** wife or widow of a duke

duchy duchies *noun* territory of a duke or duchess

duck ducks ducking ducked *noun* **1** water bird with short legs, webbed feet and a broad blunt bill **2** its flesh, used as food **3** female of this bird **4** *Cricket* score of nothing ▷ *verb* **5** to move (the head or body) quickly downwards, to avoid being seen or to dodge a blow **6** to plunge suddenly under water **7** *informal* to dodge (a duty or responsibility)

duckling *noun* young duck

duct *noun* **1** tube, pipe or channel through which liquid or gas is conveyed **2** bodily passage conveying secretions or excretions

dud *informal noun* **1** ineffectual person or thing ▷ *adjective* **2** bad or useless

due *adjective* **1** expected or scheduled to be present or arrive **2** owed as a debt **3** fitting or proper **4** **due to** attributable to or caused by ▷ *noun* **5** something that is owed or required **6** **dues** charges for membership of a club or organization ▷ *adverb* **7** directly or exactly: *due south*

duel duels duelling duelled *noun* **1** formal fight with deadly weapons between two people to settle a quarrel ▷ *verb* **2** to fight in a duel

duet *noun* piece of music for two performers

dug *verb* past of **dig**

dugong *noun* whalelike mammal of tropical waters

dugout *noun* 1 *Brit* (at a sports ground) covered bench where managers and substitutes sit 2 canoe made by hollowing out a log 3 *Military* covered excavation to provide shelter

duke *noun* 1 nobleman of the highest rank 2 prince or ruler of a small principality or duchy

dull *adjective* 1 not interesting 2 (of an ache) not acute 3 (of weather) not bright or clear 4 lacking in spirit 5 not very intelligent 6 (of a blade) not sharp ▷ *verb* 7 to make or become dull > **dullness** *noun* > **dully** *adverb*

duly *adverb* 1 in a proper manner 2 at the proper time

dumb *adjective* 1 lacking the power to speak 2 silent 3 *informal* stupid

dumbfounded *adjective* speechless with astonishment

dummy dummies *noun* 1 figure representing the human form, used for displaying clothes etc 2 copy of an object, often lacking some essential feature of the original 3 rubber teat for a baby to suck 4 *informal* stupid person ▷ *adjective* 5 imitation or substitute

dump *verb* 1 to drop or let fall in a careless manner 2 *informal* to get rid of (someone or something no longer wanted) ▷ *noun* 3 place where waste materials are left 4 *informal* dirty unattractive place 5 *Military* place where weapons or supplies are stored

dumpling *noun* 1 small ball of dough cooked and served with stew 2 round pastry case filled with fruit

dunce *noun* person who is stupid or slow to learn

dune *noun* mound or ridge of drifted sand

dung *noun* faeces from animals such as cattle

dungarees *plural noun* trousers which have a bib covering the chest and straps over the shoulders

dungeon *noun* underground prison cell

dunk *verb* 1 to dip (a biscuit or bread) in a drink or soup before eating it 2 to put (something) in liquid

duo duos *noun* 1 pair of performers 2 *informal* pair of closely connected people

dupe dupes duping duped *verb* 1 to deceive or cheat ▷ *noun* 2 person who is easily deceive

duplicate duplicates duplicating duplicated *adjective* 1 copied exactly from an original ▷ *noun* 2 exact copy ▷ *verb* 3 to make an exact copy of 4 to do again (something that has already been done) > **duplication** *noun*: *unnecessary duplication of work*

durable *adjective* long-lasting > **durability** *noun*

duration *noun* length of time that something lasts

duress *noun* compulsion by use of force or threats

during *preposition* throughout or within the limit of (a period of time)

dusk *noun* time just before nightfall, when it is almost dark

dust *noun* 1 small dry particles of earth, sand or dirt ▷ *verb* 2 to remove dust from (furniture) by wiping 3 to sprinkle (something) with a powdery substance

dustbin *noun* large container for household rubbish

duster *noun* cloth used for dusting

dustman dustmen *noun* *Brit* man whose job is to collect household rubbish

dusty dustier dustiest *adjective* covered with dust

Dutch *adjective* **1** of the Netherlands ▷ *noun* **2** main language spoken in the Netherlands ▷ *plural* **3 the Dutch** the people who come from the Netherlands ▷ *adverb* **4 go Dutch** *informal* to share the expenses on an outing

Dutch courage *noun* false courage gained from drinking alcohol

dutiful *adjective* doing what is expected > **dutifully** *adverb*

duty duties *noun* **1** work or a task performed as part of your job **2** task that a person feels morally bound to do **3** government tax on imports **4 on duty** at work

duty-free *adjective* untaxed and therefore cheaper than normal: *duty-free vodka*

duvet *noun* kind of quilt used in bed instead of blankets

DVD DVDs *abbreviation* Digital Versatile (or Video) Disk

dwarf dwarfs or **dwarves; dwarfs dwarfing dwarfed** *noun* **1** person who is smaller than average **2** (in folklore) small ugly manlike creature, often possessing magical powers ▷ *adjective* **3** (of an animal or plant) much smaller than the usual size for the species ▷ *verb* **4** to cause (someone or something) to seem small by being much larger

dwell dwells dwelling dwelled or **dwelt** *verb literary* to live as a permanent resident > **dwell on** *verb* to think, speak or write at length about

dwelling *noun* place of residence

dwindle dwindles dwindling dwindled *verb* to grow less in size, strength or number

dye dyes dyeing dyed *noun* **1** colouring substance **2** colour produced by dyeing ▷ *verb* **3** to colour (hair or fabric) by applying a dye

dying *verb* present participle of **die**

dyke or **dike** *noun* wall built to prevent flooding

dynamic *adjective* **1** full of energy, ambition and new ideas **2** *Physics* of energy or forces that produce motion > **dynamically** *adverb*

dynamics *noun* **1** branch of mechanics concerned with the forces that change or produce the motions of bodies ▷ *plural* **2** forces that produce change in a system **3** degrees of loudness needed in the performance of a piece of music or the symbols indicating these in written music

dynamite dynamites dynamiting dynamited *noun* **1** explosive made of nitroglycerine **2** *informal* dangerous or exciting person or thing ▷ *verb* **3** to blow (something) up with dynamite

dynamo dynamos *noun* device for converting mechanical energy into electrical energy

dynasty dynasties *noun* sequence of hereditary rulers

dysentery *noun* infection of the intestine causing severe diarrhoea

dyslexia *noun* disorder causing impaired ability to read > **dyslexic** *adjective*: *a dyslexic child*

e

e- *prefix meaning* electronic: *e-mail*

each *adjective, pronoun* every (one) taken separately

> Wherever you use *each other* you could also use *one another*

eager *adjective* showing or feeling great desire; keen **> eagerly** *adverb* **> eagerness** *noun*

eagle *noun* **1** large bird of prey with keen eyesight **2** *Golf* score of two strokes under par for a hole

ear *noun* **1** organ of hearing, especially the external part of it **2** head of corn

eardrum *noun* thin piece of skin inside the ear which enables you to hear sounds

earl *noun* British nobleman ranking next below a marquess

early earlier earliest *adjective, adverb* **1** before the expected or usual time **2** in the first part of a period **3** in a period far back in time

earmark *verb* to set (something) aside for a specific purpose

earn *verb* **1** to obtain (something) by work or merit **2** (of investments etc) to gain (interest) **> earner** *noun*: *a wage earner*

earnest *adjective* **1** serious and

sincere ▷ *noun* **2 in earnest** seriously **> earnestly** *adverb*

earnings *plural noun* money earned

earphone *noun* receiver for a radio etc, held to or put in the ear

earring *noun* piece of jewellery worn in the ear lobe

earshot *noun* hearing range

earth *noun* **1** planet that we live on **2** land, the ground **3** soil **4** fox's hole **5** wire connecting an electrical apparatus with the earth ▷ *verb* **6** to connect (a circuit) to earth

earthenware *noun* pottery made of baked clay

earthly *adjective* concerned with life on earth rather than heaven or life after death

earthquake *noun* violent vibration of the earth's surface

earthworm *noun* worm that burrows in the soil

earthy earthier earthiest *adjective* **1** coarse or crude **2** of or like earth

earwig *noun* small insect with a pincer-like tail

ease eases easing eased *noun* **1** freedom from difficulty, discomfort or worry **2** rest or leisure ▷ *verb* **3** to lessen **4** to move carefully or gradually

easel *noun* frame to support an artist's canvas or a blackboard

easily *adverb* **1** without difficulty **2** without a doubt

east *noun* **1** (direction towards) the part of the horizon where the sun rises **2** region lying in this direction ▷ *adjective* **3** to or in the east **4** (of a wind) from the east ▷ *adverb* **5** in, to or towards the east

Easter *noun* Christian spring festival celebrating the Resurrection of Jesus Christ

easterly *adjective* **1** to or towards

the east **2** (of a wind) blowing from the east

eastern *adjective* in or from the east

eastward *adjective, adverb* towards the east

eastwards *adverb* towards the east

easy easier easiest *adjective* **1** not needing much work or effort **2** free from pain, care or anxiety **3** easy-going

> Although *easy* is an adjective, it can be used as an adverb in fixed phrases like *take it easy*

eat eats eating ate eaten *verb* **1** to take (food) into the mouth and swallow it **2** to have a meal > **eat away** *verb* (also **eat away at**) to destroy (something) slowly

eaves *plural noun* overhanging edges of a roof

eavesdrop eavesdrops eavesdropping eavesdropped *verb* to listen secretly to a private conversation

ebb *verb* **1** (of tide water) to flow back **2** to fall away or decline ▷ *noun* **3** flowing back of the tide **4** **at a low ebb** in a state of weakness

ebony *noun* **1** hard black wood ▷ *adjective* **2** deep black

ebullient *adjective* full of enthusiasm or excitement > **ebullience** *noun*

EC *abbreviation* European Community: a former name for the European Union

eccentric *adjective* **1** odd or unconventional ▷ *noun* **2** eccentric person > **eccentrically** *adverb* > **eccentricity** *noun: unusual to the point of eccentricity*

ecclesiastical *adjective* of the Christian Church or clergy

echelon *noun* level of power or responsibility

echidna echidnas or **echidnae** *noun* Australian spiny egg-laying mammal

echo echoes echoing echoed *noun* **1** repetition of sounds by reflection of sound waves off a surface **2** close imitation ▷ *verb* **3** to be repeated as an echo **4** to repeat or express agreement with

eclectic *adjective* selecting from various styles, ideas or sources

eclipse *noun* temporary obscuring of one star or planet by another

eco- *prefix indicating* of or relating to ecology or the environment

ecology *noun* study of the relationships between living things and their environment > **ecological** *adjective* **1** of ecology **2** intended to protect the environment > **ecologically** *adverb* > **ecologist** *noun*

e-commerce or **ecommerce** *noun* business transactions done on the Internet

economic *adjective* **1** concerning the management of the money, industry and trade in a country **2** profitable **3** *informal* inexpensive or cheap

economical *adjective* spending money carefully and sensibly > **economically** *adverb*

economic migrant *noun* person emigrating to improve his or her standard of living

economics *noun* **1** the study of the production and distribution of goods, services and wealth in a society and the organization of its money, industry and trade ▷ *plural* **2** financial aspects

economist *noun* specialist in economics

economize economizes economizing economized; also spelt **economise** *verb* to reduce expenses

economy economies *noun*
1 system that a country uses to
organize and manage its money,
industry and trade 2 wealth that
a country gets from business and
industry 3 careful use of money or
resources to avoid waste

ecosystem *noun* system involving
interactions between a community
and its environment

ecstasy ecstasies *noun* 1 state
of intense delight 2 *informal*
powerful drug that can produce
hallucinations > **ecstatic**
adjective very happy and excited
> **ecstatically** *adverb*

eczema *noun* skin disease that
causes the skin surface to become
rough and itchy

eddy eddies eddying eddied *noun*
1 circular movement of air, water,
etc ▷ *verb* 2 to move with a circular
motion

edge edges edging edged *noun*
1 border or line where something
ends or begins 2 cutting side of a
blade 3 **have the edge on** to have
an advantage over (someone) 4 **on
edge** nervous or irritable ▷ *verb*
5 to provide an edge or border for
(something) 6 to push (your way)
gradually

edgy edgier edgiest *adjective*
nervous or irritable

edible *adjective* fit to be eaten

edifice *noun* large building

edit *verb* 1 to make changes, cuts and
corrections (to a piece of writing,
book, film, etc) so that it is fit for
publication or broadcast 2 to be in
charge of (a newspaper, magazine,
etc) or a section of it

edition *noun* number of copies
of a new publication printed at
one time

editor *noun* 1 person who edits
2 person in charge of a newspaper
or magazine or a section of it

editorial *noun* 1 newspaper article
stating the opinion of the editor
▷ *adjective* 2 relating to editing or
editors > **editorially** *adverb*

**educate educates educating
educated** *verb* to teach (someone)

educated *adjective* having a high
standard of learning and culture

education *noun* 1 gaining
knowledge and understanding
through learning 2 system of
teaching people at school or
university > **educational** *adjective*:
*educational materials; It would be very
educational* > **educationally** *adverb*

eel *noun* snakelike fish

eerie eerier eeriest *adjective*
uncannily frightening or disturbing
> **eerily** *adverb*: *eerily quiet*

effect *noun* 1 change or result
caused by someone or something
2 overall impression 3 **take effect**
to start to happen or to produce
results: *The law will take effect
next year*

Remember that *effect* is a *noun*
and *affect* is a verb

effective *adjective* 1 producing
a desired result 2 coming into
operation or beginning officially
> **effectively** *adverb*

effeminate *adjective* (of a man)
displaying characteristics thought
to be typical of a woman

efficient *adjective* functioning
effectively and with little waste of
effort > **efficiency** *noun* ability to
function effectively and with little
waste of effort > **efficiently** *adverb*

effigy effigies *noun* statue or model
of a person

effluent *noun* liquid waste that
comes out of factories or sewage

works

effluvium effluvia *noun*
unpleasant smell or gas given off by
something

effort *noun* **1** physical or mental
exertion **2** attempt

effortless *adjective* done easily and
well > **effortlessly** *adverb*

e.g. *abbreviation* (*Latin: exempli gratia*)
for example

egalitarian *adjective* favouring
equality for all people

egg *noun* **1** oval or round object laid
by the females of birds and other
creatures, containing a developing
embryo **2** hen's egg used as food
3 (also **ovum**) cell produced in
a female animal's body that can
develop into a baby if it is fertilized
> **egg on** *verb* to encourage
(someone) to do something foolish
or daring

eggplant *noun* US, Canadian,
Aust, NZ dark purple pear-shaped
vegetable; aubergine

ego egos *noun* self-esteem

egocentric *adjective* only thinking
of oneself

egoism or **egotism** *noun*
1 excessive concern for one's own
interests **2** excessively high opinion
of oneself > **egoist** or **egotist** *noun*
egotistical person > **egotistic** or
egotistical or **egoistic** *adjective*
having an excessive concern for
one's own interests

Egyptian *adjective* **1** belonging or
relating to Egypt ▷ *noun* **2** someone
from Egypt

eight *adjective, noun* the number 8
> **eighth** *adjective, noun*

eighteen *adjective, noun* the number
18 > **eighteenth** *adjective, noun*

eighty eighties *adjective, noun* the
number 80 > **eightieth** *adjective,
noun*

either *adjective, pronoun* **1** one or
the other (of two) **2** each of two
▷ *conjunction* **3** used preceding two
or more possibilities joined by *or*
▷ *adverb* **4** likewise: *I don't eat meat
and he doesn't either*

**ejaculate ejaculates ejaculating
ejaculated** *verb* **1** to discharge
semen **2** to utter (something)
abruptly > **ejaculation** *noun* act of
ejaculating

eject *verb* to force out or expel
> **ejection** *noun*: *the ejection of
hecklers from the meeting*

**elaborate elaborates
elaborating elaborated**
adjective **1** with a lot of fine detail;
fancy ▷ *verb* **2** to add more
information or detail about
(something) > **elaborately** *adverb*
> **elaboration** *noun* adding more
detail about something

eland *noun* large antelope of
southern Africa

elapse elapses elapsing elapsed
verb (of time) to pass by

elastic *adjective* **1** able to stretch
easily **2** adapting easily to change
▷ *noun* **3** rubber material that
stretches and returns to its original
shape > **elasticity** *noun*: *to restore
the skin's elasticity*

elated *adjective* extremely happy
and excited > **elation** *noun* great
happiness

elbow *noun* **1** joint between your
upper arm and forearm ▷ *verb* **2** to
shove or strike (someone) with
your elbow

elder *adjective* **1** (of brother, son,
daughter, etc) older ▷ *noun* **2** older
person **3** small tree with white
flowers and black berries > **eldest**
adjective (of brother, son, daughter,
etc) oldest

elderly *adjective* (fairly) old

elect *verb* **1** to choose (someone) by voting **2** to decide (to do something) ▷ *adjective* **3** appointed but not yet in office: *president elect*

election *noun* **1** choosing of representatives by voting **2** act of choosing > **electoral** *adjective*: *electoral reform*

elector *noun* someone who has the right to vote in an election

electorate *noun* people who have the right to vote

electric *adjective* **1** powered or produced by electricity **2** exciting or tense

electrical *adjective* using or producing electricity > **electrically** *adverb*

electrician *noun* person trained to install and repair electrical equipment

electricity *noun* **1** form of energy associated with stationary or moving electrons or other charged particles **2** electric current or charge

electrified *adjective* connected to a supply of electricity

electrifying *adjective* very exciting

electro- *prefix meaninng* operated by or caused by electricity

electrocute electrocutes electrocuting electrocuted *verb* to kill or injure (someone) by electricity > **electrocution** *noun*: *death by electrocution*

electrode *noun* conductor through which an electric current enters or leaves a battery, vacuum tube, etc

electron *noun* elementary particle in all atoms that has a negative electrical charge

electronic *adjective* having transistors or silicon chips which control an electric current > **electronically** *adverb*

electronic mail see **e-mail**

electronics *noun* technology concerned with the development of electronic devices and circuits

elegant *adjective* pleasing or graceful in dress, style or design > **elegance** *noun*: *understated elegance* > **elegantly** *adverb*

elegy elegies *noun* mournful poem, especially a lament for the dead

element *noun* **1** component part **2** substance that cannot be separated into other substances by ordinary chemical techniques **3** section of people within a larger group: *the rowdy element* **4** heating wire in an electric kettle, stove, etc **5 in your element** in a situation where you are happiest **6 elements a** basic principles of something **b** weather conditions, especially wind, rain and cold

elemental *adjective* simple and basic, but powerful

elementary *adjective* simple and straightforward

elephant *noun* huge four-footed thick-skinned animal with ivory tusks and a long trunk

elevate elevates elevating elevated *verb* **1** to raise (someone) in rank or status **2** to lift (something) up

elevation *noun* **1** raising of someone or something to a higher level or position **2** height above sea level

elevator *noun* *Aust, US, Canadian* lift for carrying people

eleven *adjective, noun* **1** the number 11 ▷ *noun* **2** *Sport* team of eleven people > **eleventh** *adjective, noun*

elf elves *noun* (in folklore) small mischievous fairy

elicit *verb* **1** to bring about (a response or reaction) **2** to find

out (information) by careful
questioning

eligible *adjective* meeting the
requirements or qualifications
needed > **eligibility** *noun*: *eligibility
for benefits*

**eliminate eliminates
eliminating eliminated** *verb* to
get rid of > **elimination** *noun*: *the
elimination of chemical weapons*

elite *noun* most powerful, rich or
gifted members of a group

Elizabethan *adjective* of the reign
of Elizabeth I of England (1558–1603)

elk *noun* large deer of N Europe
and Asia

ellipse *noun* a regular oval shape,
like a circle seen from an angle

elm *noun* tall tree with broad leaves

elocution *noun* art of speaking
clearly in public

elongated *adjective* long and thin

elope elopes eloping eloped *verb*
(of two people) to run away secretly
to get married

eloquent *adjective* able to speak
or write skilfully and with ease
> **eloquence** *noun* fluent powerful
use of language > **eloquently** *adverb*

else *adjective, adverb* **1** in addition or
more: *what else can I do?* **2** other or
different: *It was unlike anything else
that had happened*

elsewhere *adverb* in or to another
place

elude eludes eluding eluded
verb **1** to escape from (someone
or something) by cleverness or
quickness **2** to baffle (someone)

elusive *adjective* difficult to catch
or remember

elves *noun* plural of **elf**

em- *prefix* another form of the
prefix **en-**

  em- is the form used before the
  letters *b*, *m* and *p*

emaciated *adjective* extremely
thin and weak, because of illness or
lack of food

e-mail or **email** *noun* **1** (also
electronic mail) sending of
messages between computer
terminals ▷ *verb* **2** to communicate
with (someone) in this way

emancipation *noun* freeing
someone from harmful or
unpleasant restrictions

embalm *verb* to preserve (a
corpse) from decay by the use of
chemicals etc

embankment *noun* man-made
ridge that carries a road or railway
or holds back water

**embargo embargoes
embargoing embargoed** *noun*
1 order by a government prohibiting
trade with a country ▷ *verb* **2** to put
an embargo on (goods)

embark *verb* **1** to board a ship or
aircraft **2** (followed by *on*) to begin
(a new project)

**embarrass embarrasses
embarrassing embarrassed**
verb to cause (someone) to feel
self-conscious or ashamed
> **embarrassed** *adjective*
> **embarrassing** *adjective*
> **embarrassment** *noun*

embassy embassies *noun*
1 offices or official residence of an
ambassador **2** ambassador and
his staff

embedded *adjective* **1** fixed firmly
and deeply **2** (of a journalist)
assigned to accompany an active
military unit

embellish *verb* **1** to decorate **2** to
add colourful details to (a story)

ember *noun* glowing piece of wood
or coal in a dying fire

**embezzle embezzles embezzling
embezzled** *verb* to steal (money

that has been entrusted to you)
> **embezzlement** *noun*

embittered *adjective* feeling anger
as a result of misfortune

emblazoned *adjective* decorated
(with something)

emblem *noun* object or design
that symbolizes a quality, type
or group

**embody embodies embodying
embodied** *verb* 1 to be an example
or expression of (a quality or idea)
2 to comprise or include (a number
of things) > **embodiment** *noun: the
embodiment of vulnerability*

embossed *adjective* (of a design
or pattern) standing out from a
surface

**embrace embraces embracing
embraced** *verb* 1 to clasp
(someone) in your arms; hug 2 to
accept (an idea) eagerly ▷ *noun*
3 act of embracing

embroider *verb* to decorate (fabric)
with needlework > **embroidery**
noun

embroiled *adjective* deeply involved
and entangled (in an argument
or conflict)

embryo embryos *noun* unborn
creature in the early stages of
development > **embryonic**
adjective at an early stage

emerald *noun* 1 bright green
precious stone ▷ *adjective* 2 bright
green

**emerge emerges emerging
emerged** *verb* 1 to come into view
2 (followed by *from*) to come out of
(a difficult or bad experience) 3 to
become known > **emergence** *noun*
coming into existence > **emergent**
adjective coming into existence

emergency emergencies *noun*
sudden unforeseen occurrence
needing immediate action

emigrant *noun* person who goes
and settles in another country

**emigrate emigrates emigrating
emigrated** *verb* to go and settle
in another country > **emigration**
noun process of emigrating

eminent *adjective* well-known
and respected > **eminence** *noun*
position of superiority or fame
> **eminently** *adverb* very

emir *noun* Muslim ruler

emission *noun* release of
something such as gas or radiation
into the atmosphere

emit emits emitting emitted *verb*
1 to give out (heat, light or a smell)
2 to utter (a sound)

emoticon *noun Computers* same
as **smiley**

emotion *noun* strong feeling

emotional *adjective* readily affected
by or appealing to the emotions
> **emotionally** *adverb*

emotive *adjective* tending to arouse
emotion

**empathize empathizes
empathizing empathized**; also
spelt **empathise** *verb* (followed by
with) to understand the feelings of
(someone) > **empathy** *noun* ability
to understand someone else's
feelings as if they were your own

emperor *noun* ruler of an empire

emphasis emphases *noun*
1 special importance or
significance 2 stress on a word or
phrase in speech

**emphasize emphasizes
emphasizing emphasized**; also
spelt **emphasise** *verb* to make it
known that (something) is very
important

emphatic *adjective* showing
emphasis > **emphatically** *adverb*

empire *noun* 1 group of countries
under the rule of one state or

person **2** large organization that is directed by one person or group

employ employs employing employed *verb* **1** to hire (someone) **2** to provide work or occupation for (someone) **3** to use (something)

employee *noun* person who works for another person or for an organization

employer *noun* person or organization that employs someone

employment *noun* **1** state of being employed **2** work done by a person to earn money

empower *verb* to enable or authorize (someone) to do something

empress empresses *noun* woman who rules an empire, or the wife of an emperor

empty emptier emptiest; empties emptying emptied *adjective* **1** containing nothing **2** unoccupied **3** without purpose or value **4** (of words) insincere ▷ *verb* **5** to make (something) empty > **empties** *plural noun* empty boxes, bottles, etc > **emptiness** *noun*

emu emus or **emu** *noun* large Australian flightless bird with long legs

emulate emulates emulating emulated *verb* to attempt to equal or surpass (someone or something) by imitating > **emulation** *noun*: *a role model worthy of emulation*

emulsion *noun* a water-based paint

emu oil *noun* oil derived from emu fat, used as a liniment by native Australians

en- *prefix meaning* **1** to surround or cover: *enclose; encrusted* **2** to cause to be in a certain state or condition: *enamoured; endanger*

enable enables enabling

enabled *verb* to provide (someone) with the means, opportunity or authority (to do something)

enact *verb* **1** to establish (a law or bill) by law **2** to perform (a story or play) by acting > **enactment** *noun*: *the enactment of the Bill of Rights*

enamel enamels enamelling enamelled *noun* **1** glasslike coating applied to metal etc to preserve the surface ▷ *verb* **2** to cover (an object) with enamel > **enamelled** *adjective* covered with enamel

enamoured *adjective* **be enamoured of** to like (someone or something) very much

encapsulate encapsulates encapsulating encapsulated *verb* to contain or represent (facts or ideas) in a small space

encased *adjective* surrounded or covered with a substance: *encased in plaster*

enchanted *adjective* fascinated or charmed

enchanting *adjective* attractive, delightful or charming

encircle encircles encircling encircled *verb* to form a circle around (something or someone)

enclave *noun* part of a country entirely surrounded by foreign territory

enclose encloses enclosing enclosed *verb* **1** to surround (an object or area) completely **2** to include (something) along with something else > **enclosed** *adjective* **1** surrounded completely **2** included

enclosure *noun* area of land surrounded by a wall or fence and used for a particular purpose

encompass encompasses encompassing encompassed *verb* to include all of (a number of things)

encore *interjection* **1** again, once more ▷ *noun* **2** short extra performance due to enthusiastic demand

encounter *verb* **1** to meet (someone) unexpectedly **2** to be faced with (a difficulty) ▷ *noun* **3** unexpected meeting

encourage encourages encouraging encouraged *verb* **1** to inspire (someone) with confidence **2** to spur (someone) on > **encouragement** *noun: My friends gave me a great deal of encouragement* > **encouraging** *adjective*

encroach encroaches encroaching encroached *verb* (followed by) (on) to intrude gradually on (a person's rights or land) > **encroachment** *noun* intruding gradually on something

encrusted *adjective* covered with a layer of something: *a necklace encrusted with gold*

encyclopedia or **encyclopaedia** *noun* book or set of books containing facts about many subjects, usually in alphabetical order

encyclopedic or **encyclopaedic** *adjective* knowing or giving information about many different things

end *noun* **1** furthest point or part **2** limit **3** last part of something **4** fragment **5** death or destruction **6** purpose **7** *Sport* either of the two defended areas of a playing field ▷ *verb* **8** to come or bring (something) to a finish

endanger *verb* to put (something) in danger

endear *verb* (followed by *to*) to cause (someone) to be liked > **endearing** *adjective: an endearing*

personality > **endearingly** *adverb*

endeavour *verb* **1** to try ▷ *noun* **2** effort

ending *noun* final part of something, especially a film, play or book

endless *adjective* having or seeming to have no end > **endlessly** *adverb*

endorse endorses endorsing endorsed *verb* **1** to give approval to **2** to sign the back of (a cheque) **3** to record a conviction on (a driving licence)

endorsement *noun* **1** statement or action showing support or approval for someone or something **2** *Brit* note on someone's driving licence showing that he or she has been found guilty of a driving offence

endowed *adjective* **endowed with** provided with (a quality or ability)

endurance *noun* act or power of enduring

endure endures enduring endured *verb* **1** to bear (hardship) patiently **2** to last for a long time > **enduring** *adjective: an enduring friendship*

enema *noun* liquid put into a person's rectum to cause their bowels to empty

enemy enemies *noun* hostile person or nation, opponent

energetic *adjective* having energy or enthusiasm; lively > **energetically** *adverb* with great energy

energy energies *noun* **1** capacity for intense activity **2** capacity to do work and overcome resistance **3** source of power, such as electricity

enforce enforces enforcing enforced *verb* to cause (a law or rule) to be obeyed > **enforceable** *adjective* > **enforcement** *noun:*

stricter enforcement of laws

engage engages engaging engaged *verb* **1** to take part or participate **2** to involve (a person or his or her attention) intensely

engaged *adjective* **1** having agreed to be married **2** in use

engagement *noun* appointment with someone

engine *noun* **1** any machine that converts energy into mechanical work **2** railway locomotive

engineer *noun* **1** person trained in any branch of engineering ▷ *verb* **2** to plan (an event or situation) in a clever manner

engineering *noun* profession of applying scientific principles to the design and construction of engines, cars, buildings or machines

English *noun* **1** official language of Britain, Ireland, Australia, New Zealand, South Africa, Canada, the US and several other countries ▷ *plural* **2** **the English** the people of England ▷ *adjective* **3** relating to England

Englishman Englishmen *noun* a man from England > **Englishwoman** *noun*

engrave engraves engraving engraved *verb* to carve (a design) onto a hard surface > **engraver** *noun*

engraving *noun* print made from an engraved plate

engrossed *adjective* having all your attention taken up: *engrossed in a video game*

engulf *verb* to cover or surround (something) completely

enhance enhances enhancing enhanced *verb* to increase the quality, value or attractiveness of (something) > **enhancement** *noun* increase in quality, value or

attractiveness

enigma *noun* puzzling thing or person

enigmatic *adjective* mysterious, puzzling or difficult to understand > **enigmatically** *adverb*

enjoy enjoys enjoying enjoyed *verb* **1** to take pleasure in **2** to experience

enjoyable *adjective* giving pleasure or satisfaction

enjoyment *noun* pleasure or satisfaction from doing something enjoyable

enlarge enlarges enlarging enlarged *verb* **1** to make (something) larger **2** (followed by *on*) to speak or write about (a subject) in greater detail

enlargement *noun* **1** making something bigger **2** something, especially a photograph, that has been made bigger

enlighten *verb* to give information to (someone) > **enlightening** *adjective*: *an enlightening talk* > **enlightenment** *noun*

enlightened *adjective* well informed and willing to consider different opinions

enlist *verb* **1** to enter the armed forces **2** to obtain support or help from (someone)

enliven *verb* to make (something) lively or cheerful

en masse *adverb* French in a group or all together

enormity enormities *noun* **1** great wickedness **2** gross offence **3** *informal* great size

enormous *adjective* very big, vast > **enormously** *adverb* very

enough *adjective* **1** as much or as many as necessary ▷ *noun* **2** sufficient quantity ▷ *adverb* **3** sufficiently **4** fairly or quite: *That's* *a common enough experience*

enquire enquires enquiring enquired; also spelt **inquire** *verb* to seek information or ask (about)

enquiry enquiries *noun* **1** question **2** investigation

enrage enrages enraging enraged *verb* to makes (someone) very angry > **enraged** *adjective*

enrich enriches enriching enriched *verb* to improve the quality of (something) > **enriched** *adjective* > **enrichment** *noun*: *the enrichment of society*

enrol enrols enrolling enrolled *verb* (to cause) to become a member > **enrolment** *noun* act of enrolling

en route *adverb* French on the way

ensconced *adjective* settled firmly or comfortably

ensemble *noun* **1** all the parts of something taken together **2** company of actors or musicians **3** *Music* group of musicians playing together

enshrine enshrines enshrining enshrined *verb* to cherish or treasure (something)

ensign *noun* **1** naval flag **2** *US* naval officer

ensue ensues ensuing ensued *verb* to come next or result > **ensuing** *adjective* following or resulting

ensure ensures ensuring ensured *verb* to make certain or sure (that something happens)

entail *verb* to involve or bring about

entangled *adjective* involved or caught up: *entangled in international politics*

enter *verb* **1** to come or go into (a place) **2** to join (an organization) **3** to become involved in or take part in (a competition or examination) **4** to record (an item) in a journal etc

enterprise *noun* **1** company or firm **2** bold or difficult undertaking > **enterprising** *adjective* full of boldness and initiative

entertain *verb* **1** to amuse (people) **2** to receive (people) as guests > **entertainer** *noun* person who amuses audiences, *eg* a comedian or singer > **entertaining** *adjective* amusing > **entertainment** *noun* anything that people watch for pleasure, *eg* shows and films

enthral enthrals enthralling enthralled *verb* to hold the attention of (someone) > **enthralling** *adjective* fascinating

enthuse enthuses enthusing enthused *verb* to show enthusiasm

enthusiasm *noun* ardent interest, eagerness

enthusiastic *adjective* showing great excitement, eagerness or approval > **enthusiastically** *adverb*

entice entices enticing enticed *verb* to tempt (someone) to do something

enticing *adjective* extremely attractive and tempting

entire *adjective* including every detail, part or aspect of something > **entirely** *adverb* wholly and completely > **entirety** *noun*: *This message will now be repeated in its entirety*

entitle entitles entitling entitled *verb* to give a right to (someone) > **entitlement** *noun*: *their entitlement to benefit*

entitled *adjective* having as a title

entity entities *noun* separate distinct thing

entourage *noun* group of people who follow or travel with a famous or important person

entrails *plural noun* **1** intestines

2 innermost parts of something

entrance¹ noun **1** way into a place **2** act of entering **3** right of entering

entrance² entrances entranced entrancing verb **1** to delight (someone) **2** to put (someone) into a trance > **entrancing** adjective fascinating

entrant noun person who enters a university, contest, etc

entrenched adjective (of a belief, custom or power) firmly established

entrepreneur noun business person who attempts to make a profit by risk and initiative > **entrepreneurial** adjective: his entrepreneurial spirit

entrust verb to put (something) into the care or protection of (someone)

entry entries noun **1** entrance, way in **2** entering **3** item entered in a journal etc

envelop verb to wrap (something) up, enclose (something)

envelope noun folded gummed paper cover for a letter

enviable adjective arousing envy; fortunate

envious adjective full of envy > **enviously** adverb

environment noun external conditions and surroundings in which people, animals, or plants live > **environmental** adjective: environmental damage > **environmentally** adverb: environmentally friendly goods

> There is an n before the m in environment

environmentalist noun person concerned with the protection of the natural environment

envisage envisages envisaging envisaged verb to conceive of (something) as a possibility

envoy envoys noun **1** messenger **2** diplomat ranking below an ambassador

envy envies envying envied noun **1** feeling of discontent aroused by another's good fortune ▷ verb **2** to grudge (someone) his or her good fortune, success or qualities

enzyme noun a chemical substance, usually a protein, produced by cells in the body

ephemeral adjective short-lived

epic noun **1** long poem, book or film about heroic events or actions ▷ adjective **2** very impressive or ambitious

epicentre noun point on the earth's surface immediately above the origin of an earthquake

epidemic noun **1** widespread occurrence of a disease **2** rapid spread of something

epigram noun short witty remark or poem

epigraph noun **1** quotation at the start of a book **2** inscription

epilepsy noun disorder of the nervous system causing loss of consciousness and sometimes convulsions > **epileptic** adjective **1** of or having epilepsy ▷ noun **2** person who has epilepsy

episode noun **1** incident in a series of incidents **2** section of a serialized book, television programme, etc

epistle noun letter, especially of an apostle

epitaph noun commemorative inscription on a tomb

epithet noun descriptive word or name

epitome noun typical example

> Do not use epitome to mean 'the peak of something'. It means 'the most typical example of something'

epoch *noun* long period of time

eponymous *adjective* after whom a book, play, etc is named: *the eponymous hero of 'Eric the Viking'*

equal equals equalling equalled *adjective* **1** identical in size, quantity, degree, etc **2** having identical rights or status **3** evenly balanced **4** (followed by *to*) having the necessary ability (for) ▷ *noun* **5** person or thing equal to another ▷ *verb* **6** to be equal to (something) > **equality** *noun* state of being equal > **equally** *adverb*

equalize equalizes equalizing equalized; also spelt **equalise** *verb* **1** to make (something) equal or become equal **2** to reach the same score as your opponent

equate equates equating equated *verb* to make or regard (something) as equivalent to something else

equation *noun* mathematical statement that two expressions are equal

equator *noun* imaginary circle round the earth, lying halfway between the North and South Poles > **equatorial** *adjective* near or at the equator

equestrian *adjective* relating to horses and riding

equilateral *adjective* (of a triangle) having equal sides

equilibrium *noun* steadiness or stability

equine *adjective* relating to horses

equinox equinoxes *noun* time of year when day and night are of equal length

equip equips equipping equipped *verb* to provide (someone or something) with supplies, components, etc

equipment *noun* set of tools or devices used for a particular purpose; apparatus

equitable *adjective* fair and reasonable

equity *noun* fairness

equivalent *adjective* **1** equal in use, size, value or effect ▷ *noun* **2** something that has the same use, size, value or effect as something else > **equivalence** *noun* state of being equivalent

era *noun* period of time considered as distinctive

eradicate eradicates eradicating eradicated *verb* to destroy (something) completely > **eradication** *noun*: *the eradication of corruption*

erase erases erasing erased *verb* to remove (something) > **eraser** *noun* object for erasing something written

erect *verb* **1** to build (something) ▷ *adjective* **2** in a straight and upright position; vertical > **erection** *noun* **1** process of erecting something **2** something that has been erected **3** stiff swollen penis in an upright position

ermine *noun* expensive white fur

erode erodes eroding eroded *verb* to wear (something) away

erosion *noun* gradual wearing away and destruction of something

erotic *adjective* involving or arousing sexual desire > **erotically** *adverb*

err *verb* to make a mistake

errand *noun* short trip to do something for someone

erratic *adjective* irregular or unpredictable > **erratically** *adverb*

erroneous *adjective* incorrect, mistaken > **erroneously** *adverb*

error *noun* mistake, inaccuracy or misjudgment

erudite *adjective* having great

academic knowledge

erupt *verb* **1** (of a volcano) to throw out a lot of hot lava and ash suddenly and violently **2** to burst forth suddenly and violently > **eruption** *noun*: *volcanic eruptions*

escalate escalates escalating escalated *verb* to increase in extent or intensity

escalator *noun* moving staircase

escapade *noun* mischievous adventure

escape escapes escaping escaped *verb* **1** to get free of **2** to avoid **3** (of a gas, liquid, etc) to leak gradually ▷ *noun* **4** act of escaping **5** means of relaxation

escapee *noun* person who has escaped

escapism *noun* taking refuge in fantasy to avoid unpleasant reality > **escapist** *adjective*: *escapist fantasy*

eschew *verb* to avoid or keep away from (something)

escort *noun* **1** people or vehicles accompanying another person for protection or as an honour **2** person who accompanies a person of the opposite sex to a social event ▷ *verb* **3** to act as an escort to (someone)

Eskimo Eskimos *noun offensive* a name that was formerly used for the Inuit people and their language

especially *adverb* particularly

espionage *noun* spying

espouse espouses espousing espoused *verb* to adopt or give support to (a cause etc)

espresso espressos *noun* strong coffee made by forcing steam or boiling water through ground coffee beans

The second letter of *espresso* is s and not x

ess- *suffix indicating* a female: *lioness*

Special words for a woman doing a particular activity such as *actress*, *authoress* and *poetess* are better avoided in favour of *actor*, *author* and *poet*

essay essays *noun* **1** short literary composition **2** short piece of writing on a subject done as an exercise by a student

essence *noun* **1** most important feature of a thing which gives it its identity **2** concentrated liquid used to flavour food

essential *adjective* **1** vitally important **2** basic or fundamental ▷ *noun* **3** something fundamental or indispensable > **essentially** *adverb* fundamentally

establish establishes establishing established *verb* **1** to set (something) up on a permanent basis **2** to make (yourself) secure or permanent in a certain place, job, etc **3** to prove (a fact) > **established** *adjective*

establishment *noun* **1** act of establishing **2** commercial or other institution **3** **the Establishment** group of people having authority within a society

estate *noun* **1** large area of privately owned land in the country and all the property on it **2** large area of property development, especially of new houses or factories **3** property of a deceased person

estate agent *noun* person who works for a company that sells houses and land

esteem *noun* **1** high regard ▷ *verb* **2** to think highly of (someone or something) > **esteemed** *adjective* greatly admired and respected

estimate estimates estimating estimated *verb* **1** to calculate (an amount or quantity) roughly **2** to form an opinion about (something) ▷ *noun* **3** approximate calculation **4** statement from a workman etc of the likely charge for a job **5** opinion

estimation *noun* considered opinion

estranged *adjective* no longer living with your husband or wife

estrogen *noun* female sex hormone that regulates the reproductive cycle

estuary estuaries *noun* mouth of a river

etc *abbreviation* et cetera

et cetera *Latin* **1** and the rest or and others **2** or the like

As *etc* means 'and the rest', you should not write *and etc*

etch etches etching etched *verb* **1** to cut (a design or pattern) on a surface by using acid or a sharp tool **2** to imprint (something) vividly on someone's mind > **etched** *adjective*

etching *noun* picture printed from a metal plate that has had a design cut into it

eternal *adjective* lasting forever or seeming to last forever > **eternally** *adverb*

eternity eternities *noun* **1** infinite time **2** timeless existence after death **3** period of time that seems to go on forever

ether *noun* colourless sweet-smelling liquid used as an anaesthetic

ethereal *adjective* extremely delicate

ethical *adjective* in agreement with accepted principles of behaviour that are thought to be right > **ethically** *adverb*

ethics *noun* **1** code of behaviour ▷ *plural* **2** study of morals

Ethiopian *adjective* **1** belonging

to or relating to Ethiopia ▷ *noun* **2** someone from Ethiopia

ethnic *adjective* **1** relating to a people or group that shares a culture, religion or language **2** belonging or relating to such a group, especially one that is a minority group in a particular place > **ethnically** *adverb*

ethos *noun* distinctive spirit and attitudes of a people, culture, etc

etiquette *noun* conventional code of conduct

etymology *noun* study of the sources and development of words

EU *abbreviation* European Union

eucalyptus or **eucalypt eucalyptuses** or **eucalypts** *noun* tree, mainly grown in Australia, that provides timber, gum and medicinal oil from the leaves

Eucharist *noun* religious ceremony in which Christians remember and celebrate Christ's last meal with his disciples

eulogy eulogies *noun* speech or writing in praise of a person

eunuch *noun* castrated man, especially (formerly) a guard in a harem

euphemism *noun* inoffensive word or phrase substituted for one considered offensive or upsetting > **euphemistic** *adjective*: *a euphemistic way of saying that someone has been lying* > **euphemistically** *adverb*

euphoria *noun* sense of elation > **euphoric** *adjective* intensely happy and excited

euro euros *noun* unit of the single currency of the European Union

Europe *noun* second smallest continent, having Asia to the east, the Arctic to the north, the Atlantic to the west, and the Mediterranean and Africa to the south

European *noun* **1** someone from Europe ▷ *adjective* **2** of or relating to Europe

European Union *noun* economic and political association of a number of European nations

euthanasia *noun* act of killing someone painlessly, especially to relieve his or her suffering

evacuate evacuates evacuating evacuated *verb* **1** to send (someone) away from a place of danger **2** to empty (a place) > **evacuation** *noun*: *the evacuation of the sick and wounded* > **evacuee** *noun* person who has been sent away from a place of danger

evade evades evading evaded *verb* **1** to get away from or avoid (a problem or question) **2** to elude (someone or something)

evaluate evaluates evaluating evaluated *verb* to find or judge the value of > **evaluation** *noun* assessing the strengths and weaknesses of something

evangelical *adjective* of certain Protestant sects which maintain the doctrine of salvation by faith

evangelist *noun* travelling preacher > **evangelism** *noun* teaching and spreading of the Christian gospel > **evangelize** *verb* to preach the gospel

evaporate evaporates evaporating evaporated *verb* to change from a liquid or solid to a vapour > **evaporation** *noun*

evasion *noun* deliberately avoiding doing something: *evasion of arrest*

evasive *adjective* deliberately trying to avoid talking about or doing something

eve *noun* **1** evening or day before some special event **2** period

immediately before an event

even *adjective* **1** flat or smooth **2** (followed by *with*) on the same level (as) **3** equally balanced **4** divisible by two ▷ *adverb* **5** equally **6** simply **7** nevertheless > **evenly** *adverb*

evening *noun* **1** end of the day or early part of the night ▷ *adjective* **2** of or in the evening

event *noun* **1** anything that takes place; happening **2** planned and organized occasion **3** contest in a sporting programme

eventful *adjective* full of exciting incidents

eventual *adjective* ultimate

eventuality eventualities *noun* possible event

eventually *adverb* at the end of a situation or process

ever *adverb* **1** at any time **2** always

evergreen *noun, adjective* (tree or shrub) having leaves throughout the year

everlasting *adjective* never coming to an end

every *adjective* **1** each without exception **2** all possible

everybody *pronoun* every person

everyday *adjective* usual or ordinary

everyone *pronoun* every person

everything *pronoun* **1** all or the whole of something **2** the most important thing

everywhere *adverb* in all places

evict *verb* to legally expel (someone) from his or her home > **eviction** *noun*: *They were facing eviction*

evidence *noun* **1** reason for belief **2** matter produced before a law court to prove or disprove a point **3** sign, indication

evident *adjective* easily seen or understood > **evidently** *adverb*

evil *noun* **1** wickedness **2** wicked deed ▷ *adjective* **3** harmful **4** morally bad **5** very unpleasant

evoke evokes evoking evoked *verb* to call or summon up (a memory, feeling, etc)

evolution *noun* gradual change in the characteristics of living things over successive generations, especially to a more complex form > **evolutionary** *adjective*: *an evolutionary process*

evolve evolves evolving evolved *verb* **1** to develop gradually **2** (of an animal or plant species) to undergo evolution

ewe *noun* female sheep

ex- *prefix meaning* former: *ex-wife*

exacerbate exacerbates exacerbating exacerbated *verb* to make (pain, emotion or a situation) worse

exact *adjective* **1** correct and complete in every detail **2** precise, as opposed to approximate ▷ *verb* **3** to demand (something) from someone > **exactly** *adverb*

exaggerate exaggerates exaggerating exaggerated *verb* **1** to regard or represent (something) as greater than is true **2** to make (something) greater or more noticeable > **exaggeration** *noun* act of exaggerating

exalted *adjective* very important

exam *noun* short for **examination**

examination *noun* **1** examining **2** test of a candidate's knowledge or skill

examine examines examining examined *verb* **1** to look at (something or someone) closely **2** to test the knowledge of **3** to ask questions of

examiner *noun* person who sets or marks an examination

example *noun* **1** specimen typical of its group; sample **2** person or thing worthy of imitation **3** punishment regarded as a warning to others

exasperate exasperates exasperating exasperated *verb* to cause great irritation to > **exasperating** *adjective* > **exasperation** *noun*

excavate excavates excavating excavated *verb* **1** to remove earth from the ground by digging **2** to dig up (buried objects) from a piece of land to learn about the past > **excavation** *noun*: *the excavation of a bronze-age boat*

exceed *verb* **1** to be greater than (something) **2** to go beyond (a limit) > **exceedingly** *adverb* very

excel excels excelling excelled *verb* to be outstandingly good at something

Excellency Excellencies *noun* title used to address a high-ranking official, such as an ambassador

excellent *adjective* exceptionally good; superb > **excellence** *noun*: *the top award for excellence*

except *preposition* **1** (sometimes followed by *for*) other than, not including **2 except that** but for the fact that ▷ *verb* **3** not to include > **exception** *noun* **1** excepting **2** thing that is excluded from or does not conform to the general rule > **exceptional** *adjective* **1** not ordinary **2** much above the average > **exceptionally** *adverb*

excerpt *noun* passage taken from a book, speech, etc

excess excesses *noun* **1** state or act of exceeding the permitted limits **2** immoderate amount **3** amount by which a thing exceeds the permitted limits

excessive *adjective* too great in

amount or degree > **excessively** *adverb* too

exchange exchanges exchanging exchanged *verb* **1** to give or receive (something) in return for something else ▷ *noun* **2** act of exchanging **3** thing given or received in place of another **4** centre in which telephone lines are interconnected **5** *Finance* place where securities or commodities are traded **6** transfer of sums of money of equal value between different currencies

Exchequer *noun Brit* government department in charge of state money

excise excises excising excised *noun* **1** tax on goods produced for the home market ▷ *verb* **2** to cut (something) out or away

excitable *adjective* easily excited

excite excites exciting excited *verb* **1** to arouse (someone) to strong emotion; thrill **2** to arouse or evoke (an emotion) > **excited** *adjective* happy and unable to relax > **excitedly** *adverb* > **excitement** *noun* state of being excited > **exciting** *adjective*

exclaim *verb* to speak suddenly or cry out

exclamation *noun* word or phrase spoken suddenly to express a strong feeling

exclamation mark *noun* punctuation mark (!) used after exclamations

exclude excludes excluding excluded *verb* **1** to keep or leave (someone) out **2** to leave (something) out of consideration > **exclusion** *noun: women's exclusion from political power*

exclusive *adjective* **1** excluding everything else **2** not shared

3 catering for a privileged minority ▷ *noun* **4** story reported in only one newspaper > **exclusively** *adverb*

excrement *noun* solid waste matter discharged from the body

excrete excretes excreting excreted *verb* to discharge (waste matter) from the body > **excretion** *noun: the excretion of this drug from the body*

excruciating *adjective* **1** agonizing **2** hard to bear > **excruciatingly** *adverb*

excursion *noun* short journey, especially for pleasure

excuse excuses excusing excused *noun* **1** explanation offered to justify a fault etc ▷ *verb* **2** to put forward a reason or justification for (a fault etc) **3** to forgive (a person) or overlook (a fault etc) **4** to free (someone) from a duty or responsibility **5** to allow (someone) to leave

execute executes executing executed *verb* **1** to kill (someone) as a punishment for a crime **2** to carry it out or perform (a plan or an action) > **execution** *noun* > **executioner** *noun* person who executes criminals

executive *noun* **1** person employed by a company at a senior level **2** (in an organization) committee having authority to make decisions and ensure that they are carried out ▷ *adjective* **3** concerned with making important decisions and ensuring that they are carried out

executor *noun* person appointed to perform the instructions of a will

exemplary *adjective* **1** being a good example **2** serving as a warning

exemplify exemplifies exemplifying exemplified *verb* to be a typical example of

exempt *adjective* **1** not subject to an obligation or rule ▷ *verb* **2** to release (someone) from an obligation or rule > **exemption** *noun* being excused from an obligation or rule

exercise exercises exercising exercised *noun* **1** activity to train the body or mind **2** set of movements or tasks designed to improve or test a person's ability **3** performance of a function ▷ *verb* **4** to make use of (something): *to exercise your rights* **5** to take exercise or perform exercises

exert *verb* **1** to use (influence, authority, etc) forcefully or effectively **2** **exert yourself** to make a special effort > **exertion** *noun* vigorous physical effort or exercise

exhale exhales exhaling exhaled *verb* to breathe out

exhaust *verb* **1** to tire (someone) out **2** to use up (a supply of something) **3** to discuss (a subject) thoroughly ▷ *noun* **4** gases ejected from an engine as waste products **5** pipe through which an engine's exhaust fumes pass > **exhaustion** *noun* **1** extreme tiredness **2** exhausting

exhaustive *adjective* thorough and complete > **exhaustively** *adverb*

exhibit *verb* **1** to display (things) to the public **2** to show (a quality or feeling) ▷ *noun* **3** object exhibited to the public

exhibition *noun* **1** public display of art, skills, etc **2** exhibiting

exhibitor *noun* person whose work is being shown in an exhibition

exhilarating *adjective* exciting and thrilling

exhort *verb* to urge earnestly

exile exiles exiling exiled *noun* **1** prolonged, usually enforced, absence from your country **2** person banished or living away from his or her country ▷ *verb* **3** to expel (someone) from his or her country

exist *verb* **1** to have being or reality **2** to live

existence *noun* **1** state of being or existing **2** way of living or being: *an idyllic existence*

exit *noun* **1** way out **2** going out **3** actor's going off stage ▷ *verb* **4** to go out **5** to go offstage: used as a stage direction

exodus exoduses *noun* departure of a large number of people

exorcize exorcizes exorcizing exorcized; also spelt **exorcise** *verb* to expel (evil spirits) by prayers and religious rites > **exorcism** *noun*: *a priest performing an exorcism*

exotic *adjective* **1** having a strange allure or beauty **2** originating in a foreign country

expand *verb* **1** to become larger or make (something) larger **2** (followed by *on*) to give more details about > **expansion** *noun*

expanse *noun* uninterrupted wide area

expansive *adjective* **1** wide or extensive **2** friendly and talkative

expatriate *adjective* **1** living outside your native country ▷ *noun* **2** person living outside his or her native country

expect *verb* **1** to regard (something) as probable **2** to look forward to or await **3** to require (something) as an obligation

expectancy *noun* feeling of anticipation

expectant *adjective* **1** expecting or hopeful **2** pregnant > **expectantly** *adverb*

expectation *noun* **1** act or state of expecting **2** something looked forward to **3** attitude of anticipation or hope

expedient *noun* **1** something that achieves a particular purpose ▷ *adjective* **2** suitable to the circumstances; appropriate **> expediency** *noun* doing what is convenient rather than what is morally right

expedition *noun* **1** organized journey, especially for exploration **2** people and equipment comprising an expedition **3** pleasure trip or excursion **> expeditionary** *adjective* relating to an expedition, especially a military one

expel expels expelling expelled *verb* **1** to force out (a gas or liquid) from a place **2** to dismiss (someone) from a school etc permanently

expend *verb* to spend or use up (energy, time or money)

expendable *adjective* no longer useful or necessary, and therefore able to be got rid of

expenditure *noun* **1** something expended, especially money **2** amount expended

expense *noun* **1** cost **2** (cause of) spending **3** **expenses** money spent while doing something connected with work and paid back by your employer

expensive *adjective* high-priced **> expensively** *adverb*

experience experiences experiencing experienced *noun* **1** direct personal participation **2** particular incident, feeling, etc that a person has undergone **3** accumulated knowledge ▷ *verb* **4** to participate in or undergo **5** to be affected by (an emotion)

experiment *noun* **1** test to provide evidence to prove or disprove a theory **2** attempt at something

new ▷ *verb* **3** to carry out an experiment **> experimental** *adjective*: *an experimental system* **> experimentally** *adverb* **> experimentation** *noun*: *experimentation on animals*

expert *noun* **1** person with extensive skill or knowledge in a particular field; authority ▷ *adjective* **2** skilful or knowledgeable **> expertly** *adverb*

expertise *noun* special skill or knowledge

expire expires expiring expired *verb* **1** to finish or run out **2** *literary* to die **> expiry** *noun* end, especially of a contract period

explain *verb* **1** to make (something) clear and intelligible **2** to account for (something) **> explanation** *noun*: *There was no apparent explanation for the crash* **> explanatory** *adjective*: *a series of explanatory notes*

explicit *adjective* **1** precisely and clearly expressed **2** shown in realistic detail **> explicitly** *adverb*: *She has been talking very explicitly about AIDS to these groups*

explode explodes exploding exploded *verb* **1** to burst with great violence, blow up **2** to react suddenly with emotion **3** to increase rapidly

exploit *verb* **1** to take advantage of (someone) for your own purposes **2** to make the best use of (something) ▷ *noun* **3** notable feat or deed **> exploitation** *noun*: *the exploitation of workers*

explore *verb* **explores exploring explored 1** to think carefully about (an idea) **2** to travel into (unfamiliar regions), especially for scientific purposes **> exploration** *noun* act of exploring **> exploratory** *adjective*:

exploratory surgery > **explorer** *noun* person who explores unfamiliar regions

explosion *noun* sudden violent burst of energy, for example one caused by a bomb

explosive *adjective* **1** tending to explode ▷ *noun* **2** substance that causes explosions

exponent *noun* **1** person who advocates an idea, cause, etc **2** skilful performer, especially a musician

export *noun* **1** selling or shipping of goods to a foreign country **2** product shipped or sold to a foreign country ▷ *verb* **3** to sell or ship (goods) to a foreign country > **exporter** *noun* country, firm or person that sells or ships goods to a foreign country

expose exposes exposing exposed *verb* **1** to uncover or reveal (something) **2** to make (someone) vulnerable, leave (someone) unprotected **3** to subject (a photographic film) to light

exposition *noun* detailed explanation of a particular subject

exposure *noun* **1** exposing **2** lack of shelter from the weather, especially the cold **3** appearance before the public, as on television

express expresses expressing expressed *verb* **1** to put (an idea or feeling) into words **2** to show (an emotion) **3** to indicate (a quantity) by a symbol or formula ▷ *adjective* **4** of or for rapid transport of people, mail, etc ▷ *noun* **5** fast train or bus stopping at only a few stations ▷ *adverb* **6** by express delivery

expression *noun* **1** expressing **2** word or phrase **3** showing or communication of emotion **4** look on the face that indicates mood

5 *Maths* variable, function, or some combination of these

expressive *adjective* **1** showing feelings clearly **2** full of expression

expressway expressways *noun Aust* road designed for fast-moving traffic

expulsion *noun* act of officially banning someone from a place or institution

exquisite *adjective* **1** of extreme beauty or delicacy **2** intense in feeling

extend *verb* **1** to continue and stretch into the distance **2** to draw (something) out or stretch (something) **3** to last for a certain time **4** to increase in size or scope **5** to offer (something): *extend your sympathy* > **extension** *noun* **1** room or rooms added to an existing building **2** additional telephone connected to the same line as another **3** extending

extensive *adjective* having a large extent or widespread > **extensively** *adverb*: *to travel extensively*

extent *noun* range over which something extends; area

exterior *noun* **1** part or surface on the outside **2** outward appearance ▷ *adjective* **3** of, on or coming from the outside

exterminate exterminates exterminating exterminated *verb* to destroy (animals or people) completely > **extermination** *noun*

external *adjective* of, situated on or coming from the outside > **externally** *adverb*: *Externally, it is in good condition*

extinct *adjective* **1** having died out **2** (of a volcano) no longer liable to erupt > **extinction** *noun*: *to save a species from extinction*

extinguish extinguishes extinguishing extinguished verb to put out (a fire or light)

extinguisher noun device for extinguishing a fire or light

extol extols extolling extolled verb to praise (the virtues, benefits or quality of something) highly

extort verb to get (something) by force or threats > **extortion** noun: He admitted extortion and kidnapping

extortionate adjective (of prices) excessive

extra adjective 1 more than is usual, expected or needed; additional ▷ noun 2 additional person or thing 3 something for which an additional charge is made 4 Films actor hired for crowd scenes ▷ adverb 5 unusually or exceptionally

extra- prefix meaning outside or beyond an area or scope: extraordinary

extract verb 1 to take or get (something) out, often by force 2 to get (information) from someone with difficulty ▷ noun 3 something extracted, such as a passage from a book etc 4 preparation containing the concentrated essence of a substance: beef extract > **extraction** noun 1 country or people that your family originally comes from: of Australian extraction 2 process of taking or getting something out of a place

extraordinary adjective unusual or surprising > **extraordinarily** adverb

extravagant adjective 1 spending money excessively 2 going beyond reasonable limits > **extravagance** noun excessive spending > **extravagantly** adverb

extravaganza noun elaborate and lavish entertainment, display, etc

extreme adjective 1 of a high or the highest degree or intensity 2 severe 3 immoderate 4 farthest or outermost ▷ noun 5 either of the two limits of a scale or range > **extremely** adverb very

extremist noun 1 person who favours immoderate methods ▷ adjective 2 holding extreme opinions > **extremism** noun: right-wing extremism

extremity extremities noun 1 farthest point 2 **extremities** hands and feet or fingers and toes

extricate extricates extricating extricated verb to free (someone) from complication or difficulty

extrovert noun lively outgoing person

exuberant adjective high-spirited > **exuberance** noun: a burst of exuberance > **exuberantly** adverb

exude exudes exuding exuded verb to make (something) apparent by mood or behaviour: exude ability

eye eyes eyeing or **eying eyed** noun 1 organ of sight 2 ability to judge or appreciate: a good eye for detail 3 hole at one end of a sewing needle through which you pass thread ▷ verb 4 to look at (something) carefully or warily

eyeball noun ball-shaped part of the eye

eyebrow noun line of hair on the bony ridge above the eye

eyelash eyelashes noun short hair that grows out from the eyelid

eyelid noun fold of skin that covers the eye when it is closed

eyesight noun ability to see

eyesore noun ugly object

eyewitness eyewitnesses noun person who was present at an event and can describe what happened

eyrie noun nest of an eagle

fable *noun* **1** story with a moral **2** false or fictitious account **3** legend

fabled *adjective* made famous in legend

fabric *noun* **1** cloth **2** walls, roof and basic structure of a building **3** structure, laws and customs of society

fabricate fabricates fabricating fabricated *verb* **1** to make up (a story or lie) **2** to make or build > **fabrication** *noun*

fabulous *adjective* **1** *informal* wonderful or very impressive **2** not real but told of in stories and legends

facade *noun* **1** front of a building **2** (false) outward appearance

face faces facing faced *noun* **1** front of the head **2** facial expression **3** distorted expression **4** outward appearance **5** front or side, especially the most important side **6** dial of a clock **7** dignity or self-respect ▷ *verb* **8** to be opposite (something or someone) **9** to look or turn towards (something or someone) **10** to be confronted by (something) > **face up to** *verb* to accept (an unpleasant fact or reality)

faceless *adjective* impersonal or anonymous

face-lift *noun* **1** operation to tighten facial skin, to remove wrinkles **2** improvement or new look

facet *noun* **1** aspect **2** cut surface of a precious stone

facetious *adjective* witty or amusing but in a rather silly or inappropriate way

facial *adjective* **1** of the face ▷ *noun* **2** beauty treatment for the face

facilitate facilitates facilitating facilitated *verb* to make (something) easier

facility facilities *noun* **1** talent or ability **2 facilities** means or equipment for an activity

fact *noun* **1** event or thing known to have happened or existed **2** provable truth **3 in fact** actually or really > **factual** *adjective*: *factual errors* > **factually** *adverb*: *It was factually incorrect*

faction *noun* (dissenting) minority group within a larger body

fact of life facts of life *noun* **1** something inescapable **2 facts of life** details of sex and reproduction

factor *noun* **1** something that helps to cause a result **2** *Maths* one of two or more whole numbers that when multiplied together give a given number. For example, 2 and 5 are factors of 10

factory factories *noun* building or group of buildings where goods are manufactured

faculty faculties *noun* **1** physical or mental ability **2** department in a university or college

fad *noun* temporary fashion

fade fades fading faded *verb* **1** to lose or cause something to lose brightness, colour or strength **2** to vanish slowly

faeces *plural noun* solid waste matter excreted from a person's or animal's body

fag *noun Brit informal* cigarette

Fahrenheit *noun* a scale of temperature in which the freezing point of water is 32• and the boiling point is 212•

fail *verb* **1** to be unsuccessful **2** to stop working **3** to be or to judge (someone) to be below the required standard in a test **4** to disappoint or be useless to (someone) **5** to neglect or be unablae (to do something) ▷ *noun* **6** instance of not passing an exam or test **7 without fail a** regularly **b** definitely

failing *noun* **1** weak point ▷ *preposition* **2** in the absence of

failure *noun* **1** act or instance of failing **2** unsuccessful person or thing **3 someone's failure to do something** fact of someone not having done something

faint *adjective* **1** (of sound, colour or image) not easy to hear or see owing to a lack of volume, brightness or definition **2** dizzy or weak **3** slight ▷ *verb* **4** to lose consciousness temporarily; to black out or pass out ▷ *noun* **5** temporary loss of consciousness **> faintly** *adverb*

fair *adjective* **1** unbiased, reasonable and just **2** quite large: *a fair amount of money* **3** quite good: *a fair attempt* **4** having light-coloured hair or pale skin **5** (of weather) fine ▷ *noun* **6** travelling entertainment with sideshows, rides and amusements **7** exhibition of goods produced by a particular industry ▷ *adverb* **8** fairly **> fairness** *noun*

fairground *noun* open space used for a fair

fairly *adverb* **1** moderately **2** to a great degree or extent **3** as deserved; reasonably

fairway fairways *noun Golf* smooth area between the tee and the green

fairy fairies *noun* (in stories) small supernatural creature with magic powers

fairy tale or **story** *noun* **1** story about fairies or magic **2** unbelievable story or explanation

faith *noun* **1** confidence or trust **2** religion

faithful *adjective* **1** loyal **2** accurate and reliable **> faithfully** *adverb* **> faithfulness** *noun*

fake fakes faking faked *noun* **1** imitation of something meant to trick people into thinking that it is genuine; copy or sham ▷ *adjective* **2** imitation and not genuine; artificial ▷ *verb* **3** to pretend to have (an illness, emotion, etc); feign **4** to cause (something not genuine) to appear real or more valuable by fraud

falcon *noun* small bird of prey that can be trained to hunt other birds or small animals

fall falls falling fell fallen *verb* **1** (also **fall over**) to lose balance and tumble towards the ground **2** to drop from a higher to a lower place through the force of gravity **3** to land **4** to go down or decrease in number or quality **5** to pass into a specified condition; become: *He fell ill* **6** (of a soldier) to be killed **7** to occur or happen ▷ *noun* **8** act of falling **9** thing or amount that falls **10** decrease or reduction in value or number **11** decline in power or influence **12** *US* autumn **13 falls** waterfall **> fall down** *verb* (of an argument or idea) to fail > **fall for** verb **1** informal to fall in love with **2** to be deceived by (a lie or trick) > **fall out** verb to quarrel; have a disagreement > **fall through** verb (of an arrangement or plan) to fail or be abandoned

fallacy fallacies noun false belief > **fallacious** adjective: It is a fallacious argument

fall guy noun **1** informal victim of a confidence trick **2** scapegoat

fallible adjective (of a person) liable to make mistakes > **fallibility** noun: reminders of human fallibility

fallopian tube noun one of two tubes in a woman's or female mammal's body along which the eggs pass from the ovaries to the uterus

fallout noun radioactive particles that fall to the earth after a nuclear explosion

fallow adjective (of land) ploughed but not planted so as to recover and regain fertility

false adjective **1** untrue or incorrect **2** artificial or fake **3** deceptive: false promises > **falsely** adverb > **falseness** noun: the obvious falseness of their position > **falsity** noun: efforts to establish the truth or falsity of these claims

falsehood noun **1** quality of being untrue **2** lie

falsify falsifies falsifying falsified verb to alter fraudulently > **falsification** noun: deliberate falsification of evidence

falter verb **1** to be hesitant, weak or unsure **2** to lose power momentarily **3** to talk hesitantly **4** to move unsteadily

fame noun state of being widely known or recognized

famed adjective very well-known; famous

familiar adjective **1** well-known **2** too informal and friendly **3** intimate or friendly **4** (followed by with) acquainted > **familiarity** noun > **familiarize** verb to acquaint (someone) fully with a particular subject > **familiarly** adverb

family families noun **1** group consisting of parents and their children **2** group descended from a common ancestor **3** group of related objects or beings ▷ adjective **4** suitable for parents and children together > **familial** adjective: social and familial relationships

family planning noun practice of controlling the number of children you have, usually by using contraception

famine noun severe shortage of food

famished adjective informal very hungry

famous adjective very well-known

famously adverb old-fashioned informal very well

fan fans fanning fanned noun **1** informal enthusiastic follower of a pop star, sport or hobby **2** hand-held or mechanical device used to create a cooling draught ▷ verb **3** to blow or cool (someone or something) with a fan > **fan out** verb to spread out like a fan

fanatic noun person who is very extreme in their support for a cause or in their enthusiasm for a particular activity > **fanaticism** noun: the evils of religious fanaticism

fanatical adjective extreme and obsessive in your support or enthusiasm for something > **fanatically** adverb

fanciful adjective **1** not based on fact: Mother's fanciful tales of elves *and fairies* **2** excessively elaborate

**fancy fancies fancying fancied;
fancier fanciest** *verb* **1** *informal*
to have a wish for; want **2** *informal*
to be sexually attracted to **3** to
suppose **4 fancy yourself** *informal*
to have a high opinion of yourself
▷ *noun* **5** sudden irrational liking or
desire **6** uncontrolled imagination
▷ *adjective* **7** not plain; elaborate

fancy dress *noun* party costume
representing a historical figure,
animal, etc

fanfare *noun* short loud tune played
on brass instruments

fang *noun* long pointed tooth

fantail *noun* **1** a pigeon with a large
tail that can be opened out like a
fan **2** small Australian and
New Zealand bird with a fan-
shaped tail

**fantasize fantasizes fantasizing
fantasized**; also spelt **fantasise**
verb to imagine pleasant but
unlikely events or situations;
daydream

fantastic *adjective* **1** *informal* very
good **2** unrealistic or absurd
3 extremely large in degree or
amount **4** strange and difficult
to believe > **fantastically**
adverb

fantasy fantasies *noun* **1** imagined
story or situation; daydream
2 far-fetched notion **3** imagination
unrestricted by reality **4** fiction
with a large fantasy content

FAQ FAQs *abbreviation Computers*
frequently asked question *or*
questions

**far farther farthest; further
furthest** *adverb* **1** at, to or from a
great distance **2** at or to a remote
time **3** very much: *far more important*
4 so far up to now ▷ *adjective* **5** a
long way away in space or time

6 further away or more distant
When you are talking about a
physical distance you can use
farther and *farthest* or *further*
and *furthest*. If you are talking
about extra effort or time, use
further and *furthest*: *A further
delay is likely*

farce *noun* **1** humorous play in which
ridiculous and unlikely situations
occur **2** disorganized and ridiculous
or ludicrous situation > **farcical**
adjective ludicrous > **farcically**
adverb

fare fares faring fared *noun*
1 charge for a passenger's journey
2 passenger **3** food provided ▷ *verb*
4 to get on (in a particular way): *We
fared badly*

Far East *noun* the countries of East
Asia, including China, Japan and
Malaysia > **Far Eastern** *adjective*

farewell *interjection* **1** goodbye
▷ *noun, adjective* **2** (of event) related
to leaving: *a farewell speech*

far-fetched *adjective* unlikely to
be true

farm *noun* **1** area of land together
with the buildings on it that forms
a unit and is used for growing
crops or rearing livestock ▷ *verb*
2 to run a farm by rearing livestock
and/or cultivating the land **3** to
cultivate (land) **4** to rear (livestock)
> **farming** *noun*

farmer *noun* person who owns or
runs a farm

farmhouse *noun* the main house
on a farm

farmyard *noun* area surrounded by
farm buildings

farrier *noun* person who shoes
horses

farther *or* **farthest** comparative
and superlative forms of **far**

fascinate fascinates fascinating

fascinated *verb* to attract and interest (someone) strongly > **fascinating** *adjective*: *a fascinating place to visit* > **fascination** *noun*: *her fascination with politics*

fascism *noun* extreme right-wing political ideology or system of government with a powerful dictator and state control of most activities. Nationalism is encouraged and political opposition not allowed > **fascist** *adjective, noun*

fashion *noun* **1** style of dress or way of behaving that is popular at a particular time; vogue **2** way something happens or is done ▷ *verb* **3** to make or shape

fashionable *adjective* currently popular; in vogue > **fashionably** *adverb*

fast *adjective* **1** (capable of) acting or moving quickly **2** done in or lasting a short time **3** (of a clock or watch) showing a time later than the correct time **4** (of colour or dye) not likely to run when wet ▷ *adverb* **5** quickly **6** soundly or deeply: *fast asleep* **7** tightly and firmly ▷ *verb* **8** to go without food, especially for religious reasons ▷ *noun* **9** period of fasting

fasten *verb* to close, do up or fix (something) in place

fastener or **fastening** *noun* device that fastens

fast food *noun* hot food, such as hamburgers, that is prepared and served quickly after you have ordered it

fastidious *adjective* **1** very fussy about details **2** excessively concerned with cleanliness

fast-track *adjective* **1** taking the quickest but most competitive route to success: *fast-track executives*

▷ *verb* **2** to speed up the progress of (a project or person)

fat fatter fattest; fats *adjective* **1** carrying too much weight on your body; overweight **2** (of meat) containing a lot of fat **3** thick ▷ *noun* **4** extra flesh on the body **5** greasy solid or liquid substance obtained from animals or plants and often used in cooking > **fatness** *noun* > **fatty** *adjective* containing fat

fatal *adjective* **1** causing death **2** very damaging; disastrous > **fatally** *adverb*

fatality fatalities *noun* death caused by an accident or disaster

fate *noun* **1** power supposed by some to control events; destiny **2** fortune that awaits a person or thing

fateful *adjective* having an important, often disastrous, effect

father *noun* **1** male parent **2** man who starts, creates or invents something: *the father of Italian painting* **3** **Father a** God **b** form of address for a priest in some Christian churches ▷ *verb* **4** to be the father of (a child) > **fatherhood** *noun*: *the joys of fatherhood* > **fatherly** *adjective*: *a few words of fatherly advice*

father-in-law fathers-in-law *noun* father of your husband or wife

fathom *noun* **1** unit of length, used in navigation, equal to six feet (1.83 metres) ▷ *verb* **2** to understand

fatigue fatigues fatiguing fatigued *noun* **1** extreme physical or mental tiredness **2** weakening of a material due to stress ▷ *verb* **3** to tire out

fatten *verb* to feed (an animal) so that it puts on weight

fatuous *adjective* foolish

faucet *noun* US tap

fault *noun* **1** responsibility for

something wrong **2** weakness, defect or flaw **3** mistake or error **4** *Geology* large crack in rock caused by movement of the earth's crust **5** *Tennis, squash, etc* incorrect and invalid serve ▷ *verb* **6** to criticize > **faultless** *adjective: an almost faultless performance* > **faulty** *adjective: faulty wiring*

fauna *noun* animals of a given place or time

favour *noun* **1** approving attitude **2** act of goodwill or generosity **3** **in someone's favour** of help or advantage to someone **4** **in favour of a** feeling approval for **b** to the benefit of ▷ *verb* **5** to prefer (someone or something) **6** to support or recommend

favourable *adjective* **1** encouraging or advantageous: *a favourable review* **2** useful or beneficial: *favourable weather conditions* **3** giving consent: *They got a favourable response from the bank* > **favourably** *adverb*

favourite *adjective* **1** most liked ▷ *noun* **2** preferred person or thing **3** *Sport* competitor expected to win

favouritism *noun* practice of giving special treatment to a person or group

fawn *adjective* **1** light yellowish-brown ▷ *noun* **2** young deer ▷ *verb* **3** **fawn on** to seek the approval of (someone) by flattering them

fax faxes faxing faxed *noun* **1** exact copy of a document sent electronically along a telephone line **2** electronic system for sending exact copies of documents by telephone ▷ *verb* **3** to send (a document) by this system

FBI *abbreviation US* Federal Bureau of Investigation: the agency of the American Department of Justice that investigates crimes in which American national law is broken

fear *noun* **1** distress or alarm caused by approaching danger or pain **2** thought that something undesirable or unpleasant might happen ▷ *verb* **3** to be afraid of **4** to be afraid (that something may happen) > **fear for** *verb* to feel anxious about the safety of

fearful *adjective* **1** feeling fear **2** *informal* very unpleasant > **fearfully** *adverb*

fearless *adjective* without fear > **fearlessly** *adverb*

fearsome *adjective* terrible or frightening

feasible *adjective* able to be done; possible > **feasibility** *noun: the feasibility of constructing a new bypass* > **feasibly** *adverb*

feast *noun* **1** large and special meal for a lot of people **2** annual religious celebration ▷ *verb* **3** to eat a feast **4** **feast on** to eat a large amount of

feat *noun* impressive and difficult achievement

feather *noun* one of the light fluffy things covering a bird's body > **feathered** *adjective* > **feathery** *adjective*

feature features featuring featured *noun* **1** interesting or important part or characteristic of something **2** part of your face, such as your eyes or nose **3** special article or programme dealing with a particular subject **4** main film in a cinema programme ▷ *verb* **5** to have (someone or something) as a feature or to be a feature in (something) > **featureless** *adjective: a featureless landscape*

February *noun* second month of the year

fed *verb* past of **feed**

federal *adjective* relating to a system

of government in which a group of states is controlled by a central government, but each state has its own local powers

federalism *noun* **1** belief in or support for a federal system of government **2** federal system of government > **federalist** *noun* someone who believes in or supports a federal system of government

federation *noun* group of organizations or states that have joined together for a common purpose

fed up *adjective informal* bored or dissatisfied

fee *noun* charge or payment for a job, service or activity

feeble feebler feeblest *adjective* **1** lacking physical or mental power **2** unconvincing

feed feeds feeding fed *verb* **1** to give food to (a person or animal) **2** to give (something) to (a person or animal) as food **3** to eat **4** to supply (what is needed): *The information was fed into a computer database* > *noun* **5** act of feeding **6** food, especially for babies or animals

feedback *noun* **1** comments and information about the quality or success of something **2** condition in which some of the power, sound or information produced by electronic equipment goes back into it

feel feels feeling felt *verb* **1** to experience (an emotion, sensation or effect of something) **2** to believe **3** to become aware of (something or someone) by touch **4** to touch (something) **5** (of things) to give the impression of being (cold, hard, soft, etc) **6 feel like** to wish for

or want > *noun* **7** way something feels **8** act of feeling **9** impression **10** instinctive aptitude

feeler *noun* organ of touch in some animals; antenna

feeling *noun* **1** emotion or reaction **2** physical sensation **3** ability to experience physical sensations **4** opinion **5** impression **6** sympathy or understanding **7 feelings** emotions or beliefs

feet *noun* plural of **foot**

feign *verb* to pretend to experience (something)

feline *adjective* **1** belonging or relating to the cat family **2** catlike

fell *verb* **1** past tense of **fall 2** to cut down (a tree)

fellow *noun* **1** *old-fashioned* man or boy **2** senior member of a learned society or a university college **3** comrade, associate or person in the same group or condition > *adjective* **4** (of a person) in the same group or condition: *his fellow editors*

fellowship *noun* **1** feeling of friendliness and companionship experienced by those doing something together **2** group with shared aims or interests **3** paid research post in a college or university

felt *verb* **1** past of **feel** > *noun* **2** matted fabric made by bonding fibres by pressure

female *noun* **1** person or animal that belongs to the sex that can have babies or young > *adjective* **2** concerning or relating to females

feminine *adjective* **1** having qualities traditionally regarded as suitable for, or typical of, women **2** relating to women **3** belonging to a particular class of nouns, adjectives, pronouns or endings in some languages > **femininity** noun: Pink emphasizes femininity

feminism noun belief that women should have the same rights and opportunities as men > **feminist** noun, adjective

fen noun Brit low-lying flat marshy land

fence fences fencing fenced noun 1 wooden or wire barrier between two areas of land 2 barrier or hedge for horses to jump over in horse racing or show jumping ▷ verb 3 to surround (an area of land) with a fence 4 to fight with swords as a sport > **fencer** noun

fencing noun sport of fighting with swords

fend verb **fend for yourself** to look after yourself > **fend off** verb to defend yourself against (a verbal or physical attack or attacker)

fender noun 1 low metal frame in front of a fireplace 2 Chiefly US wing of a car

feral adjective wild

ferment noun, verb (of wine, beer or fruit) to change chemically, often producing alcohol > **fermentation** noun: chemicals produced during fermentation

fern noun plant with long feathery leaves and no flowers

ferocious adjective violent and fierce > **ferociously** adverb > **ferocity** noun

ferret noun 1 small fierce animal related to the weasel and kept for hunting rats and rabbits ▷ verb 2 to search around > **ferret out** verb to find out (information) by searching

ferry ferries ferrying ferried noun 1 boat for transporting people and vehicles ▷ verb 2 to carry (people or goods) by ferry

fertile adjective 1 capable of

producing young, crops or vegetation 2 creative: a fertile mind > **fertility** noun

fertilize fertilizes fertilizing fertilized; also spelt **fertilise** verb 1 to cause (an animal or plant) to begin the process of reproduction by supplying sperm or pollen 2 to feed (soil or land) with nutrients > **fertilization** noun

fertilizer or **fertiliser** noun substance added to the soil to improve plant growth

fervent or **fervid** adjective intensely passionate, enthusiastic and sincere > **fervently** adverb

fervour noun very strong feeling for or belief in something

fester verb 1 (of a situation or problem) to grow worse and increasingly hostile 2 (of a wound) to become infected and form pus

festival noun 1 organized series of events or performances 2 day or period of celebration

festive adjective full of happiness and celebration

festivity festivities noun happy celebration

festooned adjective **festooned with** adorned with

fetch fetches fetching fetched verb 1 to go to get (someone or something) 2 to be sold for (a sum of money)

fetching adjective attractive

fete fetes feting feted; also spelt **fête** noun 1 outdoor event with competitions, displays and goods for sale ▷ verb 2 to honour or entertain (someone) regally

fetid adjective stinking

fetter noun chain or shackle for the foot

fetus another spelling of **foetus**

feud noun 1 long-term and very

bitter quarrel, especially between families ▷ *verb* **2** to carry on a feud

feudalism *noun* social and political system that was common in the Middle Ages in Europe. Under this system, ordinary people were given land and protection by a lord, and in return they worked and fought for him > **feudal** *adjective* relating to or resembling feudalism

fever *noun* **1** (illness causing) high body temperature **2** nervous excitement

feverish *adjective* **1** suffering from fever **2** in a state of nervous excitement > **feverishly** *adverb*

few *adjective, pronoun* **1** not many **2** **a few** a small number (of) **3** **quite a few** or **a good few** several

> You use *few* and *fewer* to talk about things that can be counted: *fewer than five visits.* When you are talking about amounts that can't be counted you should use *little* and *less*: *less work*

fiancé *noun* man engaged to be married

fiancée *noun* woman engaged to be married

fiasco fiascos *noun* event or attempt that fails completely, especially in a ridiculous or disorganized way

fib fibs fibbing fibbed *noun* **1** small unimportant lie ▷ *verb* **2** to tell a small lie

fibre *noun* **1** thread that can be spun into yarn **2** part of plants that can be eaten but not digested and that helps food pass quickly through the body > **fibrous** *adjective*

fickle *adjective* changeable or inconstant

fiction *noun* **1** stories about people and events that have been invented

by the author **2** invented story

fictional *adjective* (of a character or event) existing only in fiction

fictitious *adjective* **1** not genuine; made up **2** (of a character or event) existing only in fiction

fiddle fiddles fiddling fiddled *verb* **1** (often followed by *with*) to move or touch something restlessly **2** to falsify (accounts) ▷ *noun* **3** *informal* dishonest action or scheme **4** violin > **fiddler** *noun*

fiddly fiddlier fiddliest *adjective* awkward to do or use

fidelity *noun* faithfulness

fidget *verb* **1** to move about restlessly ▷ *noun* **2** someone who fidgets > **fidgety** *adjective*

field *noun* **1** enclosed piece of land where crops are grown or animals are kept **2** marked-off area for sports: *a hockey field* **3** area rich in a specified natural resource: *an oil field* **4** subject or area of interest; sphere ▷ *verb* **5** *Sport* to catch and return (a ball) **6** to deal with (a question) successfully

field day *noun* **have a field day** to have a pleasant time doing something that you have been given the opportunity to do

fielder *noun* *Sport* player whose task is to field the ball

field events *plural noun* throwing and jumping events in athletics

field marshal *noun* army officer of the highest rank

field sports *plural noun* hunting, shooting and fishing

fieldwork *noun* study of something in the environment where it naturally lives or occurs, rather than in a class or laboratory

fiend *noun* **1** evil spirit **2** cruel or wicked person **3** *informal* person devoted to something: *a fitness fiend*

fierce fiercer fiercest *adjective*
1 wild or aggressive **2** intense
or strong > **fiercely** *adverb*
> **fierceness** *noun*

fiery fierier fieriest *adjective*
1 consisting of or like fire **2** showing
great anger, energy or passion

fifteen *adjective, noun* the number 15
> **fifteenth** *adjective, noun*

fifth *adjective, noun* **1** (coming as)
number 5 in a series ▷ *noun* **2** one of
five equal parts

fifty fifties *adjective, noun* the
number 50 > **fiftieth** *adjective, noun*

fifty-fifty *adverb* **1** divided equally
into two portions ▷ *adjective*
2 just as likely not to happen as to
happen: *You've got a fifty-fifty chance
of being right*

fig *noun* **1** soft sweet fruit full of tiny
seeds. It grows in hot countries and
is often eaten dried **2** tree bearing it

fight fights fighting fought *verb*
1 to take part in a battle, a war, a
boxing match or some other form
of physical combat **2** to battle
against (someone) **3** to struggle
to overcome someone or obtain
something **4** to carry on (a battle
or contest) **5** to make (your way)
somewhere with difficulty ▷ *noun*
6 situation in which people
hit or try to hurt each other
7 determined attempt to prevent
or achieve something: *the fight for
independence* > **fighter** *noun* **1** boxer
2 determined person **3** aircraft
designed to destroy other aircraft
> **fight off** *verb* **1** to drive away (an
attacker) **2** to struggle to avoid

figment *noun* **figment of your
imagination** imaginary thing

figure figures figuring figured
noun **1** written number **2** amount
expressed in numbers **3** *Maths*
geometrical shape **4** diagram or

table in a written text **5** shape
of a person whom you cannot
see clearly **6** shape of your body
7 person **8** representation in
painting or sculpture of a human
form ▷ *verb* **9** (usually followed by
in) to be included (in) **10** *informal*
to guess or conclude > **figure
out** *verb* to solve (something)
or to understand (something or
someone)

figurative *adjective* (of language)
abstract, imaginative or symbolic
> **figuratively** *adverb*

figurehead *noun* **1** someone who is
the leader in name of a movement
or organization but who has no real
power **2** carved wooden model of a
person or creature decorating the
front of a sailing ship

**figure of speech figures of
speech** *noun* expression such as a
simile or idiom in which words do
not have their literal meaning

filament *noun* fine wire in a light
bulb that gives out light

file files filing filed *noun* **1** box or
folder used to keep documents
in order **2** documents in a file
3 information about a person
or subject **4** line of people one
behind the other **5** *Computers*
organized collection of related
material **6** tool with a rough
surface, used for smoothing or
shaping hard material ▷ *verb* **7** to
place (a document) in a file **8** to
place (a legal document) on an
official record **9** to bring a lawsuit,
especially for divorce **10** to walk
or march in a line **11** to smooth or
shape (something) with a file

fill *verb* **1** to make (something) full or
to become full **2** to occupy (a space
or gap) completely **3** to plug (a gap)
4 to satisfy (a need) **5** to hold and

perform the duties of (a position)
6 to appoint someone to (a job or
position) ▷ *noun* **7 have your fill**
to have enough for your needs or
wants > **fill in** *verb* **1** to complete (a
form) **2** to update (someone)

fillet *noun* **1** boneless piece of meat
or fish ▷ *verb* **2** to remove the bones
from (meat or fish)

filling *noun* **1** soft food mixture
inside a sandwich, cake or pie
2 small amount of metal or
plastic put into a hole in a tooth
by a dentist ▷ *adjective* **3** (of food)
substantial and satisfying

filly fillies *noun* young female horse

film *noun* **1** series of moving pictures
projected onto a screen and shown
at the cinema or on television
2 thin flexible strip of plastic used
in a camera to record images when
exposed to light **3** thin sheet or
layer ▷ *verb* **4** to record (someone or
something) using a movie or video
camera **5** to make a film of (a scene,
story, etc) ▷ *adjective* **6** connected
with films or the cinema

filter *noun* **1** device that allows some
substances, lights or sounds to pass
through it, but not others ▷ *verb*
2 to pass (a substance) through
a filter **3** to pass slowly or faintly
> **filtration** *noun*

filth *noun* **1** disgusting dirt
2 offensive material or language
> **filthy** *adjective*

fin *noun* **1** a thin flat structure
sticking out of a fish's body and
helping it to balance and swim
2 part of the tail of an aircraft that
sticks up

final *adjective* **1** last in a series
or happening at the end of
something **2** (of a decision) having
no possibility of further change,
action or discussion ▷ *noun* **3** the

last game or contest in a series
which decides the overall winner
4 finals last and most important
examinations in a university or
college course

finale *noun* last section of a piece of
music or show

finalist *noun* competitor in a final

**finalize finalizes finalizing
finalized**; also spelt **finalise** *verb* to
complete the remaining details of
(something)

finally *adverb* **1** eventually or at last
2 lastly or in conclusion

**finance finances financing
financed** *verb* **1** to provide or obtain
funds for (a project, purchase)
▷ *noun* **2** management of money,
loans or investments **3** funds for
paying for something **4 finances**
money resources

financial *adjective* relating to or
involving money > **financially**
adverb

financial year *noun* specific period
of twelve months according to
which budgets, profits and other
financial matters are planned
and assessed. In Britain the main
financial year starts on 5th April

financier *noun* person or
organization providing the funds
for a project or for business

finch finches *noun* small songbird
with a short strong beak

find finds finding found *verb*
1 to discover or come across
(something or someone) by chance
or after a search **2** to become aware
of or realize **3** to consider (someone
or something) to have a particular
quality **4** *Law* to pronounce (the
defendant) guilty or not guilty **5** to
provide (money or time), especially
with difficulty ▷ *noun* **6** valuable
or useful person or thing > **finder**

noun > **find out** *verb* **1** to learn or discover (something), either by chance or after research **2** to learn about something bad, criminal or negligent done by (someone)

findings *plural noun* conclusions from an investigation

fine finer finest; fines fining fined *adjective* **1** very good **2** (of weather) clear and dry **3** in good health **4** satisfactory **5** of delicate workmanship **6** very narrow or thin **7** subtle or abstruse: *a fine distinction* **8** (of a net or sieve) having very small holes **9** (of dust or powder) consisting of very small particles ▷ *adverb* **10** very well ▷ *noun* **11** payment imposed as a penalty or punishment ▷ *verb* **12** to impose a fine on (a person or organization)

finery *noun* very beautiful clothing and jewellery

finesse *noun* **1** delicate skill **2** subtlety and tact

finger *noun* **1** one of the four long jointed parts of the hand **2** part of a glove that covers a finger ▷ *verb* **3** to touch or handle (something) with your fingers

fingernail *noun* any of the hard coverings on the upper part of the ends of your fingers

fingerprint *noun* mark made showing the pattern on the skin at the tip of a person's finger

finish *verb* **1** to reach the end (of) **2** to come to an end or stop **3** to use (something) up ▷ *noun* **4** end or last part **5** texture or appearance of the surface of something

finite *adjective* having limits in space, time or size

Finn *noun* someone from Finland

Finnish *adjective* **1** belonging or relating to Finland ▷ *noun* **2** the main language spoken in Finland

fir *noun* tall pointed evergreen tree that has needle-like leaves and produces cones

fire fires firing fired *noun* **1** flames produced when something burns **2** pile or mass of burning material **3** piece of equipment used as a heater **4** incident involving unwanted destructive burning **5** shooting of guns **6** **open fire** to begin shooting ▷ *verb* **7** to operate (a weapon) so that a bullet or missile is released **8** *informal* to dismiss from employment **9** to bake (ceramics etc) in a kiln

firearm *noun* gun

fire brigade *noun* organized body of people whose job is to put out fires

fire engine *noun* vehicle carrying equipment for putting out fires

fire escape *noun* metal staircase or ladder down the outside of a building for escape in the event of fire

fire extinguisher *noun* metal cylinder containing water or foam for spraying onto a fire to put it out

firefighter *noun* member of a fire brigade

firefly fireflies *noun* insect that glows in the dark

fireplace *noun* opening beneath a chimney where a fire can be lit

fireproof *adjective* resistant to fire

fire station *noun* building where firefighters are stationed

firewall *noun* *Computers* system that prevents unauthorized access to a computer from the Internet

firework *noun* small container of gunpowder and other chemicals which explodes and produces spectacular explosions and coloured sparks when lit

firing squad *noun* group of

soldiers ordered to shoot a person condemned to death

firm *adjective* **1** not soft or yielding **2** securely in position **3** definite **4** having or showing determination and authority ▷ *adverb* **5** in an unyielding manner: *hold firm* ▷ *noun* **6** business; company > **firmly** *adverb* > **firmness** *noun*

first *adjective* **1** earliest in time or order **2** graded or ranked above all others ▷ *noun* **3** person or thing coming before all others **4** outset or beginning **5** first-class honours degree at university **6** lowest forward gear in a car or other vehicle ▷ *adverb* **7** before anything else **8** for the first time > **firstly** *adverb*

first aid *noun* immediate medical assistance given to an injured person

first-class *adjective* **1** of the highest quality or standard **2** *Travel* (of a ticket, seat or accommodation) relating to the best and most expensive facilities **3** (of postage) quicker but more expensive

first cousin *noun* son or daughter of your uncle or aunt

first-hand *adjective* **1** obtained directly from the original source ▷ *adverb* **2** directly from the original source

First Lady First Ladies *noun* the wife of the president of a country

first person *noun Grammar* the *I* or *we* form of a pronoun or verb

first-rate *adjective* excellent

fiscal *adjective* of government or public money, especially taxes

fish fishes fishing fished *noun* **1** cold-blooded creature living in water that has a spine, gills, fins and a scaly skin **2** the flesh of such a creature eaten as food ▷ *verb* **3** to

try to catch fish **4** **fish for** to try to get (information) in an indirect way > **fishing** *noun*

▎ The plural of *fish* can be either *fish* or *fishes*, but *fish* is more common

fisherman fishermen *noun* person who catches fish for a living or for pleasure

fishery fisheries *noun* area of the sea used for fishing

fishmonger *noun* seller of fish

fishnet *noun* open mesh fabric resembling netting

fish slice *noun* kitchen tool with a broad flat slatted blade attached to a long handle

fishy fishier fishiest *adjective* **1** smelling of fish **2** *informal* suspicious or questionable

fission *noun* **1** splitting **2** (also **nuclear fission**) splitting of an atomic nucleus with the release of a large amount of energy

fissure *noun* deep crack, especially in rock

fist *noun* clenched hand with the fingers curled tightly towards the palm

fit fits fitting fitted; fitter fittest *verb* **1** to be of the correct size or shape (for) **2** to fix or put (something) in place **3** to be appropriate or suitable for (a situation, person or thing) **4** to correspond with the facts or circumstances **5** to adjust (something) to make it the right size and shape ▷ *noun* **6** way in which something fits **7** sudden attack or convulsion, such as an epileptic seizure **8** sudden short burst or spell of laughter, coughing or panic ▷ *adjective* **9** suitable or appropriate **10** in good health **11** worthy or deserving > **fit in**

verb **1** to make a place or time for (someone or something) **2** to conform or manage to belong > **fitness** *noun* > **fit out** *verb* to provide (someone or something) with the necessary equipment

fitful *adjective* happening at irregular intervals and not continuous > **fitfully** *adverb*

fitter *noun* person who assembles or installs machinery

fitting *adjective* **1** appropriate or suitable ▷ *noun* **2** accessory or part **3** session trying on clothes that are being adjusted to ensure a correct fit **4 fittings** furnishings and accessories in a building

five *adjective, noun* the number 5

fix fixes fixing fixed *verb* **1** to mend or repair **2** to place permanently **3** to settle definitely **4** to direct (your attention) steadily **5** to arrange or organize **6** *informal* to influence the outcome of (something) unfairly ▷ *noun* **7** *informal* **a** difficult situation **b** unfair or dishonest arrangement **c** injection of a drug such as heroin > **fixed** *adjective* > **fixedly** *adverb* steadily > **fix up** *verb* **1** to arrange **2** (followed by *with*) to provide (someone) with

fixation *noun* extreme and obsessive interest in something

fixture *noun* **1** permanently fitted piece of household equipment **2** sports match or the date fixed for it

fizz fizzes fizzing fizzed *verb* **1** to make a hissing or bubbling noise **2** to give off small bubbles

fizzle fizzles fizzling fizzled *verb* to make a weak hissing or bubbling sound > **fizzle out** *verb informal* to come to nothing or fail

fizzy fizzier fizziest *adjective*

(of drink) bubbly, owing to the presence of carbon dioxide

fjord *noun* long narrow inlet of the sea between cliffs, especially in Norway

flab *noun informal* unsightly body fat

flabbergasted *adjective* completely astonished

flabby flabbier flabbiest *adjective* having flabby flesh

flaccid *adjective* soft and limp > **flaccidity** *noun*

flag flags flagging flagged *noun* **1** rectangular or square cloth which has a particular colour and design, and is used as the symbol of a nation or as a signal **2** (also **flagstone**) flat paving-stone ▷ *verb* **3** to lose enthusiasm or vigour **4** to mark with a flag or sticker > **flag down** *verb* to signal (a vehicle) to stop by waving your arm

flagon *noun* large wide bottle or a narrow-necked jug for wine or cider

flagrant *adjective* openly outrageous > **flagrantly** *adverb*

flagship *noun* ship carrying the commander of the fleet

flagstone *noun* flat paving-stone

flail *verb* to wave about wildly

flair *noun* **1** natural ability **2** stylishness

flak *noun* **1** anti-aircraft fire **2** *informal* severe criticism

flake flakes flaking flaked *noun* **1** small thin piece, especially chipped off something ▷ *verb* **2** to peel off in flakes > **flaked** *adjective*: *flaked almonds* > **flake out** *verb informal* to collapse or fall asleep from exhaustion > **flaky** *adjective*: *flaky pastry*

flamboyant *adjective* **1** behaving in a very noticeable, extravagant way **2** very bright and showy > **flamboyance** *noun*

flame *noun* **1** luminous burning gas coming from burning material **2 old flame** *informal* former boyfriend or girlfriend

flamenco *noun* type of rhythmical Spanish dancing or the guitar music that accompanies it

flamingo flamingos or **flamingoes** *noun* long-legged wading bird with pink or white feathers and a long neck

flammable *adjective* easily set on fire

flan *noun* open sweet or savoury tart with a pastry or cake base

flank *noun* **1** part of the side between the hips and ribs ▷ *verb* **2** to be at or to move along the side of

flannel *noun* **1** *Brit* small piece of cloth for washing your face **2** soft woollen fabric for clothing **3 flannels** trousers made of flannel

flap flaps flapping flapped *verb* **1** to move back and forwards or up and down with a snapping sound ▷ *noun* **2** action or sound of flapping **3** piece of something such as paper, fabric or skin, attached by one edge only

flapjack *noun* chewy biscuit made with oats

flare flares flaring flared *noun* **1** device that produces a brightly coloured flame, used especially as an emergency signal **2 flares** flared trousers ▷ *verb* **3** to start to burn much more vigorously **4** *informal* (of temper, violence or trouble) to break out suddenly **5** (of a skirt or trousers) to become wider towards the bottom **> flared** *adjective* (of a skirt or trousers) becoming wider towards the bottom

flash flashes flashing flashed *noun* **1** sudden short burst of light or flame **2** burst (of intuition or emotion) **3** very short time **4** brief unscheduled news announcement ▷ *verb* **5** to give out or to cause (a torch, headlight, etc) to give out light suddenly or repeatedly **6** to move very fast **7** *informal* to show (something) briefly or arrogantly

flashback *noun* scene in a book, play or film that returns to earlier events

flashlight *noun* *US* torch

flashpoint *noun* critical point beyond which a situation will inevitably erupt into violence

flashy flashier flashiest *adjective* expensive-looking and showy, in a vulgar way

flask *noun* **1** container for keeping drinks hot **2** flat bottle for carrying alcoholic drink in the pocket

flat flats flatting flatted; flatter flattest *noun* **1** self-contained set of rooms, usually on one level, for living in **2** *Music* note or key a semitone lower than that described by the same letter. It is represented by the symbol (♭) **3** punctured tyre **4** mud bank exposed at low tide ▷ *verb* **5** *Aust, NZ* to live in a flat **6 go flatting** *NZ* to leave home and live with others in a shared house or flat ▷ *adjective* **7** level and horizontal **8** even and smooth **9** (of a tyre or ball) deflated **10** outright **11** (of a rate, fee, etc) fixed **12** without variation or emotion **13** (of a drink) no longer fizzy **14** (of a battery) with no electrical charge **15** *Music* below the true pitch ▷ *adverb* **16** in or into a flat position **17** completely or absolutely **18** *Music* too low in pitch **> flatly** *adverb* **> flatness** *noun*

flatfish *noun* sea fish, such as the sole, which has a flat body

▮ The plural of *flatfish* is *flatfish*

flathead *noun* common Australian

edible fish

flatten *verb* to become or make (something) flat or flatter

flatter *verb* 1 to praise (someone) insincerely 2 to make (someone) appear more attractive 3 **flatter yourself** to believe something good about yourself that others doubt > **flattered** *adjective* feeling pleased and special > **flattering** *adjective*: *a flattering colour*

flattery *noun* flattering words or behaviour

flatulence *noun* condition of having too much gas in your stomach or intestines

flaunt *verb* to display (yourself or your possessions) arrogantly

flautist *noun* flute player

flavour *noun* 1 distinctive taste 2 distinctive characteristic or quality ▷ *verb* 3 to add flavour to (food) > **flavouring** *noun* substance used to flavour food

flaw *noun* 1 fault or mark 2 mistake that makes a plan or argument invalid > **flawed** *adjective* > **flawless** *adjective*

flax *noun* plant used for making rope and cloth

flay flays flaying flayed *verb* 1 to strip the skin off (a dead animal) 2 to criticize (someone) severely

flea *noun* small wingless jumping bloodsucking insect

fleck *noun* small mark, streak or speck > **flecked** *adjective*: *The wall was flecked with blood*

fled *verb* past of **flee**

fledgling *noun* 1 young bird ▷ *adjective* 2 new or inexperienced

flee flees fleeing fled *verb* to run away (from)

fleece fleeces fleecing fleeced *noun* 1 sheep's coat of wool 2 sheepskin used as a lining

for coats etc 3 warm polyester fabric 4 *Brit* jacket or top made of this fabric ▷ *verb* 5 to defraud or overcharge (someone)

fleet *noun* group of ships or vehicles owned by the same organization or travelling together

fleeting *adjective* lasting for a very short time > **fleetingly** *adverb*

Flemish *noun* language spoken in many parts of Belgium

flesh *noun* 1 soft part of a human or animal body 2 *informal* excess fat 3 thick soft part of a fruit or vegetable 4 human body as opposed to the soul > **fleshy** *adjective* 1 plump 2 like flesh

flew *verb* past tense of **fly**

flex flexes flexing flexed *noun* 1 flexible insulated electric cable ▷ *verb* 2 to bend (your muscles)

flexible *adjective* 1 easily bent 2 adaptable > **flexibility** *noun*

flick *verb* 1 to move (something) with a quick jerk of your finger 2 to move with a short sudden movement, often repeatedly ▷ *noun* 3 quick or sharp movement

flicker *verb* 1 to shine unsteadily or intermittently ▷ *noun* 2 unsteady brief light 3 momentary feeling

flier *noun* same as **flyer**

flight *noun* 1 journey by air 2 act or manner of flying through the air 3 ability to fly 4 aircraft flying on a scheduled journey 5 set of stairs between two landings 6 act of running away

flight attendant *noun* person who looks after passengers on an aircraft

flightless *adjective* (of certain birds or insects) unable to fly

flimsy flimsier flimsiest *adjective* 1 not strong or substantial 2 thin 3 not very convincing

flinch flinches flinching flinched
verb to draw back or wince, as
from pain

fling flings flinging flung *verb*
1 to throw, send or move forcefully
or hurriedly ▷ *noun* **2** spell of
self-indulgent enjoyment **3** brief
romantic or sexual relationship

flint *noun* **1** hard grey stone **2** piece
of this

flip flips flipping flipped *verb* **1** to
turn (something small or light) over
or move (something) with a quick
movement **2** to hit (something)
sharply with your finger or thumb
▷ **flip through** *verb* to look at (a
book or magazine) quickly or idly

flip-flop *noun Brit, S Afr* rubber-soled
sandal held on by a strip of rubber,
plastic, etc between the big toe and
the next toe

flippant *adjective* showing an
inappropriate lack of seriousness
▷ **flippancy** *noun*

flipper *noun* **1** broad flat limb of a
sea animal adapted for swimming
2 one of a pair of broad flat pieces of
rubber that you can attach to your
feet to help you swim

flirt *verb* **1** to behave as if sexually
attracted to someone but without
serious intentions ▷ *noun* **2** person
who flirts ▷ **flirtation** *noun*
▷ **flirtatious** *adjective* ▷ **flirt with**
verb to consider lightly; toy with

flit flits flitting flitted *verb*
1 *informal* to depart hurriedly and
secretly ▷ *noun* **2** act of flitting

float *verb* **1** to be supported by a
liquid **2** to move lightly and freely,
supported by the air **3** to launch
(a company) as a public company,
with shares available on the stock
market ▷ *noun* **4** light object used
to help someone or something
float **5** indicator on a fishing line

that moves when a fish bites
6 decorated truck in a procession
7 *Brit* small delivery vehicle **8** *Aust*
vehicle for transporting horses
9 sum of money used for minor
expenses or to provide change
▷ **floating** *adjective* **1** moving about
or changing: *a floating population*
2 (of a voter) not committed to
one party

flock *noun* **1** group (of birds, sheep
or goats) **2** *Christianity* congregation

flog flogs flogging flogged *verb*
1 to beat (someone) with a whip or
stick **2** *Brit, NZ, S Afr informal* to sell
3 *NZ informal* to steal ▷ **flogging**
noun

flood *noun* **1** large amount of water
covering an area that is usually
dry ▷ *verb* **2** to cover (something)
or to become covered with water
3 to come in large numbers or
quantities

floodgates *plural noun* **open the
floodgates** to give a lot of people
the opportunity suddenly to do
something they could not do before

floodlight *noun* powerful outdoor
lamp used to light up public
buildings and sports grounds
▷ **floodlit** *adjective*

floor *noun* **1** the part of a room you
walk on **2** one of the levels of a
building **3** flat bottom surface of
something **4** (right to speak in)
a legislative hall ▷ *verb* **5** *informal*
(of remark or question) to cause
(someone) to be disconcerted and
unable to respond adequately

floorboard *noun* one of the long
planks of wood from which a floor
is made

flop flops flopping flopped *verb*
1 to bend, fall or collapse loosely or
carelessly **2** *informal* to fail ▷ *noun*
3 *informal* failure

floppy floppier floppiest
adjective tending to hang loosely
downwards

floppy disk or **disc** *noun* Computers
flexible magnetic disk on which
computer data is stored

flora *noun* plants of a given place
or time

floral *adjective* made from or
decorated with flowers

florid *adjective* **1** highly elaborate
and extravagant; ornate: *florid
language* **2** with a red or flushed
complexion

florist *noun* person or shop selling
flowers

floss *noun* **1** see **dental floss** **2** fine
silky fibres

flotation *noun* **1** launching of a
business enterprise as a public
company, with shares available on
the stock market **2** act of floating

flotilla *noun* small fleet or fleet of
small ships

flotsam *noun* wreckage or rubbish
floating at sea or washed up on
the shore

**flounce flounces flouncing
flounced** *verb* **1** to walk with
exaggerated movements
suggesting anger or impatience
about something: *She flounced out of
the office* ▷ *noun* **2** ornamental frill

**flounder flounders floundering
floundered** *verb* **1** to move with
difficulty, as in mud **2** to find it
difficult to decide what to do or say
▷ *noun* **3** edible flatfish

flour *noun* powder made by grinding
grain, usually wheat, and used
for baking and cooking > **floured**
adjective > **floury** *adjective*

**flourish flourishes flourishing
flourished** *verb* **1** to be active,
successful, healthy or widespread
2 to wave (something) dramatically

▷ *noun* **3** bold sweeping or waving
motion > **flourishing** *adjective*:
Business is flourishing

flout *verb* to deliberately disobey (a
rule, law, etc)

flow *verb* **1** (of liquid) to move in a
stream **2** (of blood or electricity) to
circulate **3** to hang loosely ▷ *noun*
4 act, rate or manner of flowing
5 continuous stream of something

flow chart *noun* diagram showing
the sequence of steps that lead to
various results

flower *noun* **1** part of a plant
containing the reproductive
organs from which the fruit or
seeds develop **2** plant grown for
its colourful flowers ▷ *verb* **3** to
produce flowers; bloom

flowery *adjective* (of language or
style) elaborate

flown *verb* past participle of **fly**

flu *noun* illness similar to a very bad
cold, which causes headaches,
sore throat, weakness and aching
muscles; short for **influenza**

**fluctuate fluctuates fluctuating
fluctuated** *verb* to change
frequently and erratically: *fluctuating
between feeling well and not so well*

flue *noun* passage or pipe which
takes fumes and smoke away from
a stove or boiler

fluent *adjective* **1** able to speak a
foreign language correctly and
without hesitation **2** able to
speak or write easily and without
hesitation **3** spoken or written with
ease > **fluency** *noun* > **fluently**
adverb

fluff *noun* **1** mass of soft light woolly
threads or fibres ▷ *verb* **2** (often
followed by *up*) to brush or shake
(something) to make it seem larger
and lighter > **fluffy** *adjective*

fluid *noun* **1** liquid ▷ *adjective* **2** (of

movement) smooth and flowing
> **fluidity** *noun*

fluke *noun* accidental success or stroke of luck

flung *verb* past of **fling**

fluorescent *adjective* **1** having a very bright appearance when light is shone on it, as if it is shining itself: *fluorescent yellow dye* **2** (of a light or lamp) in the form of a tube and shining with a hard bright light

fluoride *noun* mixture of chemicals that is meant to prevent tooth decay

flurry flurries *noun* short rush of activity or movement

flush flushes flushing flushed *verb* **1** to blush or to cause (someone) to blush **2** to send water through (a toilet or pipe) so as to clean it **3** to drive (someone or something) out of a hiding place ▷ *noun* **4** rosy red colour; blush **5** pleasure and excitement **6** (in card games) hand all of one suit ▷ *adjective* **7** level with the surrounding surface **8** *informal* having plenty of money > **flushed** *adjective*

fluster *verb* **1** to make (someone) confused and nervous by rushing them ▷ *noun* **2** confused and nervous state > **flustered** *adjective* confused, nervous and rushed

flute *noun* **1** wind instrument consisting of a tube with sound holes and a hole for blowing across. It is held sideways **2** tall narrow wineglass

fluted *adjective* having decorative grooves

flutter *verb* **1** to flap or wave with small quick movements **2** to move (something) quickly and irregularly **3** (of the heart) to beat abnormally quickly ▷ *noun* **4** nervous agitation

5 *informal* small bet

flux *noun* state of constant change

fly flies flying flew flown *noun* **1** insect with two pairs of wings **2** (*often plural*) *Brit* fastening at the front of trousers **3** (also **fly sheet**) flap forming the entrance to a tent ▷ *verb* **4** to move through the air on wings or in an aircraft **5** to pilot (a plane) **6** to float, flutter or be displayed in the air **7** to transport (someone or something) or to be transported by air **8** to move quickly or suddenly **9** (of time) to pass rapidly **10** to flee ▷ *adjective* **11** *informal* sharp and cunning > **flying** *adjective, noun*

flyer or **flier** *noun* **1** small advertising leaflet **2** aviator

fly-fishing *noun* method of freshwater fishing using imitation flies as bait

flying *adjective* hurried and brief

flying fox flying foxes *noun* **1** large fruit-eating bat, found in Australia and Africa **2** *Aust, NZ* cable car used to carry people over rivers and gorges

flying saucer *noun* unidentified disc-shaped flying object, supposedly from outer space

flyover *noun* structure carrying one road over another at a junction or intersection

foal *noun* **1** young horse ▷ *verb* **2** to give birth to a foal

foam *noun* **1** mass of tiny bubbles **2** light spongy material used, for example, in furniture or packaging ▷ *verb* **3** to produce foam

fob off fobs off fobbing off fobbed off *verb* to stop (someone) asking questions or complaining by offering excuses, telling them half truths or giving them something of inferior quality

focal *adjective* **1** of or at a focus **2** very important

focal point *noun* the part of something that receives most attention

focus focuses or **focusses focusing** or **focussing focused** or **focussed; focuses** or **foci** *verb* **1** to adjust (your eyes, a camera or a lens, etc) in order to see or view something clearly **2 focus on a** to concentrate on **b** to look at ▷ *noun* **3** centre of interest or activity

> When *focuses* is a plural noun, always spell it with a single s in the middle. When it is a verb form, you can alternatively spell it with a double s

focus group *noun* group of people gathered by a market-research company to discuss and assess a product or service

fodder *noun* food for farm animals or horses

foe *noun* enemy

foetus foetuses; also spelt **fetus** *noun* an unborn child or animal in the womb ▷ **foetal** *adjective*

fog fogs fogging fogged *noun* **1** thick mist of water droplets suspended in the air ▷ *verb* **2** (often followed by *up*) to cover or become covered with steam ▷ **foggy** *adjective*: *a foggy morning*

foible *noun* minor weakness or slight peculiarity in a person's character

foil foils foiling foiled *verb* **1** to ruin (someone's plan) ▷ *noun* **2** metal in a thin sheet, especially for wrapping food **3** anything or anyone that shows up the qualities of something or someone else by contrast **4** thin light sword with a button on the tip, used in fencing

foist *verb* (followed by *on* or *upon*) to force or impose (something) on

fold *verb* **1** to bend (something) so that one part covers another **2** to cross (your arms) **3** *Cooking* to mix gently **4** *informal* (of a business) to fail or go bankrupt ▷ *noun* **5** mark, crease or hollow made by folding **6** folded piece or part **7** small enclosed area for sheep **8** church or its members

folder *noun* piece of folded cardboard for holding loose papers

foliage *noun* leaves

folk *noun* **1** people in general **2** race of people ▷ *plural* **3** *informal* relatives ▷ *adjective* **4** (of music, dance or art) traditional or representative of the ordinary local people

folklore *noun* traditional stories and beliefs of a community

follicle *noun* small pouchlike structure or cavity in the body, especially one from which a hair grows

follow *verb* **1** to go or come after **2** to be a logical or natural consequence of **3** to keep to the course, track or direction of (a road, river or sign) **4** to act in accordance with (instructions or advice) **5** to accept the ideas or beliefs of **6** to understand (an explanation, plot or story) **7** to have a keen interest in (something) **8** to be true or logical in consequence ▷ **follow up** *verb* **1** to investigate (a matter, suggestion or discovery) **2** to do a second, often similar, thing after (a first)

follower *noun* disciple or supporter

following *adjective* **1** about to be mentioned **2** next in time ▷ *noun* **3** group of supporters ▷ *preposition* **4** as a result of

folly follies *noun* **1** foolishness **2** foolish action or idea **3** useless extravagant building

foment *verb* to encourage or stir up (trouble)

fond *adjective* 1 tender or loving 2 (of hope or belief) foolish 3 **fond of** having a liking for > **fondly** *adverb* > **fondness** *noun*

fondle fondles fondling fondled *verb* to stroke tenderly

font *noun* 1 bowl in a church that holds water for baptisms 2 set of printing type of one style and size

food *noun* 1 what people and animals eat 2 substance that provides nourishment for plants

food chain *noun* a series of living things which are linked because each one feeds on the next one in the series. For example, a plant may be eaten by a rabbit which may be eaten by a fox

foodstuff *noun* substance used as food

food technology *noun* study of foods, what they consist of and their effect on the body

fool *noun* 1 person who behaves in a silly or stupid way 2 dessert of puréed fruit mixed with cream ▷ *verb* 3 to deceive (someone)

foolhardy *adjective* recklessly adventurous > **foolhardiness** *noun*: *the foolhardiness of travelling across the world by bike*

foolish *adjective* unwise, silly or absurd > **foolishly** *adverb* > **foolishness** *noun*: *He felt ashamed of his foolishness*

foolproof *adjective* unable to fail

foot feet; foots footing footed *noun* 1 part of the leg below the ankle 2 lowest part of anything: *the foot of the mountain* 3 unit of length equal to twelve inches or about 30.5 centimetres 4 *Poetry* basic unit of rhythm containing two or three syllables ▷ *adjective* 5 (of a brake, pedal or pump) operated by your foot ▷ *verb* 6 **foot the bill** to pay the entire cost 7 **foot it** *informal* to walk

footage *noun* amount or length of film

football *noun* 1 any of various games in which the ball can be kicked, such as soccer, rugby, Australian Rules and American football 2 ball used in any of these games > **footballer** *noun*

footfall *noun* sound of a footstep

foothills *plural noun* hills at the foot of a mountain

foothold *noun* 1 place where you can put your foot when climbing 2 secure position from which progress may be made

footing *noun* 1 secure grip by or for the feet 2 basis or foundation of a relationship or situation

footman footmen *noun* male servant in a large house who wears a uniform

footnote *noun* note printed at the foot of a page

footpath *noun* 1 narrow path for walkers only 2 *Aust* raised space alongside a road, for pedestrians

footprint *noun* mark left by a foot

footstep *noun* 1 step taken when walking 2 sound made by walking

for *preposition* 1 indicating the person or thing receiving or benefiting from something: *a gift for you* 2 indicating the destination of something: *the train for Liverpool* 3 indicating a length of time or distance: *for three weeks; for five miles* 4 indicating the reason, cause or purpose of something: *This is my excuse for going to Italy* 5 indicating the person or thing represented by someone: *playing for his country*

forage forages foraging foraged

verb to search about (for food)

foray forays *noun* **1** brief attempt to do or get something **2** brief raid or attack

forbid forbids forbidding forbade forbidden *verb* to prohibit or refuse to allow: *He forbade her to leave the house* > **forbidden** *adjective*

force forces forcing forced *verb* **1** to make (someone) do something; compel **2** to break open ▷ *noun* **3** strength or power **4** compulsion **5** *Physics* pushing or pulling influence that changes a body from a state of rest to one of motion, or changes its rate of motion **6** mental or moral strength **7** person or thing with strength or influence **8** vehemence or intensity **9** group of people organized for a particular task or duty **10 in force a** having legal validity **b** in great numbers

forceful *adjective* powerful and convincing > **forcefully** *adverb*

forceps *plural noun* pair of long tongs or pincers used by a doctor

forcible *adjective* **1** involving physical force or violence **2** strong and convincing > **forcibly** *adverb*

ford *noun* **1** shallow place where a river may be crossed ▷ *verb* **2** to cross (a river) at a ford

fore *adjective* **1** in, at or towards the front ▷ *noun* **2 come to the fore** to become important or popular: *Environmental issues have come to the fore lately*

forearm *noun* arm from the wrist to the elbow

forebear *noun* ancestor

foreboding *noun* feeling that something bad is about to happen

forecast forecasts forecasting forecast or **forecasted** *verb* **1** to predict (weather, events, etc) ▷ *noun* **2** prediction

foreclose forecloses foreclosing foreclosed *verb* to take possession of property bought with borrowed money which has not been repaid

forecourt *noun* courtyard or open space in front of a building

forefather *noun* ancestor

forefinger *noun* finger next to your thumb

forefront *noun* leading or most active position

forego foregoes foregoing forewent foregone; also spelt **forgo** *verb* to do without or give up

foregoing *adjective formal* going before; preceding

foregone conclusion *noun* inevitable result

foreground *noun* part of a view, especially in a picture, nearest the observer

forehand *noun Tennis, Squash, Badminton* stroke made with the palm of your hand facing in the direction that you hit the ball

forehead *noun* area of your face above your eyebrows and below your hairline

foreign *adjective* **1** belonging to or involving countries other than your own **2** unfamiliar or uncharacteristic **3** in an abnormal place or position: *foreign matter* > **foreigner** *noun*

foreman foremen *noun* **1** person in charge of a group of workers **2** leader of a jury

foremost *adjective, adverb* first in time, place or importance

forename *noun* first name

forensic *adjective* **1** relating to or involving the scientific examination of objects involved in a crime **2** relating to or involving the legal profession

forensic medicine *noun* use

of medical knowledge for the purposes of the law

forerunner *noun* something or someone that precedes, influences or is an early sign of subsequent developments in the area

foresee foresees foreseeing foresaw foreseen *verb* to see or know beforehand; predict > **foreseeable** *adjective*: *He will continue as chairman for the foreseeable future*

foreshadow foreshadows foreshadowing foreshadowed *verb* to be a sign of (something); presage

foreshorten *verb* to represent (an object) in a picture as shorter than it really is, in accordance with perspective

foresight *noun* ability to anticipate and provide for future needs

foreskin *noun* fold of skin covering the tip of the penis

forest *noun* large area of trees growing close together

forestall *verb* to prevent (someone) from doing something by taking prior action

forestry *noun* **1** science of planting and caring for trees **2** management of forests

foretaste *noun* early limited experience of something to come

foretell foretells foretelling foretold *verb* to predict

forethought *noun* careful thought and planning about future actions and consequences

forever or **for ever** *adverb* permanently or continually

forewarn *verb* to warn (someone) beforehand

foreword *noun* introduction to a book

forfeit *verb* **1** to lose (something) as a penalty ▷ *noun* **2** thing lost or given up as a penalty

forge forges forging forged *noun* **1** place where a blacksmith works making metal goods by hand; smithy **2** furnace for melting metal ▷ *verb* **3** to make an illegal copy of (a painting, document or money, etc) **4** to shape (metal) by heating and hammering it **5** to create (a relationship etc) > **forge ahead** *verb* to progress quickly

forger *noun* person who makes an illegal copy of something

forgery forgeries *noun* **1** illegal copy of something **2** crime of forging money, documents or paintings

forget forgets forgetting forgot forgotten *verb* **1** to fail to remember (something) **2** to neglect **3** to leave (something) behind by mistake **4** **forget yourself** to behave in an unacceptable way > **forgetful** *adjective* tending to forget > **forgetfulness** *noun*

forget-me-not *noun* plant with clusters of small blue flowers

forgive forgives forgiving forgave forgiven *verb* to stop resenting (someone for something they have done); pardon > **forgiveness** *noun* > **forgiving** *adjective*

forgo *verb* same as **forego**

forgot *verb* past tense of **forget**

forgotten *verb* past participle of **forget**

fork *noun* **1** tool for eating food, with prongs and a handle **2** large similarly-shaped garden tool **3** point where a road, river, etc divides into two branches **4** one of the branches ▷ *verb* **5** to pick up, dig, etc (something) with a fork **6** to branch **7** to take one or

other branch at a fork in the road
> **forked** *adjective* > **fork out** *verb*
informal to pay

fork-lift truck *noun* vehicle with a
forklike device at the front which
can be raised or lowered to move
loads

forlorn *adjective* **1** lonely and
unhappy **2** (of hope or attempt)
desperate and without any
expectation of success > **forlornly**
adverb

form *noun* **1** type or kind **2** shape
or appearance **3** mode in which
something appears **4** printed
document with spaces for details
5 physical or mental condition
6 previous record of an athlete,
racehorse, etc **7** class in school
▷ *verb* **8** to come into existence; be
made **9** to create, organize or start
10 to make up: *events that were to
form the basis of her novel*

formal *adjective* **1** correct, serious
and conforming to accepted
conventions: *a very formal letter of
apology* **2** of or for formal occasions
3 stiff in manner **4** organized
5 official and publicly recognized:
the first formal agreement of its kind
> **formally** *adverb*

formaldehyde *noun* a poisonous
strong-smelling gas, used for
preserving specimens in biology

formality formalities *noun*
1 requirement of custom or
etiquette **2** necessary procedure
without real importance

**format formats formatting
formatted** *noun* **1** style in which
something is arranged ▷ *verb* **2** to
arrange (something) in a format

formation *noun* **1** process of
developing and creating something
2 structure or shape of something
3 arrangement of people or things

acting as a unit

formative *adjective* having an
important and lasting influence on
character and development

former *adjective* **1** happening or
existing before now or in the past
▷ *noun* **2** **the former** the first
mentioned of two > **formerly**
adverb

formidable *adjective* **1** frightening
because difficult to overcome or
manage **2** extremely impressive
> **formidably** *adverb*

formula formulae or **formulas**
noun **1** group of numbers, letters
or symbols expressing a scientific
or mathematical rule **2** list of
quantities of substances that when
mixed make another substance,
for example in chemistry **3** method
or rule for doing or producing
something

**formulate formulates
formulating formulated** *verb*
to create and express (a plan or
thought) in a clear and precise way

fornication *noun formal* sin of
having sex with someone without
being married to them

**forsake forsakes forsaking
forsook forsaken** *verb* to give up
or abandon (someone)

fort *noun* **1** strong building built for
defence **2** **hold the fort** *informal*
to keep things going during
someone's absence

forte *noun* something that someone
does really well; speciality

forth *adverb* forwards, out or away

forthcoming *adjective* **1** about to
appear or happen **2** available **3** (of a
person) communicative

forthright *adjective* direct and
outspoken

fortieth *adjective, noun* see **forty**

fortification *noun* building, wall or

ditch used to protect a place

fortify fortifies fortifying fortified *verb* **1** to strengthen (a place) against attack, by building walls **2** to make (someone) feel stronger or more prepared **3** to add vitamins etc to (food) **4** to add alcohol to (wine) to make sherry or port

fortitude *noun* calm and patient courage in times of trouble or when suffering

fortnight *noun* two weeks > **fortnightly** *adverb, adjective*

fortress fortresses *noun* large fort or fortified town

fortuitous *adjective* happening by chance or good luck > **fortuitously** *adverb*

fortunate *adjective* **1** having good luck; lucky **2** occurring by good luck > **fortunately** *adverb*

fortune *noun* **1** luck, especially when favourable **2** wealth or large sum of money **3** (*often plural*) person's destiny

forty forties *adjective, noun* the number 40 > **fortieth** *adjective, noun*

forum forums or **fora** *noun* **1** place, meeting or medium in which people can exchange ideas and discuss public issues **2** square in Roman towns where people met to discuss business and politics

forward forwards forwarding forwarded *adverb* **1** same as **forwards** ▷ *adjective* **2** directed or moving ahead **3** in, at or near the front **4** presumptuous **5** well developed or advanced **6** relating to the future ▷ *noun* **7** attacking player in various team games, such as soccer or hockey ▷ *verb* **8** to send (a letter etc) on to an ultimate destination > **forwards** *adverb*

1 towards or at a place further ahead in space or time **2** towards the front

fossick *verb Aust, NZ* to search, especially for gold or precious stones

fossil *noun* the remains or impression of an animal or plant from a previous age, preserved in rock > **fossilize** *verb* to turn into a fossil

fossil fuel *noun* fuel such as coal, oil or natural gas, formed by the rotting of animals and plants from millions of years ago

foster *verb* **1** to bring up (someone else's child) without becoming the legal parent **2** to promote the growth or development of > **foster child** *noun* > **foster home** *noun* > **foster parent** *noun*

fought *verb* past of **fight**

foul *adjective* **1** dirty, wicked or obscene ▷ *verb* **2** to make (something) dirty or polluted, especially with faeces **3** *Sport* to break the rules to the disadvantage of (an opponent) ▷ *noun* **4** *Sport* act of breaking the rules

found *verb* **1** past of **find 2** to start or set up (an organization or institution) **3** to lay the foundation of

foundation *noun* **1** basis or base **2** part of a building or wall below the ground **3** act of founding **4** organization set up by money left in someone's will for research or charity **5** cosmetic used as a base for make-up

founder *noun* **1** person responsible for setting up an institution or organization ▷ *verb* **2** to break down or fail **3** (of a ship) to sink

foundry foundries *noun* factory where metal is melted and cast

fountain *noun* **1** jet of water **2** structure from which such a jet spurts

fountain pen *noun* pen supplied with ink from a container inside it

four *adjective, noun* **1** the number 4 ▷ *noun* **2** **on all fours** on hands and knees

four-poster *noun* bed with four posts supporting a canopy and curtains

fourteen *adjective, noun* the number 14 > **fourteenth** *adjective, noun*

fourth *adjective, noun* **1** (coming as) number 4 in a series ▷ *noun* **2** quarter

fowl fowl or **fowls** *noun* bird such as a chicken or duck that is kept for its meat or eggs or hunted for its meat

fox foxes foxing foxed *noun* **1** dog-like wild animal with reddish-brown fur, a pointed face and ears, and a thick tail **2** cunning person ▷ *verb* **3** *informal* to puzzle or perplex

foxglove *noun* tall plant with purple or white trumpet-shaped flowers

foxhound *noun* breed of dog used for hunting foxes

foyer *noun* large area just inside the main doors of a theatre, cinema or hotel

fracas *noun* noisy quarrel

　The plural of *fracas* is *fracas*

fraction *noun* **1** part of a whole number **2** tiny amount, fragment or piece of something > **fractional** *adjective* > **fractionally** *adverb*

fractious *adjective* easily upset or angered

fracture fractures fracturing fractured *noun* **1** crack or break in something, especially a bone ▷ *verb* **2** to break

fragile *adjective* **1** easily broken or damaged **2** in a weakened physical state > **fragility** *noun*

fragment *noun* **1** small piece broken off something ▷ *verb* **2** to break into pieces > **fragmentation** *noun* > **fragmented** *adjective*

fragmentary *adjective* made up of small pieces or parts that are not connected: *fragmentary notes in a journal*

fragrance *noun* **1** sweet or pleasant smell **2** perfume or scent

fragrant *adjective* smelling sweet or pleasant

frail *adjective* **1** physically weak **2** easily damaged > **frailty** *noun* physical or moral weakness

frame frames framing framed *noun* **1** structure surrounding a door, window or picture **2** structure giving shape or support **3** person's build **4** one of the many separate photographs of which a cinema film is made up **5** **frames** the part of a pair of glasses that holds the lenses ▷ *verb* **6** to put (a picture) into a frame **7** to put (something) into words; express **8** *informal* to incriminate (a person) on a false charge

framework *noun* **1** supporting structure **2** set of rules, beliefs or ideas which you use to decide what to do

franc *noun* monetary unit of Switzerland, various African countries and formerly of France and Belgium

franchise *noun* **1** right to vote **2** authorization to sell a company's goods

frank *adjective* **1** open, honest and straightforward in what you say ▷ *noun* **2** official mark on a letter permitting delivery ▷ *verb* **3** to put such a mark on (a letter) > **frankly** *adverb* > **frankness** *noun*

frantic *adjective* **1** made wild and

uncontrolled through anxiety or fear **2** hurried and disorganized > **frantically** adverb

fraternal adjective of a brother; brotherly

fraternity fraternities noun **1** brotherhood **2** group of people with shared interests, aims, etc **3** US male social club at college

fraternize fraternizes fraternizing fraternized; also spelt **fraternise** verb to associate on friendly terms

fraud noun **1** crime of getting money by deceit or trickery **2** something that deceives people in an illegal or immoral way **3** person who is not what he or she pretends to be

fraudulent adjective dishonest or deceitful

fraught adjective **1** tense or anxious **2 fraught with** involving or filled with (problems or dificulties)

fray frays fraying frayed verb **1** to become or make (something) ragged at the edge **2** to become strained ▷ noun **3** Brit, Aust, NZ noisy quarrel or fight

freak noun **1** abnormal person or thing ▷ adjective **2** very unusual and unlikely to happen

freckle noun small brown spot on the skin > **freckled** adjective marked with freckles

free freer freest; frees freeing freed adjective **1** (of person, group) able to act at will; not forced, restrained or imprisoned **2** (of activity, event) not controlled or limited: the free flow of aid; free trade **3** (of an object, event or activity) costing nothing **4** (of a person) not busy **5** (of a place, seat or machine) not in use ▷ verb **6** to release or liberate **7** to make available or usable

-free suffix meaning without: a trouble-free journey

freedom noun **1** being free **2** right or privilege of unlimited access: the freedom of the city

freehold noun right to own a house or piece of land for life without conditions

freelance adjective **1** self-employed ▷ adverb **2** as a self-employed person ▷ noun **3** self-employed person doing specific pieces of work for various employers

freely adverb without restriction

free-range adjective kept or produced in natural conditions

freestyle noun sports competitions, especially swimming, in which competitors can use any style or method

freeway freeways noun US, Aust motorway

free will noun **of your own free will** by choice and without pressure being exerted

freeze freezes freezing froze frozen verb **1** (of a liquid) to become solid because of the cold **2** to preserve (food etc) by extreme cold **3** to be very cold **4** to become suddenly very still or quiet with fear, shock, etc **5** Drama to stop (the action in a film) at a particular frame **6** to fix (prices or wages) at a particular level ▷ noun **7** period of very cold weather **8** official action taken to prevent wages or prices from rising

freezer noun large refrigerator which freezes and stores food for a long time

freezing adjective informal very cold

freight noun **1** cargo transported by lorries, ships, etc **2** commercial transport of goods **3** cost of this

French adjective **1** belonging

or relating to France ▷ *noun*
2 language of France, also spoken
in parts of Belgium, Canada and
Switzerland ▷ *plural* **3 the French**
the people of France

French bean *noun* green pod eaten
as a vegetable, which grows on
a climbing plant with white or
mauve flowers

French fries *plural noun* potato
chips

French horn *noun* brass wind
instrument with a coiled tube

Frenchman Frenchmen *noun*
man from France > **Frenchwoman**
noun

French window *noun* one of a
pair of glass doors that lead into a
garden or onto a balcony

frenetic *adjective* wild and excited
> **frenetically** *adverb*

frenzy frenzies *noun* wild and
uncontrolled state > **frenzied**
adjective

frequency frequencies *noun*
1 how often something happens
2 *Physics* the rate at which a sound
wave or radio wave vibrates

frequent *adjective* **1** happening
often ▷ *verb* **2** to visit (a place) often
> **frequently** *adverb*

fresco frescoes or **frescos** *noun*
picture painted on wet plaster
on a wall

fresh *adjective* **1** newly made,
acquired, etc **2** original **3** further or
additional **4** (of food) not preserved
5 (of water) not salty **6** (of weather)
brisk or invigorating **7** not tired
8 fresh from having recently
experienced (something) > **freshly**
adverb > **freshness** *noun*

freshwater *adjective* **1** (of a lake or
pool) containing water that is not
salty **2** (of a fish or animal) living in
a river, lake or pool that is not salty

fret frets fretting fretted *verb* **1** to
be worried ▷ *noun* **2** small bar on
the fingerboard of a guitar etc

fretful *adjective* showing signs of
worry or unhappiness

Freudian slip *noun* something
that you say or do that reveals your
unconscious thoughts

friar *noun* member of a male Roman
Catholic religious order

friary friaries *noun* building in
which friars live

friction *noun* **1** force that stops
things from moving freely when
they rub against each other
2 rubbing **3** clash of wills or
personalities

Friday Fridays *noun* day between
Thursday and Saturday

fridge *noun* electrically cooled
container in which you store food
and drinks to keep them fresh;
refrigerator

fried *verb* past of **fry**

friend *noun* person you know well
and like

friendly friendlies; friendlier
friendliest *adjective* **1** showing
or expressing liking **2** not hostile;
on the same side ▷ *noun* **3** *Sport*
match played for its own sake
and not as part of a competition
> **friendliness** *noun*

-friendly *suffix indicating* good
or easy for the person or thing
specified: *user-friendly*

friendship *noun* **1** relationship that
you have with a friend **2** state of
being friends with someone

frieze *noun* decorative band on
a wall

frigate *noun* medium-sized fast
warship

fright *noun* **1** sudden fear or alarm
2 sudden alarming shock

frighten *verb* to scare or

terrify > **frightened** adjective
> **frightening** adjective

frightful adjective 1 horrifying
2 informal very great > **frightfully**
adverb

frigid adjective 1 (of a woman)
sexually unresponsive 2 cold and
unfriendly

frill noun strip of cloth with many
folds, attached to something
as a decoration > **frilly** adjective
decorated with frills or lace

fringe noun 1 hair that is cut to
hang down over your forehead
2 ornamental edge of hanging
threads, tassels, etc 3 outer edge
4 less important parts of an activity
or group ▷ adjective 5 (of theatre)
unofficial or unconventional
> **fringed** adjective

frisk verb informal to search (a
person) for concealed weapons etc

frisky friskier friskiest adjective
lively or high-spirited

fritter noun piece of food fried in
batter > **fritter away** verb to waste

frivolous adjective 1 not serious
or sensible 2 enjoyable but trivial
> **frivolity** noun

frizzy frizzier frizziest adjective (of
hair) having small tight wiry curls

frock noun old-fashioned dress

frog noun small amphibious
creature with smooth skin,
prominent eyes, and long back legs
which it uses for jumping

frolic frolics frolicking frolicked
verb to run around and play in a
lively way

from preposition 1 indicating the
origin or source of something
or someone: a call from a public
telephone; people from a city 100 miles
away 2 indicating a starting point
or point of departure: She fled from
the room 3 indicating the start

of a range: a score from one to five
4 indicating a cause: the wreckage
from the bomb blast 5 indicating a
sum or amount that is reduced by
another sum or amount: The money
is deducted from her salary every month

frond noun long feathery leaf

front noun 1 part of something that
faces forward 2 position directly
before or ahead 3 place where two
armies are fighting 4 Meteorology
dividing line between a mass of
cold air and a mass of warm air
5 outward appearance 6 informal
cover for another, usually criminal,
activity 7 particular field of activity:
on the economic front 8 **in front**
ahead or further forward 9 **in front
of a** in the presence of **b** before
▷ adjective 9 of or at the front
> **frontal** adjective: the frontal region
of the brain

frontage noun (of a building) wall
facing onto a street, river or public
place; facade

frontier noun border between two
countries

frontispiece noun illustration
facing the title page of a book

frost noun 1 white frozen dew or
mist 2 atmospheric temperature
below freezing point

frostbite noun damage to your
fingers, toes or ears caused by
extreme cold

frosting noun Chiefly US sugar icing

frosty frostier frostiest adjective
1 below freezing 2 unfriendly
> **frostily** adverb

froth noun 1 mass of small bubbles
▷ verb 2 to foam > **frothy** adjective

frown verb 1 to wrinkle your brows
in worry, anger or thought ▷ noun
2 cross frowning expression

froze verb past tense of **freeze**

frozen verb 1 past participle of

freeze ▷ *adjective* **2** extremely cold

fructose *noun* type of sugar found in many fruits and in honey

frugal *adjective* **1** spending very little money; thrifty **2** (of a meal) small and cheap **> frugality** *noun* **> frugally** *adverb*

fruit *noun* **1** part of a plant containing seeds, especially if edible **2** (*often plural*) good result of an action or effort

fruitful *adjective* useful or productive

fruitless *adjective* useless or unproductive

fruit machine *noun* coin-operated gambling machine

fruit salad *noun* mixture of pieces of different fruits served in a juice as a dessert

fruity fruitier fruitiest *adjective* **1** of or like fruit **2** (of a voice) rich and deep

frustrate frustrates frustrating frustrated *verb* **1** to make (someone) angry or upset by not allowing or preventing them from doing what they want **2** to hinder or prevent (a plan) **> frustrated** *adjective*: *frustrated motorists, desperate to get moving* **> frustrating** *adjective*: *a frustrating day at work* **> frustration** *noun*: *his frustration at being left out of the team*

fry fries frying fried *verb* to cook or be cooked in fat or oil

fuchsia *noun* plant or bush with pink, purple or white flowers that hang downwards

fudge fudges fudging fudged *noun* **1** soft brown sweet made from butter, milk and sugar ▷ *verb* **2** to avoid making a firm statement or decision about (something)

fuel fuels fuelling fuelled *noun* **1** substance such as coal or petrol that is burned to provide heat or power ▷ *verb* **2** to provide (a device or vehicle) with fuel

fug *noun* hot stale atmosphere **> fuggy** *adjective*

fugitive *noun* person who flees, especially from arrest or pursuit

-ful *suffix* **1** used to form adjectives with the meaning 'full of': *careful* **2** used to form nouns which mean 'the amount needed to fill': *spoonful*

fulcrum fulcrums or **fulcra** *noun* the point at which something is balancing or pivoting

fulfil fulfils fulfilling fulfilled *verb* **1** to carry out or achieve (a promise, duty, dream or hope) **2** (of work, activity) to satisfy (someone or yourself) completely **> fulfilling** *adjective*: *a happy and fulfilling life* **> fulfilment** *noun*: *It was the fulfilment of a dream*

full *adjective* **1** containing as much or as many as possible **2** complete or whole **3** (of clothes) loose and made from a lot of fabric **4** having had enough to eat **5** (of a figure) plump **6** (of a sound or flavour) rich and strong ▷ *adverb* **7** completely **8** directly ▷ *noun* **9 in full** completely **> fullness** *noun* **> fully** *adverb*

full-blooded *adjective* vigorous or enthusiastic

full-blown *adjective* fully developed

full moon *noun* phase of the moon when it looks round and complete

full stop *noun* punctuation mark (.) used at the end of a sentence and after abbreviations or initials

full-time *adjective* **1** involving work for the whole of each normal working week ▷ *noun* **2** *Sport* the end of a match ▷ *adverb* **3** (also **full time**) during the whole of each normal working week

fully-fledged *adjective* completely developed: *I was a fully-fledged and mature human being*

fulmar *noun* Arctic sea bird

fulsome *adjective* exaggerated and elaborate, and often sounding insincere

fumble fumbles fumbling fumbled *verb* to handle something awkwardly

fume fumes fuming fumed *verb* to be very angry > **fumes** *plural noun* gases, vapours or smoke which are released from certain chemicals or burning substances and which smell unpleasant and may be toxic

fumigate fumigates fumigating fumigated *verb* to disinfect with fumes

fun *noun* **1** enjoyment or amusement **2 make fun of** to mock or tease

function *noun* **1** purpose something exists for **2** role or job **3** way something works **4** large or formal social event **5** *Maths* quantity whose value depends on the varying value of another ▷ *verb* **6** to operate or work **7 function as** to fill the role of

functional *adjective* **1** relating to the way something works **2** practical rather than decorative **3** in working order

fund *noun* **1** stock of money for a special purpose **2** supply or store **3 funds** money resources ▷ *verb* **4** to provide money for (something or someone) > **funding** *noun*: *Where are they going to get the funding?*

fundamental *adjective* **1** essential or primary **2** basic ▷ *noun* **3** basic rule or fact > **fundamentally** *adverb*

fundamentalism *noun* literal or strict interpretation of a religion > **fundamentalist** *noun, adjective*

fundraising *noun* activity involved in raising money for a cause > **fundraiser** *noun* someone who raises money for a cause

funeral *noun* ceremony or religious service for the burial or cremation of a dead person

funereal *adjective* gloomy or sombre

funfair *noun* place or event provided for outdoor entertainment, having stalls and rides on machines

fungicide *noun* substance that destroys fungi

fungus fungi or **funguses** *noun* organism such as a mushroom, toadstool or mould that does not have leaves and grows on other living things > **fungal** *adjective*: *a fungal infection*

funicular *noun* cable railway on a mountainside or cliff

funk *verb* **1** *old-fashioned informal* to avoid (doing something) through fear ▷ *noun* **2** style of music with a strong rhythm based on jazz and blues

funky funkier funkiest *adjective* (of music) having a strong beat

funnel funnels funnelling funnelled *noun* **1** tube with a cone shape at the top for pouring liquids into a narrow opening **2** metal chimney on a ship or steam engine ▷ *verb* **3** to move or cause to move through or as if through a funnel

funny funnier funniest *adjective* **1** odd, strange or puzzling **2** causing amusement or laughter > **funnily** *adverb*

fur *noun* **1** soft thick body hair of many animals **2** animal skin with the fur left on **3** coat made from this > **furry** *adjective*: *a furry toy*

furious *adjective* **1** very angry **2** involving great energy, effort or speed > **furiously** *adverb*

furlong *noun* unit of length equal to

220 yards (201.168 metres)

furnace *noun* enclosed chamber containing a very hot fire used, for example, in the steel industry for melting ore

furnish furnishes furnishing furnished *verb* **1** to provide (a house or room) with furniture **2** to supply or provide (someone with something)

furnishings *plural noun* furniture, carpets and fittings

furniture *noun* large movable articles such as chairs and wardrobes: *a few pieces of furniture*

furore *noun* angry and excited reaction

furrow *noun* **1** long shallow trench made by a plough **2** groove, especially a wrinkle on the forehead ▷ *verb* **3** **furrow your brow** to frown

further *adjective* **1** additional or more **2** more distant ▷ *adverb* **3** in addition **4** to a greater distance or extent ▷ *verb* **5** to assist the progress of (something)

further education *noun* Brit education beyond school other than at a university

furthermore *adverb formal* besides

furthermost *adjective* most distant

furthest *adjective* **1** most distant ▷ *adverb* **2** to the greatest distance or extent

furtive *adjective* sly and secretive > **furtively** *adverb*

fury *noun* violent or extreme anger

fuse fuses fusing fused *noun* **1** safety device for electric circuits, containing a wire that melts and breaks the connection when the circuit is overloaded **2** long cord attached to some types of simple bomb which is lit to detonate the bomb ▷ *verb* **3** to stop working or cause (something) to stop working as a result of a blown fuse **4** to join or combine

fuselage *noun* body of an aircraft

fusion *noun* **1** something new created by a mixture of qualities, ideas or things **2** the joining together of two or more things to form one thing **3** the melting together of two substances **4** (also **nuclear fusion**) combination of the nucleus of two atoms with the release of energy

fuss fusses fussing fussed *noun* **1** needless activity, worry or attentiveness **2** complaint or objection ▷ *verb* **3** to show unnecessary concern or attention over unimportant things

fussy fussier fussiest *adjective* **1** inclined to fuss **2** overparticular **3** overelaborate

futile *adjective* having no chance of success: *a futile attempt to calm the storm* > **futility** *noun*: *the futility of war*

future *noun* **1** time to come **2** what will happen **3** prospects ▷ *adjective* **4** yet to come or be **5** of or relating to time to come **6** (of a verb tense) indicating that the action specified has not yet taken place

futuristic *adjective* (of a design) very modern and strange, as if belonging to a time in the future

fuzz *noun* mass of fine or curly hairs or fibres

g *symbol* **1** gram(s) **2** (acceleration due to) gravity

gabble gabbles gabbling gabbled *verb* **1** to speak rapidly and indistinctly ▷ *noun* **2** rapid indistinct speech

gable *noun* triangular upper part of a wall between sloping roofs

gadget *noun* small mechanical device or appliance > **gadgetry** *noun* gadgets

Gaelic *noun* any of the Celtic languages of Ireland and the Scottish Highlands

gaffe *noun* social blunder

gaffer *noun Brit informal* foreman or boss

gag gags gagging gagged *verb* **1** to choke and nearly vomit **2** to stop up the mouth of (someone) with a strip of cloth **3** to deprive (someone) of free speech ▷ *noun* **4** strip of cloth tied across the mouth **5** *informal* joke

gaggle *noun* **1** *informal* disorderly crowd **2** flock of geese

gaiety *noun* **1** cheerfulness **2** merrymaking

gaily *adverb* merrily

gain *verb* **1** to acquire or obtain (something) **2** (followed by *from*) to get an advantage from a situation **3** (of a watch or clock) to be or become too fast ▷ *noun* **4** profit or advantage **5** increase > **gain on** or **upon** *verb* to get nearer to or catch up with (someone)

gait *noun* manner of walking

gala *noun* **1** festival **2** competitive sporting event

galactic *adjective* relating to a galaxy

galah *noun Aust* **1** cockatoo with a pink breast and a grey back and wings **2** *informal* stupid person

galaxy galaxies *noun* system of stars

gale *noun* strong wind

gall *noun* **1** *informal* impudence ▷ *verb* **2** to annoy (someone)

gallant *adjective* **1** brave and noble **2** (of a man) attentive to women > **gallantly** *adverb* > **gallantry** *noun* **1** showy attentive treatment of women **2** bravery

gall bladder *noun* organ next to the liver that stores bile

galleon *noun* large three-masted sailing ship of the 15th–17th centuries

gallery galleries *noun* **1** room or building for displaying works of art **2** balcony in a church, theatre, etc

galley galleys *noun* **1** kitchen of a ship or aircraft **2** *History* ship propelled by oars, usually rowed by slaves

Gallic *adjective literary* French

gallium *noun Chemistry* soft grey metallic element used in semiconductors

gallon *noun* liquid measure of eight pints, equal to 4.55 litres

gallop *noun* **1** horse's fastest pace **2** galloping ▷ *verb* **3** to go or ride at a gallop **4** to move or progress rapidly

gallows *noun* wooden structure used for hanging criminals

gallstone *noun* small painful lump formed in the gall bladder or its ducts

galore *adverb* in abundance: *chocolates galore*

galoshes *plural noun* Brit, Aust, NZ waterproof shoes for wearing on top of ordinary shoes

galvanized or **galvanised** *adjective* (of metal) coated with zinc by an electrical process to protect it from rust

gambit *noun* 1 opening line or move intended to secure an advantage 2 *Chess* opening move involving the sacrifice of a pawn

gamble gambles gambling gambled *verb* 1 to bet money on the result of a game or race; wager 2 to risk losing (something) in the hope of gaining an advantage ▷ *noun* 3 risky undertaking > **gambler** *noun* person who gambles regularly > **gambling** *noun* activity of betting money

gambol gambols gambolling gambolled *verb* 1 to jump about playfully, frolic ▷ *noun* 2 frolic

game *noun* 1 amusement or pastime 2 contest for amusement 3 single period of play in a contest 4 animals or birds hunted for sport or food 5 scheme or trick ▷ *adjective* 6 willing to try something unusual or difficult > **gamely** *adverb*: *He gamely defended the decision* > **gaming** *noun* gambling

gamekeeper *noun* Brit, Aust, S Afr person employed to look after game animals and birds on a country estate

gammon *noun* cured or smoked ham

gamut *noun* whole range or scale (of music, emotions, etc)

gander *noun* male goose

gang *noun* group of people who join together for some purpose, *eg* to commit a crime > **gang up on** *verb* to join together to oppose (someone)

gangplank *noun* portable bridge for boarding or leaving a ship

gangrene *noun* decay of body tissue as a result of disease or injury > **gangrenous** *adjective*: *gangrenous limbs*

gangster *noun* member of a criminal gang

gangway gangways *noun* 1 passage between rows of seats 2 gangplank

gannet *noun* large sea bird

gaol *noun* same as **jail**

gap *noun* 1 break or opening 2 great difference: *the gap between fantasy and reality*

gape gapes gaping gaped *verb* 1 to stare with your mouth open in surprise 2 to be wide open > **gaping** *adjective*: *gaping holes in the wall*

garage *noun* 1 building where cars are kept 2 place for the refuelling, sale and repair of cars

garb *noun* formal clothes

garbage *noun* 1 rubbish, especially household rubbish 2 nonsense

garbled *adjective* (of a story etc) jumbled and confused

garden *noun* 1 piece of land for growing flowers, fruit or vegetables 2 **gardens** ornamental park > **gardener** *noun* person who looks after a garden as a job or hobby > **gardening** *noun* looking after a garden as a job or hobby

garden centre *noun* place selling plants and gardening equipment

gargle gargles gargling gargled

verb to wash the throat with a liquid by breathing out slowly through the liquid

gargoyle *noun* waterspout carved in the form of a grotesque face, especially on a church

garish *adjective* crudely bright or colourful

garland *noun* circle of flowers worn or hung as a decoration

garlic *noun* pungent bulb of a plant of the onion family, used in cooking

garment *noun* article of clothing

garnet *noun* red semiprecious stone

garnish garnishes garnishing garnished *verb* 1 to decorate (food) ▷ *noun* 2 decoration for food

garret *noun* attic in a house

garrison *noun* 1 troops stationed in a town or fort 2 fortified place

garrotte garrottes garrotting garrotted; also spelt **garotte** *verb* to strangle (someone) with a piece of wire

garter *noun* band worn round the leg to hold up a sock or stocking

gas gases; gasses gassing gassed *noun* 1 airlike substance that is not liquid or solid 2 fossil fuel in the form of a gas, used for heating 3 *Chiefly US* petrol ▷ *verb* 4 to poison (people or animals) with gas

The plural of the noun *gas* is *gases*. The verb forms of *gas* are spelt with a double *s*

gas chamber *noun* airtight room which is filled with poison gas to kill people or animals

gash gashes gashing gashed *verb* 1 to make a long deep cut in (something) ▷ *noun* 2 long deep cut

gas mask *noun* mask with a chemical filter to protect the wearer against poison gas

gasoline *noun* US petrol

gasp *verb* 1 to draw in breath sharply or with difficulty ▷ *noun* 2 convulsive intake of breath

gastric *adjective* of the stomach

gate *noun* 1 movable barrier, usually hinged, in a wall or fence 2 number of people attending a sporting event

gateau gateaux *noun* rich layered cake with cream in it

gatecrash gatecrashes gatecrashing gatecrashed *verb* to enter (a party) uninvited

gateway gateways *noun* 1 entrance with a gate 2 means of access: *New York is the gateway to America*

gather *verb* 1 to come together in a group; assemble 2 to collect (a number of things) gradually 3 to increase (something) gradually 4 to learn (something) from information given

gathering *noun* meeting of people who have come together for a particular purpose

gauche *adjective* socially awkward

gaudy gaudier gaudiest *adjective* vulgarly bright or colourful

gauge gauges gauging gauged *verb* 1 to estimate or calculate (something) ▷ *noun* 2 measuring instrument 3 scale or standard of measurement 4 distance between the rails of a railway track

gaunt *adjective* lean and haggard

gauntlet *noun* 1 heavy glove with a long cuff 2 **run the gauntlet** to be exposed to criticism or unpleasant treatment 3 **throw down the gauntlet** to offer a challenge

gave *verb* past tense of **give**

gay gayer gayest; gays *adjective* 1 homosexual 2 *old-fashioned* carefree and merry ▷ *noun*

3 homosexual person

> The most common meaning of *gay* now is 'homosexual'. In some older books it may have its old-fashioned meaning of 'carefree and merry'

gaze gazes gazing gazed *verb* to look fixedly

gazelle *noun* small graceful antelope

gazette *noun* official publication containing announcements

gazillion *noun informal* extremely large unspecified amount

GB *abbreviation* Great Britain

GCE GCEs *abbreviation* (in Britain) General Certificate of Education

GCSE GCSEs *abbreviation* (in Britain) General Certificate of Secondary Education

gear *noun* **1** set of toothed wheels connecting with another or with a rack to change the direction or speed of transmitted motion **2** mechanism for transmitting motion by gears **3** setting of a gear to suit engine speed: *first gear* **4** clothing or belongings **5** equipment ▷ *verb* **6** (followed by *to*) to prepare (someone) or organize (something) for a particular event or purpose

geek *noun informal* **1** boring unattractive person **2** person highly knowledgeable in computing > **geeky** *adjective*

geese *noun* plural of **goose**

gel gels gelling gelled *noun* **1** jelly-like substance, especially one used to set a hairstyle ▷ *verb* **2** to form a gel **3** *informal* to take on a definite form

gelatine or **gelatin** *noun* **1** substance made by boiling animal bones **2** edible jelly made of this

gelding *noun* castrated horse

gem *noun* **1** precious stone or jewel **2** highly valued person or thing

Gemini *noun* third sign of the zodiac, represented by a pair of twins

gemsbok gemsbok or **gemsboks** *noun S Afr* type of large antelope with straight horns

gen *noun informal* information

gender *noun* **1** state of being male or female **2** *Grammar* classification of nouns in certain languages as masculine, feminine or neuter

gene *noun* part of a cell which determines inherited characteristics

genealogy *noun* the study of the history and descent of a family or families > **genealogical** *adjective* > **genealogist** *noun*

general *adjective* **1** common or widespread **2** of or affecting all or most **3** not specific **4** including or dealing with various or miscellaneous items **5** highest in authority or rank: *general manager* ▷ *noun* **6** very senior army officer **7** **in general** mostly or usually > **generally** *adverb* usually

general election *noun* election in which everyone old enough to vote can vote for the candidate he or she wants to represent them in Parliament

generalize generalizes generalizing generalized; also spelt **generalise** *verb* to say that something is true in most cases, ignoring minor details > **generalization** *noun*: *That's rather a sweeping generalization*

general practitioner *noun* doctor who works in the community rather than in a hospital

generate generates generating generated *verb* to produce (something) or bring (something) into being

generation noun 1 all the people born about the same time 2 average time between two generations (about 30 years)

generator noun machine for converting mechanical energy into electrical energy

generic adjective of a class, group or genus > **generically** adverb

generous adjective 1 very willing to give money or time 2 very large; ample > **generosity** noun state of being generous > **generously** adverb

genesis noun formal beginning or origin

genetic adjective relating to genes or genetics > **genetically** adverb > **genetics** noun study of heredity and variation in organisms

genial adjective cheerful and friendly > **genially** adverb in a cheerful and friendly manner

genie noun (in fairy tales) servant who appears by magic and grants wishes

genital adjective relating to the sexual organs or reproduction

genitals or **genitalia** plural noun external sexual organs

genius geniuses noun (person with) exceptional ability in a particular field

genocide noun murder of a race of people

genre noun style of literary, musical or artistic work

genteel adjective very polite and refined

gentile adjective, noun non-Jewish (person)

gentility noun excessive politeness and refinement

gentle gentler gentlest adjective

1 mild or kindly 2 not rough or severe 3 gradual 4 easily controlled, tame > **gentleness** noun: the gentleness with which she treated her pregnant mother > **gently** adverb

gentleman gentlemen noun 1 polite well-bred man 2 man of high social position 3 polite name for a man > **gentlemanly** adjective (of a man) having good manners

gentry plural noun people just below the nobility in social rank

genuine adjective 1 not fake, authentic 2 sincere > **genuinely** adverb > **genuineness** noun: the genuineness of their intentions

genus genera noun Biology group into which a family of animals or plants is divided

geo- prefix meaning earth: geography; geologist

geography noun study of the earth's physical features, climate, population, etc > **geographical** or **geographic** adjective relating to geography > **geographically** adverb

geology noun study of the earth's origin, structure and composition > **geological** adjective relating to geology > **geologist** noun person who studies geology

geometry noun branch of mathematics dealing with points, lines, curves and surfaces > **geometric** or **geometrical** adjective 1 consisting of regular lines and shapes, such as squares, triangles and circles 2 involving geometry > **geometrically** adverb in a geometric pattern

Georgian adjective of the time of any of the four kings of Britain called George, esp. 1714–1830

geranium noun cultivated plant with red, pink or white flowers

gerbil *noun* burrowing desert rodent of Asia and Africa

geriatrics *noun* branch of medicine dealing with old age and its diseases > **geriatric** *adjective, noun* old (person)

germ *noun* **1** very small organism that causes disease **2** *formal* beginning from which something may develop

German *noun* **1** language of Germany, Austria and part of Switzerland **2** person from Germany ▷ *adjective* **3** of Germany or its language > **Germanic** *adjective* typical of Germany or the German people

German measles *noun* contagious disease accompanied by a cough, sore throat and red spots

German shepherd *noun* Alsatian

germinate germinates germinating germinated *verb* **1** (of a seed) to start to grow **2** (of an idea or plan) to start to develop > **germination** *noun*: *the germination of a seed*

gerrymander *verb* to alter political boundaries in an area to give unfair advantage to a particular party and make it more likely that its candidate(s) will do well in elections > **gerrymandering** *noun*

gestation *noun* period of carrying of young in the womb between conception and birth

gesticulate gesticulates gesticulating gesticulated *verb* to make expressive movements with the hands and arms > **gesticulation** *noun*

gesture gestures gesturing gestured *noun* **1** movement to convey meaning **2** thing said or done to show your feelings ▷ *verb*

3 to move your hands or head in order to communicate a message or feeling

get gets getting got *verb* **1** to obtain or receive **2** to bring or fetch **3** to become as specified: *get wet* **4** to understand **5** (often followed by *to*) to come to or arrive (at a place) **6** to go on board (a plane, bus, etc) **7** to persuade (someone to do something) > **get across** *verb* to cause (something) to be understood > **get at** *verb* **1** to imply or mean (something) **2** to criticize (someone) > **get away with** *verb* not to be found out or punished for doing (something dishonest) > **get by** *verb* to manage in spite of difficulties > **get on** *verb* **1** (of two people) to like each other's company **2** (often followed by *with*) to continue or start doing (something) > **get over with** *verb* to be finished with (something unpleasant) > **get through to** *verb* **1** to make (someone) understand what you are saying **2** to contact (someone) by telephone

getaway getaways *noun* escape made by criminals

get-together *noun* *informal* informal meeting or party

geyser *noun* **1** spring that discharges steam and hot water **2** *Brit, S Afr* domestic gas water heater

Ghanaian *adjective* **1** of Ghana ▷ *noun* **2** person from Ghana

ghastly ghastlier ghastliest *adjective* extremely horrible and unpleasant

gherkin *noun* small pickled cucumber

ghetto ghettos or **ghettoes** *noun* part of a city where many poor people of a particular race live

ghost *noun* spirit of a dead person, believed to haunt people or places

ghoulish *adjective* very interested in unpleasant things such as death and murder

giant *noun* **1** mythical being of superhuman size ▷ *adjective* **2** much larger than other similar things: *giant prawns*

gibberish *noun* speech that makes no sense at all

gibbon *noun* ape with very long arms

gibe gibes gibing gibed *noun, verb* same as **jibe**

giddy giddier giddiest *adjective* feeling unsteady on your feet usually because of illness > **giddily** *adverb* dizzily

gift *noun* **1** present **2** natural talent > **gifted** *adjective* talented

gig *noun* **1** rock or jazz concert **2** light two-wheeled horse-drawn carriage

gigantic *adjective* enormous

giggle giggles giggling giggled *verb* **1** to laugh in a nervous or embarrassed way ▷ *noun* **2** short nervous laugh > **giggly** *adjective* laughing in a nervous or embarrassed way

gilded *adjective* covered with a thin layer of gold

gill¹ *noun* liquid measure of quarter of a pint, equal to 0.142 litres

gill² *noun* organs on the sides of a fish that it uses for breathing

gilt *adjective* **1** covered with a thin layer of gold ▷ *noun* **2** thin layer of gold used as decoration

gimmick *noun* something designed to attract attention or publicity > **gimmicky** *adjective* designed to attract attention or publicity

gin *noun* strong colourless alcoholic drink made from grain and juniper berries

ginger *noun* **1** plant root with a hot spicy flavour, used in cooking ▷ *adjective* **2** bright orange or red: *ginger hair*

gingerbread *noun* moist cake flavoured with ginger

ginger group *noun* Brit, Aust, NZ group within a larger group that agitates for a more active policy

gingerly *adverb* cautiously

gingham *noun* checked cotton cloth

Gipsy Gipsies *noun* same as **Gypsy**

giraffe *noun* a tall four-legged African mammal with a very long neck

girder *noun* large metal beam used in the construction of a bridge or a building

girdle *noun* woman's corset

girl *noun* female child > **girlhood** *noun* period of being a girl > **girlish** *adjective* like a young girl

girlfriend *noun* girl or woman with whom a person is romantically or sexually involved

giro giros *noun* **1** (in some countries) system of transferring money within a post office or bank directly from one account to another **2** Brit informal social security payment by giro cheque

girth *noun* measurement round something

gist *noun* substance or main point of a matter

give gives giving gave given *verb* **1** to present (something) to another person **2** to utter or emit (something) **3** to organize or host (a party or meal) **4** to yield or break under pressure ▷ *noun* **5** resilience or elasticity > **give in** *verb* to admit defeat > **give out** *verb* to stop working: *the electricity gave out* > **give up** *verb* **1** to stop doing

(something) **2** to admit defeat
3 to let the police know where
(someone) is hiding

given *verb* **1** the past participle of
give ▷ *adjective* **2** fixed or specified:
*My style can change at any given
moment*

glacé *adjective* preserved in a thick
sugary syrup: *glacé cherries*

glacier *noun* slow-moving mass
of ice formed by accumulated
snow > **glaciation** *noun Geography*
condition of being covered with
sheet ice

glad gladder gladdest *adjective*
1 pleased and happy **2** **glad to** very
willing to (do something) > **gladly**
adverb > **gladness** *noun*: *a night of
joy and gladness*

glade *noun* open space in a forest

gladiator *noun* (in ancient Rome)
man trained to fight in arenas to
provide entertainment

gladiolus gladioli *noun* garden
plant with sword-shaped leaves

glamour *noun* alluring charm or
fascination > **glamorous** *adjective*
alluring

glance glances glancing glanced
verb **1** to look rapidly or briefly
▷ *noun* **2** brief look > **glance off** *verb*
to strike and be deflected off (an
object) at an oblique angle

gland *noun* organ that produces and
secretes substances in the body
> **glandular** *adjective*: *glandular
tissue*

glare glares glaring glared *verb*
1 to stare angrily ▷ *noun* **2** angry
stare **3** unpleasant brightness

glass glasses *noun* **1** hard,
transparent substance that is easily
broken, used to make windows and
bottles **2** tumbler > **glassy** *adjective*
1 like glass **2** expressionless

glasses *plural noun* spectacles

glaze glazes glazing glazed *verb*
1 to fit a sheet of glass into the
frame of (a window) **2** to cover
(pottery or food) with a smooth
shiny surface ▷ *noun* **3** smooth
shiny surface on pottery or food
> **glaze over** *verb* (of eyes) to
become dull and expressionless, as
when someone is bored

glazed *adjective* (of a facial
expression) looking bored

gleam *noun* **1** small beam or glow
of light **2** brief or faint indication
▷ *verb* **3** to shine and reflect light

glean *verb* to gather (facts etc)
bit by bit

glee *noun old-fashioned* triumph and
delight > **gleeful** *adjective* happy
and excited, often at someone else's
bad luck > **gleefully** *adverb* in a
gleeful manner

glen *noun* deep narrow valley,
especially in Scotland

glib glibber glibbest *adjective*
fluent but insincere or superficial
> **glibly** *adverb*

glide glides gliding glided *verb* **1** to
move easily and smoothly **2** (of an
aircraft) to move without the use
of engines

glider *noun* aircraft without an
engine which floats on air currents

glimmer *verb* **1** to shine faintly,
flicker ▷ *noun* **2** faint gleam **3** faint
indication

**glimpse glimpses glimpsing
glimpsed** *noun* **1** brief or
incomplete view ▷ *verb* **2** to catch a
glimpse of (someone or something)

glint *verb* **1** to gleam brightly ▷ *noun*
2 quick flash of light **3** brightness
in someone's eye expressing some
emotion: *a glint of mischief*

glisten *verb* to gleam or sparkle

glitter *verb* **1** to shine with bright
flashes ▷ *noun* **2** sparkle or

brilliance **3** tiny pieces of shiny decorative material

gloat *verb* to cruelly show your pleasure about your own success or someone else's failure

global *adjective* worldwide

globalization *noun* trend towards the existence of a single world market dominated by multinational companies

global warming *noun* increase in the overall temperature worldwide believed to be caused by the greenhouse effect

globe *noun* **1** sphere with a map of the earth on it **2** spherical object **3** *Aust, NZ, S Afr* light bulb **4 the globe** the earth

gloom *noun* **1** melancholy or depression **2** darkness > **gloomy gloomier gloomiest** *adjective* **1** melancholy or unhappy **2** dark or dim > **gloomily** *adverb*

glorify glorifies glorifying glorified *verb* to make (something) seem more worthy than it is > **glorification** *noun*: *the glorification of violence*

glorious *adjective* **1** brilliantly beautiful **2** delightful **3** involving great fame and success > **gloriously** *adverb*

glory glories glorying gloried *noun* **1** praise or honour **2** something considered splendid or admirable ▷ *verb* **3** (followed by *in*) to take great delight in (something)

glory box glory boxes *noun Aust, NZ old-fashioned* chest in which a young woman stores household goods and linen for her marriage

gloss glosses glossing glossed *noun* **1** bright shine on a surface **2** attractive appearance that may hide less attractive qualities > **gloss over** *verb* to try to cover up

or pass over (a fault or error)

glossary glossaries *noun* list of words with their explanations or translations, usually found at the back of a book

glossy glossier glossiest *adjective* **1** smooth and shiny **2** (of a magazine) printed on shiny paper

glove *noun* covering for the hand with individual sheaths for each finger and the thumb

glow *verb* **1** to shine with a dull steady light **2** to have a strong feeling of pleasure or happiness ▷ *noun* **3** dull steady light **4** strong feeling of pleasure or happiness

glower *verb, noun* (to) scowl

glowing *adjective* (of description, report, etc) full of praise

glucose *noun* kind of sugar found in fruit

glue glues gluing or **glueing glued** *noun* **1** substance used for sticking things together ▷ *verb* **2** to stick (objects) together using glue

glum glummer glummest *adjective* sullen or gloomy > **glumly** *adverb*

glut *noun* excessive supply

gluten *noun* sticky protein found in cereal grain

glutton *noun* **1** greedy person **2** person with a great capacity for something > **gluttony** *noun* state of being greedy

gnarled *adjective* rough, twisted and knobbly

gnash gnashes gnashing gnashed *verb* to grind (your teeth) together in anger or pain

gnat *noun* small biting two-winged fly

gnaw *verb* **1** to bite or chew (something) steadily **2** (followed by *at*) to cause constant distress to (someone)

gnome *noun* imaginary creature like a little old man

gnu *noun* oxlike S African antelope

go goes going went gone *verb* **1** to move to or from a place **2** to depart **3** to be, do or become as specified: *She felt she was going mad* **4** (often followed by *with*) to blend or harmonize (with something) **5** to fail or break down **6** to be got rid of ▷ *noun* **7** attempt > **go back on** *verb* to break (a promise etc) > **go down** *verb* to get a particular kind of reception: *His speech went down well* > **go for** *verb* **1** to like (something) very much **2** to attack (someone) > **go off** *verb* **1** (of a bomb) to explode **2** *informal* to stop liking (someone or something) > **go on** *verb* **1** to continue (doing something) **2** to keep talking about (something) in a rather boring way **3** to be happening > **go through** *verb* **1** to experience (an unpleasant event) **2** (of a law or agreement) to be approved and become official > **go through with** *verb* to do (something), even though it is unpleasant

goad *verb* to provoke (someone) to take some kind of action, usually in anger

go-ahead *noun* permission to do something

goal *noun* **1** *Sport* posts through which the ball or puck has to be propelled to score **2** score made in this way **3** aim or purpose

goalkeeper *noun Sport* player whose task is to stop shots entering the goal

goanna *noun* large Australian lizard

goat *noun* animal like a sheep with coarse hair, a beard and horns

go-away bird *noun S Afr* grey lourie, a type of bird that lives in open grassland

gob *noun Brit, Aust, NZ informal* mouth

gobble gobbles gobbling gobbled *verb* **1** to eat (food) hastily and greedily **2** to make the rapid gurgling cry of the male turkey

gobbledygook or **gobbledegook** *noun* language or jargon that is impossible to understand

goblet *noun* drinking cup without handles

goblin *noun* ugly mischievous creature in fairy stories

god *noun* **1** spirit or being worshipped as having supernatural power **2** object of worship, idol **3 God** (in religions such as Islam, Christianity and Judaism) the Supreme Being, creator and ruler of the universe **4 the gods** top balcony in a theatre

godchild godchildren *noun* child for whom a person stands as godparent > **goddaughter** *noun* girl for whom a person stands as godparent > **godson** *noun* boy for whom a person stands as godparent

goddess goddesses *noun* female god

godparent *noun* person who promises at a child's baptism to bring the child up as a Christian > **godfather** *noun* **1** male godparent **2** head of a criminal, especially Mafia, organization > **godmother** *noun* female godparent

godsend *noun* something unexpected but welcome

goggles *plural noun* protective spectacles

going *noun* condition of the ground for walking or riding over

gold *noun* 1 yellow precious metal 2 coins or articles made of this ▷ *adjective* 3 gold-coloured

golden *adjective* 1 made of gold 2 gold-coloured 3 very successful or promising

golden rule *noun* important principle

golden wedding *noun* fiftieth wedding anniversary

goldfish *noun* orange fish kept in ponds or aquariums
▌ The plural of *goldfish* is *goldfish*

goldsmith *noun* person whose job is making jewellery out of gold

golf *noun* outdoor game in which a ball is struck with clubs into a series of holes > **golfer** *noun* person who plays golf

golf course *noun* area of grassy land where people play golf

gondola *noun* long narrow boat used in Venice

gone *verb* past participle of **go**

gong *noun* flat circular piece of metal that produces a note when struck

good better best *adjective* 1 pleasant, acceptable or satisfactory 2 kind, thoughtful and loving 3 skilful or successful: *good at art* 4 well-behaved 5 used to emphasize something: *a good few million pounds* 6 **as good as** virtually ▷ *noun* 7 benefit 8 positive moral qualities 9 **for good** permanently
▌ *Good* is an adjective, and should not be used as an adverb. You should say that *a person did well* not *did good*

goodbye *interjection, noun* expression used on parting

Good Friday *noun* Friday before Easter, when Christians remember the crucifixion of Christ

good-natured *adjective* friendly, pleasant and even-tempered

goodness *noun* 1 quality of being kind ▷ *interjection* 2 exclamation of surprise

goods *plural noun* 1 merchandise 2 property

goodwill *noun* kindly feeling

goody goodies *noun* 1 *informal* hero in a book or film 2 enjoyable thing

goose geese *noun* web-footed bird like a large duck

gooseberry gooseberries *noun* edible yellowy-green berry

gore gores goring gored *noun* 1 blood from a wound ▷ *verb* 2 to pierce (someone) with horns

gorge gorges gorging gorged *noun* 1 deep narrow valley ▷ *verb* 2 **gorge yourself** to eat greedily

gorgeous *adjective* 1 strikingly beautiful or attractive 2 *informal* very pleasant

gorilla *noun* very large strong ape with very dark fur

gorse *noun* prickly yellow-flowered shrub

gory gorier goriest *adjective* 1 horrific or bloodthirsty 2 involving bloodshed

gosling *noun* young goose

gospel *noun* 1 **Gospel** any of the first four books of the New Testament 2 unquestionable truth 3 Black religious music originating in the churches of the Southern US

gossip gossips gossiping gossiped *noun* 1 idle talk, especially about other people 2 person who engages in gossip ▷ *verb* 3 to engage in gossip

got *verb* 1 past of **get** 2 **have got** to possess 3 **have got to** to need or be required to

gouge gouges gouging gouged *verb* 1 to scoop or force (something) out **2** to cut (a hole or groove) in something

goulash *noun* rich stew seasoned with paprika, originally from Hungary

gourd *noun* fleshy fruit of a climbing plant

gourmet *noun* person who enjoys good food and drink and knows a lot about it

gout *noun* disease causing inflammation of the joints, especially in the toes

govern *verb* **1** to control (a country) **2** to influence (a situation)

governess governesses *noun* woman teacher in a private household

government *noun* **1** group of people who govern a country **2** control and organization of a country > **governmental** *adjective*: *a governmental agency*

governor *noun* **1** person who controls and organizes a state or an institution **2** *Aust* representative of the King or Queen in a State

governor general governors general *noun* chief representative of the King or Queen in Australia, New Zealand and other Commonwealth countries

gown *noun* **1** woman's long formal dress **2** official robe worn by judges, clergymen, etc

GP GPs *abbreviation* general practitioner

grab grabs grabbing grabbed *verb* **1** to grasp (something) suddenly, snatch (something) > *noun* **2** sudden snatch

grace graces gracing graced *noun* **1** beauty and elegance; poise **2** polite kind behaviour **3** short prayer of thanks for a meal **4 Grace** title of a duke, duchess

or archbishop > *verb* **5** to kindly agree to be present at (an event) > **graceful** *adjective*: *graceful ballerinas* > **gracefully** *adverb*

gracious *adjective* **1** kind, polite and pleasant > *interjection* **2 good gracious!** exclamation of surprise > **graciously** *adverb*

grade grades grading graded *noun* **1** place on a scale of quality, rank or size **2** mark or rating > *verb* **3** to arrange (things) in grades

gradient *noun* (degree of) slope

gradual *adjective* occurring, developing or moving in small stages > **gradually** *adverb* happening or changing slowly over a long period of time

graduate graduates graduating graduated *verb* **1** to receive a degree or diploma **2** to progress gradually from one thing towards another > *noun* **3** holder of a degree > **graduation** *noun*: *they asked what his plans were after graduation*

graffiti *(plural) noun* words or drawings scribbled or sprayed on walls etc

> Although *graffiti* is a plural in Italian, the language it comes from, in English it can be either a singular or a plural noun

graft *noun* **1** surgical transplant of skin or tissue **2** shoot of a plant set in the stalk of another **3** *informal* hard work > *verb* **4** to transplant (living tissue) surgically **5** to insert (a plant shoot) in another stalk

grain *noun* **1** seedlike fruit of a cereal plant **2** cereal plants in general **3** small hard particle **4** very small amount **5** arrangement of fibres, as in wood **6** texture or pattern resulting from this **7 go against the grain** to be contrary to your natural inclination

gram or **gramme** *noun* metric unit of mass equal to one thousandth of a kilogram

grammar *noun* branch of linguistics dealing with the form, function, and order of words

grammar school *noun* **1** *Brit* especially formerly, a secondary school providing an education with a strong academic bias **2** *Aust* private school, usually one controlled by a church

grammatical *adjective* according to the rules of grammar > **grammatically** *adverb*

gran *noun Brit, Aust, NZ informal* grandmother

granary granaries *noun* **1** storehouse for grain ▷ *adjective* **2** *trademark* (of bread) containing whole grains of wheat

grand *adjective* **1** large or impressive; imposing **2** dignified or haughty **3** *informal* excellent **4** (of a total) final ▷ *noun* **5** *informal* thousand pounds or dollars > **grandly** *adverb* in a manner intended to impress

grandad or **granddad** *noun informal* grandfather

grandchild grandchildren *noun* child of your son or daughter

granddaughter *noun* female grandchild

grandeur *noun* magnificence

grandfather *noun* male grandparent

grandfather clock *noun* tall standing clock with a pendulum and wooden case

grandiose *adjective* intended to be very impressive but seeming ridiculous

grandma *noun informal* grandmother

grandmother *noun* female grandparent

grandparent *noun* parent of your father or mother

grand piano grand pianos *noun* large harp-shaped piano with the strings set horizontally

grandson *noun* male grandchild

grandstand *noun* terraced block of seats giving the best view at a sports ground

granite *noun* very hard rock often used in building

granny grannies *noun informal* grandmother

grant *verb* **1** to allow someone to have (something) **2** to admit the truth of (something) **3 take for granted a** to accept (something) as true without proof **b** to take advantage of (someone) without due appreciation ▷ *noun* **4** sum of money provided by a government for a specific purpose, such as education

granule *noun* small grain

grape *noun* small juicy green or purple berry, eaten raw or used to produce wine, raisins, currants or sultanas

grapefruit *noun* large round yellow citrus fruit

grapevine *noun* **1** grape-bearing vine **2** *informal* unofficial way of spreading news

graph *noun* diagram in which a line shows how two sets of numbers or measurements are related

-graph *suffix meaning* writer or recorder of some sort or something made by writing, drawing or recording: *telegraph; autograph*

graphic *adjective* **1** vividly descriptive **2** of or using drawing, painting, etc > **graphically** *adverb* in a vividly descriptive fashion > **graphics** *plural noun* diagrams, graphs, etc, especially as used on a television programme or computer screen

graphite *noun* soft black form of carbon, used in pencil leads

grapple grapples grappling grappled *verb* (followed by *with*) **1** to try to cope with (something difficult) **2** to come to grips with (a person)

grasp *verb* **1** to grip (something) firmly **2** to understand (something) ▷ *noun* **3** grip or clasp **4** understanding

grass grasses *noun* common green plant that grows on lawns and in parks > **grassy** *adjective* covered in grass

grasshopper *noun* jumping insect with long hind legs

grate grates grating grated *verb* **1** to rub (food) into small bits against a grater **2** to scrape with a harsh rasping noise **3** (followed by *on*) to annoy (someone) ▷ *noun* **4** framework of metal bars for holding fuel in a fireplace

grateful *adjective* feeling or showing gratitude; thankful > **gratefully** *adverb* thankfully

grater *noun* small metal tool used for grating food

gratify gratifies gratifying gratified *verb* **1** to satisfy or please (someone) **2** to indulge (a desire or whim)

grating *adjective* **1** harsh or rasping ▷ *noun* **2** framework of metal bars covering an opening

gratis *adverb, adjective* free, for nothing

gratitude *noun* feeling of being thankful for a favour or gift; appreciation

gratuitous *adjective* unjustified: *gratuitous violence* > **gratuitously** *adverb* unnecessarily

grave[1] **graves; graver gravest** *noun* **1** hole for burying a corpse ▷ *adjective* **2** serious and solemn > **gravely** *adverb*

grave[2] *noun* accent (`) over a vowel to indicate a special pronunciation

gravel *noun* mixture of small stones and coarse sand

graven *adjective* carved or engraved

gravestone *noun* stone marking a grave

graveyard *noun* area of land where corpses are buried

gravitate gravitates gravitating gravitated *verb* to be drawn towards something

gravitation *noun* force that causes objects to be attracted to each other > **gravitational** *adjective*: *the earth's gravitational pull*

gravity *noun* **1** force of attraction of one object for another, especially of objects to the earth **2** seriousness or importance

gravy *noun* **1** juices from meat in cooking **2** sauce made from these

graze grazes grazing grazed *verb* **1** (of animals) to feed on grass **2** to scratch or scrape (a body part) ▷ *noun* **3** slight scratch or scrape

grease greases greasing greased *noun* **1** soft melted animal fat **2** any thick oily substance ▷ *verb* **3** to apply grease to (something) > **greasy** *adjective* covered with or containing grease

great *adjective* **1** large in size or number **2** important **3** *informal* excellent > **greatly** *adverb*: *People would benefit greatly from a pollution-free environment* > **greatness** *noun*: *Abraham Lincoln achieved greatness*

Great Britain *noun* largest of the British Isles, consisting of England, Scotland, and Wales

greatcoat *noun* heavy overcoat

Great Dane *noun* very large dog with short smooth hair

great-grandfather *noun* father's or mother's grandfather

great-grandmother *noun* father's or mother's grandmother

greed *noun* excessive desire for food, wealth, etc

greedy greedier greediest *adjective* wanting more of something than you really need > **greedily** *adverb* > **greediness** *noun* being greedy

Greek *noun* **1** language of Greece **2** person from Greece ▷ *adjective* **3** of Greece, the Greeks or the Greek language

green *adjective* **1** of a colour between blue and yellow **2** **Green** of or concerned with environmental issues **3** *informal* young and inexperienced ▷ *noun* **4** colour between blue and yellow **5** area of grass in the middle of a village **6** grassy area on which putting or bowls is played **7** area of smooth short grass around each hole on a golf course **8** **Green** person concerned with environmental issues **9** **greens** green vegetables > **greenery** *noun* vegetation

greenfly greenfly or **greenflies** *noun* small green insect that damages plants

greengrocer *noun* Brit shopkeeper selling vegetables and fruit

greenhouse *noun* glass building for growing plants that need to be kept warm

greenhouse effect *noun* rise in the temperature of the earth caused by heat absorbed from the sun being unable to leave the atmosphere

green paper *noun* Brit, Aust, NZ report published by the government containing proposals to be discussed before decisions are made about them

greenstone *noun* NZ type of green jade used for Maori ornaments

greet *verb* **1** to meet (someone) with expressions of welcome **2** to react to (something) in a specified manner: *This decision was greeted with dismay*

greeting *noun* something friendly that you say to someone you meet

gregarious *adjective* fond of company

grenade *noun* small bomb thrown by hand or fired from a rifle

grevillea *noun* Australian evergreen tree or shrub

grew *verb* past tense of **grow**

grey *adjective* **1** of a colour between black and white **2** dull or boring ▷ *noun* **3** grey colour > **greying** *adjective* (of hair) turning grey > **greyness** *noun*: *winter's greyness*

greyhound *noun* swift slender dog used in racing

grid *noun* **1** network of horizontal and vertical lines, bars, etc **2** national network of electricity supply cables

grief *noun* deep sadness; sorrow

grievance *noun* cause for complaint

grieve grieves grieving grieved *verb* to feel grief or cause (someone) to feel grief

grievous *adjective* very serious > **grievously** *adverb*: *grievously injured*

grill *noun* **1** device on a cooker that radiates heat downwards **2** a metal frame on which you cook food over a fire **3** grilled food ▷ *verb* **4** to cook (food) under a grill **5** to question (someone) relentlessly

grille or **grill** *noun* grating over an

opening

grim grimmer grimmest *adjective*
1 (of a person) very serious or
stern **2** (of a place) unattractive
and depressing **3** (of a situation
or piece of news) very unpleasant
and worrying ▷ **grimly** *adverb* in a
grim manner

**grimace grimaces grimacing
grimaced** *noun* **1** ugly or distorted
facial expression of pain, disgust,
etc ▷ *verb* **2** to make a grimace

grime *noun* ingrained dirt ▷ **grimy**
adjective: *a grimy industrial city*

grin grins grinning grinned *verb*
1 to smile broadly, showing the
teeth ▷ *noun* **2** broad smile

grind grinds grinding ground *verb*
1 to crush or rub (something) to a
powder; powder **2** to scrape (the
teeth) together with a harsh noise

grip grips gripping gripped *noun*
1 firm hold or grasp **2** control over
a situation **3** a handle on a bat or
a racket ▷ *verb* **4** to grasp or hold
(something) tightly

grisly grislier grisliest *adjective*
horrifying or ghastly

grit grits gritting gritted *noun*
1 rough particles of sand ▷ *verb* **2** to
spread grit on (an icy road) **3** **grit
your teeth** to decide to carry on
in a difficult situation ▷ **gritty**
adjective **1** containing or covered
with grit **2** brave and determined
3 (of a drama) realistic

grizzled *adjective* grey-haired

grizzly bear *noun* large greyish-
brown American bear

groan *noun* **1** deep sound of grief or
pain ▷ *verb* **2** to utter a groan

grocer *noun* shopkeeper who sells
many kinds of food and other
household goods

grocery groceries *noun* **1** business
or premises of a grocer **2** **groceries**

goods sold by a grocer

grog *noun* *Brit, Aust, NZ informal* any
alcoholic drink

groin *noun* place where the legs join
the abdomen

groom *noun* **1** person who looks
after horses **2** bridegroom ▷ *verb*
3 to brush or clean (a horse) **4** to
train (someone) for a future role

groove *noun* long narrow channel
in a surface ▷ **grooved** *adjective*
having deep grooves on the surface

grope gropes groping groped
verb (followed by *for*) **1** to search
for (something you cannot see)
with your hands **2** to try to think of
(something such as the solution to
a problem)

**gross grosser grossest; grosses
grossing grossed** *adjective*
1 extremely bad: *a gross betrayal*
2 (of speech or behaviour) vulgar
3 *informal* disgusting or repulsive
4 total; without deductions **5** (of
weight) including container
weight ▷ *noun* **6** twelve dozen
▷ *verb* **7** to earn (an amount of
money) in total ▷ **grossly** *adverb*:
grossly overweight

grotesque *adjective* **1** very strange
and ugly **2** exaggerated and absurd
▷ **grotesquely** *adverb*

grotto grottoes or **grottos** *noun*
small picturesque cave

ground *noun* **1** surface of the
earth **2** soil **3** area used for a
specific purpose: *rugby ground*
4 position in an argument or
controversy **5** **grounds a** enclosed
land round a house **b** reason or
motive ▷ *verb* **6** (followed by *in*)
to base or establish (something)
on something else **7** to ban (an
aircraft) from flying **8** past of **grind**

ground floor *noun* floor of a
building level with the ground

grounding *noun* basic knowledge of a subject

groundless *adjective* without reason

group *noun* 1 number of people or things regarded as a unit 2 small band of musicians or singers ▷ *verb* 3 to place or form (people or things) into a group

grouping *noun* number of things or people that are linked together in some way

grouse *noun* stocky game bird ■ The plural of *grouse* is *grouse*

grove *noun literary* small group of trees

grovel grovels grovelling grovelled *verb* to behave humbly in order to win a superior's favour

grow grows growing grew grown *verb* 1 to develop physically 2 (of a plant) to exist 3 to cultivate (plants) 4 to increase in size or degree 5 to become gradually: *It was growing dark* > **grow on** *verb informal* to gradually become liked by (someone) > **grow up** *verb* to mature

growl *verb* 1 to make a low rumbling sound 2 to utter (something) with a growl ▷ *noun* 3 growling sound

grown-up *adjective, noun* adult

growth *noun* 1 growing 2 increase 3 process by which something develops to its full size 4 tumour

grub *noun* 1 legless insect larva 2 *informal* food

grubby grubbier grubbiest *adjective* dirty

grudge grudges grudging grudged *verb* 1 to be unwilling to give or allow (someone something) ▷ *noun* 2 resentment

grudging *adjective* done or felt unwillingly: *grudging admiration* > **grudgingly** *adverb* unwillingly

gruel *noun* thin porridge

gruelling *adjective* exhausting or severe

gruesome *adjective* causing horror and disgust

gruff *adjective* rough or surly in manner or voice

grumble grumbles grumbling grumbled *verb* 1 to complain ▷ *noun* 2 complaint

grumpy grumpier grumpiest *adjective* bad-tempered and fed-up

grunt *verb* 1 to make a low short gruff sound, like a pig ▷ *noun* 2 pig's sound 3 gruff noise

guarantee guarantees guaranteeing guaranteed *noun* 1 formal assurance, especially in writing, that a product will meet certain standards 2 something that makes a specified condition or outcome certain ▷ *verb* 3 to make certain (that something will happen) > **guarantor** *noun* person who gives or is bound by a guarantee

guard *verb* 1 to watch over (someone or something) to protect or to prevent escape ▷ *noun* 2 person or group that guards 3 official in charge of a train 4 screen for enclosing anything dangerous > **guard against** *verb* to take precautions against

guardian *noun* 1 keeper or protector 2 person legally responsible for a child, mentally ill person, etc > **guardianship** *noun* position of being a guardian

guernsey guernseys *noun* 1 *Aust, NZ* jersey 2 *Aust* sleeveless top worn by an Australian Rules football player

guerrilla or **guerilla** *noun* member of an unofficial armed force fighting regular forces

guess guesses guessing guessed
verb **1** to form or express an
opinion that it is the case, without
having much information ▷ noun
2 estimate or conclusion reached
by guessing

guest noun **1** person entertained
at another's house or at another's
expense **2** invited performer or
speaker **3** customer at a hotel or
restaurant

guffaw noun **1** crude noisy laugh
▷ verb **2** to laugh in this way

guidance noun leadership,
instruction or advice

guide guides guiding guided
noun **1** person who conducts tour
expeditions **2** person who shows
the way **3** book of instruction or
information **4** **Guide** member of
an organization for girls equivalent
to the Scouts ▷ verb **5** to act as a
guide for (someone) **6** to control,
supervise or influence (someone)

guidebook noun book that gives
information about a place

guide dog noun dog trained to lead
a blind person

guideline noun set principle for
doing something

guild noun organization or club

guile noun cunning or deceit
> **guileless** adjective open and
honest

guillotine noun machine for
beheading people

guilt noun **1** fact or state of having
done wrong **2** remorse for
wrongdoing

guilty guiltier guiltiest adjective
1 responsible for an offence or
misdeed **2** feeling or showing guilt
> **guiltily** adverb

guinea noun old British unit of
money, worth 21 shillings

guinea pig noun **1** small furry

animal without a tail, often
kept as a pet **2** person used to try
something out on

guise noun misleading appearance

guitar noun stringed instrument
with a flat back and a long neck,
played by plucking or strumming
> **guitarist** noun person who plays
the guitar

gulf noun **1** large deep bay
2 large difference in opinion or
understanding

gull noun long-winged sea bird

gullet noun muscular tube through
which food passes from the mouth
to the stomach

gullible adjective easily tricked
> **gullibility** noun being gullible

gully gullies noun channel cut by
running water

gulp verb **1** to swallow (food or drink)
hastily **2** to gasp ▷ noun **3** large
quantity of food or drink swallowed
at one time

gum noun **1** firm flesh in which the
teeth are set **2** sticky substance
obtained from certain trees
3 adhesive **4** chewing gum

gumboots plural noun Chiefly Brit
Wellington boots

gum tree noun eucalypt tree

gun noun weapon that fires bullets
or shells

gunboat noun small warship

gunfire noun repeated firing of guns

gunpowder noun explosive powder
made from a mixture of potassium
nitrate and other substances

gunshot noun shot or range of a gun

gunyah noun Aust hut or shelter
in the bush

guppy guppies noun small
colourful aquarium fish

gurdwara noun Sikh place of
worship

gurgle gurgles gurgling gurgled

verb, noun (to make) a bubbling noise

guru gurus *noun* **1** Hindu or Sikh religious teacher or leader **2** leader, adviser or expert

gush gushes gushing gushed *verb* **1** to flow out in large quantities **2** to express admiration in an exaggerated way **> gushing** *adjective*

gust *noun* sudden blast of wind **> gusty** *adjective*

gusto *noun* enjoyment or zest

gut guts gutting gutted *noun* **1** intestine **2 guts a** internal organs **b** *informal* courage ▷ *verb* **3** to remove the guts from (a dead fish) **4** (of a fire) to destroy the inside of (a building)

gutter *noun* shallow channel for carrying away water from a roof or roadside **> guttering** *noun* material for gutters

guttural *adjective* (of a sound) produced at the back of the throat

guy guys *noun* **1** *informal* man or boy **2** crude model of Guy Fawkes burnt on November 5th (**Guy Fawkes Day**) **3** rope or chain to steady or secure something

guzzle guzzles guzzling guzzled *verb* to eat or drink (something) greedily

gym *noun* **1** gymnasium **2** gymnastics

gymkhana *noun* horse-riding competition

gymnasium *noun* large room with equipment for physical training

gymnast *noun* expert in gymnastics **> gymnastic** *adjective*: *gymnastic exercises*

gymnastics *plural noun* exercises to develop strength and agility

gynaecology *noun* branch of medical science concerned with the female reproductive system **> gynaecological** *adjective*: *a routine gynaecological examination* **> gynaecologist** *noun* doctor who specializes in gynaecology

Gypsy Gypsies *noun* member of a travelling people found throughout Europe

gyrate gyrates gyrating gyrated *verb* to move round in a circle

haberdashery *noun* ribbons, needles, cotton and other small articles used for sewing

habit *noun* **1** something that you do often **2** something that you keep doing and find difficult to stop doing **3** loose dress-like costume of a monk or nun

habitat *noun* natural home of an animal or plant

habitation *noun formal* **1** activity of living somewhere **2** dwelling place

habitual *adjective* done regularly and repeatedly > **habitually** *adverb*

hack *verb* **1** to cut or chop violently ▷ *noun* **2** (inferior) writer or journalist

hacker *noun informal* someone who uses a computer to break into the computer system of a company or government

hackles *plural noun* **1** hairs on the back of an animal's neck which rise when it is angry **2 make your hackles rise** to make you feel angry or hostile

hackneyed *adjective* (of a word or phrase) unoriginal and overused

hacksaw *noun* small saw with a narrow blade set in a frame

had *verb* past of **have**

haddock *noun* edible sea fish of the North Atlantic
▋ The plural of *haddock* is *haddock*

haemoglobin *noun* substance in red blood cells which carries oxygen round the body

haemophilia *noun* hereditary illness in which the blood does not clot > **haemophiliac** *noun* person who suffers from haemophilia

haemorrhage haemorrhages haemorrhaging haemorrhaged *noun* **1** (instance of) heavy bleeding ▷ *verb* **2** to bleed heavily

haemorrhoids *plural noun* painful lumps around the anus that are caused by swollen veins; piles

hag *noun offensive* ugly old woman

haggard *adjective* looking tired and ill

haggis haggises *noun* Scottish dish made from the internal organs of a sheep, boiled together with oatmeal and spices in a bag traditionally made from the sheep's stomach

haggle haggles haggling haggled *verb* to bargain or wrangle over a price

hail *noun* **1** frozen rain **2** large number of insults, missiles, blows or other things ▷ *verb* **3** to fall as or like hail **4** to call out to (someone); greet **5** to stop (a taxi) by waving **6** to acknowledge (someone or something) publicly > **hail from** *verb* to come originally from

hair *noun* **1** soft threadlike strand that grows with others from the skin of animals and humans **2** such strands collectively, especially on the head

haircut *noun* **1** the cutting of someone's hair **2** style in which it is cut

hairdo hairdos *noun informal* hairstyle

hairdresser *noun* **1** person trained to cut and style hair **2** shop where people go to have their hair cut > **hairdressing** *noun, adjective*

hairline *noun* **1** the edge of the area at the top of the forehead where your hair starts ▷ *adjective* **2** (of a crack) very fine or narrow

hairpin *noun* U-shaped wire used to hold the hair in place

hairpin bend *noun* U-shaped bend in a road

hair-raising *adjective* very frightening or exciting

hairstyle *noun* cut and arrangement of a person's hair

hairy hairier hairiest *adjective* **1** covered with hair **2** *informal* difficult, exciting and rather frightening

hajj *noun* pilgrimage a Muslim makes to Mecca

haka haka or **hakas** *noun NZ* **1** ceremonial Maori dance with chanting **2** similar dance performed by a sports team before a match

hake *noun* edible sea fish related to the cod

■ The plural of *hake* is *hake*

hakea *noun* Australian tree or shrub with hard woody fruit

halal *noun* **1** meat from animals slaughtered according to Muslim law ▷ *adjective* **2** relating to such meat

halcyon *adjective literary* **1** peaceful and happy **2 halcyon days** time of peace and happiness

half halves *noun* **1** either of two equal parts that make up a whole **2** *informal* half-pint of beer, cider etc **3** half-price ticket ▷ *adjective* **4** denoting one of two equal parts

▷ *adverb* **5** to the extent of half **6** partially or partly: *I half expected him to explode in anger*

half-baked *adjective informal* (of an idea, theory or plan) not properly thought out

half board *noun* (at a hotel) breakfast and dinner but not lunch

half-brother *noun* brother related through one parent only

half-hearted *adjective* unenthusiastic

half-life *noun Physics* amount of time taken for a radioactive substance to lose half its radioactivity

half-pie *adjective NZ informal* incomplete

half-pipe *noun* large U-shaped ramp used for skateboarding, snowboarding, etc

half-sister *noun* sister related through one parent only

half-timbered *adjective* (of a house) having a framework of wooden beams that are left exposed and visible in the walls

half-time *noun Sport* short rest period between two halves of a game

halfway *adverb, adjective* at or up to half the distance between two points in place or time; midway

halibut halibut or **halibuts** *noun* large edible flatfish of North Atlantic

hall *noun* **1** (also **hallway**) entrance passage **2** large room or building for public meetings, dances, etc **3** *Brit* large country house

hallelujah *interjection* exclamation of praise to God

hallmark *noun* **1** typical feature or quality **2** mark indicating the standard of tested gold and silver ▷ *verb* **3** to stamp with a hallmark

hallowed *adjective* respected as being holy

Halloween or **Hallowe'en** *noun* October 31, celebrated by children by dressing up as ghosts, witches, etc

hallucinate hallucinates hallucinating hallucinated *verb* to see or experience strange things in your mind because of illness or drugs > **hallucination** *noun*: *Drugs can cause hallucinations* > **hallucinatory** *adjective*: *a hallucinatory state*

halo haloes or **halos** *noun* ring of light round the head of a holy figure

halt *verb* 1 to come or bring something to a stop ▷ *noun* 2 temporary stop

halter *noun* strap round a horse's head with a rope to lead it with

halve halves halving halved *verb* 1 to divide (something) in half 2 to reduce (something) or be reduced by half

halves *noun* plural of **half**

ham *noun* 1 smoked or salted meat from a pig's thigh 2 bad actor who overacts 3 amateur radio operator

hamburger *noun* minced beef shaped into a flat disc, cooked and usually served in a bread roll

hamlet *noun* small village

hammer *noun* 1 tool with a heavy metal head and a wooden handle, used to drive in nails etc 2 heavy metal ball on a wire, thrown as a sport ▷ *verb* 3 to hit (something) repeatedly with a hammer or your fist 4 *informal* to punish or defeat (someone) utterly 5 **hammer something into someone** to keep repeating something to someone in the hope that they will remember it

hammock *noun* hanging bed made of canvas or net

hamper *noun* 1 large wicker basket with a lid 2 selection of food and drink packed as a gift ▷ *verb* 3 to make it difficult for (someone or something) to move or progress

hamster *noun* small furry rodent with a short tail and cheek pouches that is often kept as a pet
▇ There is no *p* in *hamster*

hamstring *noun* tendon at the back of your knee

hand *noun* 1 part of your body at the end of your arm, consisting of a palm, four fingers and a thumb 2 style of handwriting 3 round of applause 4 pointer on a dial, especially on a clock 5 cards dealt to a player in a card game 6 manual worker 7 unit of length of four inches (10.16 centimetres) used to measure horses 8 **have a hand in** to be involved in 9 **give someone a hand** to help someone 10 **to hand, at hand** or **on hand** nearby 11 **on the one hand** way of introducing the first part of an argument or discussion when giving two contrasting points of view 12 **on the other hand** way of introducing the second part of an argument or discussion when giving two contrasting points of view 13 **out of hand** beyond control ▷ *verb* 14 to pass or give > **hand down** *verb* to pass (something) from one generation to another

handbag *noun* woman's small bag for carrying personal articles in

handbook *noun* small reference or instruction book

handcuff *noun* one of a linked pair of metal rings designed to be locked round a prisoner's wrists by the police

handful *noun* **1** amount that can be held in the hand **2** small number **3** *informal* person or animal that is difficult to control

hand-held *adjective* **1** designed to be held in the hand ▷ *noun* **2** computer that can be held in the hand

handicap handicaps handicapping handicapped *noun* **1** physical or mental disability **2** something that makes progress difficult **3** contest in which the competitors are given advantages or disadvantages according to their skill in an attempt to equalize their chances of winning **4** advantage or disadvantage given ▷ *verb* **5** to make it difficult for (someone) to do something

handicraft *noun* **1** activity such as embroidery or pottery which involves making things with your hands **2** any of the items produced

handiwork *noun* result of someone's work or activity

handkerchief *noun* small square of fabric used for blowing your nose

handle handles handling handled *noun* **1** part of an object that is designed for holding when you use it **2** small lever or knob used to open and close a door or window ▷ *verb* **3** to hold, feel or move (something) with your hands **4** to control or deal with

handlebars *plural noun* curved metal bar used to steer a cycle

handout *noun* **1** clothing, food or money given to a needy person **2** written information given out at a talk etc

hand-picked *adjective* carefully chosen

handset *noun* part (of a telephone) that you speak into and listen with

hands-free *adjective, noun* (of) a device allowing the user to make and receive phone calls without holding the handset

handshake *noun* the grasping and shaking of a person's hand by another person as a gesture of greeting, taking leave or agreement

handsome *adjective* **1** (especially of a man) good-looking **2** large or generous > **handsomely** *adverb*

handwriting *noun* (style of) writing by hand

handy handier handiest *adjective* **1** convenient, useful or conveniently near **2** skilful

handyman handymen *noun* man who is good at making or repairing things

hang hangs hanging hung *verb* **1** to attach (something) or be attached at the top with the lower part free **2** (*past*: **hanged**) to kill (someone) by suspending them by a rope around the neck ▷ *noun* **3 get the hang of** *informal* to begin to understand > **hang about** or **hang around** *verb* **1** *informal* to wait somewhere **2 hang about with** to spend a lot of time with > **hang back** *verb* to hesitate or be reluctant > **hang on** *verb* **1** (often followed by *to*) to hold tightly **2** *informal* to wait > **hang over** *verb* (of a future event or possibility) to worry or frighten (someone) > **hang up** *verb* to put down the receiver ending a telephone call

hangar *noun* large shed for storing aircraft

hanger *noun* (also **coat hanger**) curved piece of wood, wire or plastic, with a hook, for hanging up clothes

hanger-on hangers-on *noun* unwelcome follower of an

important person

hang-glider *noun* aircraft without an engine and consisting of a large frame covered in fabric, from which the pilot hangs in a harness > **hang-gliding** *noun*

hangi hangi or **hangis** *noun* (in New Zealand) Maori oven consisting of a hole in the ground lined with hot stones

hangman hangmen *noun* man who executes people by hanging

hangover *noun* headache and sickness after drinking too much alcohol

hang-up *noun informal* emotional problem

hank *noun* coil, especially of wool

hanker *verb* (followed by *after* or *for*) to want very much > **hankering** *noun*: He has a hankering to go back to acting

hanky hankies; also spelt **hankie** *noun informal* handkerchief

Hanukkah or **Chanukah** *noun* eight-day Jewish festival of lights

haphazard *adjective* not organized or planned > **haphazardly** *adverb*

hapless *adjective literary* unlucky

happen *verb* **1** to take place; occur **2** to chance (to be or do something)

happening *noun* event or occurrence

happiness *noun* feeling of great contentment or pleasure

happy happier happiest *adjective* **1** feeling or causing joy **2** satisfied that something is right **3** willing **4** lucky or fortunate > **happily** *adverb*

happy-go-lucky *adjective* carefree and cheerful

harangue harangues haranguing harangued *verb* **1** to talk to (someone) at length angrily, passionately and forcefully about

something ▷ *noun* **2** a long, angry, passionate and forceful speech

harass harasses harassing harassed *verb* to annoy or trouble (someone) constantly > **harassed** *adjective* > **harassment** *noun*: *intimidation and harassment*

harbinger *noun* someone or something that announces the approach of something: *I hate to be the harbinger of doom*

harbour *noun* **1** sheltered port ▷ *verb* **2** to hide (someone) secretly in your house; shelter **3** to have (a feeling, hope or grudge) for a long time

hard *adjective* **1** firm, solid or rigid **2** difficult **3** requiring a lot of effort **4** unkind or unfeeling **5** causing pain, sorrow or hardship **6** (of water) containing calcium salts which stop soap lathering freely **7** (of a drug) strong and addictive **8** (of evidence or facts) provable and indisputable **9** (of drink, liquor) strong and alcoholic ▷ *adverb* **10** with great energy or effort **11** with great intensity **12** to the extent of becoming firm, solid or rigid: *The ground was baked hard* > **hardness** *noun*

hard and fast *adjective* fixed and unchangeable: *hard and fast rules*

hardback *noun* a book with a stiff cover

hard-bitten *adjective* tough and determined

hard copy hard copies *noun* paper printout

hard core *noun* (in an organization) group of people most resistant to change

harden *verb* to become hard or get harder > **hardening** *noun*

hardened *adjective* used to and no longer affected by something unpleasant: *hardened criminals*

hard labour *noun* difficult and exhausting physical work; used in some countries as a punishment for a crime

hardly *adverb* **1** scarcely or not at all **2** with difficulty

> You should not use *hardly* with a negative word like *not* or *no*: *He could hardly hear her* not *He could not hardly hear her*

hard-nosed *adjective* tough, practical and realistic

hard of hearing *adjective* unable to hear well

hardship *noun* **1** suffering **2** difficult circumstances

hard shoulder *noun* area at the edge of a motorway where you can park in the event of a breakdown

hard up *adjective informal* short of money

hardware *noun* **1** metal tools and implements **2** machinery used in a computer system **3** heavy military equipment, such as tanks and missiles

hard-wearing *adjective* strong, well-made and long-lasting

hardwood *noun* **1** strong hard wood from a tree such as oak or ash **2** the tree itself

hardy hardier hardiest *adjective* able to stand difficult conditions > **hardiness** *noun*

hare hares haring hared *noun* **1** animal like a large rabbit, with longer ears and legs ▷ *verb* **2** (usually followed by *off*) to run (away) quickly

harem *noun* **1** group of wives or mistresses of one man, especially in Muslim societies **2** place where these women live

hark *verb old-fashioned* to listen > **hark back** *verb* to return (to an

earlier subject)

harm *verb* **1** to injure or damage ▷ *noun* **2** injury or damage

harmful *adjective* causing injury or damage

harmless *adjective* **1** safe to use or be near **2** unlikely to cause problems or annoyance > **harmlessly** *adverb*

harmonic *adjective* using musical harmony

harmonica *noun* small musical instrument which you play by blowing and sucking while moving it across your lips; mouth organ

harmonious *adjective* **1** peaceful, friendly and free from disagreement **2** attractively and agreeably combined > **harmoniously** *adverb*

harmony harmonies *noun* **1** peaceful agreement and cooperation **2** pleasant combination of notes sounded at the same time **3** *Music* the structure and relationship of chords in a piece of music

harness harnesses harnessing harnessed *noun* **1** arrangement of straps for attaching a horse to a cart or plough **2** set of straps fastened round someone's body to attach something: *a safety harness* ▷ *verb* **3** to bring (something) under control in order to make use of it

harp *noun* large triangular stringed instrument played with the fingers > **harpist** *noun*

harpoon *noun* **1** barbed spear attached to a rope used for hunting whales ▷ *verb* **2** to spear (a whale or large fish) with a harpoon

harpsichord *noun* stringed keyboard instrument

harrowing *adjective* very distressing

harsh *adjective* **1** severe and difficult to cope with **2** unkind or unsympathetic **3** extremely hard, bright or rough > **harshly** adverb > **harshness** noun

harvest noun **1** (season for) the gathering of crops **2** crops gathered ▷ verb **3** to gather (a ripened crop) > **harvester** noun

has verb third person singular of the present tense of **have**

has-been noun informal person who is no longer popular or successful

hash hashes noun **1** (also **hash mark**) the character (#) **2** dish of diced cooked meat and vegetables reheated **3** informal hashish **4 make a hash of** informal to do (a job) badly

hashish noun drug made from the cannabis plant

hassle hassles hassling hassled informal noun **1** trouble or bother ▷ verb **2** to bother (someone) with repeated requests to do something; pester

haste noun **1** (excessive) quickness **2 make haste** to hurry or rush

hasten verb **1** to hurry **2** to cause (something) to happen earlier than otherwise

hasty hastier hastiest adjective (too) quick > **hastily** adverb (too) quickly

hat noun **1** covering for the head, often with a brim **2 keep something under your hat** to keep something secret

hatch hatches hatching hatched verb **1** (of a bird or reptile) to come out of the egg **2** (of an egg) to break open allowing a young bird or reptile to come out **3** to devise (a plot) ▷ noun **4** covered opening in a wall, floor or ceiling

hatchback noun car with a rear door that opens upwards

hatchet noun **1** small axe **2 bury**

the hatchet to make peace

hate hates hating hated verb **1** to dislike (someone or something) intensely ▷ noun **2** intense dislike

hatred noun intense dislike

hat trick noun three achievements in a row, especially in sport

haughty haughtier haughtiest adjective proud or arrogant > **haughtily** adverb

haul verb **1** to pull or drag (something or someone) with effort ▷ noun **2** amount gained by effort or theft **3 long haul** something that takes a lot of time and effort

haulage noun business or cost of transporting goods

haulier noun firm or person that transports goods by road

haunches plural noun buttocks and thighs

haunt verb **1** (of a ghost) to visit (a building, place) regularly **2** (of a memory or fear) to worry or trouble (someone) continually ▷ noun **3** place visited frequently

haunted adjective **1** frequented by ghosts **2** very worried or troubled

haunting adjective memorably beautiful or sad

have has having had verb **1** to possess or hold **2** to receive, take or obtain **3** to experience or be affected by **4** to cause to be done **5** to give birth to (a baby, foal, kittens etc) **6** used to form past tenses (with a past participle): *We have looked; She had done enough* **7 have to** to be obliged to; must: *I had to go* **8 had better** should or ought to > **have on** verb **1** to wear (clothing) **2** informal to tease or trick > **have up** verb to bring (someone) to trial

haven noun place of safety

havoc *noun* disorder and confusion

hawk *noun* **1** bird of prey with a short hooked bill and very good eyesight ▷ *verb* **2** to offer (goods) for sale in the street or door-to-door

hawthorn *noun* thorny shrub or tree producing white blossom and red berries

hay *noun* grass cut and dried as animal feed

hay fever *noun* allergy to pollen and grass, causing sneezing and watering eyes

haystack *noun* large firmly built pile of hay

hazard *noun* **1** something that could be dangerous ▷ *verb* **2** to put (something) at risk **3** to make (a guess) > **hazardous** *adjective*: *hazardous waste*

haze *noun* mist, often caused by heat

hazel *noun* **1** small tree producing edible nuts ▷ *adjective* **2** (of eyes) greenish-brown

hazy hazier haziest *adjective* **1** not clear; misty **2** confused or vague

he *pronoun refers to*: **1** male person or animal **2** a person or animal of unknown or unspecified sex ▷ *noun* **3** male person or animal

head *noun* **1** part of your body containing your eyes, mouth, nose and brain **2** mind and mental abilities **3** upper or most forward part of anything **4** most important end of something **5** person in charge of a group, organization or school **6** pus-filled tip of a spot or boil **7** white froth on beer **8** (of a computer or tape recorder) part that can read or write information **9** (*plural* **head**) person or animal considered as a unit **10** off your head *informal* foolish or insane **11** can't make head nor tail

of can't understand ▷ *adjective* **12** chief or principal ▷ *verb* **13** to be at the top or front of **14** to be in charge of **15** to move (in a particular direction) **16** to hit (a ball) with your head **17** to provide (something) with a heading > **head off** *verb* **1** to make (someone or something) change direction **2** to prevent (something) from happening > **heads** *adverb informal* with the side of a coin which has a portrait of a head on it uppermost

headache *noun* **1** pain in your head **2** *informal* cause of worry or annoyance

header *noun* **1** *Football* hitting a ball with your head **2** headlong fall

head-hunt *verb informal* (of a company) to approach and offer a job to (a person working for a rival company)

heading *noun* title written or printed at the top of a page

headland *noun* narrow piece of land jutting out into the sea

headlight *noun* powerful light on the front of a vehicle

headline *noun* **1** title at the top of a newspaper article, especially on the front page **2** **headlines** main points of a news broadcast

headlong *adverb, adjective* **1** with your head first **2** hastily

headmaster *noun* male head teacher

headmistress headmistresses *noun* female head teacher

headphones *plural noun* pair of small speakers which you wear over your ears to listen to a radio, CD player, etc without other people hearing

headquarters *plural noun* centre from which the operations of an organization are directed

headroom *noun* amount of space below a roof, arch, bridge etc under which an object must pass or fit

headstone *noun* memorial stone on a grave

headstrong *adjective* self-willed and obstinate

head teacher *noun* the teacher who is in charge of a school

headway *noun* progress

headwind *noun* wind blowing against you, hindering rather than helping your progress

heady headier headiest *adjective* intoxicating or exciting

heal *verb* to become well or make (someone) well > **healer** *noun*

health *noun* **1** condition of your body and the extent to which it is free from illness **2** state of being well; fitness

health food *noun* food believed to be good for you, especially food that is free from additives

healthy *adjective* **1** (of person, animal) having good health **2** (of food or an activity) good for you **3** (of an organization or system) functioning well; sound > **healthily** *adverb*

heap *noun* **1** pile of things one on top of another **2** *informal* (also **heaps**) large number or quantity ▷ *verb* **3** to gather (things) into a pile **4** (followed by *on*) to give a lot of (something) to (someone): *He was quick to heap praise on his secretary*

hear hears hearing heard *verb* **1** to pick up (a sound) with your ears **2** to listen to **3** to learn or be informed **4** *Law* to try (a case) **5 hear! hear!** exclamation of approval or agreement > **hearer** *noun* > **hear out** *verb* to listen to everything said by (someone) without interrupting

hearing *noun* **1** ability to hear **2** trial of a case

hearsay *noun* gossip or rumour

hearse *noun* funeral car used to carry a coffin

heart *noun* **1** organ that pumps blood round your body **2** centre of emotions, especially love **3** courage or spirit **4** central or most important part **5** shape representing a heart, used especially as a symbol of love **6** playing card with red heart-shaped symbols **7 by heart** from memory

heartache *noun* very great sadness and emotional suffering

heart attack *noun* serious medical condition in which the heart suddenly beats irregularly or stops completely

heartbreak *noun* intense grief > **heartbreaking** *adjective*: *a heartbreaking story* > **heartbroken** *adjective* suffering intense grief

heartburn *noun* burning sensation in the chest caused by indigestion

heartening *adjective* encouraging or uplifting

heart failure *noun* serious condition in which someone's heart does not work as well as it should, sometimes stopping completely

heartfelt *adjective* felt sincerely or strongly

hearth *noun* floor of a fireplace

heartless *adjective* cruel and unkind

heart-rending *adjective* causing great sorrow

heart-throb *noun informal* very attractive man, especially a film or pop star

heart-to-heart heart-to-hearts *noun* discussion in which two people talk about their deepest feelings

hearty heartier heartiest
adjective **1** friendly and enthusiastic
2 substantial and nourishing
3 strongly felt ▷ **heartily** *adverb*: *I'm
heartily sick of it*

heat *noun* **1** warmth or state of being
hot **2** temperature **3** hot weather
4 preliminary eliminating contest
or race to decide who will take
part in the later stages **5 on** or **in
heat** (of some female animals)
ready for mating ▷ *verb* **6** to make
(something) hot or become hot

heated *adjective* angry and excited

heater *noun* heating device

heath *noun Brit* area of open land
covered with rough grass or
heather

heathen *noun old-fashioned* person
who does not believe in one of the
established religions

heather *noun* low-growing plant
with small purple, pinkish or white
flowers, that grows on heaths and
moorland

heating *noun* **1** equipment used to
heat a building **2** process and cost
of running such equipment

heatwave *noun* period of time
when the weather is much hotter
than usual

heave heaves heaving heaved
verb **1** to lift, move or throw
(something heavy) with effort **2** to
utter (a sigh) **3** to rise and fall **4** to
vomit ▷ *noun* **5** instance of heaving

heaven *noun* **1** place believed
to be the home of God, where
good people go when they die
2 wonderful place or state **3 the
heavens** *literary* sky

heavenly *adjective* **1** of or like
heaven **2** *informal* wonderful or
beautiful

heavy heavier heaviest; heavies
adjective **1** great in weight or force
2 great in degree or amount **3** solid
and thick in appearance **4** using a
lot of something quickly **5** *informal*
serious and difficult to deal with or
understand **6 with a heavy heart**
with sadness or sorrow ▷ **heavily**
adverb ▷ **heaviness** *noun*

heavy-duty *adjective* (of
equipment or material) strong and
hard-wearing

heavy-handed *adjective* showing
a lack of care or thought and using
too much authority

heavy industry *noun* large-scale
industry in which large machinery
is used to produce large objects or
raw materials such as steel

heavyweight *noun* **1** a boxer in the
heaviest weight group **2** important
person with a lot of influence

Hebrew *noun* **1** ancient language
of the Hebrews **2** its modern form,
used in Israel **3** Hebrew-speaking
Jew living in Israel in past times
▷ *adjective* **4** relating to the
Hebrews and their customs

heckle heckles heckling heckled
verb to interrupt (a public speaker)
with comments, questions or
taunts ▷ **heckler** *noun*

hectare *noun* one hundred acres or
10 000 square metres (2.471 acres)

hectic *adjective* rushed or busy

hedge hedges hedging hedged
noun **1** row of bushes forming a
barrier or boundary ▷ *verb* **2** to
avoid answering a question or
dealing with a problem **3 hedge
your bets** to avoid the risk of
losing completely by supporting
two or more people or courses
of action

hedgehog *noun* small brown
animal with a protective covering
of sharp spikes covering its back

hedgerow *noun* bushes forming a hedge

hedonism *noun* belief that pleasure is the most important thing in life > **hedonist** *noun* > **hedonistic** *adjective*: *her hedonistic lifestyle*

heed *noun* **1** careful attention ▷ *verb* **2** to pay careful attention to

heel *noun* **1** back part of your foot **2** the part of a shoe or sock that goes under your heel **3** **down at heel** shabby and untidy ▷ *verb* **4** to repair the heel of (a shoe)

heeler *noun Aust* dog that herds cattle by biting at their heels

hefty heftier heftiest *adjective* of great size, force or weight

height *noun* **1** distance from base to top **2** distance above sea level **3** a high position or place **4** highest degree or point; peak

heighten *verb* to make (something) higher or more intense or to become higher or more intense

heinous *adjective* evil and shocking

heir *noun* person entitled to inherit property or title

heiress heiresses *noun* a woman who has inherited or is likely to inherit a large amount of money or property

heirloom *noun* object that has belonged to a family for generations

held *verb* past of **hold**

helicopter *noun* aircraft with rotating blades above it which enable it to take off vertically, hover and fly

helium *noun Chemistry* colourless odourless gas that is lighter than air and used to fill balloons

helix helixes *noun* spiral or coil

hell *noun* **1** place believed to be where wicked people go when they die **2** terrible place or state

hellbent *adjective* (followed by *on*) determined to

hellish *adjective informal* very unpleasant

hello *interjection* expression of greeting

helm *noun* **1** position from which a boat is steered **2** tiller or wheel for steering **3** **at the helm** in a position of leadership or control

helmet *noun* hard hat worn to protect your head

help *verb* **1** to make something easier, better or quicker for (someone) **2** to improve (a situation) **3** to stop yourself from: *I can't help smiling* **4** **help yourself** to take something, especially food or drink, without being served ▷ *noun* **5** assistance or support > **helper** *noun*

helpful *adjective* providing help or relief > **helpfully** *adverb*

helping *noun* single portion of food

helpless *adjective* weak, incapable or powerless > **helplessly** *adverb* > **helplessness** *noun*

hem hems hemming hemmed *noun* **1** edge (of a piece of clothing, curtain, etc) which has been turned over and sewn in place ▷ *verb* **2** to provide (something) with a hem > **hem in** *verb* to surround and prevent (someone) from moving

hemisphere *noun* one half of the earth, a brain or a sphere > **hemispherical** *adjective*

hemlock *noun* **1** poisonous plant with spotted stems and small white flowers; **2** poison made from it

hemp *noun* tall plant, some varieties of which are used to make rope, and others to produce the drug cannabis

hen *noun* **1** female chicken **2** female

of any bird

hence *formal conjunction* **1** for this reason ▷ *adverb* **2** from this time

henceforth *adverb* from now on

henchman henchmen *noun* person employed by someone powerful to carry out orders

hepatitis *noun* inflammation of the liver

her *pronoun* **1** refers to a female person or animal, or anything thought of as feminine; used as the object of a verb or preposition ▷ *adjective* **2** belonging to her

herald *noun* **1** (in the past) a messenger or announcer of important news ▷ *verb* **2** to be a sign of (a future event)

heraldry *noun* study of coats of arms and family trees > **heraldic** *adjective*

herb *noun* plant whose leaves are used in medicine or to flavour food > **herbal** *adjective*: *herbal remedies* > **herbalist** *noun* person who grows or specializes in the use of medicinal herbs

herbicide *noun* chemical used to destroy plants, especially weeds

herbivore *noun* animal that eats only plants > **herbivorous** *adjective*: *A few beetles are herbivorous*

herd *noun* **1** large group of animals feeding and living together **2** large crowd of people ▷ *verb* **3** to collect (animals or people) into a herd

here *adverb* in, at or to this place or point

hereafter *adverb* **1** *formal* after this point or time ▷ *noun* **2** **the hereafter** life after death

hereby *adverb formal* by means of this or as a result of this

hereditary *adjective* passed on to a child from a parent

heredity *noun* passing on

of characteristics from one generation to another through genes

herein *adverb formal* in this place or document

heresy heresies *noun* belief or behaviour considered wrong because it goes against accepted opinion or belief, especially religious belief

heretic *noun* person whose opinions go against accepted beliefs > **heretical** *adjective*: *heretical ideas*

herewith *adverb formal* with this letter or document

heritage *noun* possessions or traditions that have been passed from one generation to another

hermetic *adjective* sealed so as to be airtight > **hermetically** *adverb*: *hermetically sealed*

hermit *noun* person living in solitude, especially for religious reasons

hernia *noun* medical condition in which part of the intestine or another organ sticks through a weak point in the surrounding tissue

hero heroes *noun* **1** main male character in a film, book, etc **2** person who has done something exceptionally brave or good

heroic *adjective* **1** brave, courageous and determined **2** of or like a hero > **heroically** *adverb*

heroin *noun* highly addictive drug derived from morphine

heroine *noun* **1** main female character in a film, book, etc **2** woman or girl who has done something exceptionally brave or good

heroism *noun* great courage and bravery

heron *noun* wading bird with very long legs and a long beak and neck

herpes *noun* any of several inflammatory skin diseases, including shingles and cold sores

herring herrings or **herring** *noun* silvery food fish of northern seas

herringbone *noun* pattern made up of parallel rows of V-shapes within V-shapes, resembling the pattern of bones branching off the spine of a fish

hers *pronoun* object or objects belonging to or relating to a woman, girl or female animal that has already been mentioned

herself *pronoun* **1** used as an object of a verb or pronoun when the woman, girl or female animal that does an action is also the woman, girl or female animal that is directly affected by it: *She pulled herself out of the water* **2** used to emphasize *she*: *She herself knew nothing about it*

hertz *noun* *Physics* unit of frequency equal to one cycle per second
■ The plural of *hertz* is *hertz*

hesitant *adjective* undecided or uncertain about doing something > **hesitantly** *adverb*

hesitate hesitates hesitating hesitated *verb* **1** to pause or show uncertainty **2** to be reluctant (to do something) > **hesitation** *noun*: *"I know," he replied, without hesitation*

hessian *noun* thick coarse fabric used for making sacks

heterosexual *adjective* **1** (of person) sexually attracted to members of the opposite sex ▷ *noun* **2** person who is sexually attracted to people of the opposite sex

hewn *adjective* carved from a substance

hexagon *noun* six-sided shape > **hexagonal** *adjective*: *Choose*

between square and hexagonal tiles

heyday *noun* period of greatest success

hi *interjection* *informal* expression of greeting

hiatus hiatuses *noun* *formal* pause or interruption

hibernate hibernates hibernating hibernated *verb* (of an animal) to spend the winter in a state resembling deep sleep > **hibernation** *noun*: *The snakes have come out of hibernation*

hibiscus hibiscuses *noun* type of tropical shrub with brightly coloured flowers

hiccup hiccups hiccupping hiccupped; also spelt **hiccough** *noun* **1** one of a series of short uncontrolled intakes of breath, each accompanied by a gulping sound in your throat that you sometimes get especially if you have been eating or drinking too quickly **2** *informal* small problem; hitch ▷ *verb* **3** to make a hiccup

hide hides hiding hid hidden *verb* **1** to put (yourself or an object) somewhere very difficult to see or find in order to avoid discovery; conceal **2** to keep (something) secret ▷ *noun* **3** place of concealment, especially for a bird-watcher **4** skin of an animal > **hiding** *noun* **1** state of concealment: *in hiding* **2** *informal* severe beating

hideous *adjective* very ugly or unpleasant > **hideously** *adverb*

hide-out *noun* hiding place

hierarchy hierarchies *noun* system in which people or things are ranked according to how important they are > **hierarchical** *adjective*: *a hierarchical society*

hieroglyphic *noun* (also

hieroglyph) picture or symbol used in the writing system of ancient Egypt

hi-fi hi-fis *noun* set of stereo equipment on which you can play compact discs and tapes

high *adjective* **1** of a great height; tall **2** far above ground or sea level **3** greater than usual in degree, quantity or intensity **4** of great importance, quality or rank **5** (of a sound or note) close to the top of a range **6** *informal* under the influence of alcohol or drugs ▷ *adverb* **7** at or to a high level ▷ *noun* **8** a high point or level: *Morale reached a new high* **9 on a high** *informal* in a very excited and optimistic mood

highbrow *adjective* concerned with serious intellectual subjects

higher education *noun* education at colleges and universities

high jump *noun* athletics event involving jumping over a high bar

highlands *plural noun* mountainous or hilly areas

highlight *verb* **1** to give emphasis to ▷ *noun* **2** most interesting part or feature **3** lighter area of a painting, showing where light shines on things **4** lightened streak in your hair

highly *adverb* **1** extremely **2** very well

high-minded *adjective* having strong moral principles

Highness Highnesses *noun* title used to address or refer to a royal person

high-pitched *adjective* (of sound) high or rather shrill

high-rise *adjective* (of a building) having many storeys

high school *noun* secondary school

high tea *noun* early evening meal consisting of a cooked dish, bread, cakes and tea

high tide *noun* the time when the sea is at its highest level

highway highrways *noun* **1** public road **2** *US, Aust, NZ* main road

Highway Code *noun* regulations and recommendations applying to all road users

highwayman highwaymen *noun* (formerly) robber, usually on horseback, who robbed travellers at gunpoint

hijack *verb* to seize control of (an aircraft or other vehicle) during a journey > **hijacker** *noun* > **hijacking** *noun*

hike hikes hiking hiked *noun* **1** long walk in the country, especially for pleasure ▷ *verb* **2** to go for a long walk > **hiker** *noun*

hilarious *adjective* very funny > **hilariously** *adverb*

hilarity *noun* great amusement and laughter

hill *noun* raised part of land, higher than the land surrounding it, but less high than a mountain > **hilly** *adjective*: *a hilly area*

hillbilly hillbillies *noun US* unsophisticated country person

hilt *noun* handle of a sword or knife

him *pronoun* refers to a male person or animal or a person or animal of unknown or unspecified sex; used as the object of a verb or preposition

himself *pronoun* **1** used as an object of a verb or pronoun when the man, boy or male animal that does an action is also the man, boy or male animal that is directly affected by it: *He pulled himself out of the water* **2** used to emphasize *he*: *He himself knew nothing about it*

hind *adjective* **1** situated at the back ▷ *noun* **2** female deer

hinder *verb* to get in the way of

(someone or something); hamper

Hindi *noun* language spoken in northern India

hindquarters *plural noun* back parts and back legs (of an animal)

hindrance *noun* **1** someone or something that causes difficulties or is an obstruction **2** act of hindering

hindsight *noun* ability to understand an event after it has taken place: *With hindsight, I realized how odd he is*

Hindu Hindus *noun* **1** person who practises Hinduism ▷ *adjective* **2** of Hinduism > **Hinduism** *noun* dominant religion of India, which involves the worship of many gods and a belief in reincarnation

hinge hinges hinging hinged *noun* **1** movable joint which attaches a door or window to its frame ▷ *verb* **2** (followed by *on*) to depend on

hint *noun* **1** indirect suggestion, clue or helpful piece of advice **2** small amount ▷ *verb* **3** to suggest indirectly

hinterland *noun* land lying behind a coast or near a city, especially a port

hip *noun* either side of the body between the pelvis and the thigh

hippo hippos *noun informal* hippopotamus

hippopotamus hippopotamuses or **hippopotami** *noun* large African animal with thick wrinkled skin, living near rivers

hippy hippies; also spelt **hippie** *noun* (esp. in the 1960s) someone rejecting conventional society and trying to live a life based on peace and love

hire hires hiring hired *verb* **1** to

pay to have temporary use of **2** to employ (someone) to do a job ▷ *noun* **3** temporary use in exchange for money

hirsute *adjective formal* hairy

his *adjective* **1** belonging to him ▷ *pronoun* **2** object or objects belonging to or relating to a man, boy or male animal that has already been mentioned, or to any person whose sex is unkown

Hispanic *adjective* Spanish or Latin-American

hiss hisses hissing hissed *verb* **1** to make a long s sound, especially to show disapproval or aggression ▷ *noun* **2** sound like that of a long *s*

histogram *noun* statistical graph in which the frequency of values is represented by vertical bars of varying heights and widths

historian *noun* person who studies and writes about history

historic *adjective* famous or significant in history

historical *adjective* **1** occurring in the past **2** based on history > **historically** *adverb*

history histories *noun* **1** study of the past **2** past events and developments **3** record or account of past events and developments **4** record of someone's past

histrionic *adjective* excessively dramatic > **histrionics** *plural noun* excessively dramatic behaviour

hit hits hitting hit *verb* **1** to strike (someone or something) forcefully **2** to come into violent contact with **3** to affect (someone) badly **4** to reach (a point or place) **5** **hit it off** *informal* to get on well together ▷ *noun* **6** instance of hitting **7** successful record, film, etc **8** *Computers* single visit to a website > **hit on** *verb* to think of (an idea)

hit and miss *adjective* sometimes successful and sometimes not

hit-and-run *adjective* (of a car accident) in which the driver responsible for the accident drives away without stopping

hitch hitches hitching hitched *noun* **1** minor problem ▷ *verb* **2** *informal* to travel by getting lifts from passing vehicles **3** to attach > **hitch up** *verb* to pull (something) up with a jerk

hitchhike hitchhikes hitchhiking hitchhiked *verb* to travel by getting lifts from passing vehicles > **hitchhiker** *noun* > **hitchhiking** *noun*

hi tech *adjective* using very advanced technology

hither *adverb* **1** *old-fashioned* to or towards this place **2 hither and thither** in all directions

hitherto *adverb formal* until this time

hit man hit men *noun* person hired to kill someone

HIV *abbreviation* human immunodeficiency virus: cause of AIDS

hive hives hiving hived *noun* **1** same as **beehive 2 hive of activity** place where people are very busy > **hive off** *verb* to separate (something) from a larger group

hoard *verb* **1** to save or store (objects, food); stockpile ▷ *noun* **2** store of things that has been saved or hidden; stash > **hoarder** *noun*

hoarding *noun* large board for displaying advertisements by the side of the road

hoarse *adjective* **1** (of a voice) rough and unclear **2** having a rough and unclear voice > **hoarsely** *adverb*

hoax hoaxes hoaxing hoaxed *noun* **1** trick or an attempt to deceive someone ▷ *verb* **2** to deceive or play a trick on > **hoaxer** *noun*

hob *noun Brit* surface on top of a cooker containing rings, hotplates or gas burners for cooking things

hobble hobbles hobbling hobbled *verb* **1** to walk lamely **2** to tie the legs of (a horse) together to restrict its movement

hobby hobbies *noun* something that you do for enjoyment in your spare time

hobbyhorse *noun* favourite topic

hock *noun* **1** joint in the back leg of an animal such as a horse that corresponds to the human ankle **2** white German wine

hockey *noun* **1** team game played on a field with a ball and curved sticks **2** *US* ice hockey

hoe hoes hoeing hoed *noun* **1** long-handled tool with a small square blade, used for loosening soil or weeding ▷ *verb* **2** to scrape or weed with a hoe

hog hogs hogging hogged *noun* **1** castrated male pig **2 go the whole hog** to do something completely or thoroughly in a bold or extravagant way ▷ *verb* **3** *informal* to take more than your share of (something) or keep (something) for too long

Hogmanay *noun* (in Scotland) New Year's Eve

hoi polloi *noun* the ordinary people

hoist *verb* **1** to raise or lift (something) up ▷ *noun* **2** device for lifting things

hokey-pokey *noun NZ* brittle toffee sold in lumps

hold holds holding held *verb* **1** to keep or support (something) in or with your hands or arms **2** to have or possess (power, office or an opinion) **3** to arrange for (a meeting, party, election, etc) to take place **4** to consider (someone or something) to be as specified: *Who are you holding responsible?* **5** to have space for (an amount or number) **6** *informal* to wait, especially on the telephone **7** to keep back or reserve (tickets or an order) **8** to maintain (something) in a specified position or state ▷ *noun* **9** act or way of holding **10** controlling influence **11** cargo compartment on a ship or aircraft > **hold back** *verb* to prevent or keep control of > **hold down** *verb* to keep (something) or keep it under control: *How can I hold down a job like this?* > **holder** *noun* > **hold on to** *verb* to continue to have (something) in spite of difficulties > **hold out** *verb* to stand firm and resist opposition in difficult circumstances > **hold up** *verb* to delay

holdall *noun* large strong travelling bag

hold-up *noun* **1** armed robbery **2** delay

hole holes holing holed *noun* **1** gap, opening or hollow **2** animal's burrow **3** *informal* weakness or error (in a theory or argument) **4** *informal* difficult situation **5** *Golf* small holes into which you have to hit the ball ▷ *verb* **6** to make holes in **7** to hit (a golf ball) into the target hole

Holi *noun* Hindu festival celebrated in spring

holiday holidays holidaying holidayed *noun* **1** time spent away from home for rest or recreation **2** day or other period of rest from work or studies ▷ *verb* **3** to take a holiday (somewhere)

holidaymaker *noun* a person who

is away from home on holiday

holiness *noun* **1** state of being holy **2** **Your Holiness** or **His Holiness** title used to address or refer to the Pope

hollow *adjective* **1** having a hole or space inside **2** (of a sound) as if echoing in a hollow place **3** without any real value or worth ▷ *noun* **4** space **5** dip in the land ▷ *verb* **6** to form a hollow in **7** to make (something) by forming such a hollow

holly *noun* evergreen tree with prickly leaves and red berries

holocaust *noun* destruction or loss of life on a massive scale

hologram *noun* three-dimensional photographic image

holster *noun* leather case for a hand gun, hung from a belt

holy holier holiest *adjective* **1** relating to God or a god **2** (of a person) religious and living a very pure and good life

homage *noun* act of respect or honour towards someone or something

home *noun* **1** place where you live **2** place for the care of the elderly, orphans, etc ▷ *adjective* **3** connected with or involving your home or country **4** *Sport* played on your own ground ▷ *adverb* **5** to or at home

homeland *noun* native country

homeless *adjective* **1** having nowhere to live ▷ *plural noun* **2** people who have nowhere to live > **homelessness** *noun*

homely *adjective* simple, ordinary and comfortable

homeopathy *noun* treatment of disease by small doses of a drug that produces symptoms of the disease in healthy people > **homeopath** *noun* person

who practises homeopathy
> **homeopathic** adjective

homeowner noun person who owns the home in which he or she lives

home page noun Computers introductory information about a website with links to the information or services provided

homesick adjective unhappy because of being away from home and missing family and friends > **homesickness** noun

homespun adjective not sophisticated or complicated: The book is simple homespun philosophy

homestead noun house and its land and other buildings, especially a farm

home truths plural noun unpleasant facts told to a person about himself or herself

homeward adjective 1 towards home ▷ adverb 2 (also **homewards**) towards home

homework noun 1 school work done at home 2 preparatory research and work

homicide noun 1 killing of a human being 2 person who kills someone > **homicidal** adjective

homing adjective 1 (of a device) capable of guiding itself to a target 2 (of a pigeon or instinct) with or relating to the ability to find home

homogeneous or **homogenous** adjective formed of similar parts

homograph noun word spelt the same as another, but with a different meaning

homonym noun word spelt or pronounced the same as another, but with a different meaning

homophone noun word pronounced the same as another, but with a different meaning or

spelling, eg write and right

Homo sapiens noun formal scientific name for human beings as a species

homosexual adjective 1 (of person) sexually attracted to members of the same sex ▷ noun 2 person who is sexually attracted to people of the same sex > **homosexuality** noun

hone hones honing honed verb 1 to sharpen (a tool) 2 to improve and develop (a skill, ability or quality)

honest adjective 1 truthful and trustworthy 2 open and sincere > **honestly** adverb

honesty noun quality of being honest

honey noun 1 sweet edible sticky substance made by bees from nectar 2 term of endearment

honeycomb noun waxy structure of six-sided cells in which honey is stored by bees in a beehive

honeyeater noun small Australian bird that feeds on nectar from flowers

honeymoon noun holiday taken by a couple who have just got married

honeysuckle noun climbing shrub with sweet-smelling flowers

hongi noun NZ Maori greeting in which people touch noses

honk honks honking honked noun 1 sound made by a car horn 2 sound made by a goose ▷ verb 3 to make this sound 4 to cause (a horn) to make this sound

honorary adjective 1 (of a degree or title) held or given only as an honour 2 (of a job) unpaid

honour noun 1 sense of honesty and fairness 2 respect 3 award given out of respect 4 pleasure or privilege 5 **honours** class of university degree of a higher standard than a pass or ordinary degree ▷ verb **6** to give praise and attention to **7** to give an award to (someone) out of respect **8** to pay (a cheque or bill) **9** to keep (a promise)

honourable adjective worthy of respect or esteem

hood noun **1** loose head covering, often attached to a coat or jacket **2** folding roof of a convertible car or a pram **3** US, Aust car bonnet

-hood suffix added at the end of words to form nouns that indicate a state or condition: childhood

hooded adjective (of a garment) having a hood

hoof hooves or **hoofs** noun horny covering of the foot of a horse, deer, etc

hook noun **1** curved piece of metal, plastic, etc, used to catch, hang, hold or pull something **2** curving movement, for example of the fist in boxing, or of a golf ball **3 let someone off the hook** to cause someone to get out of a punishment or difficult situation ▷ verb **4** to fasten or catch (something) with or as if with a hook

hooked adjective **1** bent like a hook **2** (followed by on) informal addicted (to) or obsessed (with)

hooligan noun destructive and violent young person > **hooliganism** noun

hoop noun large ring, often used as a toy

hooray interjection same as **hurray**

hoot noun **1** sound of a car horn **2** cry of an owl **3** similar sound to that of an owl ▷ verb **4** to sound (a car horn) **5** to make a long oo sound like an owl

Hoover® noun **1** vacuum cleaner ▷ verb **2 hoover** to clean with a vacuum cleaner

hooves noun a plural of **hoof**

hop hops hopping hopped verb **1** to jump on one foot **2** to move in short jumps **3** informal to move quickly ▷ noun **4** instance of hopping **5** (often plural) climbing plant, the dried flowers of which are used to make beer

hope hopes hoping hoped verb **1** to want (something to happen or be true) ▷ noun **2** wish or feeling of desire and expectation

hopeful adjective having, expressing or inspiring hope > **hopefully** adverb **1** in a hopeful manner **2** it is hoped

❚ Some people do not like the use of hopefully to mean 'it is hoped', for example hopefully, we'll win

hopeless adjective **1** having no hope **2** certain to fail or be unsuccessful **3** unable to do something well; useless: I'm hopeless at remembering birthdays > **hopelessly** adverb > **hopelessness** noun

hopper noun large funnel-shaped container for storing substances such as grain or sand

hopscotch noun children's game of hopping in a pattern drawn on the ground

horde noun large crowd

horizon noun **1** apparent line that divides the earth and the sky **2 horizons** limits of what you want to do or are interested in: Travel broadens your horizons

horizontal adjective flat and parallel to the horizon > **horizontally** adverb

hormone noun **1** substance secreted by certain glands which stimulates certain organs of the body **2** synthetic substance with

the same effect > **hormonal**
adjective: *hormonal changes*

horn *noun* **1** one of a pair of bony growths sticking out of the heads of cattle, sheep, etc **2** substance of which horns are made **3** musical instrument with a tube or pipe of brass fitted with a mouthpiece **4** device on a vehicle sounded as a warning

hornet *noun* type of large wasp with a severe sting

horoscope *noun* prediction about a person's future based on the positions of the planets, sun and moon at his or her birth

horrendous *adjective* very unpleasant and shocking

horrible *adjective* **1** disagreeable and unpleasant **2** causing shock, fear or disgust > **horribly** *adverb*

horrid *adjective* disagreeable and unpleasant

horrific *adjective* causing horror: *a horrific attack*

horrify horrifies horrifying horrified *verb* to cause (someone) to feel horror or shock > **horrified** *adjective* > **horrifying** *adjective*

horror *noun* terror or hatred

hors d'oeuvre *noun* appetizer served before a main meal

horse *noun* **1** large animal with hooves, a mane and a tail, used for riding and pulling carts etc **2** piece of gymnastic equipment used for vaulting over

horseback *noun* **1 on horseback** riding a horse > *adjective* **2** on a horse or on horses

horsepower *noun* unit of power (equivalent to 745.7 watts), used to measure the power of an engine

horseradish *noun* strong-tasting root of a plant, often made into a sauce

horseshoe *noun* protective U-shaped piece of iron nailed to a horse's hoof, regarded as a symbol of good luck

horsey or **horsy** *adjective* very keen on horses

horticulture *noun* art or science of growing flowers, fruit and vegetables > **horticultural** *adjective*

hose hoses hosing hosed *noun* **1** flexible pipe along which liquid or gas can be passed ▷ *verb* **2** to wash or water (something) with a hose

hosiery *noun* stockings, socks and tights collectively

hospice *noun* nursing home for people who are dying

hospitable *adjective* welcoming to strangers or guests

hospital *noun* place where people who are sick or injured are looked after and treated

hospitality *noun* kindness in welcoming strangers or guests

hospitalize hospitalizes hospitalizing hospitalized; also spelt **hospitalise** *verb* to send or admit (someone) to hospital

host *noun* **1** person who entertains guests **2** place or country providing the facilities for an event **3** compere of a show **4** animal or plant on which a parasite lives **5** large number ▷ *verb* **6** to be the host of (an event or party)

Host *noun Christianity* consecrated bread used in Holy Communion or Mass

hostage *noun* person who is illegally held prisoner and threatened with injury or death unless certain demands are met by other people

hostel *noun* building providing accommodation at a low cost for a specific group of people such as students, travellers, homeless people, etc

hostess hostesses *noun* woman who entertains guests

hostile *adjective* **1** unfriendly **2** (followed by *to*) opposed (to) **3** relating to or involving the enemies of a country

hostility hostilities *noun* **1** unfriendly and aggressive feelings or behaviour **2** **hostilities** acts of warfare

hot hotter hottest *adjective* **1** having a high temperature **2** strong or spicy **3** (of news) very recent **4** (of a temper) quick to rouse **5** liked very much: *a hot favourite* **6** dangerous or difficult to deal with **7** *informal* stolen > **hotly** *adverb*

hot air *noun informal* empty talk

hotbed *noun* any place encouraging a particular activity: *hotbeds of unrest*

hot dog *noun* long roll split lengthways with a hot sausage inside

hotel *noun* building where people stay, paying for their room and meals

hothouse *noun* **1** greenhouse **2** place or situation of intense intellectual or emotional activity: *a hothouse of radical socialist ideas*

hotplate *noun* heated metal surface on an electric cooker, used for cooking food in pans

hot seat *noun* **in the hot seat** *informal* having to make difficult decisions for which you will be held responsible

hound *noun* **1** hunting dog > *verb* **2** to pursue (someone) relentlessly

hour *noun* **1** unit of time equal to sixty minutes and a twenty-fourth part of a day **2** time **3** **hours** period regularly appointed for work or business

hourly *adjective* **1** happening every hour **2** frequent > *adverb* **3** every hour **4** frequently

house houses housing housed *noun* **1** building used as a home **2** building used for some specific purpose: *the opera house* **3** business firm **4** family or dynasty **5** theatre or cinema audience > *verb* **6** to give accommodation to **7** to contain or cover

houseboat *noun* boat tied up at a particular place on a river or canal and used as a home

household *noun* **1** all the people living in a house > *adjective* **2** **household name** very well-known person

householder *noun* person who owns or rents a house

housekeeper *noun* person employed to run someone else's household

housekeeping *noun* (money for) running a household

House of Commons *noun* the more powerful of the two parts of the British Parliament. Its members are elected by the public

House of Lords *noun* the less powerful of the two parts of the British Parliament. Its members are unelected

House of Representatives *noun* **1** (in Australia) the larger of the two parts of the Federal Parliament **2** (in New Zealand) the Parliament

house-train *verb* to train (a pet) to be clean in the house and to urinate and defecate outside or in a litter tray

house-warming *noun* party to celebrate moving into a new home

housewife housewives *noun* married woman who runs her own household and does not have a paid job

housework *noun* work of running a home, such as cleaning and cooking

housing *noun* **1** houses and flats or apartments **2** the providing of houses

hovel *noun* small house or hut that is dirty or badly in need of repair

hover *verb* **1** (of a bird etc) to hang in the air **2** to stand around in a state of indecision

hovercraft hovercraft or **hovercrafts** *noun* vehicle which can travel over both land and sea on a cushion of air

how *adverb* **1** in what way or by what means **2** to what degree: *I know how hard it is; How much is it for the weekend?* **3** used to emphasize: *How odd!*

however *adverb* **1** nevertheless **2** by whatever means **3** no matter how: *However much it hurt, he could do it*

howl *verb* **1** (of wolf, dog, person) to make a long loud wailing noise ▷ *noun* **2** loud wailing cry **3** loud burst of laughter

HQ HQs *abbreviation* headquarters

hub *noun* **1** centre of a wheel, through which the axle passes **2** the most important or active part of a place or organization

hubbub *noun* great noise or confusion

huddle huddles huddling huddled *verb* **1** to keep your arms and legs close to your body often in response to cold or fear **2** (of people or animals) to crowd closely together ▷ *noun* **3** small group

hue *noun* colour or shade

hue and cry *noun* public outcry

huff *noun* **in a huff** in an angry and resentful mood ▷ **huffy** *adjective* ▷ **huffily** *adverb*

hug hugs hugging hugged *verb* **1** to clasp (someone) tightly in your arms as a gesture of affection **2** to keep close to (the ground, kerb, etc) ▷ *noun* **3** tight or fond embrace

huge *adjective* very big ▷ **hugely** *adverb*: *a hugely successful career*

hui hui or **huis** *noun NZ* **1** meeting of Maori people **2** *informal* party

hulk *noun* **1** large heavy person or thing **2** body of an abandoned ship ▷ **hulking** *adjective* bulky or unwieldy

hull *noun* main body of a boat that sits in the water

hullabaloo hullabaloos *noun* loud confused noise or clamour

hum hums humming hummed *verb* **1** to make a continuous low noise **2** to sing with the lips closed **3** *informal* (of a place) to be very busy ▷ *noun* **4** humming sound

human *adjective* **1** of or typical of people ▷ *noun* **2** person; human being ▷ **humanly** *adverb* by human powers or means

human being *noun* man, woman or child

humane *adjective* kind or merciful ▷ **humanely** *adverb*

humanism *noun* belief in mankind's ability to achieve happiness and fulfilment without the need for religion ▷ **humanist** *noun*

humanitarian *noun* **1** person who works for the welfare of mankind or who has the interests of humankind at heart ▷ *adjective* **2** concerned with the welfare of mankind ▷ **humanitarianism** *noun*

humanity humanities *noun*

1 human race 2 the quality of being human 3 kindness or mercy 4 **humanities** study of literature, philosophy and the arts

human rights plural noun rights of individuals to freedom and justice

humble humbler humblest; humbles humbling humbled adjective 1 conscious of your failings 2 modest or unpretentious 3 unimportant ▷ verb 4 to cause (someone) to feel humble; humiliate > **humbly** adverb

humbug noun 1 Brit hard striped peppermint sweet 2 speech or writing that is obviously dishonest or untrue

humdrum adjective ordinary or dull

humid adjective damp and hot

humidity noun amount of moisture in the air, or the state of being humid

humiliate humiliates humiliating humiliated verb to make (someone) feel ashamed or appear stupid in front of other people > **humiliating** adjective > **humiliation** noun

humility noun quality of being humble

hummingbird noun very small American bird whose powerful wings make a humming noise as they beat

humorous adjective funny and amusing

humour noun 1 quality of being funny 2 ability to say amusing things or find things amusing 3 state of mind; mood ▷ verb 4 to be kind and indulgent to

hump noun 1 raised piece of ground 2 large lump on the back of an animal or person ▷ verb 3 informal to carry or heave 4 **get** or **take the hump** informal to be annoyed; sulk

hunch hunches hunching hunched noun 1 feeling or suspicion not based on facts ▷ verb 2 to draw (your shoulders) up or together

hunchback noun old-fashioned person with an abnormal curvature of the spine

hundred adjective, noun 1 the number 100 ▷ noun 2 **hundreds** large but unspecified number; lots > **hundredth** adjective, noun

hung verb past of **hang** ▷ adjective 2 (of a parliament or jury) with no side having a clear majority

Hungarian adjective 1 belonging or relating to Hungary ▷ noun 2 person from Hungary 3 main language spoken in Hungary

hunger noun 1 need or desire to eat 2 desire or craving > **hunger for** verb to want very much

hunger strike noun refusal to eat, as a means of protest

hung over adjective informal suffering from sickness and a headache after having drunk too much alcohol

hungry hungrier hungriest adjective needing or wanting to eat > **hungrily** adverb

hunk noun 1 large piece 2 informal sexually attractive man

hunt verb 1 to seek out and kill (wild animals) for food or sport 2 (followed by for) to search for ▷ noun 3 instance of hunting > **hunter** noun > **hunting** adjective, noun

huntaway huntaways noun Aust, NZ sheepdog trained to drive sheep by barking

hurdle noun 1 Sport light barrier for jumping over in some races 2 problem or difficulty 3 **hurdles** race involving hurdles > **hurdler**

noun

hurl *verb* **1** to throw (something) forcefully **2** to utter (insults) forcefully

hurray or **hurrah** *interjection* exclamation of joy or applause

hurricane *noun* very violent wind or storm

hurricane lamp *noun* paraffin lamp with a glass covering

hurry hurries hurrying hurried *verb* **1** to move or do something as quickly as possible **2** to cause (something or someone) to move or do something more quickly than otherwise ▷ *noun* **3** haste or rush **> hurried** *adjective* **> hurriedly** *adverb*

hurt hurts hurting hurt *verb* **1** to injure or cause physical pain to **2** to be painful **3** to make (someone) unhappy by being unkind or thoughtless towards them ▷ *noun* **4** physical or mental pain **> hurtful** *adjective* unkind: *a hurtful remark*

hurtle hurtles hurtling hurtled *verb* to move quickly or violently

husband *noun* **1** woman's partner in marriage ▷ *verb* **2** to use (resources) economically

husbandry *noun* **1** farming **2** management of resources

hush hushes hushing hushed *verb* **1** to be silent or make (someone) silent ▷ *noun* **2** stillness or silence **> hushed** *adjective* **> hush up** *verb* to suppress information about

husk *noun* dry outer covering of certain seeds and fruits

husky huskier huskiest; huskies *adjective* **1** (of voice) slightly hoarse ▷ *noun* **2** Arctic sledge dog with thick hair and a curled tail **> huskily** *adverb*

hustle hustles hustling hustled *verb* **1** to push (someone) about; jostle ▷ *noun* **2** lively activity or bustle

hut *noun* small house, shelter or shed

hutch hutches *noun* wooden box with wire mesh at one side, for keeping pet rabbits etc

hyacinth *noun* sweet-smelling spring flower that grows from a bulb

hybrid *noun* **1** plant or animal that has been bred from two different types of plant or animal **2** anything that is a mixture of two other things ▷ *adjective* **3** of mixed origin

hydra hydras or **hydrae** *noun* microscopic freshwater creature that has a slender tubular body and tentacles round the mouth

hydrangea *noun* ornamental shrub with clusters of pink, blue or white flowers

hydrant *noun* outlet from a water main from which water can be tapped for fighting fires

hydraulic *adjective* operated by pressure forced through a pipe by a liquid such as water or oil **> hydraulically** *adverb* **> hydraulics** *noun* study of the mechanical properties of fluids as they apply to practical engineering

hydro- *prefix meaning* **1** water: *hydroelectric* **2** containing hydrogen: *hydrochloric acid*

hydroelectric *adjective* of or relating to the generation of electricity by water pressure **> hydroelectricity** *noun*

hydrogen *noun* Chemistry light flammable colourless gas that combines with oxygen to form water

hydroponics *noun* method of growing plants in water rather than soil

hyena *noun* wild doglike animal of

Africa and Asia that hunts in packs

hygiene *noun* practice of keeping yourself and your surroundings clean, especially to stop the spread of disease > **hygienic** *adjective* > **hygienically** *adverb*

hymn *noun* Christian song in praise of God

hyper- *prefix meaning* very much, over or excessively: *hyperactive*

hyperactive *adjective* (of person) unable to relax and always in a state of restless activity

hyperbole *noun* deliberate exaggeration for effect

hypertension *noun formal* high blood pressure

hyphen *noun* punctuation mark (-) indicating that two words or syllables are connected > **hyphenate** *verb* to separate (words or syllables) with a hyphen > **hyphenated** *adjective* having a hyphen > **hyphenation** *noun*

hypnosis *noun* artificially induced state of relaxation in which the mind is more than usually receptive to suggestion

hypnotic *adjective* of or (as if) producing hypnosis: *The chant had an almost hypnotic effect*

hypnotism *noun* process of producing hypnosis in someone

hypnotist *noun* person who produces hypnosis in others

hypnotize hypnotizes hypnotizing hypnotized; also spelt **hypnotise** *verb* to put (someone) into a state in which they seem to be asleep but can respond to questions and suggestions

hypo- *prefix meaning* under or below: *hypotension*

hypochondria *noun* undue preoccupation with your health

> **hypochondriac** *noun* person who continually worries about his or her health

hypocrisy hypocrisies *noun* pretence that you have beliefs or qualities that you do not really have, so that you seem a better person than you are > **hypocrite** *noun* person who pretends to be what he or she is not > **hypocritical** *adjective* > **hypocritically** *adverb*

hypodermic *noun* syringe or needle used for injecting drugs

hypotension *noun formal* low blood pressure

hypotenuse *noun* longest side of a right-angled triangle opposite the right angle

hypothermia *noun* condition in which a person's body temperature is dangerously low as a result of prolonged exposure to severe cold

hypothesis hypotheses *noun* explanation or theory which has not yet been proved to be correct

hypothetical *adjective* based on assumption rather than on fact or reality > **hypothetically** *adverb*

hysterectomy hysterectomies *noun* surgical removal of the womb

hysteria *noun* state of uncontrolled excitement or panic

hysterical *adjective* in a state of uncontrolled excitement or panic > **hysterically** *adverb*

hysterics *plural noun* **1** attack of hysteria **2** *informal* uncontrollable laughter

I *pronoun* used by a speaker or writer to refer to himself or herself as the subject of a verb

ibis ibises *noun* large wading bird with long legs

-ible *suffix* another form of the suffix **-able**

-ic or **-ical** *suffix* used to form adjectives: *ironic; ironical*

ice ices icing iced *noun* **1** frozen water **2** *Chiefly Brit* ice cream **3 break the ice** to create a relaxed atmosphere, especially between people meeting for the first time ▷ *verb* **4** (followed by *up* or *over*) to become covered with ice **5** to cover (a cake) with icing

Ice Age *noun* period lasting thousands of years when much of the earth's surface was covered in ice

iceberg *noun* large floating mass of ice

icebox iceboxes *noun US* refrigerator

icecap *noun* mass of ice permanently covering an area

ice cream *noun* cold sweet dessert or confection made from frozen and flavoured cream

ice cube *noun* small square block of ice added to a drink to cool it

iced *adjective* **1** covered with icing **2** (of a drink) containing ice

ice hockey *noun* type of hockey played on ice

Icelandic *noun* main language spoken in Iceland

ice lolly ice lollies *noun* flavoured ice on a stick

ice skate *noun* boot with a steel blade fixed to the sole, to enable the wearer to glide over ice

ice-skate ice-skates ice-skating ice-skated *verb* to move about on ice wearing ice-skates ▷ **ice-skater** *noun*

icicle *noun* piece of ice shaped like a pointed stick hanging down where water has dripped

icing *noun* mixture of powdered sugar and water or egg whites, used to decorate cakes

icing sugar *noun* finely ground sugar for making icing

icon *noun* **1** picture on a computer screen representing a program that can be activated by clicking on it **2** picture of Christ or another religious figure, regarded as holy

ICT *abbreviation* information and communications technology

icy icier iciest *adjective* **1** very cold **2** covered with ice **3** unfriendly and cold ▷ **icily** *adverb*

id *noun Psychology* basic instincts and unconscious thoughts

idea *noun* **1** plan or thought formed in the mind **2** belief or opinion **3** knowledge

ideal *adjective* **1** most suitable **2** perfect ▷ *noun* **3** principle or idea that you try to achieve because it seems perfect to you **4** perfect example (of a person or thing)

idealism *noun* tendency to seek

perfection in everything > **idealist** noun > **idealistic** adjective

idealize idealizes idealizing idealized; also spelt **idealise** verb to regard or portray (someone or something) as perfect or nearly perfect > **idealization** noun

ideally adverb **1** if everything were perfect; in a perfect world: Ideally, they'd have their own home **2** perfectly

identical adjective exactly the same > **identically** adverb

identification noun **1** act of identifying **2** document such as a driver's licence or passport, which proves who you are

identify identifies identifying identified verb to recognize (someone or something) as being or prove (someone or something) to be a particular person or thing > **identifiable** adjective: a clearly identifiable cause of stress > **identify with** verb to understand and sympathize with the feelings and ideas of (a person or group)

identity identities noun characteristics that make you who you are

ideology ideologies noun body of ideas and beliefs of a group, nation, etc > **ideological** adjective > **ideologically** adverb

idiom noun group of words whose meaning together is different from all the words taken individually. For example, It is raining cats and dogs is an idiom

idiosyncrasy idiosyncrasies noun personal peculiarity of mind, habit or behaviour > **idiosyncratic** adjective

idiot noun foolish or stupid person

idiotic adjective extremely foolish or silly > **idiotically** adverb

idle idler idlest; idles idling idled

adjective **1** not doing anything **2** not willing to work; lazy **3** not being used **4** useless or meaningless: an idle threat ▷ verb **5** (of an engine) to run slowly out of gear > **idly** adverb

idol noun **1** famous person who is loved and admired by fans **2** picture or statue which is worshipped as if it were a god

idolize idolizes idolizing idolized; also spelt **idolise** verb to love or admire (someone) excessively

idyll noun scene or time of great peace and happiness > **idyllic** adjective: an idyllic place to stay

i.e. abbreviation (Latin: id est) that is to say

if conjunction **1** on the condition that **2** whether **3** even though

igloo igloos noun dome-shaped Inuit house made of snow and ice

igneous adjective technical (of rock) formed as molten rock cools and hardens

ignite ignites igniting ignited verb to set fire to (something) or catch fire

ignition noun system that ignites the fuel-and-air mixture to start an engine

ignominious adjective shameful or considered wrong > **ignominiously** adverb

ignominy noun humiliating disgrace

ignoramus ignoramuses noun ignorant person

ignorant adjective lacking knowledge > **ignorance** noun > **ignorantly** adverb

ignore ignores ignoring ignored verb to refuse to notice (someone or something); disregard

iguana noun large tropical American lizard

il- prefix meaning not or the opposite

of: the form of *in-* that is used before
the letter *l*: *illegible*

ilk *noun* type: *others of his ilk*

ill *adjective* **1** not in good health
2 harmful or unpleasant: *ill effects*
3 **ills** difficulties or problems
▷ *adverb* **4** badly **5** hardly or with
difficulty: *I can ill afford to lose him*

ill at ease *adjective* uncomfortable
or unable to relax

illegal *adjective* against the law
> **illegality** *noun* > **illegally** *adverb*

illegible *adjective* (of writing)
unclear and difficult or impossible
to read

illegitimate *adjective* **1** born of
parents not married to each other
2 not lawful > **illegitimacy** *noun*

ill-fated *adjective* doomed to end
unhappily

illicit *adjective* **1** illegal **2** forbidden or
disapproved of by society

illiterate *adjective* **1** unable to read
or write ▷ *noun* **2** someone who is
unable to read or write > **illiteracy**
noun

illness illnesses *noun* **1** experience
of being ill **2** particular disease

illogical *adjective* **1** not reasonable or
sensible **2** not logical > **illogically**
adverb

ill-treat *verb* to treat (someone or
something) badly, causing hurt,
harm or damage > **ill-treatment**
noun

illuminate illuminates
illuminating illuminated *verb*
1 to light (something) up **2** to
make (something) clear; explain
3 *History* to decorate (a manuscript)
with brightly coloured pictures
> **illuminating** *adjective*

illumination *noun* **1** lighting
2 **illuminations** coloured lights
put up to decorate a town

illusion *noun* **1** false belief

2 deceptive impression of reality
which deceives the eye

illusory *adjective* seeming to be
true, but actually false

illustrate illustrates illustrating
illustrated *verb* **1** to explain
(something) by use of examples
2 to provide (a book or text) with
pictures **3** to be an example of
> **illustrative** *adjective*: *illustrative*
examples > **illustrator** *noun*

illustration *noun* **1** picture or
diagram **2** example

illustrious *adjective* famous and
distinguished

ill will *noun* feeling of hostility

im- *prefix meaning* not or the opposite
of: the form of *in-* used before
the letters *b*, *m* and *p*: *imbalance;*
immature

image *noun* **1** mental picture
of someone or something
2 impression people have of
a person, organization, etc
3 representation of a person or
thing in a work of art

imagery *noun* descriptive language
used in a poem or book

imaginary *adjective* existing only in
the imagination

imagination *noun* **1** the ability
to form new and exciting ideas
2 ability to make mental images of
things that you may not have seen

imaginative *adjective* having or
showing a lot of creative mental
ability > **imaginatively** *adverb*

imagine imagines imagining
imagined *verb* **1** to form a mental
image of **2** to think, believe or guess
> **imaginable** *adjective*: *hats of every*
imaginable shape and size

imam *noun* **1** leader of prayers in
a mosque **2** title of some Islamic
leaders

imbalance *noun* lack of balance or

proportion

imbecile *noun* stupid person

imitate imitates imitating imitated *verb* to copy > **imitative** *adjective* > **imitator** *noun*

imitation *noun* **1** copy of an original **2** instance of imitating

immaculate *adjective* **1** completely clean or tidy **2** without any mistakes at all > **immaculately** *adverb*

immaterial *adjective* not important or not relevant

immature *adjective* **1** not fully developed **2** lacking the wisdom and good sense expected of a person of this age > **immaturity** *noun*

immediate *adjective* **1** occurring at once **2** next or nearest in time, space or relationship > **immediacy** *noun*

immediately *adverb* **1** straight away **2** just: *immediately behind the house*

immemorial *adjective* **since or from time immemorial** longer than anyone can remember

immense *adjective* extremely large > **immensely** *adverb* to a very great degree > **immensity** *noun*

immerse immerses immersing immersed *verb* **1** to involve (someone) deeply; engross **2** to plunge (something or someone) into liquid > **immersion** *noun*: *damage due to immersion in water*

immigrant *noun* someone who has come to live permanently in a new country > **immigrate** *verb* to come to live > **immigration** *noun* coming to a foreign country in order to live there

imminent *adjective* about to happen > **imminently** *adverb* > **imminence** *noun*

immobile *adjective* **1** not moving **2** unable to move > **immobility** *noun*

immobilize immobilizes immobilizing immobilized; also spelt **immobilise** *verb* to make unable to move or work

immoral *adjective* morally wrong; corrupt > **immorality** *noun*

Do not confuse *immoral* and *amoral*. You use *immoral* to talk about people who are aware of moral standards, but go against them. *Amoral* applies to people with no moral standards

immortal *adjective* **1** living forever **2** famous for all time > **immortalize** *verb*

immortality *noun* state of living forever and never dying

immovable or **immoveable** *adjective* fixed and unable to be moved > **immovably** *adverb*

immune *adjective* **1** protected against a specific disease **2** (followed by *to*) secure (against)

immune system *noun* body's system of defence against disease

immunity *noun* **1** ability to resist disease **2** freedom from prosecution, tax, etc

immunize immunizes immunizing immunized; also spelt **immunise** *verb* to make (a person or animal) immune to a disease, usually by means of an injection > **immunization** *noun*

imp *noun* (in folklore) mischievous small creature with magical powers > **impish** *adjective*

impact *noun* **1** strong effect **2** (force of) a collision

impair *verb* to weaken or damage (something) > **impairment** *noun*

impale impales impaling impaled *verb* to pierce with a

sharp object

impart *verb formal* to pass on (information)

impartial *adjective* not favouring one side or the other; fair and objective > **impartially** *adverb* > **impartiality** *noun*

impasse *noun* situation in which progress is impossible

impassioned *adjective* full of emotion

impassive *adjective* showing no emotion > **impassively** *adverb*

impasto *noun Art* technique of painting with thick paint so that brush strokes or palette-knife marks can be seen

impatient *adjective* **1** irritable at any delay or difficulty **2** restless (to have or do something) > **impatiently** *adverb* > **impatience** *noun*

impeccable *adjective* excellent and without any faults > **impeccably** *adverb*

impede impedes impeding impeded *verb* to hinder (someone) in action or progress

impediment *noun* something that makes action, speech or progress difficult

impelled *adjective* driven (to do something)

impending *adjective* (especially of something bad) about to happen

impenetrable *adjective* **1** impossible to get through **2** impossible to understand

imperative *adjective* **1** extremely urgent or important; vital ▷ *noun* **2** *Grammar* form of a verb that is used for giving orders

imperceptible *adjective* too slight or gradual to be noticed > **imperceptibly** *adverb*

imperfect *adjective* **1** having faults or mistakes ▷ *noun* **2** *Grammar*

(also **imperfect tense**) tense of verbs describing continuous, incomplete or repeated past actions > **imperfection** *noun* > **imperfectly** *adverb*

imperial *adjective* **1** relating to an empire, emperor or empress **2** denoting a system of weights and measures that uses inches, feet, and yards, ounces and pounds, pints and gallons > **imperialism** *noun* system of rule in which a rich and powerful nation controls other nations > **imperialist** *adjective, noun*

imperious *adjective* proud and domineering > **imperiously** *adverb*

impermeable *adjective* through which liquid cannot pass

impersonal *adjective* **1** lacking human warmth or sympathy **2** not relating to any particular person; objective **3** *Grammar* (of a verb) without a personal subject, *eg It is snowing* > **impersonally** *adverb*

impersonate impersonates impersonating impersonated *verb* to pretend to be (another person) > **impersonation** *noun* > **impersonator** *noun*

impertinent *adjective* disrespectful or rude > **impertinently** *adverb* > **impertinence** *noun*

imperturbable *adjective* calm; not excitable

impervious *adjective* (followed by *to*) not affected or influenced by (a feeling, argument, etc)

impetuous *adjective* hasty and lacking in forethought; rash > **impetuosity** *noun* > **impetuously** *adverb*

impetus *noun* **1** incentive or impulse **2** *Physics* force that starts a body moving

impinge impinges impinging

impinged verb **impinge on** or **upon** to affect or restrict

implacable adjective not prepared to be appeased; unyielding > **implacability** noun > **implacably** adverb

implant verb 1 to put (something) into someone's body, usually by surgical operation 2 to fix (something) firmly in someone's mind ▷ noun 3 Medicine something put into someone's body, usually by surgical operation

implausible adjective very unlikely > **implausibly** adverb

implement verb 1 to carry out (a plan, instructions, etc) ▷ noun 2 tool or instrument > **implementation** noun

implicate implicates implicating implicated verb to show (someone) to be involved in something, especially a crime

implication noun something suggested indirectly or implied

implicit adjective 1 expressed indirectly 2 absolute and unquestioning: implicit support > **implicitly** adverb

implore implores imploring implored verb to beg (someone) earnestly

imply implies implying implied verb to suggest or hint (that something is the case)

import imports importing imported verb 1 to bring in (goods) from another country ▷ noun 2 something imported > **importation** noun > **importer** noun

important adjective 1 very valuable, necessary or significant 2 having influence or power > **importance** noun value, necessity or significance > **importantly** adverb

impose imposes imposing imposed verb 1 to force the acceptance of (something) 2 (often followed by on) to take unfair advantage (of) > **imposition** noun unreasonable demand

imposing adjective grand and impressive

impossible adjective not able to be done or to happen > **impossibility** noun > **impossibly** adverb

imposter or **impostor** noun person who pretends to be someone else in order to get things they want

impotent adjective 1 powerless 2 (of a man) incapable of having or maintaining an erection during sexual intercourse > **impotence** noun > **impotently** adverb

impound verb to take legal possession of; confiscate

impoverished adjective poor

impracticable adjective impossible to do

impractical adjective not practical, sensible or realistic

impregnable adjective impossible to break into

impregnated adjective saturated or soaked

impresario impresarios noun person who runs theatre performances, concerts, etc

impress impresses impressing impressed verb 1 to cause (someone) to feel admiration or respect 2 **impress something on someone** to make someone understand the importance of something 3 to stress or emphasize

impression noun 1 effect, especially a strong or favourable one 2 vague idea 3 impersonation for entertainment 4 mark made by pressing

impressionable *adjective* easily impressed or influenced

impressionism *noun* style of painting which is concerned with the impressions created by light and shapes, rather than with exact details > **impressionist** *noun*

impressive *adjective* making a strong impression, especially through size, importance or quality

imprint *noun* 1 lasting effect (on mind) 2 mark left by something causing pressure ▷ *verb* 3 to fix (something in someone's memory) 4 to produce (a mark) by printing or stamping

imprison *verb* to put (someone) in prison > **imprisonment** *noun*

improbable *adjective* not likely to be true or to happen > **improbability** *noun* > **improbably** *adverb*

impromptu *adjective* without planning or preparation

improper *adjective* 1 indecent or shocking 2 illegal or dishonest 3 not suitable or correct > **improperly** *adverb* > **impropriety** *noun formal* unsuitable or improper behaviour

improve improves improving improved *verb* to become better or to make (something) better > **improvement** *noun*

improvise improvises improvising improvised *verb* 1 to make use of whatever materials are available 2 to make up (a piece of music, speech, etc) as you go along > **improvisation** *noun* > **improvised** *adjective*

impudent *adjective* cheeky and disrespectful > **impudence** *noun* > **impudently** *adverb*

impulse *noun* 1 sudden urge to do something 2 *Physics* short electrical signal passing along a wire or nerve or through the air 3 **on impulse** suddenly and without planning > **impulsive** *adjective* 1 (of person) tending to do things on the spur of the moment without thinking about them carefully 2 (of action, decision, etc) carried out or taken on the spur of the moment without too much thinking > **impulsively** *adverb*

impure *adjective* 1 having dirty or unwanted substances mixed in 2 immoral or obscene

impurity impurities *noun* 1 quality of being impure 2 trace of dirt or another substance that should not be present

in *preposition* 1 indicating position inside (something): *in the box* 2 indicating state or situation, etc: *in a mess* 3 indicating time or manner: *in the afternoon; in a husky voice* ▷ *adverb* 4 indicating position inside, entry into, etc: *She stayed in; Come in* ▷ *adjective* 5 fashionable

in- *prefix* 1 added to the beginning of some words to form a word with the opposite meaning: *insincere* 2 in, into or in the course of: *infiltrate*

inability *noun* lack of means or skill to do something

inaccessible *adjective* impossible or very difficult to reach

inaccurate *adjective* not correct

inadequate *adjective* 1 not enough 2 not good enough > **inadequacy** *noun* > **inadequately** *adverb*

inadvertent *adjective* unintentional > **inadvertently** *adverb*

inane *adjective* silly or stupid > **inanely** *adverb* > **inanity** *noun*

inanimate *adjective* not living

inappropriate *adjective* not suitable > **inappropriately** *adverb*

inarticulate *adjective* unable to express yourself clearly or well

inasmuch as *conjunction* because or in so far as

inaudible *adjective* not loud enough to be heard > **inaudibly** *adverb*

inaugurate inaugurates inaugurating inaugurated *verb* 1 to open (a building) especially with ceremony 2 to begin to use (a new system) 3 formally to establish (a new leader) in office > **inaugural** *adjective* > **inauguration** *noun*

inborn *adjective* existing from birth; natural

inbred *adjective* 1 inborn or ingrained 2 (of person) having closely related ancestors

inbuilt *adjective* present from the start

incalculable *adjective* too great to be estimated

incandescent *adjective* glowing with heat > **incandescence** *noun*

incantation *noun* ritual chanting of magic words or sounds

incapable *adjective* 1 (followed by *of*) unable (to do something) 2 incompetent

incapacitate incapacitates incapacitating incapacitated *verb* to deprive (someone) of strength or ability

incarcerate incarcerates incarcerating incarcerated *verb* to imprison > **incarceration** *noun*

incarnate *adjective* in human form > **incarnation** *noun*

incendiary *adjective* (of a bomb, attack, etc) designed to cause fires

incense *noun* substance that gives off a sweet perfume when burned

incensed *adjective* extremely angry

incentive *noun* something that encourages effort or action

inception *noun formal* beginning

incessant *adjective* never stopping > **incessantly** *adverb*

incest *noun* sexual intercourse between two people too closely related to marry > **incestuous** *adjective*: *an incestuous relationship*

inch inches inching inched *noun* 1 unit of length equal to about 2.54 centimetres ▷ *verb* 2 to move slowly and gradually

incidence *noun* frequency that something occurs

incident *noun* event

incidental *adjective* occurring as a minor part of something > **incidentally** *adverb*

incinerate incinerates incinerating incinerated *verb* to burn > **incineration** *noun*

incinerator *noun* special container for burning rubbish

incipient *adjective* just starting to appear or happen

incision *noun* a sharp cut, made especially by a surgeon operating on a patient

incisive *adjective* direct and forceful

incite incites inciting incited *verb* 1 to stir up (trouble, violence, criminal behaviour, etc) 2 to provoke (someone) into doing something > **incitement** *noun*

inclination *noun* 1 liking, tendency or preference 2 slope

incline inclines inclining inclined *verb* 1 to make (someone) likely (to do something) 2 **be inclined** to tend (to do something) ▷ *noun* 3 slope

include includes including included *verb* to have (something or someone) as part of something or make them part of it > **including** *preposition*: *everybody, including me*

inclusion *noun* act of making something or someone part of

something

inclusive *adjective* including everything (specified)

incognito *adjective, adverb* in disguise or with a false identity

incoherent *adjective* unclear and impossible to understand
> **incoherence** *noun*
> **incoherently** *adverb*

income *noun* amount of money earned from work, investments, etc

income tax *noun* tax on annual income

incoming *adjective* 1 coming in 2 about to come into office

incomparable *adjective* beyond comparison; unequalled
> **incomparably** *adverb*

incompatible *adjective* unable to live or exist together because of differences > **incompatibility** *noun*

incompetent *adjective* not having the necessary ability or skill to do something > **incompetence** *noun*
> **incompetently** *adverb*

incomplete *adjective* not complete or finished > **incompletely** *adverb*

incomprehensible *adjective* not able to be understood

inconceivable *adjective* impossible to believe

inconclusive *adjective* not leading to a decision or a definite result

incongruous *adjective* inappropriate or out of place
> **incongruously** *adverb*

inconsequential *adjective* unimportant or insignificant

inconsiderate *adjective* not considerate

inconsistent *adjective* not always behaving in the same way; unpredictable > **inconsistency** *noun* > **inconsistently** *adverb*

inconspicuous *adjective* not easily seen or obvious

> **inconspicuously** *adverb*

incontinent *adjective* unable to control your bladder or bowels
> **incontinence** *noun*

incontrovertible *adjective* impossible to deny or disprove

inconvenience inconveniences inconveniencing inconvenienced *noun* 1 trouble or difficulty ▷ *verb* 2 to cause (someone) trouble or difficulty
> **inconvenient** *adjective*
> **inconveniently** *adverb*

incorporate incorporates incorporating incorporated *verb* to include (something or someone) as part of a larger unit
> **incorporation** *noun*

incorrect *adjective* wrong or untrue
> **incorrectly** *adverb*

increase increases increasing increased *verb* 1 to become or make (something) greater in size, number, etc ▷ *noun* 2 rise in number, size, etc 3 amount by which something increases
> **increasingly** *adverb*

incredible *adjective* hard to believe or imagine; amazing > **incredibly** *adverb*

incredulous *adjective* not able to believe something > **incredulity** *noun* > **incredulously** *adverb*

increment *noun* increase in money or value, especially a regular salary increase > **incremental** *adjective*

incriminate incriminates incriminating incriminated *verb* to make (someone) seem guilty of a crime > **incriminating** *adjective*

incubate incubates incubating incubated *verb* (of eggs) to be kept warm until ready to hatch
> **incubation** *noun* > **incubator** *noun* piece of hospital equipment in which sick or weak newborn babies

are kept warm

incumbent *adjective* 1 **it is incumbent on** it is the duty of (someone to do something) ▷ *noun* 2 person holding a particular office

incur incurs incurring incurred *verb* to cause (something unpleasant) to happen

incurable *adjective* not able to be cured > **incurably** *adverb*

indebted *adjective* grateful (to someone for help or favours) > **indebtedness** *noun*

indecent *adjective* 1 morally or sexually offensive 2 unsuitable or unseemly: *indecent haste* > **indecency** *noun* > **indecently** *adverb*

indeed *adverb* really or certainly

indefatigable *adjective* never getting tired

indefensible *adjective* unable to be justified

indefinite *adjective* 1 without exact limits: *for an indefinite period* 2 vague or unclear > **indefinitely** *adverb*

indefinite article *noun* grammatical term for *a* or *an*

indelible *adjective* impossible to erase or remove > **indelibly** *adverb*

indemnity indemnities *noun formal* insurance against loss or damage

indent *verb* to start (a line of writing) further in from the margin than the other lines

indentation *noun* dent or groove in a surface or edge

independence *noun* 1 not relying on anyone else 2 self-rule

independent *adjective* 1 free from the control or influence of others 2 separate 3 financially self-reliant 4 capable of acting for yourself or on your own > **independently** *adverb*

indeterminate *adjective* not certain and not fixed

index *noun* **indexes** or **indices** 1 alphabetical list of names or subjects dealt with in a book 2 alphabetical list of all the books in a library, arranged by title, author or subject

index finger *noun* finger next to your thumb

Indian *adjective* 1 belonging or relating to India ▷ *noun* 2 someone from India 3 *old-fashioned* Native American

indicate indicates indicating indicated *verb* 1 to be a sign or symptom of 2 to point (something) out 3 to state (something) briefly 4 (of a measuring instrument) to show a reading of 5 (of driver) to give a signal showing which way you are going to turn

indication *noun* a sign of what someone feels or what is likely to happen

indicative *adjective* 1 **indicative of** suggesting ▷ *noun* 2 *Grammar* mood of verbs used for making statements. Compare **subjunctive**

indicator *noun* 1 something acting as a sign or indication 2 flashing light on a vehicle showing the driver's intention to turn 3 *Chemistry* substance that shows if another substance is an acid or alkali by changing colour when it comes into contact with it

indict *verb* to charge (someone) officially with a crime > **indictable** *adjective*: *an indictable offence* > **indictment** *noun*

indifferent *adjective* 1 (often followed by *to*) showing no interest or concern (in) 2 of poor quality > **indifference** *noun* > **indifferently** *adverb*

indigenous *adjective* born in or native to a country

indigestion *noun* discomfort or pain caused by difficulty in digesting food > **indigestible** *adjective* difficult to digest

indignant *adjective* angry at something unfair or wrong > **indignantly** *adverb*

indignation *noun* anger at something unfair or wrong

indignity indignities *noun* something causing embarrassment or humiliation

indigo *noun, adjective* deep violet-blue

indirect *adjective* not direct > **indirectly** *adverb*

indiscreet *adjective* incautious or tactless in revealing secrets > **indiscretion** *noun*

indiscriminate *adjective* showing lack of careful thought or choice > **indiscriminately** *adverb*

indispensable *adjective* absolutely essential

indisputable *adjective* beyond doubt > **indisputably** *adverb*

indistinct *adjective* not clear > **indistinctly** *adverb*

individual *adjective* **1** relating to one particular person or thing **2** separate or distinct **3** distinctive or unusual ▷ *noun* **4** single person or thing > **individually** *adverb*

individualist *noun* someone who likes to do things in their own way > **individualistic** *adjective*: *a very individualistic society*

individuality *noun* quality of being different from all other things, and therefore interesting and noticeable

indoctrinate indoctrinates indoctrinating indoctrinated *verb* to teach (someone) to accept a doctrine or belief uncritically

> **indoctrination** *noun*

indomitable *adjective formal* too strong to be defeated or discouraged

Indonesian *adjective* **1** belonging or relating to Indonesia ▷ *noun* **2** someone from Indonesia **3** official language of Indonesia

indoor *adjective* inside a building

indoors *adverb* inside a building

induce induces inducing induced *verb* **1** to cause (a state or condition) **2** to persuade or influence (someone to do something) **3** *Medicine* to cause (a woman) to go into labour or bring on (labour) by the use of drugs etc

inducement *noun* something used to persuade someone to do something

indulge indulges indulging indulged *verb* **1** to allow yourself to do something that you enjoy **2** to allow (someone) to have or do what they want

indulgence *noun* **1** something allowed because it gives pleasure **2** act of indulging yourself or someone else

indulgent *adjective* showing kindness, generosity and understanding towards someone, often to an excessive degree > **indulgently** *adverb*

industrial *adjective* relating to industry

industrial action *noun* any action, such as striking or working to rule, that is used by workers as a way of protesting about their pay and conditions with the aim of bringing about change

industrialist *noun* person who owns or controls a lot of factories

industrialize industrializes industrializing industrialized;

also spelt **industrialise** *verb*
to develop large-scale industry
in (a country or region)
> **industrialization** *noun*

Industrial Revolution *noun* the
transformation of Britain and other
countries in the eighteenth and
nineteenth century into industrial
nations, through greater use of
machinery

industrious *adjective* hard-working

industry industries *noun*
1 work and processes involved in
manufacturing things in factories
2 all the people and processes
involved in manufacturing a
particular thing

inedible *adjective* not fit to be eaten

ineffectual *adjective* having very
little effect

inefficient *adjective* badly
organized, wasteful and
slow > **inefficiency** *noun*
> **inefficiently** *adverb*

ineligible *adjective* not qualified for
or entitled to something

inept *adjective* clumsy or lacking skill
> **ineptitude** *noun*

inequality inequalities *noun*
difference in size, status, wealth or
position, between different things,
groups or people

inert *adjective* **1** without the
power of motion or resistance
2 chemically unreactive
> **inertness** *noun*

inertia *noun* feeling of
unwillingness to do anything

inevitable *adjective* unavoidable
or sure to happen > **inevitability**
noun > **inevitably** *adverb*

inexhaustible *adjective* incapable
of running out or being used up

inexorable *adjective* unable to
be prevented from continuing or
progressing > **inexorably** *adverb*

inexpensive *adjective* not costing
much

inexperienced *adjective* lacking
experience of a situation or activity
> **inexperience** *noun*

inexplicable *adjective* impossible
to explain > **inexplicably** *adverb*

inextricably *adverb* without
possibility of separation

infallible *adjective* never wrong
> **infallibility** *noun*

infamous *adjective* well-known for
something bad

infancy *noun* **1** early childhood
2 early stage of development

infant *noun* very young child

infantile *adjective* childish

infantry *noun* soldiers who fight
on foot

infatuated *adjective* feeling such
intense love or passion for someone
that you cannot think sensibly
about them > **infatuation** *noun*
intense unreasoning passion

infect *verb* to give (someone or
something) a disease

infection *noun* **1** disease caused by
germs **2** being infected

infectious *adjective* **1** (of a disease)
spreading without actual contact
2 spreading from person to person:
infectious enthusiasm

infer infers inferring inferred
verb to work (something) out
from evidence > **inference** *noun*
conclusion

▮ Do not use *infer* to mean the
same as *imply*

inferior *adjective* **1** lower in quality,
position or status ▷ *noun* **2** person
of lower position or status
> **inferiority** *noun*

infernal *adjective* **1** *old-fashioned
informal* very irritating **2** relating
to hell

inferno infernos *noun* intense

raging fire

infertile *adjective* **1** (of soil) poor in quality and not good for growing plants **2** unable to produce children or young > **infertility** *noun*

infested *adjective* inhabited or overrun by a large number of animals or insects > **infestation** *noun*

infidelity infidelities *noun* being unfaithful to your husband, wife or partner

infighting *noun* quarrelling within a group

infiltrate infiltrates infiltrating infiltrated *verb* to become part of (an organization) gradually and secretly with the aim of finding out information about its activities > **infiltration** *noun* > **infiltrator** *noun*

infinite *adjective* without any limit or end > **infinitely** *adverb*

infinitive *noun* Grammar form of a verb not showing tense, person or number, *eg to sleep, to be*

infinity *noun* endless space, time or number

infirmary infirmaries *noun* hospital

inflamed *adjective* (of part of the body) red, swollen and painful because of infection

inflammable *adjective* easily set on fire

inflammation *noun* painful redness or swelling of part of the body

inflammatory *adjective* likely to provoke anger

inflate inflates inflating inflated *verb* to fill (something) with air or gas > **inflatable** *adjective* able to be inflated

inflation *noun* increase in prices and fall in the value of money

> **inflationary** *adjective*

inflection or **inflexion** *noun* Grammar change in the form of a word according to function, tense, number, etc

inflexible *adjective* **1** unwilling to be persuaded; obstinate **2** (of a policy etc) firmly fixed or unalterable

inflict *verb* to impose (something unpleasant) on

influence influences influencing influenced *noun* **1** power of a person to have an effect over others **2** effect of a person or thing on another ▷ *verb* **3** to have an effect on

influential *adjective* having a lot of influence

influenza *noun* formal flu

influx *noun* arrival or entry of many people or things

inform *verb* **1** to tell (someone) of something **2** to give information to the police revealing the involvement of a particular person in a crime > **informant** *noun* person who gives information

informal *adjective* **1** relaxed and friendly **2** appropriate for everyday life or use > **informality** *noun* > **informally** *adverb*

information *noun* knowledge or facts

information technology *noun* use of computers and electronic technology to store and communicate information

informative *adjective* giving useful information

informer *noun* person who gives information to the police revealing the involvement of a particular person in a crime

infrared *adjective* of or using rays below the red end of the visible spectrum

infrastructure *noun* basic

facilities, services and equipment needed for a country or organization to function properly

infringe infringes infringing infringed verb **1** to break (a law or agreement) **2** to interfere with (people's rights), preventing them from using them > **infringement** noun

infuriate infuriates infuriating infuriated verb to make (someone) very angry > **infuriating** adjective

infuse infuses infusing infused verb **1** to fill (someone with an emotion or quality) **2** to leave (something) to soak in hot water so that the water absorbs its flavours, etc > **infusion** noun

ingenious adjective showing cleverness and originality > **ingeniously** adverb

ingenuity noun cleverness and originality at inventing things or working out plans

ingot noun oblong block of metal, especially gold

ingrained adjective firmly fixed

ingratiate ingratiates ingratiating ingratiated verb to try to make (yourself) popular with someone > **ingratiating** adjective

ingratitude noun lack of gratitude

ingredient noun one of the things from which a dish or mixture is made

inhabit verb to live in

inhabitant noun person who lives in a place

inhale inhales inhaling inhaled verb to breathe in (air, smoke, etc) > **inhalation** noun

inherent adjective forming an inseparable part of something > **inherently** adverb

inherit verb **1** to receive (money etc) from someone who has died **2** to receive (a characteristic) from an earlier generation > **inheritance** noun > **inheritor** noun

inhibit verb **1** to prevent (someone) from doing something **2** to hinder or prevent (something) from happening

inhibited adjective finding it difficult to relax and show emotions

inhibition noun feeling of fear or embarrassment that stops you from behaving naturally

inhospitable adjective **1** difficult to live in; harsh **2** not welcoming or friendly

inhuman adjective **1** cruel or brutal **2** not human

inhumane adjective cruel or brutal > **inhumanity** noun

inimitable adjective impossible to imitate; unique

initial adjective **1** first or at the beginning ▷ noun **2** first letter, especially of a person's name > **initially** adverb

initiate initiates initiating initiated verb **1** to begin or set (something) up **2** to admit (someone) into a closed group, especially by means of a special ceremony > **initiation** noun

initiative noun **1** attempt to get something done **2** first step, commencing move **3** ability to act independently

inject verb **1** to put (a substance) into someone's body with a syringe **2** to introduce (a new element) > **injection** noun

injunction noun court order not to do something

injure injures injuring injured verb to hurt (a person or animal)

injury injuries noun hurt or damage

injustice noun **1** lack of justice

and fairness **2** unfair action **3 do someone an injustice** to criticize someone unfairly

ink *noun* coloured liquid used for writing or printing

inkling *noun* slight idea or suspicion

inlaid *adjective* decorated with small pieces of wood, metal or stone

inland *adjective, adverb* in or towards the interior of a country; away from the sea

in-laws *plural noun* the family of your husband or wife

inlay *noun* inlaid substance or pattern

inlet *noun* **1** narrow strip of water extending from the sea into the land **2** valve etc through which liquid or gas enters

inmate *noun* person living in an institution such as a prison

inn *noun* pub or small hotel, especially in the country

innards *plural noun informal* internal parts

innate *adjective* being part of someone's nature; inborn > **innately** *adverb*

inner *adjective* happening or located inside

innermost *adjective* deepest and most secret

innings *noun Sport* player's or side's turn of batting

innocent *adjective* **1** not guilty of a crime **2** without experience of evil **3** without malicious intent > **innocence** *noun* > **innocently** *adverb*

innocuous *adjective* not harmful

innovation *noun* **1** new idea or method **2** introduction of new ideas or methods > **innovative** *adjective* fresh and new

innuendo innuendos or **innuendoes** *noun* indirect reference to something rude or unpleasant

innumerable *adjective* too many to be counted

inoculate inoculates inoculating inoculated *verb* to protect against disease by injecting with a vaccine

inopportune *adjective* badly timed or unsuitable

input *noun* **1** resources put into a project etc **2** data fed into a computer

inquest *noun* official inquiry into a sudden death

inquire inquires inquiring inquired *verb* to seek information or ask (about) > **inquiring** *adjective*

inquiry inquiries *noun* **1** question **2** investigation

inquisition *noun* thorough official investigation, often using harsh methods of questioning

inquisitive *adjective* curious and keen to find out about things > **inquisitively** *adverb*

inroads *plural noun* **make inroads into** to start affecting or reducing

insane *adjective* **1** mentally ill **2** stupidly irresponsible > **insanely** *adverb* > **insanity** *noun*

insanitary *adjective* dirty or unhealthy

insatiable *adjective* unable to be satisfied > **insatiably** *adverb*

inscribe inscribes inscribing inscribed *verb* **1** to write or carve (words) on something **2** to write on or carve (something) with words

inscription *noun* words written or carved on something

inscrutable *adjective* revealing nothing or giving nothing away

insect *noun* small animal with six legs and usually wings

insecticide *noun* substance for

killing insects

insecure *adjective* **1** anxious or not confident **2** not safe or well-protected > **insecurity** *noun*

insensitive *adjective* unaware of or ignoring other people's feelings > **insensitivity** *noun*

inseparable *adjective* **1** (of two people) spending most of the time together **2** (of two things) impossible to separate

insert *verb* to put (something) inside or include (something) > **insertion** *noun*

inshore *adjective* **1** close to the shore ▷ *adjective, adverb* **2** towards the shore

inside *preposition* **1** in or into the interior of ▷ *adjective* **2** on or relating to the inside **3** by or from someone within an organization: *inside information* ▷ *adverb* **4** on, in or into the inside; indoors ▷ *noun* **5** inner side, surface or part **6 inside out** with the inside facing outwards **7 know something inside out** to know something thoroughly **8 insides** *informal* stomach and bowels

insider *noun* member of a group who has privileged knowledge about it

insidious *adjective* dangerous and developing slowly without being noticed > **insidiously** *adverb*

insight *noun* deep understanding

insignia *noun* badge or emblem of a particular organization

insignificant *adjective* small and unimportant > **insignificance** *noun*

insincere *adjective* pretending to have certain feelings; not genuine > **insincerely** *adverb* > **insincerity** *noun*

insinuate insinuates

insinuating insinuated *verb* **1** to suggest (something unpleasant) indirectly; hint at **2** to work (yourself) into a position gradually and cleverly > **insinuation** *noun*

insipid *adjective* lacking interest, spirit or flavour

insist *verb* to demand or state firmly

insistent *adjective* **1** making persistent demands **2** demanding attention > **insistence** *noun* > **insistently** *adverb*

in so far as or **insofar as** *preposition* to the extent that

insolent *adjective* rude and disrespectful > **insolence** *noun* > **insolently** *adverb*

insoluble *adjective* **1** impossible to solve **2** impossible to dissolve

insolvent *adjective* unable to pay your debts > **insolvency** *noun*

insomnia *noun* difficulty in sleeping > **insomniac** *noun* person who has difficulty in sleeping

inspect *verb* to check (someone or something) closely or officially > **inspection** *noun*

inspector *noun* **1** person who inspects **2** high-ranking police officer

inspire inspires inspiring inspired *verb* **1** to fill (someone) with enthusiasm; stimulate **2** to arouse (an emotion) > **inspiration** *noun* **1** creative influence or stimulus **2** brilliant idea > **inspired** *adjective* > **inspiring** *adjective*

instability *noun* lack of stability

install *verb* **1** to put in and prepare (equipment) for use **2** to place (a person) formally in a position or rank **3** to settle (yourself) in a place > **installation** *noun* **1** installing **2** equipment installed **3** place containing equipment for a particular purpose: *oil installations*

instalment *noun* one of a series of successive parts

instance *noun* **1** particular example **2 for instance** for example

instant *noun* **1** very brief time **2** particular moment ▷ *adjective* **3** happening at once; immediate **4** (of foods) requiring little preparation > **instantly** *adverb*

instantaneous *adjective* happening at once > **instantaneously** *adverb*

instead *adverb* in place of something

instigate instigates instigating instigated *verb* to cause (something) to happen > **instigation** *noun*: *The search was carried out at the instigation of the president* > **instigator** *noun*

instil instils instilling instilled *verb* to introduce (an idea etc) gradually into someone's mind

instinct *noun* natural tendency to behave in a certain way > **instinctive** *adjective* > **instinctively** *adverb*

institute institutes instituting instituted *noun* **1** organization set up for a specific purpose, especially for research or teaching ▷ *verb* **2** *formal* to start or establish (a rule or system)

institution *noun* **1** long-established custom **2** large important organization such as a university or bank > **institutional** *adjective*

instruct *verb* **1** to tell (someone) to do something **2** to teach (someone) how to do something > **instruction** *noun* > **instructive** *adjective* informative or helpful > **instructor** *noun*

instrument *noun* **1** tool or device used for a particular job **2** object, such as a piano or flute, played to make music **3** measuring device to show height, speed, etc

instrumental *adjective* **1** (followed by *in*) having an important role (in doing something) **2** (of music) played by or composed for musical instruments

insubordinate *adjective* not submissive to authority; disobedient > **insubordination** *noun*

insufferable *adjective* unbearable

insufficient *adjective* not enough > **insufficiently** *adverb*

insular *adjective* not open to new ideas; narrow-minded > **insularity** *noun*

insulate insulates insulating insulated *verb* **1** to cover (something) with a layer to keep it warm or to stop electricity passing through it **2** to protect (someone) from harmful things > **insulation** *noun* > **insulator** *noun*

insulin *noun* hormone produced in the pancreas that controls the amount of sugar in the blood

insult *verb* **1** to be rude and offensive to (someone) ▷ *noun* **2** rude remark or action which offends you > **insulting** *adjective*

insuperable *adjective* impossible to overcome

insurance *noun* **1** agreement by which you make regular payments to a company in exchange for compensation in case of damage, loss, etc **2** money paid to or by an insurance company **3** means of protection

insure insures insuring insured *verb* **1** to protect (something or yourself) by paying for insurance **2 insure against** to take action to prevent (something) from happening or to provide protection if it does happen

insurrection *noun* rebellion

intact *adjective* not changed or damaged in any way

intake *noun* amount or number of something taken in

integral *adjective* being an essential part of a whole

integrate integrates integrating integrated *verb* 1 (of person) to become part of a group or community 2 to combine (things) so that they become part of a whole > **integration** *noun*

integrity *noun* 1 quality of being honest and following your principles 2 quality of being united

intellect *noun* ability to think and reason

intellectual *adjective* 1 involving thought, ideas and understanding 2 intelligent and enjoying thinking about complicated ideas ▷ *noun* 3 person who enjoys thinking about complicated ideas > **intellectually** *adverb*

intelligence *noun* 1 quality of being able to understand and to learn things quickly and well 2 information about the aims and activities, especially military or terrorist ones, of an organization, government, etc 3 people or department collecting such information

intelligent *adjective* 1 able to understand, learn and think things out quickly 2 (of a computerized device) able to react to events > **intelligently** *adverb*

intelligentsia *noun* intellectual or cultured people in a society

intelligible *adjective* able to be understood > **intelligibility** *noun*

intend *verb* 1 to propose or plan (to do something) 2 **be intended to**

do something to have something as your purpose or task

intense *adjective* 1 very great in strength or amount 2 deeply emotional > **intensely** *adverb* > **intensity** *noun*

intensify intensifies intensifying intensified *verb* to become or make (something) greater or stronger > **intensification** *noun*

intensive *adjective* using or needing a lot of energy or effort over a short time

intent *noun* 1 *formal* intention ▷ *adjective* 2 **intent on doing something** determined to do something > **intently** *adverb*

intention *noun* plan

intentional *adjective* done on purpose; deliberate > **intentionally** *adverb*

inter- *prefix meaning* between or among: *international*

interact *verb* to act, work or communicate together > **interaction** *noun*

interactive *adjective* (of television, a computer, game, etc) reacting to decisions taken by the viewer, user or player

intercede intercedes interceding interceded *verb* to try to end a dispute between two people or groups

intercept *verb* to seize or stop (someone or something) on their way somewhere

interchange *noun* act or process of exchanging things or ideas > **interchangeable** *adjective*

intercom *noun* internal communication system resembling a telephone

intercourse *noun* (also **sexual intercourse**) act of having sex

interest *noun* **1** desire to know or hear more about something **2** something in which you are interested **3** (*often plural*) advantage or benefit **4** reason for wanting something to happen **5** sum paid for the use of borrowed money **6** (*often plural*) right or share ▷ *verb* **7** to attract the attention of (someone) because he or she wants to know or hear more > **interested** *adjective* **1** feeling or showing interest **2** involved in or affected by something > **interesting** *adjective* of interest > **interestingly** *adverb*

interface *noun* **1** area where two things interact or link **2** **user interface** presentation on screen of a computer program and how easy it is to operate

interfere interferes interfering interfered *verb* **1** to try to influence other people's affairs when it is not really your business to do so **2** (followed by *with*) to clash (with) or get in the way (of) > **interference** *noun* > **interfering** *adjective*

interim *adjective* temporary or provisional

interior *noun* **1** inside **2** inland region ▷ *adjective* **3** inside or inner

interjection *noun* word or phrase spoken suddenly to express surprise, pain or anger

interlude *noun* short rest or break in an activity or event

intermediary intermediaries *noun* someone who tries to get two groups of people to come to an agreement

intermediate *adjective* occurring in the middle, between two other stages

interminable *adjective* seemingly endless because boring

> **interminably** *adverb*

intermission *noun* interval between parts of a play, film, etc

intermittent *adjective* occurring at intervals > **intermittently** *adverb*

internal *adjective* happening inside a person, place or object > **internally** *adverb*

international *adjective* **1** of or involving two or more countries ▷ *noun* **2** game or match between teams of different countries > **internationally** *adverb*

Internet or **internet** *noun* worldwide computer communication network

interplay *noun* the way two things react with one another

interpret *verb* **1** to explain the meaning of **2** to translate orally what someone says in one language into another language for the benefit of others **3** to convey the meaning of (a poem, song, etc) in performance > **interpretation** *noun* > **interpreter** *noun*

interrogate interrogates interrogating interrogated *verb* to question (someone) closely > **interrogation** *noun* > **interrogator** *noun*

interrogative *adjective* **1** questioning or related to asking a question ▷ *noun* **2** word used in asking a question, such as *how* or *why*

interrupt *verb* **1** to start talking while someone else is talking **2** to break into (a conversation etc) **3** to stop (a process or activity) temporarily > **interruption** *noun*

intersect *verb* (of roads) to meet and cross > **intersection** *noun*

interspersed *adjective* scattered (among, between or on)

interval *noun* **1** time between two

particular moments or events
2 break between parts of a play,
concert, etc **3** difference in pitch
between musical notes **4 at
intervals a** repeatedly **b** with
spaces left between

**intervene intervenes
intervening intervened** *verb* to
step in to a situation, especially to
prevent conflict > **intervention**
noun

intervening *adjective* (of time) in
between

interview *noun* **1** formal discussion,
especially between an employer
and someone trying to get a job
2 questioning of a well-known
person about his or her career,
views, etc, by a reporter ▷ *verb*
3 to conduct an interview with
> **interviewee** *noun* someone
interviewed > **interviewer** *noun*
someone conducting an interview

intestine *noun* (*often plural*)
tube that carries food from your
stomach to your bowels, and in
which the food is digested

intimate¹ *adjective* **1** having a close
personal relationship **2** personal or
private **3** (of knowledge) extensive
and detailed **4** having a quiet and
friendly atmosphere > **intimacy**
noun: *the intimacy of their relationship*
> **intimately** *adverb*

intimate² **intimates intimating
intimated** *verb* to hint or suggest
> **intimation** *noun*: *the first
intimation that something could
be amiss*

**intimidate intimidates
intimidating intimidated** *verb*
to frighten (someone) deliberately
with the aim of influencing
their behaviour > **intimidated**
adjective > **intimidating** *adjective*
> **intimidation** *noun*

into *preposition* **1** indicating motion
towards the inside of something:
into the valley **2** indicating the result
of change or division: *turned into a
madman; cut into pieces* **3** indicating
destination: *Their car crashed into
a tree* **4** *informal* interested in:
Nowadays I'm really into healthy food

intolerable *adjective* more than can
be endured > **intolerably** *adverb*

intonation *noun* the way that your
voice rises and falls as you speak

**intoxicate intoxicates
intoxicating intoxicated**
verb **1** to make (someone)
drunk **2** to excite (someone) to
excess > **intoxicating** *adjective*
> **intoxication** *noun*

intoxicated *adjective* **1** drunk
2 overexcited

intra- *prefix meaning* within or
inside: *intra-European conflicts*

intractable *adjective* formal
stubborn and difficult to deal with

intranet *noun* Computers internal
network that makes use of Internet
technology

intransitive *adjective* (of a verb) not
taking a direct object

intravenous *adjective* given into a
vein > **intravenously** *adverb*

intrepid *adjective* fearless or bold
> **intrepidly** *adverb*

intricate *adjective* **1** involved or
complicated **2** full of fine detail
> **intricacy** *noun*: *the intricacy of the
design* > **intricately** *adverb*

**intrigue intrigues intriguing
intrigued** *verb* **1** to make
(someone) interested or curious
2 to plot secretly ▷ *noun* **3** secret
planning or plotting > **intriguing**
adjective

intrinsic *adjective* essential to
the basic nature of something
> **intrinsically** *adverb*

**introduce introduces
introducing introduced** verb
1 to present (someone) by name
(to another person) **2** to say a
few explanatory words at the
beginning of (a radio or television
programme) **3** to make (someone)
aware of or get them interested in
something for the first time **4** to
insert (something) > **introductory**
adjective

introduction noun **1** act of
presenting a person or thing for the
first time **2** piece of writing at the
beginning of a book, usually telling
you what the book is about

introvert noun person concerned
more with his or her thoughts and
feelings than with the outside
world > **introversion** noun
> **introverted** adjective

**intrude intrudes intruding
intruded** verb to come in or join
in without being invited: I don't
want to intrude on your parents
> **intrusion** noun > **intrusive**
adjective

intruder noun person who enters a
place without permission

intuition noun feeling you have
about something that you cannot
explain > **intuitive** adjective
> **intuitively** adverb

Inuit noun **1** member of a group
of people who live in Northern
Canada, Greenland, Alaska and
Eastern Siberia, formerly known as
Eskimos **2** language spoken by the
Inuit people

inundated adjective overwhelmed
(with letters, requests, etc)

**invade invades invading
invaded** verb **1** to enter (a country)
by force **2** to disturb (someone's
privacy) > **invader** noun

invalid¹ noun disabled or chronically

ill person > **invalidity** noun

invalid² adjective **1** (of an argument
etc) not valid because based on a
mistake **2** not acceptable legally
> **invalidate** verb to make invalid
> **invalidity** noun

invaluable adjective extremely
useful

invariably adverb almost always

invasion noun **1** entry by force;
invading **2** intrusion: an invasion
of privacy

invective noun formal abusive
language used by someone who
is angry

invent verb **1** to think up or create
(something new) **2** to make up (a
story, excuse, etc) > **invention**
noun **1** something invented
2 ability to invent > **inventive**
adjective creative and resourceful
> **inventiveness** noun > **inventor**
noun

inventory inventories noun
detailed list of all the objects in
a place

inverse adjective **1** reversed in effect,
sequence, direction, etc ▷ noun
2 exact opposite > **inversely** adverb

invert verb to turn (something)
upside down or inside out

invertebrate noun technical animal
with no backbone

inverted adjective upside down or
back to front

inverted commas plural noun
the punctuation marks " " or ' ', used
to show where speech begins and
ends; quotation marks

invest verb **1** to pay (money) into a
bank or buy shares with it in the
expectation of receiving a profit
2 to spend (money, time, etc) on
something in the hope of making
it a success > **invest in** verb to buy
> **investment** noun > **investor**

noun

investigate investigates investigating investigated *verb* to try to find out all the facts about (something) > **investigation** *noun* > **investigative** *adjective* > **investigator** *noun*

inveterate *adjective* firmly established in a habit or condition and unlikely to stop

invigilate invigilates invigilating invigilated *verb* to supervise people sitting an examination > **invigilator** *noun*

invigorated *adjective* energetic and refreshed > **invigorating** *adjective*: *an invigorating walk*

invincible *adjective* impossible to defeat > **invincibility** *noun*

invisible *adjective* not able to be seen > **invisibility** *noun* > **invisibly** *adverb*

invite invites inviting invited *verb* 1 to ask (someone) to an event 2 to ask (someone to do something) > **invitation** *noun* > **inviting** *adjective* tempting or attractive

invoice invoices invoicing invoiced *noun* 1 bill for goods or services supplied ▷ *verb* 2 to present (someone) with a bill for goods or services supplied

invoke invokes invoking invoked *verb* to use (a law) to justify something

involuntary *adjective* sudden and uncontrollable; unintentional > **involuntarily** *adverb*

involve involves involving involved *verb* 1 to include (someone or something) as a necessary part 2 to affect or concern > **involvement** *noun*

involved *adjective* 1 complicated 2 concerned or taking part

inward *adjective* 1 directed towards the inside or middle 2 situated within 3 spiritual or mental ▷ *adverb* 4 (also **inwards**) towards the inside or middle > **inwardly** *adverb*

iodine *noun* Chemistry bluish-black substance used in medicine and photography

ion *noun* electrically charged atom

iota *noun* very small amount

IQ IQs *abbreviation* intelligence quotient: level of intelligence shown by the results of a special test

ir- *prefix meaning* not or the opposite of; the form of *in-* used before the letter r, eg *irrational*

Iranian *adjective* 1 belonging or relating to Iran ▷ *noun* 2 someone from Iran 3 main language spoken in Iran; Farsi

Iraqi Iraqis *adjective* 1 belonging or relating to Iraq ▷ *noun* 2 someone from Iraq

irate *adjective* very angry

iridescent *adjective* having shimmering changing colours like a rainbow

iris irises *noun* 1 round, coloured part of your eye 2 tall plant with purple, yellow or white flowers

Irish *adjective* 1 belonging or relating to the Irish Republic, or to the whole of Ireland ▷ *noun* 2 (also **Irish Gaelic**) language spoken in some parts of Ireland ▷ *plural* **the Irish** the people of Ireland

Irishman Irishmen *noun* man from Ireland

Irishwoman Irishwomen *noun* woman from Ireland

irk *verb* to irritate or annoy > **irksome** *adjective* irritating or annoying

iron *noun* 1 hard dark metal used to make steel and things like gates and fences. Small amounts of iron are found in blood **2** device that heats up in order to press clothes **3** metal-headed golf club **4 irons** chains or restraints ▷ *adjective* **5** made of iron **6** strong, inflexible: *iron will* ▷ *verb* **7** to smooth (clothes or fabric) with an iron > **ironing** *noun* clothes to be ironed > **iron out** *verb* to solve (difficulties)

Iron Age *noun* era about three thousand years ago when people first started to make tools out of iron

ironbark *noun* Australian eucalypt with a hard rough bark

ironic or **ironical** *adjective* **1** using irony **2** odd or amusing because of being at odds with what you would expect > **ironically** *adverb*

ironmonger *noun* shopkeeper or shop dealing in hardware

irony ironies *noun* **1** mildly sarcastic use of words to imply the opposite of what is said **2** aspect of a situation that is odd or amusing because it is the opposite of what you would expect

irrational *adjective* not based on or not using logical reasoning > **irrationality** *noun* > **irrationally** *adverb*

irrefutable *adjective* impossible to deny or disprove

irregular *adjective* **1** not regular or even **2** not conforming to accepted practice **3** (of a word) not following the typical pattern of formation in a language > **irregularity** *noun* > **irregularly** *adverb*

irrelevant *adjective* not directly connected with the matter in hand > **irrelevance** *noun*

irrepressible *adjective* unfailingly lively and cheerful

irresistible *adjective* too attractive or strong to resist > **irresistibly** *adverb*

irrespective of *preposition* without taking account of

irresponsible *adjective* not giving enough thought or taking enough care about the consequences of your actions or attitudes > **irresponsibility** *noun* > **irresponsibly** *adverb*

irrevocable *adjective* not possible to change or undo > **irrevocably** *adverb*

irrigate irrigates irrigating irrigated *verb* to supply (land) with water by artificial channels or pipes > **irrigation** *noun*

irritate irritates irritating irritated *verb* **1** to annoy **2** to cause (a body part) to itch or become inflamed > **irritable** *adjective* easily annoyed > **irritably** *adverb* > **irritant** *noun, adjective* (person or thing) causing irritation > **irritation** *noun*

is *verb* third person singular present tense of **be**

-ish *suffix* used to form adjectives that mean *fairly* or *rather*: *smallish*

Islam *noun* Muslim religion teaching that there is one God and that Mohammed is his prophet. The holy book of Islam is the Koran > **Islamic** *adjective*

island *noun* piece of land surrounded by water > **islander** *noun* person who lives on an island

isle *noun literary* island

-ism *suffix* **1** used to form nouns that refer to an action or condition: *criticism; heroism* **2** used to form nouns that refer to a political or economic system or a system of beliefs: *Marxism; Sikhism* **3** used to form nouns that refer to a type of prejudice: *racism; sexism*

**isolate isolates isolating
isolated** *verb* to set (someone)
apart > **isolated** *adjective*
> **isolation** *noun*

isosceles triangle *noun* triangle
with two sides of equal length

ISP ISPs *abbreviation* Internet service
provider

Israeli Israelis *adjective* 1 belonging
or relating to Israel ▷ *noun*
2 someone from Israel

issue issues issuing issued *noun*
1 important subject that people are
talking about 2 particular edition
of a magazine or newspaper
3 reason for quarrelling ▷ *verb* 4 to
make (a statement etc) publicly 5 to
supply (someone) officially (with)
6 to produce and make available

-ist *suffix* 1 used to form nouns and
adjectives which refer to someone
who is involved in a certain activity
or who believes in a certain system
or religion: *chemist; motorist;
Buddhist* 2 used to form nouns and
adjectives which refer to someone
who has a certain prejudice: *racist*

isthmus isthmuses *noun* narrow
strip of land with water on either
side connecting two areas of land

it *pronoun* 1 refers to any inanimate
object 2 refers to a baby or
animal whose sex is unknown
or unimportant to you 3 refers
to a thing mentioned or being
discussed 4 used as the subject of
impersonal verbs: *It's windy* > **it's**
1 it is 2 it has
▮ Do not confuse *it's* with *its*

IT *abbreviation* information
technology

Italian *adjective* 1 belonging or
relating to Italy ▷ *noun* 2 someone
from Italy 3 main language spoken
in Italy

italic *adjective* (of printed letters)
sloping to the right > **italics** *plural
noun* this style of printing, used for
emphasis

itch itches itching itched *verb* 1 to
have an itch 2 **be itching to do
something** to be impatient to do
something ▷ *noun* 3 skin irritation
causing a desire to scratch > **itchy**
adjective

item *noun* 1 single thing in a list
or collection 2 newspaper or
magazine article

itinerary itineraries *noun* detailed
plan of a journey

-itis *suffix* added to names of parts
of the body to refer to a condition
involving inflammation of that
part: *appendicitis; tonsillitis*

its *adjective, pronoun* belonging to it
▮ Do not confuse *its* with *it's*

itself *pronoun* 1 used as an object of
a verb or pronoun when the thing
that does an action is also the thing
directly affected by it: *It switches
itself off* 2 used for emphasis: *The site
itself forms a large rectangle*

-ity *suffix* used to form nouns that
refer to a state or condition:
continuity; technicality

-ive *suffix* used to form adjectives
and some nouns: *massive; detective*

ivory *noun* 1 hard white bony
substance forming the tusks of
elephants ▷ *adjective* 2 yellowish-
white

ivy ivies *noun* evergreen climbing
plant

iwi *noun NZ* Maori tribe

-ize or **-ise** *suffix* used to form verbs.
▮ Most verbs can be spelt with
either ending, though there
are some that can only be spelt
with '-ise', for example *advertise,
improvise* and *revise*

J

jab jabs jabbing jabbed *verb* **1** to poke (something) sharply ▷ *noun* **2** quick punch or poke **3** *informal* injection

jabber *verb* to talk rapidly or incoherently

jabiru jabirus *noun* white and green Australian stork with red legs

jack *noun* **1** device for raising a motor vehicle or other heavy object **2** playing card with a picture of a pageboy, whose value is between a ten and a queen **3** *Bowls* small white bowl aimed at by the players **4** socket in electrical equipment into which a plug fits ▷ **jack up** *verb* **1** to raise (a motor vehicle) with a jack **2** to increase (prices or salaries) **3** *NZ informal* to organize or prepare

jackal *noun* doglike wild animal of Africa and Asia

jackaroo jackaroos; also spelt **jackeroo** *noun Aust* trainee on a sheep or cattle station

jackboot *noun* high military boot

jackdaw *noun* bird like a small crow

with black and grey feathers

jacket *noun* **1** short coat **2** skin of a baked potato **3** outer paper cover on a hardback book

jackknife jackknives; jackknifes jackknifing jackknifed *verb* **1** (of an articulated truck) to go out of control so that the trailer swings round at a sharp angle to the cab ▷ *noun* **2** knife with a blade that folds into the handle

jackpot *noun* **1** largest prize that may be won in a gambling game **2 hit the jackpot** *informal* to be very successful through luck

jade *noun* **1** hard green stone used for making jewellery and ornaments ▷ *adjective* **2** bluish-green

jaded *adjective* tired and unenthusiastic

jagged *adjective* having an uneven edge with sharp points

jaguar *noun* large member of the cat family, with spots on its back

jail or **gaol** *noun* **1** prison ▷ *verb* **2** to send to prison > **jailer** *noun* person in charge of the prisoners in a jail

jam jams jamming jammed *verb* **1** to pack tightly into a place **2** to crowd or congest **3** to make or become stuck **4** *Radio* to block (a radio signal) and prevent it from being heard properly **5 jam on the brakes** to apply the brakes fiercely ▷ *noun* **6** hold-up of traffic **7** *informal* awkward situation **8** food made from fruit boiled with sugar

Jamaican *adjective* **1** belonging or relating to Jamaica ▷ *noun* **2** someone from Jamaica

jamb *noun* side post of a door or window frame

jamboree *noun* large gathering of people enjoying themselves

jam-packed *adjective* filled to capacity

Jandal® *noun NZ* sandal with a strap between the big toe and other toes and over the foot

jangle *verb* **jangles jangling jangled 1** to (cause to) make a harsh ringing noise **2** (of nerves) to be upset or irritated

janitor *noun* caretaker of a school or other building

January *noun* first month of the year

Japanese *adjective* **1** belonging or relating to Japan ▷ *noun* **2** someone from Japan **3** main language spoken in Japan

jar jars jarring jarred *noun* **1** wide-mouthed container, usually round and made of glass **2** jolt or shock ▷ *verb* **3** to have a disturbing or unpleasant effect **4** to jolt or bump

jargon *noun* words that are used in special or technical ways by particular groups of people, often making the language difficult to understand

jarrah *noun* Australian eucalypt tree that produces valuable timber

jasmine *noun* climbing plant with sweet-smelling yellow or white flowers

jaundice *noun* disease affecting the liver, causing yellowness of the skin

jaundiced *adjective* (of an attitude or opinion) bitter or cynical

jaunt *noun* short journey for pleasure

jaunty jauntier jauntiest *adjective* expressing cheerfulness and self-confidence: *a jaunty tune* > **jauntily** *adverb*

javelin *noun* light spear thrown in sports competitions

jaw *noun* **1** one of the bones in which the teeth are set **2** **jaws a** mouth **b** gripping part of a tool

jay jays *noun* bird with a pinkish body and blue-and-black wings

jaywalker *noun* person who crosses the road in a careless or dangerous manner > **jaywalking** *noun*

jazz jazzes jazzing jazzed *noun* kind of music with an exciting rhythm, usually involving improvisation > **jazz up** *verb informal* to make (something) more lively or colourful

jazzy jazzier jazziest *adjective informal* flashy or showy

jealous *adjective* **1** fearful of losing a partner or possession to a rival **2** envious **3** suspiciously watchful > **jealously** *adverb* > **jealousy** *noun*

jeans *plural noun* casual denim trousers

Jeep® *noun* four-wheel-drive motor vehicle

jeer *verb* **1** (followed by *at*) to insult (someone) in a loud, unpleasant way ▷ *noun* **2** rude or insulting remark > **jeering** *adjective*

Jehovah *noun* name of God in the Old Testament

jell *verb* **1** to form into a jelly-like substance **2** to become more definite: *His ideas began to jell*

jelly jellies *noun* **1** soft food made of liquid set with gelatine **2** jam made from fruit juice and sugar

jellyfish *noun* small jelly-like sea animal with tentacles which may sting

▏ The plural of *jellyfish* is *jellyfish*

jeopardize jeopardizes jeopardizing jeopardized; also spelt **jeopardise** *verb* to place (something) in danger

jeopardy *noun* danger: *Setbacks have put the whole project in jeopardy*

jerk *verb* **1** to move suddenly and sharply ▷ *noun* **2** sudden sharp movement **3** *informal* stupid or ignorant person

jerkin *noun* short sleeveless jacket

jerky *adjective* (of movements) sudden and quick; not smooth > **jerkily** *adverb* > **jerkiness** *noun*

jerry-built *adjective* built badly using flimsy materials

jerry-can *noun* flat-sided can for carrying petrol or water

jersey jerseys *noun* **1** knitted jumper **2** machine-knitted fabric **3** **Jersey** breed of dairy cow that produces very rich milk

jest *verb* **1** to speak jokingly **2** ▷ *noun* joke

jester *noun* History professional clown at a royal court

Jesuit *noun* member of the Society of Jesus, a Roman Catholic order founded in the sixteenth century

jet jets jetting jetted *verb* **1** to fly by jet aircraft ▷ *noun* **2** aircraft driven by jet propulsion **3** stream of liquid or gas, especially one forced from a small hole **4** nozzle from which gas or liquid is forced **5** hard black mineral

jet-black *adjective* glossy black

jet boat *noun* motorboat propelled by a jet of water

jet lag *noun* tiredness and confusion felt by people after a long flight across different time zones

jetsam *noun* rubbish left floating on the sea or washed up on the sea shore

jet set *noun* rich and fashionable people who travel the world for pleasure

jettison *verb* **1** to abandon (something) **2** to throw (something) overboard

jetty jetties *noun* wooden platform at the edge of the sea or a river, where boats can be moored

Jew *noun* **1** person whose religion is Judaism **2** descendant of the ancient Hebrews > **Jewish** *adjective*

jewel *noun* **1** precious stone **2** special person or thing > **jewelled** *adjective*

jeweller *noun* person who makes jewellery or who sells and repairs jewellery and watches

jewellery *noun* ornaments that people wear, made of valuable metals and sometimes decorated with precious stones

jib jibs jibbing jibbed *noun* **1** triangular sail set in front of a mast **2** projecting arm of a crane or derrick > **jib at** *verb* to object to (a proposal etc)

jibe jibes jibing jibed; also spelt **gibe** *noun* **1** an insulting remark ▷ *verb* **2** to make insulting or taunting remarks

jiffy jiffies *noun* informal very short period of time: *I'll be back in a jiffy*

jig jigs jigging jigged *noun* **1** type of lively folk dance; also the music that accompanies it ▷ *verb* **2** to dance or jump around in a lively bouncy manner

jiggle jiggles jiggling jiggled *verb* to move up and down with short jerky movements

jigsaw *noun* **1** (also **jigsaw puzzle**) picture cut into interlocking pieces, which the user tries to fit together again **2** mechanical saw for cutting along curved lines

jihad *noun* Islamic holy war against those who reject the teachings of Islam

jilt *verb* to leave or reject (one's lover) > **jilted** *adjective*

jingle jingles jingling jingled *noun* **1** catchy verse or song used in a radio or television advert **2** gentle ringing sound ▷ *verb* **3** to make a gentle ringing sound

jingoism *noun* overenthusiastic and unreasonable belief in the

superiority of one's own country
> **jingoistic** *adjective*

jinks *plural noun* **high jinks** noisy
and mischievous behaviour

jinx jinxes *noun* person or thing that
is thought to bring bad luck

jinxed *adjective* considered to be
unlucky

jitters *plural noun informal* **the
jitters** worried nervousness: *I had
the jitters during my speech* > **jittery**
adjective nervous

jive jives jiving jived *noun* **1** lively
dance of the 1940s and '50s ▷ *verb*
2 to dance the jive

job *noun* **1** occupation or paid
employment **2** task to be done
3 *informal* difficult task **4** *Brit,
Aust, NZ informal* crime, especially
robbery **5** **just the job** exactly right

job centre *noun* government office
where people can find out about
job vacancies

jobless *adjective* without any work

job lot *noun* collection of items,
often cheap and of low quality, that
are sold together

**jockey jockeys jockeying
jockeyed** *noun* **1** (professional)
rider of racehorses ▷ *verb* **2** **jockey
for position** to manoeuvre in order
to obtain an advantage

jockstrap *noun* close-fitting piece
of clothing worn under shorts to
support the genitals of men or boys
who are playing sports

jocular *adjective* intended to make
people laugh: *a jocular remark*
> **jocularly** *adverb*

jodhpurs *plural noun* riding
trousers, loose-fitting above the
knee but tight below

joey joeys *noun Aust* young
kangaroo

jog jogs jogging jogged *verb* **1** to
run at a gentle pace, often as a form

of exercise **2** to nudge (something)
slightly **3** **jog someone's
memory** to remind someone
of something ▷ *noun* **4** slow run
> **jogger** *noun* > **jogging** *noun*

join *verb* **1** to become a member (of)
2 to come into someone's company
3 to take part (in) **4** to come or bring
together ▷ *noun* **5** place where two
things are joined > **join up** *verb* to
enlist in the armed services

joiner *noun* person who makes
wooden furniture, doors and
window frames

joinery *noun* work done by a joiner

joint *adjective* **1** shared by two or
more ▷ *noun* **2** place where bones
meet but can move **3** junction
of two or more parts or objects
4 piece of meat for roasting
5 *informal* house or place, especially
a disreputable bar or nightclub
6 *informal* marijuana cigarette
7 **out of joint a** disorganized
b (of a bone) knocked out of its
normal position ▷ *verb* **8** to divide
meat into joints > **jointed** *adjective*
1 having joints that move **2** (of a
large piece of meat) cut into pieces
and ready to cook > **jointly** *adverb*

joist *noun* horizontal beam that
helps support a floor or ceiling

joke jokes joking joked *noun*
1 thing said or done to cause
laughter **2** ridiculous person or
thing that is not worthy of respect:
The decision was a joke ▷ *verb* **3** to
make jokes > **jokingly** *adverb*

joker *noun* **1** person who jokes
2 extra card in a pack of cards,
counted as any other in some
games

jollity *noun* cheerful behaviour and
high spirits

**jolly jollier jolliest; jollies
jollying jollied** *adjective* **1** (of a

person) happy and cheerful **2** (of an occasion) merry and festive ▷ *verb* **3 jolly along** to try to keep (someone) cheerful by flattery or coaxing ▷ *adverb* **4** *informal* very

jolt *noun* **1** unpleasant surprise or shock **2** sudden jerk or bump ▷ *verb* **3** to surprise or shock **4** to bump against (someone or something) with a sudden violent movement

Jordanian *adjective* **1** belonging or relating to Jordan ▷ *noun* **2** someone from Jordan

joss stick *noun* stick of incense giving off a sweet smell when burnt

jostle jostles jostling jostled *verb* to knock or push against roughly

jot jots jotting jotted *verb* **1** (followed by *down*) to write a brief note of ▷ *noun* **2** very small amount > **jottings** *plural noun* notes jotted down

jotter *noun* notebook

joule *noun* *Physics* unit of work or energy

journal *noun* **1** magazine that deals with a particular subject, trade or profession **2** diary which someone keeps regularly

journalism *noun* work of collecting, writing and publishing news in newspapers, magazines and on television and radio > **journalist** *noun* person whose job is writing for newspapers and magazines > **journalistic** *adjective*

journey journeys journeying journeyed *noun* **1** act or process of travelling from one place to another ▷ *verb* **2** to travel

joust jousts jousting jousted *History noun* **1** competition in medieval times between knights fighting on horseback, using lances ▷ *verb* **2** to fight on horseback using lances

jovial *adjective* happy and cheerful > **joviality** *noun* cheerful friendliness > **jovially** *adverb*

joy joys *noun* **1** feeling of great delight or pleasure **2** something or someone that causes happiness **3** *informal* success or luck: *Any joy with your insurance claim?*

joyful *adjective* **1** causing pleasure and happiness **2** extremely happy > **joyfully** *adverb*

joyless *adjective* giving or experiencing no happiness or pleasure

joyous *adjective* *formal* extremely happy and enthusiastic > **joyously** *adverb*

joyride *noun* drive in a stolen car for pleasure > **joyrider** *noun* > **joyriding** *noun*

joystick *noun* control device for an aircraft or computer

JP JPs *abbreviation* (in Britain) Justice of the Peace

jube *noun* *Aust, NZ informal* fruit-flavoured jelly sweet

jubilant *adjective* feeling or expressing great joy or triumph > **jubilantly** *adverb*

jubilation *noun* feeling of great happiness or triumph

jubilee *noun* special anniversary, especially 25th (**silver jubilee**) or 50th (**golden jubilee**)

Judaism *noun* religion of the Jews, based on the Old Testament and the Talmud > **Judaic** *adjective*

judder *verb* **1** to shake and vibrate noisily and violently ▷ *noun* **2** violent vibration

judder bar *noun* *NZ* raised strip across a road designed to slow down vehicles

judge judges judging judged *noun* **1** public official who tries cases and passes sentence in a court of law **2** person who decides the outcome of a contest ▷ *verb* **3** to act as a judge **4** to form an opinion about (someone or something) **5** to decide the result of (a competition)

judgment or **judgement** *noun* **1** opinion reached after careful thought **2** verdict of a judge **3** ability to make sensible decisions or achieve a balanced viewpoint

judicial *adjective* relating to the legal system: *an independent judicial inquiry* > **judicially** *adverb*

judiciary *noun* branch of government concerned with justice and the legal system

judicious *adjective* well-judged and sensible > **judiciously** *adverb*

judo *noun* sport, originating from Japan, in which two opponents try to force each other to the ground using special throwing techniques

jug *noun* container for liquids, with a handle and small spout

juggernaut *noun Brit* large heavy truck

juggle juggles juggling juggled *verb* **1** to throw and catch (several objects) so that most are in the air at the same time **2** to keep (several activities) in progress at the same time > **juggler** *noun* person who juggles in order to entertain people

jugular or **jugular vein** *noun* one of three large veins of the neck that return blood from the head to the heart

juice *noun* **1** liquid part of vegetables, fruit or meat **2 juices** fluids in the body: *gastric juices*

juicy juicier juiciest *adjective* **1** full of juice **2** interesting, exciting or scandalous > **juiciness** *noun*

jujitsu *noun* Japanese form of self-defence in which two opponents try to unbalance each other

jukebox jukeboxes *noun* coin-operated machine found in cafés and pubs, on which CDs or videos can be played

July *noun* seventh month of the year

jumble jumbles jumbling jumbled *noun* **1** untidy muddle of things **2** articles for a jumble sale ▷ *verb* **3** (followed by *up*) to mix (things) untidily

jumble sale *noun* event at which cheap second-hand items are sold to raise money, often for a charity

jumbo jumbos *adjective* **1** *informal* very large ▷ *noun* **2** (also **jumbo jet**) large jet airliner

jumbuck *noun Aust old-fashioned* sheep

jump *verb* **1** to leap or spring into the air using the leg muscles **2** to move quickly and suddenly **3** to make a sudden sharp movement of surprise **4** to increase suddenly ▷ *noun* **5** act of jumping **6** sudden rise **7** break in continuity > **jump at** *verb* to accept (a chance etc) gladly > **jump on** *verb* to criticize (someone) suddenly

jumped-up *adjective* arrogant because of recent promotion

jumper *noun* sweater or pullover

jump lead *noun* electric cable to connect a flat car battery to another battery to aid starting an engine

jump suit *noun* one-piece garment of trousers and top

jumpy jumpier jumpiest *adjective* nervous and worried

junction *noun* place where routes, railway lines or roads meet

junction box junction boxes *noun* box in which electrical wires or cables are safely connected

juncture *noun* point in time which is important to a process or series of events: *Any move at this juncture would be interpreted as weakness*

June *noun* sixth month of the year

jungle *noun* **1** tropical forest of dense tangled vegetation **2** confusion or mess: *a jungle of complex rules*

junior *adjective* **1** holding a low-ranking position in an organization **2** younger **3** relating to childhood: *a junior school* ▷ *noun* **4** person who holds an unimportant position in an organization

juniper *noun* evergreen shrub with purple berries used in cooking and medicine

junk *noun* **1** discarded or useless objects **2** rubbish **3** flat-bottomed Chinese sailing boat

junket *noun* trip or visit by public officials paid for from public funds

junk food *noun* food of low nutritional value

junkie *noun informal* drug addict

junta *noun* group of military officers who seize power in a country through the use of force

Jupiter *noun* largest planet in the solar system and fifth from the sun

jurisdiction *noun formal* **1** right or power to apply laws and make legal judgments: *The Court did not have the jurisdiction to examine the case* **2** power or authority: *The airport was under French jurisdiction*

jurisprudence *noun formal* study of law and the principles on which laws are based

jurist *noun formal* expert in law

juror *noun* member of a jury

jury juries *noun* group of people in a court of law who have been chosen to listen to the facts of a case on trial, and to decide whether the accused person is guilty or not

just *adverb* **1** very recently **2** at this instant **3** merely, only **4** exactly

5 barely: *They only just won* **6** really **7** **just now** *S Afr* in a little while ▷ *adjective* **8** fair or impartial in action or judgment **9** proper or right > **justly** *adverb*

justice *noun* **1** fairness and reasonableness: *There is no justice in this world!* **2** administration of law in a country **3** judge or magistrate

Justice of the Peace Justices of the Peace *noun* (in Britain) person who is authorized to act as a judge in a local court of law

justify justifies justifying justified *verb* **1** to prove (a decision, action or idea) to be reasonable or necessary: *This decision was fully justified by economic conditions* **2** to adjust (text) so that the margins are straight > **justifiable** *adjective* acceptable or reasonable > **justifiably** *adverb* > **justification** *noun* acceptable or reasonable explanation for something

jut juts jutting jutted *verb* to stick out beyond or above a surface or edge

jute *noun* strong fibre made from the bark of an Asian plant, used to make rope and sacking

juvenile *adjective* **1** young **2** of or suitable for young people **3** immature and rather silly ▷ *noun* **4** young person or child

juvenile delinquent *noun* young person guilty of a crime > **juvenile delinquency** *noun*

juxtapose juxtaposes juxtaposing juxtaposed *verb* to put (things or ideas) close together in order to emphasize the differences > **juxtaposition** *noun*

kaffir kaffirs or **kaffir** *noun S Afr very offensive* Black person

kaftan *noun* **1** long loose Eastern garment **2** woman's dress resembling this

kale *noun* cabbage with crinkled leaves

kaleidoscope *noun* tube-shaped toy containing loose coloured pieces reflected by mirrors so that changing patterns form when the tube is twisted ▷ **kaleidoscopic** *adjective* colourful and constantly changing

kamikaze *noun* **1** (in World War II) Japanese pilot who performed a suicide mission ▷ *adjective* **2** (of an action) undertaken in the knowledge that it will kill or injure the person performing it

kangaroo kangaroos *noun* Australian animal which moves by jumping with its powerful hind legs

kaolin *noun* fine white clay used to make porcelain and in some medicines

kapok *noun* fluffy fibre from a tropical tree, used to stuff cushions etc

karaoke *noun* form of entertainment in which people sing over a prerecorded backing tape

karate *noun* Japanese system of unarmed combat using blows with the feet, hands, elbows and legs

karma *noun Buddhism, Hinduism* person's actions affecting his or her fate in future lives

Karoo Karoos; also spelt **Karroo** *noun S Afr* area of very dry land

karri karris *noun* **1** Australian eucalypt **2** its wood, used for building

katipo katipos *noun* small poisonous New Zealand spider

kauri kauri or **kauris** *noun* large New Zealand tree that produces wood used for building and making furniture

kayak *noun* **1** Inuit canoe made of sealskins stretched over a frame **2** fibreglass or canvas-covered canoe of this design

kea kea or **keas** *noun* **1** large greenish New Zealand parrot **2 the Keas** youngest members of the Scouts

kebab *noun* **1** dish of small pieces of meat grilled on skewers **2** (also **doner kebab**) grilled minced lamb served in a split slice of unleavened bread

kedgeree *noun* dish of fish with rice and eggs

keel *noun* main lengthways timber or steel support along the base of a ship ▷ **keel over** *verb* **1** to turn upside down **2** *informal* to collapse suddenly

keen *adjective* **1** eager or enthusiastic **2** intense or strong **3** intellectually acute **4** (of the senses) capable of recognizing small distinctions **5** sharp ▷ **keenly** *adverb* ▷ **keenness** *noun*

keep keeps keeping kept *verb*
1 to have or retain possession
of (something or someone) **2** to
store (something) **3** to stay or
cause (something or someone)
to stay in, on or at a place or
position **4** to continue or persist
5 to detain (someone) **6** to look
after or provide for (something or
someone) ▷ *noun* **7** cost of food and
everyday expenses > **keep up** *verb*
to maintain (something) at the
current level > **keep up with** *verb*
to move at a pace set by (someone)

keeper *noun* **1** person who looks
after animals in a zoo **2** person in
charge of a museum or collection
3 short for **goalkeeper**

keep fit *noun* exercises to promote
physical fitness

keeping *noun* **1** care or charge
2 in or **out of keeping with**
appropriate *or* inappropriate for

keepsake *noun* gift treasured for
the sake of the giver

keg *noun* small metal beer barrel

kelp *noun* large brown seaweed

kelpie *noun* Australian sheepdog
with a smooth coat and upright
ears

kelvin *noun* SI unit of temperature

Kelvin scale *noun* temperature
scale starting at absolute zero
(-273.15° Celsius)

kennel *noun* **1** hutlike shelter for a
dog **2 kennels** place for breeding,
boarding or training dogs

Kenyan *adjective* **1** belonging or
relating to Kenya ▷ *noun* **2** someone
from Kenya

kept *verb* past of **keep**

kerb *noun* edging to a pavement

kernel *noun* **1** seed of a nut, cereal or
fruit; stone **2** central and essential
part of something

kerosene *noun* US, Canadian, Aust,

NZ liquid mixture distilled from
petroleum and used as a fuel or
solvent

kestrel *noun* type of small falcon

ketchup *noun* thick cold sauce,
usually made of tomatoes

kettle *noun* container with a spout
and handle used for boiling water

kettledrum *noun* large bowl-
shaped metal drum

key keys keying keyed *noun*
1 device for locking and unlocking
a lock by moving a bolt **2** device
turned to wind a clock, operate
a machine, etc **3** any of a set of
levers or buttons pressed to use a
typewriter, computer or musical
keyboard instrument **4** *Music*
set of related notes **5** something
crucial in providing an explanation
or interpretation **6** means of
achieving a desired end **7** list of
explanations of codes, symbols, etc
▷ *adjective* **8** of great importance
▷ *verb* **9** (also **key in**) to type in
(text) using a keyboard

keyboard *noun* **1** set of keys on a
piano, computer, etc **2** musical
instrument played using a
keyboard

keystone *noun* **1** most important
part of a process, organization, etc
2 central stone of an arch which
keeps the others in position

kg *symbol* kilogram(s)

khaki *adjective* **1** dull yellowish-
brown ▷ *noun* **2** hard-wearing
fabric of this colour used for
military uniforms

khanda *noun* sword used by Sikhs in
the Amrit ceremony

Khoisan *noun* group of languages
spoken in southern Africa

kHz *symbol* kilohertz

kia ora *interjection* NZ Maori
greeting

kibbutz kibbutzim noun farm or factory in Israel where the workers live together and share everything

kick verb **1** to drive, push or strike (something or someone) with the foot **2** (of a gun) to recoil when fired **3** (followed by against) informal to object (to something) or resist (something) **4** informal to free yourself of (an addiction) **5** Rugby to score (a goal) with a kick ▷ noun **6** thrust or blow with the foot **7** recoil of a gun when fired **8** informal excitement or thrill **> kick off** verb **1** to start a game of soccer **2** informal to begin **> kick up** verb informal to create (a fuss)

kick-off noun start of a game of soccer

kid kids kidding kidded noun **1** informal child **2** young goat **3** leather made from the skin of a young goat ▷ verb **4** informal to tease or deceive (someone)

kidnap kidnaps kidnapping kidnapped verb to take (someone) away by force and hold (him or her) to ransom **> kidnapper** noun person who kidnaps someone **> kidnapping** noun

kidney kidneys noun **1** either of the pair of organs that remove waste products from the blood **2** animal kidney used as food

kidney bean noun reddish-brown kidney-shaped bean, edible when cooked

kill verb **1** to cause the death of (a person or an animal) **2** informal to cause (someone) pain or discomfort **3** to put an end to (a conversation or an activity) **4** to pass (time) ▷ noun **5** act of killing **6** animals or birds killed in a hunt **> killer** noun person who kills someone

kiln noun oven for baking or drying pottery, bricks, etc

kilo kilos noun short for **kilogram**

kilobyte noun Computers 1024 units of information

kilogram or **kilogramme** noun one thousand grams

kilohertz noun one thousand hertz

◼ The plural of kilohertz is kilohertz

kilometre noun one thousand metres

kilowatt noun Electricity one thousand watts

kilt noun knee-length pleated tartan skirt worn originally by Scottish Highlanders

kimono kimonos noun loose wide-sleeved Japanese robe, fastened with a sash

kin or **kinsfolk** plural noun person's relatives collectively

kind adjective **1** considerate, friendly and helpful ▷ noun **2** class or group with common characteristics **3** essential nature or character **4** **in kind a** (of payment) in goods rather than money **b** with something similar **5** **kind of** to a certain extent **> kindness** noun: We have been treated with such kindness

kindergarten noun class or school for children under six years old

kindle kindles kindling kindled verb **1** to set (a fire) alight **2** (of a fire) to start to burn **3** to arouse (a feeling) or (of a feeling) to be aroused

kindling noun dry wood or straw for starting fires

kindly adjective **1** having a warm-hearted nature **2** pleasant or agreeable ▷ adverb **3** in a considerate way **4** please: Will you kindly be quiet! **> kindliness** noun

kindred adjective **1** having similar qualities **2** related by blood or marriage ▷ *noun* **3** same as **kin**

kinetic *adjective* relating to or caused by motion

kinetic energy *noun* energy produced when something moves

king *noun* **1** male ruler of a monarchy **2** ruler or chief **3** best or most important of its kind **4** piece in chess that must be defended **5** playing card with a picture of a king on it

kingdom *noun* **1** country ruled by a king or queen **2** division of the natural world

kingfisher *noun* small bird, often with a bright-coloured plumage, that dives for fish

kingpin *noun* most important person in an organization

king-size or **king-sized** *adjective* larger than standard size

kink *noun* **1** twist or bend in rope, wire, hair, etc **2** *informal* quirk in someone's personality

kinky kinkier kinkiest *adjective* **1** *informal* having peculiar sexual tastes **2** full of kinks

kinship *noun* family relationship to other people

kiosk *noun* **1** small booth selling drinks, cigarettes, newspapers, etc **2** public telephone box

kip kips kipping kipped *noun, verb informal* to sleep

kipper *noun* cleaned, salted and smoked herring

kirk *noun Scot* church

kiss kisses kissing kissed *verb* **1** to touch (someone) with the lips in affection or greeting **2** to join lips with (someone) in love or desire ▷ *noun* **3** touch with the lips

kiss of life *noun* method of reviving someone by blowing air into his or her lungs

kit kits kitting kitted *noun* **1** outfit or equipment for a specific purpose **2** set of pieces of equipment sold ready to be put together **3** *NZ* flax basket > **kit out** *verb* to provide (someone) with clothes or equipment needed for a particular activity

kitchen *noun* room used for cooking

kite *noun* **1** light frame covered with a thin material flown on a string in the wind **2** large hawk with a forked tail

kith *plural noun* **kith and kin** friends and relatives

kitset *noun NZ* set of parts for putting together to make a house or a piece of furniture

kitten *noun* young cat

kitty kitties *noun* **1** fund of money given by a group of people to pay for things together **2** total amount bet in certain gambling games

kiwi kiwis *noun* **1** New Zealand bird with a long beak and no tail, which cannot fly **2 Kiwi** *informal* New Zealander

kiwi fruit *noun* edible fruit with a fuzzy brownish skin and green flesh

kleptomania *noun* uncontrollable desire to steal > **kleptomaniac** *noun* person who has an uncontrollable desire to steal

kloof *noun S Afr* gorge

km *symbol* kilometre(s)

knack *noun* **1** skilful way of doing something **2** innate ability

knapsack knapsacks *noun* soldier's or traveller's bag worn strapped on the back

knave *noun* **1** jack at cards **2** *obsolete* dishonest man

knead *verb* **1** to work (dough) into a smooth mixture with the hands **2** to squeeze or press (something) with the hands

knee knees kneeing kneed *noun*

1 joint between thigh and lower leg **2** lap **3** part of a garment covering the knee ▷ *verb* **4** to strike or push (someone) with the knee

kneecap kneecaps kneecapping kneecapped *noun* **1** bone in front of the knee ▷ *verb* **2** to shoot (someone) in the kneecap

kneel kneels kneeling knelt *verb* to fall or rest on one's knees

knell *noun* **1** sound of a bell, especially at a funeral or death **2** sign of something bad about to happen

knew *verb* past tense of **know**

knickers *plural noun* woman's or girl's undergarment covering the lower trunk and having holes for the legs; pants

knick-knack *noun* small ornament

knife knives; knifes knifing knifed *noun* **1** cutting tool or weapon consisting of a sharp-edged blade with a handle ▷ *verb* **2** to cut (something) or stab (someone) with a knife

knight *noun* **1** man who has been given a knighthood **2** *History* man who served a monarch or lord as a mounted soldier **3** chess piece shaped like a horse's head ▷ *verb* **4** to award a knighthood to (a man) > **knighthood** *noun* honorary title given to a man by the British sovereign

knit knits knitting knitted *verb* **1** to make (a garment) by working lengths of wool together using needles or a machine **2** to join closely together **3** to draw (one's eyebrows) together > **knitting** *noun* **1** garment being knitted **2** the activity of knitting

knob *noun* **1** rounded switch on a machine such as a radio **2** rounded handle on a door or drawer **3** small amount (of butter)

knobkerrie *noun* S Afr club with a rounded end

knock *verb* **1** to give a blow or push to (someone or something) **2** to tap on (something) with the knuckles **3** to make or drive (someone or something) into a certain position by striking **4** *informal* to criticize (someone) **5** (of an engine) to make a regular banging noise as a result of a fault ▷ *noun* **6** blow or rap **7** knocking sound > **knock about** or **around** *verb* **1** to wander or spend time aimlessly **2** to hit or kick (someone) brutally > **knock back** *verb informal* **1** to drink (a drink) quickly **2** to cost (someone) a certain amount **3** to reject or refuse (someone) > **knock down** *verb* **1** to demolish (a building) **2** to reduce (a price) > **knock off** *verb* **1** *informal* to cease work **2** *informal* to make or do (something) hurriedly or easily **3** to take (a specified amount) off a price **4** *Brit, Aust, NZ informal* to steal (something) > **knock out** *verb* **1** to hit (someone) so hard that he or she becomes unconscious **2** *informal* to overwhelm or amaze (someone) **3** to defeat (a competitor) in a knockout competition

knocker *noun* metal fitting for knocking on a door

knockout *noun* **1** blow so hard that it makes an opponent unconscious **2** competition in which competitors are eliminated in each round until only the winner is left **3** *informal* extremely attractive person or thing

knoll *noun* small rounded hill

knot knots knotting knotted *noun* **1** fastening made by looping and pulling tight strands of string, cord or rope **2** tangle (of hair)

3 small cluster or huddled group (of people) **4** round lump or spot in timber **5** feeling of tightness in the stomach, caused by tension or nervousness **6** unit of speed used by ships, equal to one nautical mile (1.85 kilometres) per hour ▷ *verb* **7** to tie (something) with or into a knot

know knows knowing knew known *verb* **1** to be or feel certain of the truth of (information etc) **2** to be acquainted with (a person or place) **3** to have a grasp of or understand (a skill or language) **4** to be aware of (a fact) ▷ *noun* **5 in the know** *informal* informed or aware of something few people know about

know-how *noun informal* ability to do something difficult or technical

knowing *adjective* suggesting secret knowledge > **knowingly** *adverb* **1** deliberately **2** in a way that suggests secret knowledge

knowledge *noun* **1** facts or experiences known by a person **2** state of knowing **3** specific information on a subject

knowledgeable or **knowledgable** *adjective* intelligent or well-informed

knuckle knuckles knuckling knuckled *noun* **1** bone at the finger joint **2** knee joint of a calf or pig **3 near the knuckle** *informal* rather rude or offensive > **knuckle under** *verb* to yield or give in

koala *noun* Australian animal with grey fur that lives in trees

kohanga reo or **kohanga** *noun* NZ infant class where children are taught in Maori

The plural of *kohanga reo* is *kohanga reo*

kookaburra *noun* large Australian kingfisher with a cackling cry

koppie or **kopje** *noun* S Afr small hill

Koran *noun* sacred book of Islam

Korean *adjective* **1** relating or belonging to Korea ▷ *noun* **2** someone from Korea **3** main language spoken in Korea

kosher *adjective* **1** (of food) prepared according to Jewish law **2** *informal* correct or genuine ▷ *noun* **3** kosher food

kowhai kowhai or **kowhais** *noun* small New Zealand tree with clusters of yellow flowers

kowtow *verb* (followed by *to*) to behave very humbly and respectfully (towards someone)

kph *abbreviation* kilometres per hour

kraal *noun* S African village surrounded by a strong fence

krypton *noun* Chemistry colourless gas present in the atmosphere and used in fluorescent lights

kudos *noun* fame or credit

kudu kudus; also spelt **koodoo** *noun* S Afr large African antelope with curled horns

kumara kumara or **kumaras** *noun* NZ tropical root vegetable with yellow or orange flesh

kumquat *noun* citrus fruit resembling a tiny orange

kung fu *noun* Chinese martial art combining hand, foot and weapon techniques

kura kaupapa Maori *noun* NZ primary school where the teaching is done in Maori

Kurd *noun* member of a group of people who live mainly in eastern Turkey, northern Iraq and western Iran

Kurdish *adjective* **1** belonging or relating to the Kurds ▷ *noun* **2** language spoken by the Kurds

kW *abbreviation* kilowatt(s)

l

l *symbol* litre

lab *noun informal* short for **laboratory**

label labels labelling labelled *noun* 1 piece of paper or plastic attached to something to identify it or show its destination ▷ *verb* 2 to put a label on (something)

laboratory laboratories *noun* building or room designed for scientific research or for the teaching of practical science

laborious *adjective* involving great prolonged effort > **laboriously** *adverb*

Labor Party *noun Aust* main left-wing political party in Australia

labour (*US & Aust*) or **labor** *noun* 1 physical work or exertion 2 workers in industry 3 final stage of pregnancy, leading to childbirth ▷ *verb* 4 *old-fashioned* to work hard > **labourer** *noun* person who labours, especially someone doing manual work for wages

Labour Party *noun* main left-wing political party in a number of countries including Britain and New Zealand

labrador *noun* large retriever dog with a usually gold or black coat

labyrinth *noun* complicated network of passages; maze

lace laces lacing laced *noun* 1 delicate decorative fabric made from threads woven into an open weblike pattern 2 cord drawn through eyelets and tied ▷ *verb* 3 to fasten (shoes) with laces 4 to add a small amount of alcohol, a drug, etc to (food or drink) > **lacy** *adjective* fine, like lace

lack *noun* 1 shortage or absence of something needed or wanted ▷ *verb* 2 not to be present when or where needed 3 to need or be short of (something)

lacklustre *adjective* lacking brilliance or vitality

laconic *adjective* using only a few words

lacquer *noun* hard varnish for wood or metal

lacrosse *noun* sport in which teams catch and throw a ball using long sticks with a net at the end, in an attempt to score goals

lad *noun* boy or young man

ladder *noun* 1 frame of two poles connected by horizontal steps used for climbing 2 line of stitches that have come undone in tights or stockings ▷ *verb* 3 to have such a line of undone stitches in (one's tights or stockings)

laden *adjective* (often followed by *with*) carrying a lot (of something)

ladle ladles ladling ladled *noun* 1 spoon with a long handle and a large bowl, used for serving soup etc ▷ *verb* 2 to serve out (soup etc)

lady ladies *noun* 1 woman regarded as having characteristics of good breeding or high rank 2 polite term of address for a woman 3 **Lady** title of some female members of the

British nobility

ladybird *noun* small red flying beetle with black spots

lady-in-waiting ladies-in-waiting *noun* female servant of a queen or princess

ladylike *adjective* polite and dignified

Ladyship *noun* **Your Ladyship** term of address for a woman with the title *Lady*

lag lags lagging lagged *verb* to wrap (a boiler, pipes, etc) with insulating material > **lag behind** *verb* to make slower progress than other people

lager *noun* light-coloured beer

lagoon *noun* area of water cut off from the open sea by coral reefs or sand bars

laid *verb* past of **lay**

lain *verb* past participle of **lie²**

lair *noun* resting place of a wild animal

laird *noun* landowner in Scotland

lake *noun* area of fresh water surrounded by land

lama *noun* Buddhist priest or monk

lamb *noun* **1** young sheep **2** its meat

lame *adjective* **1** having an injured or disabled leg or foot **2** (of an excuse) unconvincing; feeble > **lamely** *adverb* in an unconvincing manner > **lameness** *noun*

lament *verb* **1** to feel or express sorrow for (something) ▷ *noun* **2** passionate expression of grief **3** song or poem expressing grief at someone's death

lamentable *adjective* very disappointing

laminated *adjective* consisting of several thin sheets or layers stuck together: *laminated glass*

lamp *noun* device that produces light from electricity, oil or gas

lamppost *noun* post supporting a lamp in the street

lampshade *noun* decorative covering over an electric light bulb that prevents the bulb giving out too harsh a light

lance lances lancing lanced *noun* **1** long spear used by a mounted soldier ▷ *verb* **2** to pierce (a boil or abscess) with a sharp instrument

land *noun* **1** solid part of the earth's surface **2** ground, especially with reference to its type or use **3** country or region ▷ *verb* **4** to come to earth after a flight, jump or fall **5** *informal* to succeed in getting (something) **6** to catch (a fish) **7** (followed by *with*) to cause (someone) to have to deal with something unpleasant

landing *noun* **1** floor area at the top of a flight of stairs **2** bringing or coming to land

landlady landladies *noun* woman who owns a house or small hotel and who lets rooms to people

landlord *noun* man who owns a house or small hotel and who lets rooms to people

landmark *noun* **1** prominent feature of a landscape **2** event, decision, etc considered as an important development

landowner *noun* person who owns land, especially a large area of the countryside

landscape *noun* **1** extensive piece of inland scenery seen from one place **2** picture of it

landslide *noun* **1** (also **landslip**) falling of soil, rock, etc down the side of a mountain **2** overwhelming electoral victory

lane *noun* **1** narrow road, especially in the country **2** one of the strips on a road marked with lines to guide drivers

language *noun* **1** system of sounds, symbols, etc for communicating thought **2** particular system used by a nation or people **3** style in which a person expresses himself or herself

languid *adjective* lacking energy or enthusiasm > **languidly** *adverb*

languish languishes languishing languished *verb* to suffer neglect or hardship

lanky lankier lankiest *adjective* ungracefully tall and thin

lantana *noun* shrub with orange or yellow flowers, considered a weed in Australia

lantern *noun* light in a transparent protective case

lap laps lapping lapped *noun* **1** part between the waist and knees of a person when sitting **2** single circuit of a racecourse or track ▷ *verb* **3** to overtake (an opponent) in a race so as to be one or more circuits ahead **4** (of waves) to beat softly against a shore etc > **lap up** *verb* (of an animal) to drink (liquid) by scooping up with the tongue

lapel *noun* part of the front of a coat or jacket folded back towards the shoulders

lapse lapses lapsing lapsed *noun* **1** slight mistake **2** instance of bad behaviour by someone usually well-behaved **3** period of time between two events ▷ *verb* **4** **lapse into** to give way to (a regrettable kind of behaviour): *They lapsed into silence* **5** to end or become invalid, especially through disuse

lard *noun* fat from a pig, used in cooking

larder *noun* storeroom for food

large larger largest *adjective* **1** great in size, number or extent

▷ *noun* **2** **at large** (of a prisoner) escaped from prison > **largely** *adverb* to a great extent

lark *noun* **1** small brown songbird **2** *informal* harmless piece of mischief or fun

larrikin *noun Aust, NZ informal* mischievous or unruly person

larva larvae *noun* insect in an immature stage, often resembling a worm

laryngitis *noun* inflammation of the larynx, causing loss of voice

larynx larynxes or **larynges** *noun* part of the throat containing the vocal cords

lasagne *noun* dish made from layers of pasta in wide flat sheets, meat and cheese

laser *noun* device that produces a very narrow intense beam of light, used for cutting very hard materials and in surgery etc

lash lashes lashing lashed *noun* **1** eyelash **2** strip of leather at the end of a whip **3** sharp blow with a whip > **lash out** *verb* (followed by *at*) to make a sudden physical or verbal attack on (someone)

lass lasses *noun* girl

lasso lassoes or **lassos lassoing lassoed** *noun* **1** rope with a noose for catching cattle and horses ▷ *verb* **2** to catch (an animal) with a lasso

last *adjective, adverb* **1** coming at the end or after all others **2** most recent(ly) ▷ *adjective* **3** only remaining ▷ *verb* **4** to continue to exist or happen **5** to remain fresh, uninjured or unaltered > **lastly** *adverb*: *Lastly, let's look at sales*

last-ditch *adjective* done as a final resort

latch latches latching latched *noun* **1** fastening for a door with a bar and lever **2** lock that can only be opened from the outside with a key > **latch onto** *verb* to become attached to (a person or idea)

late later latest *adjective* **1** after the normal or expected time **2** towards the end of a period **3** recently dead ▷ *adverb* **4** after the normal or expected time > **lately** *adverb* in recent times

latent *adjective* hidden and not yet developed

lateral *adjective* of or relating to the side or sides

lathe *noun* machine for turning wood or metal while it is being shaped

lather *noun* froth of soap and water

Latin *noun* **1** language of the ancient Romans **2** member of a people who speak languages closely related to Latin, such as French, Italian, Spanish and Portuguese

Latin America *noun* parts of South and Central America whose official language is Spanish or Portuguese > **Latin American** *noun, adjective*

latitude *noun* distance north or south of the equator measured in degrees

latrine *noun* hole or trench in the ground used as a toilet at a camp

latter *adjective, noun* **1** second of two ▷ *adjective* **2** second or end: *the latter part of his career* > **latterly** *adverb formal* recently

You use *latter* to talk about the second of two items. To talk about the last of three or more items you should use *last-named*

lattice *noun* structure made of strips crossed over each other diagonally with holes in between

laudable *adjective* praiseworthy

laugh *verb* **1** to make a noise with the voice that expresses amusement or happiness ▷ *noun* **2** act or instance of laughing > **laughable** *adjective* absurd > **laughter** *noun*

laughing stock *noun* person who has been made to seem ridiculous

launch launches launching launched *verb* **1** to put (a ship or boat) into the water, especially for the first time **2** to put (a new product) on the market **3** to send (a missile or spacecraft) into space or the air ▷ *noun* **4** launching **5** open motorboat

launch pad or **launching pad** *noun* place from which space rockets take off

launder *verb old-fashioned* to wash and iron (clothes and linen)

laundry laundries *noun* **1** clothes etc for washing or that have recently been washed **2** business that washes and irons clothes and sheets

laurel *noun* evergreen tree with shiny leaves

lava *noun* molten rock thrown out by volcanoes, which hardens as it cools

lavatory lavatories *noun* toilet

lavender *noun* **1** shrub with fragrant flowers ▷ *adjective* **2** bluish-purple

lavish lavishes lavishing lavished *adjective* **1** giving or spending generously ▷ *verb* **2** (followed by *on*) to give (money, affection, etc) generously > **lavishly** *adverb*

law *noun* **1** system of rules developed by a government, which regulate what people may and may not do and deals with people who break these rules **2** one of these rules **3** profession of people such as lawyers, whose job involves the application of the laws of a country

4 scientific fact that explains how things work in the physical world > **lawful** *adjective* allowed by law > **lawfully** *adverb* as allowed by the law > **lawless** *adjective* having no regard for the law

law-abiding *adjective* obeying the laws

lawn *noun* **1** area of cultivated grass **2** fine linen or cotton fabric

lawnmower *noun* machine for cutting grass

lawsuit *noun* court case brought by one person or group against another

lawyer *noun* person who is qualified in law, and who advises people about the law and represents them in court

lax *adjective* not strict

laxative *noun* medicine taken to stop constipation

lay lays laying laid *verb* **1** to put (something) down so that it lies somewhere **2** (of a bird or reptile) to produce (an egg) out of its body **3** to arrange (a table) for a meal **4** to set (a trap) for someone **5** to put (emphasis) on something to indicate that it is very important **6** past tense of **lie²** **7** **lay odds on** to bet that (something) will happen ▷ *adjective* **8** of people who are involved with a Christian church but are not members of the clergy > **lay off** *verb* **1** to dismiss (staff) during a slack period **2** *informal* to stop doing something annoying > **lay on** *verb* to provide (a meal or entertainment)

People often get confused about *lay* and *lie*. The verb *to lay* (past tense: *laid*) takes an object: *Lay the table please; The Queen laid a wreath.* The verb *to lie* (past tense : *lay*) does not take an object: *The book was lying on the table; I lay on the bed*

lay-by lay-bys *noun* **1** stopping place for traffic beside a road **2** *Aust, NZ* system whereby a customer pays a deposit on an item in a shop so that it will be kept for him or her until the rest of the price is paid

layer *noun* single thickness of something, such as a cover or coating on a surface

layman laymen *noun* **1** person who is not a member of the clergy **2** person without specialist knowledge

layout *noun* arrangement, especially of matter for printing or of a building

laze lazes lazing lazed *verb* to be idle or lazy

lazy lazier laziest *adjective* idle and not inclined to work or make much effort > **lazily** *adverb* > **laziness** *noun* the state of being idle

lb *abbreviation* pound (weight)

lbw *abbreviation Cricket* leg before wicket

leach leaches leaching leached *verb* to remove (minerals) from rocks by a liquid passing through the rock

lead¹ leads leading led *verb* **1** to guide or conduct (someone) somewhere **2** to cause (someone) to feel, think or behave in a certain way **3** to control or direct (a group of people) **4** **lead to** to result in (something happening) ▷ *noun* **5** clue that might the police to solve a crime **6** length of leather or chain attached to a dog's collar to control it > **leading** *adjective*

lead² *noun* soft heavy grey metal

leaden *adjective* **1** heavy and slow-moving **2** dull grey

leader *noun* **1** person who leads **2** article in a newspaper expressing editorial views > **leadership**

noun **1** group of people in charge of an organization **2** ability to be a good leader

leaf leaves; leafs leafing leafed *noun* flat usually green blade attached to the stem of a plant > **leaf through** *verb* to turn the pages of (a book, magazine or newspaper) without reading them > **leafy** *adjective*: *tall leafy trees*

leaflet *noun* sheet of printed matter for distribution

league *noun* **1** association promoting the interests of its members **2** association of sports clubs organizing competitions between its members **3** measure of distance used in former times and equivalent to about three miles

leak *noun* **1** hole or defect that allows the escape or entrance of liquid, gas, radiation, etc **2** disclosure of secrets ▷ *verb* **3** to let liquid etc in or out **4** (of liquid etc) to find its way through a leak **5** to disclose (secret information) > **leakage** *noun* escape of liquid etc from a pipe or container > **leaky** *adjective*

lean leans leaning leant or **leaned; leaner leanest** *verb* **1** to bend or slope from an upright position: *He leaned forward* ▷ *adjective* **2** thin but healthy-looking **3** (of meat) lacking fat **4** (of a period) during which food or money is in short supply

leap leaps leaping leapt or **leaped** *verb* **1** to make a sudden powerful jump ▷ *noun* **2** sudden powerful jump

leap year *noun* year with February 29th as an extra day

learn learns learning learnt or **learned** *verb* **1** to gain skill or knowledge by study, practice or teaching **2** to memorize **3** to find

out about or discover > **learned** *adjective* having a lot of knowledge gained from years of study > **learner** *noun* > **learning** *noun* knowledge got by study

lease leases leasing leased *noun* **1** contract by which property is rented for a stated time by the owner to a tenant ▷ *verb* **2** to let or rent (property) by lease

leash leashes *noun* lead for a dog

least *adjective* **1** superlative of **little 2** smallest ▷ *noun* **3** smallest possible amount **4 at least** no fewer or less than ▷ *adverb* **5** in the smallest degree

leather *noun* material made from specially treated animal skins > **leathery** *adjective* like leather; tough

leave leaves leaving left *verb* **1** to go away from (a place) **2** to allow (someone) to remain somewhere, accidentally or deliberately **3** to stop being part of (a job or organization) **4** to arrange for (money or possessions) to be given to someone after one's death **5** to cause (a number) to remain after subtracting one number from another ▷ *noun* **6** period of holiday or absence from work or duty

Lebanese *adjective* **1** of Lebanon ▷ *noun* **2** person from Lebanon.
■ The plural of *Lebanese* is *Lebanese*

lecherous *adjective* constantly thinking about sex

lectern *noun* sloping reading desk, especially in a church

lecture lectures lecturing lectured *noun* **1** informative talk to an audience on a subject **2** lengthy scolding ▷ *verb* **3** to teach in a college or university

lecturer *noun* teacher in a college or university

led *verb* past of **lead¹**

ledge *noun* **1** narrow shelf sticking out from a wall **2** shelflike projection from a cliff etc

ledger *noun* book of debit and credit accounts of a firm

lee *noun* **1** sheltered part or side ▷ *adjective* **2** denoting the side of a ship away from the wind

leech leeches *noun* small worm that lives in water and feeds by sucking the blood from other animals

leek *noun* vegetable of the onion family with a long bulb and thick stem

leer *verb* **1** to look or grin at someone in a sneering or suggestive manner ▷ *noun* **2** sneering or suggestive look or grin

leeway *noun* room for free movement within limits

left *adjective* **1** of the side that faces west when the front faces north ▷ *adverb* **2** on or towards the left ▷ *noun* **3** left side or part **4** *Politics* people and political groups supporting socialism or communism rather than capitalism ▷ *verb* **5** past of **leave** > **leftist** *noun, adjective* (person) of the political left

left-handed *adjective* more adept with the left hand than with the right

leftovers *plural noun* unused bits of food or material

left-wing *adjective* supporting socialism or communism rather than capitalism > **left-winger** *noun*

leg *noun* **1** one of the limbs on which a person or animal walks, runs or stands **2** part of a garment covering the leg **3** one of the parts of an object such as a table that rest on the floor and support its weight

4 stage of a journey **5** *Sport* one of two matches played between two sports teams

legacy legacies *noun* **1** thing left in a will **2** something that exists as a result of a previous event or time: *the legacy of a Catholic upbringing*

legal *adjective* **1** allowed by the law **2** relating to law or lawyers > **legally** *adverb*

legal aid *noun* system providing the services of a lawyer free, or very cheaply, to people who cannot afford the full fees

legality *noun* (of an action) fact of being allowed by the law: *They challenged the legality of the scheme*

legalize legalizes legalizing legalized; also spelt **legalise** *verb* to make (something) legal > **legalization** *noun*

legend *noun* **1** traditional story or myth **2** famous person or event > **legendary** *adjective* **1** famous **2** of or in legend

leggings *plural noun* **1** close-fitting trousers for women or children **2** protective or waterproof covering worn over trousers

legible *adjective* easily read

legion *noun* **1** large military force **2** large number **3** infantry unit in the Roman army

legionnaire *noun* member of a legion

legislate legislates legislating legislated *verb formal* to make laws

legislation *noun* law or set of laws created by a government

legislative *adjective* of the making of new laws

legislator *noun formal* maker of laws

legislature *noun formal* parliament in a country, which is responsible for making new laws

legitimate *adjective* reasonable or acceptable according to existing laws or standards > **legitimacy** *noun* > **legitimately** *adverb*

leisure *noun* 1 time for relaxation or hobbies 2 **at (your) leisure** when you have time > **leisurely** *adjective* 1 deliberate, unhurried ▷ *adverb* 2 slowly

lekker *adjective S Afr informal* 1 attractive or nice 2 tasty

lemming *noun* small rodent of cold northern regions, reputed to run into the sea and drown during mass migrations

lemon *noun* 1 sour-tasting yellow oval fruit that grows on trees ▷ *adjective* 2 pale-yellow

lemonade *noun* lemon-flavoured soft drink, often fizzy

lend lends lending lent *verb* 1 to give someone the temporary use of (something) 2 (of a bank etc) to provide (money) temporarily, often for interest > **lender** *noun*

length *noun* 1 extent or measurement from end to end 2 period of time for which something happens 3 quality of being long 4 piece of something narrow and long 5 **at length** for a long time

lengthen *verb* to make (something) longer

lengthways or **lengthwise** *adverb* horizontally from one end to the other

lengthy lengthier lengthiest *adjective* lasting for a long time

lenient *adjective* tolerant, not strict or severe > **leniency** *noun* > **leniently** *adverb*

lens lenses *noun* 1 piece of glass or similar material with one or both sides curved, used to bring together or spread light rays in cameras, spectacles, telescopes, etc 2 transparent structure in the eye that focuses light

lent *verb* past of **lend**

Lent *noun* period of forty days leading up to Easter, during which Christians give up something they enjoy

lentil *noun* small dried red or brown seed, cooked and eaten in soups and curries

Leo *noun* fifth sign of the zodiac, represented by a lion

leopard *noun* wild Asian or African big cat, with yellow fur and black or brown spots

leotard *noun* tight-fitting costume covering the body and sometimes the legs, worn for dancing or exercise

leper *noun* person suffering from leprosy

leprosy *noun* disease attacking the nerves and skin, resulting in loss of feeling in the affected parts

lesbian *noun* homosexual woman > **lesbianism** *noun*

lesion *noun* injury or wound

less *adjective* 1 smaller in extent, degree or duration 2 not so much 3 comparative of **little** ▷ *adverb* 4 to a smaller extent or degree ▷ *preposition* 5 after deducting; minus

> You use *less* with singular words: *less time; less money*. With plural words you should use *fewer*: *fewer cars; fewer problems*

-less *suffix meaning* without: *hopeless*

lessen *verb* to be reduced in amount, size or quality; decrease

lesser *adjective* not as great in quantity, size or worth

lesson *noun* 1 single period of instruction in a subject

2 experience that makes one understand something important

lest *conjunction* so as to prevent any possibility that

let lets letting let *verb* **1** to allow (someone) to do something **2** used as an auxiliary to express a proposal, command, threat, or assumption: *let's go* **3** to grant the use of (a house or flat) for rent **4 let yourself in for** to agree to do (something you do not really want to do) > **let down** *verb* **1** to fail (someone); disappoint **2** to deflate > **let off** *verb* **1** to excuse (someone) from a punishment **2** to light (a firework) or detonate (an explosive)

lethal *adjective* deadly: *a lethal weapon*

lethargy *noun* lack of energy and enthusiasm > **lethargic** *adjective*

letter *noun* **1** written message, usually sent by post **2** alphabetical symbol

letter box letter boxes *noun* **1** slot in a door through which letters are delivered **2** box in a street or post office where letters are posted

lettering *noun* writing, especially the type of letters used: *bold lettering*

lettuce *noun* plant with large green leaves used in salads

leukaemia or **leukemia** *noun* disease caused by uncontrolled overproduction of white blood cells

level levels levelling levelled *adjective* **1** (of a surface) smooth, flat and parallel to the ground ▷ *verb* **2** to make (a piece of land) flat **3** to direct (a criticism, accusation, etc) at someone ▷ *adverb* **4 draw level with** to get closer to (someone) so that one is moving next to him or her ▷ *noun* **5** point on a scale measuring the amount, importance or difficulty

of something **6** height that a liquid comes up to in a container > **level off** or **level out** *verb* to stop increasing or decreasing

level crossing *noun* point where a railway line and road cross

level-headed *adjective* not apt to be carried away by emotion

lever *noun* **1** handle used to operate machinery **2** bar used to move a heavy object or to open something

leverage *noun* **1** action or power of a lever **2** knowledge or influence that can be used to make someone do something

leveret *noun* young hare

levy levies levying levied *verb* **1** to impose and collect (a tax) ▷ *noun* **2** *formal* amount of money that one pays in tax

lewd *adjective* lustful or indecent

lexicography *noun* the profession of writing dictionaries

liability liabilities *noun* **1** responsibility for wrongdoing **2** *informal* person who causes a lot of problems or embarrassment **3 liabilities** business debts

liable *adjective* **1** (followed by *to*) likely (to happen) **2** (followed by *for*) legally responsible (for something)

liaise liaises liaising liaised *verb* to establish and maintain communication (with a person or organization)

liaison *noun* communication and contact between groups

liar *noun* person who tells lies

libel libels libelling libelled *noun* **1** published statement falsely damaging a person's reputation ▷ *verb* **2** to falsely damage the reputation of (someone) > **libellous** *adjective*

liberal *adjective* **1** tolerant of a wide range of behaviour, standards or opinions **2** generous (with something) **3** (of a quantity) large ▷ *noun* **4** person who has liberal ideas or opinions **> liberalism** *noun* belief in democratic reforms and individual freedom **> liberally** *adverb* in large quantities

Liberal Democrat or **Lib Dem** *noun* member of the Liberal Democrats, a British political party favouring a mixed economy and individual freedom

liberate liberates liberating liberated *verb* to free (people) from prison or from an unpleasant situation **> liberation** *noun* **> liberator** *noun*

liberty *noun* freedom to choose how one wants to live, without government restrictions

libido libidos *noun* sexual drive

Libra *noun* seventh sign of the zodiac, represented by a pair of scales

librarian *noun* person in charge of a library

library libraries *noun* **1** building where books are kept for people to come and read or borrow **2** collection of books, records, etc for consultation or borrowing

Libyan *adjective* **1** of Libya ▷ *noun* **2** person from Libya

lice *noun* a plural of **louse**

licence *noun* **1** official document giving official permission to do something **2** freedom to do what one wants, especially when considered irresponsible

▇ The noun *licence* ends in *ce*

license licenses licensing licensed *verb* to give official permission for (an activity) to be carried out

▇ The verb *license* ends in *se*

lichen *noun* green moss-like growth on rocks or tree trunks

lick *verb* **1** to pass the tongue over (something) ▷ *noun* **2** licking

lid *noun* movable cover for a container

lie¹ lies lying lied *verb* **1** to say something that is not true ▷ *noun* **2** something said that is not true

lie² lies lying lay lain *verb* **1** to be in a horizontal position **2** to be situated

▌ The past tense of this verb *lie* is *lay*. Do not confuse it with the verb *to lay* (past tense *laid*) meaning 'put'

lieu *noun* **in lieu of** instead of

lieutenant *noun* junior officer in the army or navy

life lives *noun* **1** quality of being able to grow and develop, which is present in people, plants and animals **2** period between birth and death or between birth and the present time **3** amount of time something is active or functions **4** liveliness or high spirits **5** imprisonment for the rest of your life or until granted parole

life assurance *noun* insurance that provides a sum of money in the event of the policy holder's death

lifeblood *noun* most essential part of something

lifeboat *noun* **1** boat kept on shore, used for rescuing people at sea **2** small boat kept on a ship, used if the ship starts to sink

life expectancy life expectancies *noun* number of years a person can expect to live

lifeguard *noun* person whose job is to rescue people in difficulty at sea or in a swimming pool

life jacket *noun* sleeveless inflatable jacket that keeps a person afloat in water

lifeless *adjective* **1** dead **2** not lively or exciting

lifelike *adjective* (of a picture or sculpture) looking very real or alive

lifeline *noun* **1** means of contact or support **2** rope used in rescuing a person in danger

lifelong *adjective* lasting all of a person's life

lifesaver *noun Aust, NZ* person whose job is to rescue people who are in difficulty at sea

life science *noun* any science concerned with living organisms, such as biology, botany or zoology

life span *noun* **1** length of time during which a person is alive **2** length of time a product or organization exists or is useful

lifetime *noun* length of time a person is alive

lift *verb* **1** to move (something) upwards in position, status, volume, etc **2** to remove or cancel (a ban) **3** *informal* to steal (something) ▷ *noun* **4** cage raised and lowered in a vertical shaft to transport people or goods **5** ride in a car etc as a passenger

ligament *noun* band of tissue joining bones

light lights lighting lighted or **lit; lighter lightest** *noun* **1** brightness from the sun, fire or lamps, by which things are visible **2** lamp or other device that gives out brightness **3** match or lighter to light a cigarette: *Have you got a light?* ▷ *adjective* **4** (of a place) bright **5** (of a colour) pale **6** (of an object) not weighing much **7** (of a task) fairly easy **8** (of books or music) not serious or profound ▷ *verb* **9** to cause (a fire) to start burning **10** to cause (a place) to be filled with light

> **lightly** *adverb* > **lightness** *noun*

lighten *verb* **1** to become less dark **2** to make (something) less heavy

lighter *noun* device for lighting cigarettes etc

light-headed *adjective* feeling faint; dizzy

light-hearted *adjective* cheerful and carefree

lighthouse *noun* tower by the sea with a powerful light to guide ships

lighting *noun* **1** way that a room or building is lit **2** apparatus for and use of artificial light in theatres, films, etc

lightning *noun* bright flashes of light in the sky, produced by natural electricity during a thunderstorm

lightweight *noun, adjective* **1** not weighing much ▷ *noun* **2** boxer weighing up to 135lb (professional) or 60kg (amateur)

light year *noun Astronomy* distance that light travels in one year, about six million million miles

likable or **likeable** *adjective* pleasant and friendly

like likes liking liked *preposition, adjective, noun* **1** indicating similarity, comparison, etc **2** **feel like** to want to do or to have: *I feel like a walk* ▷ *verb* **3** to find (something or someone) pleasant

-like *suffix meaning* resembling or similar to: *a balloonlike object*

likelihood *noun* probability

likely likelier likeliest *adjective* probable

liken *verb* to compare (one thing) to another

likeness likenesses *noun* resemblance

likewise *adverb* similarly

liking *noun* fondness for (someone or something)

lilac *noun* **1** shrub with pale mauve

or white flowers ▷ *adjective* **2** light-purple

lilt *noun* pleasing musical quality in speaking > **lilting** *adjective*

lily lilies *noun* plant that grows from a bulb and has large, often white, flowers

limb *noun* **1** arm, leg or wing **2** main branch of a tree **3 go out on a limb** to say or do something risky

limber up *verb* to stretch your muscles in preparation for doing sport

limbo *noun* **1** West Indian dance in which dancers lean backwards to pass under a bar **2 in limbo** not knowing the result or next stage of something and powerless to influence it

lime *noun* **1** calcium compound used as a fertilizer or in making cement **2** small green citrus fruit **3** deciduous tree with heart-shaped leaves and fragrant flowers

limelight *noun* glare of publicity

limerick *noun* humorous verse of five lines

limestone *noun* white rock used in building

limit *noun* **1** boundary or extreme beyond which something cannot go: *the speed limit* ▷ *verb* **2** to prevent (something) from becoming bigger, spreading or making progress > **limited** *adjective* rather small in amount or extent

limitation *noun* **1** reducing or controlling of something **2 limitations** limits of the abilities of someone or something

limousine *noun* large luxurious car, usually driven by a chauffeur

limp *verb* **1** to walk with an uneven step because of an injured leg or foot ▷ *noun* **2** limping walk ▷ *adjective* **3** without firmness or

stiffness

limpet *noun* shellfish that sticks tightly to rocks

line lines lining lined *noun* **1** long narrow mark **2** telephone connection **3** railway track **4** course or direction of movement **5** attitude towards something **6** kind of work someone does **7** row or queue of people **8** type of product **9** row of words **10 lines** words of a theatrical part ▷ *verb* **11** to cover the inside of (something) > **line up** *verb* **1** to stand in a line **2** to arrange (something) for a special occasion

lineage *noun* all the people from whom someone is directly descended

linear *adjective* arranged in a line or in a strict sequence, or happening at a constant rate

line dancing *noun* form of dancing performed by rows of people to country and western music

linen *noun* **1** cloth or thread made from flax **2** sheets, tablecloths, etc

liner *noun* large passenger ship or aircraft

linesman linesmen *noun* (in some sports) an official who helps the referee or umpire

-ling *suffix meaning* small: *duckling*

linger *verb* to remain for a long time

lingerie *noun* women's underwear or nightwear

lingo lingoes *noun informal* foreign or unfamiliar language

linguist *noun* person who studies foreign languages or the way language works

lining *noun* any material used to line the inside of something

link *noun* **1** relationship or connection between two things: *the link between sunbathing and skin cancer* **2** person or thing forming a connection **3** any of the rings forming a chain ▷ *verb* **4** to join (people, places or things) together > **linkage** *noun*: *There is no formal linkage between the two agreements*

lino *noun* short for **linoleum**

linoleum *noun* floor covering with a shiny surface

lint *noun* soft material for dressing a wound

lion *noun* large animal of the cat family, the male of which has a shaggy mane

lip *noun* **1** either of the fleshy edges of the mouth **2** rim of a jug etc

lip-read lip-reads lip-reading lip-read *verb* to understand speech by following lip movements, often done by deaf people

lipstick *noun* cosmetic in stick form, for colouring the lips

liqueur *noun* flavoured and sweetened alcoholic spirit, usually drunk after a meal

liquid *noun* **1** substance in a physical state which can change shape but not size ▷ *adjective* **2** of or being a liquid **3** (of assets) in the form of money or easily converted into money

liquidate liquidates liquidating liquidated *verb* **1** to dissolve (a company) and share its assets among creditors **2** *informal* to wipe out or kill (someone) > **liquidation** *noun*: *The company went into liquidation* > **liquidator** *noun* official appointed to liquidate a business

liquor *noun* any strong alcoholic drink

liquorice *noun* **1** root used to flavour sweets **2** sweets flavoured with this

lira lire *noun* unit of currency of Turkey and formerly of Italy

lisp *noun* **1** speech defect in which *s* and *z* are pronounced *th* ▷ *verb* **2** to speak with a lisp

list *noun* **1** item-by-item record of names or things, usually written one below another ▷ *verb* **2** to make a list of (a number of things) **3** (of a ship) to lean to one side

listen *verb* to heed or pay attention (to something) > **listener** *noun*: *I'm a regular listener to her show*

listless *adjective* lacking interest or energy > **listlessly** *adverb* without interest or energy

lit *verb* a past of **light**

litany litanies *noun* **1** prayer with responses from the congregation **2** any tedious recital

literacy *noun* ability to read and write

literal *adjective* **1** according to the explicit meaning of a word or text; not figurative **2** (of a translation) word for word > **literally** *adverb*: *The views are literally breath-taking*

literary *adjective* of or knowledgeable about literature

literate *adjective* able to read and write

literature *noun* **1** written works such as novels, plays and poetry **2** books and writings of a country, period or subject

lithe *adjective* flexible or supple

litmus *noun* *Chemistry* blue dye turned red by acids and restored to blue by alkalis

litmus test *noun* something regarded as a simple and accurate test of a particular thing

litre *noun* unit of liquid measure equal to 1000 cubic centimetres or 1.76 pints

litter *noun* **1** untidy rubbish dropped in public places **2** group of young animals produced at one birth **3** dry material to absorb a cat's excrement ▷ *verb* **4** to scatter things about untidily in (a place)

little less least *adjective* **1** small or smaller than average ▷ *adverb* **2** not a lot or not often ▷ *noun* **3** small amount, extent or duration

live¹ lives living lived *verb* **1** to be alive **2** to reside > **live down** *verb* to wait till people forget (a past mistake or misdeed) > **live up to** *verb* to meet (one's expectations)

live² *adjective* **1** living; alive **2** (of a broadcast) transmitted during the actual performance **3** (of a wire, circuit, etc) carrying an electric current **4** causing interest or controversy **5** capable of exploding

livelihood *noun* occupation or employment

lively *adjective* full of life or vigour; energetic > **liveliness** *noun* vigour and enthusiasm

liven up *verb* to make (things) more lively

liver *noun* **1** large organ in the body that cleans the blood and aids digestion **2** animal liver as food

livestock *noun* farm animals

livid *adjective* **1** *informal* angry or furious **2** bluish-grey

living *adjective* **1** alive ▷ *noun* **2** **for a living** in order to earn money to live: *What does he do for a living?*

living room *noun* room in a house used for relaxation and entertainment

lizard *noun* four-footed reptile with a long body and tail

llama *noun* woolly animal of the camel family found in S America

load *noun* **1** something being carried **2** **loads** *informal* lots ▷ *verb* **3** to put a load onto (an animal) or into (a vehicle)

loaf loaves; loafs loafing loafed *noun* **1** shaped mass of baked bread ▷ *verb* **2** to be lazy and not do

any work

loan *noun* **1** sum of money borrowed **2** lending ▷ *verb* **3** to lend (something) to someone

loath or **loth** *adjective* unwilling or reluctant (to do something)

loathe loathes loathing loathed *verb* to hate or be disgusted by (someone or something) > **loathing** *noun* > **loathsome** *adjective*

lob lobs lobbing lobbed *Sport noun* **1** ball struck or thrown high in the air ▷ *verb* **2** to strike or throw (a ball) high in the air

lobby lobbies lobbying lobbied *noun* **1** corridor into which rooms open **2** group which tries to influence an organization ▷ *verb* **3** to try to influence (an MP or organization) in the formulation of policy > **lobbyist** *noun* person who lobbies an MP or organization

lobe *noun* **1** any rounded part of something **2** soft hanging part of the ear

lobster *noun* shellfish with a long tail and claws, which turns red when boiled

local *adjective* **1** of the area close to your home **2** (of an anaesthetic) producing loss of feeling in one part of the body ▷ *noun* **3** person belonging to a particular district **4** *informal* pub close to your home > **locally** *adverb*

locality localities *noun* neighbourhood or area

localized or **localised** *adjective* existing or happening in only one place: *localized pain*

locate locates locating located *verb* **1** to discover the whereabouts of (someone or something) **2** to situate (something) in a place

location *noun* **1** site or position

2 site of a film production away from the studio **3** S Afr Black African or coloured township

loch noun Scot lake

lock noun **1** appliance for fastening a door, case, etc **2** section of a canal shut off by gates between which the water level can be altered to aid boats moving from one level to another **3** small bunch of hair ▷ verb **4** to close and fasten (something) with a key **5** to move into place and become firmly fixed there

locker noun small cupboard with a lock

locket noun small hinged pendant for a portrait etc, worn on a chain round the neck

locksmith noun person who makes and mends locks

locomotive noun railway engine

locust noun destructive African insect that flies in swarms and eats crops

lodge lodges lodging lodged noun **1** small house in the grounds of a large country house **2** small house used for holidays ▷ verb **3** to live in another's house at a fixed charge **4** to stick or become stuck (in a place) **5** to make (a complaint) formally

lodger noun person who lives in someone's house and pays rent

lodgings plural noun rented room or rooms in another person's house

loft noun space between the top storey and roof of a building

lofty loftier loftiest adjective **1** of great height **2** very noble or important **3** proud and superior

log logs logging logged noun **1** portion of a felled tree stripped of branches **2** detailed record of a journey of a ship, aircraft, etc ▷ verb **3** to make a record of (something)

in a ship's log > **log in** verb to gain access (to a computer system) by keying in a special command > **log out** verb to leave (a computer system) by keying in a special command

logic noun **1** way of reasoning involving a series of statements, each of which must be true if the statement before it is true **2** any sensible thinking or reasonable decision

logical adjective **1** (of an argument) using logic **2** (of a course of action or a decision) sensible or reasonable in the circumstances > **logically** adverb

logistics noun detailed planning and organization of a large, especially military, operation

logo logos noun emblem used by a company or other organization

-logy suffix used to form words that refer to the study of something: biology; geology

loin noun **1** piece of meat from the back or sides of an animal **2** **loins** old-fashioned front part of the body between the waist and the thighs, especially the sexual parts

loiter verb to stand or wait aimlessly or idly

loll verb **1** to lounge lazily **2** (of a head or tongue) to hang loosely

lollipop noun hard sweet on a small wooden stick

lolly lollies noun **1** lollipop or ice lolly **2** Aust, NZ sweet

lolly scramble noun NZ sweets scattered on the ground for children to collect

lone adjective solitary or single

lonely lonelier loneliest adjective **1** sad because alone **2** (of a place) isolated and unfrequented > **loneliness** noun

loner *noun informal* person who prefers to be alone

lonesome *adjective* lonely and sad

long *adjective* 1 having length, especially great length, in space or time ▷ *adverb* 2 for an extensive period 3 **as long as** only if 4 **before long** soon 5 **no longer** not any more ▷ *verb* 6 (followed by *for*) to have a strong desire for > **longing** *noun* yearning

longevity *noun* long life

longhand *noun* ordinary writing, not shorthand or typing

longitude *noun* distance east or west from a line passing through Greenwich, measured in degrees

long jump *noun* athletics event involving jumping as far as possible after taking a long run

long-range *adjective* 1 extending into the future 2 (of vehicles, weapons, etc) designed to cover great distances

long-sighted *adjective* able to see distant objects in focus but not nearby ones

long-standing *adjective* existing for a long time

long-suffering *adjective* enduring trouble or unhappiness without complaint

long-term *adjective* lasting or effective for a long time

long-winded *adjective* speaking or writing at tedious length

loo loos *noun informal* toilet

look *verb* 1 (followed by *at*) to direct the eyes or attention towards 2 to have the appearance of being (as specified) 3 to search (for something or someone) ▷ *noun* 4 instance of looking; glance 5 facial expression 6 **looks** attractiveness > **look after** *verb* to take care of > **look down on** *verb* to treat (someone) as inferior or unimportant > **look forward to** *verb* to anticipate (something) with pleasure > **look out** *verb* to be careful > **look up** *verb* 1 to discover or confirm (information) by checking in a book 2 (of a situation) to improve 3 to visit (someone) after a long gap > **look up to** *verb* to respect (someone)

lookalike *noun* person who is the double of another

lookout *noun* 1 person who is watching for danger; guard 2 place for watching 3 **on the lookout** watching or waiting expectantly (for something)

loom *noun* 1 machine for weaving cloth ▷ *verb* 2 to appear suddenly and unclearly or threateningly 3 to seem ominously close

loony loonies *informal adjective* 1 foolish or insane ▷ *noun* 2 foolish or insane person

loop *noun* 1 rounded shape made by a curved line or rope crossing itself ▷ *verb* 2 to fasten (something) with a loop

loophole *noun* means of evading a rule without breaking it

loose looser loosest *adjective* 1 not tight, fastened, fixed or tense 2 **at a loose end** bored; with nothing to do ▷ *adverb* 3 free from captivity > **loosely** *adverb*

loosen *verb* to make (something) looser

loot *verb* 1 to steal goods from (shops and houses) during a battle or riot ▷ *noun* 2 stolen money and goods

lop lops lopping lopped *verb* to chop (something) off with one quick stroke

lopsided *adjective* greater in height, weight or size on one side

lord *noun* 1 male member of the

British nobility **2 Lord a** God or Jesus **b** (in Britain) title given to certain male officials and peers ▷ *verb* **3 lord it over** to act in a superior manner towards

Lordship *noun* (in Britain) title of some male officials and peers

lore *noun* all the traditional knowledge and stories about a subject

lorikeet *noun* small brightly coloured Australian parrot

lorry lorries *noun Brit, S Afr* large vehicle for transporting goods by road

lory lories *noun* small, brightly coloured parrot found in Australia

lose loses losing lost *verb* **1** to come to be without (something), especially by accident or carelessness **2** to be deprived of (something) **3** to be deprived of (a relative or friend) through his or her death **4** to be defeated in (a competition etc) **5** (of a business) to spend more (money) than it earns **6** to be or become engrossed: *lost in thought* > **loser** *noun* **1** person or thing that loses **2** *informal* person who seems destined to fail

loss losses *noun* **1** losing **2 at a loss** confused or bewildered

lost *verb* **1** past of **lose** ▷ *adjective* **2** unable to find your way **3** unable to be found

lot *noun* **1** item at auction **2 a lot a** a great number or quantity: *a lot of noise* **b** very much or very often: *He's out a lot* **3 the lot** or **the whole lot** the whole amount or number **4 lots** great numbers or quantities: *We took lots of photos*

loth *adjective* same as **loath**

lotion *noun* medical or cosmetic liquid for use on the skin

lottery lotteries *noun* method of raising money by selling tickets that win prizes by chance

lotus lotuses *noun* large water lily of Africa and Asia

loud *adjective* **1** having a high volume of sound **2** (of clothing) too bright > **loudly** *adverb* > **loudness** *noun*

loudspeaker *noun* piece of equipment that makes your voice louder when you speak into a microphone connected to it

lounge lounges lounging lounged *noun* **1** living room in a private house **2** more expensive bar in a pub ▷ *verb* **3** to sit, lie or stand in a relaxed manner

lourie *noun S Afr* one of two types of bird found in South Africa: the grey lourie, which lives in open grassland, and the more brightly coloured species, which lives in forests

louse lice *noun* small insect that lives on people's bodies

lousy lousier lousiest *adjective informal* **1** mean or unpleasant **2** bad, inferior **3** unwell

lout *noun* young man who behaves in an aggressive and rude way

lovable or **loveable** *adjective* having very attractive qualities and therefore easy to love

love loves loving loved *verb* **1** to have a great affection for (someone) **2** to enjoy (something) very much **3 would love to** to want very much to (do something): *I would love to live there* ▷ *noun* **4** great affection **5** *Tennis squash, etc* score of nothing **6 in love** feeling a strong emotional and sexual attraction (for someone) **7 make love** (often followed by *to*) to have sexual intercourse with (someone) > **loving** *adjective* affectionate or tender > **lovingly** *adverb*

love affair noun romantic or sexual relationship between two people who are not married to each other

love life love lives noun person's romantic or sexual relationships

lovely lovelier loveliest adjective very beautiful, attractive and pleasant > **loveliness** noun: a vision of loveliness

lover noun **1** person having a sexual relationship outside marriage **2** person who loves a specified person or thing

low adjective **1** not tall or high **2** of little or less than the usual amount, degree, quality or cost **3** coarse or vulgar **4** not loud **5** deep in pitch ▷ adverb **6** in or to a low position, level or degree ▷ noun **7** low position, level or degree

lowboy lowboys noun Aust, NZ small wardrobe or chest of drawers

lower verb **1** to move (something) downwards **2** to lessen (something)

lowlands plural noun area of flat low land > **lowland** adjective

lowly lowlier lowliest adjective low in importance, rank or status

low tide noun time, usually twice a day, when the sea is at its lowest level

loyal adjective faithful to your friends, country or government > **loyally** adverb > **loyalty** noun

loyalist noun person who remains firm in support for a government or ruler

lozenge noun **1** medicated tablet held in the mouth until it dissolves **2** diamond-shaped figure

LP LPs noun long-playing record

LSD noun lysergic acid diethylamide, a very powerful drug that causes hallucinations

Ltd abbreviation Brit Limited (Liability)

lubra noun Aust Australian Aboriginal woman

lubricate lubricates lubricating lubricated verb to oil or grease (something) to lessen friction > **lubricant** noun lubricating substance, such as oil > **lubrication** noun

lucid adjective **1** (of writing or speech) clear and easily understood **2** (of a person) able to think clearly

luck noun fortune, good or bad

luckless adjective having bad luck

lucky adjective having or bringing good luck > **luckily** adverb fortunately

lucrative adjective very profitable

ludicrous adjective absurd or ridiculous

lug lugs lugging lugged verb to carry or drag (something) with great effort

luggage noun traveller's cases, bags, etc

lukewarm adjective **1** moderately warm; tepid **2** indifferent or half-hearted

lull verb **1** to calm the fears or suspicions of (someone) by deception ▷ noun **2** brief time of quiet in a storm etc

lullaby lullabies noun quiet song to send a child to sleep

lumber noun **1** Brit unwanted disused household articles **2** Chiefly US sawn timber ▷ verb **3** to move heavily and awkwardly **4** informal to burden (someone) with something unpleasant

luminary luminaries noun literary famous person

luminous adjective glowing in the dark, usually because treated with a special substance > **luminosity** noun **1** brightness **2** (of a person's skin) healthy glow

lump *noun* **1** shapeless piece or mass
2 swelling **3** *informal* awkward or
stupid person ▷ *verb* **4** to consider
(people or things) as a single group
5 lump it *informal* to tolerate or
put up with something > **lumpy**
adjective containing or covered
with lumps

lump sum *noun* large sum of money
paid at one time

lunacy *noun* **1** extremely foolish or
eccentric behaviour **2** *old-fashioned*
severe mental illness

lunar *adjective* relating to the moon

lunatic *adjective* **1** foolish and
irresponsible ▷ *noun* **2** foolish or
annoying person **3** *old-fashioned*
insane person

lunch lunches lunching lunched
noun **1** meal taken in the middle of
the day ▷ *verb* **2** to eat lunch

luncheon *noun formal* lunch

lung *noun* organ that allows an
animal or bird to breathe air:
humans have two lungs in the chest

lunge lunges lunging lunged
noun **1** sudden forward motion
2 thrust with a sword ▷ *verb* **3** to
move with a lunge

lurch lurches lurching lurched
verb **1** to make a sudden jerky
movement ▷ *noun* **2** lurching
movement **3 leave someone in
the lurch** to abandon someone in
difficulties

lure lures luring lured *verb* **1** to
tempt or attract (someone) by the
promise of reward ▷ *noun* **2** person
or thing that lures

lurid *adjective* **1** vivid in shocking
detail; sensational **2** glaring in
colour

lurk *verb* to lie hidden or move
stealthily, especially for sinister
purposes

luscious *adjective* extremely

pleasurable to taste or smell

lush *adjective* (of grass etc) growing
thickly and healthily

lust *noun* **1** strong sexual desire **2** any
strong desire ▷ *verb* **3** (followed by
after) to have a strong desire for

lustre *noun* gloss or sheen

lute *noun* ancient guitar-like
musical instrument with a body
shaped like a half pear

luxuriant *adjective* (of plants
or gardens) large, healthy and
growing strongly

luxurious *adjective* very expensive
and full of luxury; splendid
> **luxuriously** *adverb*

luxury luxuries *noun* **1** enjoyment
of rich, very comfortable living
2 enjoyable but not essential thing

-ly *suffix* **1** forming adjectives that
describe a quality: *friendly* **2** forming
adjectives that refer to how
often something happens: *yearly*
3 forming adverbs that refer to how
something is done: *quickly; nicely*

lying *noun* telling lies ▷ *verb*
2 present participle of **lie¹** and **lie²**

lynch lynches lynching lynched
verb (of a crowd) to put (someone)
to death without a trial

lynx lynxes *noun* wildcat with
tufted ears and a short tail

lyre *noun* ancient musical
instrument like a U-shaped harp

lyric *adjective* (of poetry) expressing
personal emotion in songlike
style > **lyrical** *adjective* poetic and
romantic

lyrics *plural noun* words of a popular
song

m *symbol* **1** metre(s) **2** mile(s)

macabre *adjective* strange and horrible; gruesome

macadamia *noun* Australian tree with edible nuts

macaroni *noun* pasta in short tube shapes

macaroon *noun* small biscuit or cake made with ground almonds

mace *noun* ornamental pole carried by an official during ceremonies as a symbol of authority

machete *noun* broad heavy knife used for cutting or as a weapon

machine machines machining machined *noun* **1** apparatus, usually powered by electricity, designed to perform a particular task ▷ *verb* **2** to make or produce (something) by machine

machine gun *noun* automatic gun that fires rapidly and continuously

machinery *noun* machines or machine parts collectively

machismo *noun* exaggerated or strong masculinity

macho *adjective* strongly or exaggeratedly masculine

mackerel *noun* edible sea fish with blue and silver stripes

mackintosh mackintoshes *noun* raincoat made from specially treated waterproof cloth

mad madder maddest *adjective* **1** mentally deranged; insane **2** very foolish **3** *informal* angry **4** (followed by *about*) very enthusiastic (about someone or something) > **madly** *adverb* > **madness** *noun*

madam *noun* polite form of address to a woman

maddening *adjective* irritating or frustrating

madrigal *noun* song sung by several people without instruments

Mafia *noun* international secret criminal organization founded in Sicily

magazine *noun* **1** weekly or monthly publication with articles and photographs **2** compartment in a gun for cartridges

magenta *noun, adjective* deep reddish-purple

maggot *noun* larva of an insect

magic *noun* **1** in fairy stories, a special power that can make impossible things happen **2** art of performing tricks to entertain people > **magical** *adjective* **1** of, using or like magic **2** *informal* wonderful or marvellous > **magically** *adverb*

magician *noun* **1** person who performs tricks as entertainment **2** in fairy stories, a man with magical powers

magistrate *noun* official who acts as a judge in a law court that deals with less serious crimes

magnanimous *adjective* noble and generous

magnate *noun* influential or wealthy person, especially in industry

magnet *noun* piece of iron or steel

capable of attracting iron and pointing north when suspended

magnetic *adjective* **1** having the properties of a magnet **2** powerfully attractive > **magnetism** *noun* **1** magnetic property **2** powerful personal charm **3** science of magnetic properties

magnificent *adjective* extremely beautiful or impressive
> **magnificence** *noun*
> **magnificently** *adverb*

magnify magnifies magnifying magnified *verb* (of a microscope or lens) to makes (something) appear bigger than it actually is
> **magnification** *noun*

magnifying glass magnifying glasses *noun* lens which makes things appear bigger than they really are

magnitude *noun* relative importance or size

magnolia *noun* shrub or tree with showy white or pink flowers

magnum *noun* large wine bottle holding about 1.5 litres

magpie *noun* black-and-white bird

mahogany *noun* hard reddish-brown wood of several tropical trees

maid or **maidservant** *noun* female servant

maiden *noun* **1** *literary* young unmarried woman ▷ *adjective* **2** first: *maiden voyage*

maiden name *noun* woman's surname before marriage

mail *noun* **1** letters and packages delivered by the post office ▷ *verb* **2** to send (a letter) by mail

mail order *noun* system of buying goods by post

maim *verb* to injure (someone) very badly for life

main *adjective* **1** chief or principal

▷ *noun* **2** principal pipe or line carrying water, gas or electricity **3 mains** main distribution network for water, gas or electricity
> **mainly** *adverb* for the most part; chiefly

mainframe *noun* Computers high-speed general-purpose computer

mainland *noun* stretch of land which forms the main part of a country

mainstay *noun* most important part of something

mainstream *noun* most ordinary and conventional group of people or ideas in a society

maintain *verb* **1** to keep (something) going or keep (something) at a particular rate or level **2** to keep (something) going or keep (something) at a particular rate or level **3** to support (someone) financially **4** to assert that (something) is true

maintenance *noun* **1** process of keeping something in good condition **2** money that a person sends regularly to someone to provide for the things he or she needs

maize *noun* type of corn with spikes of yellow grains

majestic *adjective* beautiful, dignified and impressive
> **majestically** *adverb*

majesty majesties *noun* **1** great dignity and impressiveness **2 His Majesty** or **Her Majesty** way of referring to a king or queen

major *adjective* **1** greater in number, quality or extent **2** significant or serious **3** denoting the key in which most European music is written ▷ *noun* **4** middle-ranking army officer

majority majorities *noun* **1** greater

number **2** number by which the votes on one side exceed those on the other

> You should use *majority* only to talk about things that can be counted: *the majority of car owners*. To talk about an amount that cannot be counted you should use *most*: *Most of the harvest was saved*

make makes making made *verb* **1** to create, construct or establish **2** to force (someone) to do something **3** to bring about or produce **4** to perform (an action) **5 make do** to manage with an inferior alternative ▷ *noun* **6** brand, type or style > **maker** *noun* manufacturer > **make up** *verb* **1** to form or constitute **2** to invent (a story) **3** (followed by *for*) to compensate for (something that you have done wrong) **4** to apply cosmetics to **5 make it up** to settle a quarrel > **making** *noun* **1** creation or production **2 in the making** gradually becoming: *a captain in the making*

make-up *noun* **1** cosmetics **2** character or personality

maladjusted *adjective* Psychology unable to meet the demands of society

malaise *noun* vague feeling of unease, illness or depression

malaria *noun* infectious disease caused by the bite of some mosquitoes

Malaysian *adjective* **1** of Malaysia ▷ *noun* **2** person from Malaysia

male *adjective* **1** of the sex which can fertilize female reproductive cells ▷ *noun* **2** male person or animal

male chauvinist *noun* man who thinks that men are better than women

malevolent *adjective* wishing evil to others; spiteful > **malevolence** *noun*: *a streak of malevolence*

malfunction *verb* **1** to function imperfectly or fail to function ▷ *noun* **2** defective functioning or failure to function

malice *noun* desire to cause harm to others

malicious *adjective* intended to harm: *malicious gossip*

malign *verb* to say unpleasant and untrue things about (someone)

malignant *adjective* (of a tumour) harmful and uncontrollable

mallard *noun* wild duck, the male of which has a green head

mallee *noun* Aust low-growing eucalypt found in dry regions

mallet *noun* wooden hammer with a square head

malnutrition *noun* inadequate nutrition

malodorous *adjective* bad-smelling

malpractice *noun* immoral, illegal or unethical professional conduct

malt *noun* grain, such as barley, prepared for use in making beer or whisky

mammal *noun* animal of the type that suckles its young

mammoth *noun* **1** extinct elephant-like mammal ▷ *adjective* **2** colossal

man men; mans manning manned *noun* **1** adult male **2** humankind: *one of the hardest substances known to man* **3 men** people: *all men are equal* ▷ *verb* **4** to be in charge of or operate

mana *noun* NZ authority or influence

manacles *plural noun* metal rings or clamps attached to a prisoner's wrists or ankles

manage manages managing managed *verb* **1** to succeed in doing something **2** to be in charge of or administer (an organization or business)

manageable *adjective* able to be dealt with

management *noun* **1** managers collectively **2** administration or organization

manager *noun* person responsible for running a business or organization

> In business, the word *manager* can apply to either a man or a woman

manageress manageresses *noun* woman responsible for running a business or organization

managing director *noun* company director responsible for the way the company is managed

mandarin *noun* kind of small orange

mandate *noun* authorization or instruction from an electorate to its representative or government

mandatory *adjective* compulsory

mandir *noun* Hindu temple

mandolin *noun* musical instrument with four pairs of strings

mane *noun* long hair on the neck of a horse, lion, etc

manger *noun* eating trough in a stable or barn

mangle mangles mangling mangled *verb* to destroy (something) by crushing and twisting

mango mangoes or **mangos** *noun* tropical fruit with sweet juicy yellow flesh

manhole *noun* hole with a cover, through which a person can enter a drain or sewer

manhood *noun* state of being a man rather than a boy

mania *noun* **1** extreme enthusiasm:

my wife's mania for plant collecting **2** mental illness

maniac *noun* mad person who is violent and dangerous

manic *adjective* **1** energetic and excited **2** affected by mania

manicure *noun* cosmetic care of the fingernails and hands > **manicurist** *noun* person whose job is the cosmetic care of fingernails and hands

manifest *adjective* **1** easily noticed, obvious ▷ *verb* **2** to show or reveal (something): *Fear can manifest itself in many ways*

manifestation *noun* sign that something is happening or exists: *a manifestation of stress*

manifesto manifestoes or **manifestos** *noun* declaration of policy as issued by a political party

manipulate manipulates manipulating manipulated *verb* **1** to control or influence (people or events) to produce a particular result **2** to control (a piece of equipment) in a skilful way > **manipulation** *noun*: *political manipulation* > **manipulative** *adjective* influencing people to produce a desired result > **manipulator** *noun*

mankind *noun* human beings collectively

manly manlier manliest *adjective* possessing qualities that are typically masculine

manna *noun* **appear like manna from heaven** to appear suddenly as if by a miracle to help someone in a difficult situation

manner *noun* **1** way a thing happens or is done **2** person's bearing or behaviour **3** **manners** (polite) social behaviour

mannerism *noun* person's

distinctive habit or trait

manoeuvre manoeuvres manoeuvring manoeuvred *noun* **1** skilful movement **2** contrived, complicated and possibly deceptive plan or action ▷ *verb* **3** to skilfully move (something) into a place

manor *noun Brit* large country house and its lands

manpower *noun* available number of workers

mansion *noun* large house

manslaughter *noun Law* unlawful but unintentional killing of a person

mantelpiece *noun* shelf above a fireplace

mantle *noun literary* responsibilities and duties which go with a particular job or position

mantra *noun* word or short piece of sacred text or prayer continually repeated to help concentration

manual *adjective* **1** of or done with the hands **2** by human labour rather than automatic means ▷ *noun* **3** instruction book explaining how to use a machine > **manually** *adverb*

manufacture manufactures manufacturing manufactured *verb* **1** to process or make (goods) on a large scale using machinery **2** to invent or concoct (an excuse etc)

manufacturer *noun* company that manufactures goods

manure *noun* animal excrement used as a fertilizer

manuscript *noun* handwritten or typed document, especially a version of a book before it is printed

Manx *adjective* of the Isle of Man

many *adjective* **1** numerous ▷ *pronoun* **2** large number

Maori Maoris *noun* **1** person descended from the people who lived in New Zealand before Europeans arrived **2** language of the Maoris

map maps mapping mapped *noun* representation of the earth's surface or some part of it, showing geographical features > **map out** *verb* to work out (a plan)

maple *noun* tree with broad leaves, a variety of which (**sugar maple**) yields sugar

mar mars marring marred *verb* to spoil (something)

marae *noun* **1** enclosed space in front of a Maori meeting house **2** Maori meeting house and its buildings

marathon *noun* **1** long-distance race of 26 miles 385 yards (42.195 kilometres) ▷ *adjective* **2** (of a task) large and taking a long time

marble *noun* **1** kind of limestone with a mottled appearance, which can be highly polished **2** small glass ball used in a children's game **3 marbles** game of rolling these at one another

march marches marching marched *verb* **1** to walk with a military step **2** to walk quickly in a determined way ▷ *noun* **3** organized protest in which a large group of people walk somewhere together

March *noun* third month of the year

mare *noun* female horse

margarine *noun* butter substitute made from animal or vegetable fats

margin *noun* **1** blank space at each side of a printed or written page **2** additional amount or one greater than necessary **3 win by a large/ small margin** to win (a contest) by a large or small amount

marginal *adjective* **1** insignificant or unimportant **2** *Politics* (of a constituency) won by only a small margin > **marginally** *adverb* to only a small extent

marigold *noun* plant with yellow or orange flowers

marijuana *noun* dried flowers and leaves of the cannabis plant, used as a drug, especially in cigarettes

marina *noun* harbour for yachts and other pleasure boats

marinate marinates marinating marinated; also **marinade** *verb* to soak (fish or meat) in a seasoned liquid before cooking

marine *adjective* 1 of the sea or shipping ▷ *noun* 2 (especially in Britain and the US) soldier trained for land and sea combat

marital *adjective* relating to marriage

maritime *adjective* relating to shipping

marjoram *noun* herb used for seasoning food and in salads

mark *noun* 1 line, dot, scar, etc visible on a surface 2 written or printed symbol 3 letter or number used to grade academic work 4 unit of currency formerly used in Germany ▷ *verb* 5 to make a mark on (a surface) 6 to be a sign of (something) 7 to grade (academic work) 8 to stay close to (a sporting opponent) to hamper his or her play

marked *adjective* noticeable > **markedly** *adverb*

market *noun* 1 place where goods or animals are bought and sold 2 place with many small stalls selling different goods 3 demand for goods ▷ *verb* 4 to sell (a product) in an organized way

marketing *noun* part of a business that controls the way that goods or services are sold

market research *noun* research into consumers' needs and purchases

marksman marksmen *noun* person skilled at shooting

marlin *noun Aust* large fish found in tropical seas that has a very long upper jaw

marmalade *noun* jam made from citrus fruits

maroon *adjective* reddish-purple

marooned *adjective* 1 abandoned ashore, especially on an island 2 isolated without resources

marquee *noun* large tent used for a party or exhibition

marquis marquises; also spelt **marquess** *noun Brit* nobleman of the rank below a duke

marriage *noun* 1 state of being married; matrimony 2 wedding

marrow *noun* long thick striped green vegetable with whitish flesh

marry marries marrying married *verb* 1 to take (someone) as a husband or wife 2 to join (a couple) in marriage > **married** *adjective*: *a married man*

Mars *noun* fourth planet from the sun in the solar system

marsh marshes *noun* low-lying wet land

marshal marshals marshalling marshalled *noun* 1 official who organizes ceremonies or events ▷ *verb* 2 to gather (things or people) together and organize them

marshmallow *noun* spongy pink or white sweet

marsupial *noun* animal that carries its young in a pouch, such as a kangaroo

martial *adjective* of or relating to war

martial art *noun* any of various philosophies and techniques of self-defence, originating in the Far East, such as karate

Martian *noun* supposed inhabitant of Mars

martyr *noun* **1** person who dies or suffers for his or her beliefs ▷ *verb* **2** to make a martyr of (someone) > **martyrdom** *noun*: *They see martyrdom as the ultimate glory*

marvel marvels marvelling marvelled *verb* **1** to be filled with wonder ▷ *noun* **2** wonderful thing

marvellous *adjective* wonderful or excellent > **marvellously** *adverb*

Marxism *noun* political philosophy of Karl Marx, which states that society will develop towards communism through the struggle between different social classes > **Marxist** *noun* **1** person who believes in Marxism ▷ *adjective* **2** believing in Marxism

marzipan *noun* paste of ground almonds, sugar and egg whites, put on top of cakes or used to make small sweets

mascara *noun* cosmetic for darkening and lengthening the eyelashes

mascot *noun* person, animal or thing supposed to bring good luck

masculine *adjective* **1** typical of men rather than women **2** *Grammar* of the gender of nouns that includes some male animate things > **masculinity** *noun*

mash mashes mashing mashed *verb* to crush (cooked vegetables) into a soft mass

mask *noun* **1** covering for the face, as a disguise or protection ▷ *verb* **2** to hide or disguise (something)

masochism *noun* condition in which pleasure is obtained from feeling pain or from being humiliated > **masochist** *noun* someone who gets pleasure from his or her own suffering

mason *noun* person who works with stone

masonry *noun* pieces of stone forming part of a wall or building

masquerade masquerades masquerading masqueraded *verb* (followed by *as*) to pretend to be (someone or something else)

mass masses massing massed *noun* **1** large quantity **2** *Physics* amount of matter in an object **3 the masses** ordinary people ▷ *adjective* **4** involving many people ▷ *verb* **5** to gather together in a large group

Mass *noun* service of the Eucharist, especially in the Roman Catholic Church

massacre massacres massacring massacred *noun* **1** indiscriminate killing of large numbers of people ▷ *verb* **2** to kill (people) in large numbers

massage massages massaging massaged *noun* **1** rubbing and kneading of parts of the body to reduce pain or stiffness ▷ *verb* **2** to give a massage to (someone)

massive *adjective* large and heavy > **massively** *adverb* extremely

mass-produce mass-produces mass-producing mass-produced *verb* to manufacture (standardized goods) in large quantities

mast *noun* tall pole for supporting something, especially a ship's sails

master *noun* **1** person in control, such as an employer or an owner of slaves or animals **2** male teacher ▷ *adjective* **3** overall or controlling **4** main or principal ▷ *verb* **5** to acquire knowledge of or skill in (something) **6** to succeed in controlling (a difficult situation)

masterful *adjective* showing control and authority

masterly *adjective* showing great skill

mastermind *verb* 1 to plan and direct (a complex task) ▷ *noun* 2 person who plans and directs a complex task

masterpiece *noun* outstanding work of art

masturbate masturbates masturbating masturbated *verb* to stroke or rub one's genitals for sexual pleasure > **masturbation** *noun* masturbating

mat *noun* piece of fabric used as a floor covering or to protect a surface

matador *noun* man who kills the bull in bullfights

match matches matching matched *noun* 1 contest in a game or sport 2 small stick with a tip that produces a flame when scraped on a rough surface ▷ *verb* 3 to be exactly like, equal to or in harmony with (something)

matchbox matchboxes *noun* small box that contains or once contained matches

mate mates mating mated *noun* 1 *informal* friend 2 sexual partner of an animal 3 officer in a merchant ship ▷ *verb* 4 (of animals) to be paired for reproduction

material *noun* 1 substance of which a thing is made 2 cloth 3 information on which a piece of work may be based 4 **materials** equipment needed for an activity ▷ *adjective* 5 involving possessions or money > **materially** *adverb* considerably

materialism *noun* excessive interest in or desire for money and possessions > **materialistic** *adjective*: *a materialistic society*

materialize materializes

materializing materialized; also spelt **materialise** *verb* to happen in fact or appear

maternal *adjective* 1 of a mother 2 related through one's mother

maternity *adjective* of or for pregnant women

mathematics *noun* study of numbers, quantities and shapes > **mathematical** *adjective* > **mathematically** *adverb* > **mathematician** *noun* person trained in the study of numbers, quantities and shapes

maths *noun informal* mathematics

Matilda *Aust noun* 1 *old-fashioned* swagman's bundle of belongings 2 **waltz Matilda** to travel about carrying your bundle of belongings

matinée *noun* afternoon performance in a theatre or cinema

matrimony *noun formal* marriage > **matrimonial** *adjective*: *the matrimonial home*

matrix matrices *noun* 1 substance or situation in which something originates, takes form or is enclosed 2 *Maths* rectangular array of numbers or elements

matron *noun* 1 *Brit* **a** (in a nursing home or, formerly, in a hospital) senior nurse in charge of the nursing staff **b** (in a boarding school) woman responsible for looking after the health of the children 2 staid or dignified married woman

matt *adjective* dull, not shiny

matted *adjective* (of hair) tangled, with strands sticking together

matter *noun* 1 substance of which something is made 2 physical substance 3 event, situation or subject 4 written material in general 5 **what's the matter?** what is wrong? ▷ *verb* 6 to be of importance

matter-of-fact *adjective* showing no emotion

matting *noun* thick woven material such as rope or straw, used as a floor covering

mattress mattresses *noun* large stuffed flat case, often with springs, used on or as a bed

mature matures maturing matured *adjective* **1** fully developed or grown-up ▷ *verb* **2** to become mature **3** (of a bill or bond) to become due for payment > **maturely** *adverb* > **maturity** *noun* state of being mature

maudlin *adjective* foolishly or tearfully sentimental

maul *verb* (of an animal) to attack (someone) savagely

mausoleum *noun* stately tomb

mauve *adjective* pale purple

maxim *noun* general truth or principle

maximize maximizes maximizing maximized; also spelt **maximise** *verb* to increase (something) to a maximum

maximum *adjective, noun* greatest possible (amount or number)

may *verb* used as an auxiliary to express possibility, permission, opportunity, etc

May *noun* fifth month of the year

maybe *adverb* perhaps or possibly

mayhem *noun* violent destruction or confusion

mayonnaise *noun* thick salad dressing made with egg yolks, oil and vinegar

mayor *noun* person elected to lead and represent the people of a town

maze *noun* complex network of paths or lines designed to puzzle

MBE MBEs *abbreviation* (in Britain) Member of the Order of the British Empire

MD MDs *abbreviation* **1** Doctor of Medicine **2** managing director

me *pronoun* object form of **I**

meadow *noun* piece of grassland

meagre *adjective* scanty or insufficient

meal *noun* **1** occasion when food is served and eaten **2** the food itself

mealie *noun* S Afr maize

mean means meaning meant *verb* **1** to intend to convey or express **2** to signify or denote **3** to intend (to do something) **4** to have importance as specified: *It would mean a lot to them to win* ▷ *adjective* **5** miserly, ungenerous or petty **6** unkind or cruel ▷ *noun* **7** *Maths* average of a set of numbers > **meanly** *adverb* > **meanness** *noun: his meanness over money*

meander *verb* to follow a winding course

meaning *noun* **1** sense or significance **2** worth or purpose: *a challenge that gives meaning to life* > **meaningful** *adjective: a meaningful event* > **meaningfully** *adverb* > **meaningless** *adjective: a meaningless existence*

means *noun* **1** method by which something is done ▷ *plural* **2** money or income

means test *noun* inquiry into a person's finances to decide on their eligibility for financial aid

meantime *noun* intervening period

meanwhile *adverb* **1** during the intervening period ▷ *noun* **2** intervening period

measles *noun* infectious disease producing red spots

measly *adjective informal* meagre

measure measures measuring measured *noun* **1** unit of size or quantity **2** certain amount (of

something): *a measure of agreement*
3 measures actions taken ▷ *verb*
4 to determine the size or quantity
of (something) **5** to be (a specified
amount) in size or quantity

measured *adjective* **1** slow and
steady **2** carefully considered

measurement *noun* **1** measuring
2 size

meat *noun* animal flesh as food
> meaty *adjective* (tasting) of or
like meat

Mecca *noun* **1** holy city of Islam
2 place that attracts visitors
> Most Muslims dislike this form
and use the Arabic *Makkah*

mechanic *noun* person skilled in
repairing or operating machinery

mechanical *adjective* **1** of or done by
machines **2** (of an action) without
thought or feeling **> mechanically**
adverb

mechanics *noun* **1** scientific study
of motion and force ▷ *plural* **2** way
in which something works or is
done: *the mechanics of accounting*

mechanism *noun* **1** piece of
machinery **2** process or technique

medal *noun* piece of metal with an
inscription etc, given as a reward
or memento

medallion *noun* disc-shaped
ornament worn on a chain round
the neck

medallist *noun* winner of a medal

meddle meddles meddling
meddled *verb* to interfere
annoyingly

media *plural noun* television, radio
and newspapers collectively
> Although *media* is a plural noun,
it is becoming more common
for it to be used as a singular: *The
media is obsessed with violence*

mediaeval *adjective* same as
medieval

median *adjective, noun* Geometry
middle (point or line)

mediate mediates mediating
mediated *verb* to intervene in a
dispute to bring about agreement
> mediation *noun*: *United Nations
mediation between the two sides*
> mediator *noun*

medical *adjective* **1** of or relating
to the science of medicine ▷ *noun*
2 *informal* medical examination
> medically *adverb*

medication *noun* medicinal
substance

medicinal *adjective* relating to the
treatment of illness

medicine *noun* **1** substance used
to treat disease **2** science of
preventing, diagnosing or curing
disease

medieval *adjective* of the Middle
Ages

mediocre *adjective* of rather poor
quality **> mediocrity** *noun*: *the
mediocrity of television*

meditate meditates meditating
meditated *verb* **1** to reflect deeply,
especially on spiritual matters
2 (followed by *on*) to think about or
plan (something) **> meditation**
noun act of meditating

Mediterranean *noun* **1** large sea
between southern Europe and
northern Africa ▷ *adjective* **2** of the
Mediterranean or the European
countries adjoining it

medium mediums or **media**
adjective **1** midway between
extremes, average ▷ *noun* **2** means
of communicating news or
information to the public, such as
radio or newspapers **3** person who
can supposedly communicate with
the dead

medley medleys *noun*
1 miscellaneous mixture **2** musical

sequence of different tunes

meek *adjective* submissive or humble > **meekly** *adverb* > **meekness** *noun* submissiveness or humility

meet meets meeting met *verb* **1** to come together with (someone) **2** to come into contact with (someone) **3** to go to the place of arrival of (someone) **4** to satisfy (a need etc) **5** to experience (a situation, attitude or problem) **6 meet with** or **be met with** to get (a particular reaction): *I was met with silence*

meeting *noun* **1** event in which people discuss proposals and make decisions together **2** act of meeting someone

megabyte *noun Computers* 2²⁰ or 1 048 576 bytes

megahertz *noun* one million hertz ▪ The plural of *megahertz* is *megahertz*

melaleuca *noun* Australian shrub or tree with a white trunk and black branches

melancholy *noun* **1** sadness or gloom ▷ *adjective* **2** sad or gloomy

mêlée *noun* noisy confused fight or crowd

mellow *adjective* **1** (of light) soft, not harsh **2** (of a sound) smooth and pleasant to listen to ▷ *verb* **3** to become more pleasant or relaxed

melodic *adjective* relating to melody

melodious *adjective* pleasing to the ear

melodrama *noun* play full of extravagant action and emotion

melodramatic *adjective* behaving in an exaggerated emotional way; theatrical

melody melodies *noun* series of musical notes which make a tune

melon *noun* large round juicy fruit with a hard rind

melt *verb* to become liquid or cause

(a solid) to become liquid by heat

member *noun* **1** one of the people or things belonging to a group **2** individual making up a body or society ▷ *adjective* **3** (of a country or state) belonging to an international organization

Member of Parliament Members of Parliament *noun* person elected to parliament

membership *noun* **1** state of being a member of an organization **2** people belonging to an organization

membrane *noun* thin flexible tissue in a plant or animal body

memento mementos *noun* thing serving to remind; souvenir

memo memos *noun* short for **memorandum**

memoirs *plural noun* biography or historical account based on personal knowledge

memorable *adjective* worth remembering, noteworthy > **memorably** *adverb*

memorandum memorandums or **memoranda** *noun* **1** written record or communication within a business **2** note of things to be remembered

memorial *noun* **1** something serving to commemorate a person or thing ▷ *adjective* **2** serving as a memorial

memory memories *noun* **1** ability to remember **2** particular recollection **3** part of a computer that stores information

men *noun* plural of **man**

menace menaces menacing menaced *noun* **1** someone or something likely to cause serious harm **2** quality of being threatening ▷ *verb* **3** to threaten or endanger (someone) > **menacingly** *adverb*

menagerie *noun* collection of wild animals for exhibition

mend *verb* to repair or patch

menial *adjective* involving boring work of low status

meningitis *noun* inflammation of the membranes of the brain

menopause *noun* time when a woman's menstrual cycle ceases

menorah menorahs *noun* candelabra that usually has seven parts and is used in Jewish temples

menstruate menstruates menstruating menstruated *verb* (of a woman) to have an approximately monthly discharge of blood from the womb > **menstrual** *adjective: the menstrual cycle* > **menstruation** *noun* approximately monthly discharge of blood from the womb of a woman who is not pregnant

-ment *suffix indicating* state or feeling: *contentment; resentment*

mental *adjective* **1** of, in or done by the mind **2** of or for mental illness > **mentally** *adverb*

mentality mentalities *noun* way of thinking

mention *verb* **1** to refer to (something) briefly ▷ *noun* **2** brief reference to a person or thing

mentor *noun* adviser or guide

menu *noun* **1** list of dishes to be served, or from which to order **2** *Computers* list of options displayed on a screen

mercenary mercenaries *adjective* **1** mainly interested in getting money ▷ *noun* **2** soldier paid to fight for a foreign country

merchandise *noun* goods that are sold

merchant *noun* person engaged in trade; wholesale trader

merchant navy *noun* ships or crew engaged in a nation's commercial shipping

merciful *adjective* **1** compassionate and kind **2** considered to be fortunate as a relief from suffering: *Death came as a merciful release* > **mercifully** *adverb*

merciless *adjective* showing no kindness or forgiveness; heartless > **mercilessly** *adverb*

mercury *noun* silvery liquid metal

Mercury *noun* planet nearest the sun in the solar system

mercy mercies *noun* compassionate treatment of an offender or enemy who is in one's power

mere merest *adjective* nothing more than: *mere chance* > **merely** *adverb*

merge merges merging merged *verb* to combine or blend

merger *noun* combination of business firms into one

meringue *noun* baked mixture of egg whites and sugar

merino merinos *noun* breed of sheep, common in Australia and New Zealand, with fine soft wool

merit *noun* **1** excellence or worth **2 merits** admirable qualities ▷ *verb* **3** to deserve (something)

meritocracy meritocracies *noun* rule by people of superior talent or intellect

mermaid *noun* imaginary sea creature with the upper part of a woman and the lower part of a fish

merry merrier merriest *adjective* **1** cheerful or jolly **2** *informal* slightly drunk > **merrily** *adverb*

merry-go-round *noun* roundabout

mesh meshes *noun* network or net

mess messes messing messed *noun* **1** untidy or dirty confusion

2 trouble or difficulty **3** place where members of the armed forces eat ▷ *verb* **4** (followed by *about*) to potter about **> mess up** *verb* to spoil (something) or do (something) wrong

message *noun* **1** communication sent **2** meaning or moral

messaging *noun* sending messages between mobile phones, using letters and numbers to produce shortened forms of words

messenger *noun* someone who takes a message to someone for someone else

Messiah *noun* **1** Jews' promised deliverer **2** Christ

Messrs *noun* plural of **Mr**

messy messier messiest *adjective* dirty, confused or untidy

met *verb* past of **meet**

metabolism *noun* chemical processes of a living body
> metabolic *adjective*: *people with a low metabolic rate*

metal *noun* chemical element, such as iron or copper, that is malleable and capable of conducting heat and electricity **> metallic** *adjective* made of or resembling metal

metamorphic *adjective* (of rocks) changed in texture or structure by heat and pressure

metamorphosis
metamorphoses *noun* change of form or character

metaphor *noun* figure of speech in which a word is used to refer to something it does not mean literally in order to suggest a resemblance: *He is a lion in battle* **> metaphorical** *adjective*: *talking in metaphorical terms* **> metaphorically** *adverb*

meteor *noun* piece of rock or metal that burns very brightly when it enters the earth's atmosphere from space

meteoric *adjective* (of someone's rise to power or success) happening very quickly

meteorite *noun* meteor that has fallen to earth

meteorology *noun* study of the earth's atmosphere, especially for weather forecasting **> meteorological** *adjective* relating to the weather or weather forecasting

meter *noun* instrument for measuring and recording something, such as the consumption of gas or electricity

methane *noun* colourless inflammable gas

method *noun* **1** way or manner **2** technique

methodical *adjective* orderly **> methodically** *adverb*

Methodist *noun* **1** member of any of the Protestant churches originated by John Wesley and his followers ▷ *adjective* **2** of Methodists or their Church

methylated spirits *noun* alcohol with methanol added, used as a solvent and for heating

meticulous *adjective* very careful about details **> meticulously** *adverb*

metre *noun* **1** basic unit of length equal to about 1.094 yards (100 centimetres) **2** rhythm of poetry

metric *adjective* relating to the decimal system of weights and measures based on the metre

metropolis metropolises *noun* chief city of a country or region

metropolitan *adjective* of a metropolis

mettle *noun* **on your mettle** ready to do something as well as you can in a test or challenge

mew *noun* **1** cry of a cat ▷ *verb* **2** to utter this cry

mews *noun* yard or street orig. of stables, now often converted into houses

Mexican *adjective* **1** of Mexico ▷ *noun* **2** person from Mexico

mg *symbol* milligram(s)

miasma miasmas or **miasmata** *noun* unwholesome or foreboding atmosphere

mica *noun* glasslike mineral used as an electrical insulator

mice *noun* plural of **mouse**

micro- *prefix meaning* very small

microchip *noun* small wafer of silicon containing electronic circuits

microphone *noun* instrument for amplifying or transmitting sounds

microprocessor *noun* integrated circuit acting as the central processing unit in a small computer

microscope *noun* instrument with lens(es) that produces a magnified image of a very small object

microscopic *adjective* very small

microwave microwaves microwaving microwaved *noun* **1** electromagnetic wave with a wavelength of a few centimetres, used in radar and cooking **2** microwave oven ▷ *verb* **3** to cook (food) in a microwave oven

microwave oven *noun* oven using microwaves to cook food quickly

mid- *prefix indicating* middle: *mid-Atlantic; the mid-70s*

midday *noun* noon

middle *adjective* **1** equally distant from two extremes **2** medium, intermediate ▷ *noun* **3** middle point or part

middle age *noun* period of life between about 40 and 60 years

old > **middle-aged** *adjective* aged between about 40 and 60 years old

Middle Ages *plural noun* period from about 1000 AD to the 15th century

middle class middle classes *noun* social class of business and professional people > **middle-class** *adjective* belonging to the middle class

Middle East *noun* area around the eastern Mediterranean up to and including Iran

Middle English *noun* the form of the English language that existed from about 1100 AD until about 1450 AD

middle-of-the-road *adjective* (of opinions) moderate

middle school *noun* in England and Wales, a school for children aged between about 8 and 12

middling *adjective* of average quality or ability

midge *noun* small mosquito-like insect

midget *noun* very small person or thing

midnight *noun* twelve o'clock at night

midriff *noun* middle part of the body

midst *noun* **in the midst of** in the middle of

midsummer *adjective* of or relating to the period in the middle of summer

midway *adverb* halfway

midwife midwives *noun* trained nurse who assists at childbirth > **midwifery** *noun* work of a midwife

might *verb* **1** past tense or subjunctive mood of **may**: *I might stay a while; You might like to go and see it* ▷ *noun* **2** *literary* power or strength

mightily *adverb old-fashioned* to a great degree or extent

mighty mightier mightiest *adjective literary* powerful or strong

migraine *noun* severe headache, often with nausea and visual disturbances

migrant *noun* **1** person or animal that moves from one place to another ▷ *adjective* **2** moving from one place to another

migrate migrates migrating migrated *verb* **1** to move from one place to settle in another **2** (of animals) to move at a particular season to a different place > **migration** *noun* > **migratory** *adjective* (of an animal) migrating every year

mike *noun informal* microphone

mild *adjective* **1** not strongly flavoured **2** gentle **3** calm or temperate > **mildly** *adverb*

mildew *noun* destructive fungus on plants or things exposed to damp

mile *noun* unit of length equal to 1760 yards or 1.609 kilometres

mileage *noun* **1** distance travelled in miles **2** miles travelled by a motor vehicle per gallon of petrol **3** *informal* usefulness of something

militant *adjective* **1** aggressive or vigorous in support of a cause ▷ *noun* **2** person who tries to bring about extreme political or social change > **militancy** *noun*

military *adjective* **1** of or for soldiers, armies or war ▷ *noun* **2** armed services > **militarily** *adverb*

militia *noun* military force of trained citizens for use in emergency only

milk *noun* **1** white fluid produced by female mammals to feed their young **2** milk of cows, goats, etc, used by humans as food ▷ *verb* **3** to draw milk from the udders of (a cow or goat) **4** to exploit

milk teeth *noun* first set of teeth in young children

milky milkier milkiest *adjective* **1** pale creamy white **2** containing a lot of milk

Milky Way *noun* luminous band of stars stretching across the night sky

mill *noun* **1** building where grain is crushed to make flour **2** factory for making materials such as steel, wool or cotton **3** small device for grinding coffee or spices into powder

millennium millennia or **millenniums** *noun* period of a thousand years

miller *noun* person who works in a mill

milli- *prefix indicating* a thousandth part: *millisecond*

milligram *noun* thousandth of a gram

millilitre *noun* thousandth of a litre

millimetre *noun* thousandth of a metre

million *adjective, noun* **1** one thousand thousands; 1,000,000 **2** **millions** large but unspecified number; lots > **millionth** *adjective, noun: the millionth truck; a millionth of a second*

millionaire *noun* person who owns at least a million pounds, dollars, etc

millstone *noun* **millstone round your neck** unpleasant problem or responsibility that you cannot escape from

mime mimes miming mimed *noun* **1** acting without the use of words ▷ *verb* **2** to describe or express (something) in mime

mimic mimics mimicking mimicked *verb* **1** to imitate (a person or manner), especially in an amusing way ▷ *noun* **2** person who is good at mimicking > **mimicry** *noun* action of mimicking someone

minaret *noun* tall slender tower of a mosque

mince minces mincing minced *verb* **1** to cut or grind (meat) into very small pieces **2** to walk in an affected manner ▷ *noun* **3** minced meat

mind *noun* **1** ability to think **2** memory or attention **3 change your mind** to change a decision that you have made ▷ *verb* **4** to take offence at (something) **5** to take care of

mindful *adjective* (followed by *of*) heedful of (something)

mindless *adjective* stupid and destructive

mine mines mining mined *pronoun* **1** belonging to me ▷ *noun* **2** deep hole for digging out coal, ores, etc **3** bomb placed under the ground or in water ▷ *verb* **4** to dig (minerals) from a mine > **miner** *noun* person who works in a mine > **mining** *noun*

minefield *noun* area of land or water containing mines

mineral *noun* naturally occurring inorganic substance, such as metal

mineral water *noun* water that comes from a natural spring

minestrone *noun* soup containing vegetables and pasta

minesweeper *noun* ship for clearing away mines

mingle mingles mingling mingled *verb* to mix or blend

mini- *prefix indicating* smaller or less important: *a TV mini-series*

miniature *noun* **1** small portrait, model or copy ▷ *adjective* **2** small-scale

minibus minibuses *noun* small bus

minim *noun Music* note half the length of a semibreve

minimal *adjective* minimum > **minimally** *adverb* to the minimum degree

minimize minimizes minimizing minimized; also spelt **minimise** *verb* to reduce to a minimum

minimum *adjective, noun* least possible (amount or number)

minister *noun* **1** head of a government department **2** (in a Protestant church) member of the clergy

ministerial *adjective* of government a minister

ministry ministries *noun* **1** ministers collectively **2** government department

mink *noun* **1** stoatlike animal **2** its highly valued fur

minnow *noun* very small freshwater fish

minor *adjective* **1** lesser **2** *Music* (of a scale) having a semitone between the second and third notes ▷ *noun* **3** person regarded legally as a child

minority minorities *noun* **1** lesser number **2** group in a minority in any state

minstrel *noun* medieval singer or musician

mint *noun* **1** herb used for flavouring in cooking **2** peppermint-flavoured sweet **3** place where money is coined ▷ *verb* **4** to make (coins) ▷ *adjective* **5 in mint condition** in perfect condition; like new

minus minuses *preposition* **1** indicating subtraction ▷ *adjective* **2** less than zero ▷ *noun* **3** sign (-) denoting subtraction or a number less than zero **4** disadvantage

minuscule *adjective* very small indeed

minute¹ minutes minuting minuted *noun* **1** 60th part of an hour or degree **2** moment **3 minutes** record of the proceedings of a meeting ▷ *verb* **4** to write the official notes of (a meeting)

minute² *adjective* extremely small > **minutely** *adverb* in great detail

minutiae *plural noun* trifling or precise details

miracle *noun* **1** wonderful and surprising event, believed to have been caused by God **2** any very surprising and fortunate event > **miraculous** *adjective*: *He made a miraculous recovery* > **miraculously** *adverb*

mirage *noun* optical illusion, especially one caused by hot air

mire *noun literary* swampy ground or mud

mirror *noun* **1** coated glass surface for reflecting images ▷ *verb* **2** to reflect (something) in or as if in a mirror

mirth *noun literary* laughter, merriment or gaiety

mis- *prefix indicating* wrong(ly), bad(ly)

misbehave misbehaves misbehaving misbehaved *verb* to be naughty or behave badly > **misbehaviour** *noun* naughty or bad behaviour

miscarriage *noun* **1** spontaneous premature expulsion of a foetus from the womb **2** failure: *a miscarriage of justice*

miscellaneous *adjective* mixed or assorted

mischance *noun* unlucky event

mischief *noun* eagerness to have fun by teasing people or playing tricks > **mischievous** *adjective* full of mischief

misconception *noun* wrong idea or belief

misconduct *noun* bad or unacceptable behaviour by a professional person

misdemeanour *noun* minor wrongdoing

miser *noun* person who hoards money and hates spending it > **miserly** *adjective* reluctant to spend money; mean

miserable *adjective* **1** very unhappy and sad; dejected **2** causing misery > **miserably** *adverb*

misery miseries *noun* great unhappiness

misfire misfires misfiring misfired *verb* (of a plan) to fail to turn out as intended

misfit *noun* person not suited to his or her social environment

misfortune *noun* piece of bad luck

misgiving *noun* feeling of fear or doubt

misguided *adjective* mistaken or unwise

misinform *verb* to give incorrect information to > **misinformation** *noun* incorrect information

misinterpret *verb* to make an incorrect interpretation of

misjudge misjudges misjudging misjudged *verb* to judge (someone or something) wrongly or unfairly

mislay mislays mislaying mislaid *verb* to lose (something) temporarily

mislead misleads misleading misled *verb* to give false or confusing information to

misplaced *adjective* (of a feeling) inappropriate or directed at the wrong thing or person

misprint *noun* printing error

misrepresent *verb* to represent (someone) wrongly or inaccurately

> **misrepresentation** *noun*

miss misses missing missed *verb*
1 to fail to notice, hear, hit, reach, find or catch (something) **2** not to be in time for (a bus, train or plane) **3** to notice or regret the absence of **4** to fail to take advantage of (a chance or opportunity) ▷ *noun* **5** fact or instance of missing

Miss Misses *noun* title used before the name of a girl or unmarried woman

missile *noun* object or weapon thrown, shot or launched at a target

mission *noun* **1** specific task or duty **2** group of people sent on a mission **3** journey made by a military aeroplane or space rocket to carry out a task **4** building in which missionaries work

missionary missionaries *noun* person sent abroad to do religious and social work

missive *noun* old-fashioned letter

mist mists misting misted *noun* **1** thin fog ▷ *verb* **2** (of eyes) to become blurred with tears **3** (followed by *up*, *over*) (of a glass) to become opaque because covered with condensation

mistake mistakes mistaking mistook mistaken *noun* **1** error or blunder ▷ *verb* **2** to confuse (a person or thing) with another

mistaken *adjective* **1** (of a person) wrong: *I was mistaken about you* **2** (of a belief or opinion) incorrect
> **mistakenly** *adverb* incorrectly

Mister *noun* polite form of address to a man

mistletoe *noun* evergreen plant with white berries growing as a parasite on trees, used as a Christmas decoration

mistook *verb* past of **mistake**

mistreat *verb* to treat (a person or animal) badly

mistress mistresses *noun* **1** woman who has a continuing sexual relationship with a married man **2** female employer of a servant **3** female teacher

mistrust *verb* **1** to have doubts or suspicions about (someone) ▷ *noun* **2** lack of trust

misty mistier mistiest *adjective* full of or covered with mist

misunderstand misunderstands misunderstanding misunderstood *verb* to fail to understand (someone) properly
> **misunderstanding** *noun* slight quarrel or disagreement

misuse misuses misusing misused *noun* **1** incorrect, improper or careless use ▷ *verb* **2** to use (something) wrongly

mite *noun* very tiny creature that lives in the fur of animals

mitigating *adjective* formal (of circumstances) making a crime easier to understand or justify

mitten *noun* glove with one section for the thumb and one for the four fingers together

mix mixes mixing mixed *verb* to combine or blend (things) into one mass > **mix up** *verb* to confuse (two things or people)

mixed *adjective* **1** consisting of several things of the same general kind **2** involving people from two or more different races: *mixed marriages* **3** (of education or accommodation) for both males and females

mixed up *adjective* **1** confused **2** (followed by *in*) involved in (a crime or a scandal)

mixer *noun* machine used for

mixing things together

mixture *noun* **1** several different things mixed together **2** substance consisting of other substances that have been stirred or shaken together

mix-up *noun* mistake in something that was planned

ml *symbol* millilitres(s)

mm *symbol* millimetre(s)

moa *noun* large extinct flightless New Zealand bird

moan *noun* **1** low cry of pain **2** *informal* grumble ▷ *verb* **3** to make a low cry of pain **4** *informal* to grumble

moat *noun* deep wide ditch, especially round a castle

mob mobs mobbing mobbed *noun* **1** disorderly crowd ▷ *verb* **2** to surround (someone) in a disorderly crowd

mobile *adjective* **1** able to move or be moved freely and easily: *a mobile library* **2** able to travel or move about from one place to another ▷ *noun* **3** same as **mobile phone** **4** hanging structure designed to move in air currents > **mobility** *noun* condition of being mobile

mobile phone *noun* cordless phone powered by batteries

moccasin *noun* soft leather shoe

mock *verb* **1** to make fun of, mimic or ridicule (someone) ▷ *adjective* **2** sham or imitation **3** (of an examination) done as a practice before the real examination

mockery *noun* expression of scorn or ridicule

mode *noun* **1** method or manner **2** *Maths* biggest in a set of groups

model models modelling modelled *noun* **1** (miniature) representation **2** pattern **3** person or thing worthy of imitation

4 person who poses for an artist or photographer **5** person who wears clothes to display them to prospective buyers ▷ *adjective* **6** denoting a (miniature) representation of something **7** excellent: *a model pupil* ▷ *verb* **8** to display (clothes) by wearing them **9** to make (shapes or figures) out of clay or wood **10** **model yourself on** to copy the behaviour of (someone that you admire)

modem *noun* device for connecting two computers by a telephone line

moderate moderates moderating moderated *adjective* **1** not extreme **2** average ▷ *noun* **3** person of moderate views ▷ *verb* **4** to become less violent or extreme or make (something) less violent or extreme > **moderately** *adverb* > **moderation** *noun*: *a man of fairness and moderation*

modern *adjective* **1** of present or recent times **2** up-to-date > **modernity** *noun*: *the clash between tradition and modernity*

modernize modernizes modernizing modernized; also spelt **modernise** *verb* to bring (something) up to date

modest *adjective* **1** not vain or boastful **2** quite small in size or amount **3** shy and easily embarrassed > **modestly** *adverb* in a modest manner > **modesty** *noun* quality of being modest

modify modifies modifying modified *verb* to change (something) slightly in order to improve it > **modification** *noun* small change made to improve something

module *noun* **1** one of the parts that when put together form a whole unit or object **2** part of a machine or system that does a particular task **3** part of a spacecraft that can do certain things away from the main body ▷ **modular** adjective

mohair noun very soft fluffy wool obtained from angora goats

moist adjective slightly wet

moisten verb to make (something) moist

moisture noun tiny drops of water in the air or on the ground

molar noun large back tooth used for grinding

mole noun **1** small dark raised spot on the skin **2** small burrowing animal with black fur **3** informal member of an organization who is working as a spy for a rival organization

molecule noun the smallest amount of a substance that can exist ▷ **molecular** adjective: the molecular structure of fuel

molest verb to touch (a child) in a sexual way ▷ **molester** noun

mollify mollifies mollifying mollified verb to make (someone) less upset or angry

mollusc noun soft-bodied, usually hard-shelled, animal, such as a snail or oyster

molten adjective liquefied or melted

moment noun **1** very short space of time; second **2** point in time **3 at the moment** now

momentary adjective lasting only a moment ▷ **momentarily** adverb

momentous adjective of great significance

momentum noun **1** ability to keep developing: The campaign is gaining momentum **2** impetus of a moving body

monarch noun sovereign ruler of a state

monarchy monarchies noun government by or a state ruled by a sovereign

monastery monasteries noun residence of a community of monks ▷ **monastic** adjective of monks, nuns or monasteries

Monday Mondays noun day between Sunday and Tuesday

money noun medium of exchange, coins or banknotes

mongrel noun dog of mixed breed

monitor noun **1** person or device that checks, controls, warns or keeps a record of something **2** visual display unit of a computer **3** Brit, Aust, NZ pupil assisting a teacher with duties ▷ verb **4** to watch and check on (something)

monk noun member of an all-male religious community bound by vows

monkey monkeys noun animal that has a long tail and climbs trees

mono- prefix indicating one or single: monosyllable

monocle noun eyeglass for one eye only

monogamy noun custom of being married to one person at a time ▷ **monogamous** adjective being married to one person at a time

monologue noun long speech by one person during a play or a conversation

monopoly monopolies noun exclusive possession of or right to do something

monotone noun unvaried pitch in speech or sound

monotonous adjective tedious due to lack of variety ▷ **monotony** noun: to break the monotony

monotreme noun Australian mammal with a single opening in its body for the passage of eggs, sperm, faeces and urine

monounsaturated *adjective* (of an oil) made mainly from vegetable fat > **monounsaturate** *noun*

monsoon *noun* season of very heavy rain in South-east Asia

monster *noun* 1 large imaginary frightening beast 2 very wicked person ▷ *adjective* 3 huge

monstrosity monstrosities *noun* large ugly thing

monstrous *adjective* extremely shocking or unfair > **monstrously** *adverb*

montage *noun* picture or film consisting of a combination of several different items arranged to produce an unusual effect

month *noun* one of the twelve divisions of the calendar year

monthly *adjective* happening or payable once a month

monument *noun* something, especially a building or statue, that commemorates something

monumental *adjective* 1 (of a building or sculpture) very large and important 2 very large or extreme

moo moos mooing mooed *verb* to make the long deep cry of a cow

mood *noun* temporary (gloomy) state of mind

moody moodier moodiest *adjective* 1 sullen or gloomy 2 changeable in mood

moon *noun* natural satellite of the earth

moonlight moonlights moonlighting moonlighted *noun* 1 light from the moon ▷ *verb* 2 *informal* to work at a secondary job, especially illegally

moonlit *adjective* lit by the light of the moon: *a moonlit evening*

moor *noun* 1 high area of open land ▷ *verb* 2 to secure (a ship) with ropes etc

mooring *noun* place for mooring a ship

moose *noun* large N American deer ▪ The plural of *moose* is *moose*

moot *verb* to bring (something) up for discussion

mop mops mopping mopped *noun* 1 long stick with twists of cotton or a sponge on the end, used for washing floors 2 thick mass of hair ▷ *verb* 3 to clean (a surface) with or as if with a mop

mope mopes moping moped *verb* to feel miserable and not interested in anything

moped *noun* type of small motorcycle

mopoke *noun* small spotted owl found in Australia and New Zealand

moral *adjective* 1 concerned with right and wrong conduct ▷ *noun* 2 lesson to be obtained from a story or event 3 **morals** values based on beliefs about the correct and acceptable way to behave > **morality** *noun* 1 good moral conduct 2 moral goodness or badness > **morally** *adverb*

morale *noun* degree of confidence or hope of a person or group

morbid *adjective* unduly interested in death or unpleasant events

more *adjective* 1 greater in amount or degree 2 comparative of **much** or **many** 3 additional or further ▷ *adverb* 4 to a greater extent 5 in addition ▷ *pronoun* 6 greater or additional amount or number

moreover *adverb* in addition to what has already been said

morepork *noun* NZ same as **mopoke**

morgue *noun* building where dead bodies are kept before being buried or cremated

moribund *adjective* without force or vitality

morning *noun* **1** part of the day before noon **2** part of the day between midnight and noon

Moroccan *adjective* **1** of Morocco ▷ *noun* **2** person from Morocco

moron *noun informal* foolish or stupid person > **moronic** *adjective*

morose *adjective* sullen or moody

morphine *noun* drug extracted from opium, used as an anaesthetic and sedative

Morse or **Morse code** *noun* code used for sending messages in which each letter is represented by a series of dots and dashes

morsel *noun* small piece of food

mortal *adjective* **1** unable to live forever **2** (of a wound) causing death ▷ *noun* **3** human being

mortality *noun* **1** state of being mortal **2** great loss of life **3** death rate

mortar *noun* **1** small cannon with a short range **2** mixture of lime, sand and water for holding bricks and stones together

mortgage mortgages mortgaging mortgaged *noun* **1** loan from a bank or a building society to buy a house ▷ *verb* **2** to use (your house) as a guarantee to a company in order to borrow money

mortifying *adjective* embarrassing or humiliating

mortuary mortuaries *noun* building where corpses are kept before burial or cremation

mosaic *noun* design or decoration using small pieces of coloured stone or glass

Moslem *noun, adjective* same as **Muslim**

mosque *noun* Muslim temple

mosquito mosquitoes or **mosquitos** *noun* blood-sucking flying insect

moss mosses *noun* small flowerless plant growing in masses on moist surfaces > **mossy** *adjective*

most *noun* **1** greatest number or degree ▷ *adjective* **2** greatest in number or degree **3** superlative of **much** or **many** ▷ *adverb* **4** in the greatest degree

mostly *adverb* for the most part; generally

MOT MOTs *noun* (in Britain) compulsory annual test of the roadworthiness of vehicles over a certain age

motel *noun* roadside hotel for motorists

moth *noun* insect like a butterfly which usually flies at night

mother *noun* **1** female parent ▷ *verb* **2** to look after (someone) as a mother

motherhood *noun* state of being a mother

mother-in-law mothers-in-law *noun* mother of your husband or wife

motif *noun* (recurring) theme or design

motion *noun* **1** process, action or way of moving **2** action or gesture **3** proposal in a meeting ▷ *verb* **4** to direct (someone) by gesture

motionless *adjective* not moving

motivate motivates motivating motivated *verb* **1** to inspire (someone) to behave in a particular way **2** to make (someone) feel determined to do something > **motivated** *adjective: highly motivated employees* > **motivation** *noun: his lack of motivation at work*

motive *noun* reason for a course of action

motley *adjective* miscellaneous

motor *noun* **1** engine, especially of a vehicle **2** machine that converts electrical energy into mechanical energy ▷ *verb* **3** to travel by car

motorboat *noun* boat with an engine

motorcar *noun* car

motorcycle *noun* two-wheeled vehicle with an engine that is ridden like a bicycle **> motorcyclist** *noun* person who rides a motorcycle

motoring *adjective* relating to cars and driving: *a motoring correspondent*

motorist *noun* person who drives a car

motorway motorways *noun* main road for fast-moving traffic

mottled *adjective* marked with blotches

motto mottoes or **mottos** *noun* saying expressing an ideal or rule of conduct

mould *noun* **1** hollow container in which metal etc is cast **2** fungal growth caused by dampness ▷ *verb* **3** to shape **4** to influence or direct **> mouldy** *adjective* covered with mould

moult *verb* to shed feathers, hair or skin to make way for new growth

mound *noun* **1** heap, especially of earth or stones **2** small hill

mount *verb* **1** to climb or ascend (something) **2** to get up on (a horse etc) **3** to increase or accumulate **4** to fix (an object) in a particular place to display it **5** to organize (a campaign or event) ▷ *noun* **6** mountain

mountain *noun* **1** hill of great size **2** large heap

mountaineer *noun* person who climbs mountains

mountainous *adjective* full of mountains

mourn *verb* to feel or express sorrow for (a dead person or lost thing)

mourner *noun* person attending a funeral

mournful *adjective* sad or dismal

mourning *noun* conventional symbols of grief for death, such as the wearing of black

mouse mice *noun* **1** small long-tailed rodent **2** *Computers* hand-held device for moving the cursor without keying

mousse *noun* dish of flavoured cream whipped and set

moustache *noun* hair on a man's upper lip

mouth *noun* **1** opening in the head for eating and issuing sounds **2** entrance to a cave or a hole **3** point where a river enters the sea ▷ *verb* **4** to form (words) with the lips without speaking

mouthful *noun* amount of food or drink put into the mouth at any one time when eating or drinking

mouthpiece *noun* **1** part of a telephone into which a person speaks **2** part of a wind instrument into which the player blows **3** spokesperson

movable or **moveable** *adjective* able to be moved from one place to another

move moves moving moved *verb* **1** to change in place or position **2** to change the place or position of (something) **3** to change (one's house etc) **4** to stir the emotions of (someone) **5** to suggest (a proposal) formally ▷ *noun* **6** moving **7** act of putting a piece or counter in a game in a different position: *It's your move next*

movement *noun* **1** action or process of moving **2** group with a common aim: *the peace movement*

3 division of a piece of classical music **4 movements** *formal* everything that you do during a period of time

moving *adjective* causing you to feel deep sadness or emotion > **movingly** *adverb*

mow mows mowing mowed mown *verb* to cut (grass or crops) > **mow down** *verb* to kill (people) in large numbers > **mower** *noun* machine for cutting grass

MP MPs *abbreviation* Member of Parliament

mpg *abbreviation* miles per gallon

mph *abbreviation* miles per hour

Mr title used before a man's name

Mrs title used before a married woman's name

Ms title used instead of Miss or Mrs

MSP MSPs *abbreviation* (in Britain) Member of the Scottish Parliament

much *adjective* **1** large amount or degree of ▷ *noun* **2** large amount or degree ▷ *adverb* **3** to a great degree **4** often: *It didn't rain much*

muck *noun* **1** *informal* dirt or filth **2** manure > **muck about** *verb* *informal* to behave stupidly and waste time > **mucky** *adjective* *informal* very dirty

mucus *noun* liquid produced in parts of the body, *eg* the nose

mud *noun* wet soft earth

muddle muddles muddling muddled *verb* **1** to confuse (someone) **2** to mix (things) up ▷ *noun* **3** state of confusion

muddy muddier muddiest *adjective* **1** covered in mud **2** (of a colour) dull and not clear

muesli *noun* mixture of grain, nuts and dried fruit, eaten with milk

muffin *noun* a small round cake eaten hot

muffled *adjective* (of a sound) quiet or difficult to hear: *a muffled explosion*

mug mugs mugging mugged *noun* **1** large drinking cup **2** *informal* gullible person ▷ *verb* **3** *informal* to attack and rob (someone) > **mugger** *noun* > **mugging** *noun*

muggy muggier muggiest *adjective* (of weather) unpleasantly warm and damp

mule *noun* offspring of a horse and a donkey

mulga *noun* **1** Australian acacia shrub growing in desert regions **2** *Aust informal* the outback
▋ The plural of *mulga* is *mulga*

mull *verb* **mull over** to think (something) over or ponder (something)

mullet *noun* common edible fish found in Australian and New Zealand waters

mulloway mulloways *noun* large edible fish found in Australian waters

multi- *prefix indicating* many: *multicultural; multistorey*

multimedia *noun* **1** *Computing* sound, pictures, film and ordinary text used to convey information **2** TV, computers and books used as teaching aids

multinational *noun* very large company with branches in many countries

multiple *adjective* **1** having many parts ▷ *noun* **2** quantity which contains another an exact number of times

multiple sclerosis *noun* serious disease that attacks the nervous system

multiplex multiplexes *noun* purpose-built complex containing several cinemas and usually restaurants and bars

multiplication *noun* **1** process of multiplying one number by another **2** large increase in number

multiplicity *noun* large number or great variety

multiply multiplies multiplying multiplied *verb* **1** to increase in number, quantity or degree **2** to add (a number or quantity) to itself a given number of times

multipurpose *adjective* having many uses

multitude *noun formal* very large number of people or things

mum *noun informal* mother

mumble mumbles mumbling mumbled *verb* to speak indistinctly, mutter

mummy mummies *noun* **1** child's word for **mother 2** body embalmed and wrapped for burial in ancient Egypt

mumps *noun* infectious disease with swelling in the glands of the neck

munch munches munching munched *verb* to chew (food) noisily and steadily

mundane *adjective* very ordinary and not interesting or unusual

municipal *adjective* relating to a city or town

munitions *plural noun* military stores

mural *noun* picture painted on a wall

murder *noun* **1** unlawful intentional killing of a human being ▷ *verb* **2** to kill (someone) in this way > **murderer** *noun* person who has murdered someone > **murderous** *adjective* **1** likely to murder someone **2** *informal* dangerous, difficult or unpleasant

murky murkier murkiest *adjective* dark or gloomy

murmur *verb* **1** to speak in a quiet indistinct way ▷ *noun* **2** something that someone says that can hardly be heard

muscle muscles muscling muscled *noun* tissue in the body which produces movement by contracting > **muscle in on** *verb informal* to force your way into (a situation where you are not wanted)

muscular *adjective* **1** with well-developed muscles **2** of muscles

muse muses musing mused *verb literary* to think about something for a long time

museum *noun* building where natural, artistic, historical or scientific objects are exhibited and preserved

mush *noun* soft pulpy mass

mushroom *noun* **1** edible fungus with a stem and cap ▷ *verb* **2** to grow rapidly

mushy mushier mushiest *adjective* **1** (of fruits or vegetables) too soft **2** *informal* (of a story) too sentimental

music *noun* **1** art form using a melodious and harmonious combination of notes **2** written or printed form of this

musical *adjective* **1** of or like music **2** talented in or fond of music ▷ *noun* **3** play or film with songs and dancing > **musically** *adverb*

musician *noun* person who plays a musical instrument

musk *noun* scent obtained from a gland of the musk deer or produced synthetically > **musky** *adjective* (of a smell) strong, warm and sweet

musket *noun History* long-barrelled gun

Muslim or **Moslem** *noun* **1** follower of the religion of Islam ▷ *adjective*

2 of or relating to Islam

muslin *noun* fine cotton fabric

mussel *noun* edible shellfish with a dark hinged shell

must *verb* **1** used as an auxiliary to express obligation, certainty or resolution ▷ *noun* **2** essential or necessary thing

mustard *noun* paste made from the powdered seeds of a plant, used as a condiment

muster *verb* to gather together (energy, support, etc)

musty mustier mustiest *adjective* smelling mouldy and stale

mutate mutates mutating mutated *verb* to change and develop in a new way, especially genetically ▷ **mutant** *noun*, *adjective*

mutation *noun* (genetic) change

mute *adjective formal* not giving out sound or speech

muted *adjective* **1** (of sound or colour) softened **2** (of a reaction) subdued

muti *noun S Afr informal* medicine, especially herbal medicine

mutilate mutilates mutilating mutilated *verb* **1** to deprive of a limb or other part **2** to damage (a book or text) ▷ **mutilation** *noun*

mutiny mutinies mutinying mutinied *noun* **1** rebellion against authority, especially by soldiers or sailors ▷ *verb* **2** to commit mutiny

mutter *verb* **1** to speak indistinctly **2** to grumble

mutton *noun* flesh of a sheep, used as food

mutton bird *noun* **1** *Aust* sea bird with dark plumage **2** *NZ* any of a number of migratory sea birds, the young of which are a Maori delicacy

mutual *adjective* **1** felt or expressed by each of two people about the other **2** common to both or all ▷ **mutually** *adverb*

muzzle muzzles muzzling muzzled *noun* **1** animal's mouth and nose **2** cover for a dog's muzzle to prevent biting **3** open end of a gun ▷ *verb* **4** to put a muzzle on

my *adjective* belonging to me

mynah bird *noun* tropical bird that can mimic human speech

myriad *adjective* **1** very many ▷ *noun* **2** large indefinite number

myrrh *noun* fragrant substance used in perfume and incense

myself *pronoun* emphatic or reflexive form of **I** or **me**

mysterious *adjective* **1** strange and not well understood **2** secretive ▷ **mysteriously** *adverb*

mystery mysteries *noun* something that is not understood or known about

mystic *noun* **1** person who seeks spiritual knowledge ▷ *adjective* **2** mystical ▷ **mystical** *adjective* having a spiritual or religious significance beyond human understanding ▷ **mysticism** *noun* religious practice in which people search for truth and closeness to God through meditation and prayer

mystify *verb* **mystifies mystifying mystified** to bewilder or puzzle (someone)

mystique *noun* atmosphere of mystery or power

myth *noun* **1** tale with supernatural characters, usually of how the world and humankind began **2** untrue idea or explanation

mythical *adjective* imaginary, untrue or existing only in myths

mythology *noun* myths collectively ▷ **mythological** *adjective*

n

naartjie *noun S Afr* tangerine

nab nabs nabbing nabbed *verb informal* **1** to arrest **2** to catch (someone) in wrongdoing

nag nags nagging nagged *verb* **1** to scold or find fault constantly **2** to be a constant source of discomfort or worry to ▷ *noun* **3** person who nags > **nagging** *adjective, noun*

nail nails nailing nailed *noun* **1** pointed piece of metal with a head, hit with a hammer to join two objects together **2** hard covering of the upper tips of the fingers and toes **3** **hit the nail on the head** to say something exactly correct ▷ *verb* **4** to attach (something) with nails **5** *informal* to catch or arrest

naïve or **naïve** *adjective* **1** innocent and easily fooled **2** simple and unsophisticated > **naively** *adverb* > **naivety** *noun*

naked *adjective* **1** without clothes **2** without any covering **3** **the naked eye** the eye unassisted by binoculars, telescope, etc > **nakedness** *noun*

name names naming named *noun* **1** word by which a person or thing is known **2** reputation, especially a good one **3** **call someone names** to use insulting words to describe someone ▷ *verb* **4** to give a name to **5** to refer to (someone or something) by name **6** to fix or specify

nameless *adjective* **1** without a name **2** unspecified **3** too horrible to be mentioned

namely *adverb* that is to say

namesake *noun* person with the same name as another

nanny nannies *noun* woman whose job is looking after young children

nap naps napping napped *noun* **1** short sleep ▷ *verb* **2** to have a short sleep

napalm *noun* highly inflammable jellied petrol, used in bombs

nape *noun* back of the neck

naphthalene *noun* white crystalline product distilled from coal tar or petroleum, used in disinfectants, mothballs and explosives

napkin *noun* piece of cloth or paper for wiping your mouth or protecting your clothes while eating

nappy nappies *noun* piece of absorbent material fastened round a baby's bottom to absorb urine and faeces

narcotic *noun, adjective* (of) a drug, such as morphine or opium, designed to produce numbness and drowsiness

narrate narrates narrating narrated *verb* **1** to tell (a story) **2** to speak words that accompany and explain what is happening in a film or TV programme > **narration** *noun*

narrative *noun* account or story

narrator *noun* 1 person who tells a story 2 person who speaks the words accompanying and explaining a film or TV programme

narrow *adjective* 1 small in breadth in comparison to length 2 limited in range, extent or outlook 3 with little margin: *a narrow escape* 4 **narrows** narrow part of a strait, river or current ▷ *verb* 5 to make or become narrow 6 (often followed by *down*) to limit or restrict > **narrowly** *adverb* > **narrowness** *noun*

narrow-minded *adjective* intolerant or bigoted

nasal *adjective* 1 of the nose 2 (of a sound) pronounced with air passing through the nose > **nasally** *adverb*

nasty nastier nastiest *adjective* 1 unpleasant 2 (of an injury) dangerous or painful 3 spiteful or unkind > **nastily** *adverb* > **nastiness** *noun*

natal *adjective* of or relating to birth

nation *noun* people of one or more cultures or races organized as a single state

national *adjective* 1 typical of a particular nation ▷ *noun* 2 citizen of a nation > **nationally** *adverb*

national anthem *noun* official song of a country

nationalism *noun* 1 policy of national independence 2 patriotism, sometimes to an excessive degree > **nationalist** *noun, adjective* > **nationalistic** *adjective*

nationality nationalities *noun* 1 fact of being a citizen of a particular nation 2 group of people of the same race

nationalize nationalizes nationalizing nationalized; also spelt **nationalise** *verb* to put (an industry or a company) under state control > **nationalization** *noun*

National Party *noun* major political party in Australia and New Zealand

national service *noun* compulsory military service

nationwide *adjective, adverb* happening all over a country

native *adjective* 1 relating to a place where a person was born 2 born in a specified place 3 (followed by *to*) originating (in) 4 inborn ▷ *noun* 5 person born in a specified place 6 indigenous animal or plant 7 member of the original race of a country

Nativity *noun* Christianity birth of Jesus Christ

natter *informal verb* 1 to talk idly or chatter ▷ *noun* 2 long idle chat

natural *adjective* 1 normal or to be expected 2 genuine or spontaneous 3 of, according to, existing in or produced by nature 4 not created by human beings 5 not synthetic ▷ *noun* 6 person with an inborn talent or skill > **naturally** *adverb* 1 of course 2 in a natural or normal way 3 instinctively

naturalist *noun* student of natural history

nature *noun* 1 whole system of the existence, forces and events of the physical world that are not controlled by human beings 2 fundamental or essential qualities 3 kind or sort

naught *noun lit* nothing

naughty naughtier naughtiest *adjective* 1 disobedient or mischievous 2 mildly indecent > **naughtily** *adverb* > **naughtiness** *noun*

nausea *noun* feeling of being about

to vomit > **nauseous** *adjective* **1** as if about to vomit **2** sickening

nautical *adjective* of the sea or ships

naval *adjective* of or relating to a navy or ships

navel *noun* hollow in the middle of the abdomen where the umbilical cord was attached

navigate navigates navigating navigated *verb* **1** to direct or plot the path or position of a ship, aircraft or car **2** to travel over or through > **navigation** *noun* > **navigator** *noun*

navvy navvies *noun Brit* labourer employed on a road or a building site

navy navies *noun* **1** branch of a country's armed services that fights at sea **2** warships of a nation ▷ *adjective* **3** very dark blue; also **navy-blue**

Nazi *noun* **1** member of the fascist National Socialist Party, which held power in Germany under Adolf Hitler ▷ *adjective* **2** of or relating to the Nazis > **Nazism** *noun*

NB *abbreviation* (Latin: *nota bene*) note well

Neanderthal *adjective* of a type of primitive man that lived in Europe before 12 000 BC

near *preposition, adverb, adjective* **1** indicating a place or time not far away ▷ *adjective* **2** almost being the thing specified: *a near disaster* ▷ *verb* **3** to draw close (to) > **nearness** *noun*

nearby *adjective* not far away

nearly *adverb* almost

neat *adjective* **1** tidy and clean **2** smoothly or competently done **3** undiluted > **neatly** *adverb* > **neatness** *noun*

necessarily *adverb* inevitably or certainly

necessary *adjective* **1** needed to achieve the desired result: *the necessary skills* **2** certain or unavoidable: *the necessary consequences*

necessity necessities *noun* **1** circumstances that inevitably require a certain result **2** something needed

neck *noun* **1** part of the body joining the head to the shoulders **2** part of a garment round the neck **3** long narrow part of a bottle or violin ▷ *verb* **4** *informal* to kiss and cuddle

necklace *noun* **1** decorative piece of jewellery worn around the neck **2** *S Afr* burning petrol-filled tyre placed round someone's neck to kill him or her

nectar *noun* **1** sweet liquid collected from flowers by bees **2** drink of the gods

nectarine *noun* smooth-skinned peach

née *preposition* indicating the surname that a woman had before marrying

need needs needing needed *verb* **1** to require or be in want of **2** to be obliged (to do something) ▷ *noun* **3** condition of lacking something **4** requirement or necessity **5** poverty

needle needles needling needled *noun* **1** thin pointed piece of metal with an eye through which thread is passed for sewing **2** long pointed rod used in knitting **3** pointed part of a hypodermic syringe **4** small pointed part in a record player that touches the record and picks up the sound signals; stylus **5** pointer on a measuring instrument or compass **6** long narrow stiff leaf ▷ *verb* **7** *informal* to goad or provoke

needless *adjective* unnecessary

> **needlessly** adverb

needlework noun sewing and embroidery

needy needier neediest adjective poor and in need of financial support

negative adjective 1 expressing a denial or refusal 2 lacking positive qualities 3 (of an electrical charge) having the same electrical charge as an electron ▷ noun 4 negative word or statement 5 Photography image with a reversal of tones or colours from which positive prints are made > **negatively** adverb

neglect verb 1 to take no care of 2 to fail (to do something) through carelessness 3 to disregard ▷ noun 4 neglecting or being neglected > **neglectful** adjective

negligent adjective neglectful or careless > **negligence** noun > **negligently** adverb

negligible adjective very small or unimportant

negotiable adjective able to be negotiated

negotiate negotiates negotiating negotiated verb 1 to discuss in order to reach (an agreement) 2 to succeed in passing round or over (a place or problem) > **negotiation** noun > **negotiator** noun

Negro Negroes noun old-fashioned member of any of the Black peoples originating in Africa

neigh noun 1 loud high-pitched sound made by a horse ▷ verb 2 to make this sound

neighbour noun person who lives or is situated near another

neighbourhood noun 1 district 2 surroundings 3 people of a district

neighbouring adjective situated nearby

neither adjective, pronoun 1 not one nor the other ▷ conjunction 2 nor

neo- prefix meaning new, recent or a modern form of: neo-fascism

neo-conservatism noun (in the US) a right-wing tendency that originated amongst supporters of the political left > **neo-conservative** adjective, noun

neon noun Chemistry colourless odourless gaseous element used in illuminated signs and lights

nephew noun son of your brother or sister

nepotism noun favouritism in business shown to relatives and friends

Neptune noun eighth planet from the sun in the solar system

nerve noun 1 cordlike bundle of fibres that conducts impulses between the brain and other parts of the body 2 bravery and determination 3 impudence 4 **nerves a** anxiety or tension **b** ability or inability to remain calm in a difficult situation

nerve-racking adjective very distressing or harrowing

nervous adjective 1 apprehensive or worried 2 of or relating to the nerves > **nervously** adverb > **nervousness** noun

nervous breakdown noun mental illness in which someone suffers from severe depression and needs psychiatric treatment

nervous system noun nerves, brain and spinal cord

nest noun 1 place or structure in which birds or certain animals lay eggs or give birth to young 2 secluded place 3 set of things of graduated sizes designed to fit together ▷ verb 4 to make or inhabit a nest

nestle nestles nestling nestled
verb **1** to snuggle **2** to be in a
sheltered position

nestling *noun* bird too young to
leave the nest

net nets netting netted *noun*
1 fabric of meshes of string, thread
or wire with many openings **2** piece
of net used to protect or hold things
or to trap animals **3** Internet ▷ *verb*
4 to catch (a fish or animal) in a net

netball *noun* team game in which
a ball has to be thrown through a
net hanging from a ring at the top
of a pole

netting *noun* material made of net

nettle *noun* plant with stinging
hairs on the leaves

network *noun* **1** system of
intersecting lines, roads, etc
2 interconnecting group or
system **3** group of broadcasting
stations that all transmit the same
programmes at the same time

neuron or **neurone** *noun* cell
carrying nerve impulses in the
nervous system

neurosis neuroses *noun* mental
disorder producing hysteria,
anxiety, depression or obsessive
behaviour

neurotic *adjective* **1** emotionally
unstable **2** suffering from neurosis
▷ *noun* **3** neurotic person

neuter *adjective* **1** (of grammatical
inflections in some languages)
neither masculine nor feminine
▷ *verb* **2** to remove the reproductive
organs of (an animal)

neutral *adjective* **1** taking neither
side in a war or dispute **2** of or
belonging to a neutral party or
country **3** (of a colour) not definite
or striking ▷ *noun* **4** neutral
person or nation **5** neutral gear
> **neutrality** *noun*

neutron *noun* electrically neutral
elementary particle of about the
same mass as a proton

never *adverb* at no time

nevertheless *adverb* in spite
of that

new *adjective* **1** not existing before
2 recently acquired **3** having lately
come into some state **4** additional
5 (followed by *to*) unfamiliar
> **newness** *noun*

newborn *adjective* recently or
just born

newcomer *noun* recent arrival or
participant

newly *adverb* recently: *the newly
arrived visitors*

new moon *noun* moon when it
appears as a narrow crescent at the
beginning of its cycle

news *noun* **1** important or
interesting new happenings
2 information about such events
reported in the media

newsagent *noun Brit* shopkeeper
who sells newspapers and
magazines

newspaper *noun* weekly or daily
publication containing news

newt *noun* small amphibious
creature with a long slender body
and tail

New Testament *noun* second
main division of the Bible

newton *noun* unit of force

New Year *noun* beginning of a
calendar year

New Zealander *noun* person from
New Zealand

next *adjective, adverb* **1** immediately
following **2** nearest

next door *adjective, adverb* in or to
the adjacent house

next-of-kin *noun* closest relative
The plural of *next-of-kin* is
next-of-kin

NHS *abbreviation* (in Britain)
National Health Service

nib *noun* writing point of a pen

nibble nibbles nibbling nibbled
verb **1** to take little bites (of) ▷ *noun*
2 little bite

nice nicer nicest *adjective* **1** pleasant
2 kind **3** good or satisfactory
4 subtle: *a nice distinction* > **nicely**
adverb > **niceness** *noun*

nicety niceties *noun* **1** subtle point
2 refinement or delicacy

niche *noun* **1** hollow area in a wall
2 suitable position for a particular
person

nick *verb* **1** to make a small cut in
2 *Chiefly Brit informal* to steal **3** *Chiefly
Brit informal* to arrest ▷ *noun* **4** small
cut **5** *informal* prison or police
station

nickel *noun* **1** *Chemistry* silvery-white
metal often used in alloys **2** US coin
worth five cents

**nickname nicknames
nicknaming nicknamed** *noun*
1 familiar name given to a person
or place ▷ *verb* **2** to call (someone or
something) by a nickname

nicotine *noun* addictive substance
found in tobacco

niece *noun* daughter of your brother
or sister

nifty niftier niftiest *adjective*
informal neat or smart

Nigerian *adjective* **1** of Nigeria
▷ *noun* **2** person from Nigeria

niggle niggles niggling niggled
verb **1** to worry (someone) slightly
2 to continually find fault with
▷ *noun* **3** small worry or doubt

night *noun* time of darkness
between sunset and sunrise

nightclub *noun* place for dancing,
music, etc, open late at night

nightdress nightdresses *noun*
woman's loose dress worn in bed

nightfall *noun* time when it starts
to get dark

nightie *noun informal* nightdress

nightingale *noun* small bird with a
musical song usually heard at night

nightly *adjective* **1** happening every
night ▷ *adverb* **2** every night

nightmare *noun* **1** very bad dream
2 very unpleasant experience
> **nightmarish** *adjective*

nil *noun* nothing or zero

nimble nimbler nimblest *adjective*
1 agile and quick **2** mentally alert or
acute > **nimbly** *adverb*

nimbus *noun* dark grey rain cloud

nincompoop *noun informal* stupid
person

nine *adjective, noun* the number 9
> **ninth** *adjective, noun*

nineteen *adjective, noun* the
number 19 > **nineteenth** *adjective,
noun*

ninety *adjective, noun* the number
90 > **ninetieth** *adjective, noun*

nip nips nipping nipped *verb*
1 *informal* to hurry **2** to pinch or
squeeze **3** to bite lightly ▷ *noun*
4 pinch or light bite **5** sharp
coldness

nipple *noun* projection in the centre
of a breast

nirvana *noun Buddhism, Hinduism*
absolute spiritual enlightenment
and bliss

nit *noun* egg or larva of a louse

nitpicking *adjective informal* too
concerned with insignificant
detail, especially to find fault

nitrogen *noun Chemistry* colourless
odourless gas that forms four fifths
of the air

no noes or **nos** *interjection*
1 expresses denial, disagreement
or refusal ▷ *adjective* **2** not any or
not a ▷ *adverb* **3** not at all ▷ *noun*
4 negative answer or vote against

something

no. *abbreviation* number

nobility *noun* 1 quality of being noble 2 class of people holding titles and high social rank

noble nobler noblest; nobles *adjective* 1 showing or having high moral qualities 2 of the nobility 3 impressive and magnificent ▷ *noun* 4 member of the nobility > **nobly** *adverb*

nobleman noblemen *noun* man who is a member of the nobility > **noblewoman** *noun*

nobody nobodies *pronoun* 1 no person ▷ *noun* 2 person of no importance

nocturnal *adjective* 1 of the night 2 active at night

nod nods nodding nodded *verb* 1 to lower and raise (your head) briefly in agreement or greeting ▷ *noun* 2 act of nodding > **nod off** *verb informal* to fall asleep

node *noun* 1 point on a plant stem from which leaves grow 2 point at which a curve crosses itself

nodule *noun* 1 small knot or lump 2 rounded mineral growth on the root of a plant

noise *noun* sound, usually a loud or disturbing one

noisy noisier noisiest *adjective* 1 making a lot of noise 2 full of noise > **noisily** *adverb* > **noisiness** *noun*

nomad *noun* member of a tribe with no fixed dwelling place; wanderer > **nomadic** *adjective*

nominal *adjective* 1 in name only 2 very small in comparison with real worth > **nominally** *adverb*

nominate nominates nominating nominated *verb* 1 to suggest as a candidate 2 to appoint to an office or position > **nomination** *noun*

non- *prefix indicating* 1 negation: *nonexistent* 2 refusal or failure: *noncooperation* 3 exclusion from a specified class: *nonfiction* 4 lack or absence: *nonevent*

nonagenarian *noun* person aged between ninety and ninety-nine

nonchalant *adjective* casually unconcerned or indifferent > **nonchalance** *noun* > **nonchalantly** *adverb*

noncombatant *noun* member of the armed forces whose duties do not include fighting

noncommissioned officer *noun* (in the armed forces) subordinate officer, risen from the ranks

nondescript *adjective* lacking outstanding features

none *pronoun* 1 not any 2 no-one

nonetheless *adverb* despite that, however

nonfiction *noun* writing that is factual rather than about imaginary events

nonplussed *adjective* perplexed

nonsense *noun* 1 something that has or makes no sense 2 absurd language 3 foolish behaviour > **nonsensical** *adjective*

nonstop *adjective, adverb* without a stop

noodles *plural noun* long thin strips of pasta

nook *noun* sheltered place

noon *noun* twelve o'clock midday

no-one or **no one** *pronoun* nobody

noose *noun* loop in the end of a rope, tied with a slipknot

nor *conjunction* and not

norm *noun* standard that is regarded as normal

normal *adjective* 1 usual, regular or typical 2 meeting standards or conventions > **normality** *noun*

normally *adverb* 1 usually 2 in a

normal way

north *noun* **1** direction towards the North Pole, opposite south **2** area lying in or towards the north ▷ *adjective* **3** to or in the north **4** (of a wind) from the north ▷ *adverb* **5** in, to or towards the north

North America *noun* continent consisting of Canada, the United States and Mexico > **North American** *adjective*

northeast *noun* **1** direction midway between north and east **2** area lying in or towards the northeast ▷ *adjective* **3** to or in the northeast **4** (of a wind) from the northeast ▷ *adverb* **5** in, to or towards the northeast

northeasterly northeasterlies *adjective, adverb* **1** in, towards or from the northeast ▷ *noun* **2** wind blowing from the northeast

northeastern *adjective* in or from the northeast

northerly northerlies *adjective, adverb* **1** in, towards or from the north ▷ *noun* **2** wind blowing from the north

northern *adjective* in or from the north

North Pole *noun* northernmost point on the earth's axis

northward *adjective, adverb* in or towards the north

northwards *adverb* towards the north

northwest northwesterlies *noun* **1** direction midway between north and west **2** area lying in or towards the northwest ▷ *adjective* **3** to or in the northwest **4** (of a wind) from the northwest ▷ *adverb* **5** in, to or towards the northwest

northwesterly *adjective, adverb* **1** in, towards or from the northwest ▷ *noun* **2** wind blowing from the northwest

northwestern *adjective* in or from the northwest

Norwegian *adjective* **1** of Norway ▷ *noun* **2** person from Norway **3** language of Norway

nose noses nosing nosed *noun* **1** organ of smell, used also in breathing **2** front part of a vehicle ▷ *verb* **3** to move forward slowly and carefully **4** to pry or snoop

nosey *adjective* same as **nosy**

nostalgia *noun* sentimental longing for the past > **nostalgic** *adjective*

nostril *noun* either of the two openings at the end of the nose

nosy nosier nosiest; also spelt **nosey** *adjective informal* prying or inquisitive

not *adverb* expressing negation, refusal or denial

notable *adjective* **1** worthy of being noted; remarkable ▷ *noun* **2** person of distinction > **notably** *adverb*

notch notches notching notched *noun* **1** V-shaped cut **2** *informal* step or level ▷ *verb* **3** to make a notch in

note notes noting noted *noun* **1** short letter **2** brief comment or record **3** banknote **4** (symbol for) a musical sound **5** hint or mood ▷ *verb* **6** to notice or pay attention to **7** to record (something) in writing **8** to remark upon (something) > **note down** *verb* to write (something) down to have as a record

notebook *noun* book for writing in

noted *adjective* well-known

nothing *pronoun* **1** not anything **2** matter of no importance **3** figure o ▷ *adverb* **4** not at all

notice notices noticing noticed *noun* **1** observation or attention

2 sign giving warning or an announcement **3** advance warning of intention to end a contract of employment ▷ *verb* **4** to observe or become aware of **5** to point out or remark upon

noticeable *adjective* easily seen or detected; appreciable > **noticeably** *adverb*

noticeboard *noun* board where notices are displayed

notify notifies notifying notified *verb* to inform > **notification** *noun*

notion *noun* **1** idea or opinion **2** whim

notorious *adjective* well known for something bad > **notoriety** *noun* > **notoriously** *adverb*

notwithstanding *preposition* in spite of

nougat *noun* chewy sweet containing nuts and fruit

nought *noun* **1** figure o **2** nothing

noun *noun* word that refers to a person, place or thing

nourish nourishes nourishing nourished *verb* **1** to feed **2** to encourage or foster (an idea or feeling)

nourishing *adjective* providing the food necessary for life and growth

nourishment *noun* food necessary for life and growth

novel *noun* **1** long fictitious story in book form ▷ *adjective* **2** fresh, new or original

novelist *noun* person who writes novels

novelty novelties *noun* **1** newness **2** something new or unusual

November *noun* eleventh month of the year

novice *noun* **1** beginner **2** person who has entered a religious order but has not yet taken vows

now *adverb* **1** at or for the present time **2** immediately ▷ *conjunction* **3** seeing that, since

nowadays *adverb* in these times

nowhere *adverb* not anywhere

noxious *adjective* **1** poisonous or harmful **2** extremely unpleasant

nozzle *noun* projecting spout through which fluid is discharged

nuance *noun* subtle difference in colour, meaning or tone

nub *noun* point or gist (of a story etc)

nubile *adjective* (of a young woman) **1** sexually attractive **2** old enough to get married

nuclear *adjective* **1** of nuclear weapons or energy **2** of a nucleus, especially the nucleus of an atom

nuclear reactor *noun* device in which a nuclear reaction is maintained and controlled to produce nuclear energy

nucleus nuclei *noun* **1** central part of an atom or cell **2** basic central part of something

nude *adjective* **1** naked ▷ *noun* **2** naked figure in painting, sculpture or photography > **nudity** *noun*

nudge nudges nudging nudged *verb* **1** to push gently, especially with the elbow ▷ *noun* **2** gentle push or touch

nudist *noun* person who believes in not wearing clothes > **nudism** *noun*

nugget *noun* **1** small lump of gold in its natural state **2** something small but valuable

nuisance *noun* something or someone that causes annoyance or bother

null *adjective* **null and void** not legally valid

nulla-nulla *noun* wooden club used by Australian Aborigines

numb *adjective* **1** without feeling, as through cold, shock or fear ▷ *verb*

2 to make numb

numbat *noun* small Australian marsupial with a long snout and tongue

number *noun* **1** sum or quantity **2** word or symbol used to express a sum or quantity; numeral **3** numeral or string of numerals used to identify a person or thing **4** one of a series, such as a copy of a magazine **5** song or piece of music **6** group of people **7** *Grammar* classification of words depending on how many persons or things are referred to ▷ *verb* **8** to count **9** to give a number to **10** to amount to **11** to include in a group

numberplate *noun* plate on a car showing the registration number

numeral *noun* word or symbol used to express a sum or quantity

numerical *adjective* measured or expressed in numbers > **numerically** *adverb*

numerous *adjective* existing or happening in large numbers

nun *noun* female member of a religious order

nurse nurses nursing nursed *noun* **1** person whose job is looking after sick people, usually in a hospital **2** woman whose job is looking after children ▷ *verb* **3** to look after (a sick person) **4** to breast-feed (a baby) **5** to try to cure (an ailment) **6** to harbour or foster (a feeling)

nursery nurseries *noun* **1** room where children sleep or play **2** place where children are taken care of while their parents are at work **3** place where plants are grown for sale

nursery school *noun* school for children from 3 to 5 years old

nursing home *noun* private hospital or home for old people

nurture nurtures nurturing nurtured *noun* **1** act or process of promoting the development of a child or young plant ▷ *verb* **2** to promote or encourage the development of

nut *noun* **1** fruit consisting of a hard shell and a kernel **2** small piece of metal that screws onto a bolt **3** *informal* insane or eccentric person **4** *informal* head

nutmeg *noun* spice made from the seed of a tropical tree

nutrient *noun* substance that provides nourishment

nutrition *noun* **1** process of taking in and absorbing nutrients **2** process of being nourished > **nutritional** *adjective* > **nutritionist** *noun* professional advising on diet

nutritious or **nutritive** *adjective* nourishing

nutty nuttier nuttiest *adjective* **1** containing or resembling nuts **2** *informal* insane or eccentric

nuzzle nuzzles nuzzling nuzzled *verb* to push or rub gently with the nose or snout

nylon *noun* **1** synthetic material used for clothing etc **2** **nylons** *old-fashioned* stockings made of nylon

oaf *noun* stupid or clumsy person

oak *noun* 1 deciduous forest tree 2 its wood, used for furniture

OAP OAPs *abbreviation* (in Britain) old-age pensioner

oar *noun* pole with a broad blade, used for rowing a boat

oasis oases *noun* fertile area in a desert

oat *noun* 1 hard cereal grown as food 2 **oats** grain of this cereal

oath *noun* solemn promise, especially to be truthful in court

oatmeal *noun* rough flour made from oats

OBE OBEs *abbreviation* (in Britain) Officer of the Order of the British Empire

obedient *adjective* obeying or willing to obey > **obedience** *noun: unquestioning obedience* > **obediently** *adverb*

obelisk *noun* four-sided stone column tapering to a pyramid at the top, built in honour of a person or event

obese *adjective* very fat > **obesity** *noun: Obesity rates among children are increasing*

obey obeys obeying obeyed *verb* to carry out instructions or orders

obituary obituaries *noun* announcement of someone's death, especially in a newspaper

object *noun* 1 physical thing 2 focus of thoughts or action 3 aim or purpose 4 *Grammar* word that a verb or preposition affects ▷ *verb* 5 to express disapproval

objection *noun* 1 expression or feeling of opposition or disapproval 2 reason for opposing something

objectionable *adjective* unpleasant and offensive

objective *noun* 1 aim or purpose ▷ *adjective* 2 not biased 3 existing in the real world outside the human mind > **objectively** *adverb* > **objectivity** *noun: The press strives for balance and objectivity*

obligated *adjective* obliged to do something

obligation *noun* duty

obligatory *adjective* required by a rule or law

oblige obliges obliging obliged *verb* 1 to compel (someone) morally or by law to do something 2 to do a favour for (someone)

obliging *adjective* ready to help other people > **obligingly** *adverb*

oblique *adjective* 1 slanting 2 indirect > **obliquely** *adverb*

obliterate obliterates obliterating obliterated *verb* to destroy every trace of > **obliteration** *noun: the obliteration of three rainforests*

oblivion *noun* 1 state of being forgotten 2 state of being unaware or unconscious

oblivious *adjective* unaware > **obliviously** *adverb*

oblong *adjective* 1 having two long sides, two short sides and four right angles ▷ *noun* 2 oblong figure

obnoxious *adjective* offensive

oboe *noun* double-reeded woodwind instrument > **oboist** *noun*

obscene *adjective* **1** portraying sex offensively **2** disgusting > **obscenely** *adverb*

obscenity obscenities *noun* **1** art, language or behaviour that is sexual and offends or shocks people **2** very offensive word or expression

obscure obscures obscuring obscured *adjective* **1** not well known **2** hard to understand **3** indistinct ▷ *verb* **4** to make (something) obscure > **obscurity** *noun*: She was plucked from obscurity

observance *noun* observing of a custom

observant *adjective* quick to notice things

observation *noun* **1** action or habit of observing **2** remark

observatory observatories *noun* building equipped for studying the weather and the stars

observe observes observing observed *verb* **1** to see or notice **2** to watch (someone or something) carefully **3** to remark **4** to act according to (a law or custom) > **observable** *adjective*: This had no observable effect on their behaviour

observer *noun* person who observes, especially one who watches someone or something carefully

obsess obsesses obsessing obsessed *verb* to preoccupy (someone) compulsively > **obsessed** *adjective*: obsessed with gangster movies > **obsessive** *adjective*: obsessive about motor racing

obsession *noun* something that preoccupies a person to the exclusion of other things

> **obsessional** *adjective*: She became almost obsessional about the way she looked

obsolescent *adjective* becoming obsolete > **obsolescence** *noun*: the rapid obsolescence of technological products

obsolete *adjective* no longer in use

obstacle *noun* something that makes progress difficult

obstetrics *noun* branch of medicine concerned with pregnancy and childbirth > **obstetric** *adjective*: obstetric care > **obstetrician** *noun*: an appointment to see the obstetrician

obstinate *adjective* **1** stubborn **2** difficult to remove or change > **obstinacy** *noun*: the streak of obstinacy in me that would not let me stop > **obstinately** *adverb*

obstruct *verb* to block with an obstacle > **obstruction** *noun*: vehicles causing an obstruction > **obstructive** *adjective*: She was obstructive and refused to follow procedure

obtain *verb* to acquire intentionally > **obtainable** *adjective*: It's obtainable from most health shops

obtrusive *adjective* unpleasantly noticeable

obtuse *adjective* **1** mentally slow **2** *Maths* (of an angle) between 90° and 180° **3** not pointed

obvious *adjective* easy to see or understand; evident > **obviously** *adverb*

occasion *noun* **1** time at which a particular thing happens **2** reason: no occasion for complaint **3** special event ▷ *verb formal* **4** to cause

occasional *adjective* happening sometimes > **occasionally** *adverb*

occult *adjective* **1** relating to the supernatural ▷ *noun* **2** **the occult** knowledge or study of the supernatural

occupancy occupancies *noun*
(length of) a person's stay in a
specified place

occupant *noun* person occupying a
specified place

occupation *noun* **1** profession
2 activity that occupies your
time **3** control of a country by a
foreign military power **4** being
occupied > **occupational** *adjective*:
occupational health and safety issues

**occupy occupies occupying
occupied** *verb* **1** to live or work in (a
building) **2** to take up the attention
of (someone) **3** to take up (space
or time) **4** to take possession of (a
place) by force > **occupier** *noun*: *the
occupier of the flat*

occur occurs occurring occurred
verb **1** to happen **2** to exist **3** **occur
to** to come to the mind of

occurrence *noun* **1** something that
occurs **2** fact of occurring

ocean *noun* **1** vast area of sea
between continents **2** *literary* sea
> **oceanic** *adjective*: *oceanic islands*

o'clock *adverb* used after a number
to specify an hour

octagon *noun* geometric figure
with eight sides > **octagonal**
adjective: *an octagonal box*

octave *noun* Music (interval
between the first and) eighth note
of a scale

October *noun* tenth month of
the year

octopus octopuses *noun* sea
creature with a soft body and eight
tentacles

odd *adjective* **1** unusual **2** occasional
3 not divisible by two **4** not part
of a set **5** **odds** (ratio showing)
the probability of something
happening > **oddly** *adverb*
> **oddness** *noun*: *the oddness of his*

opinions

oddity oddities *noun* odd person
or thing

oddments *plural noun* things
left over

odds and ends *plural noun* small
miscellaneous items

ode *noun* lyric poem, usually
addressed to a particular subject

odious *adjective* offensive

odium *noun formal* widespread
dislike

odour *noun* particular smell
> **odorous** *adjective*: *odorous air
emissions*

odyssey odysseys *noun* long
eventful journey

oesophagus oesophagi *noun*
passage between the mouth and
stomach

oestrogen *noun* female hormone
that controls the reproductive cycle

of *preposition* **1** belonging to
2 consisting of **3** connected with
4 characteristic of

off *preposition* **1** away from ▷ *adverb*
2 away ▷ *adjective* **3** not operating
4 cancelled **5** (of food) gone bad

offal *noun* edible organs of an
animal, such as liver or kidneys

off colour *adjective* slightly ill

offence *noun* **1** (cause of) hurt
feelings or annoyance **2** illegal act
3 **give offence** to cause to feel
upset or angry **4** **take offence** to
feel hurt or offended

offend *verb* **1** to hurt the feelings
of (a person) **2** *formal* to commit
a crime

offender *noun* person who commits
a crime

offensive *adjective* **1** disagreeable
2 insulting **3** aggressive ▷ *noun*
4 position or action of attack
> **offensively** *adverb*

offer *verb* **1** to present (something)

for acceptance or rejection **2** to provide **3** to be willing (to do something) **4** to propose as payment ▷ *noun* **5** instance of offering something

offering *noun* thing offered

offhand *adjective* **1** casual, curt ▷ *adverb* **2** without preparation

office *noun* **1** room or building where people work at desks **2** department of a commercial organization **3** formal position of responsibility **4** place where tickets or information can be obtained

officer *noun* **1** person in authority in the armed services **2** member of the police force **3** person with special responsibility in an organization

official *adjective* **1** of a position of authority **2** approved or arranged by someone in authority ▷ *noun* **3** person who holds a position of authority > **officially** *adverb*

officialdom *noun* officials collectively

officiate officiates officiating officiated *verb* to act in an official role

offing *noun* **in the offing** likely to happen soon

off-licence *noun* Brit shop licensed to sell alcohol for drinking elsewhere

offline *adjective* (of a computer) not connected to the Internet

off-road *adjective* (of a motor vehicle) designed for use away from public roads

offset offsets offsetting offset *verb* to cancel out or compensate for

offshoot *noun* something developed from something else

offshore *adjective, adverb* in or from the part of the sea near the shore

offside *adjective, adverb* **1** Sport (positioned) illegally ahead of the ball ▷ *noun* **2** side of a vehicle that is furthest from the pavement

offspring *noun* immediate descendant or descendants of a person or animal

often *adverb* frequently, much of the time

ogle ogles ogling ogled *verb* to stare at (someone) lustfully

ogre *noun* **1** giant that eats human flesh **2** monstrous or cruel person

ohm *noun* unit of electrical resistance

oil *noun* **1** viscous liquid, insoluble in water and usually flammable **2** same as **petroleum 3** petroleum derivative, used as a fuel or lubricant **4 oils** oil-based paints used in art ▷ *verb* **5** to lubricate (a machine) with oil

oilfield *noun* area containing oil reserves

oil painting *noun* picture painted using oil-based paints

oil rig *noun* platform constructed for drilling oil wells

oilskin *noun* (garment made from) waterproof material

oily oilier oiliest *adjective* **1** covered with or containing oil **2** like oil

ointment *noun* greasy substance used for healing skin or as a cosmetic

OK or **okay** *informal interjection* **1** expression of approval ▷ *noun* **2** approval

okra *noun* tropical plant with edible green pods

old *adjective* **1** having lived or existed for a long time **2** of a specified age: *two years old* **3** former

olden *adjective* old: *in the olden days*

Old English *noun* form of the English language that existed from the fifth century AD until about 1100; also called **Anglo-Saxon**

old-fashioned *adjective* **1** no longer commonly used or valued **2** favouring or denoting the styles or ideas of a former time

Old Norse *noun* language spoken in Scandinavia and Iceland from about 700 AD to about 1350 AD and from which many English words are derived

Old Testament *noun* part of the Bible recording Hebrew history

oleander *noun* Mediterranean flowering evergreen shrub

olive *noun* **1** small green or black fruit used as food or pressed for its oil **2** tree on which this fruit grows ▷ *adjective* **3** greyish-green

-ology *suffix* used to form words that refer to the study of something: *biology; geology*

Olympic Games *plural noun* four-yearly international sports competition

ombudsman *noun* official who investigates complaints against government organizations

omelette *noun* dish of eggs beaten and fried

omen *noun* happening or object thought to foretell success or misfortune

ominous *adjective* worrying, seeming to foretell misfortune > **ominously** *adverb*

omission *noun* **1** something that has not been included or done **2** act of missing out or failing to do something

omit omits omitting omitted *verb* **1** to leave out **2** to neglect (to do something)

omnibus omnibuses *noun* **1** several books or TV or radio programmes made into one **2** *old-fashioned* bus

omnipotent *adjective* having unlimited power > **omnipotence** *noun: the omnipotence of God*

omnivore *noun* animal that eats all kinds of food, including meat and plants > **omnivorous** *adjective*: *Brown bears are omnivorous*

on *preposition* **1** touching or attached to: *lying on the ground; a puppet on a string; on the coast* **2** inside: *on a train* **3** indicating when: *on Mondays* **4** using: *on the phone* **5** about: *a talk on dictionary skills* ▷ *adverb* **6** in operation: *He left the lights on* **7** continuing: *He stayed on after his family left* **8** forwards: *from that day on* ▷ *adjective* **9** operating: *All the lights were on* **10** taking place: *What's on at the cinema?*

once *adverb* **1** on one occasion **2** formerly ▷ *conjunction* **3** as soon as ▷ *noun* **4** one occasion or case **5 at once a** immediately **b** simultaneously

one *adjective, noun* **1** the number 1 ▷ *pronoun* **2** any person; you **3** referring back to something or someone already mentioned or known about: *I'll get one; Which one?* ▷ *adjective* **4** single or lone **5** used emphatically to mean *a* or *an*: *They got one almighty shock* ▷ *noun* **6** single unit

one-off *noun* something that happens or is made only once

onerous *adjective* (of a task) difficult to carry out

oneself *pronoun* reflexive form of **one**

one-sided *adjective* **1** considering only one point of view **2** having all the advantage on one side

one-way *adjective* moving or allowing travel in one direction only

ongoing *adjective* in progress, continuing

onion *noun* strongly flavoured edible bulb

online *adjective* relating to the Internet: *online shopping*

onlooker *noun* person who watches without taking part

only *adjective* 1 alone of its kind ▷ *adverb* 2 exclusively 3 merely 4 no more than 5 **only too** extremely ▷ *conjunction* 6 but

onomatopoeia *noun* use of a word which imitates the sound it represents, such as *hiss* > **onomatopoeic** *adjective*: *'Buzz' is an onomatopoeic word*

onset *noun* beginning

onslaught *noun* violent attack

onto *preposition* 1 to a position on 2 aware of: *She's onto us*

onus onuses *noun formal* responsibility or burden

onward *adjective* 1 directed or moving forward ▷ *adverb* 2 (also **onwards**) ahead, forward

onyx *noun* type of quartz with coloured layers

ooze oozes oozing oozed *verb* 1 to flow slowly ▷ *noun* 2 soft mud at the bottom of a lake or river

opal *noun* iridescent precious stone

opaque *adjective* 1 not able to be seen through, not transparent 2 difficult to understand

open *adjective* 1 not closed 2 not covered 3 unfolded 4 ready for business 5 free from obstruction, accessible 6 frank ▷ *verb* 7 to (cause to) become open 8 to begin ▷ *noun* 9 **in the open a** outdoors **b** not secret

opening *noun* 1 opportunity 2 hole 3 first part ▷ *adjective* 4 first

openly *adverb* without concealment

open-minded *adjective* receptive to new ideas

open-plan *adjective* (of a house or office) having few interior walls

opera *noun* 1 drama in which the text is sung to an orchestral accompaniment 2 plural of **opus** > **operatic** *adjective*: *an amateur operatic society*

operate operates operating operated *verb* 1 to work 2 to control the working of (a machine) 3 to perform a surgical operation (on a person or animal)

operation *noun* 1 method or procedure of working 2 medical procedure in which the body is worked on to repair a damaged part 3 **in operation** working or being used

operational *adjective* 1 in working order 2 occurring while a plan is being carried out

operative *adjective* 1 working ▷ *noun* 2 worker with a special skill

operator *noun* 1 someone who works at a telephone exchange or on a switchboard 2 someone who operates a machine 3 someone who runs a business: *a tour operator*

opinion *noun* personal belief or judgment

opinionated *adjective* having strong opinions

opinion poll see **poll**

opium *noun* addictive narcotic drug made from poppy seeds

opponent *noun* person you are competing, fighting or arguing against in a contest, battle or argument

opportune *adjective formal* happening at a suitable time

opportunism *noun* doing whatever is advantageous without regard for principles > **opportunist** *noun*

opportunity opportunities *noun* 1 favourable time or condition

2 good chance

oppose opposes opposing opposed *verb* **1** to work against **2 be opposed to** to disagree with or disapprove of

opposed *adjective* **1 opposed to** against (something or someone) in speech or action **2** opposite or very different **3 as opposed to** in strong contrast with

opposite *adjective* **1** situated on the other side **2** facing **3** completely different ▷ *noun* **4** person or thing that is opposite ▷ *preposition* **5** facing ▷ *adverb* **6** on the other side

opposition *noun* **1** obstruction or hostility **2** group opposing another **3 the Opposition** political parties not in power

oppressed *adjective* treated cruelly or unfairly > **oppression** *noun*: *political oppression* > **oppress** *verb* > **oppressor** *noun*: *They tried to resist their oppressors by non-violent means*

oppressive *adjective* **1** tyrannical **2** uncomfortable or depressing **3** (of weather) hot and humid > **oppressively** *adverb*

opt *verb* **1** to show preference (for) or choose (to do something) **2 opt out** to choose not to be part (of)

optic *adjective* relating to the eyes or sight

optical *adjective* **1** concerned with vision, light or images **2** relating to the appearance of things: *an optical illusion*

optician *noun* **1** (also **ophthalmic optician**) person qualified to prescribe glasses **2** (also **dispensing optician**) person who supplies and fits glasses

optimal *adjective* best or most favourable

optimism *noun* tendency to take the most hopeful view > **optimist**

noun: *Optimists predict the economy will grow steadily* > **optimistic** *adjective*: *She was in a jovial and optimistic mood* > **optimistically** *adverb*

optimum optima or **optimums** *noun* **1** best possible conditions ▷ *adjective* **2** most favourable

option *noun* **1** choice **2** thing chosen **3** right to buy or sell something at a specified price within a given time

optional *adjective* possible but not compulsory

optometrist *noun* person qualified to prescribe glasses > **optometry** *noun*

opulent *adjective* having or indicating wealth > **opulence** *noun*: *the elegant opulence of the German embassy*

opus opuses or **opera** *noun* artistic creation, especially a musical work

or *conjunction* **1** used to join alternatives: *tea or coffee* **2** used to introduce a warning: *Do as I say or else I'll shoot*

-or *suffix* used to form nouns from verbs: *actor; conductor*

oracle *noun* **1** shrine of an ancient god **2** prophecy, often obscure, revealed at a shrine **3** person believed to make infallible predictions

oral *adjective* **1** spoken **2** (of a drug) to be taken by mouth ▷ *noun* **3** spoken examination > **orally** *adverb*

orange *noun* **1** reddish-yellow citrus fruit ▷ *adjective* **2** reddish-yellow

orang-utan or **orang-utang** *noun* large reddish-brown ape with long arms

orator *noun* skilful public speaker

oratorio oratorios *noun* musical composition for choir and orchestra, usually with a religious theme

oratory oratories noun 1 art of making speeches 2 small private chapel

orbit noun 1 curved path of a planet, satellite or spacecraft around another body 2 sphere of influence ▷ verb 3 to move in an orbit around 4 to put (a satellite or spacecraft) into orbit

orchard noun area where fruit trees are grown

orchestra noun 1 large group of musicians, especially playing a variety of instruments 2 (also **orchestra pit**) area of a theatre in front of the stage, reserved for the musicians > **orchestral** adjective: an orchestral concert

orchestrate orchestrates orchestrating orchestrated verb 1 to arrange (music) for orchestra 2 to organize (something) to produce a particular result > **orchestration** noun: Mahler's imaginative orchestration

orchid noun plant with flowers that have unusual lip-shaped petals

ordain verb to make (someone) a member of the clergy

ordeal noun painful or difficult experience

order noun 1 instruction to be carried out 2 methodical arrangement or sequence 3 established social system 4 condition of a law-abiding society 5 request for goods to be supplied 6 kind, sort 7 religious society of monks or nuns 8 **in order** so that it is possible ▷ verb 9 to command or instruct (to do something) 10 to request (something) to be supplied in return for payment

orderly orderlies adjective 1 well-organized 2 well-behaved ▷ noun 3 male hospital attendant

ordinal number noun number showing a position in a series: first; second. Compare **cardinal number**

ordinarily adverb usually

ordinary adjective 1 usual or normal 2 dull or commonplace

ordination noun act of making someone a member of the clergy

ordnance noun weapons and military supplies

ore noun (rock containing) a mineral which yields metal

oregano noun sweet-smelling herb used in cooking

organ noun 1 part of an animal or plant that has a particular function, such as the heart or lungs 2 musical keyboard instrument in which notes are produced by forcing air through pipes

organic adjective 1 of or produced from animals or plants 2 grown without artificial fertilizers or pesticides 3 Chemistry relating to compounds of carbon > **organically** adverb

organism noun any living animal or plant

organist noun organ player

organization noun 1 group of people working together 2 act of organizing > **organizational** adjective: organizational skills

organize organizes organizing organized; also spelt **organise** verb 1 to plan and arrange (something) 2 to arrange systematically > **organized** adjective: organized resistance > **organizer** noun: She is a good organizer

orgasm noun most intense point of sexual pleasure

orgy orgies noun 1 party involving promiscuous sexual activity 2 unrestrained indulgence: an orgy *of destruction*

orient *verb* **1** to position (yourself) according to your surroundings **2** to position (a map) in relation to the points of the compass

Orient *noun* **the Orient** *literary* eastern and south-eastern Asia

Oriental *adjective* relating to eastern or south-eastern Asia: *Oriental carpets*

orientate orientates orientating orientated *verb* same as **orient**

orientation *noun* **1** activities and aims that a person or organization is interested in **2** position of an object with relation to the points of the compass or other specific directions

oriented or **orientated** *adjective* interested (in) or directed (toward something): *Medical care needs to be oriented towards prevention* > **-oriented** or **-orientated** *suffix*: *career-oriented women*

orienteering *noun* sport in which competitors hike over a course using a compass and map

origin *noun* **1** point from which something develops **2** ancestry

original *adjective* **1** first or earliest **2** new, not copied or based on something else **3** able to think up new ideas ▷ *noun* **4** first version, from which others are copied > **originality** *noun*: *ideas of startling originality* > **originally** *adverb*

originate originates originating originated *verb* to come or bring into existence > **originator** *noun*: *the originator of the theory of relativity*

ornament *noun* **1** decorative object ▷ *verb* **2** to decorate

ornamental *adjective* designed to be attractive rather than useful

ornamentation *noun* decoration

on a building, a piece of furniture or a work of art

ornate *adjective* highly decorated, elaborate

ornithology *noun* study of birds > **ornithological** *adjective*: *an ornithological society* > **ornithologist** *noun*: *a keen amateur ornithologist*

orphan *noun* **1** child whose parents are dead ▷ *verb* **2** to cause (someone) to become an orphan

orphanage *noun* children's home for orphans

orphaned *adjective* having no living parents

orthodox *adjective* conforming to established views > **orthodoxy** *noun*: *He rebelled against religious orthodoxy*

Orthodox Church *noun* dominant Christian Church in Eastern Europe

osmosis *noun* **1** movement of a liquid through a membrane from a lower to a higher concentration **2** process of subtle influence

osprey ospreys *noun* large fish-eating bird of prey

ostensible *adjective* apparent, seeming > **ostensibly** *adverb* seemingly

ostentatious *adjective* **1** intended to impress people, for example by looking expensive **2** flaunting your wealth or making a show of your importance > **ostentation** *noun*: *a notable lack of ostentation* > **ostentatiously** *adverb*

osteopathy *noun* medical treatment involving manipulation of the joints > **osteopath** *noun*: *Perhaps you should see an osteopath*

ostinato ostinatos *noun* Music musical phrase that is continuously repeated throughout a piece

ostracize ostracizes ostracizing

ostracized; also spelt **ostracise**
verb to exclude (a person) from a
group: *She was ostracized for being fat*

ostrich ostriches *noun* large
African bird that runs fast but
cannot fly

other *adjective* **1** different from
the ones specified or understood
2 additional **3 the other day** a
few days ago ▷ *noun* **4** other person
or thing

otherwise *conjunction* **1** or else,
if not ▷ *adverb* **2** differently, in
another way

otter *noun* small brown freshwater
mammal that eats fish

ouch *interjection* exclamation of
sudden pain

ought *verb used to express:*
1 obligation: *You ought to pay*
2 advisability: *You ought to diet*
3 probability: *You ought to know
by then*

ounce *noun* unit of weight equal
to one sixteenth of a pound (28.4
grams)

our *adjective* belonging to us

ours *pronoun* thing(s) belonging
to us

ourselves *pronoun* emphatic and
reflexive form of **we** or **us**

oust *verb* to force (someone) out of
a position

out *adverb* **1** towards the outside
of a place: *Two dogs rushed out
of the house* **2** not at home **3** in
the open air: *They are playing out
in bright sunshine* **4** no longer
shining or burning: *The lights
went out* ▷ *adjective* **5** on strike:
*1000 construction workers are out
in sympathy* **6** unacceptable or
unfashionable: *Miniskirts are out*
7 incorrect: *Logan's timing was out in
the first two rounds*

out- *prefix meaning* **1** surpassing:

outlive; outdistance **2** on the outside
or away from the centre: *outpost*

out-and-out *adjective* entire or
complete: *an out-and-out lie*

outback *noun* remote bush country
of Australia

outboard motor *noun* engine
externally attached to the stern
of a boat

outbreak *noun* sudden occurrence
(of something unpleasant)

outburst *noun* sudden expression
of emotion

outcast *noun* person rejected by a
particular group

outclassed *adjective* surpassed
in quality

outcome *noun* result

outcrop *noun* part of a rock
formation that sticks out of the
earth

outcry outcries *noun* vehement or
widespread protest

outdated *adjective* no longer in
fashion

**outdo outdoes outdoing outdid
outdone** *verb* to be more successful
or better than (someone or
something) in performance

outdoor *adjective* happening or
used outside

outdoors *adverb* **1** in(to) the open
air ▷ *noun* **2** the open air

outer *adjective* on the outside

outer space *noun* space beyond the
earth's atmosphere

outfit *noun* **1** matching set of clothes
2 *informal* group of people working
together

outgoing *adjective* **1** leaving
2 sociable **3 outgoings** expenses

**outgrow outgrows outgrowing
outgrew outgrown** *verb* to
become too large or too old for

outhouse *noun* building near a
main building

outing *noun* leisure trip

outlandish *adjective* extremely unconventional

outlaw *verb* **1** to make (something) illegal ▷ *noun* **2** *History* criminal deprived of legal protection

outlay outlays *noun* expenditure

outlet *noun* **1** means of expressing emotion **2** market for a product **3** place where a product is sold **4** opening or way out

outline outlines outlining outlined *noun* **1** short general explanation **2** line defining the shape of something ▷ *verb* **3** to give the main features or general idea of (something) **4** to show the general shape of an object but not its details

outlive outlives outliving outlived *verb* to live longer than someone

outlook *noun* **1** attitude **2** probable outcome

outlying *adjective* distant from the main area

outmoded *adjective* no longer fashionable or accepted

outnumber *verb* to exceed in number

out of *preposition* **1** because of: *She went along out of curiosity* **2** from (a material or source): *old instruments made out of wood* **3** no longer in a specified state or condition: *out of work* **4** at or to a point outside: *The train pulled out of the station* **5** away from, not in: *out of focus*

out-of-date *adjective* old-fashioned

out of doors *adverb* outside

outpatient *noun* patient who does not stay in hospital overnight

outpost *noun* outlying settlement

output ouputs outputting outputted or **output** *noun* **1** amount produced **2** power, voltage or current delivered by an electrical circuit **3** *Computers* data produced ▷ *verb* **4** *Computers* to produce (data) at the end of a process

outrage outrages outraging outraged *noun* **1** great moral indignation **2** gross violation of morality ▷ *verb* **3** to cause deep indignation, anger or resentment in (someone)

outrageous *adjective* **1** shocking **2** offensive > **outrageously** *adverb*

outright *adjective, adverb* **1** absolute(ly) **2** open(ly) and direct(ly)

outset *noun* beginning

outshine outshines outshining outshone *verb* to surpass (someone) in excellence

outside *preposition, adjective, adverb* **1** indicating movement to or position on the exterior ▷ *adjective* **2** unlikely: *an outside chance* **3** coming from outside ▷ *noun* **4** external area or surface

outsider *noun* **1** person outside a specific group **2** contestant thought unlikely to win

outsize or **outsized** *adjective* larger than normal

outskirts *plural noun* outer areas, especially of a town

outspoken *adjective* **1** tending to say what you think, regardless of how others may react **2** said openly

outstanding *adjective* **1** excellent **2** still to be dealt with or paid

outstretched *adjective* extended or stretched out as far as possible

outstrip outstrips outstripping outstripped *verb* **1** to surpass (someone) in a particular activity **2** to go faster than (someone)

outward *adjective* **1** apparent ▷ *adverb* **2** same as **outwards**

> **outwardly** *adverb*

outwards *adverb* away from a place or towards the outside: *The door opened outwards*

outweigh *verb* to be more important, significant or influential than

outwit outwits outwitting outwitted *verb* to get the better of (someone) by cunning

ova *noun* plural of **ovum**

oval *adjective* **1** egg-shaped ▷ *noun* **2** anything that is oval in shape

ovary ovaries *noun* female egg-producing organ

ovation *noun* enthusiastic round of applause

oven *noun* heated compartment or container for cooking or for drying or firing ceramics

over *preposition, adverb* **1** indicating position on the top of, movement to the other side of, amount greater than, etc: *a room over the garage; climbing over the fence; over fifty pounds* ▷ *adjective* **2** finished ▷ *noun* **3** *Cricket* series of six balls bowled from one end

over- *prefix meaning* **1** too much: *overeat* **2** above: *overlord* **3** on top: *overshoe*

overall *adjective, adverb* **1** in total ▷ *noun* **2 overalls** protective garment consisting of trousers with a jacket or bib and braces attached

overawe overawes overawing overawed *verb* to fill (someone) with respect or fear > **overawed** *adjective*: *He had been overawed to meet the Prime Minister*

overbearing *adjective* unpleasantly forceful: *a difficult relationship with his overbearing father*

overboard *adverb* **1** from a boat into the water **2 go overboard** to go to extremes, especially in enthusiasm

overcast *adjective* (of the sky) covered by clouds

overcoat *noun* heavy coat

overcome overcomes overcoming overcame overcome *verb* **1** to gain control over after an effort **2** (of an emotion) to affect strongly

overcrowded *adjective* containing more people or things than is desirable

overdo overdoes overdoing overdid overdone *verb* **1** to do to excess **2** to exaggerate (something)

overdose overdoses overdosing overdosed *noun* **1** excessive dose of a drug ▷ *verb* **2** to take more of a drug than is safe, either accidentally or deliberately

overdraft *noun* **1** overdrawing **2** amount overdrawn

overdrawn *adjective* **1** having taken out more money than you had in your bank account **2** (of an account) in debit

overdrive *noun* extra, higher gear in a vehicle, which is used at high speeds to reduce engine wear and save petrol

overdue *adjective* still due after the time allowed

overestimate overestimates overestimating overestimated *verb* to believe something or someone to be bigger, more important, or better than is the case

overflow overflows overflowing overflowed or **overflown** *verb* **1** to flow over (a brim) **2** to be filled beyond capacity so as to spill over ▷ *noun* **3** outlet that enables surplus liquid to be drained off

overgrown *adjective* thickly covered with plants and weeds

overhang overhangs
overhanging overhung *verb*
1 to project or hang over beyond
(something) ▷ *noun* **2** overhanging
part or object

overhaul *verb* **1** to examine (a
system or an idea) carefully
for faults **2** to make repairs or
adjustments to (a vehicle or
machine)

overhead *adverb, adjective* above
your head

overheads *plural noun* general cost
of maintaining a business

overhear overhears
overhearing overheard *verb*
to hear (a speaker or remark)
unintentionally or without the
speaker's knowledge

overjoyed *adjective* extremely
pleased

overlaid *adjective*: **overlaid with**
covered with

overland *adjective, adverb* by land

overlander *noun Aust history* man
who drove cattle or sheep long
distances through the outback

overlap overlaps overlapping
overlapped *verb* **1** to share part of
the same space or period of time
(as) ▷ *noun* **2** area overlapping

overleaf *adverb* on the back of the
current page

overload *verb* to put too large a load
on or in (something)

overlook *verb* **1** to fail to notice **2** to
ignore (misbehaviour or a fault)

overly *adverb* excessively

overnight *adjective, adverb*
1 (taking place) during one night
2 (happening) very quickly

overpower *verb* **1** to subdue or
overcome (someone) **2** to have
a such a strong effect on as to
make helpless or ineffective
> **overpowering** *adjective*:

overpowering anger

overrate overrates overrating
overrated *verb* to have too high an
opinion of > **overrated** *adjective*:
The food here is overrated

overreact *verb* to react more
strongly or forcefully than is
necessary

overriding *adjective* more
important than anything else

overrule overrules overruling
overruled *verb* to reverse the
decision of (a person with less
power)

overrun overruns overrunning
overran overrun *verb* **1** to
conquer (territory) rapidly by
force of number **2** to spread over (a
place) rapidly **3** to extend beyond
a set limit

overseas *adverb, adjective* to, of or
from a distant country

oversee oversees overseeing
oversaw overseen *verb* to watch
over from a position of authority
> **overseer** *noun*: *I was promoted
to overseer*

overshadow *verb* to reduce the
significance of (a person or thing)
by comparison

oversight *noun* mistake caused by
not noticing something

overspill *noun Brit* rehousing of
people from crowded cities in
smaller towns

overstate overstates
overstating overstated *verb* to
state (something) too strongly

overstep oversteps
overstepping overstepped *verb*
overstep the mark to go too far
and behave in an unacceptable way

overt *adjective* open, not hidden
> **overtly** *adverb*

overtake overtakes overtaking
overtook overtaken *verb* to move

past (a vehicle or person) travelling in the same direction

overthrow **overthrows**
overthrowing **overthrew**
overthrown *verb* to defeat and replace (a ruler or government) by force

overtime *noun, adverb* (paid work done) in addition to your normal working hours

overtones *plural noun* additional meaning: *the political overtones of the trial*

overture *noun* 1 *Music* orchestral introduction 2 **overtures** opening moves in a new relationship

overturn *verb* 1 to turn upside down 2 to overrule (a legal decision)

overview *noun* general understanding or description of a situation

overweight *adjective* weighing more than is healthy

overwhelm *verb* 1 to overpower the thoughts, emotions or senses of (someone) 2 to overcome (people) with irresistible force
> **overwhelming** *adjective*: *an overwhelming majority*
> **overwhelmingly** *adverb*

overwork *verb* to work too hard or too long

overwrought *adjective* nervous and agitated

ovulate **ovulates** **ovulating**
ovulated *verb* to produce or release an egg cell from an ovary

ovum **ova** *noun* unfertilized egg cell

owe **owes** **owing** **owed** *verb* 1 to be obliged to pay (a sum of money) to (a person) 2 to feel an obligation to do or give

owl *noun* night bird of prey

own *adjective* 1 used to emphasize possession: *my own idea* ▷ *pronoun*

2 the one or ones belonging to a particular person: *I had one of my own* 3 **on your own a** alone **b** without help ▷ *verb* 4 to have (something) as your possession

owner *noun* person to whom something belongs

ownership *noun* state or fact of being an owner

ox **oxen** *noun* castrated bull

oxide *noun* compound of oxygen and one other element

oxidize **oxidizes** **oxidizing**
oxidized; also spelt **oxidise**
verb to combine chemically with oxygen, as in burning or rusting
> **oxidation** *noun*: *the oxidation of metals*

oxygen *noun* *Chemistry* gaseous element essential to life and combustion

oxymoron *noun* figure of speech that combines two apparently contradictory ideas: *cruel kindness*

oyster *noun* edible shellfish

oz. *abbreviation* ounce

ozone *noun* strong-smelling form of oxygen

ozone layer *noun* layer of ozone in the upper atmosphere that filters out ultraviolet radiation

p *abbreviation* **1** *Brit, Aust, NZ* penny **2** *Brit* pence

p. pp. *abbreviation* page

pa pa or **pas** *noun* Maori village or settlement

pace paces pacing paced *noun* **1** single step in walking **2** length of a step **3** rate of progress ▷ *verb* **4** to walk up and down, especially in anxiety **5 pace out** to cross or measure with steps

pacemaker *noun* electronic device surgically implanted in a person with heart disease to regulate the heartbeat

pachyderm *noun* thick-skinned animal such as an elephant

Pacific *noun* ocean separating North and South America from Asia and Australia

pacifist *noun* person who refuses on principle to take part in war > **pacifism** *noun*

pacify pacifies pacifying pacified *verb* to soothe or calm

pack *verb* **1** to put (clothes etc) together in a suitcase or bag **2** to put (goods) into containers or parcels **3** to fill with people or things ▷ *noun* **4** bag carried on a person's or animal's back **5** *Chiefly US* same as **packet 6** set of playing cards **7** group of dogs or wolves that hunt together > **pack in** *verb informal* to stop doing (something) > **pack up** *verb* **1** to put (your things) in a bag because you are leaving **2** (of machine) to stop working

package packages packaging packaged *noun* **1** small parcel **2** (also **package deal**) deal in which separate items are presented together as a unit ▷ *verb* **3** to put (something) into a package

packaging *noun* container or wrapping in which an item is sold or sent

packed *adjective* very full

packet *noun* **1** small container (and contents) **2** small parcel **3** *informal* large sum of money

pact *noun* formal agreement

pad pads padding padded *noun* **1** piece of soft material used for protection, support, absorption of liquid, etc **2** number of sheets of paper fastened at the edge **3** fleshy underpart of an animal's paw **4** place for launching rockets **5** *informal* home ▷ *verb* **6** to protect or fill (something) with soft material **7** to walk with soft steps

padding *noun* **1** soft material used to pad something **2** unnecessary words put into a speech or written work to make it longer

paddle paddles paddling paddled *noun* **1** short oar with a broad blade at one or each end ▷ *verb* **2** to move (a canoe etc) with a paddle **3** to walk barefoot in shallow water

paddock *noun* small field or enclosure for horses

paddy paddies *noun* **1** *Brit informal*

fit of temper **2** same as **paddy field**

paddy field or **paddy** *noun* field where rice is grown

padlock *noun* **1** detachable lock with a hinged hoop fastened over a ring on the object to be secured ▷ *verb* **2** to fasten (something) with a padlock

padre *noun* chaplain to the armed forces

paediatrician *noun* doctor who specializes in treating children

paediatrics *noun* branch of medicine concerned with diseases of children > **paediatric** *adjective*

paedophile *noun* person who is sexually attracted to children

pagan *adjective* **1** not belonging to one of the world's main religions ▷ *noun* **2** someone who believes in a pagan religion > **paganism** *noun*

page pages paging paged *noun* **1** (one side of) a sheet of paper forming a book etc **2** screenful of information from a website or teletext service **3** (also **pageboy**) small boy who attends a bride at her wedding **4** *History* boy in training for knighthood ▷ *verb* **5** to summon (someone) by bleeper or loudspeaker, in order to pass on a message

pageant *noun* parade or display of people in costume, usually illustrating a scene from history

pagoda *noun* pyramid-shaped Asian temple or tower

paid *verb* **1** past of **pay 2 put paid to** *informal* to end or destroy

pail *noun* (contents of) a bucket

pain *noun* **1** physical or mental suffering **2 pains** trouble or effort **3 on pain of** subject to the penalty of

painful *adjective* causing emotional or physical pain > **painfully** *adverb*

painkiller *noun* drug that relieves pain

painless *adjective* not causing emotional or physical pain: *a painless death* > **painlessly** *adverb*

painstaking *adjective* extremely thorough and careful

paint *noun* **1** coloured substance, spread on a surface with a brush or roller ▷ *verb* **2** to colour or coat with paint **3** to use paint to make a picture of

painter *noun* **1** artist who paints pictures **2** person who paints surfaces of building as a trade **3** rope at the front of a boat, for tying it up

painting *noun* **1** picture produced by using paint **2** art of producing pictures by applying paints to paper or canvas

pair *noun* **1** set of two things matched for use together ▷ *verb* **2** to group or be grouped in twos

paisley pattern *noun* pattern of small curving shapes, used in fabric

Pakeha Pakeha or **Pakehas** *noun* NZ New Zealander of European rather than Maori descent

Pakistani Pakistanis *adjective* **1** belonging or relating to Pakistan ▷ *noun* **2** someone from Pakistan

pal *noun informal* friend

palace *noun* **1** residence of a king, bishop, etc **2** large grand building

Palagi Palagi or **Palagis** *noun* Samoan name for a **Pakeha**

palatable *adjective* pleasant to taste

palate *noun* **1** roof of the mouth **2** sense of taste

palaver *noun* time-wasting fuss

pale paler palest; pales paling paled *adjective* **1** light, whitish **2** whitish in the face, especially through illness or shock ▷ *noun*

3 beyond the pale outside the limits of social acceptability ▷ *verb* **4** to become pale or paler

Palestinian *adjective* **1** belonging or relating to the region formerly called Palestine or its people ▷ *noun* **2** Arab from this region

palette *noun* artist's flat board for mixing colours on

pall *noun* **1** cloth spread over a coffin **2** dark cloud (of smoke) **3** depressing oppressive atmosphere ▷ *verb* **4** to become boring

pallet *noun* **1** portable platform for storing and moving goods **2** straw-filled mattress or bed

palm *noun* **1** inner surface of the hand **2** tropical tree with long pointed leaves growing out of the top of a straight trunk ▷ *verb* **3 palm off** to get rid of (an unwanted thing or person), especially by deceit

Palm Sunday *noun* Sunday before Easter

palmtop *adjective* **1** (of a computer) small enough to be held in the hand ▷ *noun* **2** computer small enough to be held in the hand

palpable *adjective* **1** obvious: *a palpable hit* **2** so intense as to seem capable of being touched: *The tension was almost palpable* **> palpably** *adverb*

paltry paltrier paltriest *adjective* (of an amount) very small

pamper *verb* to treat (someone) with great indulgence, spoil

pamphlet *noun* thin paper-covered booklet

pan pans panning panned *noun* **1** wide long-handled metal container used in cooking **2** bowl of a toilet ▷ *verb* **3** to sift gravel from (a river) in a pan to search for gold

4 *informal* to criticize harshly **5** (of a film camera) to be moved slowly so as to cover a whole scene or follow a moving object **> pan out** *verb* to work out

pan- *prefix indicating* all: *pan-American*

panacea *noun* remedy for all diseases or problems

panache *noun* confident elegant style

pancake *noun* thin flat circle of fried batter

pancreas *noun* large gland behind the stomach that produces insulin and helps digestion

panda *noun* large black-and-white bearlike mammal from China

panda car *noun* Brit police patrol car

pandemonium *noun* wild confusion, uproar

pander *verb* **pander to** to indulge (a person or his or her desires)

pane *noun* sheet of glass in a window or door

panel panels panelling panelled *noun* **1** flat distinct section of a larger surface, for example in a door **2** group of people as a team in a quiz etc **3** list of jurors, doctors, etc **4** board or surface containing switches and controls to operate equipment ▷ *verb* **5** to cover or decorate with panels **> panelled** *adjective*

panelling *noun* panels collectively, especially on a wall

pang *noun* sudden sharp feeling of pain or sadness

panic panics panicking panicked *noun* **1** sudden overwhelming fear, often affecting a whole group of people ▷ *verb* **2** to feel or cause to feel panic

panorama *noun* wide unbroken view of a scene **> panoramic**

adjective: *panoramic views*

pansy pansies *noun* small garden flower with velvety purple, yellow or white petals

pant *verb* to breathe quickly and noisily during or after exertion

panther *noun* leopard, especially a black one

panties *plural noun* women's underpants; pants

pantomime *noun* play based on a fairy tale, performed at Christmas time

pantry pantries *noun* small room or cupboard for storing food

pants *plural noun* **1** undergarment for the lower part of the body **2** *US, Canadian, Aust, NZ* trousers

papaya or **pawpaw** *noun* large sweet tropical fruit

paper *noun* **1** material made in sheets from wood pulp or other fibres **2** printed sheet of this **3** newspaper **4** set of examination questions **5** article or essay **6 papers** personal documents ▷ *verb* **7** to cover (walls) with wallpaper

paperback *noun* book with covers made of flexible card

paperweight *noun* heavy decorative object placed on top of loose papers

paperwork *noun* clerical work, such as writing reports and letters

papier-mâché *noun* material made from paper mixed with paste and moulded when moist

paprika *noun* mild powdered seasoning made from red peppers

par *noun* **1** usual or average condition: *feeling under par* **2** *Golf* expected standard score **3** face value of stocks and shares **4 on a par with** equal to

parable *noun* story that illustrates a religious teaching

parachute parachutes parachuting parachuted *noun* **1** large fabric canopy that slows the descent of a person or object from an aircraft ▷ *verb* **2** to land or drop by parachute > **parachutist** *noun*

parade parades parading paraded *noun* **1** procession or march **2** street or promenade ▷ *verb* **3** to display or flaunt **4** to march in procession

paradise *noun* **1** heaven **2** place or situation that is near-perfect

paradox paradoxes *noun* statement that seems self-contradictory but may be true > **paradoxical** *adjective*

paraffin *noun* *Brit, S Afr* liquid mixture distilled from petroleum and used as a fuel or solvent

paragon *noun* model of perfection

paragraph *noun* section of a piece of writing starting on a new line

parallel parallels paralleling or **parallelling paralleled** or **parallelled** *adjective* **1** separated by an equal distance at every point **2** exactly corresponding ▷ *noun* **3** line separated from another by an equal distance at every point **4** thing with similar features to another **5** line of latitude ▷ *verb* **6** to correspond to

parallelogram *noun* *Maths* four-sided geometric figure with opposite sides parallel

paralyse paralyses paralysing paralysed *verb* **1** to affect with paralysis **2** to make temporarily unable to move or take action

paralysis *noun* inability to move or feel, because of damage to the nervous system

paramedic *noun* person working in support of the medical profession

parameter *noun* limiting factor or boundary

paramilitary *adjective* organized on military lines

paramount *adjective* of the greatest importance

paranoia *noun* 1 mental illness causing delusions of grandeur or persecution 2 *informal* intense fear or suspicion

paranoid *adjective* having undue suspicion or fear of persecution

parapet *noun* low wall or railing along the edge of a balcony or roof

paraphernalia *noun* personal belongings or bits of equipment

paraphrase paraphrases paraphrasing paraphrased *verb* to put (a statement or text) into other words

parasite *noun* 1 animal or plant living in or on another 2 person who lives at the expense of others
> **parasitic** *adjective*

parasol *noun* umbrella-like sunshade

paratroops or **paratroopers** *plural noun* soldiers trained to be dropped by parachute into a battle area

parcel parcels parcelling parcelled *noun* 1 something wrapped up; a package ▷ *verb* 2 **parcel up** to wrap up 3 **parcel out** to divide into parts

parched *adjective* 1 very hot and dry 2 *informal* thirsty

parchment *noun* thick smooth writing material made from animal skin

pardon pardons pardoning pardoned *verb* 1 to forgive or excuse ▷ *noun* 2 forgiveness 3 official release from punishment for a crime

pare pares paring pared *verb*

1 to cut off the skin or top layer of
2 **pare down** to reduce in size or amount

parent *noun* father or mother
> **parental** *adjective*: *parental duties*

parentage *noun* ancestry or family

parenthesis parentheses *noun*
1 word or sentence inserted into a passage, marked off by brackets or dashes 2 **parentheses** round brackets, ( )

parish *noun* area that has its own church and a priest or pastor

parishioner *noun* inhabitant of a parish

parity *noun formal* equality or equivalence

park *noun* 1 area of open land for recreational use by the public 2 area containing a number of related enterprises: *a business park* 3 *Brit* area of private land around a large country house ▷ *verb* 4 to stop and leave (a vehicle) temporarily
> **parked** *adjective*: *parked cars*
> **parking** *noun*: *free parking*

parliament *noun* law-making assembly of a country
> **parliamentary** *adjective*: *parliamentary debates*

parlour *noun* old-fashioned living room for receiving visitors

parlous *adjective* old-fashioned 1 dire 2 dangerously bad

parochial *adjective* 1 narrow in outlook 2 of a parish

parody parodies parodying parodied *noun* 1 exaggerated and amusing imitation of someone else's style ▷ *verb* 2 to make a parody of

parole paroles paroling paroled *noun* 1 early freeing of a prisoner on condition that he or she behaves well 2 **on parole** (of a prisoner) released on condition that he or she behaves well ▷ *verb* **3** to place (a person) on parole

parrot *noun* **1** tropical bird with a short hooked beak and an ability to imitate human speech ▷ *verb* **2** to repeat without thinking

parry parries parrying parried *verb* **1** to ward off (an attack) **2** to avoid (an awkward question) in a clever way

parsley *noun* herb used for seasoning and decorating food

parsnip *noun* long tapering cream-coloured root vegetable

parson *noun* **1** Anglican parish priest **2** any member of the clergy

part *noun* **1** one of the pieces that make up a whole **2** one of several equal divisions **3** actor's role **4** component of a vehicle or machine **5 parts** region or area ▷ *verb* **6** to divide or separate from one another **7** (of people) to leave each other > **part with** *verb* to give away or hand over

partake partaking partook partaken *verb* **1 partake of** to take (food or drink) **2 partake in** to take part in

partial *adjective* **1** not complete **2** prejudiced **3 partial to** having a liking for > **partially** *adverb*

participate participates participating participated *verb* to become actively involved in > **participant** *noun*: *participants in the course* > **participation** *noun*

participle *noun* form of a verb used in compound tenses, *eg written* or *writing*

particle *noun* **1** extremely small piece or amount **2** *Physics* minute piece of matter, such as a proton or electron

particular *adjective* **1** relating to one person or thing

2 exceptional or special **3** very exact **4** difficult to please, fastidious ▷ *noun* **5 particulars** items of information; details > **particularly** *adverb*

parting *noun* **1** occasion when one person leaves another **2** line of scalp between sections of hair combed in opposite directions **3** dividing or separating

partisan *noun* **1** strong supporter of a party or group **2** member of a resistance movement ▷ *adjective* **3** prejudiced or one-sided

partition *noun* **1** screen or thin wall that divides a room **2** division of a country into independent parts ▷ *verb* **3** to divide (something) into separate parts

partly *adverb* not completely

partner *noun* **1** either member of a couple in a relationship or activity **2** member of a business partnership ▷ *verb* **3** to be the partner of

partnership *noun* joint business venture between two or more people

part of speech parts of speech *noun* particular grammatical class of words, such as noun or verb

partook the past tense of **partake**

partridge *noun* game bird of the grouse family

part-time *adjective* occupying or working less than the full working week

party parties *noun* **1** social gathering for pleasure **2** group of people travelling or working together **3** group of people with a common political aim **4** *formal* person or people forming one side in a lawsuit or dispute

pass passes passing passed *verb* **1** to go by, past or through **2** to be successful in (a test or examination) **3** to spend (time) or (of time) to go by **4** to give or hand **5** to be inherited by **6** Sport to hit, kick or throw (the ball) to another player **7** (of a law-making body) to agree to (a law) **8** to exceed ▷ noun **9** successful result in a test or examination **10** permit or licence **11** **make a pass at** informal to make sexual advances to ▷ **pass away** verb to die ▷ **pass out** verb informal to faint

passable adjective **1** (just) acceptable **2** (of a road) capable of being travelled along

passage noun **1** channel or opening providing a way through **2** hall or corridor **3** section of a book etc **4** journey by sea **5** right or freedom to pass

passé adjective out-of-date

passenger noun **1** person travelling in a vehicle driven by someone else **2** member of a team who does not pull his or her weight

passer-by **passers-by** noun person who is walking past something

passing adjective **1** brief or transitory **2** cursory or casual

passion noun **1** intense sexual love **2** any strong emotion **3** great enthusiasm **4** **Passion** Christianity the suffering of Christ

passionate adjective expressing very strong feelings about something ▷ **passionately** adverb

passion fruit noun edible fruit of the **passionflower**, a tropical American plant

passive adjective **1** not playing an active part **2** submissive and receptive to outside forces **3** Grammar (of a verb) in a form indicating that the subject receives the action, eg was jeered in He was jeered by the crowd ▷ **passively**

adverb ▷ **passivity** noun: the passivity of the public under military occupation

Passover noun Jewish festival commemorating the sparing of the Jews in Egypt

passport noun official document of nationality granting permission to travel abroad

password noun **1** secret word or phrase that ensures admission **2** a sequence of characters that must be keyed in order to get access to some computers or computer files

past adjective **1** of the time before the present **2** ended, gone by **3** Grammar (of a verb tense) indicating that the action specified took place earlier ▷ noun **4** period of time before the present **5** person's earlier life, especially a disreputable period **6** Grammar past tense ▷ adverb **7** by, along ▷ preposition **8** beyond **9** **past it** informal unable to do the things you could do when younger

pasta noun type of food, such as spaghetti, that is made in different shapes from flour and water

paste **pastes** **pasting** **pasted** noun **1** moist soft mixture, such as toothpaste **2** adhesive, especially for paper **3** shiny glass used to make imitation jewellery ▷ verb **4** to fasten with paste **5** Computers to insert

pastel noun **1** coloured chalk crayon for drawing **2** picture drawn in pastels **3** pale delicate colour ▷ adjective **4** pale and delicate in colour

pasteurized adjective (of food or drinks) treated with a special heating process to kill bacteria

pastime noun activity that makes time pass pleasantly

pastor noun member of the clergy in

charge of a congregation

pastoral *adjective* **1** of or depicting country life **2** of or relating to the duties of the clergy and the needs of their flock

past participle *noun Grammar* the form of a verb, usually ending in *ed* or *en*, that is used to make some past tenses and the passive. For example *killed* in *She has killed the goldfish* and *broken* in *A window had been broken* are past participles

pastry pastries *noun* **1** baking dough made of flour, fat and water **2** cake or pie

past tense *noun Grammar* tense of a verb that is used mainly to refer to things that happened or existed before the time of writing or speaking

pasture *noun* grassy land for farm animals to graze on

pasty¹ pastier pastiest *adjective* (of a complexion) pale and unhealthy

pasty² pasties *noun* round of pastry folded over a savoury filling

pat pats patting patted *verb* **1** to tap lightly ▷ *noun* **2** gentle tap or stroke **3** small shaped mass of butter etc ▷ *adjective* **4** quick, ready or glib **5** **off pat** learned thoroughly

patch patches patching patched *noun* **1** piece of material sewn on a garment **2** small contrasting section **3** plot of ground **4** protective pad for the eye ▷ *verb* **5** to mend with a patch > **patch up** *verb* **1** to repair clumsily **2** to make up (a quarrel)

patchwork *noun* needlework made of pieces of different materials sewn together

patchy patchier patchiest *adjective* of uneven quality or intensity

pâté *noun* spread of finely minced liver etc

patent *noun* **1** document giving the exclusive right to make or sell an invention ▷ *adjective* **2** obvious: *It's patent nonsense* ▷ *verb* **3** to obtain a patent for (an invention) > **patently** *adverb*

paternal *adjective* **1** fatherly **2** related through your father

paternity *noun* fact or state of being a father

path *noun* **1** surfaced walk or track **2** course of action

pathetic *adjective* **1** causing feelings of pity or sadness **2** distressingly inadequate > **pathetically** *adverb*

pathname *noun Computers* file name listing the sequence of directories leading to a particular file or directory

pathological *adjective* **1** of pathology **2** *informal* extreme and uncontrollable > **pathologically** *adverb*

pathology *noun* scientific study of diseases > **pathologist** *noun*: *an experienced pathologist*

pathos *noun* power of arousing pity or sadness

pathway pathways *noun* path

patience *noun* **1** quality of being patient **2** card game for one

patient *adjective* **1** enduring difficulties or delays calmly ▷ *noun* **2** person receiving medical treatment > **patiently** *adverb*

patio patios *noun* paved area adjoining a house

patriarch *noun* **1** male head of a family or tribe **2** highest-ranking bishop in Orthodox Churches

patriarchy patriarchies *noun* society in which men have most of the power > **patriarchal** *adjective*: *a* *patriarchal society*

patrician *formal noun* member of the nobility

patriot *noun* person who loves his or her country and supports its interests > **patriotic** *adjective*: *patriotic songs* > **patriotism** *noun*: *He joined the army out of a sense of patriotism*

patrol patrols patrolling patrolled *noun* **1** regular circuit by a guard **2** person or small group patrolling **3** unit of Scouts or Guides > *verb* **4** to carry out a patrol of (a place)

patron *noun* **1** person who gives financial support to charities, artists, etc **2** regular customer of a shop, pub, etc

patronage *noun* support given by a patron

patronize patronizes patronizing patronized; also spelt **patronise** *verb* **1** to treat in a condescending way **2** to be a patron of > **patronizing** *adjective*

patron saint *noun* saint regarded as the guardian of a country or group

patter *verb* **1** to make repeated soft tapping sounds > *noun* **2** quick succession of taps **3** glib rapid speech

pattern *noun* **1** arrangement of repeated parts or decorative designs **2** regular way that something is done **3** diagram or shape used as a guide to make something

patterned *adjective* decorated with a pattern

paunch paunches *noun* protruding belly

pauper *noun* old-fashioned very poor person

pause pauses pausing paused *verb* **1** to stop for a time > *noun* **2** stop or rest in speech or action

pave paves paving paved *verb* to form (a surface) with stone or brick

pavement *noun* paved path for pedestrians

pavilion *noun* **1** building on a playing field etc **2** building for housing an exhibition etc

paw *noun* **1** animal's foot with claws and pads > *verb* **2** to scrape with the paw or hoof **3** *informal* to touch in a rough or overfamiliar way

pawn *verb* **1** to deposit (an article) as security for money borrowed > *noun* **2** chessman of the lowest value **3** person manipulated by someone else

pawnbroker *noun* lender of money on goods deposited

pawpaw *noun* same as a **papaya**

pay pays paying paid *verb* **1** to give money etc in return for goods or services **2** to settle a debt or obligation **3** to compensate (for) **4** to give **5** to be profitable to > *noun* **6** wages or salary

payable *adjective* due to be paid

payment *noun* **1** act of paying **2** money paid

payroll *noun* list of paid employees of an organization

PC PCs *abbreviation* **1** personal computer **2** (in Britain) Police Constable **3** politically correct

PDA PDAs *abbreviation* personal digital assistant

PDF *abbreviation* Computers portable document format: a format in which documents may be viewed

PE *abbreviation* physical education

pea *noun* **1** climbing plant with seeds growing in pods **2** its seed, eaten as a vegetable

peace *noun* **1** calm, quietness **2** absence of anxiety **3** freedom from war **4** harmony between people

peaceable *adjective* inclined towards peace > **peaceably** *adverb*

peaceful *adjective* quiet and calm > **peacefully** *adverb*

peach peaches *noun* **1** soft juicy fruit with a stone and a downy skin ▷ *adjective* **2** pinkish-orange

peacock *noun* large male bird with a brilliantly coloured fanlike tail

peak *noun* **1** pointed top, especially of a mountain **2** point of greatest development etc **3** projecting piece on the front of a cap ▷ *verb* **4** to form or reach a peak ▷ *adjective* **5** of or at the point of greatest demand

peaked *adjective* having a peak

peal *noun* **1** long loud echoing sound, especially of bells or thunder ▷ *verb* **2** to sound with a peal or peals

peanut *noun* **1** pea-shaped nut that ripens underground **2** **peanuts** *informal* trifling amount of money

pear *noun* sweet juicy fruit with a narrow top and rounded base

pearl *noun* hard round shiny object found inside some oyster shells and used as a jewel

peasant *noun* person working on the land, especially in poorer countries or in the past

peat *noun* decayed vegetable material found in bogs, used as fertilizer or fuel

pebble *noun* small roundish stone

peck *verb* **1** to strike or pick up with the beak **2** *informal* to kiss quickly **3** **peck at** to nibble or eat reluctantly ▷ *noun* **4** pecking movement

peckish *adjective informal* slightly hungry

peculiar *adjective* **1** strange **2** distinct, special **3** belonging exclusively to > **peculiarly** *adverb*

peculiarity peculiarities

noun **1** oddity, eccentricity **2** distinguishing trait

pedal pedals pedalling pedalled *noun* **1** foot-operated lever used to control a vehicle or machine, or to modify the tone of a musical instrument ▷ *verb* **2** to propel (a bicycle) by using its pedals

pedantic *adjective* excessively concerned with details and rules, especially in academic work

peddle peddles peddling peddled *verb* to sell (goods) from door to door

pedestal *noun* base supporting a column, statue, etc

pedestrian *noun* **1** person who walks ▷ *adjective* **2** dull, uninspiring

pedestrian crossing *noun* place marked where pedestrians may cross a road

pediatrician another spelling of **paediatrician**

pediatrics another spelling of **paediatrics**

pedigree *noun* register of ancestors, especially of a purebred animal

peek *verb* **1** to glance quickly or secretly ▷ *noun* **2** quick look at something

peel *verb* **1** to remove the skin or rind of (a vegetable or fruit) **2** (of skin or a surface) to come off in flakes ▷ *noun* **3** rind or skin

peelings *plural noun* strips of skin or rind that have been peeled off

peep *verb* **1** to look slyly or quickly **2** to make a small shrill noise ▷ *noun* **3** peeping look **4** small shrill noise

peer *verb* **1** to look closely and intently ▷ *noun* **2** (*feminine* **peeress**) (in Britain) member of the nobility **3** person of the same status, age, etc

peerage *noun* **Brit 1** whole body of peers **2** rank of a peer

peer group *noun* group of people of

similar age, status, etc

peerless *adjective* so magnificent or perfect that nothing can equal it

peewee *noun* black-and-white Australian bird

peg pegs pegging pegged *noun* **1** pin or clip for joining, fastening, marking, etc **2** hook or knob for hanging things on **3 off the peg** (of clothes) ready-to-wear, not tailor-made ▷ *verb* **4** to fasten with pegs **5** to stabilize (prices)

peggy square *noun NZ* small hand-knitted square

pejorative *adjective* (of words etc) with an insulting or critical meaning

Pekinese *noun* small dog with a short wrinkled muzzle

■ The plural of *Pekinese* is *Pekinese*

pelican *noun* large water bird with a pouch beneath its bill for storing fish

pellet *noun* small ball of something

pelt *verb* **1** to throw (missiles) at **2 pelt along** to run fast or rush **3** to rain heavily ▷ *noun* **4** skin and fur of an animal **5 at full pelt** at top speed

pelvis pelvises *noun* framework of bones at the base of the spine, to which the hips are attached > **pelvic** *adjective*: *the pelvic bone*

pen pens penning penned *noun* **1** instrument for writing in ink **2** small enclosure for domestic animals ▷ *verb* **3** to write or compose **4** to enclose (animals) in a pen **5 penned in** trapped or confined

penal *adjective* of or used in punishment

penalize penalizes penalizing penalized; also spelt **penalise** *verb* **1** to impose a penalty on **2** to handicap or hinder

penalty penalties *noun* **1** punishment for a crime or offence **2** *Sport* handicap or disadvantage imposed for breaking a rule, such as a free shot at goal by the opposition

penance *noun* voluntary self-punishment to make amends for wrongdoing

pence *noun Brit* a plural of **penny**

penchant *noun formal* inclination or liking

pencil pencils pencilling pencilled *noun* **1** thin cylindrical instrument containing graphite, for writing or drawing ▷ *verb* **2** to draw, write or mark with a pencil

pendant *noun* ornament worn on a chain round the neck

pending *formal preposition* **1** while waiting for ▷ *adjective* **2** not yet decided or settled

pendulum *noun* suspended weight swinging to and fro, especially as a regulator for a clock

penetrate penetrates penetrating penetrated *verb* **1** to find or force a way into or through **2** to arrive at the meaning of

penetrating *adjective* **1** (of a sound) loud and unpleasant **2** quick to understand

penetration *noun* **1** act or an instance of penetrating **2** keen insight or perception

pen friend *noun* friend with whom a person corresponds without meeting

penguin *noun* flightless black-and-white sea bird of the southern hemisphere

penicillin *noun* antibiotic drug effective against a wide range of diseases and infections

peninsula *noun* strip of land nearly surrounded by water

penis penises *noun* male organ

used for urinating and having sexual intercourse

penitent *adjective* **1** feeling sorry for having done wrong ▷ *noun* **2** someone who is penitent > **penitence** *noun*

penknife penknives *noun* small knife with blade(s) that fold into the handle

pennant *noun* triangular flag, especially one used by ships as a signal

penniless *adjective* very poor

penny pence pennies *noun* **1** British bronze coin worth one hundredth of a pound **2** former British and Australian coin worth one twelfth of a shilling

pension *noun* regular payment to people above a certain age, retired employees, widows, etc

pensioner *noun* person receiving a pension

pensive *adjective* deeply thoughtful, often with a tinge of sadness

pentagon *noun* geometric figure with five sides

pentathlon *noun* sports contest in which athletes compete in five different events

penthouse *noun* flat built on the roof or top floor of a building

pent-up *adjective* (of an emotion) not released, repressed

penultimate *adjective* second last

peony peonies *noun* garden plant with showy red, pink or white flowers

people peoples peopling peopled *plural noun* **1** persons generally **2** the community **3** your family ▷ *noun* **4** race or nation ▷ *verb* **5** to provide with inhabitants

pep peps pepping pepped *noun* **1** high spirits, energy or enthusiasm ▷ *verb* **2** **pep up** to stimulate or invigorate

pepper *noun* **1** sharp hot condiment made from the fruit of an East Indian climbing plant **2** colourful tropical fruit used as a vegetable ▷ *verb* **3** to season with pepper **4** to sprinkle or dot

peppermint *noun* **1** plant that yields an oil with a strong sharp flavour **2** sweet flavoured with this

per *preposition* **1** for each **2** **as per** in accordance with

perceive perceives perceiving perceived *verb* **1** to become aware of (something) through the senses **2** to understand

per cent *adverb* in each hundred

percentage *noun* proportion or rate per hundred

perceptible *adjective* able to be perceived, recognizable

perception *noun* **1** act of perceiving **2** intuitive judgment

perceptive *adjective* able to realize or notice things that are not obvious > **perceptively** *adverb*

perch perches perching perched *noun* **1** resting place for a bird **2** any of various edible fishes ▷ *verb* **3** to alight, rest or place on or as if on a perch

percolator *noun* coffeepot in which boiling water is forced through a tube and filters down through coffee

percussion *noun* **1** striking of one thing against another **2** percussion instruments collectively

percussion instrument *noun* musical instrument played by being struck, such as drums or cymbals

percussionist *noun* person who plays percussion instruments

perennial *adjective* **1** lasting through many years ▷ *noun* **2** plant lasting more than two years

perfect *adjective* **1** having all the essential elements **2** faultless **3** correct or precise **4** utter or absolute **5** excellent ▷ *noun* **6** *Grammar* (also **perfect tense**) tense formed using *have/has* and the past participle: *I have lost my purse* ▷ *verb* **7** to improve **8** to make fully correct > **perfectly** *adverb*

perfection *noun* state of being perfect

perfectionist *noun* person who demands the highest standards of excellence

perforated *adjective* pierced with holes > **perforation** *noun*: *perforation of the eardrum*

perform *verb* **1** to carry out (an action) **2** to act, sing or present a play before an audience **3** to fulfil (a request etc) > **performer** *noun*: *a world-class performer*

performance *noun* **1** act of performing **2** artistic or dramatic production **3** manner of quality of functioning: *his poor performance*

perfume perfumes perfuming perfumed *noun* **1** liquid cosmetic worn for its pleasant smell **2** fragrance ▷ *verb* **3** to give a pleasant smell to > **perfumed** *adjective*: *a perfumed envelope*

perfunctory *adjective* done only as a matter of routine, superficial

perhaps *adverb* possibly, maybe

peril *noun* great danger > **perilous** *adjective*: *a perilous journey* > **perilously** *adverb*

perimeter *noun* (length of) the outer edge of an area

period *noun* **1** particular portion of time **2** single occurrence of menstruation **3** division of time at school etc when a particular subject is taught **4** *US* full stop ▷ *adjective* **5** (of furniture, dress, a play, etc) dating from or in the style of an earlier time

periodic *adjective* recurring at intervals > **periodically** *adverb*

periodical *noun* **1** magazine issued at regular intervals ▷ *adjective* **2** periodic

periodic table *noun* *Chemistry* chart of the elements, arranged to show their relationship to each other

peripheral *adjective* **1** unimportant, not central **2** on or relating to the edge of an area

periphery peripheries *noun* **1** boundary or edge **2** fringes of a field of activity

perish perishes perishing perished *verb* **1** to be destroyed or die **2** to decay or rot

perishable *adjective* liable to rot quickly

perjure perjures perjuring perjured *verb* **perjure yourself** to lie deliberately while under oath in a court

perjury perjuries *noun* *Law* act or crime of lying while under oath in a court

perk *noun* *informal* incidental benefit gained from a job, such as a company car > **perk up** *verb* to cheer up

perky *adjective* lively or cheerful

perm *noun* **1** long-lasting curly hairstyle produced by treating the hair with chemicals ▷ *verb* **2** to give (hair) a perm

permanent *adjective* lasting forever > **permanence** *noun*: *belief in the permanence of nature* > **permanently** *adverb*

permeable *adjective* *formal* able to be permeated, especially by liquid

permeate permeates permeating permeated *verb* to

penetrate or spread throughout (something)

permissible *adjective* allowed by the rules

permission *noun* authorization to do something

permissive *adjective* tolerant or lenient, especially in sexual matters > **permissiveness** *noun*

permit permits permitting permitted *verb* 1 to give permission, allow ▷ *noun* 2 document giving permission to do something

permutation *noun* any of the ways a number of things can be arranged or combined

pernicious *adjective formal* 1 wicked 2 extremely harmful, deadly

peroxide *noun* 1 hydrogen peroxide used as a hair bleach 2 oxide containing a high proportion of oxygen

perpendicular *adjective* 1 at right angles to a line or surface 2 upright or vertical ▷ *noun* 3 line or plane at right angles to another

perpetrate perpetrates perpetrating perpetrated *verb* to commit or be responsible for (a wrongdoing) > **perpetrator** *noun*

perpetual *adjective* 1 lasting forever 2 continually repeated > **perpetually** *adverb*

perpetuate perpetuates perpetuating perpetuated *verb* to cause to continue or be remembered

perpetuity perpetuities *noun* 1 eternity 2 state of being perpetual 3 **in perpetuity** forever

perplexed *adjective* puzzled or bewildered

persecute persecutes persecuting persecuted *verb* 1 to treat cruelly because of race, religion, etc 2 to subject to persistent harassment > **persecution** *noun*: *political persecution* > **persecutor** *noun*: *They rose up against their persecutors*

persevere perseveres persevering persevered *verb* to keep making an effort despite difficulties > **perseverance** *noun*: *This will require enormous patience and perseverance*

Persian *adjective, noun* old word for Iranian, used especially when referring to the older forms of the language

persimmon *noun* sweet red tropical fruit

persist persists persisting persisted *verb* 1 to continue to be or happen 2 to continue in spite of obstacles or objections > **persistence** *noun*: *Skill only comes with practice and persistence* > **persistent** *adjective*

person people or **persons** *noun* 1 human being 2 body of a human being 3 *Grammar* form of pronouns and verbs that shows if a person is speaking, spoken to, or spoken of 4 **in person** actually present

The usual plural of *person* is *people*. *Persons* is much less common, and is used only in formal or official English

personal *adjective* 1 individual or private 2 of the body: *personal hygiene* 3 (of a remark etc) offensive

personal computer *noun* small computer used for word processing or computer games

personality personalities *noun* 1 person's distinctive characteristics 2 celebrity

personally *adverb* 1 directly, not by delegation to others 2 in one's own opinion

personal pronoun *noun* pronoun such as *I* or *she* that stands for a definite person

personification *noun* **1** form of imagery in which something inanimate is described as if it has human qualities **2** living example of a particular quality: *the personification of evil*

personify personifies personifying personified *verb* **1** to give human characteristics to **2** to be an example of, typify

personnel *noun* **1** people employed in an organization **2** department in an organization that appoints or keeps records of employees

perspective *noun* **1** view of the relative importance of situations or facts **2** method of drawing that gives the effect of solidity and relative distances and sizes

perspiration *noun* sweat

perspire perspires perspiring perspired *verb* to sweat

persuade persuades persuading persuaded *verb* **1** to make (someone) do something by argument, charm, etc **2** to convince

persuasion *noun* **1** act of persuading **2** way of thinking or belief > **persuasive** *adjective*: *a persuasive argument*

pertaining *adjective formal*
pertaining to about or concerning

pertinent *adjective* relevant

perturbed *adjective* greatly worried

peruse peruses perusing perused *verb* to read (something) in a careful or leisurely manner > **perusal** *noun*

Peruvian *adjective* **1** belonging or relating to Peru ▷ *noun* **2** someone from Peru

pervade pervades pervading pervaded *verb* to spread right

through (something) > **pervasive** *adjective*: *a pervasive sense of fear*

perverse *adjective* deliberately doing something different from what is thought normal or proper > **perversely** *adverb* > **perversity** *noun*

perversion *noun* **1** sexual act or desire considered abnormal **2** act of perverting

pervert *verb* **1** to use or alter for a wrong purpose **2** to lead into abnormal (sexual) behaviour ▷ *noun* **3** person who practises sexual perversion

perverted *adjective* **1** having disgusting or unacceptable behaviour or ideas, especially sexual behaviour or ideas **2** completely wrong: *a perverted sense of value*

peseta *noun* unit of currency formerly used in Spain

peso pesos *noun* main unit of currency in several South American countries

pessimism *noun* tendency to expect the worst in all things > **pessimist** *noun*: *I'm a natural pessimist* > **pessimistic** *adjective*

pest *noun* **1** annoying person **2** insect or animal that damages crops

pester *verb* to annoy or nag continually

pesticide *noun* chemical for killing insect pests

pet pets petting petted *noun* **1** animal kept for pleasure and companionship **2** person favoured or indulged ▷ *adjective* **3** particularly cherished ▷ *verb* **4** to treat as a pet **5** to pat or stroke affectionately

petal *noun* one of the brightly coloured outer parts of a flower

peter out *verb* to come gradually

to an end

petite *adjective* (of a woman) small and slim

petition *noun* **1** formal request, especially one signed by many people and presented to a government or other authority ▷ *verb* **2** to present a petition to (a government or someone in authority)

petrified *adjective* very frightened

petrol *noun* flammable liquid obtained from petroleum, used as fuel in internal-combustion engines

petroleum *noun* thick dark oil found underground

petticoat *noun* woman's skirt-shaped undergarment

petty pettier pettiest *adjective* **1** unimportant or trivial **2** small-minded **3** on a small scale: *petty crime*

petulant *adjective* childishly irritable or peevish > **petulance** *noun* > **petulantly** *adverb*

petunia *noun* garden plant with funnel-shaped flowers

pew *noun* fixed benchlike seat in a church

pewter *noun* greyish metal made of tin and lead

pH *noun Chemistry* measure of the acidity of a solution

phalanger *noun* long-tailed Australian tree-dwelling marsupial

phallus phalluses or **phalli** *noun* penis, especially as a symbol of reproductive power in primitive rites > **phallic** *adjective*: *a phallic symbol*

phantom *noun* **1** ghost **2** unreal vision

pharaoh *noun* king (of ancient Egypt)

pharmaceutical *adjective* connected with the industrial production of medicines

pharmacist *noun* person who is qualified to prepare and sell medicines

pharmacy pharmacies *noun* **1** preparation and dispensing of drugs and medicines **2** pharmacist's shop

phase phases phasing phased *noun* **1** any distinct or characteristic stage in a development or chain of events ▷ *verb* **2** to arrange or carry out in stages or to coincide with something else > **phase in** *verb* to introduce gradually > **phase out** *verb* to discontinue gradually

PhD PhDs *abbreviation* Doctor of Philosophy: degree awarded to someone who has done advanced research in a subject

pheasant *noun* game bird with bright plumage

phenomenal *adjective* extraordinarily great or good > **phenomenally** *adverb*

phenomenon phenomena *noun* **1** anything appearing or observed **2** remarkable person or thing

| Use the plural form *phenomena* only when referring to more than one *phenomenon*

philanthropist *noun* someone who freely gives help or money to people in need > **philanthropic** *adjective*: *philanthropic organizations* > **philanthropy** *noun*

philistine *adjective, noun* person who is hostile towards culture and the arts

philosophical or **philosophic** *adjective* **1** of philosophy **2** calm in the face of difficulties or disappointments

philosophy philosophies *noun* **1** study of the meaning of life, knowledge, thought, etc **2** theory or set of ideas held by a particular philosopher **3** person's outlook on life > **philosopher** *noun*

phlegm *noun* thick yellowish substance formed in the nose and throat during a cold

phobia *noun* intense and unreasoning fear or dislike > **phobic** *adjective*: *He is phobic about getting in lifts*

-phobia *suffix indicating* fear of: *claustrophobia*

phoenix phoenixes *noun* legendary bird said to set fire to itself and rise anew from its ashes

phone phones phoning phoned *informal noun* **1** telephone ▷ *verb* **2** to call or talk to (a person) by telephone

-phone *suffix meaning* giving off sound: *telephone*

phonetic *adjective* **1** of speech sounds **2** (of spelling) written as it is sounded > **phonetically** *adverb*

phoney phoneys or **phonies; phonier phoniest** *informal adjective* **1** not genuine **2** insincere ▷ *noun* **3** phoney person or thing

photo photos *noun* short for **photograph**

photo- *prefix meaning* light or using light: *photography*

photocopy photocopies photocopying photocopied *noun* **1** photographic reproduction ▷ *verb* **2** to make a photocopy of > **photocopier** *noun*

photogenic *adjective* always looking attractive in photographs

photograph *noun* **1** picture made by the chemical action of light on sensitive film ▷ *verb* **2** to take a photograph of

photographer *noun* person who takes photographs, especially

professionally > **photography** *noun*

photographic *adjective* **1** connected with photography **2** (of a person's memory) able to retain facts or appearances in precise detail

photosynthesis *noun* process by which a green plant uses sunlight to build up carbohydrate reserves

phrasal verb *noun* verb such as *take over* or *break in*, which is made up of a verb and an adverb or preposition

phrase phrases phrasing phrased *noun* **1** group of words forming a unit of meaning, especially within a sentence **2** short effective expression ▷ *verb* **3** to express in words

physical *adjective* **1** of the body, as contrasted with the mind or spirit **2** of material things or nature **3** of physics > **physically** *adverb*

physical education *noun* training and practice in sports and gymnastics

physician *noun* doctor of medicine

physics *noun* science of the properties of matter and energy > **physicist** *noun*: *a nuclear physicist*

physio- *prefix meaning* to do with the body or natural functions: *physiotherapy*

physiology *noun* science of the normal function of living things

physiotherapy *noun* treatment of disease or injury by physical means such as massage, rather than by drugs > **physiotherapist** *noun*

physique *noun* person's bodily build and muscular development

pi *noun Maths* a number, approximately 3.142 and symbolized by the Greek letter π. It is the ratio of the circumference of a circle to its diameter

piano pianos noun (also **pianoforte**) musical instrument with strings which are struck by hammers worked by a keyboard > **pianist** noun

piccolo piccolos noun small flute

pick verb 1 to choose 2 to remove (flowers or fruit) from a plant 3 to take hold of and move with the fingers 4 to provoke (a fight etc) deliberately 5 to open (a lock) by means other than a key ▷ noun 6 choice 7 best part 8 tool with a curved iron crossbar and wooden shaft, for breaking up hard ground or rocks > **pick on** verb to continually treat someone unfairly > **pick out** verb 1 to select for use or special consideration 2 to recognize (a person or thing) > **pick up** verb 1 to raise or lift 2 to collect 3 to improve

pickaxe noun large pick

picket noun 1 person or group standing outside a workplace to deter would-be workers during a strike ▷ verb 2 to form a picket outside (a workplace)

pickings plural noun money easily acquired

pickle pickles pickling pickled noun 1 food preserved in vinegar or salt water 2 informal awkward situation ▷ verb 3 to preserve in vinegar or salt water

pickpocket noun thief who steals from someone's pocket

picnic picnics picnicking picnicked noun 1 informal meal out of doors ▷ verb 2 to have a picnic

pictorial adjective of or in painting or pictures

picture pictures picturing pictured noun 1 drawing or painting 2 photograph 3 mental image 4 beautiful or picturesque object 5 image on a TV screen 6 **the pictures** the cinema ▷ verb 7 to visualize or imagine 8 to represent in a picture

picturesque adjective 1 (of a place or view) pleasant to look at 2 (of language) forceful or vivid

pie noun dish of meat, fruit, etc baked in pastry

piece pieces piecing pieced noun 1 separate bit or part 2 instance: a piece of luck 3 example or specimen 4 literary or musical composition 5 coin 6 small object used in draughts, chess, etc > **piece together** verb to make or assemble bit by bit

piecemeal adverb bit by bit

pie chart noun circular diagram with sectors representing quantities

pier noun 1 platform on stilts sticking out into the sea 2 pillar, especially one supporting a bridge

pierce pierces piercing pierced verb 1 to make a hole in or through with a sharp instrument 2 to make a way through

piercing adjective 1 (of a sound) shrill and high-pitched 2 (of eyes or a stare) intense and penetrating

piety noun deep devotion to God and religion

pig noun 1 animal kept and killed for pork, ham and bacon 2 informal greedy, dirty or rude person

pigeon noun bird with a heavy body and short legs, sometimes trained to carry messages

pigeonhole pigeonholes pigeonholing pigeonholed noun 1 compartment for papers in a desk etc ▷ verb 2 to classify

piggyback noun 1 ride on someone's shoulders ▷ adverb 2 carried on someone's shoulders

piglet *noun* young pig

pigment *noun* colouring matter, paint or dye ▷ **pigmentation** *noun*: *the pigmentation of the skin*

Pigmy Pigmies *noun* same as **Pygmy**

pigsty pigsties *noun* hut with a small enclosed area where pigs are kept

pigtail *noun* plait of hair hanging from the back or either side of the head

pike *noun* **1** large freshwater fish with strong teeth **2** *History* pointed metal blade attached to a long pole, used as a weapon

pilchard *noun* small edible sea fish of the herring family

pile piles piling piled *noun* **1** number of things lying on top of each other **2** *informal* large amount **3** fibres of a carpet or a fabric, especially velvet, that stand up from the weave ▷ *verb* **4** to collect into a pile

piles *plural noun* swollen veins in the rectum

pile-up *noun informal* traffic accident involving several vehicles

pilfer *verb* to steal (minor items) in small quantities

pilgrim *noun* person who journeys to a holy place ▷ **pilgrimage** *noun*: *the pilgrimage to Mecca*

pill *noun* **1** small ball of medicine swallowed whole **2** **the pill** pill taken by a woman to prevent pregnancy

pillage pillages pillaging pillaged *verb* **1** to steal property by violence in war ▷ *noun* **2** violent seizure of goods, especially in war

pillar *noun* **1** upright post, usually supporting a roof **2** strong supporter

pillar box pillar boxes *noun* (in Britain) red pillar-shaped letter box in the street

pillory pillories pillorying pilloried *verb* to ridicule publicly

pillow *noun* stuffed cloth bag for supporting the head in bed

pillowcase or **pillowslip** *noun* removable cover for a pillow

pilot *noun* **1** person qualified to fly an aircraft or spacecraft **2** person employed to steer a ship entering or leaving a harbour ▷ *adjective* **3** experimental and preliminary ▷ *verb* **4** to act as the pilot of **5** to guide or lead (a project or people)

pilot light *noun* small flame lighting the main one in a gas appliance

pimp *noun* man who gets customers for a prostitute in return for a share of his or her earnings

pimple *noun* small pus-filled spot on the skin ▷ **pimply** *adjective*

pin pins pinning pinned *noun* **1** short thin piece of stiff wire with a point and head, for fastening things **2** wooden or metal peg or stake ▷ *verb* **3** to fasten with a pin **4** to seize and hold fast ▷ **pin down** *verb* **1** to force (someone) to make a decision, take action, etc **2** to define clearly

pinafore *noun* **1** apron **2** dress with a bib top

pincers *plural noun* **1** tool consisting of two hinged arms, for gripping **2** claws of a lobster etc

pinch pinches pinching pinched *verb* **1** to squeeze (something) between finger and thumb **2** to cause pain by being too tight **3** *informal* to steal ▷ *noun* **4** act of pinching **5** as much as can be taken up between the finger and thumb **6** **at a pinch** if absolutely necessary

pinched *adjective* (of someone's face) thin and pale

pine pines pining pined *verb* **1 pine for** to feel great longing (for) ▷ *noun* **2** evergreen coniferous tree with very thin leaves **3** its wood

pineapple *noun* large tropical fruit with juicy yellow flesh and a hard skin

Ping-Pong® *noun* table tennis

pink *noun* **1** pale reddish colour **2** fragrant garden plant **3 in the pink** in good health ▷ *adjective* **4** of the colour pink

pinnacle *noun* **1** highest point of fame or success **2** mountain peak

pinpoint *verb* **1** to locate or identify exactly ▷ *adjective* **2** exact: *pinpoint accuracy*

pinstripe *noun* **1** very narrow stripe in fabric **2** the fabric itself

pint *noun* liquid measure, 1/8 gallon (.568 litre)

pioneer *noun* **1** explorer or early settler of a new country **2** originator or developer of something new ▷ *verb* **3** to be the pioneer or leader of

pious *adjective* deeply religious

pip *noun* **1** small seed in a fruit **2** high-pitched sound used as a time signal on radio

pipe pipes piping piped *noun* **1** tube for conveying liquid or gas **2** tube with a small bowl at the end for smoking tobacco **3** tubular musical instrument **4 the pipes** bagpipes ▷ *verb* **5** to convey (a liquid such as oil) by pipe

pipeline *noun* **1** long pipe for transporting oil, water, etc **2** means of communication

piper *noun* player on a pipe or bagpipes

piping *noun* **1** system of pipes **2** fancy edging on clothes etc

piracy *noun* robbery carried out at sea

piranha *noun* small fierce freshwater fish of tropical America

pirate pirates *noun* sea robber

pirouette *noun* spinning turn balanced on the toes of one foot

Pisces *noun* twelfth sign of the zodiac, represented by two fish

pistil *noun* seed-bearing part of a flower

pistol *noun* short-barrelled handgun

piston *noun* cylindrical part in an engine that slides to and fro in a cylinder

pit pits pitting pitted *noun* **1** deep hole in the ground **2** coal mine **3** dent or depression **4 pits** servicing and refuelling area on a motor-racing track ▷ *verb* **5** to mark with small dents or scars

pitch pitches pitching pitched *verb* **1** to throw or hurl **2** to set up (a tent) **3** to fall headlong **4** (of a ship or plane) to move with the front and back going up and down alternately **5** to set the level or tone of ▷ *noun* **6** area marked out for playing sport **7** degree or angle of slope **8** degree of highness or lowness of a (musical) sound **9** dark sticky substance obtained from tar

pitcher *noun* large jug with a narrow neck

pitfall *noun* hidden difficulty or danger

pith *noun* soft white lining of the rind of oranges etc

pitiful *adjective* **1** arousing pity **2** woeful, contemptible

pitiless *adjective* feeling no pity or mercy ▷ **pitilessly** *adverb*

pittance *noun* very small amount of money

pitted *adjective* covered in small hollows

pity pities pitying pitied *noun*
1 sympathy or sorrow for others'
suffering **2** regrettable fact ▷ *verb*
3 to feel pity for

pivot *noun* **1** central shaft on which
something turns ▷ *verb* **2** to provide
with or turn on a pivot

pivotal *adjective* of crucial
importance

pixie *noun* (in folklore) fairy

pizza *noun* flat disc of dough covered
with a wide variety of savoury
toppings and baked

placard *noun* notice that is carried
or displayed in public

placate placates placating
placated *verb* to make (someone)
stop feeling angry or upset

place places placing placed *noun*
1 particular part of an area or space
2 particular town, building, etc
3 position or point reached **4** seat
or space **5** usual position **6 take**
place to happen ▷ *verb* **7** to put
in a particular place **8** to identify,
put in context **9** to make (an order,
bet, etc)

placebo placebos or **placeboes**
noun substance given to a patient
in place of a drug and from which,
though it has no active ingredients,
the patient may imagine they get
some benefit

placenta *noun* organ formed in the
womb during pregnancy, providing
nutrients for the fetus

placid *adjective* not easily excited or
upset, calm **> placidly** *adverb*

plagiarism *noun* copying ideas
or passages from someone else's
work and pretending it is your own
> plagiarist *noun*

plagiarize plagiarizes
plagiarizing plagiarized; also
spelt **plagiarise** *verb* to steal (ideas
or passages from another's work)

and present them as your own

plague plagues plaguing
plagued *noun* **1** fast-spreading fatal
disease **2** *History* bubonic plague
3 overwhelming number of things
that afflict or harass ▷ *verb* **4** to
trouble or annoy continually

plaice *noun* edible European flatfish

plaid *noun* tartan cloth or pattern

plain *adjective* **1** easy to see or
understand **2** expressed honestly
and clearly **3** without decoration
or pattern **4** not beautiful **5** simple
or ordinary ▷ *noun* **6** large stretch
of level country ▷ *adverb* **7** clearly or
simply: *plain stupid* **> plainly** *adverb*

plain clothes *plural noun* ordinary
clothes, as opposed to uniform

plaintiff *noun* person who sues in a
court of law

plaintive *adjective* sad and
mournful **> plaintively** *adverb*

plait *noun* **1** intertwined length of
hair ▷ *verb* **2** to intertwine separate
strands in a pattern

plan plans planning planned *noun*
1 way thought out to do or achieve
something **2** diagram showing
the layout or design of something
▷ *verb* **3** to arrange beforehand **4** to
make a diagram of

plane planes planing planed *noun*
1 aeroplane **2** *Maths* flat surface
3 level of attainment etc **4** tool
for smoothing wood ▷ *adjective*
5 perfectly flat or level ▷ *verb* **6** to
smooth (wood) with a plane

planet *noun* large body in space that
revolves round the sun or another
star **> planetary** *adjective*: *planetary*
systems

plank *noun* long flat piece of sawn
timber

plankton *noun* minute animals and
plants floating in the surface water
of a sea or lake

planner *noun* **1** person who makes plans, especially for the development of a town, building, etc **2** chart for recording future developments, etc

plant *noun* **1** living organism that grows in the ground and has no power to move **2** equipment or machinery used in industrial processes **3** factory or other industrial premises ▷ *verb* **4** to set (seeds or crops) into the ground to grow **5** to place firmly in position

plantation *noun* **1** estate for the cultivation of tea, tobacco, etc **2** wood of cultivated trees

planter *noun* decorative pot for house plants

plaque *noun* **1** flat piece of metal which is fixed to a wall and has an inscription in memory of a famous person or event **2** filmy deposit on teeth that causes decay

plasma *noun* clear liquid part of blood

plaster *noun* **1** mixture of lime, sand, etc for coating walls **2** adhesive strip of material for dressing cuts etc ▷ *verb* **3** to coat (a wall or ceiling) with plaster **4** to coat thickly > **plasterer** *noun*

plastered *adjective* **1 plastered to** stuck to **2 plastered with** covered with

plastic *noun* **1** synthetic material that can be moulded when soft but sets in a hard long-lasting shape **2** credit cards etc as opposed to cash ▷ *adjective* **3** made of plastic **4** easily moulded, pliant

plastic surgery *noun* repair or reconstruction of missing or malformed parts of the body

plate plates plating plated *noun* **1** shallow dish for holding food **2** flat thin sheet of metal, glass, etc

3 thin coating of metal on another metal ▷ *verb* **4** to coat (a metal surface) with a thin coating of another metal

plateau plateaus or **plateaux** *noun* **1** area of level high land **2** stage when there is no change or development

platform *noun* **1** raised floor **2** raised area in a station from which passengers board trains **3** structure in the sea which holds machinery, stores, etc for drilling an oil well **4** programme of a political party

platinum *noun Chemistry* valuable silvery-white metal

platitude *noun* remark that is true but not interesting or original

platonic *adjective* (of a relationship) friendly or affectionate but not sexual

platoon *noun* smaller unit within a company of soldiers

platter *noun* large dish

platypus platypuses *noun* (also **duck-billed platypus**) Australian egg-laying amphibious mammal, with dense fur, webbed feet and a ducklike bill

plaudits *plural noun* expressions of approval

plausible *adjective* **1** apparently true or reasonable **2** persuasive but insincere > **plausibility** *noun* > **plausibly** *adverb*

play plays playing played *verb* **1** to occupy yourself in (a game or recreation) **2** to compete against (someone) in a game or sport **3** to act (a part) on the stage **4** to perform on (a musical instrument) **5** to cause (a radio, CD player, etc) to give out sound ▷ *noun* **6** story performed on stage or broadcast **7** activities children take part in for amusement **8** playing of a game

9 conduct: *fair play* **10** (scope for) freedom of movement

playboy playboys *noun* rich man who lives only for pleasure

player *noun* **1** person who plays a game or sport **2** actor or actress **3** person who plays a musical instrument

playful *adjective* **1** friendly and light-hearted **2** lively > **playfully** *adverb*

playground *noun* outdoor area for children to play in

playgroup *noun* regular meeting of very young children for supervised play

playing card *noun* one of a set of 52 cards used in card games

playing field *noun* extensive piece of ground for sport

playschool *noun* nursery group for young children

playwright *noun* author of plays

plaza *noun* **1** open space or square **2** modern shopping complex

plea *noun* **1** serious or urgent request, entreaty **2** statement of a prisoner or defendant **3** excuse

plead *verb* **1** to ask urgently or with deep feeling **2** to give as an excuse **3** *Law* to declare yourself to be guilty or innocent of a charge made against you

pleasant *adjective* pleasing or enjoyable > **pleasantly** *adverb*

pleasantry pleasantries *noun* polite or joking remark

please pleases pleasing pleased *verb* **1** to give pleasure or satisfaction to (someone) > *adverb* **2** polite word of request > **pleased** *adjective*: *I'm pleased to be going home*

pleasing *adjective* attractive, satisfying or enjoyable

pleasurable *adjective* giving pleasure > **pleasurably** *adverb*

pleasure *noun* **1** feeling of

happiness and satisfaction **2** something that causes this

pleat *noun* **1** fold made by doubling material back on itself > *verb* **2** to arrange (material) in pleats

plebiscite *noun* decision by direct voting of the people of a country

pledge pledges pledging pledged *noun* **1** solemn promise **2** something valuable given as a guarantee that a promise will be kept or a debt paid > *verb* **3** to promise solemnly **4** to bind by or as if by a pledge

plentiful *adjective* existing in large amounts or numbers > **plentifully** *adverb*

plenty *noun* **1** large amount or number **2** quite enough

plethora *noun* excess

pleurisy *noun* inflammation of the membrane covering the lungs

pliable *adjective* **1** easily bent **2** easily influenced

pliers *plural noun* tool with hinged arms and jaws for gripping

plight *noun* difficult or dangerous situation

plinth *noun* slab forming the base of a statue, column, etc

plod plods plodding plodded *verb* **1** to walk with slow heavy steps **2** to work slowly but determinedly

plonk *verb* to put (something) down heavily and carelessly

plop plops plopping plopped *noun* **1** sound of an object falling into water without a splash > *verb* **2** to make this sound

plot plots plotting plotted *noun* **1** secret plan to do something illegal or wrong **2** story of a film, novel, etc **3** small piece of land > *verb* **4** to plan secretly, conspire **5** to mark the position or course of (a ship or aircraft) on a map **6** to mark and join up (points on a graph)

plough *noun* **1** agricultural tool for turning over soil ▷ *verb* **2** to turn over (earth) with a plough

ploy *noun* manoeuvre designed to gain an advantage

pluck *verb* **1** to pull or pick off **2** to pull out the feathers of (a bird for cooking) **3** to sound the strings of (a guitar etc) with the fingers ▷ *noun* **4** bravery or courage

plucky *adjective* brave or courageous > **pluckily** *adverb*

plug plugs plugging plugged *noun* **1** thing fitting into and filling a hole **2** device connecting an appliance to an electricity supply ▷ *verb* **3** to block or seal (a hole or gap) with a plug **4** *informal* to advertise (a product etc) by constant repetition

plum *noun* **1** oval usually dark red fruit with a stone in the middle ▷ *adjective* **2** dark purplish-red

plumage *noun* bird's feathers

plumber *noun* person who fits and repairs pipes and fixtures for water and drainage systems

plumbing *noun* pipes and fixtures used in water and drainage systems

plume *noun* feather, especially one worn as an ornament

plummet *verb* to plunge downwards

plump *adjective* moderately fat > **plumpness** *noun*

plunder *verb* **1** to seize (valuables) from (a place) by force, especially in wartime ▷ *noun* **2** things plundered, spoils

plunge plunges plunging plunged *verb* **1** to put or throw forcibly or suddenly (into) **2** to descend steeply **3** **plunge into** to become deeply involved in ▷ *noun* **4** plunging, dive

Plunket Society *noun NZ*

organization for the care of mothers and babies, now called the Royal New Zealand Society for the Health of Women and Children

plural *adjective* **1** of or consisting of more than one ▷ *noun* **2** word indicating more than one

pluralism *noun* existence and toleration of a variety of peoples, opinions, etc in a society > **pluralist** *adjective*: *a pluralist democracy*

plus pluses or **plusses** *preposition, adjective* **1** indicating addition ▷ *adjective* **2** more than zero **3** positive **4** advantageous ▷ *noun* **5** sign (+) denoting addition **6** advantage

plush *noun* **1** fabric with long velvety pile ▷ *adjective* **2** (also **plushy**) luxurious

Pluto *noun* smallest planet in the solar system and farthest from the sun

plutonium *noun Chemistry* radioactive metallic element used especially in nuclear reactors and weapons

ply plies plying plied *verb* **1** to work at (a job or trade) **2** to use (a tool) **3** **ply with** to supply with or subject to persistently ▷ *noun* **4** thickness of wool, fabric, etc

plywood *noun* board made of thin layers of wood glued together

p.m. *abbreviation* (*Latin*: *post meridiem*) after noon

pneumatic *adjective* worked by or inflated with wind or air

pneumonia *noun* inflammation of the lungs

poach poaches poaching poached *verb* **1** to catch (animals) illegally on someone else's land **2** to simmer (food) gently in liquid

poacher *noun* person who catches

animals illegally on someone else's land

pocket *noun* **1** small bag sewn into clothing for carrying things **2** pouchlike container, especially for catching balls at the edge of a snooker table **3** isolated or distinct group or area ▷ *verb* **4** to put (something) into your pocket **5** to take (something) secretly or dishonestly

pocket money *noun* small regular allowance given to children by parents

pod *noun* long narrow seed case of peas, beans, etc

poddy poddies *noun Aust* calf or lamb that is being fed by hand

podium podiums or **podia** *noun* small raised platform for a conductor or speaker

poem *noun* imaginative piece of writing in rhythmic lines

poet *noun* writer of poems

poetic *adjective* of or like poetry > **poetically** *adverb*

poetry *noun* **1** poems **2** art of writing poems

poignant *adjective* sharply painful to the feelings > **poignancy** *noun*

point *noun* **1** main idea in a discussion, argument, etc **2** aim or purpose **3** detail or item **4** characteristic **5** particular position, stage or time **6** dot indicating decimals **7** sharp end **8** unit for recording a value or score **9** one of the direction marks of a compass **10** electrical socket **11** **on the point of** very shortly going to ▷ *verb* **12** to show the direction or position of something or draw attention to it by extending a finger or other pointed object towards it **13** to direct or face towards

point-blank *adjective* **1** fired at a very close target **2** (of a remark or question) direct, blunt ▷ *adverb* **3** directly or bluntly

pointed *adjective* **1** having a sharp end **2** (of a remark) obviously directed at a particular person > **pointedly** *adverb*

pointer *noun* helpful hint

pointless *adjective* meaningless or irrelevant > **pointlessly** *adverb*

point of view points of view *noun* way of considering something

poise *noun* calm dignified manner

poised *adjective* **1** absolutely ready **2** behaving with or showing poise

poison *noun* **1** substance that kills or injures when swallowed or absorbed ▷ *verb* **2** to give poison to someone **3** to have a harmful or evil effect on

poisonous *adjective* **1** containing a harmful substance that could kill you or make you ill **2** (of an animal) producing a venom that can cause death or illness in anyone bitten or stung by it

poke pokes poking poked *verb* **1** to jab or prod with your finger, a stick, etc **2** to thrust forward or out ▷ *noun* **3** poking

poker *noun* **1** metal rod for stirring a fire **2** card game in which players bet on the hands dealt

polar *adjective* of or near either of the earth's poles

polar bear *noun* white bear that lives in the regions around the North Pole

polarize polarizes polarizing polarized; also spelt **polarise** *verb* to form or cause (people) to form groups with directly opposite views > **polarization** *noun*

pole *noun* **1** long rounded piece of wood etc **2** point furthest north or south on the earth's axis of rotation

3 either of the opposite ends of a magnet or electric cell

Pole *noun* someone from Poland

pole vault *noun* athletics event in which contestants jump over a high bar using a long flexible pole to lift themselves into the air

police polices policing policed *noun* **1** organized force in a state which keeps law and order ▷ *verb* **2** to control or watch over with police or a similar body

policeman policemen *noun* member of a police force > **policewoman** *noun*

policy policies *noun* **1** plan of action adopted by a person, group or state **2** document containing an insurance contract

polio *noun* (also **poliomyelitis**) disease affecting the spinal cord, which often causes paralysis

polish polishes polishing polished *verb* **1** to make smooth and shiny by rubbing **2** to make more nearly perfect ▷ *noun* **3** substance used for polishing **4** pleasing elegant style

Polish *adjective* **1** belonging or relating to Poland ▷ *noun* **2** main language spoken in Poland

polished *adjective* **1** accomplished **2** done or performed well or professionally

polite *adjective* **1** showing consideration for others in your manners, speech, etc **2** socially correct or refined > **politely** *adverb* > **politeness** *noun*

political *adjective* of the state, government or public administration > **politically** *adverb*

politician *noun* person actively engaged in politics, especially a member of parliament

politics *noun* **1** winning and using

of power to govern society **2** (study of) the art of government **3** person's beliefs about how a country should be governed

polka *noun* **1** lively 19th-century dance **2** music for this

poll *noun* **1** (also **opinion poll**) questioning of a random sample of people to find out general opinion **2** voting **3** number of votes recorded **4** **the polls** political election ▷ *verb* **5** to receive (votes) **6** to question (a person) in an opinion poll

pollen *noun* fine dust produced by flowers to fertilize other flowers

pollinate pollinates pollinating pollinated *verb* to fertilize by the transfer of pollen > **pollination** *noun*

pollutant *noun* something that pollutes

pollute pollutes polluting polluted *verb* to contaminate with something poisonous or harmful > **polluted** *adjective*: *polluted rivers*

pollution *noun* harmful or poisonous substances introduced into an environment

polo *noun* game like hockey played by teams of players on horseback

polo-neck *noun* sweater with high turned-over collar

poly- *prefix meaning* many, much

polyester *noun* man-made material used to make plastics and clothes

polygamy *noun* practice of having more than one husband or wife at the same time > **polygamous** *adjective*: *polygamous societies*

polygon *noun* geometrical figure with three or more angles and sides

polystyrene *noun* synthetic material used especially as white rigid foam for packing and insulation

polythene *noun* light plastic used

for bags etc

polyunsaturated *adjective* of a group of fats that do not form cholesterol in the blood > **polyunsaturate** *noun: spreads containing polyunsaturates*

pomegranate *noun* round tropical fruit with a thick rind containing many seeds in a red pulp

pomp *noun* stately display or ceremony

pompous *adjective* foolishly serious and grand, self-important > **pomposity** *noun* > **pompously** *adverb*

pond *noun* small area of still water

ponder *verb* to think thoroughly or deeply (about)

ponderous *adjective* **1** serious and dull **2** heavy and unwieldy **3** (of movement) slow and clumsy > **ponderously** *adverb*

pong *noun informal* strong unpleasant smell

pontiff *noun formal* the Pope

pony ponies *noun* small horse

ponytail *noun* long hair tied in one bunch at the back of the head

pony trekking *noun* leisure activity in which people ride across country on ponies

poodle *noun* dog with curly hair often clipped fancifully

pool *noun* **1** small body of still water **2** swimming pool **3** shared fund or group of workers or resources **4** game in which players try to hit coloured balls into pockets around the table using long sticks called cues **5 the pools** form of gambling in which people try to guess the results of football matches ▷ *verb* **6** to put in a common fund

poor *adjective* **1** having little money and few possessions **2** less, smaller or weaker than is needed

or expected **3** inferior **4** unlucky, pitiable

poorly *adverb* **1** in a poor manner ▷ *adjective* **2** not in good health

pop pops popping popped *verb* **1** to make or cause to make a small explosive sound **2** *informal* to go, put or come unexpectedly or suddenly ▷ *noun* **3** music of general appeal, especially to young people **4** small explosive sound **5** *Brit* nonalcoholic fizzy drink

popcorn *noun* grains of maize heated until they puff up and burst

Pope *noun* head of the Roman Catholic Church

poplar *noun* tall slender tree

poppy poppies *noun* plant with a large red flower

populace *noun formal* the ordinary people

popular *adjective* **1** widely liked and admired **2** of or for the public in general > **popularity** *noun* > **popularly** *adverb*

popularize popularizes popularizing popularized; also spelt **popularise** *verb* **1** to make popular **2** to make (something technical or specialist) easily understood

populate populates populating populated *verb* **1** to live in, inhabit **2** to fill with inhabitants

population *noun* **1** all the people who live in a particular place **2** the number of people living in a particular place

porcelain *noun* **1** fine china **2** objects made of it

porch porches *noun* covered approach to the entrance of a building

porcupine *noun* animal covered with long pointed quills

pore pores poring pored *noun*

tiny opening in the skin or in the surface of a plant > **pore over** *verb* to examine or study intently

pork *noun* pig meat

pornography *noun* writing, films or pictures designed to be sexually exciting > **pornographic** *adjective*

porous *adjective* allowing liquid to pass through gradually

porpoise *noun* fishlike sea mammal

porridge *noun* breakfast food made of oatmeal cooked in water or milk

port *noun* **1** (town with) a harbour **2** left side of a ship or aircraft when facing the front of it **3** strong sweet wine, usually red

-port *suffix relating to* carrying: *transport*

portable *adjective* easily carried

porter *noun* **1** man who carries luggage **2** hospital worker who transfers patients between rooms **3** doorman or gatekeeper of a building

portfolio portfolios *noun* **1** (flat case for carrying) examples of an artist's work **2** area of responsibility of a government minister **3** list of investments held by an investor

porthole *noun* small round window in a ship or aircraft

portion *noun* **1** part or share **2** helping of food for one person **3** destiny or fate

portrait *noun* **1** picture of a person **2** lifelike description

portray portrays portraying portrayed *verb* to describe or represent by artistic means, as in writing or film > **portrayal** *noun*: *his portrayal of Hamlet*

Portuguese *adjective* **1** of Portugal, its people or their language ▷ *noun* **2** person from Portugal **3** language of Portugal and Brazil

The plural of *Portuguese* is *Portuguese*

pose poses posing posed *verb* **1** to place in or take up a particular position to be photographed or drawn **2** to raise (a problem) **3** to ask (a question) **4 pose as** to pretend to be ▷ *noun* **5** position while posing **6** behaviour adopted for effect

poser *noun* **1** puzzling question **2** poseur

poseur *noun* person who behaves in an affected way to impress others

posh *adjective informal* **1** smart, luxurious **2** upper-class

position *noun* **1** place **2** usual or expected place **3** way in which something is placed or arranged **4** attitude, point of view **5** job ▷ *verb* **6** to place

positive *adjective* **1** feeling no doubts, certain **2** confident, hopeful **3** helpful, providing encouragement **4** absolute, downright **5** *Maths* greater than zero **6** (of an electrical charge) having a deficiency of electrons > **positively** *adverb*

possess possesses possessing possessed *verb* **1** to have or own (something) **2** (of a feeling, belief, etc) to have complete control of, dominate > **possessor** *noun*

possession *noun* **1** state of possessing; ownership **2 possessions** things a person possesses

possessive *adjective* **1** wanting all the attention or love of another person **2** (of a word) indicating the person or thing that something belongs to

possibility possibilities *noun* something that might be true or might happen

possible *adjective* **1** able to exist, happen or be done **2** worthy of consideration ▷ *noun* **3** person or thing that might be suitable or chosen

possibly *adverb* perhaps, not necessarily

possum *noun Aust, NZ* phalanger, a marsupial with thick fur and a long tail

post *noun* **1** official system of delivering letters and parcels **2** (single collection or delivery of) letters and parcels sent by this system **3** length of wood, concrete, etc fixed upright to support or mark something **4** job ▷ *verb* **5** to send by post **6** to put up (a notice) in a public place **7** to send (a person) to a new place to work to supply someone regularly with the latest information

post- *prefix meaning* after or later than: *postwar*

postage *noun* charge for sending a letter or parcel by post

postal *adjective* of a mail-delivery service

postal order *noun Brit* written money order sent by post and cashed at a post office by the person who receives it

postbox postboxes *noun* metal box with a hole in it which you put letters into for collection by the postman

postcard *noun* card for sending a message by post without an envelope

postcode *noun* system of letters and numbers used to aid the sorting of mail

poster *noun* large picture or notice stuck on a wall

posterior *noun* **1** buttocks ▷ *adjective* **2** behind, at the back of

posterity *noun formal* future generations, descendants

posthumous *adjective* occurring after a person's death > **posthumously** *adverb*

postman postmen *noun* person who collects and delivers post

postmortem *noun* medical examination of a body to establish the cause of death

post office *noun* **1** place where postal business is conducted **2 Post Office** *Brit* national organization responsible for postal services

postpone postpones postponing postponed *verb* to put off to a later time > **postponement** *noun*

posture postures posturing postured *noun* **1** position or way in which someone stands, walks, etc ▷ *verb* **2** to behave in an exaggerated way to get attention

posy posies *noun* small bunch of flowers

pot pots potting potted *noun* **1** round deep container **2** teapot ▷ *verb* **3** to put (a plant) in soil in a flowerpot

potassium *noun Chemistry* silvery metallic element

potassium nitrate *noun* white chemical compound used to make gunpowder, fireworks and fertilizers; also **saltpetre**

potato potatoes *noun* roundish starchy vegetable that grows underground

potent *adjective* **1** effective or powerful **2** (of a male) capable of having sexual intercourse > **potency** *noun*

potential *adjective* **1** possible but not yet actual ▷ *noun* **2** ability or talent not yet fully used > **potentially** *adverb*

potential energy *noun* energy

stored in something

pothole *noun* **1** hole in the surface of a road **2** deep hole in a limestone area

potion *noun* dose of medicine or poison

potted *adjective* **1** grown in a pot **2** (of meat or fish) cooked or preserved in a pot

potter *noun* **1** person who makes pottery ▷ *verb* **2** **potter about, around** *or* **away** to be busy in a pleasant but aimless way

pottery potteries *noun* **1** articles made from baked clay **2** craft of making pottery

potty potties; pottier pottiest *noun* **1** bowl used by a small child as a toilet ▷ *adjective* **2** *informal* crazy or silly

pouch pouches *noun* **1** small bag **2** baglike pocket of skin on an animal

poultry *noun* domestic fowls

pounce pounces pouncing pounced *verb* **1** **pounce on** to spring upon suddenly to attack or capture ▷ *noun* **2** pouncing

pound *noun* **1** monetary unit of Britain and some other countries **2** unit of weight equal to 0.454 kg **3** enclosure for stray animals or officially removed vehicles ▷ *verb* **4** to hit heavily and repeatedly **5** to crush to pieces or powder **6** (of the heart) to throb heavily **7** to run heavily

pour *verb* **1** to flow or cause to flow out in a stream **2** to rain heavily **3** to come or go in large numbers

pout *verb* **1** to thrust out (the lips) sullenly or provocatively ▷ *noun* **2** pouting look

poverty *noun* **1** state of being without enough food or money **2** lack of, scarcity

powder *noun* **1** substance in the form of tiny loose particles **2** medicine or cosmetic in this form ▷ *verb* **3** to cover or sprinkle with powder > **powdery** *adjective*

power *noun* **1** ability to do or act **2** strength **3** position of authority or control **4** *Maths* product from continuous multiplication of a number by itself **5** *Physics* rate at which work is done **6** electricity supply **7** particular form of energy: *nuclear power* ▷ *verb* **8** to supply with power

power cut *noun* temporary interruption in the supply of electricity

powerful *adjective* strong, influential or effective: *a powerful car* > **powerfully** *adverb*

powerless *adjective* unable to control or influence events

power station *noun* installation for generating and distributing electric power

pp. *abbreviation* pages

PR *abbreviation* **1** proportional representation **2** public relations

practicable *adjective* **1** capable of being done successfully **2** usable

practical *adjective* **1** involving experience or actual use rather than theory **2** sensible, useful and effective **3** good at making or doing things **4** in effect though not in name ▷ *noun* **5** examination in which something has to be done or made > **practicality** *noun*: *the practicalities of everyday life*

practically *adverb* **1** almost but not completely or exactly **2** in a practical way

practice *noun* **1** something done regularly or habitually **2** repetition of something so as to gain skill

3 doctor's or lawyer's place of work

   ■ The noun *practice* ends in *ce*

practise practises practising practised *verb* **1** to do repeatedly so as to gain skill **2** to take part in, follow (a religion etc) **3** to work at: *to practise medicine* **4** to do habitually

   ■ The verb *practise* ends in *se*

practised *adjective* expert or skilled as a result of long experience

practitioner *noun* person who practises a profession

pragmatic *adjective* concerned with practical consequences rather than theory > **pragmatically** *adverb* > **pragmatism** *noun*

prairie *noun* large treeless area of grassland, especially in N America and Canada

praise praises praising praised *verb* **1** to express approval or admiration of (someone or something) **2** to express honour and thanks to (one's God) ▷ *noun* **3** something said or written to show approval or admiration

pram *noun* four-wheeled carriage for a baby, pushed by hand

prance prances prancing pranced *verb* to walk with exaggerated bouncing steps

prank *noun* mischievous trick

prattle prattles prattling prattled *verb* **1** to chatter in a childish or foolish way ▷ *noun* **2** childish or foolish talk

prawn *noun* edible shellfish like a large shrimp

pray prays praying prayed *verb* **1** to say prayers (to God) **2** to ask earnestly

prayer *noun* **1** thanks or appeal addressed to God **2** set form of words used in praying **3** earnest request

pre- *prefix meaning* before, beforehand: *prenatal; prerecorded*

preach preaches preaching preached *verb* **1** to give a talk on a religious theme as part of a church service **2** to speak in support of (an idea, principle, etc)

preacher *noun* person who preaches, especially in church

precarious *adjective* (of a position or situation) dangerous or insecure > **precariously** *adverb*

precaution *noun* action taken in advance to prevent something bad happening > **precautionary** *adjective*: *a precautionary measure*

precede precedes preceding preceded *verb* to go or be before (someone or something) in time, place or rank > **preceding** *adjective* coming before: *the preceding day*

precedence *noun* formal order of rank or position

precedent *noun* previous case or occurrence regarded as an example to be followed

precinct *noun* **1** Brit, Aust, S Afr area in a town closed to traffic **2** Brit, Aust, S Afr enclosed area round a building **3** US administrative area of a city **4 precincts** surrounding region

precious *adjective* **1** of great value and importance **2** loved and treasured

precipice *noun* very steep face of cliff or rockface

precipitate precipitates precipitating precipitated *verb formal* to cause to happen suddenly

precipitation *noun formal* rain, snow, sleet or hail

precise *adjective* **1** exact, accurate in every detail **2** strict in observing rules or standards > **precisely** *adverb* > **precision** *noun*

**preclude precludes precluding
precluded** *verb formal* to make
impossible to happen

precocious *adjective* having
developed or matured early or
too soon

preconceived *adjective* (of
an idea) formed without real
experience or reliable information
> **preconception** *noun*:
preconceptions about accountants

precondition *noun* something
that must happen or exist before
something else can

precursor *noun* something
that precedes and is a signal of
something else; a forerunner

predator *noun* animal that kills and
eats other animals > **predatory**
adjective: *predatory birds*

predecessor *noun* 1 person who
precedes another in an office or
position 2 ancestor

predetermined *adjective* decided
in advance

predicament *noun* embarrassing
or difficult situation

predict *verb* to tell about in advance;
prophesy > **predictable** *adjective*:
a predictable outcome > **prediction**
noun forecast or prophecy

predominant *adjective* more
important or more noticeable than
anything else in a particular set of
people or things > **predominance**
noun: *the predominance of English*
> **predominantly** *adverb*

**predominate predominates
predominating predominated**
verb to be the main or controlling
element

pre-eminent *adjective* excelling
all others, outstanding > **pre-
eminence** *noun*

pre-empt *verb formal* to prevent an
action by doing something which

makes it pointless or impossible

preen *verb* (of a bird) to clean or trim
(feathers) with the beak

**preface prefaces prefacing
prefaced** *noun* 1 introduction
to a book ▷ *verb* 2 to serve as an
introduction to (a book, speech,
etc)

prefect *noun* senior pupil in a
school, with limited power over
others

**prefer prefers preferring
preferred** *verb* to like better

preferable *adjective* more desirable
or suitable: *Delay is preferable to error*
> **preferably** *adverb*

preference *noun* 1 liking for one
thing above another or above the
rest 2 person or thing preferred

preferential *adjective* showing
preference

prefix prefixes *noun* letter or group
of letters put at the beginning of a
word to make a new word, such as
un- in *unhappy*

pregnant *adjective* carrying a fetus
in the womb > **pregnancy** *noun*

prehistoric *adjective* of the period
before written history begins

**prejudice prejudices prejudicing
prejudiced** *noun* 1 unreasonable or
unfair dislike or preference ▷ *verb*
2 to cause (someone) to have a
prejudice > **prejudiced** *adjective*
> **prejudicial** *adjective*

preliminary preliminaries
adjective 1 happening before and in
preparation; introductory ▷ *noun*
2 preliminary remark, contest, etc

prelude *noun* event preceding and
introducing something else

premature *adjective* 1 happening or
done before the normal or expected
time 2 (of a baby) born before
the end of the normal period of
pregnancy > **prematurely** *adverb*

premeditated *adjective* planned in advance

premier *noun* **1** prime minister **2** *Aust* leader of a State government ▷ *adjective* **3** considered to be the best or most important

première *noun* first performance of a play, film, etc

premise *noun* statement assumed to be true and used as the basis of reasoning

premises *plural noun* house or other building and its land

premium *noun* **1** additional sum of money, as on a wage or charge **2** (regular) sum paid for insurance

premonition *noun* feeling that something unpleasant is going to happen

preoccupation *noun* something that holds the attention completely

preoccupied *adjective* absorbed in something, especially your own thoughts

preparation *noun* **1** preparing **2** something done in readiness for something else

preparatory *adjective* preparing for

prepare prepares preparing prepared *verb* to make or get ready

prepared *adjective* **1** willing **2** ready

preposition *noun* word used before a noun or pronoun to show its relationship with other words, such as *by* in *go by bus*

preposterous *adjective* utterly absurd

prerequisite *noun formal* something required before something else is possible

prerogative *noun formal* special power or privilege

prescribe prescribes prescribing prescribed *verb* to recommend the use of (a medicine)

prescription *noun* written instructions from a doctor for the making up and use of a medicine

presence *noun* **1** fact of being in a specified place **2** impressive dignified appearance

present *adjective* **1** being in a specified place **2** existing or happening now **3** *Grammar* (of a verb tense) indicating that the action specified is taking place now ▷ *noun* **4** present time or tense **5** something given to bring pleasure to another person ▷ *verb* **6** to introduce formally or publicly **7** to introduce and compere (a TV or radio show) **8** to cause: *present a difficulty* **9** to give or offer formally

presentable *adjective* attractive, neat, fit for people to see

presentation *noun* **1** act of presenting or a way of presenting something **2** manner of presenting **3** formal ceremony in which an award is made **4** talk or demonstration

present-day *adjective* existing or happening now

presenter *noun* person introducing a TV or radio show

presentiment *noun* sense of something unpleasant about to happen

presently *adverb* **1** soon **2** *US, Scot* at the moment

present participle *noun Grammar* the form of a verb that ends in *-ing*, used to form some tenses and to form adjectives and nouns from a verb

present tense *noun Grammar* tense of a verb that is used mainly to talk about things that happen or exist at the time of writing or speaking

preservative *noun* chemical that prevents decay

preserve preserves preserving

preserved *verb* **1** to keep from being damaged, changed or ended **2** to treat (food) to prevent it decaying ▷ *noun* **3** area of interest restricted to a particular person or group **4** fruit preserved by cooking in sugar > **preservation** *noun*: *the preservation of natural resources*

preside presides presiding presided *verb* to be in charge, especially of a meeting

presidency presidencies *noun* office or term of a president

president *noun* **1** head of state in many countries **2** head of a society, institution, etc > **presidential** *adjective*: *presidential elections*

press presses pressing pressed *verb* **1** to apply force or weight to **2** to squeeze **3** to smooth by applying pressure or heat **4** to urge (someone) insistently **5** to crowd or push ▷ *noun* **6 the press a** news media collectively, especially newspapers **b** journalists collectively **7** printing machine

press conference *noun* interview for reporters given by a celebrity

pressing *adjective* urgent

pressure pressures pressuring pressured *noun* **1** force produced by pressing **2** urgent claims or demands **3** *Physics* force applied to a surface per unit of area ▷ *verb* **4** to persuade forcefully

pressurize pressurizes pressurizing pressurized; also spelt **pressurise** *verb* to put pressure on (someone) in an attempt to persuade them to do something

prestige *noun* high status or respect resulting from success or achievements > **prestigious** *adjective*: *one of the country's most prestigious schools*

presumably *adverb* one supposes (that)

presume presumes presuming presumed *verb* **1** to take (something) for granted **2** to dare (to)

presumption *noun* **1** bold insolent behaviour **2** strong probability

presumptuous *adjective* doing things you have no right to do

pretence *noun* behaviour intended to deceive

pretend *verb* to claim or give the appearance of (something untrue) to deceive or in play

pretender *noun* person who makes a false or disputed claim to a position of power

pretension *noun* false claim to merit or importance

pretentious *adjective* making (unjustified) claims to special merit or importance

pretext *noun* false reason given to hide the real one

pretty prettier prettiest *adjective* **1** pleasing to look at ▷ *adverb* **2** fairly, moderately: *I'm pretty certain* > **prettily** *adverb* > **prettiness** *noun*: *the prettiness of the village*

prevail *verb* **1** to gain mastery **2** to be generally established

prevailing *adjective* **1** widespread **2** predominant

prevalent *adjective* widespread, common > **prevalence** *noun*

prevent *verb* to keep from happening or doing > **preventable** *adjective*: *preventable illnesses* > **prevention** *noun*: *crime prevention*

preventive *adjective* intended to help prevent things such as disease or crime

preview *noun* **1** advance showing of a film or exhibition before it is shown to the public **2** part of a computer program which allows the user to look at what has been keyed or added to a document or spreadsheet as it will appear when it is printed

previous *adjective* coming before > **previously** *adverb*

prey preys preying preyed *noun* **1** animal hunted and killed for food by another animal **2** victim ▷ *verb* **3 prey on a** to hunt and kill for food **b** to worry or obsess

price prices pricing priced *noun* **1** amount of money for which a thing is bought or sold ▷ *verb* **2** to fix or ask the price of

priceless *adjective* **1** very valuable **2** *informal* very funny

pricey pricier priciest *adjective informal* expensive

prick *verb* **1** to pierce lightly with a sharp point **2** to cause to feel mental pain ▷ *noun* **3** sudden sharp pain caused by pricking **4** mark made by pricking

prickle prickles prickling prickled *noun* **1** thorn or spike on a plant ▷ *verb* **2** to feel a tingling or pricking sensation

prickly *adjective* **1** having prickles **2** tingling or stinging **3** touchy or irritable

pride prides priding prided *noun* **1** feeling of pleasure and satisfaction when you have done well **2** too high an opinion of yourself **3** sense of dignity and self-respect **4** something that causes you to feel pride **5** group of lions ▷ *verb* **6 pride yourself on** to feel proud about

priest *noun* **1** (in the Christian church) a person who can administer the sacraments and preach **2** (in some other religions) an official who performs religious

ceremonies > **priestly** *adjective*

priestess priestesses *noun* a female priest in a non-Christian religion

priesthood *noun* position of being a priest

prim primmer primmest *adjective* formal, proper and rather prudish

prima donna *noun* **1** leading female opera singer **2** *informal* temperamental person

primaeval *adjective* same as **primeval**

primarily *adverb* chiefly or mainly

primary *adjective* **1** chief, most important **2** being the first stage; elementary

primary colours *plural noun* (in physics) red, green and blue or (in art) red, yellow and blue, from which all other colours can be produced by mixing

primary school *noun* school for children from five to eleven years or (in New Zealand) between five to thirteen years

primate *noun* **1** member of an order of mammals including monkeys and humans **2** archbishop

prime primes priming primed *adjective* **1** main or most important **2** of the highest quality ▷ *noun* **3** time when someone is at his or her best or most vigorous ▷ *verb* **4** to give (someone) information in advance to prepare them for something **5** to prepare (a gun, pump, etc) for use

Prime Minister *noun* leader of a government

prime number *noun* number that can be divided exactly only by itself and 1

primeval *adjective* of the earliest age of the world

primitive *adjective* **1** of an early

simple stage of development **2** basic, crude

primrose *noun* pale yellow spring flower

primula *noun* type of primrose with brightly coloured flowers

prince *noun* **1** male member of a royal family, especially the son of the king or queen **2** male ruler of a small country

princely *adjective* **1** of or like a prince **2** generous, lavish or magnificent

princess princesses *noun* female member of a royal family, especially the daughter of the king or queen

principal *adjective* **1** main or most important ▷ *noun* **2** head of a school or college **3** person taking a leading part in something **4** sum of money lent on which interest is paid ▷ **principally** *adverb*

Do not confuse *principal* with *principle*

principality principalities *noun* territory ruled by a prince

principle *noun* **1** moral rule guiding behaviour **2** general or basic truth **3** scientific law concerning the working of something

Do not confuse *principle* with *principal*

print *verb* **1** to reproduce (a newspaper, book, etc) in large quantities by mechanical or electronic means **2** to reproduce (text or pictures) by pressing ink onto paper etc **3** to write in letters that are not joined up **4** to stamp (fabric) with a design **5** *Photography* to produce (pictures) from negatives ▷ *noun* **6** printed words etc **7** printed copy of a painting **8** printed lettering **9** photograph **10** printed fabric **11** mark left on a surface by something that has pressed against it

printer *noun* **1** person or company engaged in printing **2** machine that prints

printing *noun* **1** process of producing printed matter **2** printed text **3** all the copies of a book printed at one time **4** form of writing in which the letters are not joined together

print-out *noun* printed information from a computer

prior *adjective* **1** earlier **2** **prior to** before ▷ *noun* **3** head monk in a priory

prioress prioresses *noun* deputy head nun in a convent

prioritize prioritizes prioritizing prioritized; also spelt **prioritise** *verb* to arrange (items to be attended to) in order of their relative importance

priority priorities *noun* **1** most important thing that must be dealt with first **2** right to be or go before others

priory priories *noun* place where certain orders of monks or nuns live

prise prises prising prised *verb* to force open by levering

prism *noun* transparent block usually with triangular ends and rectangular sides, used to disperse light into a spectrum or refract it in optical instruments

prison *noun* building where criminals and accused people are held

prisoner *noun* person held captive

pristine *adjective* clean, new and unused

private *adjective* **1** for the use of one person or group only **2** secret **3** personal or unconnected with your work **4** owned or paid for by individuals rather than by the government **5** quiet, not likely to be disturbed ▷ *noun* **6** soldier of the lowest rank > **privacy** *noun*: *an invasion of privacy* > **privately** *adverb*

private school *noun* school that does not receive money from the government, and parents pay for their children to attend

privatize privatizes privatizing privatized; also spelt **privatise** *verb* to sell (a publicly owned company) to individuals or a private company > **privatization** *noun*

privet *noun* bushy evergreen shrub used for hedges

privilege *noun* advantage or favour that only some people have

privileged *adjective* enjoying a special right or immunity

privy *adjective* sharing knowledge of something secret

prize prizes prizing prized *noun* **1** reward given for success in a competition etc ▷ *adjective* **2** winning or likely to win a prize ▷ *verb* **3** to value highly **4** same as **prise**

pro pros *preposition* **1** in favour of ▷ *noun* **2** *informal* professional **3 pros and cons** arguments for and against

pro- *prefix meaning* in favour of: *pro-Russian*

probability probabilities *noun* **1** condition of being probable **2** event or other thing that is likely to happen or be true **3** *Maths* measure of the likelihood of an event happening

probable *adjective* likely to happen or be true

probably *adverb* in all likelihood

probation *noun* **1** system of dealing with law-breakers, especially juvenile ones, by placing them under supervision **2** period when

someone is assessed for suitability for a job etc > **probationary** *adjective*: *a probationary period*

probe probes probing probed *verb* **1** to search into or examine closely ▷ *noun* **2** surgical instrument used to examine a wound, cavity, etc

probiotic *adjective, noun* (of) a bacterium that protects the body from harmful bacteria

problem *noun* **1** something difficult to deal with or solve **2** question or puzzle set for solution > **problematic** *adjective*: *Getting there will be problematic*

procedure *noun* way of doing something, especially the correct or usual one > **procedural** *adjective*: *The judge rejected the case on procedural grounds*

proceed *verb* **1** to start or continue doing **2** *formal* to walk or go

proceedings *plural noun* **1** organized or related series of events **2** minutes of a meeting **3** legal action

proceeds *plural noun* money obtained from an event or activity

process processes processing processed *noun* **1** series of actions or changes **2** method of doing or producing something ▷ *verb* **3** to handle or prepare by a special method of manufacture

procession *noun* line of people or vehicles moving forward together in order

processor *noun* central chip in a computer which controls its operations

proclaim *verb* to declare publicly > **proclamation** *noun*

procure procures procuring procured *verb* to get or provide

prod prods prodding prodded *verb* **1** to poke with something pointed ▷ *noun* **2** prodding

prodigy prodigies *noun* person with some marvellous talent

produce produces producing produced *verb* **1** to bring (something) into existence **2** to present to view **3** to make or manufacture ▷ *noun* **4** food grown for sale

producer *noun* **1** person with control over the making of a film, record, etc **2** person or company that produces something

product *noun* **1** something produced **2** number resulting from multiplication

production *noun* **1** process of manufacturing or growing something in large quantities **2** amount of goods manufactured or food grown by a country or company **3** presentation of a play, opera, etc

productive *adjective* **1** producing large quantities **2** useful or profitable

productivity *noun* rate at which things are produced or dealt with

profane *adjective* showing disrespect for religion or holy things

profess professes professing professed *verb formal* **1** to claim (something to be true), sometimes falsely **2** to declare or express

profession *noun* **1** type of work, such as being a doctor, that needs special training **2** all the people employed in a profession: *the legal profession*

professional *adjective* **1** working in a profession **2** taking part in an activity, such as sport or music, for money **3** very competent ▷ *noun* **4** person who works in a profession **5** person paid to take part in sport,

music, etc > **professionally** *adverb*

professor *noun* teacher of the highest rank in a university > **professorial** *adjective*

proficient *adjective* skilled, expert > **proficiency** *noun*: *proficiency in English*

profile *noun* **1** outline, especially of the face, as seen from the side **2** brief biographical sketch

profit *noun* **1** money gained **2** benefit obtained ▷ *verb* **3** to gain or benefit

profitable *adjective* making profit > **profitability** *noun*: *efforts to increase profitability* > **profitably** *adverb*

profound *adjective* **1** showing or needing great knowledge **2** strongly felt, intense > **profoundly** *adverb* > **profundity** *noun*: *His work lacks profundity*

profuse *adjective* plentiful > **profusely** *adverb* > **profusion** *noun*: *a profusion of wild flowers*

program programs programming programmed *noun* **1** sequence of coded instructions for a computer ▷ *verb* **2** to arrange (data) so that it can be processed by a computer **3** to feed a program into (a computer) > **programmer** *noun*

programmable *adjective* capable of being programmed to perform a function automatically

programme *noun* **1** planned series of events **2** broadcast on radio or television **3** list of items or performers in an entertainment

progress progresses progressing progressed *noun* **1** improvement or development **2** movement forward **3** **in progress** taking place ▷ *verb* **4** to become more advanced or skilful

5 to move forward > **progression**
noun: *Both drugs slow the progression
of the disease*

progressive adjective **1** favouring
political or social reform
2 happening gradually

prohibit verb to forbid or prevent
from happening

prohibition noun **1** act of forbidding
2 ban on the sale or drinking of
alcohol

prohibitive adjective (of prices)
too high to be affordable
> **prohibitively** adverb

project noun **1** planned scheme to
do or examine something over a
period ▷ verb **2** to make a forecast
based on known data **3** to make (a
film or slide) appear on a screen **4** to
communicate (an impression) **5** to
stick out beyond a surface or edge
> **projection** noun: *sales projections*

projector noun apparatus for
projecting photographic images,
films or slides on a screen

proletariat noun formal working
class > **proletarian** adjective

proliferate proliferates
proliferating proliferated verb
to increase rapidly in numbers
> **proliferation** noun

prolific adjective very productive: *a
prolific writer* > **prolifically** adverb

prologue noun introduction to a
play or book

prolong verb to make (something)
last longer > **prolonged** adjective

prom noun informal concert at which
some of the audience stand; also
promenade concert

promenade noun Chiefly Brit paved
walkway along the seafront at a
holiday resort

prominent adjective **1** very
noticeable **2** famous, widely
known > **prominence** noun

> **prominently** adverb

promiscuous adjective having
many casual sexual relationships
> **promiscuity** noun: *male
promiscuity*

promise promises promising
promised verb **1** to say that you will
definitely do or not do something
2 to show signs of; seem likely
▷ noun **3** undertaking to do or not
to do something **4** indication of
future success

promising adjective likely to
succeed or turn out well

promontory promontories
noun point of high land jutting out
into the sea

promote promotes promoting
promoted verb **1** to help to make
(something) happen or increase
2 to raise to a higher rank or
position **3** to encourage the sale
of (a product) by advertising
> **promotion** noun: *promotion
through the ranks* > **promotional**
adjective: *promotional material*

promoter noun person who
organizes or finances an event etc

prompt verb **1** to cause (an action)
2 to remind (an actor or speaker) of
words that he or she has forgotten
▷ adjective **3** done without delay
▷ adverb **4** exactly: *six o'clock prompt*
> **promptly** adverb

prone adjective **1** **prone to** likely to
do or be affected by (something)
2 lying face downwards

prong noun one spike of a fork or
similar instrument

pronoun noun word, such as *she* or
it, used to replace a noun

pronounce pronounces
pronouncing pronounced verb
1 to form the sounds of (words or
letters), especially clearly or in a
particular way **2** to declare formally

or officially

pronounced *adjective* very noticeable

pronouncement *noun* formal announcement

pronunciation *noun* way in which a word or language is pronounced

proof *noun* 1 evidence that shows that something is true or has happened 2 copy of something printed, such as the pages of a book, for checking before final production ▷ *adjective* 3 able to withstand: *proof against criticism* 4 denoting the strength of an alcoholic drink: *seventy proof*

prop props propping propped *verb* 1 to support (something) so that it stays upright or in place ▷ *noun* 2 pole, beam, etc used as a support 3 movable object used on the set of a film or play

propaganda *noun* (organized promotion of) information to assist or damage the cause of a government or movement

propagate propagates propagating propagated *verb* 1 to spread (information and ideas) 2 to reproduce, breed or grow > **propagation** *noun*

propel propels propelling propelled *verb* to cause to move forward

propeller *noun* revolving shaft with blades for driving a ship or aircraft

propensity propensities *noun* *formal* natural tendency

proper *adjective* 1 real or genuine 2 suited to a particular purpose 3 correct in behaviour 4 *Brit, Aust, NZ informal* complete > **properly** *adverb*

proper noun *noun* name of a person, place or institution

property properties *noun*

1 something owned 2 possessions collectively 3 land or buildings owned by somebody 4 quality or attribute

prophecy prophecies *noun* 1 prediction 2 message revealing God's will

▋ The noun *prophecy* ends in *cy*

prophesy prophesies prophesying prophesied *verb* to foretell

▋ The verb *prophesy* ends in *sy*

prophet *noun* 1 person supposedly chosen by God to spread His word 2 person who predicts the future

prophetic *adjective* correctly predicting what will happen > **prophetically** *adverb*

proportion *noun* 1 relative size or extent 2 correct relation between connected parts 3 part considered with respect to the whole 4 **proportions** dimensions or size 5 **in proportion a** comparable in size, rate of increase, etc **b** without exaggerating ▷ *verb* 6 to adjust in relative amount or size

proportional or **proportionate** *adjective* being in proportion > **proportionally** or **proportionately** *adverb*

proportional representation *noun* system of voting in elections in which the number of representatives of each party is in proportion to the number of people who voted for it

proposal *noun* 1 plan that has been suggested 2 offer of marriage

propose proposes proposing proposed *verb* 1 to put forward (a plan) for consideration 2 to nominate (someone) for a position 3 to intend or plan (to do) 4 to make an offer of marriage

proposition *noun* 1 offer

2 statement or assertion **3** *informal* thing to be dealt with

proprietor *noun* owner of a business establishment

propriety *noun formal* correct conduct

propulsion *noun* **1** method by which something is propelled **2** act of propelling or state of being propelled

prose *noun* ordinary speech or writing in contrast to poetry

prosecute prosecutes prosecuting prosecuted *verb* **1** to bring a criminal charge against (someone) **2** to continue to do (something) > **prosecutor** *noun*

prosecution *noun* **1** bringing of criminal charges against someone **2** lawyers who try to prove that a person on trial is guilty

prospect *noun* **1** something anticipated **2 prospects** probability of future success ▷ *verb* **3** to explore, especially for gold or oil > **prospector** *noun*

prospective *adjective* **1** future **2** expected

prospectus *noun* booklet giving details of a university, company, etc

prosper *verb* to be successful > **prosperous** *adjective*: *a prosperous family*

prosperity *noun* success and wealth

prostitute *noun* person who offers sexual intercourse in return for payment > **prostitution** *noun*

prostrate *adjective* **1** lying face downwards **2** physically or emotionally exhausted

protagonist *noun formal* **1** supporter of a cause **2** leading character in a play or a story

protea *noun* African shrub with showy flowers

protect *verb* to defend from trouble, harm or loss > **protection** *noun*

protective *adjective* **1** giving protection: *protective clothing* **2** tending or wishing to protect someone

protector *noun* person or thing that protects

protégé *noun* person who is protected and helped by another > **protégée** *noun* woman or girl who is protected and helped by another person

protein *noun* any of a group of complex organic compounds that are essential for life

protest *noun* **1** declaration or demonstration of objection ▷ *verb* **2** to object or disagree **3** to assert formally

Protestant *noun* **1** follower of any of the Christian churches that split from the Roman Catholic Church in the sixteenth century ▷ *adjective* **2** of or relating to such a church

protestation *noun* strong declaration

proto- *prefix meaning* first: *protohuman*

protocol *noun* rules of behaviour for formal occasions

proton *noun* positively charged particle in the nucleus of an atom

prototype *noun* original or model to be copied or developed

protracted *adjective* lengthened or extended

protractor *noun* instrument for measuring angles

protrude protrudes protruding protruded *verb* to stick out or project > **protrusion** *noun*: *a protrusion of rock*

proud *adjective* **1** feeling pleasure and satisfaction **2** feeling honoured **3** thinking yourself superior to

other people **4** dignified > **proudly**
adverb

prove proves proving proved
or **proven** *verb* **1** to establish the
validity of **2** to demonstrate or test
3 to be found to be

proven *adjective* known from
experience to work

proverb *noun* short saying that
expresses a truth or gives a warning
> **proverbial** *adjective*: *the proverbial
man in the street*

**provide provides providing
provided** *verb* **1** to make
available **2** **provide for a** to take
precautions (against) **b** to support
financially > **provider** *noun*

provided that or **providing**
conjunction on condition that

providence *noun* God or nature
seen as a protective force that
arranges people's lives

province *noun* **1** area governed as a
unit of a country or empire **2** area of
learning, activity, etc **3** **provinces**
parts of a country outside the
capital

provincial *adjective* **1** of a province
or the provinces **2** unsophisticated
and narrow-minded

provision *noun* **1** act of supplying
something **2** something supplied
3 *Law* condition incorporated in a
document **4** **provisions** food

provisional *adjective* temporary or
conditional > **provisionally** *adverb*

proviso provisos or **provisoes**
noun condition in an agreement

provocation *noun* act done
deliberately to annoy someone

provocative *adjective* **1** intended to
annoy people or make them react
2 intended to make someone feel
sexual desire

**provoke provokes provoking
provoked** *verb* **1** to deliberately

anger **2** to cause (an adverse
reaction)

prow *noun* bow of a vessel

prowess *noun* superior skill or
ability

prowl *verb* to move stealthily
around a place as if in search of prey
or plunder

proximity *noun formal* **1** nearness
in space or time **2** nearness or
closeness in a series

proxy proxies *noun* **1** person
authorized to act on behalf of
someone else **2** authority to act on
behalf of someone else

prude *noun* person who is
excessively modest, prim or proper
> **prudish** *adjective*

prudent *adjective* cautious, discreet
and sensible > **prudence** *noun*
> **prudently** *adverb*

prune prunes pruning pruned
noun **1** dried plum **2** to cut off dead
parts or excessive branches from
(a tree or plant) ▷ *verb* **3** to shorten
or reduce

pry pries prying pried *verb* to
make an impertinent or uninvited
inquiry (about a private matter)

PS *abbreviation* postscript

psalm *noun* sacred song

pseudo- *prefix indicating* false,
pretending or unauthentic:
pseudoclassical

pseudonym *noun* fictitious name
adopted especially by an author

psyche *noun* human mind or soul

psychiatry *noun* branch of
medicine concerned with mental
disorders > **psychiatric** *adjective*
> **psychiatrist** *noun*

psychic *adjective* **1** having mental
powers which cannot be explained
by natural laws **2** relating to the
mind ▷ *noun* **3** person with psychic
powers

psychoanalyse psychoanalyses psychoanalysing psychoanalysed verb to examine or treat (a person) by psychoanalysis

psychoanalysis noun method of treating mental and emotional disorders by discussion and analysis of the person's thoughts and feelings > **psychoanalyst** noun

psychological adjective **1** of or affecting the mind **2** of psychology > **psychologically** adverb

psychology psychologies noun **1** study of human and animal behaviour **2** informal person's mental make-up > **psychologist** noun: She trained as a psychologist

psychopath noun person afflicted with a personality disorder causing him or her to commit antisocial or violent acts > **psychopathic** adjective: a psychopathic killer

psychosis psychoses noun severe mental disorder in which the sufferer's contact with reality becomes distorted > **psychotic** adjective: psychotic disorders

psychotherapy noun treatment of nervous disorders by psychological methods > **psychotherapist** noun

pterodactyl noun extinct flying reptile with batlike wings

PTO abbreviation please turn over

pub noun building with a bar licensed to sell alcoholic drinks

puberty noun beginning of sexual maturity

pubic adjective of the lower abdomen: pubic hair

public adjective **1** of or concerning the people as a whole **2** for use by everyone **3** well-known **4** performed or made openly ▷ noun **5** the community, people in general

> **publicly** adverb

publican noun Brit, Aust, NZ person who owns or runs a pub

publication noun **1** publishing of a printed work **2** printed work: medical publications

publicist noun person, especially a press agent or journalist, who publicizes something

publicity noun **1** process or information used to arouse public attention **2** public interest so aroused

publicize publicizes publicizing publicized; also spelt **publicise** verb to bring to public attention

public school noun private fee-paying school in Britain

public servant noun Aust, NZ someone who works in the public service

public service noun Aust, NZ government departments responsible for the administration of the country

publish publishes publishing published verb **1** to produce and issue (printed matter) for sale **2** to announce formally or in public > **publishing** noun

publisher noun company or person that publishes books, periodicals, music, etc

puck noun small rubber disc used in ice hockey

pudding noun **1** dessert, especially a cooked one served hot **2** savoury dish with pastry or batter **3** sausage-like mass of meat

puddle noun small pool of water, especially of rain

puerile adjective silly and childish

puff noun **1** (sound of) a short blast of breath, wind, etc **2** act of inhaling cigarette smoke **3 out of puff** out of breath ▷ verb **4** to blow or

breathe in short quick draughts
5 to take draws at (a cigarette)
6 puff up or **out** to swell > **puffy**
adjective: *dark-ringed puffy eyes*
puffin *noun* black-and-white sea
bird with a brightly-coloured beak
pug *noun* small snub-nosed dog
puja *noun* variety of practices which
make up Hindu worship
puke pukes puking puked *informal*
verb **1** to vomit ▷ *noun* **2** vomited
matter
pull *verb* **1** to exert force on (an
object) to move it towards the
source of the force **2** to strain or
stretch **3** to remove or extract **4** to
attract ▷ *noun* **5** act of pulling
6 force used in pulling **7** *informal*
power, influence > **pull down** *verb*
to destroy or demolish
pulley pulleys *noun* wheel with a
grooved rim in which a belt, chain
or piece of rope runs in order to lift
weights by a downward pull
pullover *noun* sweater that is pulled
on over the head
pulmonary *adjective formal* of
the lungs
pulp *noun* **1** soft wet substance made
from crushed or beaten matter
2 flesh of a fruit
pulpit *noun* raised platform for a
preacher
pulse pulses pulsing pulsed *noun*
1 regular beating of blood through
the arteries at each heartbeat **2** any
regular beat or vibration **3** edible
seed of a pod-bearing plant such as
a bean or pea ▷ *verb* **4** to beat, throb
or vibrate
puma *noun* large American wild cat
with a greyish-brown coat
pumice *noun* light porous stone
used for scouring
**pummel pummels pummelling
pummelled** *verb* to strike

repeatedly with or as if with
the fists
pump *noun* **1** machine used to
force a liquid or gas to move in
a particular direction **2** light
flat-soled shoe ▷ *verb* **3** to raise
or drive (air, liquid, etc) with a
pump **4 pump into** to supply
(something) to (something) in
large amounts: *pumping money into
the economy*
pumpkin *noun* large round fruit
with an orange rind, soft flesh and
many seeds
pun *noun* use of words to exploit
double meanings for humorous
effect
**punch punches punching
punched** *verb* **1** to strike at with a
clenched fist ▷ *noun* **2** blow with
a clenched fist **3** tool or machine
for shaping, piercing or engraving
4 drink made from a mixture of
wine, spirits, fruit, sugar and spices
punctual *adjective* arriving
or taking place at the correct
time > **punctuality** *noun*: *train
punctuality* > **punctually** *adverb*
**punctuate punctuates
punctuating punctuated** *verb*
1 to put punctuation marks into
(a written text) **2** to interrupt at
frequent intervals
punctuation *noun* (use of) marks
such as commas, colons, etc in
writing, to assist in making the
sense clear
**puncture punctures puncturing
punctured** *noun* **1** small hole made
by a sharp object, especially in
a tyre ▷ *verb* **2** to pierce a hole in
(something) with a sharp object
pungent *adjective* having a strong
sharp bitter flavour > **pungency**
noun: *the pungency of dried garlic*
punish punishes punishing

punished *verb* to cause (someone) to suffer or undergo a penalty for some wrongdoing

punishing *adjective* harsh or difficult

punishment *noun* something unpleasant done to someone because they have done something wrong

punitive *adjective* relating to punishment

Punjabi Punjabis *adjective* **1** belonging or relating to the Punjab, a state in north-western India ▷ *noun* **2** someone from the Punjab **3** language spoken in the Punjab

punk *noun* **1** aggressive style of rock music **2** follower of this music

punt *noun* open flat-bottomed boat propelled by a pole

puny punier puniest *adjective* small and feeble

pup *noun* young of certain animals, such as dogs and seals

pupil *noun* **1** person who is taught by a teacher **2** round dark opening in the centre of the eye

puppet *noun* small doll or figure moved by strings or by the operator's hand

puppy puppies *noun* young dog

purchase purchases purchasing purchased *verb* **1** to obtain (goods) by payment ▷ *noun* **2** thing that is bought **3** act of buying > **purchaser** *noun*

pure purer purest *adjective* **1** unmixed or untainted **2** innocent **3** complete: *pure delight* **4** concerned with theory only: *pure mathematics*

purée *noun* food which has been mashed or blended to a thick, smooth consistency

purely *adverb* involving only one feature and not including anything else

Purgatory *noun* (in Roman Catholic belief) place where spirits of the dead are sent to suffer for their sins before going to Heaven

purge purges purging purged *verb* **1** to rid (something) of undesirable qualities **2** to rid (an organization, etc) of undesirable people

purify purifies purifying purified *verb* to free (something) of harmful or inferior matter > **purification** *noun*: *a water purification plant*

purist *noun* person concerned with strict obedience to the traditions of a subject

puritan *noun* someone who believes in strict moral principles and avoids physical pleasures > **puritanical** *adjective*

purity *noun* state or quality of being pure: *a voice of great purity*

purple *noun* **1** colour between red and blue ▷ *adjective* **2** of this colour

purport purports purporting purported *verb* to claim (to be or do something)

purpose *noun* **1** reason for which something is done or exists **2** determination **3** practical advantage or use: *Use the time to good purpose* **4** on purpose intentionally

purposeful *adjective* having or showing determination to do something

purposely *adverb* intentionally

purr *verb* **1** (of cats) to make low vibrant sound, usually when pleased ▷ *noun* **2** this sound

purse purses pursing pursed *noun* **1** small bag for money **2** US, NZ handbag ▷ *verb* **3** to draw (your lips) together into a small round shape

purser *noun* ship's officer who keeps the accounts

pursue pursues pursuing pursued *verb* 1 to follow (a person, vehicle or animal) in order to capture or overtake 2 to follow (a goal) 3 to engage in > **pursuer** *noun*: *He shook off his pursuers*

pursuit *noun* 1 pursuing 2 occupation or pastime

purveyor *noun formal* person who sells or provides goods or services

pus *noun* yellowish matter produced by infected tissue

push pushes pushing pushed *verb* 1 to move or try to move by steady force 2 to drive or spur (yourself or another person) to do something 3 *informal* to sell (drugs) illegally ▷ *noun* 4 act of pushing 5 special effort 6 **the push** *informal* dismissal from a job or relationship > **push off** *verb informal* to go away

pushchair *noun* small folding chair on wheels in which a baby or toddler can be wheeled around

pusher *noun informal* person who sells illegal drugs

pushing *preposition* almost or nearly (a certain age, speed, etc): *pushing sixty*

pushover *noun informal* 1 something that is easy 2 someone who is easily persuaded or defeated

pushy pushier pushiest *adjective informal* too assertive or ambitious

pussy pussies *noun informal* cat

put puts putting put *verb* 1 to cause to be (in a position or place) 2 to cause to be (in a state or condition) 3 to lay (blame, emphasis, etc) on a person or thing 4 to express 5 to estimate or judge ▷ *noun* 6 throw in putting the shot > **put down** *verb* 1 *informal* to belittle or humiliate 2 to put (a sick animal) to death > **put off** *verb* 1 to postpone 2 to cause to lose interest in > **put out** *verb* 1 to extinguish (a fire, light, etc) 2 to annoy or anger 3 to dislocate: *He put his back out gardening* > **put up** *verb* 1 to build or erect 2 to accommodate 3 **put up with** *informal* to endure or tolerate

putt *Golf noun* 1 stroke on the putting green to roll the ball into or near the hole ▷ *verb* 2 to strike (the ball) in this way

putter *noun* golf club for putting

putting *noun* golf played with a putter on a course of very short holes

putty *noun* adhesive used to fix glass into frames and fill cracks in woodwork

puzzle puzzles puzzling puzzled *verb* 1 to perplex and confuse or be perplexed or confused ▷ *noun* 2 problem that cannot be easily solved 3 toy, game or question that requires skill or ingenuity to solve > **puzzled** *adjective* > **puzzlement** *noun* > **puzzling** *adjective*

PVC *abbreviation* polyvinyl chloride: plastic material used in clothes etc

Pygmy Pygmies *noun* 1 member of one of the very short peoples of Equatorial Africa ▷ *adjective* 2 **pygmy** very small

pyjamas *plural noun* loose-fitting trousers and top worn in bed

pylon *noun* steel tower-like structure supporting electrical cables

pyramid *noun* 1 solid figure with a flat base and triangular sides sloping upwards to a point 2 building of this shape, especially an ancient Egyptian one

pyre *noun* pile of wood for burning a corpse on

python *noun* large nonpoisonous snake that crushes its prey

q

quack *verb* **1** (of a duck) to make the loud harsh sound that ducks make ▷ *noun* **2** sound made by a duck **3** unqualified person who claims medical knowledge

quad *noun* **1** short for **quadrangle** **2** short for **quadruplet**

quad bike *noun* vehicle like a small motorcycle with four large wheels

quadrangle *noun* (also **quad**) rectangular courtyard with buildings on all four sides

quadri- *prefix meaning* four: *quadrilateral*

quadriceps *noun* large muscle in four parts at the front of your thigh

The plural of *quadriceps* is *quadriceps*

quadrilateral *noun Maths* polygon with four sides

quadruped *noun* four-legged animal

quadruple quadruples quadrupling quadrupled *verb* **1** (of an amount or number) to become four times as large as previously **2** to make (an amount or number) four times as large as previously; multiply by four

quadruplet *noun* one of four children born at the same time to the same mother

quagmire *noun* soft wet area of land

quail *noun* **1** small game bird of the partridge family ▷ *verb* **2** to feel or look afraid

quaint *adjective* attractively unusual, especially in an old-fashioned style > **quaintly** *adverb*

quake quakes quaking quaked *verb* to tremble with fear

Quaker *noun* member of a Christian sect, the Society of Friends

qualification *noun* **1** official record of achievement in a course or examination **2** quality or skill needed for a particular activity **3** something you add to a statement to make it less strong

qualify qualifies qualifying qualified *verb* **1** to pass the necessary examinations or tests to do a particular job or to take part in a sporting event **2** to make (someone) suitable for something **3** to moderate or restrict (a statement) by adding a detail or explanation to make it less strong

quality qualities *noun* **1** how good something is **2** characteristic

qualm *noun* **1** pang of conscience **2** sudden sensation of misgiving

quandary quandaries *noun* difficult situation or dilemma

quango quangos *noun* independent but government-appointed and -financed body responsible for a particular area of public administration; short for *quasi-autonomous non-governmental organization*

quantify quantifies quantifying quantified *verb* to express (something) as a number or an amount > **quantifiable** *adjective*

quantity quantities *noun*
1 amount you can measure or count
2 amount of something that there
is: *quantity rather than quality*

quarantine *noun* period or state of
isolation to prevent the spread of
disease between people or animals

**quarrel quarrels quarrelling
quarrelled** *noun* 1 angry argument
▷ *verb* 2 to have an angry argument

**quarry quarries quarrying
quarried** *noun* 1 place where stone
is dug from the surface of the earth
2 person or animal that is being
hunted ▷ *verb* 3 to extract (stone)
from a quarry

quart *noun* unit of liquid measure
equal to two pints (1.136 litres)

quarter *noun* 1 one of four equal
parts of something 2 *US* 25-cent
piece 3 region or district of a town
or city 4 fourth part of a year
5 *informal* unit of weight equal to 4
ounces 6 **quarters** lodgings

quarterfinal *noun* round before the
semifinal in a competition

quarterly quarterlies *adjective*
1 occurring, due or issued every
three months ▷ *noun* 2 magazine or
journal issued every three months

quartet *noun* 1 group of four
performers 2 music for such a group

quartz *noun* kind of hard, shiny
crystal used in making very
accurate watches and clocks

**quash quashes quashing
quashed** *verb* to throw out (a
decision or judgment)

quasi- *prefix meaning* almost but not
really: *quasi-religious*

quaver *verb* 1 (of a voice) to quiver
or tremble ▷ *noun* 2 *Music* note (♪)
half the length of a crotchet and an
eighth the length of a semibreve.

quay quays *noun* place where boats

are tied up and loaded or unloaded

queasy queasier queasiest
adjective feeling slightly sick
> **queasiness** *noun*

queen *noun* 1 female monarch or a
woman married to a king 2 only
female bee, wasp or ant in a colony
that can lay eggs 3 most powerful
piece in chess

queen mother *noun* widow of a
king and the mother of the reigning
monarch

queer *adjective* very strange

quell *verb* 1 to put an end to or
suppress (a rebellion or riot) 2 to
overcome (a feeling)

**quench quenches quenching
quenched** *verb* to satisfy (your
thirst)

query queries querying queried
noun 1 question 2 question mark
▷ *verb* 3 to express uncertainty,
doubt or an objection concerning

quest *noun* long and difficult search

question *noun* 1 sentence which
asks for information 2 problem
that needs to be discussed; matter
3 difficulty or uncertainty 4 **out
of the question** impossible 5 **in
question** under discussion ▷ *verb*
6 to put a question or questions to
7 to express uncertainty about

questionable *adjective* of
disputable value or authority

question mark *noun* punctuation
mark (?) written at the end of
questions

questionnaire *noun* set of
questions on a form, used to collect
information from people

queue queues queuing or
queueing queued *noun* 1 line
of people or vehicles waiting for
something ▷ *verb* 2 (often followed
by *up*) to form or remain in a line
while waiting

quibble quibbles quibbling quibbled verb 1 to make trivial objections ▷ noun 2 trivial objection

quiche noun savoury tart with an egg custard filling to which vegetables etc are added

quick adjective 1 speedy, fast 2 lasting or taking a short time 3 happening without any delay 4 intelligent and able to understand things easily ▷ noun 5 area of sensitive flesh under a nail > **quickly** adverb

quicksand noun area of deep wet sand that you sink into if you walk on it

quid noun Brit informal pound
▆ The plural of quid is quid

quiet adjective 1 making little or no noise 2 calm or peaceful 3 involving very little fuss or publicity ▷ noun 4 quietness > **quietly** adverb

quieten verb to make (someone) quiet

quill noun 1 pen made from the feather of a bird's wing or tail 2 stiff hollow spine of a porcupine or hedgehog

quilt noun padded covering for a bed

quilted adjective consisting of two layers of fabric with a layer of soft material between them

quin noun short for **quintuplet**

quince noun acid-tasting fruit

quintessence noun formal most perfect representation of a quality or state > **quintessential** adjective

quintet noun 1 group of five performers 2 music for such a group

quintuplet noun one of five children born at the same time to the same mother

quip quips quipping quipped noun 1 witty remark ▷ verb 2 to make a witty remark

quirk noun 1 odd habit or characteristic 2 unexpected event or development: a quirk of fate > **quirky** adjective

quit quits quitting quit verb 1 to stop (doing something) 2 to give up (a job) 3 to depart from (a place)

quite adverb 1 fairly but not very: She's quite pretty 2 absolutely or completely: You're quite right 3 emphasizing how large or impressive something is: It was quite a party ▷ interjection 4 expression of agreement

quiver verb 1 to shake with a tremulous movement ▷ noun 2 shaking or trembling 3 case for arrows

quiz quizzes quizzing quizzed noun 1 game in which the competitors are asked questions to test their knowledge ▷ verb 2 to question (someone) closely about something

quizzical adjective amused and questioning: a quizzical look

quota noun number or quantity of something which is officially allowed

quotation noun 1 extract from a book or speech which is quoted 2 statement of how much a piece of work will cost

quotation marks plural noun raised commas used in writing to mark the beginning and end of a quotation or passage of speech

quote quotes quoting quoted verb 1 to repeat (words) exactly from (an earlier work, speech or conversation) 2 to state (a price) for goods or a job of work ▷ noun 3 quotation 4 **quotes** informal the same as **quotation marks**

Qur'an another spelling of **Koran**

RAAF *abbreviation* Royal Australian Air Force

rabbi rabbis *noun* Jewish spiritual leader

rabbit *noun* small burrowing mammal with long ears

rabble *noun* disorderly crowd of noisy people

rabid *adjective* **1** fanatical **2** having rabies

rabies *noun* usually fatal viral disease transmitted by dogs and certain other animals

raccoon *noun* small N American mammal with a long striped tail

race races racing raced *noun* **1** contest of speed **2** group of people of common ancestry with distinguishing physical features, such as skin colour ▷ *verb* **3** to take part in a contest of speed with someone **4** to run swiftly > **racer** *noun*

racecourse *noun* grass track, sometimes with jumps, along which horses race

racehorse *noun* horse trained to run in races

racetrack *noun* circuit used for races between cars, bicycles or runners

racial *adjective* relating to the different races that people belong to > **racially** *adverb*

racing *noun* contests of speed between animals or vehicles

racism or **racialism** *noun* hostile attitude or behaviour to members of other races, based on a belief in the innate superiority of one's own race > **racist** or **racialist** *adjective, noun: a racist attack; He's a racist*

rack *noun* **1** framework for holding particular articles, such as coats or luggage **2 go to rack and ruin** to be destroyed ▷ *verb* **3** to cause great suffering to **4 rack your brains** *informal* to try very hard to remember

racket *noun* **1** noisy disturbance **2** occupation by which money is made illegally **3** another spelling of **racquet**

racquet or **racket** *noun* bat with strings across it used in tennis and similar games

racy racier raciest *adjective* **1** slightly shocking **2** spirited or lively

radar *noun* device for tracking distant objects by bouncing high-frequency radio pulses off them

radiant *adjective* **1** looking happy **2** shining **3** emitting radiation > **radiance** *noun*

radiate radiates radiating radiated *verb* **1** to spread out from a centre **2** to show (an emotion or quality) to a great degree

radiation *noun* **1** transmission of energy from one body to another **2** particles or waves emitted in nuclear decay **3** process of radiating

radiator *noun* **1** *Brit* arrangement of pipes containing hot water or steam to heat a room **2** tubes containing water as cooling apparatus for a car engine **3** *Aust, NZ* electric fire

radical *adjective* **1** fundamental **2** thorough **3** advocating fundamental change ▷ *noun* **4** person advocating fundamental (political) change **> radicalism** *noun: a long tradition of radicalism* **> radically** *adverb*

radii *noun* a plural of **radius**

radio radios radioing radioed *noun* **1** system of sending sound over a distance by transmitting electrical signals **2** piece of equipment for listening to radio programmes **3** communications device for sending and receiving messages using radio waves **4** broadcasting of programmes to the public by radio ▷ *verb* **5** to transmit (a message) by radio

radioactive *adjective* emitting radiation as a result of nuclear decay **> radioactivity** *noun: high levels of radioactivity*

radiotherapy *noun* treatment of disease, especially cancer, by radiation **> radiotherapist** *noun*

radish radishes *noun* small hot-flavoured root vegetable eaten raw in salads

radium *noun Chemistry* radioactive metallic element

radius radii or **radiuses** *noun* (length of) a straight line from the centre to the circumference of a circle

RAF *abbreviation* (in Britain) Royal Air Force

raffia *noun* prepared palm fibre for weaving mats etc

raffle raffles raffling raffled *noun* **1** lottery with goods as prizes ▷ *verb* **2** to offer as a prize in a raffle

raft *noun* floating platform of logs,

planks, etc

rafter *noun* one of the main beams of a roof

rag *noun* **1** fragment of cloth **2** *informal* newspaper **3 rags** tattered clothing

rage rages raging raged *noun* **1** violent anger or passion ▷ *verb* **2** to feel or show intense anger **3** to proceed violently and without restraint

ragged *adjective* **1** (of clothes) old and torn **2** untidy

raid *noun* **1** sudden surprise attack or search ▷ *verb* **2** to make a raid on **3** to sneak into (a place) in order to steal **> raider** *noun*

rail *noun* **1** horizontal bar, especially as part of a fence or track **2** railway considered as a means of transport ▷ *verb* **3 rail at** or **against** to complain bitterly or loudly about

railing *noun* fence made of rails supported by posts

railway railways *noun* **1** track of iron rails on which trains run **2** company operating a railway

rain *noun* **1** water falling in drops from the clouds ▷ *verb* **2** to fall or pour down as rain **3** to fall rapidly and in large quantities

rainbird *noun* South African bird whose call is believed to be a sign that it will rain

rainbow *noun* arch of colours in the sky

raincoat *noun* water-resistant overcoat

rainfall *noun* amount of rain

rainforest *noun* dense forest in tropical and temperate areas

rainwater *noun* rain that has been stored

rainy rainier rainiest *adjective* (of day, season, weather etc) characterized by having a lot of rain

raise raises raising raised *verb* **1** to lift up **2** to set upright **3** to increase in amount or intensity **4** to collect or levy **5** to bring up (a family) **6** to put forward for consideration

raisin *noun* dried grape

rake rakes raking raked *noun* **1** tool with a long handle and a crosspiece with teeth, used for smoothing earth or gathering leaves, hay, etc ▷ *verb* **2** to gather or smooth with a rake **3** to search (through) **> rake up** *verb* to revive memories of (a forgotten unpleasant event)

rally rallies rallying rallied *noun* **1** large gathering of people for a meeting **2** marked recovery of strength **3** *Tennis etc* lively exchange of strokes **4** car-driving competition on public roads ▷ *verb* **5** to bring or come together after dispersal or for a common cause **6** to regain health or strength

ram rams ramming rammed *noun* **1** adult male sheep ▷ *verb* **2** to strike against with force **3** to force or drive

RAM *abbreviation Computers* random access memory: storage space which can be filled with data but which loses its contents when the machine is switched off

Ramadan *noun* **1** 9th Muslim month **2** strict fasting from dawn to dusk observed during this time

ramble rambles rambling rambled *verb* **1** to walk without a definite route **2** to talk in a confused way ▷ *noun* **3** long walk in the countryside

rambler *noun* person who rambles

ramifications *plural noun* consequences resulting from an action

ramp *noun* slope joining two level surfaces

rampage rampages rampaging rampaged *verb* **1** to rush about violently ▷ *noun* **2** **go on the rampage** to behave violently or destructively

rampant *adjective* growing or spreading uncontrollably

rampart *noun* mound or wall for defence

ramshackle *adjective* tumbledown

ran *verb* past tense of **run**

ranch ranches *noun* large cattle farm in the American West

rancid *adjective* (of butter, bacon, etc) stale and having an offensive smell

rancour *noun* deep bitter hate **> rancorous** *adjective*: *a series of rancorous disputes*

rand *noun* monetary unit of South Africa

random *adjective* **1** made or done by chance or without plan **2** **at random** haphazard(ly) **> randomly** *adverb*

rang *verb* past tense of **ring**

range ranges ranging ranged *noun* **1** limits of effectiveness or variation **2** distance that a missile or plane can travel **3** distance of a mark shot at **4** whole set of related things **5** chain of mountains **6** place for shooting practice or rocket testing ▷ *verb* **7** to vary between one point and another **8** to cover or extend over **9** to roam (over)

ranger *noun* official in charge of a nature reserve etc

rank *noun* **1** relative place or position **2** status **3** social class **4** row or line **5** **rank and file** ordinary people or members **6** **the ranks** common soldiers ▷ *verb* **7** to have a specific rank or position **8** to arrange in rows or lines ▷ *adjective* **9** complete or absolute: *rank favouritism*

10 smelling offensively strong

ransack *verb* **1** to search through every part of (a place or thing) **2** to pillage or plunder

ransom *noun* money demanded in return for the release of someone who has been kidnapped

rant *verb* to talk in a loud and excited way

rap raps rapping rapped *verb* **1** to hit with a sharp quick blow **2** to utter (a command) abruptly **3** to perform a rhythmic monologue with musical backing ▷ *noun* **4** quick sharp blow **5** rhythmic monologue performed to music > **rapper** *noun*

rape rapes raping raped *verb* **1** to force (someone) to submit to sexual intercourse ▷ *noun* **2** act of raping **3** plant with oil-yielding seeds, also used as fodder > **rapist** *noun: a convicted rapist*

rapid *adjective* **1** quick or swift ▷ *noun* **2** **rapids** part of a river with a fast turbulent current > **rapidity** *noun* > **rapidly** *adverb*

rapier *noun* fine-bladed sword

rapport *noun* harmony or agreement

rapt *adjective* engrossed or spellbound

rapture *noun* feeling of extreme delight > **rapturous** *adjective: a rapturous welcome* > **rapturously** *adverb*

rare *adjective* **1** uncommon **2** infrequent **3** of uncommonly high quality **4** (of meat) lightly cooked > **rarely** *adverb* seldom

rarefied *adjective* **1** highly specialized, exalted **2** (of air) thin

raring *adjective* **raring to** enthusiastic, willing or ready to

rarity rarities *noun* **1** something that is valuable because it is

unusual **2** state of being rare

rascal *noun* **1** rogue **2** naughty (young) person

rash rashes *adjective* **1** hasty, reckless or incautious ▷ *noun* **2** eruption of spots or patches on the skin **3** outbreak of (unpleasant) occurrences > **rashly** *adverb*

rasher *noun* thin slice of bacon

rasp *noun* **1** harsh grating noise **2** coarse file ▷ *verb* **3** to make a harsh grating noise

raspberry raspberries *noun* red juicy edible berry

Rastafarian *noun, adjective* (member) of a religion originating in Jamaica and regarding Haile Selassie as God; also **Rasta**

rat *noun* **1** small rodent **2** *informal* contemptible person, especially a deserter or informer

rate rates rating rated *noun* **1** degree of speed or progress **2** proportion between two things **3** charge **4** **at any rate** in any case **5** **rates** (in some countries) local tax on business or property ▷ *verb* **6** to consider or value **7** to estimate the value of

rather *adverb* **1** to some extent **2** more truly or appropriately **3** more willingly

ratify ratifies ratifying ratified *verb* to give formal approval to > **ratification** *noun: the ratification of the treaty*

rating *noun* **1** valuation or assessment **2** classification **3** **ratings** size of the audience for a TV programme

ratio ratios *noun* relationship between two numbers or amounts expressed as a proportion

ration *noun* **1** fixed allowance of food etc **2** **rations** fixed daily allowance of food, such as that given to a soldier ▷ *verb* **3** to restrict the distribution of (something)

rational *adjective* **1** reasonable or sensible **2** capable of reasoning > **rationality** *noun*: *We live in an era of rationality* > **rationally** *adverb*

rationale *noun* reason for an action or decision

rattle rattles rattling rattled *verb* **1** to give out a succession of short sharp sounds **2** to shake briskly causing sharp sounds **3** *informal* to confuse or fluster ▷ *noun* **4** short sharp sound **5** baby's toy that rattles when shaken

rattlesnake *noun* poisonous snake with loose horny segments on the tail that make a rattling sound

raucous *adjective* hoarse or harsh

ravage ravages ravaging ravaged *formal verb* **1** to cause extensive damage to ▷ *noun* **2 ravages** damaging effects

rave raves raving raved *verb* **1** to talk in a wild or incoherent manner **2** *informal* to write or speak (about) with great enthusiasm ▷ *noun* **3** *informal* large-scale party with electronic dance music ▷ *adjective* **4 rave review** *informal* enthusiastic praise

raven *noun* **1** black bird like a large crow ▷ *adjective* **2** (of hair) shiny black

ravenous *adjective* very hungry

ravine *noun* narrow steep-sided valley worn by a stream

raving *adjective* **1** delirious **2** *informal* exceptional: *a raving beauty* ▷ *noun* **3 ravings** frenzied or wildly extravagant talk

ravioli *plural noun* small squares of pasta with a savoury filling

ravishing *adjective* lovely or entrancing

raw *adjective* **1** uncooked **2** not manufactured or refined **3** inexperienced **4** chilly **5 raw deal** unfair or dishonest treatment

raw material *noun* natural substance used to make something

ray rays *noun* **1** single line or narrow beam of light **2** small amount that makes an unpleasant situation seem slightly better; glimmer: *a ray of hope* **3** large sea fish with a flat body and a whiplike tail

raze razes razing razed *verb* to destroy (buildings or a town) completely

razor *noun* sharp instrument for shaving

razor blade *noun* small sharp flat piece of metal fitted into a razor for shaving

RC *abbreviation* Roman Catholic

re- *prefix indicating* repetition or return: *re-enter; retrial; renewal*

reach reaches reaching reached *verb* **1** to arrive at or get to (a place) **2** to make a movement (towards), as if to grasp or touch **3** to succeed in touching **4** to make contact or communication with **5** to extend as far as (a point or place) ▷ *noun* **6** distance that you can reach

react *verb* **1** to act in response (to) **2 react against** to act in an opposing or contrary manner

reaction *noun* **1** physical or emotional response to a stimulus **2** any action resisting another **3** opposition to change **4** chemical or nuclear change, combination or decomposition

reactionary reactionaries *adjective* **1** opposed to change, especially in politics ▷ *noun* **2** person opposed to change

reactor *noun* apparatus in which a nuclear reaction is maintained and controlled to produce nuclear energy

read reads reading read *verb* **1** to look at and understand or take in (written or printed matter) **2** to look at and say aloud **3** to interpret in a specified way **4** (of an instrument) to register **5** to undertake a course of study in (a subject) ▷ *noun* **6** matter suitable for reading: *a good read*

reader *noun* **1** person who reads **2** textbook **3** *Chiefly Brit* senior university lecturer

readership *noun* readers of a publication collectively

readily *adverb* **1** willingly and eagerly **2** easily done or quickly obtainable > **readiness** *noun*: *readiness to help out*

reading *noun* **1** activity of reading books **2** figure or measurement shown on a meter or gauge

readjust *verb* to adapt to a new situation

ready readier readiest *adjective* **1** prepared for use or action **2** willing, prompt **3** easily produced or obtained: *ready cash*

ready-made *adjective* for immediate use by any customer

reaffirm *verb* to state again

real *adjective* **1** existing in fact **2** actual **3** genuine

real estate *noun* property consisting of land and houses

realism *noun* recognition of the true nature of a situation > **realist** *noun*

realistic *adjective* seeing and accepting things as they really are > **realistically** *adverb*

reality *noun* state of things as they are

realize realizes realizing realized; *also spelt* **realise** *verb* **1** to become aware or grasp the significance of **2** *formal* to achieve

(a plan, hopes, etc) **3** to convert (property or goods) into money > **realization** *noun*

really *adverb* **1** very **2** truly ▷ *interjection* **3** exclamation of dismay, doubt or surprise

realm *noun formal* **1** kingdom **2** sphere of interest

reap *verb* **1** to cut and gather (a harvest) **2** to receive as the result of a previous activity

reaper *noun* person who reaps or a machine for reaping

reappear *verb* to appear again > **reappearance** *noun*

reappraisal *noun formal* the assessment again of the value or quality of a person or thing

rear *noun* **1** back part **2** part of an army, procession, etc behind the others ▷ *verb* **3** to care for and educate (children) **4** to breed (animals) **5** (of a horse) to rise on its hind feet

rear admiral *noun* high-ranking naval officer

rearrange rearranges rearranging rearranged *verb* to organize differently

reason *noun* **1** cause or motive **2** faculty of rational thought **3** sanity ▷ *verb* **4** to think logically in forming conclusions **5** **reason with** to persuade by logical argument into doing something

reasonable *adjective* **1** sensible **2** not excessive **3** logical > **reasonably** *adverb*

reasoning *noun* process by which you draw conclusions from facts or evidence

reassess reassesses reassessing reassessed *verb* to reconsider the value or importance of > **reassessment** *noun*

reassure reassures reassuring

reassured verb to relieve (someone) of anxieties
> **reassurance** noun: She needed some reassurance

rebate noun discount or refund

rebel rebels rebelling rebelled verb 1 to revolt against the ruling power 2 to reject accepted conventions ▷ noun 3 person who rebels

rebellion noun organized open resistance to authority

rebellious adjective unwilling to obey and likely to rebel against authority

rebuff verb 1 to reject or snub ▷ noun 2 blunt refusal, snub

rebuild rebuilds rebuilding rebuilt verb to build (a building or town again) after severe damage

rebuke rebukes rebuking rebuked verb 1 to scold sternly ▷ noun 2 stern scolding

recall verb 1 to recollect or remember 2 to order to return 3 to annul or cancel

recap recaps recapping recapped verb informal to recapitulate

recapitulate recapitulates recapitulating recapitulated verb to state again briefly

recapture recaptures recapturing recaptured verb 1 to relive (a former experience or sensation) 2 to capture again

recede recedes receding receded verb 1 to move to a more distant place 2 (of the hair) to stop growing at the front

receipt noun 1 written acknowledgment of money or goods received 2 receiving or being received 3 **receipts** money taken in over a particular period by a shop or business

receive receives receiving received verb 1 to get (something offered or sent to you) 2 to experience 3 to greet (guests) 4 to react to: The news was well received

received adjective generally accepted

receiver noun 1 part of telephone that is held to the ear 2 equipment in a telephone, radio or television that converts electrical signals into sound 3 person appointed by a court to manage the property of a bankrupt

recent adjective 1 having happened lately 2 new > **recently** adverb

reception noun 1 area for receiving guests, clients, etc 2 formal party 3 manner of receiving 4 welcome 5 (in broadcasting) quality of signals received

receptionist noun person who receives guests, clients, etc

receptive adjective willing to accept new ideas, suggestions, etc

recess recesses noun 1 niche or alcove 2 holiday between sessions of work

recession noun period of economic difficulty when little is being bought or sold

recharge recharges recharging recharged verb to charge (a battery) with electricity again after it has been used

recipe noun 1 directions for cooking a dish 2 method for achieving something

recipient noun person who receives something

reciprocal adjective 1 mutual 2 given or done in return
> **reciprocally** adverb

reciprocate reciprocates reciprocating reciprocated verb 1 to give or feel in return 2 (of a machine part) to move backwards and forwards

recital *noun* **1** musical performance by a soloist or soloists **2** act of reciting

recitation *noun* recital, usually from memory, of poetry or prose

recite recites reciting recited *verb* to repeat (a poem etc) aloud to an audience

reckless *adjective* heedless of danger > **recklessly** *adverb* > **recklessness** *noun*

reckon *verb* **1** to be of the opinion **2** to consider **3** to calculate **4** to expect **5 reckon with** or **without** to take into account or fail to take into account

reckoning *noun* **1** counting or calculating **2** retribution for your actions

reclaim *verb* **1** to regain possession of **2** to convert (unsuitable or submerged land) into land suitable for farming or building on > **reclamation** *noun*: *the reclamation of land from the marshes*

recline reclines reclining reclined *verb* to rest in a leaning position

recluse *noun* person who avoids other people > **reclusive** *adjective*: *a reclusive billionaire*

recognize recognizes recognizing recognized; also spelt **recognise** *verb* **1** to identify (someone) as a person or thing already known **2** to accept or be aware of (a fact or problem) **3** to acknowledge formally the status or legality of (someone or something) **4** to show appreciation of (something) > **recognition** *noun*: *Her work has received popular recognition* > **recognizable** *adjective* > **recognizably** *adverb*

recommend *verb* **1** to advise or counsel **2** to praise or commend **3** to make acceptable > **recommendation** *noun*: *the committee's recommendations*

reconcile reconciles reconciling reconciled *verb* **1** to harmonize (conflicting beliefs etc) **2** to re-establish friendly relations with (a person or people) or between (people) **3** to accept or cause to accept (an unpleasant situation) > **reconciliation** *noun*: *hopes for a reconciliation between them*

reconnaissance *noun* survey for military or engineering purposes

reconsider *verb* to think about again > **reconsideration** *noun*

reconstruct *verb* **1** to rebuild **2** to form a picture of (a past event, especially a crime) > **reconstruction** *noun*

record *noun* **1** document or other thing that preserves information **2** disc with indentations which a record player transforms into sound **3** best recorded achievement **4** known facts about a person's past ▷ *verb* **5** to put in writing **6** to preserve (sound, TV programmes, etc) on plastic disc, magnetic tape, etc, for reproduction on a playback device **7** to show or register

recorder *noun* **1** person or machine that records, especially a video, cassette or tape recorder **2** type of flute, held vertically

recording *noun* **1** something that has been recorded **2** process of storing sounds or visual signals for later use

recount *verb* to tell in detail

re-count *verb* **1** to count again ▷ *noun* **2** second or further count, especially of votes

recoup *verb* to regain or make good

(a loss)

recourse *noun formal* **1** source of help **2** **have recourse to** to turn to a source of help or course of action

recover *verb* **1** (of a person) to regain health, spirits or composure **2** to regain a former condition **3** to find again or obtain the return of (something lost) **4** to get back (a loss or expense)

recovery recoveries *noun* **1** act of recovering from sickness, a shock or a setback **2** restoration to a former and better condition **3** regaining of something lost

recreate recreates recreating recreated *verb* to make happen or exist again

recreation *noun* agreeable or refreshing occupation, relaxation or amusement > **recreational** *adjective*: *recreational activities*

recrimination *noun* mutual blame

recruit *verb* **1** to enlist (new soldiers, members, etc) ▷ *noun* **2** newly enlisted soldier, member or supporter > **recruitment** *noun*: *the recruitment of civil servants*

rectangle *noun* oblong four-sided figure with four right angles > **rectangular** *adjective*: *a rectangular box*

rectify rectifies rectifying rectified *verb formal* to put right or correct

rector *noun* **1** clergyman in charge of a parish **2** head of certain academic institutions

rectory rectories *noun* rector's house

rectum rectums or **recta** *noun* final section of the large intestine

recuperate recuperates recuperating recuperated *verb* to recover from illness > **recuperation** *noun*: *powers of recuperation*

recur recurs recurring recurred *verb* to happen again

recurrence *noun* repetition > **recurrent** *adjective*: *a recurrent theme*

recurring *adjective* **1** happening or occurring many times **2** (of a digit) repeated over and over again after the decimal point in a decimal fraction

recycle recycles recycling recycled *verb* to reprocess (used materials) for further use > **recyclable** *adjective*

red redder reddest; reds *adjective* **1** of a colour varying from crimson to orange and seen in blood, fire, etc **2** flushed in the face from anger, shame, etc ▷ *noun* **3** red colour **4** **in the red** *informal* in debt

redback *noun* small Australian spider with a poisonous bite

redcurrant *noun* small round edible red berry

redeem *verb* **1** to make up for **2** to reinstate (yourself) in someone's good opinion **3** *Christianity* to free from sin

redemption *noun* state of being redeemed

red-handed *adjective informal* (caught) in the act of doing something wrong or illegal

red-hot *adjective* **1** glowing red **2** extremely hot

redress redresses redressing redressed *formal verb* **1** to make amends for ▷ *noun* **2** compensation or amends

red tape *noun* excessive adherence to official rules

reduce reduces reducing reduced *verb* **1** to bring down or lower **2** to lessen or weaken

reduction *noun* **1** act of reducing

2 amount by which something is reduced

redundancy redundancies noun **1** state of being redundant **2** person or job made redundant

redundant adjective **1** (of a worker) no longer needed **2** superfluous

reed noun **1** tall grass that grows in swamps and shallow water **2** tall straight stem of this plant **3** Music vibrating cane or metal strip in certain wind instruments

reedy adjective harsh and thin in tone

reef noun ridge of rock or coral near the surface of the sea part of a sail which can be rolled up to reduce its area

reek verb **1** to smell strongly **2** **reek of** to give a strong suggestion of ▷ noun **3** strong unpleasant smell

reel noun **1** cylindrical object on which film, tape, thread or wire is wound **2** winding apparatus, as of a fishing rod **3** lively Scottish dance ▷ verb **4** to move unsteadily or spin around **5** to be in a state of confusion or stress > **reel off** verb to recite or write fluently or quickly

re-elect verb to vote for (someone) to retain his or her position, for example as a Member of Parliament

refer refers referring referred verb **refer to 1** to allude (to) **2** to be relevant (to) **3** to send (to) for information **4** to submit (to) for decision

referee noun **1** umpire in sports, especially soccer or boxing **2** person willing to testify to someone's character etc

reference noun **1** act of referring **2** citation or direction in a book **3** written testimonial regarding character or capabilities **4** **with reference to** concerning

referendum referendums or **referenda** noun direct vote of the electorate on an important question

refill verb **1** to fill (something) again ▷ noun **2** second or subsequent filling **3** replacement supply of something in a permanent container

refine refines refining refined verb **1** to purify **2** to improve

refined adjective **1** cultured or polite **2** purified

refinement noun **1** improvement or elaboration **2** fineness of taste or manners

refinery refineries noun place where sugar, oil, etc is refined

reflect verb **1** (of a surface or object) to throw back light, heat or sound **2** (of a mirror) to form an image of (something) by reflection **3** to show **4** to consider carefully

reflection noun **1** act of reflecting **2** return of rays of heat, light, etc from a surface **3** image of an object given back by a mirror etc **4** conscious thought or meditation **5** Maths transformation of a shape in which right or left, or top and bottom, are reversed

reflective adjective **1** quiet, contemplative **2** capable of reflecting images > **reflectively** adverb

reflex reflexes noun **1** involuntary response to a stimulus or situation ▷ adjective **2** (of a muscular action) involuntary **3** reflected **4** (of an angle) more than 180°

reflexive adjective Grammar denoting a verb whose subject is the same as its object, eg He's cut himself

reform noun **1** improvement ▷ verb **2** to improve (a law or institution) by correcting abuses **3** to give up or cause to give up a bad habit or way of life > **reformer** *noun*

reformation *noun* **1** act or instance of something being reformed **2 Reformation** religious movement in 16th-century Europe that resulted in the establishment of the Protestant Churches

refract *verb* to change the course of (light etc) passing from one medium to another > **refraction** *noun*: *the refraction of light in water*

refrain *verb* **1 refrain from** to keep yourself from (doing something) **2** ▷ *noun* frequently repeated part of a song

refresh refreshes refreshing refreshed *verb* **1** to revive or reinvigorate, as through food, drink or rest **2** to stimulate (the memory)

refreshing *adjective* **1** having a reviving effect **2** pleasantly different or new

refreshment *noun* something that refreshes, especially food or drink

refrigerator *noun* full name for **fridge**

refuel refuels refuelling refuelled *verb* to supply or be supplied with fresh fuel

refuge *noun* **1** (source of) shelter or protection **2** place, person or thing that offers protection or help

refugee *noun* person who seeks refuge, especially in a foreign country

refund *verb* **1** to give back (money) ▷ *noun* **2** return of money **3** amount returned

refurbish refurbishes refurbishing refurbished *verb* *formal* to renovate and brighten up > **refurbishment** *noun*: *The office is in need of complete refurbishment*

refusal *noun* denial of anything demanded or offered

refuse¹ refuses refusing refused *verb* **1** to be determined not (to do something) **2** to decline to give or allow (something) to (someone)

refuse² *noun* rubbish or useless matter

refute refutes refuting refuted *verb* to prove (a statement or theory) to be false

regain *verb* **1** to get back or recover **2** to reach again

regal *adjective* of or like a king or queen > **regally** *adverb*

regard *verb* **1** to look upon or think of in a specified way **2** to look closely at (something or someone) **3** to take notice of **4 as regards** on the subject of ▷ *noun* **5** respect or esteem **6** attention **7 regards** expression of goodwill

regardless *adverb* **1** in spite of everything **2 regardless of** taking no notice of

regatta *noun* meeting for yacht or boat races

regency regencies *noun* period when a country is ruled by a regent

regenerate regenerates regenerating regenerated *verb* **1** to (cause to) undergo spiritual, economic or physical renewal **2** to come or bring into existence once again > **regeneration** *noun*

regent *noun* **1** ruler of a kingdom during the absence, childhood or illness of its monarch ▷ *adjective* **2** ruling as a regent: *prince regent*

reggae *noun* style of Jamaican popular music with a strong beat

regime *noun* **1** system of government **2** particular administration

regiment *noun* organized body of troops as a unit of the army > **regimental** *adjective*

regimented *adjective* very strictly controlled > **regimentation** *noun*: *bureaucratic regimentation*

region *noun* **1** administrative division of a country **2** area **3 in the region of** approximately > **regional** *adjective*: *regional government* > **regionally** *adverb*

register *noun* **1** (book containing) an official list or record of things **2** range of a voice or instrument **3** style of speaking or writing, such as slang, used in particular circumstances ▷ *verb* **4** to enter (an event, person's name, ownership, etc) in a register **5** to show on a scale or other measuring instrument **6** to show on a person's face > **registration** *noun*: *compulsory registration of dogs*

registrar *noun* **1** keeper of official records **2** senior hospital doctor, junior to a consultant **3** senior administrative official at a university

registration number *noun* numbers and letters displayed on a vehicle to identify it

registry registries *noun* place where official records are kept

registry office *noun* place where births, marriages and deaths are recorded, and where people can marry without a religious ceremony

regret regrets regretting regretted *verb* **1** to feel sorry about **2** to express apology or distress ▷ *noun* **3** feeling of repentance, guilt or sorrow > **regretful** *adjective*: *a regretful smile* > **regretfully** *adverb*

regrettable *adjective* unfortunate and undesirable > **regrettably** *adverb*

regular *adjective* **1** normal, customary or usual **2** symmetrical or even **3** done or occurring according to a rule **4** periodical **5** employed continuously in the armed forces ▷ *noun* **6** regular soldier **7** *informal* frequent customer > **regularity** *noun*: *monotonous regularity* > **regularly** *adverb*

regulate regulates regulating regulated *verb* **1** to control by means of rules **2** to adjust slightly

regulation *noun* **1** rule **2** regulating

regulator *noun* **1** device that automatically controls pressure, temperature, etc **2** person or organization appointed by a government to regulate an industry

regurgitate regurgitates regurgitating regurgitated *verb* **1** to vomit **2** (of some birds and animals) to bring back (partly digested food) into the mouth **3** to reproduce (ideas, facts, etc) without understanding them

rehabilitate rehabilitates rehabilitating rehabilitated *verb* to help (a person) to readjust to society after illness, imprisonment, etc > **rehabilitation** *noun*: *the rehabilitation of young offenders*

rehearsal *noun* practice of a performance in preparation for the actual event

rehearse rehearses rehearsing rehearsed *verb* **1** to practise (a play, concert, etc) **2** to repeat aloud

reign *noun* **1** period of a sovereign's rule ▷ *verb* **2** to rule (a country) **3** to be supreme

rein *noun* **1 reins a** narrow straps attached to a bit to guide a horse **b** means of control **2 keep a tight rein on** to control carefully

reincarnation *noun* **1** rebirth of a soul in successive bodies **2** one of a series of such transmigrations

reindeer reindeer or **reindeers**

noun deer of arctic regions with large branched antlers

reinforce reinforces reinforcing reinforced *verb* **1** to give added emphasis to (an idea or feeling) **2** to make physically stronger or harder

reinforcement *noun* **1** reinforcing of something **2 reinforcements** additional soldiers sent to join an army in battle

reinstate reinstates reinstating reinstated *verb* **1** to restore to a former position **2** to cause to exist or be important again > **reinstatement** *noun*

reiterate reiterates reiterating reiterated *verb formal* to repeat again and again > **reiteration** *noun*

reject *verb* **1** to refuse to accept or believe **2** to deny to (a person) the feelings hoped for **3** to discard as useless ▷ *noun* **4** person or thing rejected as not up to standard > **rejection** *noun*

rejoice rejoices rejoicing rejoiced *verb* to feel or express great happiness

rejoin *verb* to come together with (someone or something) again

rejuvenate rejuvenates rejuvenating rejuvenated *verb* to restore youth or vitality to > **rejuvenation** *noun*

relapse relapses relapsing relapsed *verb* **1** to fall back into bad habits, illness, etc ▷ *noun* **2** return of bad habits, illness, etc

relate relates relating related *verb* **1** to establish a relation between **2** to have reference or relation to **3** to have an understanding (of people or ideas) **4** to tell (a story) or describe (an event)

related *adjective* **1** connected or associated **2** linked by kinship or marriage

relation *noun* **1** connection between things **2** relative **3** connection by blood or marriage **4** act of relating (a story) **5 relations a** social or political dealings **b** family

relationship *noun* **1** dealings and feelings between people or countries **2** emotional or sexual affair **3** connection between two things

relative *adjective* **1** dependent on relation to something else, not absolute **2** having reference or relation (to) ▷ *noun* **3** person connected by blood or marriage

relative pronoun *noun* pronoun that replaces a noun that links two parts of a sentence, for example, *who* in *the boy who left*

relax relaxes relaxing relaxed *verb* **1** to make or become looser, less tense or less rigid **2** to ease up from effort or attention **3** to make (rules or discipline) less strict **4** to become more friendly > **relaxation** *noun*

relay relays relaying relayed *noun* **1** race between teams in which each runner races part of the distance ▷ *verb* **2** to pass on (a message) **3** to broadcast (a performance or event) as it happens

release releases releasing released *verb* **1** to free (a person or animal) from captivity or imprisonment **2** to free (something) from (your grip) **3** to issue (a record, film, etc) for sale or public showing **4** to give out heat, energy, etc ▷ *noun* **5** setting free **6** statement to the press **7** act of issuing for sale or publication **8** newly issued film, record, etc

relegate relegates relegating relegated *verb* **1** to put in a less important position **2** to demote

(a sports team) to a lower league
> **relegation** noun

relent verb **1** to change your mind about some decision **2** to become milder less severe

relentless adjective **1** never stopping and never becoming less intense **2** merciless > **relentlessly** adverb

relevant adjective to do with the matter in hand > **relevance** noun: a fact of little relevance

reliable adjective able to be trusted; dependable > **reliability** noun: her car's reliability > **reliably** adverb

reliant adjective dependent > **reliance** noun: reliance on public transport

relic noun **1** something that has survived from the past **2** body or possession of a saint, regarded as holy **3** **relics** remains or traces

relief noun **1** gladness at the end or removal of pain, distress, etc **2** release from monotony or duty **3** money or food given to victims of disaster, poverty, etc

relief map noun map showing the shape and height of land by shading

relieve relieves relieving relieved verb **1** to lessen (pain, distress, boredom, etc) **2** to bring assistance to (someone in need) **3** to free (someone) from an obligation **4** to take over the duties of (someone) **5** **relieve yourself** to urinate or defecate

religion noun system of belief in and worship of a supernatural power or god

religious adjective **1** of religion **2** pious or devout **3** scrupulous or conscientious

religiously adverb regularly as a duty: he stuck religiously to the rules

relinquish relinquishes

relinquishing relinquished verb **1** to give up **2** to renounce (a claim or right)

relish relishes relishing relished verb **1** to savour or enjoy (an experience) to the full ▷ noun **2** liking or enjoyment **3** appetizing savoury food, such as pickle

relive relives reliving relived verb to remember (a past experience) very vividly, imagining it happening again

relocate relocates relocating relocated verb to move to a new place to live or work > **relocation** noun: relocation to London

reluctant adjective unwilling or disinclined > **reluctance** noun > **reluctantly** adverb

rely relies relying relied verb **rely on** or **upon** **a** to be dependent on **b** to have trust in

remain verb **1** to continue to be **2** to stay behind or in the same place **3** to be left after use or the passage of time **4** to be left to be done, said, etc

remainder noun **1** part which is left **2** amount left over after subtraction or division

remains plural noun **1** relics, especially of ancient buildings **2** dead body

remand verb **1** to send (a prisoner or accused person) back into custody or put on bail before trial ▷ noun **2** **on remand** in custody or on bail before trial

remark verb **1** to make a casual comment (on) **2** to say **3** to observe or notice ▷ noun **4** observation or comment

remarkable adjective **1** worthy of note or attention **2** striking or unusual > **remarkably** adverb

remarry remarries remarrying

remarried *verb* to marry again

remedial *adjective* **1** intended to correct a specific disability, handicap, etc **2** designed to improve someone's ability in something

remedy remedies remedying remedied *noun* **1** means of curing pain or disease **2** means of solving a problem ▷ *verb* **3** to put right or improve

remember *verb* **1** to become aware of (something forgotten) again **2** to keep (an idea, intention, etc) in your mind

remembrance *noun* **1** memory **2** honouring of the memory of a person or event

remind *verb* **1** to cause to remember **2** to put in mind (of)

reminder *noun* **1** something that recalls the past **2** note to remind a person of something not done

reminiscent *adjective* reminding or suggestive (of)

remission *noun* **1** reduction in the length of a prison term **2** easing of intensity, as of an illness

remit *noun* area of competence or authority

remittance *noun formal* money sent as payment

remnant *noun* **1** small piece, especially of fabric, left over **2** surviving trace

remorse *noun formal* feeling of sorrow and regret for something you did > **remorseful** *adjective*

remote remoter remotest *adjective* **1** far away, distant **2** aloof **3** slight or faint > **remoteness** *noun*: *the remoteness of the farmhouse*

remote control *noun* control of an apparatus from a distance by an electrical device

remotely *adverb* used to emphasize a negative statement

removal *noun* removing, especially changing residence

remove removes removing removed *verb* **1** to take away **2** to take (clothing) off **3** to get rid of **4** to dismiss (someone) from office > **removable** *adjective*

renaissance *noun* **1** revival or rebirth **2** **Renaissance** revival of learning in the 14th–16th centuries

renal *adjective* of the kidneys

rename renames renaming renamed *verb* to give (something) a new name

render *verb* **1** to cause to become **2** to give or provide (aid, a service, etc) **3** to represent in painting, music or acting

rendezvous rendezvous *noun* **1** appointment **2** meeting place
  The plural of *rendezvous* is *rendezvous*

rendition *noun formal* **1** performance **2** translation

renew *verb* **1** to begin again **2** to make valid again **3** to restore to a former state > **renewal** *noun*: *the renewal of my licence*

renewable *adjective* **1** able to be renewed ▷ *noun* **2** **renewables** sources of alternative energy, such as wind and wave power

renounce renounces renouncing renounced *verb formal* **1** to give up (a belief, habit, etc) voluntarily **2** to give up (a title or claim) formally > **renunciation** *noun*: *their renunciation of terrorism*

renovate renovates renovating renovated *verb* to restore to good condition > **renovation** *noun*: *The property needs extensive renovation*

renowned *adjective* well-known for something good > **renown** *noun*: *a singer of some renown*

rent *verb* **1** to give or have use of (land, a building, a machine, etc) in return for regular payments ▷ *noun* **2** regular payment for use of land, a building, machine, etc

rental *noun* **1** concerned with the renting out of goods and services **2** sum payable as rent

renunciation *noun* see **renounce**

reorganize reorganizes reorganizing reorganized; also spelt **reorganise** *verb* to organize in a new and more efficient way > **reorganization** *noun*: *the reorganization of the legal system*

rep *noun* **1** short for **representative**: *a sales rep* **2** short for **repertory company**

repair *verb* **1** to restore (something damaged or broken) to good condition **2** to make up for (a mistake or injury) **3** to go to (a place) ▷ *noun* **4** act of repairing **5** repaired part

repay repays repaying repaid *verb* **1** to pay back or refund **2** to make a return for (something): *repay hospitality* > **repayment** *noun*: *monthly repayments*

repeal *verb* **1** to cancel (a law) officially ▷ *noun* **2** act of repealing

repeat *verb* **1** to say, write or do again **2** to tell to another person (the secrets told to you by someone else) **3** to happen again ▷ *noun* **4** act or instance of repeating **5** programme broadcast again > **repeated** *adjective*: *repeated reminders* > **repeatedly** *adverb*

repel repels repelling repelled *verb* **1** to cause (someone) to feel disgusted **2** to force or drive back **3** to reject or spurn

repellent *adjective* **1** distasteful **2** resisting water etc ▷ *noun* **3** something that repels, especially a chemical to repel insects

repent *verb formal* to feel regret for (a deed or omission) > **repentance** *noun*: *They showed no repentance* > **repentant** *adjective*

repercussions *plural noun* indirect effects, often unpleasant

repertoire *noun* stock of plays, songs, etc that a player or company can give

repertory repertories *noun* **1** repertoire **2** theatre involving a quick succession of plays performed by the same actors

repertory company repertory companies *noun* permanent theatre company producing a succession of plays

repetition *noun* **1** act of repeating **2** thing repeated

repetitive or **repetitious** *adjective* full of repetition

replace replaces replacing replaced *verb* **1** to take the place of **2** to substitute a person or thing for (another) **3** to put (something) back in its rightful place

replacement *noun* **1** act or process of replacement **2** person or thing that replaces another

replay replays replaying replayed *noun* **1** (also **action replay**) immediate reshowing on TV of an incident in sport, especially in slow motion **2** second sports match, especially one following an earlier draw ▷ *verb* **3** to play (a match, recording, etc) again

replenish replenishes replenishing replenished *verb formal* to make full or complete again by supplying what has been used up

replica *noun* exact copy

replicate replicates replicating replicated *verb* to make or be a copy of

reply replies replying replied
verb **1** to make answer (to) in words or writing or by an action **2** to say (something) in answer ▷ *noun* **3** answer or response

report *verb* **1** to give an account of **2** to make a report (on) **3** to make a formal complaint about **4** to present yourself (to) **5** to be responsible (to) ▷ *noun* **6** account or statement **7** rumour **8** written statement of a child's progress at school

reportedly *adverb* according to rumour

reported speech *noun* report of what someone said that gives the content of the speech without repeating the exact words

reporter *noun* person who gathers news for a newspaper, TV, etc

repossess repossesses repossessing repossessed *verb* (of a lender) to take back (property) from a customer who is behind with payments

represent *verb* **1** to act as a delegate or substitute for (a person, country, etc) **2** to stand as an equivalent of **3** to be a means of expressing **4** to display the characteristics of **5** to portray, as in art

representation *noun* **1** state of being represented by someone **2** anything that represents, such as a pictorial portrait **3** **representations** formal requests or complaints made to an official body

representative *noun* **1** person chosen to stand for a group **2** (travelling) salesperson ▷ *adjective* **3** typical

repress represses repressing repressed *verb* **1** to keep (feelings)

in check **2** to restrict the freedom of > **repression** *noun*

repressive *adjective* restricting freedom by the use of force

reprieve reprieves reprieving reprieved *verb* **1** to postpone the execution of (a condemned person) **2** to give temporary relief to ▷ *noun* **3** (document granting) postponement or cancellation of a punishment **4** temporary relief

reprimand *verb* **1** to rebuke (someone) officially for a fault ▷ *noun* **2** official rebuke

reprisal *noun* retaliation

reproach reproaches reproaching reproached *verb* **1** to express disapproval (of someone's actions) ▷ *noun* **2** blame **3** **beyond reproach** beyond criticism > **reproachful** *adjective*: *a reproachful look* > **reproachfully** *adverb*

reproduce reproduces reproducing reproduced *verb* **1** to produce a copy of **2** to produce offspring **3** to recreate

reproduction *noun* **1** process of reproducing **2** facsimile, as of a painting etc **3** quality of sound from an audio system

reproductive *adjective* relating to the reproduction of living things

reptile *noun* cold-blooded egg-laying vertebrate with horny scales or plates, such as a snake or tortoise > **reptilian** *adjective*

republic *noun* **1** form of government in which the people or their elected representatives possess the supreme power **2** country in which a president is the head of state > **republican** *noun*, *adjective* > **republicanism** *noun*

Republican *noun* **1** member or supporter of the Republican

Party, the more conservative of the two main political parties in the US **2** supporter of the belief that Northern Ireland should be governed by the Republic of Ireland rather than the United Kingdom

repulse repulses repulsing
  repulsed verb **1** to be disgusting to **2** to drive (an army) back **3** to reject with coldness or discourtesy

repulsion noun **1** distaste or aversion **2** Physics force separating two objects

repulsive adjective horrible and disgusting

reputable adjective of good reputation; respectable

reputation noun estimation in which a person is held

reputed adjective supposed
  > **reputedly** adverb: He reputedly earns £30,000 per week

request verb **1** to ask for ▷ noun **2** asking **3** thing asked for

Requiem noun **1** Mass for the dead **2** music for this

require requires requiring
  required verb **1** to want or need **2** to be a necessary condition

requirement noun **1** essential condition **2** specific need or want

requisite formal adjective **1** necessary, essential ▷ noun **2** essential thing

rescue rescues rescuing
  rescued verb **1** to bring (someone or something) out of danger or trouble ▷ noun **2** rescuing
  > **rescuer** noun

research researches researching
  researched noun **1** systematic investigation to discover facts or collect information ▷ verb **2** to carry out investigations into (a subject)
  > **researcher** noun

resemblance noun similarity

resemble resembles resembling
  resembled verb to be or look like

resent verb to feel bitter about
  > **resentment** noun: resentment against his supervisor

resentful adjective bitter and angry
  > **resentfully** adverb

reservation noun **1** doubt **2** exception or limitation **3** seat, room, etc that has been reserved **4** area of land reserved for use by a particular group **5** Brit strip of ground separating the two carriageways of a dual carriageway or motorway

reserve reserves reserving
  reserved verb **1** to set aside, keep for future use **2** to obtain by arranging beforehand, book **3** to keep (something) for yourself ▷ noun **4** something, especially money or troops, kept for emergencies **5** area of land reserved for a particular purpose **6** Sport substitute **7** concealment of feelings or friendliness

reserved adjective **1** not showing your feelings; lacking friendliness **2** set aside for use by a particular person

reservoir noun natural or artificial lake storing water for community supplies

reshuffle noun reorganization

reside resides residing resided verb formal to live permanently (in a place)

residence noun formal home or house

resident noun **1** person who lives in a place ▷ adjective **2** living in a place

residential adjective **1** (of part of a town) consisting mainly of houses **2** providing living accommodation

residue noun what is left; remainder
  > **residual** adjective: residual

radiation

resign verb 1 to give up office, a job, etc 2 to reconcile (yourself) to

resignation noun 1 resigning 2 passive endurance of difficulties

resigned adjective content to endure

resilient adjective 1 (of a person) recovering quickly from a shock etc 2 able to return to normal shape after stretching etc > **resilience** noun: the resilience of children

resin noun 1 sticky substance from plants, especially pines 2 similar synthetic substance

resist verb 1 to withstand or oppose 2 to refrain from despite temptation 3 to be proof against

resistance noun 1 act of resisting 2 capacity to withstand something 3 Electricity opposition offered by a circuit to the passage of a current through it

resistant adjective 1 opposed to something and wanting to prevent it 2 not harmed or affected by

resit resits resitting resat verb 1 to take (an exam) again ▷ noun 2 exam that has to be taken again

resolute adjective firm in purpose > **resolutely** adverb

resolution noun 1 firmness of conduct or character 2 thing resolved upon 3 decision of a court or vote of an assembly 4 act of resolving

resolve resolves resolving resolved verb 1 to decide with an effort of will 2 to form (a resolution) by a vote ▷ noun 3 absolute determination

resolved adjective determined

resonance noun 1 echoing, especially with a deep sound 2 sound produced in one object by sound waves coming from another

object

resonant adjective (of a sound) deep and strong

resonate resonates resonating resonated verb to vibrate and produce a deep, strong sound

resort verb 1 to have recourse (to) for help etc ▷ noun 2 place for holidays 3 the use of something as a means or aid

resounding adjective 1 echoing 2 clear and emphatic

resource noun 1 thing resorted to for support 2 ingenuity 3 means of achieving something 4 **resources a** sources of economic wealth **b** stock that can be drawn on; funds

resourceful adjective capable and full of initiative > **resourcefulness** noun: a person of great resourcefulness

respect noun 1 consideration 2 deference or esteem 3 point or aspect 4 reference or relation: with respect to 5 **in respect of** or **with respect to** in reference or relation to ▷ verb 6 to treat with esteem 7 to show consideration for

respectable adjective 1 worthy of respect 2 fairly good > **respectability** noun > **respectably** adverb

respectful adjective showing respect for someone > **respectfully** adverb

respecting preposition concerning

respective adjective relating separately to each of those in question > **respectively** adverb

respiration noun breathing

respiratory adjective of breathing

respire respires respiring respired verb to breathe

respite noun formal 1 pause or interval of rest 2 delay

respond responds responding responded verb 1 to state or utter (something) in reply **2** to act in answer to any stimulus **3** to react favourably

respondent *noun* **1** person who answers a questionnaire or a request for information **2** *Law* defendant

response *noun* **1** answer **2** reaction to a stimulus

responsibility responsibilities *noun* **1** state of being responsible **2** person or thing for which you are responsible

responsible *adjective* **1** having control and authority **2** reporting or accountable (to) **3** sensible and dependable **4** involving responsibility > **responsibly** *adverb*

responsive *adjective* readily reacting to some influence

rest *noun* **1** freedom from exertion etc **2** repose **3** pause, especially in music **4** object used for support **5** what is left **6** others ▷ *verb* **7** to take a rest **8** to give a rest (to) **9** to be supported **10** to place for support or steadying

restaurant *noun* commercial establishment serving meals

restaurateur *noun* person who owns or runs a restaurant

restful *adjective* relaxing or soothing

restless *adjective* finding it hard to remain still or relaxed because of boredom or impatience > **restlessly** *adverb* > **restlessness** *noun*: *restlessness in the audience*

restore restores restoring restored *verb* **1** to return (a building, painting, etc) to its original condition **2** to cause to recover health or spirits **3** to return (something lost or stolen) to its owner **4** to reinforce or re-establish > **restoration** *noun*: *the restoration of old houses*

restrain *verb* **1** to hold (someone) back from action **2** to control or restrict

restrained *adjective* not displaying emotion

restraint *noun* **1** control, especially self-control **2** something that restrains

restrict *verb* to confine to certain limits > **restrictive** *adjective*

restriction *noun* rule or situation that limits what you can do

result *noun* **1** outcome or consequence **2** score **3** number obtained from a calculation **4** exam mark or grade ▷ *verb* **5** **result from** to be the outcome or consequence (of) **6** **result in** to end in > **resultant** *adjective*: *civil war and the resultant famine*

resume resumes resuming resumed *verb* **1** to begin again or go on with (something interrupted) **2** to occupy or take again > **resumption** *noun*: *a resumption of negotiations*

resurgence *noun* rising again to vigour > **resurgent** *adjective*: *resurgent extremism*

resurrect *verb* **1** to restore to life **2** to use once more (something discarded etc)

resurrection *noun* **1** rising again (especially from the dead) **2** revival **3** **the Resurrection** *Christianity* the coming back to life of Jesus Christ three days after he had been killed

resuscitate resuscitates resuscitating resuscitated *verb* to restore to consciousness > **resuscitation** *noun*: *mouth-to-mouth resuscitation*

retail *noun* **1** selling of goods individually or in small amounts to the public ▷ *adverb* **2** by retail ▷ *verb*

3 to sell or be sold retail

retailer *noun* person or company that sells goods to the public

retain *verb* to keep in your possession

retaliate retaliates retaliating retaliated *verb* to repay an injury or wrong in kind > **retaliation** *noun*: *retaliation for the bombings*

retarded *adjective* underdeveloped, especially mentally

retention *noun* the keeping of something: *votes for the retention of the death penalty*

rethink rethinks rethinking rethought *verb* to consider again, especially with a view to changing your tactics

reticent *adjective* not willing to say or tell much > **reticence** *noun*

retina *noun* light-sensitive membrane at the back of the eye

retinue *noun* band of attendants

retire retires retiring retired *verb* **1** to (cause to) give up office or work, especially through age **2** *formal* to go away or withdraw **3** to go to bed

retired *adjective* having retired from work etc > **retirement** *noun*

retort *verb* **1** to reply quickly, wittily or angrily ▷ *noun* **2** quick, witty or angry reply

retract *verb* **1** to withdraw (a statement etc) **2** to draw in (a part or appendage) > **retraction** *noun*: *a retraction of his comments*

retractable or **retractile** *adjective* able to be retracted

retreat *verb* **1** to move back from a position, withdraw ▷ *noun* **2** act of or military signal for retiring or withdrawal **3** place to which anyone retires; refuge

retribution *noun* punishment or vengeance for evil deeds

retrieve retrieves retrieving retrieved *verb* **1** to fetch back again **2** to restore to a better state **3** to recover (information) from a computer > **retrieval** *noun*

retriever *noun* large dog often used by hunters to bring back birds and animals which have been shot

retro- *prefix meaning* back or backwards: *retrospective*

retrospect *noun* **in retrospect** when looking back on the past

retrospective *adjective* **1** looking back in time **2** applying from a date in the past > **retrospectively** *adverb*

return *verb* **1** to go or come back **2** to give, put or send back **3** to hit, throw or play (a ball) back **4** (of a jury) to deliver (a verdict) ▷ *noun* **5** returning **6** (thing) being returned **7** profit **8** official report, as of taxable income **9** return ticket **10** **in return** in exchange

reunion *noun* meeting of people who have been apart

reunite reunites reuniting reunited *verb* to bring or come together again after a separation

rev revs revving revved *informal noun* **1** revolution (of an engine) ▷ *verb* **2** **rev up** to increase the speed of revolution of (an engine)

Rev. or **Revd.** *abbreviation* Reverend

revamp *verb* to renovate or restore

reveal *verb* **1** to disclose or divulge (a secret) **2** to expose to view (something concealed)

revel revels revelling revelled *verb* **1** to take pleasure (in something) **2** to make merry

revelation *noun* **1** surprising or interesting fact made known to people **2** person or experience that proves to be different from expectations

revelry *noun* festivity

revenge revenges revenging revenged *noun* **1** retaliation for wrong done ▷ *verb* **2** to avenge (yourself or another)

revenue *noun* income, especially of a state

revered *adjective* respected and admired

reverence *noun* awe mingled with respect and esteem

Reverend *adjective* title of respect for a clergyman

reverse reverses reversing reversed *verb* **1** to turn upside down or the other way round **2** to change completely **3** to move (a vehicle) backwards ▷ *noun* **4** opposite **5** back side **6** change for the worse **7** reverse gear ▷ *adjective* **8** opposite or contrary > **reversal** *noun: a reversal of previous policy*

reverse gear *noun* mechanism enabling a vehicle to move backwards

reversible *adjective* **1** capable of being reversed **2** (of clothing) made so that either side may be used as the outer side

revert *verb formal* **1** to return to a former state **2** to come back to a subject

review *noun* **1** critical assessment of a book, concert, etc **2** publication with critical articles **3** general survey ▷ *verb* **4** to hold or write a review of **5** to examine, reconsider or look back on

reviewer *noun* writer of reviews

revise revises revising revised *verb* **1** to change or alter **2** to study (work) again in preparation for an examination > **revision** *noun*

revival *noun* reviving or renewal

revive revives reviving revived *verb* to bring or come back to life, vigour, use, etc

revolt *noun* **1** uprising against authority ▷ *verb* **2** to rise up in rebellion **3** to cause to feel disgust

revolting *adjective* disgusting and horrible

revolution *noun* **1** overthrow of a government by the governed **2** great change **3** complete rotation

revolutionary revolutionaries *adjective* **1** advocating or engaged in revolution **2** radically new or different ▷ *noun* **3** person advocating or engaged in revolution

revolve revolves revolving revolved *verb* **1** to move or cause to move around a centre **2** **revolve around** to be centred on

revolver *noun* small gun held in the hand

revulsion *noun* strong disgust

reward *noun* **1** something given in return for a service **2** sum of money offered for finding a criminal or missing property ▷ *verb* **3** to pay or give something to (someone) for a service, information, etc

rewarding *adjective* giving personal satisfaction; worthwhile

rewind rewinds rewinding rewound *verb* to run (a tape or film) back to an earlier point in order to replay

rhapsody rhapsodies *noun* freely structured emotional piece of music

rhetoric *noun* **1** art of effective speaking or writing **2** artificial or exaggerated language

rhetorical *adjective* **1** (of a question) not requiring an answer **2** (of language) intended to be grand and impressive

rheumatic *adjective* affected by rheumatism

rheumatism *noun* painful inflammation of joints or muscles

rhino *noun* short for **rhinoceros**

rhinoceros rhinoceroses or **rhinoceros** *noun* large thick-skinned animal with one or two horns on its nose

rhododendron *noun* evergreen flowering shrub

rhombus rhombuses or **rhombi** *noun* parallelogram with sides of equal length but no right angles; diamond-shaped figure

rhubarb *noun* garden plant of which the fleshy stalks are cooked as fruit

rhyme rhymes rhyming rhymed *noun* **1** sameness of the final sounds at the ends of lines of verse, or in words **2** word identical in sound to another in its final sounds **3** verse marked by rhyme ▷ *verb* **4** (of a rhyme) to form a rhyme with another word

rhythm *noun* **1** any regular movement or beat **2** arrangement of the durations of and stress on the notes of a piece of music, usually grouped into a regular pattern **3** (in poetry) arrangement of words to form a regular pattern of stresses > **rhythmic** *adjective*: *rhythmic breathing* > **rhythmically** *adverb*

rib *noun* **1** one of the curved bones forming the framework of the upper part of the body **2** cut of meat including the rib(s) **3** curved supporting part, as in the hull of a boat > **ribbed** *adjective*

ribbon *noun* narrow band of fabric used for trimming, tying, etc

ribcage *noun* bony structure of ribs enclosing the lungs

rice *noun* **1** cereal plant grown on wet ground in warm countries **2** its seeds as food

rich *adjective* **1** owning a lot of money or property, wealthy **2** abounding **3** fertile **4** (of food) containing much fat or sugar **5** (of colours, smells and sounds) strong and pleasant > **richness** *noun*: *the richness of life*

riches *plural noun* valuable possessions or desirable substances

richly *adverb* **1** elaborately **2** fully

rick *noun* **1** stack of hay etc ▷ *verb* **2** to sprain or wrench (a joint)

rickets *noun* disease of children marked by softening of the bones, bow legs, etc, caused by vitamin D deficiency

rickety *adjective* shaky or unstable

rickshaw *noun* light two-wheeled man-drawn Asian vehicle

ricochet ricochets ricocheting or **ricochetting ricocheted** or **ricochetted** *verb* **1** (of a bullet) to rebound from a solid surface ▷ *noun* **2** such a rebound

rid rids ridding rid *verb* **1** *formal* to relieve (oneself) or make a place free of (something undesirable) **2 get rid of** to free yourself of (something undesirable)

riddance *noun* **good riddance** relief at getting rid of something or someone

ridden *verb* past participle of **ride** ▷ *adjective* **2** afflicted or affected by the thing specified: *disease-ridden*

riddle riddles riddling riddled *noun* **1** puzzling question designed to test people's ingenuity **2** puzzling person or thing ▷ *verb* **3** to pierce with many holes **4 riddled with** full of (something undesirable)

ride rides riding rode ridden *verb* **1** to sit on and control or propel (a horse, bicycle, etc) **2** to go on horseback or in a vehicle **3** to travel over ▷ *noun* **4** journey on a horse etc or in a vehicle

rider *noun* **1** person who rides **2** supplementary clause added to a document

ridge *noun* **1** long narrow hill **2** long narrow raised part on a surface **3** line where two sloping surfaces meet **4** *Meteorology* elongated area of high pressure

ridicule ridicules ridiculing ridiculed *noun* **1** treatment of a person or thing as ridiculous ▷ *verb* **2** to laugh at, make fun of

ridiculous *adjective* deserving to be laughed at; absurd > **ridiculously** *adverb*

rife *adjective* **1** widespread or common **2 rife with** full of

rifle rifles rifling rifled *noun* **1** firearm with a long barrel ▷ *verb* **2** to search (a house or safe) and steal from it

rift *noun* **1** break in friendly relations **2** crack, split or cleft

rig rigs rigging rigged *verb* **1** to arrange in a dishonest way for profit or advantage ▷ *noun* **2** apparatus for drilling for oil and gas > **rig up** *verb* to set up or build temporarily

right *adjective* **1** just **2** true or correct **3** proper **4** in a satisfactory condition **5** of the side that faces east when the front is turned to the north **6** of the outer side of a fabric ▷ *adverb* **7** properly **8** straight or directly **9** on or to the right side ▷ *noun* **10** claim, title, etc allowed or due **11** what is just or due **12 in the right** morally or legally correct **13 Right** conservative political party or group ▷ *verb* **14** to bring or come back to a normal or correct state

right angle *noun* angle of 90°

right away *adverb* immediately

righteous *adjective* **1** upright, godly or virtuous **2** morally justified

rightful *adjective* **1** in accordance with what is right **2** having a legally or morally just claim > **rightfully** *adverb*

right-handed *adjective* using or for the right hand

rightly *adverb* **1** in accordance with the true facts or justice **2** with good reason

right-wing *adjective* believing more strongly in capitalism or conservatism, or less strongly in socialism, than other members of the same party or group > **right-winger** *noun: a veteran right-winger*

rigid *adjective* **1** inflexible or strict **2** unyielding or stiff > **rigidity** *noun: the rigidity of government policy* > **rigidly** *adverb*

rigorous *adjective* harsh, severe or stern > **rigorously** *adverb*

rigour *noun* **1** harshness, severity or strictness **2** hardship

rim *noun* **1** edge or border **2** outer ring of a wheel > **rimmed** *adjective: rimmed with gold*

rimu rimu or **rimus** *noun* New Zealand tree whose wood is used for building and furniture

rind *noun* tough outer coating of fruits, cheese or bacon

ring rings ringing rang rung *verb* **1** to give out a clear resonant sound, as a bell **2** to cause (a bell) to sound **3** to call (a person) by telephone **4** (of a building or place) to be filled with sound **5** to put a ring round ▷ *noun* **6** ringing **7** telephone call **8** circle of gold etc, especially for a finger **9** any circular band, coil or rim **10** circle of people **11** enclosed area, especially a circle for a circus or a roped-in square for boxing

12 group operating (illegal) control of a market > **ring off** *verb* to end a telephone call > **ring up** *verb* **1** to telephone **2** to record on a cash register

ringbark *verb Aust* to kill (a tree) by cutting away a strip of bark from around its trunk

ringer *noun* **1** *informal* person or thing apparently identical to another **2** *Aust* person who works on a sheep farm **3** *Aust, NZ* fastest shearer in a woolshed

ring-in *noun informal* **1** *Aust* person or thing that is not normally a member of a particular group **2** *Aust, NZ* someone who is brought in at the last minute as a replacement for someone else

ringleader *noun* instigator of a mutiny, riot, etc

ringtone *noun* tune played by a mobile phone when it receives a call

rink *noun* **1** sheet of ice for skating or curling **2** floor for roller-skating

rinse rinses rinsing rinsed *verb* **1** to remove soap from (washed clothes, hair, etc) by applying clean water **2** to wash lightly ▷ *noun* **3** rinsing **4** liquid to tint hair

riot *noun* **1** disorderly unruly disturbance ▷ *verb* **2** to take part in a riot **3 run riot** to behave without restraint

rip rips ripping ripped *verb* **1** to tear or be torn violently **2** to remove hastily or roughly **3** *informal* to move violently or hurriedly ▷ *noun* **4** split or tear > **rip off** *verb informal* to cheat (someone) by overcharging

RIP *abbreviation* rest in peace

ripe riper ripest *adjective* **1** ready to be reaped, eaten, etc **2** matured **3** ready or suitable **4 ripe old age** an elderly but healthy age

> **ripeness** *noun*

ripen ripens ripening ripened *verb* **1** to make or become ripe **2** to mature

ripper *noun Aust, NZ informal* excellent person or thing

ripple ripples rippling rippled *noun* **1** slight wave or ruffling of a surface **2** sound like ripples of water: *a ripple of applause* ▷ *verb* **3** to flow or form into little waves (on)

rise rises rising rose risen *verb* **1** to get up from a lying, sitting or kneeling position **2** to get out of bed **3** to move upwards **4** (of the sun or moon) to appear above the horizon **5** to reach a higher level **6** (of an amount or price) to increase **7** to rebel **8** (of a court) to adjourn ▷ *noun* **9** rising **10** upward slope **11** increase, especially of wages

riser *noun* person who rises, especially from bed

rising *noun* **1** revolt ▷ *adjective* **2** increasing in rank or maturity

risk *noun* **1** chance of disaster or loss **2** person or thing considered as a potential hazard ▷ *verb* **3** to act in spite of the possibility of (injury or loss) **4** to expose to danger or loss

risky riskier riskiest *adjective* full of risk, dangerous

rite *noun* formal practice or custom, especially religious

ritual *noun* **1** prescribed order of rites **2** regular repeated action or behaviour ▷ *adjective* **3** concerning rites

ritualistic *adjective* like a ritual

rival rivals rivalling rivalled *noun* **1** person or thing that competes with or equals another for favour, success, etc ▷ *adjective* **2** in the position of a rival ▷ *verb* **3** to (try to) equal

rivalry rivalries *noun* keen competition

river *noun* **1** large natural stream of water **2** plentiful flow

rivet *noun* **1** bolt for fastening metal plates, the end being put through holes and then beaten flat ▷ *verb* **2** to fasten with rivets **3** to cause a person's attention to be fixed, as in fascination

riveting *adjective* very interesting and exciting

road *noun* **1** way prepared for passengers, vehicles, etc **2** route in a town or city with houses along it **3** way or course: *the road to fame*

road map *noun* **1** map for drivers **2** plan or guide for future actions

road rage *noun* aggressive behaviour by a driver as a reaction to the behaviour of another driver

road train *noun Aust* line of linked trailers pulled by a truck, used for transporting cattle or sheep

roadworks *plural noun* repairs to a road, especially blocking part of the road

roadworthy *adjective* (of a vehicle) mechanically sound

roam *verb* to walk about with no fixed purpose or direction

roar *verb* **1** to make a very loud noise **2** (of lions, etc) to make loud growling cries **3** to shout (something) as in anger **4** to laugh loudly ▷ *noun* **5** such a sound

roast *verb* **1** to cook (food) by dry heat, as in an oven **2** to make or be very hot ▷ *noun* **3** roasted joint of meat ▷ *adjective* **4** roasted

rob robs robbing robbed *verb* **1** to take something from (a person or place) illegally **2** to deprive, especially of something deserved

robber *noun* criminal who steals money or property using force or threats ▷ **robbery** *noun*: *a bank robbery*

robe *noun* long loose outer garment

robin *noun* small brown bird with a red breast

robot *noun* **1** automated machine, especially one performing functions in a human manner **2** person of machine-like efficiency **3** S Afr set of coloured lights at a junction to control the traffic flow ▷ **robotic** *adjective*

robust *adjective* very strong and healthy ▷ **robustly** *adverb*

rock *noun* **1** hard mineral substance that makes up part of the earth's crust; stone **2** large rugged mass of stone **3** hard sweet in sticks **4** (also **rock music**) style of pop music with a heavy beat **5** **on the rocks a** (of a marriage) about to end **b** (of an alcoholic drink) served with ice ▷ *verb* **6** to (cause to) sway to and fro

rock and roll or **rock'n'roll** *noun* style of pop music blending rhythm and blues and country music

rocket *noun* **1** self-propelling device powered by the burning of explosive contents (used as a firework, weapon, etc) **2** vehicle propelled by a rocket engine, as a weapon or carrying a spacecraft **3** firework that explodes when it is high in the air ▷ *verb* **4** to increase rapidly

rocking chair *noun* chair allowing the sitter to rock backwards and forwards

rock melon *noun US, Aust, NZ* kind of melon with sweet orange flesh

rocky rockier rockiest *adjective* **1** shaky or unstable **2** having many rocks

rod *noun* **1** slender straight bar, stick **2** cane

rode *verb* past tense of **ride**

rodent *noun* animal with teeth specialized for gnawing, such as a rat, mouse or squirrel

rodeo rodeos *noun* display of skill by cowboys, such as bareback riding

roe *noun* **1** mass of eggs in a fish, sometimes eaten as food **2** small species of deer

rogue *noun* **1** dishonest or unprincipled person **2** mischief-loving person ▷ *adjective* **3** (of a wild beast) having a savage temper and living apart from the herd

role or **rôle** *noun* **1** task or function **2** actor's part

roll *verb* **1** to move along by turning over and over **2** to move along on wheels or rollers **3** to curl or make by curling into a ball or tube **4** to move along in an undulating movement **5** to smooth out with a roller **6** to rotate wholly or partially: *He rolled his eyes* **7** (of a ship or aircraft) to turn from side to side about a line from nose to tail ▷ *noun* **8** act of rolling over or from side to side **9** piece of paper etc rolled up **10** small round individually baked piece of bread **11** list or register **12** continuous sound, as of drums, thunder, etc **13** swaying unsteady movement or gait

roll call *noun* calling out of a list of names to check who is present

roller *noun* **1** rotating cylinder used for smoothing or supporting a thing to be moved, spreading paint, etc **2** small tube around which hair may be wound in order to make it curly

Rollerblade® *noun* type of roller skate that has the wheels set in one straight line

roller coaster *noun* (at a funfair) narrow railway with steep slopes

roller-skate roller-skates roller-skating roller-skated *noun* **1** shoe with four small wheels that enable the wearer to glide swiftly over a flat surface ▷ *verb* **2** to move on roller-skates

rolling pin *noun* cylindrical roller for flattening pastry

ROM *abbreviation Computers* read only memory: storage device that holds data permanently and cannot be altered by the programmer

Roman Catholic *adjective* **1** of that section of the Christian Church that acknowledges the supremacy of the Pope ▷ *noun* **2** person who belongs to the Roman Catholic church > **Roman Catholicism** *noun: the spread of Roman Catholicism*

romance *noun* **1** love affair **2** mysterious or exciting quality **3** novel or film dealing with love, especially sentimentally

Romanian or **Rumanian** *adjective* **1** belonging or relating to Romania ▷ *noun* **2** someone from Romania **3** main language spoken in Romania

Roman numerals *plural noun* the letters I, V, X, L, C, D, M, used to represent numbers

romantic *adjective* **1** of or dealing with love **2** idealistic but impractical **3** (of literature, music, etc) displaying passion and imagination rather than order and form ▷ *noun* **4** romantic person or artist > **romantically** *adverb* > **romanticism** *noun*

rondavel *noun S Afr* small circular building with a conical roof

roo roos *noun Aust informal* kangaroo

roof *noun* outside upper covering of a building, car, etc

roofing *noun* material used for covering roofs

rooftop *noun* outside part of the roof of a building

rook *noun* **1** Eurasian bird of the crow family **2** chess piece shaped like a castle

room *noun* **1** enclosed area in a building **2** unoccupied space **3** scope or opportunity **4 rooms** lodgings

roomy roomier roomiest *adjective* spacious

roost *noun* **1** place where birds rest or sleep ▷ *verb* **2** to rest or sleep on a roost

root *noun* **1** part of a plant that grows down into the earth obtaining nourishment **2** plant with an edible root, such as a carrot **3** part of a tooth, hair, etc below the skin **4** source or origin **5** form of a word from which other words and forms are derived **6 roots** person's sense of belonging ▷ *verb* **7** to establish a root and start to grow **8** to dig or burrow

rooted *adjective* developed from or strongly influenced by something

rope ropes roping roped *noun* **1** thick cord ▷ *verb* **2** to tie with a rope

rosary rosaries *noun* **1** series of prayers **2** string of beads for counting these prayers

rose *noun* **1** shrub or climbing plant with prickly stems and fragrant flowers **2** flower of this plant **3** pink colour ▷ *adjective* **4** pink ▷ *verb* **5** past tense of **rise**

rosella *noun* type of Australian parrot

rosemary *noun* **1** fragrant flowering shrub **2** its leaves as a herb

rosette *noun* large badge of coloured ribbons gathered into a circle, which is worn as a prize in a competition or to support a political party

Rosh Hashanah or **Rosh Hashana** *noun* festival celebrating the Jewish New Year

roster *noun* list of people and their turns of duty

rostrum rostrums or **rostra** *noun* platform or stage

rosy rosier rosiest *adjective* **1** pink-coloured **2** hopeful or promising

rot rots rotting rotted *verb* **1** to decay or cause to decay **2** to deteriorate slowly, physically or mentally ▷ *noun* **3** decay

rota *noun* list of people who take it in turn to do a particular task

rotary *adjective* **1** revolving **2** operated by rotation

rotate rotates rotating rotated *verb* **1** to (cause to) move round a centre or on a pivot **2** to (cause to) follow a set sequence > **rotation** *noun*: *the daily rotation of the earth*

rotor *noun* **1** revolving portion of a dynamo, motor or turbine **2** rotating device with long blades that provides thrust to lift a helicopter

rotten *adjective* **1** decaying **2** *informal* very bad **3** corrupt

Rottweiler *noun* large sturdy dog with a smooth black and tan coat

rouble *noun* monetary unit of Russia and Tajikistan

rough *adjective* **1** uneven or irregular **2** not careful or gentle **3** difficult or unpleasant **4** approximate **5** violent, stormy or boisterous **6** in preliminary form **7** lacking refinement ▷ *verb* **8** to make rough ▷ *noun* **9** rough state or area **10** *Golf* part of the course where the grass is uncut > **roughly** *adverb* > **roughness** *noun*

roulette *noun* gambling game in which a ball is dropped onto a revolving wheel with numbered holes in it

round *adjective* **1** spherical, cylindrical, circular or curved ▷ *adverb, preposition* **2** indicating an encircling movement, presence on all sides, etc: *tied round the waist; books scattered round the room* ▷ *verb* **3** to move round ▷ *noun* **4** customary course, as of a milkman **5** game (of golf) **6** stage in a competition **7** one of several periods in a boxing match etc **8** number of drinks bought at one time **9** bullet or shell for a gun **> round up** *verb* to gather (people or animals) together

roundabout *noun* **1** road junction at which traffic passes round a central island **2** revolving circular platform on which people ride for amusement ▷ *adjective* **3** not straightforward

rounded *adjective* curved in shape, without any points or sharp edges

rounders *noun* bat-and-ball team game

round-the-clock *adjective* throughout the day and night

rouse rouses rousing roused *verb* **1** to wake up **2** to provoke or excite

rouseabout *noun Aust, NZ* labourer who does odd jobs, especially on a farm

rout *noun* **1** overwhelming defeat **2** disorderly retreat ▷ *verb* **3** to defeat and put to flight

route *noun* **1** roads taken to reach a destination **2** chosen way

routine *noun* **1** usual or regular method of procedure **2** set sequence ▷ *adjective* **3** ordinary or regular **> routinely** *adverb*

roving *adjective* **1** wandering or roaming **2** not restricted to any particular location or area

row¹ *noun* **1** straight line of people or things ▷ *verb* **2** to propel (a boat) by oars

row² *informal noun* **1** dispute **2** disturbance **3** reprimand ▷ *verb* **4** to quarrel noisily

rowdy rowdier rowdiest *adjective* disorderly, noisy and rough

rowing boat *noun* boat propelled by oars

royal *adjective* **1** of, befitting or supported by a king or queen **2** splendid ▷ *noun* **3** *informal* member of a royal family

royalist *noun* supporter of monarchy

royalty royalties *noun* **1** royal people **2** rank or power of a monarch **3** payment to an author, musician, inventor, etc

rub rubs rubbing rubbed *verb* **1** to apply pressure and friction to (something) with a circular or backwards-and-forwards movement **2** to clean, polish or dry by rubbing **3** to chafe or fray through rubbing **4 rub it in** to emphasize an unpleasant fact **> rub out** *verb* to remove or be removed with a rubber

rubber *noun* **1** strong waterproof elastic material, originally made from the dried sap of a tropical tree, now usually synthetic **2** piece of rubber used for erasing writing **3** series of matches ▷ *adjective* **4** made of or producing rubber

rubbery *adjective* soft and elastic, like rubber

rubbish *noun* **1** waste matter **2** anything worthless **3** nonsense

rubble *noun* fragments of broken stone, brick, etc

rubric *noun formal* set of instructions at the beginning of an official document

ruby rubies *noun* **1** red precious gemstone ▷ *adjective* **2** deep red

rucksack *noun* large pack carried on the back

rudder *noun* vertical hinged piece at the stern of a boat or at the rear of an aircraft, for steering

rude ruder rudest *adjective* **1** impolite or insulting **2** coarse, vulgar or obscene **3** unexpected and unpleasant **4** roughly made **5** robust > **rudely** *adverb* > **rudeness** *noun*

rudimentary *adjective formal* basic, elementary

rudiments *plural noun* simplest and most basic stages of a subject

ruff *noun* **1** starched and frilled collar **2** natural collar of feathers, fur, etc on certain birds and animals

ruffle ruffles ruffling ruffled *verb* **1** to disturb the calm of **2** to annoy or irritate ▷ *noun* **3** frill or pleat

rug *noun* **1** small carpet **2** thick woollen blanket

rugby *noun* form of football played with an oval ball which may be handled by the players. Rugby League is played with 13 players in each side, Rugby Union is played with 15 players in each side

rugged *adjective* **1** rocky or steep **2** uneven and jagged **3** strong-featured **4** tough and sturdy

rugger *noun Chiefly Brit informal* rugby

ruin *verb* **1** to destroy or spoil completely **2** to cause (someone) to lose money ▷ *noun* **3** destruction or decay **4** loss of wealth, position, etc **5** broken-down unused building

rule rules ruling ruled *noun* **1** statement of what is allowed, for example in a game or procedure **2** what is usual **3** government, authority or control **4** measuring device with a straight edge **5 as a rule** usually ▷ *verb* **6** to govern (people or a political unit) **7** to be pre-eminent or superior **8** to give a formal decision > **rule out** *verb* to dismiss from consideration

ruler *noun* **1** person who governs **2** measuring device with a straight edge

ruling *noun* formal decision

rum *noun* strong alcoholic drink distilled from sugar cane

Rumanian another spelling of **Romanian**

rumble rumbles rumbling rumbled *verb* **1** to make a low continuous noise **2** *Brit informal* to discover the (disreputable) truth about ▷ *noun* **3** deep resonant sound

rummage rummages rummaging rummaged *verb* **1** to search untidily and at length ▷ *noun* **2** untidy search through a collection of things

rumour *noun* **1** unproved statement **2** gossip or common talk

rumoured *adjective* suggested by rumour

rump *noun* **1** buttocks **2** rear of an animal

run runs running ran run *verb* **1** to move with a more rapid gait than walking **2** to take part in (a race) **3** to travel according to schedule **4** to function **5** to manage **6** to stand as a candidate for political or other office **7** to continue in a particular direction or for a specified period **8** to expose yourself to (a risk) **9** to flow **10** to spread ▷ *noun* **11** act or spell of running **12** ride in a car **13** continuous period **14** series of unravelled stitches; ladder **15** *Cricket* score of one made by a batsman

> **run away** *verb* to make your escape; flee > **run down** *verb* **1** to be rude about **2** to reduce in number or size **3** to stop working > **run out** *verb* to use up or (of a supply) to be used up > **run over** *verb* to knock down (a person) with a moving vehicle

runaway runaways *noun* person or animal that has run away

run-down *adjective* **1** exhausted **2** shabby or dilapidated ▷ *noun* **rundown 3** reduction in number or size **4** brief overview or summary

rung *noun* **1** crossbar on a ladder ▷ *verb* **2** past participle of **ring**

runner *noun* **1** competitor in a race **2** messenger **3** part underneath an ice skate etc, on which it slides **4** slender horizontal stem of a plant, such as a strawberry, running along the ground and forming new roots at intervals **5** long strip of carpet or decorative cloth

runner bean *noun* long green pod eaten as a vegetable

runner-up runners-up *noun* person who comes second in a competition

running *adjective* **1** continuous **2** consecutive **3** (of water) flowing ▷ *noun* **4** act of moving or flowing quickly **5** management of a business etc

runny runnier runniest *adjective* **1** tending to flow **2** exuding moisture

runt *noun* smallest animal in a litter

runway runways *noun* hard level roadway where aircraft take off and land

rupee *noun* monetary unit of India and Pakistan

rupture ruptures rupturing ruptured *noun* **1** breaking, breach **2** hernia ▷ *verb* **3** to break, burst or sever

rural *adjective* in or of the countryside

ruse *noun formal* trick

rush rushes rushing rushed *verb* **1** to move or do very quickly **2** to force (someone) to act hastily **3** to make a sudden attack upon (a person or place) ▷ *noun* **4** sudden quick or violent movement **5** marsh plant with a slender pithy stem **6** **rushes** first unedited prints of a scene for a film ▷ *adjective* **7** done with speed, hasty

rush hour *noun* period at the beginning and end of the working day, when many people are travelling to or from work

rusk *noun* hard brown crisp biscuit, used especially for feeding babies

Russian *adjective* **1** belonging or relating to Russia ▷ *noun* **2** someone from Russia **3** main language spoken in Russia

rust *noun* **1** reddish-brown coating formed on iron etc that has been exposed to moisture ▷ *adjective* **2** reddish-brown ▷ *verb* **3** to become coated with rust

rustic *adjective* simple in a way considered to be typical of the countryside

rustle rustles rustling rustled *verb* to make a low whispering sound > **rustling** *adjective, noun*

rusty rustier rustiest *adjective* **1** coated with rust **2** of a rust colour **3** out of practice

rut *noun* **1** furrow made by wheels **2** dull settled habits or way of living

ruthless *adjective* pitiless or merciless > **ruthlessly** *adverb* > **ruthlessness** *noun*

rye *noun* kind of grain used for fodder and bread

S

Sabbath *noun* day for worship and rest in some religions: Saturday for Jews, Sunday for Christians

sabbatical *noun* period of special leave for studying or travelling

sable *noun* dark fur from a small weasel-like Arctic animal

sabotage sabotages sabotaging sabotaged *noun* **1** damage done to machinery, systems, etc in order to cause disruption ▷ *verb* **2** to damage in order to disrupt

saboteur *noun* person who commits sabotage

sabre *noun* **1** heavy curved sword **2** *Fencing* light sword

saccharin or **saccharine** *noun* artificial sweetener

sachet *noun* small envelope or bag containing a single portion of something

sack *noun* **1** large bag without handles **2** plundering (of a captured town) **3 the sack** *informal* dismissal ▷ *verb* **4** *informal* to dismiss **5** to plunder (a captured town)

sacrament *noun* a ceremony of the Christian Church, especially Communion

sacred *adjective* holy or connected with religion holiness

sacrifice sacrifices sacrificing sacrificed *noun* **1** giving up (of something valuable or important) to help someone or something else **2** thing given up **3** killing (of an animal) as an offering to a god **4** thing offered ▷ *verb* **5** to give up (something valuable or important) for the good of someone or something else **6** to kill (an animal) as an offering to a god > **sacrificial** *adjective*: *sacrificial offerings*

sacrilege *noun* behaviour that shows great disrespect for something holy or worthy of respect > **sacrilegious** *adjective*: *It would be sacrilegious to waste this*

sacrosanct *adjective* regarded as too important to be criticized or changed

sad sadder saddest *adjective* **1** unhappy, filled with sorrow **2** causing unhappiness or sorrow: *a sad story* **3** very bad: *a sad day for democracy* **4** *Brit informal* pathetic and inadequate: *What a sad person!* > **sadly** *adverb* > **sadness** *noun*: *His joy was tinged with sadness*

sadden *verb* to make (someone) sad

saddle saddles saddling saddled *noun* **1** rider's seat on a horse or bicycle **2** joint (of meat) ▷ *verb* **3** to put a saddle on (a horse) **4** to burden (with a responsibility)

sadism *noun* gaining of pleasure from making someone suffer > **sadist** *noun* person who gains pleasure from causing suffering > **sadistic** *adjective*: *a sadistic bully* > **sadistically** *adverb*

safari safaris *noun* expedition for hunting or observing wild animals, especially in Africa

safari park *noun* park where wild

animals such as lions and elephants roam freely

safe safer safest; safes *adjective* **1** not in danger **2** not harmful or dangerous ▷ *noun* **3** strong lockable container > **safely** *adverb* > **safety** *noun: a threat to public safety*

safeguard *verb* **1** to protect ▷ *noun* **2** protection

safekeeping *noun* keeping or being held in a place of safety; protection

safety belt *noun* strap fixed to an aeroplane or car seat that you fasten round yourself to hold you in

saffron *noun* orange-coloured flavouring obtained from a type of crocus

sag sags sagging sagged *verb* to sink in the middle or hang loosely > **sagging** *adjective*

saga *noun* **1** legend of Norse heroes **2** any long story or series of events

sage *noun* **1** herb used in cooking **2** *literary* very wise person

Sagittarius *noun* ninth sign of the zodiac, represented by a half-horse half-man creature with a bow and arrow

said *verb* past of **say**

sail *noun* **1** sheet of fabric that when raised on the mast of a sailing vessel catches the wind and causes it to be blown along **2** one of the arms of a windmill that move round in the wind ▷ *verb* **3** to travel by water **4** to begin a voyage **5** to move smoothly

sailor *noun* member of the crew of a ship or boat

saint *noun* **1** *Christianity* dead person honoured by the Church for their holy life **2** very good person

saintly *adjective* behaving in a very good or holy way

sake *noun* **1** benefit **2** purpose

salacious *adjective* too concerned with sex

salad *noun* mixture of raw vegetables

salami *noun* kind of sausage that is eaten cold

salary salaries *noun* regular monthly payment to an employee > **salaried** *adjective* with a salary

sale *noun* **1** exchange of goods for money **2** event at which goods are sold for unusually low prices **3** auction > **saleable** *adjective* fit to be sold

salesman salesmen *noun* man who sells products for a company > **saleswoman saleswomen** *noun*

salient *adjective formal* prominent or noticeable

saline *adjective* containing salt

saliva *noun* liquid that forms in the mouth and helps you chew food

salivate salivates salivating salivated *verb* to produce a lot of saliva, especially when smelling or seeing food

sallow *adjective* (of skin) pale and unhealthy

sally sallies sallying sallied *noun* **1** witty remark ▷ *verb* **2** (followed by *forth*) to go out

salmon *noun* large silver-coloured fish with orange-pink flesh

▌The plural of *salmon* is *salmon*

salmonella *noun* kind of bacterium that causes severe food poisoning

salon *noun* place where hairdressers or beauticians work

saloon *noun* **1** car with a fixed roof and a separate boot **2** in America, a place where alcoholic drinks are sold and drunk

salt *noun* **1** white substance, found naturally in sea water, used to flavour and preserve food **2** chemical compound formed from an acid base ▷ *verb* **3** to season or preserve (food) with salt

salty saltier saltiest *adjective* containing salt or tasting of salt

salubrious *adjective formal*
1 pleasant and healthy
2 respectable

salutary *adjective formal* leading to improvement

salute salutes saluting saluted *noun* 1 formal sign of respect that in the army, navy, etc involves raising your right hand to your forehead 2 firing of guns as a military greeting of honour ▷ *verb* 3 to greet with a salute 4 to make a salute

salvage salvages salvaging salvaged *verb* 1 to save (something) from destruction or waste ▷ *noun* 2 ships or cargoes that are saved or reclaimed from the sea 3 goods that are saved from destruction

salvation *noun* fact or state of being saved from harm or the consequences of sin

salver *noun* (silver) tray on which something is presented

salvo salvos or **salvoes** *noun* 1 firing of several guns or missiles at the same time 2 burst (of applause or questions)

same *adjective, pronoun* 1 identical, not different or unchanged 2 just mentioned

Samoan *adjective* 1 belonging or relating to Samoa ▷ *noun* 2 person from Samoa

sample samples sampling sampled *noun* 1 small amount of something for trying or testing 2 *Music* short extract from an existing recording mixed into a backing track to produce a new recording ▷ *verb* 3 to try a sample of 4 *Music* to take a short extract from (one recording) and mix it into a

backing track 5 to record (a sound) and feed it into a computerized synthesizer so that it can be reproduced at any pitch

samurai *noun* member of an ancient Japanese warrior class
█ The plural of *samurai* is *samurai*

sanatorium sanatoriums or **sanatoria** *noun* place providing medical treatment for the sick as well as care for those recovering from serious illnesses

sanctimonious *adjective* pretending to be religious and virtuous

sanction *noun* 1 official approval 2 punishment or penalty intended to make a person, group or country obey a particular rule or law ▷ *verb* 3 to authorize or permit

sanctity *noun* quality of being important and deserving respect

sanctuary sanctuaries *noun* 1 place where you are safe from harm or danger 2 place where wildlife is protected

sand *noun* 1 substance consisting of small grains of rock. Beaches are made of sand ▷ *verb* 2 to smooth with sandpaper

sandal *noun* open shoe with straps

sandalwood *noun* 1 sweet-smelling wood of an Asian tree 2 perfumed oil extracted from this wood

sandpaper *noun* strong paper coated with sand and used for smoothing surfaces

sandshoe *noun* Brit, Aust, NZ light canvas shoe with a rubber sole

sandstone *noun* type of rock formed from sand

sandwich sandwiches sandwiching sandwiched *noun* 1 two slices of bread with a layer of food between ▷ *verb* 2 to insert between two other things: *a shop sandwiched between two pubs*

sandy sandier sandiest *adjective* **1** covered with sand **2** (of hair) reddish-fair

sane saner sanest *adjective* **1** of sound mind **2** sensible, rational

sang *verb* past tense of **sing**

sanguine *adjective formal* cheerful and confident

sanitary *adjective* concerned with cleanliness and hygiene

sanitary towel *noun* absorbent pad worn by women during their periods

sanitation *noun* sanitary measures, especially drainage or sewerage

sanity *noun* ability to think and act in a mentally stable way

sank *verb* past tense of **sink**

sap saps sapping sapped *noun* **1** watery liquid found in plants ▷ *verb* **2** to undermine, weaken or destroy

sapling *noun* young tree

sapphire *noun* blue gemstone

sarcasm *noun* mocking or insulting irony

sarcastic *adjective* relating to or involving the mocking or insulting use of irony > **sarcastically** *adverb*

sarcophagus sarcophagi or **sarcophaguses** *noun* stone coffin

sardine *noun* small sea fish of the herring family

sardonic *adjective* mocking or scornful > **sardonically** *adverb*

sari saris *noun* long piece of cloth draped around the body and over one shoulder, worn by Hindu women

sarmie *noun* S Afr informal sandwich

sartorial *adjective formal* relating to men's clothes

sash sashes *noun* decorative strip

of cloth worn round the waist or over one shoulder

sash window *noun* window consisting of two separate frames that can be opened by sliding one over the other

sat *verb* past of **sit**

Satan *noun* **1** the Devil **2 Great Satan** radical Islamic term for the United States

satanic *adjective* caused by or influenced by Satan

satchel *noun* bag with a shoulder strap, for carrying books

satellite *noun* **1** man-made device orbiting the earth and collecting and relaying information **2** natural object in space that moves round a planet or star **3** country that is dependent on a more powerful one

satin *noun* silky fabric with a glossy surface on one side

satire *noun* **1** use of mocking or ironical humour, especially in literature, to show how foolish or bad someone or something is **2** play, novel or poem that does this > **satirical** *adjective*: *a satirical magazine*

satirist *noun* writer who uses satire

satirize satirizes satirizing satirized; also spelt **satirise** *verb* to criticize or ridicule (someone or something) using satire

satisfaction *noun* feeling of pleasure you have when you do or achieve something you wanted or needed to do

satisfactory *adjective* acceptable or adequate > **satisfactorily** *adverb*

satisfy satisfies satisfying satisfied *verb* **1** to make (someone) content or pleased by doing something well enough or by giving them enough of something **2** to provide enough for **3** to convince or persuade > **satisfied** *adjective*: *He is satisfied with my work*

satisfying *adjective* pleasing or fulfilling

satsuma *noun* fruit like a small orange

saturated *adjective* **1** very wet **2** containing the maximum possible number or amount of something

saturation *noun* state of containing the maximum possible number or amount of something

Saturday Saturdays *noun* day between Friday and Sunday

Saturn *noun* sixth planet from the sun in the solar system

sauce *noun* one of many kinds of thin or thick, sweet or savoury liquids served with food

saucepan *noun* deep metal cooking pot with a handle

saucer *noun* small round dish put under a cup

saucy saucier sauciest *adjective* cheeky in an amusing way

Saudi Saudis *adjective* **1** belonging or relating to Saudi Arabia ▷ *noun* **2** person from Saudi Arabia

sauna *noun* **1** activity of alternately sitting in a steamy room sweating then having a cold bath or shower **2** place where you do this

saunter *verb* **1** to walk in a leisurely manner; stroll ▷ *noun* **2** leisurely walk

sausage *noun* minced meat in an edible tube-shaped skin

sauté sautés sautéing or **sautéeing sautéed** *verb* to fry quickly in a little fat

savage savages savaging savaged *adjective* **1** wild or untamed **2** cruel and violent ▷ *noun* **3** violent and uncivilized person

▷ *verb* **4** to attack ferociously
> **savagely** *adverb*

savagery *noun* cruel and violent behaviour

savanna *noun* area of open flat grassland in Africa

save saves saving saved *verb* **1** to rescue or preserve from harm; protect **2** to keep for the future; set aside **3** to spare or prevent (someone having to do something) **4** *Sport* to prevent the scoring of (a goal) ▷ *noun* **5** *Sport* act of preventing a goal ▷ *preposition* **6** *formal* (often followed by *for*) except: *I was alone save for the cat* > **saver** *noun* person who saves money

saving *noun* **1** reduction in the amount of time or money used **2** **savings** money you have saved

saviour *noun* person who rescues you

Saviour *noun* Christ

savour *verb* to enjoy fully; relish

savoury savouries *adjective* **1** salty or spicy **2** pleasant or respectable ▷ *noun* **3** (*usually plural*) savoury dish served before or after a meal

saw¹ saws sawing sawed sawn *noun* **1** tool, with a blade with sharp teeth along one edge, for cutting wood ▷ *verb* **2** to cut with a saw

saw² *verb* past tense of **see**

sawdust *noun* fine powdery wood fragments produced when you saw wood

saxophone *noun* brass wind instrument with keys and a curved body often played in jazz bands

say says saying said *verb* **1** to express in words; utter **2** to give as your opinion **3** to suppose ▷ *noun* **4** right or chance to speak or influence a decision

saying *noun* well-known phrase or

proverb that tells you something about human life

scab *noun* **1** crust that forms over a wound **2** *offensive* someone that works when his or her colleagues are on strike; a blackleg > **scabby** *adjective*

scabbard *noun* sheath for a sword or dagger

scabies *noun* infectious skin disease caused by a parasite

scaffold *noun* raised platform where criminals were hanged or executed

scaffolding *noun* framework of poles and boards used by workmen to stand on when working on the outside of a building

scald *verb* **1** to burn with hot liquid or steam ▷ *noun* **2** burn caused by scalding

scale scales scaling scaled *noun* **1** size or extent (of something): *the sheer scale of the disaster* **2** set of levels or numbers used for measuring things: *The earthquake measured 3.5 on the Richter scale* **3** relationship between the size of something on a map, plan or in a model and its size in the real world: *a scale of 1:10,000* **4** upward or downward sequence of eight musical notes **5** one of the small pieces of hard skin that form the skin of fishes and reptiles **6** coating that forms in kettles etc due to hard water **7 scales** piece of equipment used for weighing things ▷ *verb* **8** to climb

scalene *adjective* (of a triangle) with sides that are all of different lengths

scallop *noun* edible shellfish with two flat fan-shaped shells

scalp *noun* **1** skin under the hair on your head **2** piece of skin and hair removed when someone is scalped ▷ *verb* **3** to cut off the skin and hair from the head of (someone) in one piece

scalpel *noun* small surgical knife

scaly *adjective* covered with scales

scamper *verb* to run about quickly and lightly, perhaps in play

scampi *plural noun* large prawns, often eaten fried in breadcrumbs

scan scans scanning scanned *verb* **1** to look at (something) carefully **2** to glance over (something) quickly **3** to examine or search (something) by X-raying it or by passing a radar or sonar beam over it **4** (of verse) to conform to metrical rules ▷ *noun* **5** examination or search by a scanner

scandal *noun* situation or event considered shocking and immoral > **scandalous** *adjective*

scandalize scandalizes scandalizing scandalized; also spelt **scandalise** *verb* to shock and horrify

Scandinavia *noun* name given to a group of countries in Northern Europe, including Norway, Sweden, Denmark and sometimes Finland and Iceland > **Scandinavian** *noun*, *adjective*

scanner *noun* **1** machine used to examine, identify or record things by means of a beam of light or X-rays **2** machine that converts text or images into a form that can be stored on a computer

scant *adjective* barely enough; meagre

scanty scantier scantiest *adjective* small in size, amount or number > **scantily** *adverb*: *a group of scantily dressed women*

scapegoat *noun* someone made to bear the blame for something that may not be their fault

scar scars scarring scarred *noun*
1 mark left after a wound has healed
2 permanent emotional damage
left by a bad experience ▷ *verb* **3** to
leave a permanent mark on **4** to
have a permanent effect on

scarce scarcer scarcest *adjective*
1 not enough to meet demand **2** not
common or rarely found **3 make
yourself scarce** *informal* to leave
quickly > **scarcity** *noun*: *the scarcity
of housing*

scarcely *adverb* hardly

As *scarcely* already has a negative
sense, it is followed by *ever* or
any, and not by *never* or *no*

scare scares scaring scared
verb **1** to frighten (someone) or be
frightened ▷ *noun* **2** fright **3** panic
> **scared** *adjective*: *I was really scared*

scarecrow *noun* figure dressed in
old clothes, set up to scare birds
away from crops

scarf scarfs or **scarves** *noun* piece
of material worn round the neck,
head or shoulders

scarlet *adjective, noun* bright red

scary scarier scariest *adjective*
informal frightening

scathing *adjective* harshly critical:
They were scathing about his idea

scatter *verb* **1** to throw or drop
(things) all over an area **2** to move
away in different directions

scattering *noun* small number (of
things) spread over a large area

**scavenge scavenges scavenging
scavenged** *verb* to search for
(anything usable) among discarded
material

scavenger *noun* **1** person who
scavenges **2** animal that feeds on
decaying matter

scenario scenarios *noun*
1 summary of the plot of a play

or film **2** way a situation might
develop in the future

scene *noun* **1** place where a real or
imaginary event happens **2** part
of a play or film in which a series
of events happens in one place
3 picture or view: *a village scene*
4 display of emotion: *Don't make a
scene* **5** *informal* area of activity: *the
fashion scene* **6 behind the scenes
a** backstage **b** in secret

scenery *noun* **1** natural features of a
landscape **2** painted backcloths or
screens used on stage to represent
the scene of action

scenic *adjective* with nice views,
picturesque

scent *noun* **1** smell, especially a
pleasant one **2** series of clues
3 perfume ▷ *verb* **4** to detect by
smell **5** to fill with fragrance

sceptic *noun* person who doubts
things that are widely believed
> **sceptical** *adjective*: *She was
sceptical about the idea* > **scepticism**
noun: *his scepticism about such claims*

sceptre *noun* ornamental rod
symbolizing royal power

**schedule schedules scheduling
scheduled** *noun* **1** plan listing
events or tasks together with the
times they are to happen; timetable
2 list ▷ *verb* **3** to plan and arrange
(something) for a particular time

schema schemata *noun* **1** *technical*
outline of a plan or theory **2** mental
model used by the mind to
understand new experiences or
view the world

scheme *noun* **1** plan or arrangement
2 secret plot ▷ *verb* **3** to plan in an
underhand manner

schism *noun* split or division in a
group or organization

schizophrenia *noun* serious
mental illness in which the sufferer

has thoughts and feelings that do not relate to reality

schizophrenic *adjective* **1** having or showing signs of schizophrenia ▷ *noun* **2** person with schizophrenia

scholar *noun* **1** a learned person **2** a student receiving a scholarship **3** *S Afr* pupil

scholarly *adjective* having or showing a lot of knowledge; learned

scholarship *noun* **1** award given to a student in recognition of their academic ability in order to finance their studies **2** academic knowledge and learning

school *noun* **1** place where children are educated or instruction is given in a subject **2** group of artists, thinkers, etc with shared beliefs or methods **3** shoal (of fish, whales, dolphins, etc) ▷ *verb* **4** to educate or train

schoolchild schoolchildren *noun* child who goes to school > **schoolboy** *noun* > **schoolgirl** *noun*

schoolie *noun Aust* schoolteacher or high-school student

schooling *noun* the education you receive at school

schooner *noun* sailing ship

sciatica *noun* severe pain in the large nerve in the back of the leg

science *noun* **1** study of and knowledge about natural and physical phenomena **2** a branch of science, for example physics or biology

science fiction *noun* stories about events happening in the future or in other parts of the universe

scientific *adjective* **1** relating to science or to a particular science **2** systematic > **scientifically** *adverb*

scientist *noun* person who studies or practises a science

scintillating *adjective* lively and witty

scissors *plural noun* cutting tool with two crossed blades

scoff *verb* **1** to speak scornfully **2** *informal* to eat (food) quickly and greedily

scold *verb* to rebuke, reprimand or tell (someone) off

scone *noun* small plain cake made from flour and fat and usually eaten with butter

scoop *verb* **1** (often followed by *up*) to pick up or remove using a spoon, shovel or the palm of your hand ▷ *noun* **2** tool like a large spoon or shovel used for picking up ice cream, mashed potato and other substances **3** important news story reported in one newspaper before it appears elsewhere

scooter *noun* **1** light motorcycle **2** a simple vehicle consisting of a platform on wheels and a handlebar; to make it work you stand on the platform on one leg and use your other leg to push on the ground

scope *noun* **1** opportunity for doing something **2** range of activity

-scope *suffix* used to form nouns which refer to an instrument used for observing or detecting: *microscope; telescope*

scorch scorches scorching scorched *verb* to burn the surface of

scorching *adjective* extremely hot

score scores scoring scored *verb* **1** to gain (a point, goal, run) in a game **2** to record the score obtained by the players **3** to cut a line in **4** to achieve (a success, victory, etc) **5** (followed by *out*) to cross out

▷ *noun* **6** number of points, goals or runs gained by each competitor or competing team in a game or competition **7** written version of a piece of music showing parts for each musician **8** grievance: *settle old scores* **9** *old-fashioned* twenty or about twenty **10** **scores** lots: *scores of celebrities* > **scorer** *noun*

scorn *noun* **1** open contempt ▷ *verb* **2** to despise **3** *formal* to reject with contempt

scornful *adjective* showing contempt; contemptuous > **scornfully** *adverb*

Scorpio *noun* eighth sign of the zodiac, represented by a scorpion

scorpion *noun* small lobster-shaped animal with a poisonous sting at the end of a jointed tail

Scot *noun* person from Scotland > **Scots** *adjective* Scottish

scotch *noun* whisky made in Scotland

Scotsman Scotsmen *noun* man from Scotland > **Scotswoman** *noun*

Scottish *adjective* belonging or relating to Scotland

scoundrel *noun* *old-fashioned* cheat or deceiver

scour *verb* **1** to clean or polish by rubbing with something rough **2** to carry out a thorough search of (a place)

scourge scourges scourging scourged *noun* **1** person or thing causing severe suffering **2** whip ▷ *verb* **3** to cause severe suffering to **4** to whip

scout *noun* **1** person sent out to see what an area is like and to find out the position of things **2** member of the Scout Association, an organization for boys which aims to develop character and promotes outdoor activities ▷ *verb* **3** to act as a scout **4** (especially followed by *around*) to look around (for something)

scowl *verb* **1** to frown in an angry or sullen way ▷ *noun* **2** an angry or sullen expression

scrabble scrabbles scrabbling scrabbled *verb* to scrape at with the hands, feet or claws

Scrabble® *noun* word game played with letters on a board

scramble scrambles scrambling scrambled *verb* **1** to climb or crawl hastily or awkwardly using your hands to help you **2** to mix and cook (a mixture of eggs and milk) ▷ *noun* **3** motorcycle race over rough ground **4** rough climb

scrap scraps scrapping scrapped *noun* **1** small piece **2** (also **scrap metal**) waste metal collected for reprocessing **3** *informal* fight or quarrel **4** **scraps** leftover food ▷ *verb* **5** to get rid of

scrapbook *noun* book with blank pages in which you stick things such as pictures or newspaper articles

scrape scrapes scraping scraped *verb* **1** to clean (something off) using something rough or sharp: *scraping the fallen snow off the track* **2** to rub (against something) with a harsh noise: *The chair scraped across the floorboards.* ▷ *noun* **3** act or sound of scraping **4** mark or wound caused by scraping

scratch scratches scratching scratched *verb* **1** to mark or cut with claws, nails or anything rough or sharp **2** to rub at (your skin) with your nails and fingertips to relieve itching ▷ *noun* **3** a small cut or mark **4** **from scratch** from the very beginning **5** **up to scratch** up to standard

scratchcard *noun* ticket with a surface that you scratch off to show whether or not you have won a prize in a competition

scrawl *verb* **1** to write (words, etc) carelessly or hastily ▷ *noun* **2** careless or untidy writing

scrawny scrawnier scrawniest *adjective* thin and bony

scream *verb* **1** to shout or cry in a loud high-pitched voice, especially when afraid or in pain ▷ *noun* **2** shrill piercing cry **3** *informal* very funny person or thing

scree *noun* mass of loose shifting stones on the sloping side of a mountain

screech screeches screeching screeched *verb* **1** to give a shrill cry or a high-pitched sound ▷ *noun* **2** shrill cry

screen *noun* **1** vertical surface on which pictures or films are shown or projected **2** a movable vertical panel used to separate different parts of a room or to protect something ▷ *verb* **3** to show (a film or television programme) **4** to shelter or conceal (someone or something) with or as if with a screen **5** to investigate (a person or group) to check their suitability for a task

screenplay screenplays *noun* script (of a film)

screw *noun* **1** metal pin with a spiral ridge round its shaft and a slot for a screwdriver on its head. used for fastening things together ▷ *verb* **2** to fasten with screws **3** to twist (something) round and round in order to fasten it onto something else: *He screwed the top on the bottle* > **screw up** *verb* **1** to twist or squeeze (something) into a

distorted shape **2** *informal* to bungle or spoil

screwdriver *noun* tool for turning screws

scribble scribbles scribbling scribbled *verb* **1** to write (something) hastily or illegibly **2** to make meaningless or illegible marks ▷ *noun* **3** something written or drawn quickly or roughly

scribe *noun* person who copied manuscripts before the invention of printing

scrimp *verb* to live cheaply, spending as little money as possible

script *noun* **1** text of a film, play or TV programme **2** system of writing: *Arabic script*

scripture *noun* sacred writings, especially the Bible > **scriptural** *adjective*: *scriptural references*

scroll *noun* **1** roll of parchment or paper **2** ornamental carving shaped like a scroll ▷ *verb* **3** to move (text) up or down on a VDU screen in order to find something

scrotum scrota or **scrotums** *noun* pouch of skin containing the testicles

scrounge scrounges scrounging scrounged *verb* *informal* to get (something) by cadging or begging > **scrounger** *noun* someone who makes a habit of scrounging

scrub scrubs scrubbing scrubbed *verb* **1** to clean by rubbing, often with a hard brush and water ▷ *noun* **2** act of scrubbing: *Give them a scrub* **3** low trees and bushes **4** area of land covered with scrub

scruff *noun* back (of your neck or collar)

scruffy scruffier scruffiest *adjective* dirty and untidy or shabby

scrum *noun* *Rugby* restarting of play in which groups of opposing forwards push against each other to gain possession of the ball

scrunchie *noun* a loop of elastic loosely covered with material which is used to hold hair in a ponytail

scruple *noun* moral principle that make you unwilling to do something that seems wrong

scrupulous *adjective* **1** very conscientious or honest about what you do **2** very careful or precise > **scrupulously** *adverb*

scrutinize scrutinizes scrutinizing scrutinized; also spelt **scrutinise** *verb* to examine very carefully

scrutiny *noun* close examination

scuba diving *noun* sport of swimming underwater using tanks of compressed air and breathing apparatus

scuff *verb* **1** to drag (your feet) while walking **2** to scrape (your shoes) by doing so

scuffle scuffles scuffling scuffled *noun* **1** short disorderly fight > *verb* **2** to fight in a disorderly manner

scullery sculleries *noun* small room next to a kitchen where washing and cleaning are done

sculpt *verb* to carve or shape (figures and objects) using materials such as stone, wood or clay

sculptor *noun* someone who makes sculptures

sculpture *noun* **1** work of art produced by carving or shaping materials such as stone, wood or clay **2** art of making figures or designs in wood, stone, clay, etc

scum *noun* **1** layer of a dirty substance on the surface of a liquid **2** *informal* worthless people

scurrilous *adjective* offensive and damaging to someone's good name

scurry scurries scurrying scurried *verb* to run quickly with short steps

scurvy *noun* disease caused by a lack of vitamin C

scut *noun* short tail of the hare, rabbit or deer

scuttle scuttles scuttling scuttled *verb* **1** to run with short quick steps **2** to make a hole in (a ship) to sink it > *noun* **3** fireside container for coal

scythe *noun* **1** long-handled tool with a curved blade for cutting grass > *verb* **2** to cut with a scythe

sea *noun* **1** the salty water that covers three quarters of the earth's surface **2** particular area of this **3** large mass (of people or things) **4** **at sea a** in a ship on the ocean **b** confused or bewildered

seagull *noun* common bird with white, grey and black plumage that lives near the sea; gull

seahorse *noun* small fish that swims upright, with a head that looks like a horse's head

seal *noun* **1** amphibious mammal with flippers as limbs **2** official mark or stamped piece of wax on a document which shows that it is genuine **3** embossed piece of wax or lead fixed over the opening part of a container or envelope to show that it has not been tampered with **4** device used to close an opening tightly > *verb* **5** to stick down (an evelope) **6** to close with or as if with a seal **7** to make (something) airtight or watertight > **seal off** *verb* to enclose or isolate (a place) completely

sealant *noun* any substance used for sealing

sea lion *noun* a type of large seal

seam *noun* **1** line of stitches joining

two pieces of cloth **2** thin layer of coal or ore

seaman seamen *noun* sailor

seance *noun* meeting at which people try to communicate with the dead

search searches searching searched *verb* **1** to examine (someone or something) closely in order to find something **2** to look (for someone or something); seek ▷ *noun* **3** attempt to find something

search engine *noun Computers* Internet service enabling users to search for items of interest

searching *adjective* keen or thorough: *searching questions*

searchlight *noun* powerful light with a beam that can be shone in any direction

searing *adjective* (of pain) very sharp

seashore *noun* the land along the edge of the sea

seasick *adjective* feeling sick because of the movement of a boat > **seasickness** *noun*

seaside *noun* area next to the sea

season *noun* **1** any of the four periods of the year (spring, summer, autumn or winter), each having their own typical weather conditions **2** period of the year when something usually happens: *the football season* **3** fitting or proper time (for something) ▷ *verb* **4** to add salt, pepper or spices to (a dish)

seasonable *adjective* appropriate for the season

seasonal *adjective* depending on or varying with the seasons: *seasonal work*

seasoned *adjective* very experienced: *a seasoned professional*

seasoning *noun* salt, herbs and other flavourings and condiments that are added to food to enhance its flavour

season ticket *noun* ticket for something that you can use as many times as you like within a certain period

seat *noun* **1** something you can sit on **2** the part (of a piece of clothing) that covers your bottom **3** buttocks **4** membership of a legislative or administrative body: *winning a seat in parliament* ▷ *verb* **5** to cause (someone) to sit **6** to provide seating for: *The theatre seats 570 people*

seat belt *noun* strap fixed to an aeroplane or car seat that you fasten round yourself to hold you in

seating *noun* the number of seats or the way seats are arranged in a place

seaweed *noun* plant growing in the sea

secateurs *plural noun* small pruning shears

secluded *adjective* private or sheltered

seclusion *noun* state of being secluded or the act of causing to be secluded

second[1] *adjective* **1** following the first **2** alternate or additional ▷ *noun* **3** one of the sixty parts that a minute is divided into **4** moment **5** person or thing coming second **6** someone who attends to the needs of one of the participants in a duel or boxing match **7** (*usually plural*) slightly defective product sold cheaply ▷ *verb* **8** to express formal support for (a proposal) > **secondly** *adverb*

second[2] *verb* to transfer (a person) temporarily to another job > **secondment** *noun* temporary transfer to another job: *She was on secondment from the local authority*

secondary *adjective* **1** of less importance **2** coming after or derived from what is primary or first **3** relating to the education of pupils between the ages of 11 and 18 or, in New Zealand, between 13 and 18

secondary school *noun* a school for pupils between the ages of 11 and 18

second-class *adjective* **1** inferior **2** cheaper, slower or less comfortable than first-class ▷ *adverb* **3** by second-class mail, transport, etc

second cousin *noun* child of your parent's first cousin

second-hand *adjective* **1** not bought or acquired when new but after someone else's use: *a second-hand car* ▷ *adverb* **2** following use by someone else: *We bought it second-hand* **3** indirectly: *I heard it second-hand*

second-rate *adjective* of poor quality

second sight *noun* supposed ability to predict events

secret *adjective* **1** kept from the knowledge of others ▷ *noun* **2** something kept secret **3** underlying explanation: *the secret of my success* **4** **in secret** without other people knowing > **secrecy** *noun* > **secretly** *adverb*

secret agent *noun* spy

secretary secretaries *noun* **1** person employed by an organization to keep records, write letters and do office work **2** **Secretary** head of a state department: *the Health Secretary* > **secretarial** *adjective*: *secretarial work*

secrete secretes secreting secreted *verb* **1** (of an organ,

gland, etc) to produce and release (a substance) **2** *formal* to hide or conceal

secretion *noun* **1** substance produced by an organ or gland **2** process of producing and releasing a substance (from an organ or gland)

secretive *adjective* inclined to keep things secret

secret service *noun* government department in charge of espionage

sect *noun* religious or political group which has broken away from a larger group

sectarian *adjective* strongly supporting a particular sect: *sectarian violence*

section *noun* **1** part or subdivision of something **2** cross-section ▷ *verb* **3** to cut or divide into sections

sector *noun* **1** part or subdivision (of something) **2** three-sided part of a circle bounded by a section of the circumference and two lines going from the circumference to the centre of the circle

secular *adjective* not connected with religion or the church

secure secures securing secured *adjective* **1** locked or well protected **2** free from danger **3** free from anxiety **4** firmly fixed ▷ *verb* **5** *formal* to obtain: *They secured the rights to her story* **6** to fasten (something) firmly > **securely** *adverb*

security securities *noun* **1** state of being secure **2** precautions against theft, espionage or other danger **3** something given or pledged to guarantee payment of a loan **4** **securities** stocks, shares, bonds or other investments ▷ *adjective* **5** relating to precautions against theft, espionage or other danger: *Security forces arrested one man*

sedate *adjective* **1** calm and dignified **2** slow or unhurried ▷ *verb* **3** to give (someone) a drug to calm him or her down or make him or her sleep > **sedately** *adverb* > **sedation** *noun*: *under sedation*

sedative *adjective* **1** having a soothing or calming effect ▷ *noun* **2** sedative drug

sedentary *adjective* done sitting down or involving little exercise

sediment *noun* **1** solid material that settles at the bottom of a liquid **2** material deposited by water, ice or wind

sedimentary *adjective* (of rocks such as sandstone and limestone) formed from fragments of compressed shells or rocks

sedition *noun* speech or action encouraging rebellion against the government > **seditious** *adjective*: *seditious pamphlets*

seduce *verb* **1** to persuade (someone) to have sex **2** to tempt (someone) into wrongdoing > **seduction** *noun* > **seductive** *adjective*: *a seductive offer* > **seductively** *adverb*

see sees seeing saw seen *verb* **1** to observe: *He saw us on TV* **2** to meet or visit: *I went to see my dentist* **3** to understand: *I see what you mean* **4** to watch: *She wanted to see a horror movie* **5** to find out: *I'll see what's happening* **6** to make sure (of something): *I'll see that she gets it* **7** to make an effort, try: *I'll see if I can find it* **8** to have experience of; witness: *The next couple of years saw two momentous developments* **9** to accompany (someone to a place): *He offered to see her home* ▷ *noun* **10** diocese of a bishop > **see through** *verb* to understand the real nature of > **see to** *verb* to deal

with: *I'll see to your breakfast*

seed *noun* **1** the grain of a plant from which a new plant can grow **2** origin or beginning: *the seeds of mistrust* **3** *Sport* tennis player ranked according to his or her ability

seedling *noun* young plant grown from a seed

seedy seedier seediest *adjective* shabby: *a seedy hotel*

seeing or **seeing that** or **seeing as** *conjunction* in view of the fact that

seek seeks seeking sought *verb* **1** to try to find or obtain (someone or something) **2** to try (to do something)

seem *verb* to appear to be: *He seemed such a quiet chap*

seeming *adjective* appearing to be real or genuine; apparent > **seemingly** *adverb*

seen *verb* past participle of **see**

seep *verb* to trickle slowly (through something, into something, etc)

seersucker *noun* light cotton fabric with a slightly crinkled surface

seesaw *noun* **1** plank balanced in the middle so that two people seated on either end ride up and down alternately ▷ *verb* **2** to move up and down

seething *adjective* **1** very agitated and angry **2** crowded and full of restless activity

segment *noun* **1** one of several sections into which something may be divided **2** one of the two parts of a circle formed when you draw a straight line across it ▷ *verb*

segregate segregates segregating segregated *verb* to set apart > **segregated** *adjective* > **segregation** *noun*

seismic *adjective* relating to earthquakes

seismology *noun* study of

earthquakes

seize seizes seizing seized verb 1 to take hold of forcibly or quickly 2 to take immediate advantage of > **seize on** verb to show great and sudden interest in: *MPs have seized on a new report* > **seize up** verb 1 (of body parts) to become stiff and painful 2 (of mechanical parts) to become jammed through overheating

seizure noun 1 sudden violent attack of an illness, especially a heart attack or an illness 2 act of seizing or being seized: *the largest seizure of drugs in US history*

seldom adverb not often; rarely: *They seldom speak to each other*

select verb 1 to pick out or choose ▷ adjective 2 chosen in preference to others: *an invitation to a select few* 3 restricted to a particular group; exclusive: *one of a select band of players* > **selector** noun

selection noun 1 selecting: *the selection of parliamentary candidates* 2 things or people that have been selected 3 range from which something may be selected

selective adjective choosing carefully; choosy: *I am selective about what I eat* > **selectively** adverb

self selves noun 1 distinct individuality or identity of a person or thing 2 your basic nature 3 your own welfare or interests

self- prefix meaning 1 done to yourself or by yourself: *self-help; self-control* 2 automatic(ally): *a self-loading rifle*

self-assured adjective confident

self-centred adjective thinking only about yourself and not about other people

self-confessed adjective by your own admission

self-confident adjective confident of your own abilities or worth > **self-confidence** noun: *her lack of self-confidence*

self-conscious adjective nervous, easily embarrassed and worried about what other people think of you > **self-consciously** adverb

self-control noun ability to restrain yourself and not show your feelings

self-defence noun knowledge of and ability to use means to protect yourself if attacked

self-employed adjective working for yourself, with responsibility for your own tax payments, rather than working for an employer

self-esteem noun your good opinion of yourself

self-evident adjective obvious without proof

self-indulgent adjective being in the habit of allowing yourself treats or letting yourself do things you enjoy

self-interest noun personal advantage

selfish adjective caring too much about yourself and not enough about other people > **selfishly** adverb > **selfishness** noun

selfless adjective putting other people's interests before your own; unselfish

self-made adjective rich and successful through your own efforts

self-possessed adjective calm, confident and in control of your emotions

self-raising adjective (of flour) containing baking powder to make baking rise

self-respect noun confidence and pride in your own abilities and worth

self-righteous adjective thinking

yourself more virtuous than others > **self-righteousness** noun

self-service adjective (of shops, cafés or garages) requiring you to serve yourself and then pay a cashier

self-sufficient adjective able to provide for yourself without help

sell sells selling sold verb **1** to exchange (something) for money **2** to stock or deal in **3** (of goods) to be sold **4 to sell for** to be priced at **5** informal to persuade (someone) to accept (something) **6 sell yourself** to present yourself well, so that people have confidence in your ability: You've got to sell yourself at the interview > **seller** noun: a newspaper seller > **sell out** verb to sell your entire stock (of something)

sell-by date noun Brit date on packaged food after which it should not be sold

Sellotape® noun type of adhesive tape

selves noun plural of **self**

semaphore noun system of signalling by holding two flags in different positions to represent letters of the alphabet

semblance noun outward or superficial appearance: an effort to restore a semblance of normality

semen noun sperm-carrying fluid produced by men and male animals

semester noun either of two divisions of the academic year

semi- prefix meaning **1** half: semicircle **2** partly or almost: semiskilled

semibreve noun musical note (o) four beats long

semicircle noun half of a circle, or something with this shape > **semicircular** adjective

semicolon noun the punctuation mark (;)

semidetached adjective (of a house) joined to another on one side

semifinal noun match or round before the final > **semifinalist** noun competitor or competing team that has reached the match or round before the final

seminar noun meeting of a group of students for discussion

seminary seminaries noun college for priests

semipermeable adjective (of materials) allowing certain substances with small enough molecules to go through while providing a barrier for substances with larger molecules

semiprecious adjective (of gemstones) having less value than precious stones

semiquaver noun musical note half the length of a quaver

Semite noun member of the group of peoples including Jews and Arabs

Semitic adjective of the group of peoples including Jews and Arabs

semitone noun smallest interval between two notes in Western music

semolina noun hard grains of wheat left after the milling of flour, used to make puddings and pasta

Senate noun the smaller, more important of the two councils in the government of some countries, for example Australia, Canada and the USA

senator noun member of a Senate

send sends sending sent verb **1** to cause (a person or thing) to go to or be taken or transmitted to a place **2** to bring into a specified state or condition: The blow sent him tumbling to the ground > **send for** verb to ask (someone) to

come and see you > **send up** *verb*
informal to make fun of (someone or
something) by imitating

senile *adjective* mentally or
physically weak because of old age
> **senility** *noun: the onset of senility*

senior *adjective* **1** superior in rank
or standing **2** older **3** of or for older
pupils ▷ *noun* **4** senior person
> **seniority** *noun: Promotion
appeared to be based on seniority*

senior citizen *noun* an elderly
person, especially one receiving an
old-age pension

sensation *noun* **1** physical feeling
2 general feeling or awareness
3 ability to feel things physically
4 exciting person or thing

sensational *adjective* **1** causing
intense shock, anger or
excitement **2** *informal* very good
> **sensationally** *adverb*

sense senses sensing sensed
noun **1** any of the faculties of
perception or feeling (sight,
hearing, touch, taste or smell)
2 feeling: *a sense of guilt* **3** ability
to think and behave sensibly
4 meaning **5 make sense** to be
understandable or seem sensible
▷ *verb* **6** to become aware of;
perceive

senseless *adjective* **1** (of an act)
without meaning or purpose **2** (of a
person) unconscious

sensibility sensibilities *noun*
ability to experience deep feelings

sensible *adjective* **1** having or
showing good sense **2** practical
> **sensibly** *adverb*

sensitive *adjective* **1** responsive and
able to react with understanding
2 easily hurt or offended **3** (of
a subject) liable to arouse
controversy or strong feelings if
not dealt with carefully **4** capable

of being affected or harmed **5** (of an
instrument) responsive to slight
changes > **sensitively** *adverb*
> **sensitivity** *noun: a matter that
needs to be handled with sensitivity*.

sensor *noun* device that detects
or measures the presence of
something, such as radiation,
light or heat

sensual *adjective* **1** having a strong
liking for physical pleasures
2 giving pleasure to the body
and senses rather than the mind
> **sensuality** *noun* > **sensually**
adverb

sensuous *adjective* pleasing to the
senses > **sensuously** *adverb*

sent *verb* past of **send**

sentence *noun* **1** sequence of words
capable of standing alone as a
statement, question or command
2 punishment passed on a criminal
▷ *verb* **3** to pass sentence on (a
convicted person)

sentient *adjective* capable of feeling

sentiment *noun* **1** feeling, attitude
or opinion **2** feelings such as
tenderness or sadness: *There's no
room for sentiment in business*

sentimental *adjective* **1** excessively
romantic or nostalgic **2** relating
to a person's emotions
> **sentimentalism** *noun*
> **sentimentality** *noun*

sentinel *noun* sentry

sentry *noun* soldier on guard duty

separate *adjective* **1** not the same,
different **2** set apart **3** not shared;
individual ▷ *verb* **4** (of a couple) to
stop living together **5** to act as a
barrier between **6** to distinguish
between **7** to divide up into parts
> **separately** *adverb* > **separation**
noun **1** separating or being
separated **2** *Law* living apart of a
married couple without divorce

sepia *adjective, noun* reddish-brown (pigment)

September *noun* ninth month of the year

septic *adjective* (of a wound) infected

sepulchre *noun literary* tomb or burial vault

sequel *noun* **1** novel, play or film that continues the story of an earlier one **2** consequence or result

sequence *noun* **1** string (of events) **2** arrangement of two or more things in successive order: *Do things in the right sequence*

sequin *noun* small shiny metal disc sewn on clothes to decorate them

Serbian *adjective* **1** of Serbia ▷ *noun* **2** person from Serbia **3** form of Serbo-Croat spoken in Serbia

Serbo-Croat *adjective, noun* the main language spoken in Serbia and Croatia

serenade serenades serenading serenaded *noun* **1** music played or sung outside a woman's window to a woman by a lover ▷ *verb* **2** to sing or play a serenade to (someone)

serendipity *noun formal* gift of making fortunate discoveries by accident

serene *adjective* calm or peaceful > **serenely** *adverb* > **serenity** *noun*: *It is a place of peace and serenity*

serf *noun* medieval farm labourer who could not leave the land he worked on

sergeant *noun* **1** noncommissioned officer in the army or air force **2** police officer ranking between constable and inspector

sergeant major *noun* noncommissioned army officer of the highest rank

serial *noun* story or play produced in successive instalments: *a television serial*

serial number *noun* a number given on a product that identifies it and distinguishes it from other products of the same kind

series *noun* **1** group or succession of related things, usually arranged in order **2** set of radio or TV programmes about the same subject or characters

▇ The plural of *series* is *series*

serious *adjective* **1** giving cause for concern: **2** concerned with important matters **3** not cheerful; grave **4** sincere; not joking > **seriously** *adverb* > **seriousness** *noun*

sermon *noun* **1** talk on a religious or moral subject given as part of a church service **2** long moralizing speech

serpent *noun literary* snake

serrated *adjective* having an edge like a saw with toothlike points

servant *noun* person employed to do household work for another

serve serves serving served *verb* **1** to do useful work for (a person, community, country or cause) **2** to attend to (customers) **3** to dish out food or pour out drinks for (someone) **4** to provide with a service **5** to be a member of the armed forces **6** to spend (time) in prison **7** to act or be used: *the room that served as their office* **8** *Tennis etc* to put (the ball) into play ▷ *noun* **9** *Tennis, Badminton* act of serving the ball

server *noun Computers* computer or computer program that supplies data to other machines on a network

service services servicing serviced *noun* **1** system that provides something needed by the public: *the bus service* **2** government organization: *the diplomatic service* **3** help and efforts: *services to the community* **4** overhaul of a machine or vehicle **5** formal religious ceremony **6** *Tennis etc* act, manner or right of serving the ball **7** set of matching plates or cups and saucers and so on **8 services a** armed forces **b** (on a motorway etc) garage, eating and toilet facilities **9 be of service** to help **10 in service** available for use or in use ▷ *verb* **11** to examine and repair (a machine or vehicle)

service area *noun* area beside a motorway with garage, restaurant and toilet facilities

serviceman serviceman *noun* member of the armed forces > **servicewoman** *noun*

service station *noun* garage selling fuel for motor vehicles

serviette *noun* square of cloth or paper used to protect your clothes or wipe your mouth when eating; table napkin

servile *adjective* too eager to obey people; obsequious > **servility** *noun*

serving *noun* **1** helping (of food) ▷ *adjective* **2** (of a spoon or dish) used for serving food **3** (of an officer or soldier) on active service

servitude *noun* slavery

sesame *noun* tropical plant cultivated for its seeds and oil, which are used in cooking

session *noun* **1** period spent in an activity **2** meeting of a court, parliament, council or other official group **3** a period during which meetings are held regularly: *the end of the parliamentary session* **4** period during which an activity takes place: *a drinking session*

set sets setting set *noun* **1** number of things or people that belong together or form a group **2** *Maths* group of numbers or objects that satisfy a given condition or share a property **3** television or radio **4** *Tennis* a group of six or more games played as part of a match **5** scenery used in a play or film ▷ *verb* **6** to put in a specified position or state **7** to make ready **8** to make or become firm, solid or hard **9** to establish or arrange **10** to prescribe or assign **11** (of the sun) to go down ▷ *adjective* **12** fixed or established beforehand **13** rigid or inflexible **14 set on** determined to (do something): *He is set on becoming a wrestler* > **set about** *verb* to start > **set back** *verb* **1** to delay (something) **2** *informal* to cost (someone): *A short taxi ride will set you back £12.50* > **set off** *verb* **1** to start a journey **2** to cause (something) to start > **set out** *verb* **1** to start a journey **2** to give yourself the task of (doing something): *I didn't set out to be controversial* > **set up** *verb* to make all the preparations for: *He has set up a website*

setback *noun* anything that delays progress

set square *noun* flat right-angled triangular instrument used for drawing angles and lines

settee *noun* padded seat with arms at either end for two or three people to sit on; sofa

setter *noun* long-haired gun dog

setting *noun* **1** background or surroundings **2** time and place where a film, book, etc is supposed to have taken place **3** plates and cutlery for a single place at table **4** position or level to which the controls of a machine can be adjusted

settle settles settling settled
verb **1** to arrange or put in order **2** to
come to rest **3** to set up home **4** to
make quiet, calm or stable **5** to pay
(a bill) **6 settle for** or **on** to opt
for or agree to: *We settled for orange
juice and coffee* > **settle down** *verb*
1 to start living quietly in one place,
especially on getting married **2** to
become quiet or calm

settlement *noun* **1** official
agreement between people who
have been involved in a conflict
2 place where people have settled
and built homes **3** subsidence (of
a building) **4** long wooden bench
with high back and arms

settler *noun* someone who settles
in a new country

seven *adjective, noun* the number 7
> **seventh** *adjective, noun*

seventeen *adjective, noun* the
number 17 > **seventeenth** *adjective,
noun*

seventy seventies *adjective, noun*
the number 70 > **seventieth**
adjective, noun

sever *verb* **1** to cut through or off **2** to
break off (a relationship)

several *adjective* **1** some or a few
2 various or separate

severe *adjective* **1** extremely bad
or unpleasant **2** stern, strict or
harsh **3** plain, sober and forbidding
> **severely** *adverb* > **severity** *noun*

sew sews sewing sewed sewn
verb to join, make or embroider
items using a needle and thread or
a sewing machine > **sewing** *noun*

sewage *noun* waste matter or
excrement carried away in sewers

sewer *noun* drain to remove waste
water and sewage

sewerage *noun* system of sewers

sewn *verb* a past participle of **sew**

sex sexes *noun* **1** male or female
group: *the two sexes* **2** state of
being male or female; gender: *We
didn't want to know the sex of the
baby* **3** sexual intercourse **4** sexual
feelings or behaviour

sexism *noun* discrimination on the
basis of a person's sex

sexist *adjective* **1** involving or
indulging in discrimination on
the basis of a person's sex: *sexist
attitudes* ▷ *noun* **2** person who
discriminates on the basis of
people's sex

sextet *noun* **1** group of six
performers **2** music for such a group

sexton *noun* official in charge of a
church and churchyard

sextuplet *noun* one of six children
born to the same mother from the
same pregnancy

sexual *adjective* **1** connected with
the act of sex or with people's desire
for sex: *sexual attraction* **2** relating to
the difference between males and
females: *sexual equality* **3** relating
to the biological process by which
people and animals produce young:
sexual reproduction > **sexually**
adverb

sexual intercourse *noun* physical
act of sex between two people

sexuality *noun* **1** the ability to
experience sexual feelings **2** the
state of being heterosexual,
homosexual or bisexual

sexy sexier sexiest *adjective*
1 sexually exciting or attractive
2 *informal* exciting or trendy

shabby shabbier shabbiest
adjective **1** old and worn in
appearance **2** mean or unfair
> **shabbily** *adverb*

shack *noun* rough hut

**shackle shackles shackling
shackled** *noun* **1** one of a pair of

metal rings joined by a chain, for fastening around a person's wrists or ankles ▷ *verb* **2** to fasten with shackles **3** *literary* to restrict or hamper

shade shades shading shaded *noun* **1** an area of darkness and coolness sheltered from direct sunlight **2** cover used to provide protection from a direct source of light **3** particular hue, tone or variety of a colour **4 shades** *informal* sunglasses ▷ *verb* **5** to screen (something or someone) from light

shadow *noun* **1** dark shape cast on a surface when something stands between the surface and a source of light **2** patch of shade **3 be a shadow of your former self** to be much weaker or less impressive than you used to be ▷ *verb* **4** to follow secretly

shadow cabinet *noun* those members of the main opposition party in Parliament who would be ministers if their party were in power

shadowy *adjective* **1** (of a place) dark and full of shadows **2** (of a figure or shape) difficult to make out

shady shadier shadiest *adjective* **1** situated in or giving shade **2** of doubtful honesty or legality

shaft *noun* **1** long straight and narrow part (of a tool or weapon) **2** ray of light **3** revolving rod that transmits power in a machine: *the drive shaft* **4** vertical passageway: *a lift shaft* **5** one of the bars between which a horse, donkey, etc is harnessed to a cart

shaggy shaggier shaggiest *adjective* **1** covered with rough hair or wool **2** (of hair or fur) long and untidy

shake shakes shaking shook shaken *verb* **1** to move quickly up and down or back and forth **2** to move (your head) from side to side in order to say 'no' **3** to make unsteady **4** to tremble **5** to grasp (someone's hand) in greeting or agreement **6** to shock or upset ▷ *noun* **7** shaking **8** vibration

shaky shakier shakiest *adjective* weak and unsteady > **shakily** *adverb*

shall *verb* **1** used as an auxiliary verb to form the future tense or to indicate intention or inevitability: *I shall ring him later; We shall be late* **2** used as an auxiliary verb when making suggestions or asking what to do: *Shall I check?*

shallow *adjective* **1** not deep **2** not given to deep thought or understanding; superficial > **shallowness** *noun*

shallows *plural noun* area of shallow water

sham shams shamming shammed *noun* **1** thing or person that is not genuine ▷ *adjective* **2** not genuine ▷ *verb* **3** to fake or feign

shambles *noun* confused and disorganized situation or event

shame shames shaming shamed *noun* **1** guilt and embarrassment that comes from realizing that you have done something bad or foolish **2** capacity to feel such guilt and embarrassment **3** cause of shame: *There is no shame in that* **4** cause for regret: *It's a shame you can't come* ▷ *verb* **5** to cause to feel shame **6** to compel by shame: *They shamed their parents into giving up cigarettes* ▷ *interjection* **7** *S Afr informal* exclamation of sympathy

shameful *adjective* causing or deserving shame > **shamefully**

adverb

shameless *adjective* with no sense of shame > **shamelessly** *adverb*

shampoo shampoos shampooing shampooed *noun* **1** soapy liquid used for washing hair, carpets or upholstery **2** wash with shampoo ▷ *verb* **3** to wash (something) with shampoo

shamrock *noun* plant with three round leaves on each stem used as the national emblem of Ireland

shanghai shanghais shanghaiing shanghaied *verb* **1** to force or trick (someone) into doing something ▷ *noun* **2** *Aust, NZ* catapult

shank *noun* **1** lower leg **2** long thin straight part of something

shan't shall not

shanty shanties *noun* **1** shack or crude dwelling **2** sailor's traditional song

shanty town *noun* town or area consisting of shanties

shape shapes shaping shaped *noun* **1** outward form of an object **2** pattern or mould **3** way in which something is organized **4 in good shape** in good condition or in a good state of health ▷ *verb* **5** to form or mould **6** to influence the development of

shapeless *adjective* without a definite shape

shapely *adjective* (of woman) having an attractive figure

shard *noun* broken piece of pottery or glass

share shares sharing shared *verb* **1** to hold (something) jointly or join with others in doing, using or having (something): *We shared a bottle of champagne* **2** to divide (something) up equally: *We could share the cost between us* ▷ *noun* **3** part of something that belongs to or is contributed by a person **4** one of the equal parts into which the capital stock of a public company is divided > **share out** *verb* to divide (something) equally among a group of people

shareholder *noun* a person who owns shares in a company

share-milker *noun* *NZ* person who works on a dairy farm and shares the profit from the sale of its produce

shark *noun* **1** large powerful fish with sharp teeth **2** person who cheats others

sharp *adjective* **1** (of knife, needle) having a fine edge or point that is good for cutting or piercing things **2** not gradual **3** clearly defined **4** quick-witted **5** shrill **6** bitter or sour in taste **7** *Music* above the true pitch ▷ *adverb* **8** promptly **9** *Music* too high in pitch ▷ *noun* **10** *Music* note, or the symbol for it (♯), that is one semitone above the natural pitch > **sharply** *adverb* > **sharpness** *noun*

sharpen *verb* to make or become sharp or sharper

sharpener *noun* device for sharpening things

shatter *verb* **1** to break into pieces **2** to destroy completely

shattered *adjective informal* **1** completely exhausted **2** badly upset

shattering *adjective* causing shock or exhaustion

shave shaves shaving shaved *verb* **1** to remove (hair) from (the face, head or body) with a razor or shaver **2** to pare away ▷ *noun* **3** instance of shaving **4 close shave** *informal* narrow escape

shaven *adjective* shaved

shaver *noun* electric razor

shavings *plural noun* small, very thin pieces of wood cut off a larger piece; parings

shawl *noun* piece of cloth worn over a woman's head or shoulders or wrapped around a baby

she *pronoun refers to:* **1** female person or animal previously mentioned **2** something regarded as female, such as a car, ship or nation

sheaf sheaves *noun* **1** bundle (of papers) **2** tied bundle (of reaped corn)

shear shears shearing sheared shorn *verb* **1** to clip hair or wool from (a sheep) **2** to cut through

shearer *noun* someone whose job is to shear sheep

shears *plural noun* large cutting tool shaped rather like a pair of scissors used especially for cutting grass

sheath *noun* **1** close-fitting cover, especially for a knife or sword **2** *Brit, Aust, NZ* condom

shed sheds shedding shed *noun* **1** building used for storage, shelter or as a workshop ▷ *verb* **2** to cast off (skin, hair or leaves) **3** to weep (tears) **4** *formal* to get rid of: *The firm is to shed 700 jobs* **5** to drop (a load): *A lorry had shed a load* **6** **shed light (on)** to make clearer

sheen *noun* soft shine on the surface of something

sheep *noun* farm animal bred for wool and meat

▌The plural of *sheep* is *sheep*

sheep-dip *noun* liquid disinfectant used to keep sheep clean and free of pests

sheepdog *noun* type of dog often used for herding sheep

sheepish *adjective* embarrassed because of feeling foolish ▷ **sheepishly** *adverb*

sheepskin *noun* skin of a sheep with the fleece still on, used for making rugs and coats

sheer *adjective* **1** absolute or complete: *sheer folly* **2** perpendicular or steep: *a sheer cliff* **3** (of material) so fine as to be transparent

sheet *noun* **1** large piece of fine cloth used under blankets or duvets as bedding **2** fine rectangular piece of any material

sheikh or **sheik** *noun* Arab chief

shelf shelves *noun* flat piece of wood, metal or glass fixed horizontally and used for putting things on

shell *noun* **1** hard outer covering of an egg, nut or certain animals **2** external frame of something: *The room was just an empty shell* **3** explosive device fired from a large gun ▷ *verb* **4** to remove the shell or outer covering from (peas, nuts) **5** to fire at (a place) with artillery shells

shellfish shellfish or **shellfishes** *noun* a small, usually edible, sea creature with a shell

shell shock *noun* mental illness affecting some soldiers who have been exposed to war and battle conditions

shell suit *noun* *Brit* lightweight tracksuit made of a waterproof nylon layer over a cotton layer

shelter *noun* **1** building or structure providing protection from danger or the weather **2** protection ▷ *verb* **3** to give shelter to **4** to take shelter

sheltered *adjective* **1** (of a place) protected from wind and rain **2** (of a life) away from unpleasant or upsetting things **3** (of accommodation for the elderly or handicapped) offering specially equipped and monitored facilities

shelve shelves shelving shelved
verb to put aside or postpone

shepherd *noun* **1** person who tends
sheep ▷ *verb* **2** to guide or watch
over (people)

sherbet *noun* **1** *Brit, Aust, NZ*
fruit-flavoured fizzy powder **2** *US,
Canadian, S Afr* flavoured water ice

sheriff *noun* **1** (in the US) chief law
enforcement officer of a county
2 (in England and Wales) person
appointed by the king or queen to
carry out ceremonial duties **3** (in
Scotland) chief judge of a district
4 (in Australia) officer of the
Supreme Court

sherry sherries *noun* pale or dark
brown fortified wine

shield *noun* **1** piece of armour carried
on the arm to protect the body from
blows or missiles **2** anything that
protects ▷ *verb* **3** to protect

shift *verb* **1** to move **2** to transfer
(blame or responsibility) **3** to
remove or be removed **4** (of an
opinion or situation) to change
▷ *noun* **5** set period during which
different groups of people work in a
factory or the people assigned to a
particular period: *the night shift*

shifty shiftier shiftiest *adjective* sly
and deceitful in appearance

shilling *noun* former British,
Australian and New Zealand coin
worth one-twentieth of a pound; in
Britain replaced by the 5p piece

shimmer *verb* **1** to shine with a faint
flickering light ▷ *noun* **2** a faint
flickering light

shin *noun* **1** front of the lower leg
▷ *verb* **2** to climb (a pole or tree)
quickly, gripping with your arms
and legs

shine shines shining shone *verb*
1 to give out or reflect light **2** to aim

(a light or torch) **3** to be very good
(at something) ▷ *noun* **4** brightness
or lustre

shingle *noun* **1** small pebble found
on beaches **2** small wooden roof tile

shingles *noun* disease causing a
painful rash of small blisters along
a nerve

shining *adjective* **1** bright or
gleaming **2** **shining example** very
good or typical example

shiny shinier shiniest *adjective*
bright and polished-looking

ship ships shipping shipped
noun **1** large boat which carries
passengers or cargo; vessel ▷ *verb*
2 to send or transport (something
or someone) somewhere,
sometimes by ship

-ship *suffix* used to form nouns that
refer to a condition or position:
fellowship

shipment *noun* **1** a quantity of
goods transported somewhere: *a
shipment of olive oil* **2** transporting
(of cargo)

shipping *noun* **1** business of
transporting cargo on ships **2** ships
collectively

shipwreck *noun* **1** destruction of
a ship through storm or collision
2 wrecked ship ▷ *verb* **3** to leave
(someone) a survivor of a shipwreck

shipyard *noun* place where ships
are built

shiralee *noun Aust old-fashioned*
bundle of possessions carried by a
swagman

shire *noun* **1** *Brit old-fashioned* county
2 *Aust* rural area with an elected
council

shirk *verb* to avoid (duty or work)

shirt *noun* lightweight blouse-like
piece of clothing worn especially
by men and boys, typically having
a collar, sleeves and buttons down

the front

shiver *verb* **1** to tremble, as from cold or fear ▷ *noun* **2** slight tremble, as from cold or fear

shoal *noun* large number of fish swimming together

shock *noun* **1** sudden upsetting experience **2** something causing this **3** sudden violent blow or impact **4** serious medical condition in which the blood cannot circulate properly brought about by physical or mental shock **5** pain and muscular spasm caused by an electric current passing through the body **6** bushy mass (of hair) ▷ *verb* **7** to horrify or astonish **8** to offend or scandalize > **shocked** *adjective* > **shocker** *noun* > **shocking** *adjective* **1** *informal* very bad **2** rude or immoral

shock absorber *noun* one of the devices fitted near a vehicle's wheels to help prevent it bouncing up and down

shod *verb* past of **shoe**

shoddy shoddier shoddiest *adjective* made or done badly

shoe shoes shoeing shod *noun* **1** type of protective footwear that covers the foot, ends below the ankle and has a hard sole **2** horseshoe ▷ *verb* **3** to fit (a horse) with a horseshoe or horseshoes

shoestring *noun* **on a shoestring** using a very small amount of money

shone *verb* past of **shine**

shook *verb* past tense of **shake**

shoot shoots shooting shot *verb* **1** to hit, wound or kill (a person or animal) by firing a gun at them **2** to fire (an arrow or a bolt) from a bow or crossbow **3** to hunt **4** to send out or move rapidly: *They shot back into Green Street* **5** (of a plant)

to sprout **6** to photograph or film: *The whole film was shot in California* **7** *Sport* to take a shot at goal ▷ *noun* **8** new branch or sprout of a plant **9** hunting expedition

shooting *noun* incident in which someone is shot

shooting star *noun* meteor

shop shops shopping shopped *noun* **1** place where things are sold **2** workshop: *a bicycle repair shop* **3** **talk shop** to discuss work, especially on a social occasion ▷ *verb* **4** to go to the shops to buy things **5** *Brit, Aust, NZ informal* to inform against > **shopper** *noun*: *Christmas shoppers*

shopkeeper *noun* someone who owns or manages a small shop

shoplifter *noun* person who steals from a shop

shoplifting *noun* practice of stealing goods from shops

shopping *noun* **1** goods bought from shops **2** activity of buying things

shop steward *noun* (in some countries) trade-union official elected to represent his or her fellow workers

shore shores shoring shored *noun* **1** edge of a sea or lake ▷ *verb* **2** **shore up** to reinforce, strengthen or prop (something) up

shoreline *noun* the edge of a sea, lake or wide river

shorn *verb* **1** a past participle of **shear** ▷ *adjective* **2** (of grass, hair) cut very short

short *adjective* **1** not long: *a short distance* **2** not tall: *He's short and plump* **3** not lasting long; brief: *a short time* **4** deficient: *short of cash* **5** abrupt or rude: *She was a bit short with me* **6** (of a drink) consisting chiefly of a spirit **7** (of pastry) crumbly ▷ *adverb* **8** abruptly ▷ *noun* **9** drink of spirits **10** short film **11** *informal* short circuit

shortage *noun* deficiency

shortbread or **shortcake** *noun* crumbly biscuit made with butter

short-change short-changes short-changing short-changed *verb* to give (someone) less than the correct amount of change

short circuit *noun* electrical fault that occurs when two points accidentally become connected and the electricity travels directly between them rather than through the complete circuit

shortcoming *noun* failing or defect

shortcut *noun* quicker route or method

shorten *verb* to make (something) shorter or become shorter

shortfall *noun* smaller amount than needed

shorthand *noun* system of rapid writing using symbols to represent words

short list *noun* selected list of candidates for a job or prize, from which the final choice will be made

short-list short-lists short-listing short-listed *verb* to put on a short list

shortly *adverb* **1** soon **2** rudely

shorts *plural noun* short trousers

short shrift *noun* brief and unsympathetic treatment: *People who disagree with him are given short shrift*

short-sighted *adjective* **1** unable to see distant things clearly **2** not taking account of possible future events

short-term *adjective* happening or having an effect within a short time or for a short time

shot *verb* **1** past of **shoot** ▷ *noun* **2** shooting **3** small lead pellets used in a shotgun **4** person with specified skill in shooting: *a good shot* **5** *informal* attempt: *I'll have a shot at it* **6** *Sport* act or instance of hitting, kicking or throwing the ball **7** photograph **8** uninterrupted film sequence **9** *informal* injection **10** **like a shot** *informal* quickly and eagerly

shotgun *noun* gun for firing a lot of small pellets at once

shot put *noun* athletic event in which contestants throw a heavy metal ball as far as possible > **shot-putter** *noun* person who takes part in shot-putting events

should *verb* **1** ought to: *He should have done better* **2** to be likely to: *He should have heard by now* **3** *formal* would: *I should like to express my thanks* **4** sometimes used in subordinate clauses after *that*: *It is inevitable that you should go* **5** was to or were to: *if he should die prematurely*

shoulder *noun* **1** part of the body to which an arm, foreleg or wing is attached **2** part of a piece of clothing that covers your shoulders **3** side of a road ▷ *verb* **4** to bear (a burden or responsibility) **5** to put on your shoulder

shoulder blade *noun* either of the two large flat triangular bones in the upper part of your back, below your shoulders

shouldn't should not

shout *noun* **1** loud cry ▷ *verb* **2** to cry out loudly > **shout down** *verb* to silence (someone) or to prevent (someone) from being heard by shouting

shove shoves shoving shoved *verb* **1** to push roughly **2** *informal* to put ▷ *noun* **3** rough push > **shove**

off *verb informal* to go away

shovel shovels shovelling shovelled *noun* **1** spade-like tool for lifting or moving loose material ▷ *verb* **2** to lift or move (something) as with a shovel

show shows showing showed shown *verb* **1** to make, be or become noticeable or visible: *He showed his dislike* **2** to exhibit or display: *Show me your passport* **3** to indicate or prove: *This shows that I was right* **4** to demonstrate: *Show me how it works.* **5** to guide or lead: *I'll show you to your room.* **6** to reveal or display (an emotion) ▷ *noun* **7** public exhibition **8** entertainment on television or at the theatre and so on **9** mere display or pretence > **show off** *verb* **1** *informal* to try to impress people by behaving in a flamboyant manner **2** to allow others to see (something) to invite admiration > **show up** *verb* **1** *informal* to arrive **2** to reveal or be revealed clearly **3** to expose the faults or defects of **4** *informal* to embarrass

show business *noun* the entertainment industry

showcase *noun* **1** situation in which something is displayed to best advantage **2** glass case used to display objects

showdown *noun informal* confrontation that settles a dispute

shower *noun* **1** device for washing that sprays you with water **2** wash under such a device **3** short period of rain, hail or snow **4** sudden fall of a lot of objects ▷ *verb* **5** to wash in a shower **6** to give (a lot of things) or present (someone) with a lot of things

showing *noun* public presentation or viewing (of a film or television programme)

showjumping *noun* competitive sport of riding horses to demonstrate skill in jumping

shown *verb* past participle of **show**

show-off *noun informal* person who tries to impress people with their knowledge or skills

showroom *noun* room in which goods for sale are on display

showy showier showiest *adjective* large or bright and intended to impress; ostentatious

shrank *verb* past tense of **shrink**

shrapnel *noun* **1** artillery shell filled with pellets which scatter on explosion **2** fragments from this

shred shreds shredding shredded *noun* **1** long narrow strip torn from something **2** small amount ▷ *verb* **3** to tear to shreds

shrew *noun* **1** small mouselike animal **2** *offensive* bad-tempered nagging woman

shrewd *adjective* clever and perceptive > **shrewdly** *adverb* > **shrewdness** *noun*

shriek *noun* **1** shrill cry ▷ *verb* **2** to utter (with) a shriek

shrift *noun* See **short shrift**

shrill *adjective* (of a sound) sharp and high-pitched > **shrillness** *noun* > **shrilly** *adverb*

shrimp *noun* small edible shellfish

shrine *noun* place of worship associated with a sacred person or object

shrink shrinks shrinking shrank shrunk *verb* **1** to become or make smaller **2** to recoil or withdraw ▷ *noun* **3** *informal* psychiatrist > **shrinkage** *noun* decrease in size, value or weight

shrivel shrivels shrivelling shrivelled *verb* to shrink and wither

shroud *noun* **1** piece of cloth used to wrap a dead body **2** anything which conceals ▷ *verb* **3** to conceal: *shrouded in mystery*

Shrove Tuesday *noun* day before Ash Wednesday

shrub *noun* a low bushy plant

shrug shrugs shrugging shrugged *verb* **1** to raise and then drop (the shoulders) as a sign of indifference, ignorance or doubt ▷ *noun* **2** act of shrugging your shoulders

shrunk *verb* past participle of **shrink**

shrunken *adjective formal* reduced in size: *a shrunken old man*

shudder *verb* **1** to shake or tremble violently, especially with horror ▷ *noun* **2** shiver of fear or horror

shuffle shuffles shuffling shuffled *verb* **1** to walk without lifting your feet properly **2** **shuffle about** to move about and fidget **3** to mix (cards) up thoroughly ▷ *noun* **4** act of shuffling

shun shuns shunning shunned *verb* to avoid

shunt *verb* to move (objects or people) to a different position

shush *interjection* be quiet!

shut shuts shutting shut *verb* to close > **shut down** *verb* to close permanently > **shut up** *verb* *informal* to stop talking

shutter *noun* **1** hinged doorlike cover for closing off a window **2** device in a camera that opens to allow light through the lens when a photograph is taken

shuttle *noun* **1** plane or other vehicle that goes to and fro between two places ▷ *adjective* **2** (of services) involving a plane, bus or train service that travels to and fro between two places

shuttlecock *noun* feathered object used as a ball in the game of badminton

shy shyer shyest; shies shying shied *adjective* **1** nervous and uncomfortable in company; timid **2** **shy of** cautious or wary of ▷ *verb* **3** (of horse) to move away suddenly because startled or afraid **4** **shy away from** to avoid (doing something) through fear or lack of confidence > **shyly** *adverb* > **shyness** *noun*

Siamese twins *plural noun* twins born joined to each other at some part of the body; conjoined twins

sibling *noun formal* brother or sister

sibyl *noun* (in ancient Greece and Rome) prophetess

sick *adjective* **1** ill **2** **feel sick** to feel nauseous and likely to vomit **3** **be sick** to vomit **4** *informal* (of a person, story or joke) showing an unpleasant and frivolous disrespect for something sad **5** **sick of** *informal* disgusted by or weary of > **sickness** *noun*

sicken sickens sickening sickened *verb* to make (someone) nauseated or disgusted > **sickening** *adjective*: *a string of sickening attacks*

sickle *noun* tool with a short handle and a curved blade for cutting grass or grain

sickly sicklier sickliest *adjective* **1** unhealthy or weak **2** causing revulsion or nausea

side sides siding sided *noun* **1** either of two halves into which something can be divided **2** either surface of a flat object **3** surface or edge of something, especially when neither the front nor the back **4** area immediately next to a person or thing **5** aspect or part

6 one of two opposing groups or teams **7** slope (of a hill) **8** television channel **9 on the side a** as an extra **b** unofficially ▷ *adjective* **10** at or on the side: *the side door* **11** of lesser importance: *a side road* > **side with** *verb* to support (one side in a dispute)

sideboard *noun* a long, low cupboard for plates and glasses in a dining room

sideburns or **sideboards** *plural noun* areas of hair growing on a man's cheeks in front of his ears

side effect *noun* (of drug) additional undesirable effect

sidekick *noun informal* close friend or associate

sidelight *noun* either of two small lights on the front of a vehicle

sideline *noun* **1** extra interest or source of income **2** *Sport* line marking the boundary of a playing area

sideshow *noun* stall at a fairground

sidestep sidesteps sidestepping sidestepped *verb* to dodge (an issue)

sidetrack *verb* to divert from the main topic

sidewalk *noun US* paved path for pedestrians, at the side of a road; pavement

sideways *adverb* **1** to or from the side **2** obliquely

siding *noun* short stretch of railway track beside the main tracks where engines and carriages are left when not in use

sidle sidles sidling sidled *verb* to walk in a furtive manner

siege *noun* military operation in which an army surrounds a place and prevents food or help from reaching the people inside

siesta *noun* afternoon nap

sieve sieves sieving sieved *noun* **1** utensil with mesh through which a substance can be sifted or strained ▷ *verb* **2** to sift or strain through a sieve

sift *verb* **1** to pass (a substance) through a sieve to remove lumps **2** to examine (information or evidence) to select what is important

sigh *noun* **1** long audible breath expressing sadness, tiredness, relief or longing ▷ *verb* **2** to let out a sigh

sight *noun* **1** ability to see **2** range of vision **3** something seen: *It was a ghastly sight* **4** thing worth seeing: *Tim was eager to see the sights.* **5** device for guiding the eye while using a gun or optical instrument ▷ *verb* **6** to catch sight of

Do not confuse the spellings of *sight* and *site*

sighted *adjective* able to see

sighting *noun* instance of something rare or unexpected being seen

sight-read sight-reads sight-reading sight-read *verb* to play or sing (printed music) without previous preparation

sightseeing *noun* visiting places that tourists usually visit > **sightseer** *noun*: *For centuries, sightseers have flocked to this site*

sign *noun* **1** indication of something not immediately or outwardly observable **2** gesture, mark or symbol conveying a meaning **3** notice displayed to advertise, inform or warn **4** omen ▷ *verb* **5** to write (your name) on (a document or letter) to show its authenticity or your agreement **6** to communicate using sign language **7** to make a sign or gesture > **sign on** *verb* to register as unemployed > **sign**

up *verb* to sign a document committing yourself to a job, course, etc

signal signals signalling signalled *noun* **1** sign or gesture to convey information **2** piece of equipment beside a railway track which tells train drivers whether to stop or not **3** sequence of electrical impulses or radio waves transmitted or received ▷ *verb* **4** to convey (information) by signal

signatory signatories *noun* one of the people signing a document

signature *noun* **1** person's name written by himself or herself in his or her usual style when signing **2** sign at the start of a piece of music to show the key or tempo

signature tune *noun* tune used to introduce or identify a particular television or radio programme

significant *adjective* **1** important **2** having or expressing a meaning **3** (of amount) large > **significance** *noun* > **significantly** *adverb*

signify signifies signifying signified *verb* **1** to indicate or suggest **2** to be a symbol or sign for

sign language or **signing** *noun* system of communication by gestures, as used by deaf people

signpost *noun* road sign with information on it such as the name of a town and how far away it is

Sikh *noun* person who believes in Sikhism, an Indian religion which separated from Hinduism in the sixteenth century and which teaches that there is only one God > **Sikhism** *noun*

silage *noun* fodder crop harvested while green and partially fermented in a silo or plastic bags

silence silences silencing silenced *noun* **1** absence of noise or speech ▷ *verb* **2** to make (someone or something) silent

silent *adjective* **1** not saying a word; uncommunicative **2** not making a sound; quiet > **silently** *adverb*

silhouette *noun* outline of a dark shape seen against a light background > **silhouetted** *adjective*: *chimney-stacks silhouetted against the sky*

silicon *noun* brittle nonmetallic element widely used in chemistry and the computing and electronics industries

silk *noun* **1** fibre made by the silkworm **2** thread or fabric made from this

silkworm *noun* larva of a particular kind of moth

silky or **silken** *adjective* of or like silk; smooth and soft

sill *noun* ledge at the bottom of a window or door

silly sillier silliest *adjective* foolish

silo silos *noun* tall metal tower for storing silage or grains

silt *noun* **1** mud deposited by moving water ▷ *verb* **2** **silt up** (of a river or lake) to fill or be choked with silt

silver *noun* **1** valuable greyish-white metallic element used for making jewellery and ornaments **2** coins or articles made of silver or silver-coloured metal ▷ *adjective* **3** silver-coloured or made of silver

silverbeet *noun Aust, NZ* leafy green vegetable with white stalks

silver fern *noun* tall fern found in New Zealand. It is the symbol of New Zealand national sports teams

silverfish silverfishes or **silverfish** *noun* small silver-coloured insect with no wings

silver jubilee *noun* 25th anniversary of an important event

silver medal *noun* a medal

made from silver, or something resembling this, awarded to the competitor who comes second in a competition

silver wedding *noun* 25th wedding anniversary

silvery *adjective* having the appearance or colour of silver

similar *adjective* 1 alike but not identical 2 *Geometry* (of triangles) having the same angles > **similarly** *adverb*

similarity similarities *noun* similar quality; resemblance

simile *noun* figure of speech comparing one thing to another, using *as* or *like*: *He's as white as a sheet; She runs like a deer*

simmer *verb* 1 to cook gently at just below boiling point 2 to be in a state of suppressed rage

simper *verb* 1 to smile in a silly or affected way 2 to utter (something) with a simper ▷ *noun* 3 simpering smile

simple simpler simplest *adjective* 1 easy to understand or do 2 plain or unpretentious 3 not combined or complex 4 having some degree of mental retardation 5 no more than; mere > **simplicity** *noun* quality of being simple

simple-minded *adjective* not very intelligent or sophisticated

simplify simplifies simplifying simplified *verb* to make less complicated > **simplification** *noun*

simplistic *adjective* too simple or naive

simply *adverb* 1 merely or just 2 in a way that is easy to understand 3 plainly or unpretentiously

simulate simulates simulating simulated *verb* 1 to make a pretence of 2 to reproduce the characteristics of 3 to have the

appearance of > **simulation** *noun* > **simulator** *noun* device designed to reproduce actual conditions, for example in order to train pilots or astronauts

simultaneous *adjective* occurring at the same time > **simultaneously** *adverb*

sin sins sinning sinned *noun* 1 wicked and immoral behaviour 2 offence against a principle or standard, especially a religious one 3 **live in sin** *old-fashioned* (of an unmarried couple) to live together as if married ▷ *verb* 4 to do something wicked and immoral

since *preposition* 1 during the entire period of time from: *I've been waiting here since 3.30* ▷ *conjunction* 2 from the time when: *We've known each other since we were kids* 3 for the reason that: *I'm forever on a diet, since I put on weight easily* ▷ *adverb* 4 from that time: *He has since remarried*

sincere *adjective* without pretence or deceit > **sincerity** *noun*: *There is no doubting their sincerity*

sincerely *adverb* 1 genuinely 2 **Yours sincerely** ending for formal letters addressed and written to a named person

sinew *noun* 1 tough fibrous tissue joining muscle to bone 2 muscles or strength

sinful *adjective* wicked and immoral

sing sings singing sang sung *verb* 1 to make musical sounds with the voice 2 to perform (a song) 3 (of a bird or insect) to make a humming or whistling sound > **singer** *noun* person who sings, especially professionally

singe singes singeing singed *verb* 1 to burn the surface of ▷ *noun* 2 a slight burn

single singles singling singled

adjective **1** one only **2** unmarried **3** designed for one user: *a single bed* **4** (of a ticket) valid for an outward journey only **5 in single file** (of people or things) arranged in one line ▷ *noun* **6** single ticket **7** recording of one or two short pieces of music on a record, CD or cassette **8 singles** game between two players > **single out** *verb* to pick out from others > **singly** *adverb* on your own or one by one

single-handed *adjective* without assistance

single-minded *adjective* having one aim only

singsong *noun* informal singing session

singular *adjective* **1** (of a word or form) denoting one person or thing **2** remarkable or unusual ▷ *noun* **3** singular form of a word > **singularity** *noun* > **singularly** *adverb*

sinister *adjective* seeming evil or harmful

sink sinks sinking sank sunk *noun* **1** a basin with taps supplying water, usually in a kitchen ▷ *verb* **2** to move or cause to move downwards, especially through water: *An Indian cargo ship sank in icy seas* **3** to descend or cause to descend: *He sank into black despair* **4** to decline in value or amount **5** to become weaker **6** to dig or drill (a hole or shaft) **7** to make (a knife or your teeth) go deeply into something **8** to invest (money) > **sink in** *verb* (of a fact) to penetrate the mind

sinner *noun* person who has committed a sin

sinuous *adjective* curving or twisting

sinus sinuses *noun* air passage in the skull

sip sips sipping sipped *verb* **1** to drink in small mouthfuls ▷ *noun* **2** amount sipped

siphon *verb* to draw (a liquid) out of something through a tube and transfer it to another place

sir *noun* **1** polite term of address for a man **2 Sir** title of a knight or baronet

sire sires siring sired *verb* **1** to father ▷ *noun* **2** respectful term of address to a king

siren *noun* **1** device making a loud wailing noise as a warning **2** *literary* dangerously alluring woman

sirloin *noun* prime cut of loin of beef

sis or **sies** *interjection S Afr informal* exclamation of disgust

sister *noun* **1** girl or woman with the same parents as another person **2** female fellow-member of a group **3** senior nurse **4** nun ▷ *adjective* **5** closely related or similar

sisterhood *noun* strong feeling of companionship between women

sister-in-law sisters-in-law *noun* **1** the sister of your husband or wife **2** your brother's wife

sit sits sitting sat *verb* **1** to have your body bent at the hips so that your weight is on your buttocks rather than your feet **2** (also **sit down**) to lower yourself to a sitting position **3** to perch **4** (of an official body) to hold a session **5** to take (an examination)

sitcom *noun* *informal* a television comedy series which shows characters in amusing situations; situation comedy

site sites siting sited *noun* **1** piece of ground where a particular thing happens or is situated **2** same as **website** ▷ *verb* **3** to provide with a site

Do not confuse the spellings of *site* and *sight*

sit-in *noun* protest in which demonstrators occupy a place and refuse to move

sitting *noun* 1 one of the times when a meal is served 2 one of the occasions when a parliament or law court meets and carries out its work

sitting room *noun* room in a house where people sit and relax; living room

situated *adjective* located

situation *noun* 1 state of affairs 2 *old-fashioned* location and surroundings 3 position of employment

Siva *noun* Hindu god and one of the Trimurti

six sixes *adjective, noun* the number 6

sixteen *adjective, noun* the number 16 > **sixteenth** *adjective, noun*

sixth *adjective, noun* 1 (coming as) number 6 in a series ▷ *noun* 2 one of six equal parts

sixth sense *noun* instinctive awareness

sixty sixties *adjective, noun* the number 60 > **sixtieth** *adjective, noun*

sizable or **sizeable** *adjective* quite large

size sizes sizing sized *noun* 1 dimensions or bigness 2 one of a series of standard measurements of goods > **size up** *verb informal* to assess

sizzle sizzles sizzling sizzled *verb* to make a hissing sound like frying fat

sjambok *noun* S Afr long whip made from animal hide

skate skates skating skated *noun* 1 boot with a steel blade attached to the sole for gliding over ice; ice skate 2 item of footwear with a set of wheels attached for gliding over a hard surface; roller skate 3 large edible sea fish ▷ *verb* 4 to glide on or as if on skates > **skate over** or **round** *verb* to avoid discussing or dealing with (a matter) fully

skateboard *noun* narrow board on small wheels for riding on while standing up

skein *noun* 1 loosely coiled length of wool or thread 2 flock of geese in flight

skeleton *noun* 1 framework of bones inside a person's or animal's body ▷ *adjective* 2 (of staff or a workforce) reduced to a minimum

sketch sketches sketching sketched *noun* 1 quick rough drawing 2 brief description 3 short humorous play ▷ *verb* 4 to make a sketch of (something or someone) 5 to give a brief description of

sketchy sketchier sketchiest *adjective* incomplete or inadequate

skew or **skewed** *adjective* slanting or crooked

skewer *noun* 1 long pin to hold meat together during cooking ▷ *verb* 2 to push a skewer through

ski skis skiing skied *noun* 1 one of a pair of long runners fastened to boots for gliding over snow or water ▷ *verb* 2 to travel on skis > **skier** *noun* person who skis

skid skids skidding skidded *verb* 1 (of a moving vehicle) to slide sideways uncontrollably ▷ *noun* 2 instance of skidding

skilful *adjective* having or showing skill; able > **skilfully** *adverb*

skill *noun* 1 special ability or expertise 2 something requiring special training or expertise

skilled *adjective* 1 having the knowledge and ability to do something well 2 (of work) requiring special training

skim skims skimming skimmed
verb **1** to remove floating matter
from the surface of (a liquid) **2** to
glide smoothly over (a surface) **3** to
read (a book) quickly

skimmed milk *noun* milk from
which the cream has been removed

skimp *verb* not to invest enough
time, money, material, etc

skimpy skimpier skimpiest
adjective scanty or insufficient

skin skins skinning skinned
noun **1** outer covering of the body
2 complexion **3** outer layer or
covering **4** film on a liquid **5** animal
skin used as a material or container
▷ *verb* **6** to remove the skin of (an
animal)

skinny skinnier skinniest *adjective*
very thin

skip skips skipping skipped *verb*
1 to leap lightly from one foot to the
other **2** to jump over a rope as it is
swung under you **3** *informal* to pass
over or omit ▷ *noun* **4** little jump
from one foot to the other **5** large
metal container for holding rubbish
and rubble

skipper *noun informal* captain
(of ship)

skirmish *noun* brief or minor fight
or argument

skirt *noun* **1** piece of woman's
clothing that hangs down over
the legs from the waist ▷ *verb* **2** to
border **3** to go round **4** to avoid
dealing with (an issue)

skirting board *noun* narrow
board round the bottom of an
interior wall

skit *noun* brief satirical sketch

skite skites skiting skited *Aust,
NZ informal verb* **1** to boast ▷ *noun*
2 boaster

skittish *adjective* playful or lively

skittle *noun* bottle-shaped object

used as a target in some games

skittles *noun* game in which players
try to knock over bottle-shaped
objects (skittles) by rolling a ball
at them

skivvy skivvies *noun Brit* female
servant who does menial work

skulduggery *noun informal* trickery

skulk *verb* **1** to move stealthily
2 to lurk

skull *noun* bony part of the head
surrounding the brain

skunk *noun* small black-and-white
North American mammal which
lets out a foul-smelling fluid when
attacked

sky skies *noun* the space around the
earth which you can see when you
look upwards

skylight *noun* window in a roof
or ceiling

skyline *noun* **1** line where earth and
the sky appear to meet **2** outline of
buildings, trees, etc against the sky

skyscraper *noun* very tall building

slab *noun* thick flat piece of
something

slack *adjective* **1** not tight **2** not busy
3 not thorough; negligent ▷ *noun*
4 part (of rope) that is not taut
▷ *verb* **5** to neglect your work or
duty > **slackness** *noun*

slacken *verb* to make or become
slack

slacks *plural noun* casual trousers

slag slags slagging slagged *noun*
1 waste material left when ore has
been melted down to remove the
metal ▷ *verb* **2** **slag off** *informal*
to criticize

slain *verb* past participle of **slay**

slalom *noun* skiing competition in
which competitors have to twist
and turn quickly to avoid obstacles

slam slams slamming slammed
verb **1** to shut, put down or hit

(something) violently and noisily ▷ *noun* **2** act or sound of slamming

slander *noun* **1** false and potentially damaging claim about a person **2** crime of making such a statement ▷ *verb* **3** to make false and potentially damaging claims about a person > **slanderous** *adjective*

slang *noun* very informal language

slant *verb* **1** to lean at an angle; slope **2** to present (information) in a biased way ▷ *noun* **3** slope **4** point of view, especially a biased one

slap slaps slapping slapped *noun* **1** blow with the open hand or a flat object ▷ *verb* **2** to strike with the open hand or a flat object **3** *informal* to put (someone or something somewhere) forcefully or carelessly

slapdash *adjective* careless and hasty

slapstick *noun* boisterous knockabout comedy

slash slashes slashing slashed *verb* **1** to cut with a long sweeping stroke **2** to reduce drastically ▷ *noun* **3** a diagonal line used for separating letters, words or numbers (/); stroke

slat *noun* narrow strip of wood or metal > **slatted** *adjective*: *slatted wooden blinds*

slate slates slating slated *noun* **1** rock which splits easily into thin layers **2** piece of this for covering a roof or, formerly, for writing on ▷ *verb* **3** *informal* to criticize (something or someone) harshly

slaughter *verb* **1** to kill (animals) for food **2** to kill (people) savagely or indiscriminately ▷ *noun* **3** mass killing; massacre

slave slaves slaving slaved *noun* **1** person owned by another person and forced to work for him or her ▷ *verb* **2** to work like a slave

> **slavery** *noun* **1** state or condition of being a slave **2** practice of owning slaves

slay slays slaying slew slain *verb* *literary* to kill

sleazy sleazier sleaziest *adjective* run-down or sordid

sled *noun* sledge

sledge *noun* vehicle on runners for sliding on snow

sledgehammer *noun* large heavy hammer

sleek *adjective* **1** glossy, smooth and shiny **2** (of person) rich and elegant in appearance

sleep sleeps sleeping slept *noun* **1** natural state of rest in which your eyes are closed and you are unconscious **2** period spent sleeping; nap **3** **put to sleep** to kill (a sick or injured animal) painlessly ▷ *verb* **4** to be asleep **5** (of a house, flat, etc) to have beds for (a specified number of people)

sleeper *noun* **1** person who sleeps in a specified way: *I'm a very heavy sleeper* **2** bed on a train **3** railway car fitted for sleeping in **4** beam supporting the rails of a railway **5** ring worn in a pierced ear to stop the hole from closing up

sleeping bag *noun* padded bag for sleeping in

sleeping pill *noun* pill which you take to help you sleep

sleepout *noun* **1** *Aust* area of a veranda or porch closed off for use as a bedroom **2** *NZ* small building for sleeping in

sleepover *noun* *informal* overnight stay at someone else's house

sleepwalk *verb* to walk around while asleep

sleepy sleepier sleepiest *adjective* **1** tired and ready to go to sleep **2** (of town or village) very quiet

> **sleepily** adverb > **sleepiness** noun

sleet noun mixed rain and snow or hail

sleeve noun 1 part of a piece of clothing that covers your arms or upper arms 2 tubelike cover 3 (record) cover > **sleeveless** adjective: a sleeveless pullover

sleigh noun sledge

slender adjective 1 attractively slim 2 small in amount

slept verb past of **sleep**

sleuth noun detective

slew slews slewing slewed verb 1 past tense of **slay** 2 (of a vehicle) to skid or swing round

slice slices slicing sliced noun 1 thin flat piece cut from something 2 kitchen utensil with a broad flat blade 3 Sport instance of hitting a ball so that it goes to one side rather than straight ahead ▷ verb 4 to cut into slices 5 Sport to hit (a ball) with a slice 6 **slice through** to cut or move through (something) quickly, like a knife

slick adjective 1 (of an action) skilfully and quickly done 2 (of a person) persuasive but insincere 3 (of a book or film) well-made and attractive, but superficial ▷ noun 4 patch of oil on water

slide slides sliding slid verb 1 to slip smoothly along (a surface) ▷ noun 2 small piece of photographic film which can be projected onto a screen so that you can see the picture 3 small piece of glass on which you put something for viewing under a microscope 4 structure with a steep slippery slope for children to slide down 5 ornamental hair clip

slight adjective 1 small in quantity or extent 2 not important 3 slim and delicate ▷ verb 4 to snub ▷ noun 5 snub > **slightly** adverb

slim slimmer slimmest; slims slimming slimmed adjective 1 not heavy or stout; thin 2 slight ▷ verb 3 to make or become slim by diet and exercise > **slimmer** noun

slime noun unpleasant thick slippery substance

slimy slimier slimiest adjective 1 like slime or covered with slime 2 showing excessive and insincere helpfulness and friendliness

sling slings slinging slung noun 1 bandage hung from the neck to support an injured hand or arm 2 rope or strap for lifting something 3 strap with a string at each end for throwing a stone ▷ verb 4 to throw or put as if with a sling

slink slinks slinking slunk verb to move furtively or guiltily

slip slips slipping slipped verb 1 to slide accidentally, losing your balance 2 to go smoothly, easily or quietly: She slipped out of the house 3 to put something (somewhere) easily or quickly 4 to pass out of (your mind): It slipped my mind ▷ noun 5 act of slipping 6 mistake 7 piece of clothing worn under a dress or skirt; petticoat 8 small piece (of paper) 9 **give someone the slip** to escape from someone > **slip up** verb to make a mistake

slipped disc noun painful condition in which one of the discs connecting the bones of your spine moves out of its position

slipper noun loose soft shoe for indoor wear

slippery adjective 1 smooth, wet or greasy and therefore difficult to hold or walk on 2 (of a person) untrustworthy

slippery dip noun Aust informal

children's slide at a playground or funfair

slip rail *noun Aust, NZ* fence that can be slipped out of place to make an opening

slip road *noun* narrow road leading onto a motorway

slipstream *noun* the flow of air behind a fast-moving object, such as a car or plane

slit slits slitting slit *noun* **1** long narrow cut or opening ▷ *verb* **2** to make a long straight cut in

slither *verb* to slide in an uneven manner

sliver *noun* small thin piece

slob *noun informal* lazy and untidy person

slobber *verb* to dribble or drool

sloe *noun* small sour blue-black fruit

slog slogs slogging slogged *verb* to work hard and steadily

slogan *noun* a short easily-remembered phrase used in politics or advertising; catch-phrase

slop slops slopping slopped *verb* **1** to splash or spill ▷ *noun* **2 slops** dirty water or liquid waste

slope slopes sloping sloped *noun* **1** surface that is higher at one end than at the other; incline **2** the angle at which something slopes; gradient **3 slopes** hills ▷ *verb* **4** (of a surface) to be higher at one end than at the other **5** to lean to one side: *sloping handwriting*

sloppy sloppier sloppiest *adjective* **1** careless or untidy **2** foolishly sentimental > **sloppily** *adverb* > **sloppiness** *noun*

slot slots slotting slotted *noun* **1** narrow opening for putting something in **2** *informal* place in a schedule, scheme or organization ▷ *verb* **3** to fit into a slot

sloth *noun* **1** laziness **2** a South

and Central American animal that moves very slowly and hangs upside down from the branches of trees

slot machine *noun* automatic machine worked by placing a coin in a slot

slouch slouches slouching slouched *verb* to sit, stand or move with a drooping posture

slouch hat *noun Aust* hat with a wide flexible brim, especially an Australian army hat with the left side of the brim turned up

Slovak *adjective* **1** belonging to or relating to Slovakia ▷ *noun* **2** someone from Slovakia **3** language spoken in Slovakia

slovenly *adjective* **1** dirty or untidy **2** careless

slow *adjective* **1** taking a longer time than is usual or expected **2** not fast **3** (of a clock or watch) showing a time earlier than the correct one **4** not clever ▷ *verb* **5** (often followed by *down* or *up*) to become less fast **6** to reduce the speed (of) > **slowly** *adverb* > **slowness** *noun*

slow motion *noun* movement that is much slower than normal, especially in a film

sludge *noun* **1** thick mud **2** sewage

slug slugs slugging slugged *noun* **1** small slow-moving creature with a slimy body, like a snail without a shell **2** *informal* mouthful (of an alcoholic drink) **3** bullet

sluggish *adjective* slow-moving or lacking energy

sluice sluices sluicing sluiced *noun* **1** channel carrying off water **2** (also **sluicegate**) sliding gate used to control the flow of water in this ▷ *verb* **3** to pour water over or through

slum slums slumming slummed

noun **1** squalid overcrowded house or area ▷ *verb* **2** to be temporarily experiencing poorer places or conditions than usual

slumber *literary noun* **1** sleep ▷ *verb* **2** to sleep

slump *verb* **1** (of prices or demand) to fall suddenly and dramatically **2** (of a person) to sink or fall heavily ▷ *noun* **3** a sudden severe drop in prices or demand **4** time of unemployment and economic decline

slung *verb* past of **sling**

slunk *verb* past of **slink**

slur slurs slurring slurred *verb* **1** to pronounce or say (words) indistinctly **2** *Music* to sing or play (notes) smoothly without a break ▷ *noun* **3** slurring of words **4** remark intended to discredit someone **5** *Music* **a** slurring of notes **b** curved line indicating notes to be slurred

slurp *informal verb* **1** to eat or drink noisily ▷ *noun* **2** slurping sound

slush *noun* **1** wet melting snow **2** *informal* sloppy sentimental talk or writing > **slushy** *adjective*: *a slushy romance*

slut *noun offensive* **1** dirty, untidy woman **2** immoral woman

sly slyer or **slier slyest** or **sliest** *adjective* **1** crafty **2** secretive and cunning **3** roguish ▷ *noun* **4** **on the sly** secretly > **slyly** *adverb*

smack smacks smacking smacked *verb* **1** to slap (someone) sharply **2** **smack your lips** to open and close (your lips) loudly in enjoyment or anticipation **3** **smack of** to suggest or be reminiscent of: *His tale smacks of fantasy* ▷ *noun* **4** sharp slap **5** slapping sound **6** small fishing boat ▷ *adverb* **7** *informal* squarely or directly: *smack in the middle*

small *adjective* **1** not large in size, number or amount **2** unimportant ▷ *noun* **3** narrow part of the lower back

smallholding *noun* small area of farming land

smallpox *noun* serious contagious disease with blisters that leave scars

small talk *noun* light social conversation

smarmy smarmier smarmiest *adjective informal* unpleasantly polite and flattering

smart *adjective* **1** neat and tidy **2** clever **3** fashionable **4** brisk ▷ *verb* **5** to feel or cause stinging pain > **smartly** *adverb* > **smartness** *noun*

smart aleck *informal noun* irritatingly clever person

smart card *noun* plastic card used for storing and processing computer data

smarten *verb* to make or become smart

smash smashes smashing smashed *verb* **1** to break violently and noisily **2** to strike (against something) violently **3** to destroy ▷ *noun* **4** act or sound of smashing **5** violent collision of vehicles **6** *informal* (also **smash hit**) popular success **7** *Sport* powerful overhead shot

smashing *adjective informal* excellent

smattering *noun* slight knowledge

smear *noun* **1** dirty greasy mark or smudge **2** untrue and malicious rumour **3** *Medicine* bodily sample smeared on to a slide for examination under a microscope ▷ *verb* **4** to spread (something) with a greasy or sticky substance **5** to rub (something) so that it produces a dirty mark or smudge **6** to slander

smell smells smelling smelled
or **smelt** *noun* **1** odour or scent
2 ability to perceive odours by the
nose ▷ *verb* **3** to have or give off a
smell: *He smelled of tobacco and garlic*
4 to have an unpleasant smell **5** to
sniff (something) **6** to perceive (a
scent or odour) by means of the
nose **7** to detect by instinct

smelly smellier smelliest *adjective*
having a nasty smell

smelt smelts smelting smelted
verb **1** a past of **smell 2** to extract (a
metal) from (an ore) by heating

smile smiles smiling smiled
verb **1** to turn up the corners of
your mouth slightly because you
are pleased or amused or want
to convey friendliness ▷ *noun*
2 turning up of the corners of
the mouth to show pleasure,
amusement or friendliness

smiley smileys *noun* symbol
depicting a smile or other facial
expression, used in e-mail

smirk *noun* **1** smug smile ▷ *verb* **2** to
give a smirk

smith *noun* worker in metal

smitten *adjective* in love (with
someone) or very enthusiastic
(about them)

smock *noun* **1** loose top resembling
a long blouse ▷ *verb* **2** to gather
(material) by sewing in a
honeycomb pattern

smog *noun* mixture of smoke
and fog

smoke smokes smoking smoked
noun **1** cloudy mixture of gas and
small particles sent into the air
when something burns **2** act of
smoking tobacco ▷ *verb* **3** to give
off smoke **4** to suck in and blow out
smoke from (a cigarette, cigar or
pipe) **5** to use cigarettes, cigars or a

pipe habitually **6** to cure (meat, fish
or cheese) by treating with smoke
▷ **smoker** *noun* ▷ **smoking** *noun*

smoky smokier smokiest *adjective*
full of smoke

smooth *adjective* **1** even and
without roughness, holes or
lumps **2** without obstructions or
difficulties **3** charming and polite
but possibly insincere **4** free from
jolts **5** not harsh in taste ▷ *verb* **6** to
make smooth ▷ **smoothly** *adverb*
▷ **smoothness** *noun*

smoothie *noun* thick drink made
from milk, blended fruit and ice

smother *verb* **1** to kill (someone)
by covering their mouth and nose
so that they cannot breathe **2** to
provide (someone with love and
protection) to an excessive degree
3 to suppress or stifle (an emotion)
4 to cover (something) thickly with
something

smoulder *verb* **1** to burn slowly with
smoke but no flame **2** (of feelings)
to exist in a suppressed state

SMS *abbreviation* short message
service: used for sending data to
mobile phones

**smudge smudges smudging
smudged** *verb* **1** to make or become
dirty or messy through contact
with something ▷ *noun* **2** dirty or
blurred mark

smug smugger smuggest
adjective self-satisfied ▷ **smugly**
adverb ▷ **smugness** *noun*

**smuggle smuggles smuggling
smuggled** *verb* **1** to import or
export (goods) secretly and illegally
2 to take (something or someone)
somewhere secretly

smuggler *noun* someone who
smuggles goods illegally into a
country

smut *noun* **1** stories, jokes or

pictures that are considered to be indecent or rather obscene **2** speck of soot or dark mark left by soot

snack *noun* light quick meal

snag snags snagging snagged *noun* **1** small problem or disadvantage **2** hole in fabric caused by a sharp object **3** *Aust, NZ informal* sausage ▷ *verb* **4** to catch or tear (clothing on a point)

snail *noun* **1** small slow-moving creature with a long shiny body and a shell on its back **2** **at a snail's pace** at a very slow speed

snail mail *noun informal* conventional post, as opposed to e-mail

snake snakes snaking snaked *noun* **1** long thin scaly reptile without limbs ▷ *verb* **2** to move in a winding course like a snake

snap snaps snapping snapped *verb* **1** to break suddenly **2** to (cause to) make a sharp cracking sound **3** to bite (at) suddenly **4** to speak sharply and angrily **5** to take a snapshot of ▷ *noun* **6** act or sound of snapping **7** *informal* snapshot; photo **8** sudden brief spell of cold weather **9** card game in which the word *snap* is called when two similar cards are put down ▷ *adjective* **10** (of a decision) made on the spur of the moment > **snap up** *verb* to take eagerly and quickly

snapper *noun* type of edible fish, found in waters around Australia and New Zealand

snapshot *noun* photograph taken quickly and casually

snare snares snaring snared *noun* **1** trap for catching birds or small animals involving a noose ▷ *verb* **2** to catch (an animal or bird) in or as if in a snare

snarl *verb* **1** (of an animal) to growl with bared teeth **2** to speak or utter fiercely **3** to make tangled ▷ *noun* **4** act or sound of snarling

snatch snatches snatching snatched *verb* **1** to seize or try to seize suddenly **2** to take (food, a rest, etc) hurriedly ▷ *noun* **3** act of snatching **4** fragment (of conversation or a song)

snazzy snazzier snazziest *adjective informal* stylish and flashy

sneak *verb* **1** to move furtively **2** to bring, take or put furtively **3** *informal* to tell tales ▷ *noun* **4** someone who reports other people's bad behaviour or naughtiness to those in authority

sneakers *plural noun* casual shoes with rubber soles

sneaking *adjective* (of a feeling) slight but persistent and a little worrying

sneaky sneakier sneakiest *adjective informal* underhand

sneer *noun* **1** scornful and contemptuous expression or remark, intended to show your low opinion of someone or something ▷ *verb* **2** (often followed by *at*) to show contempt for someone or something by giving a sneer

sneeze sneezes sneezing sneezed *verb* **1** to react to a tickle in the nose by involuntarily letting out air and droplets of water from the nose and mouth suddenly and noisily ▷ *noun* **2** act or sound of sneezing

snide *adjective* (of comment, remark) critical in an unfair and nasty way

sniff *verb* **1** to breathe in through the nose in short breaths that can be heard **2** to smell (something) by sniffing ▷ *noun* **3** act or sound of sniffing > **sniff at** *verb* to express contempt for

snigger *noun* **1** sly disrespectful laugh, especially one partly stifled ▷ *verb* **2** to let out a snigger

snip snips snipping snipped *verb* **1** to cut in small quick strokes with scissors or shears ▷ *noun* **2** *informal* bargain **3** act or sound of snipping

sniper *noun* person who shoots at people from cover

snippet *noun* (of information, news) small piece

snob *noun* **1** someone who admires upper-class people and looks down on lower-class people **2** someone who believes that he or she is better than other people > **snobbery** *noun: intellectual snobbery* > **snobbish** *adjective*

snooker *noun* game played on a large table covered with smooth green cloth. Players score points by hitting different coloured balls into side pockets using a long stick called a cue

snoop *informal verb* **1** to pry ▷ *noun* **2** act of snooping > **snooper** *noun*

snooty snootier snootiest *adjective informal* haughty or snobbish

snooze snoozes snoozing snoozed *informal verb* **1** to sleep lightly for a short time, especially during the day ▷ *noun* **2** short light sleep

snore snores snoring snored *verb* **1** to make snorting sounds while sleeping ▷ *noun* **2** sound of snoring

snorkel snorkels snorkelling snorkelled *noun* **1** tube allowing a swimmer to breathe while face down in the water ▷ *verb* **2** to swim using a snorkel > **snorkelling** *noun*

snort *verb* **1** to breathe out noisily through the nostrils **2** to express contempt or anger by snorting ▷ *noun* **3** act or sound of snorting

snot *noun informal* mucus from the nose

snout *noun* (of an animal) nose and jaws

snow *noun* **1** flakes of ice crystals which fall from the sky in cold weather ▷ *verb* **2** to fall as or like snow

snowball *noun* **1** snow shaped into a ball for throwing ▷ *verb* **2** to increase rapidly

snowdrift *noun* deep pile of snow formed by the wind

snowdrop *noun* small white bell-shaped spring flower

snowman snowmen *noun* figure shaped out of snow

snub snubs snubbing snubbed *verb* **1** to insult (someone) deliberately, especially by making an insulting remark or by ignoring them ▷ *noun* **2** deliberate insult ▷ *adjective* **3** (of a nose) short and turned-up

snuff *noun* **1** powdered tobacco for sniffing up the nostrils ▷ *verb* **2** to put out (a candle)

snuffle snuffles snuffling snuffled *verb* to breathe noisily or with difficulty

snug snugger snuggest *adjective* **1** warm and comfortable **2** comfortably close-fitting > **snugly** *adverb*

snuggle snuggles snuggling snuggled *verb* to nestle into a person or thing for warmth or from affection

so *adverb* **1** to such an extent: *Why are you so cruel?* **2** very: *I'm so tired* **3** also or too: *He laughed, and so did Jarvis* **4** in such a manner: *She's a good student and we'd like her to remain so* **5** that is the case: *Have you locked the car? If so, where were the keys?* **6** **so**

much, so many limited: *There are only so many questions we can ask* **7 so long a** for a limited time **b** goodbye ▷ *conjunction* **8** therefore **9** (often followed by *that*) **a** in order that: *He left for work late so that he could talk to the children* **b** with the result that: *We were late leaving so that it was dark when we arrived* **10 so as to** in order to ▷ *interjection* **11** exclamation of surprise, triumph or realization: *So! You finally made it*

soak *verb* **1** to make (something) thoroughly wet **2** to put (something) in liquid or to lie in liquid so as to become thoroughly wet **3** (of liquid) to go into, permeate or saturate ▷ *noun* **4** soaking > **soak up** *verb* to absorb

soaked *adjective* extremely wet

soaking *adjective* If something is soaking, it is very wet

so-and-so *noun* **1** *informal* person whose name you have forgotten **2** unpleasant person or thing

soap *noun* **1** substance made of natural oils and fats and used for washing **2** *informal* soap opera ▷ *verb* **3** to apply soap to (a person or thing) > **soapy** *adjective*

soap opera *noun* radio or television serial dealing with people's daily lives

soar *verb* **1** (of a value, price or amount) to increase suddenly **2** to rise or fly upwards > **soaring** *adjective*: *soaring temperatures*

sob sobs sobbing sobbed *verb* **1** to cry noisily, with gasps and short breaths **2** to say while sobbing ▷ *noun* **3** act or sound of sobbing

sober *adjective* **1** not drunk **2** serious and thoughtful **3** (of colours) plain and dull > **soberly** *adverb* > **sober up** *verb* to become sober after being drunk

sobering *adjective* causing you to become serious and thoughtful: *the sobering lesson of the last year*

so-called *adjective* misleadingly called

soccer *noun* football played by two teams of eleven players kicking a ball in an attempt to score goals

sociable *adjective* **1** friendly or companionable **2** (of an occasion) providing companionship > **sociability** *noun*: *man's natural sociability*

social *adjective* **1** relating to society or how it is organized **2** living in a community **3** sociable **4** relating to activities that involve meeting others > **socially** *adverb*

socialism *noun* political system or ideas promoting public ownership of industries, resources and transport > **socialist** *noun, adjective*

socialize socializes socializing socialized; also spelt **socialise** *verb* to meet others socially

social security *noun* **1** payments made to the unemployed, elderly or sick by the state **2** system responsible for making such payments

social work *noun* work which involves helping or advising people with serious financial or family problems > **social worker** *noun*

society societies *noun* **1** human beings considered as a group within a particular country or region **2** organization for people who have the same interest or aim: *the school debating society* **3** rich, upper-class or fashionable people collectively **4** companionship

sociology *noun* study of human societies > **sociological** *adjective* > **sociologist** *noun*

sock *noun* piece of clothing that

covers your foot and ankle

socket *noun* **1** place on a wall or on a piece of electrical equipment into which you can put a plug or bulb **2** hollow part or opening into which another part fits: *eye sockets*

sod *noun literary* surface of the ground, together with the grass and roots growing in it; turf

soda *noun* **1** same as **soda water 2** sodium in the form of crystals or powder, used for baking or cleaning

soda water *noun* fizzy drink made from water charged with carbon dioxide

sodden *adjective* soaked

sodium *noun* silvery-white chemical element which combines with other chemicals. Salt is a sodium compound

sofa *noun* padded seat with arms at either end for two or three people to sit on; settee

soft *adjective* **1** not hard, stiff, firm or rough **2** (of a voice or sound) not loud or harsh; quiet **3** (of a colour or light) not bright **4** (of a breeze or climate) mild **5** (of a person) (too) lenient **6** (of a person) weak and easily influenced **7** (of drugs) not liable to cause addiction > **softly** *adverb*

soft drink *noun* any cold, nonalcoholic drink

soften *verb* **1** to make (something) soft or softer or to become soft or softer **2** (of a person) to become more sympathetic and less critical

software *noun* computer programs

soggy soggier soggiest *adjective* unpleasantly wet or full of water

soil *noun* **1** top layer of earth in which plants grow ▷ *verb* **2** to make (something) dirty > **soiled** *adjective*

solace *noun literary* comfort when sad or distressed

solar *adjective* **1** relating or belonging to the sun **2** using the energy of the sun

solar system *noun* the sun and the planets, comets and asteroids that go round it

sold *verb* past of **sell**

solder *verb* **1** to join (two pieces of metal) using molten metal ▷ *noun* **2** soft metal alloy used to join two metal surfaces

soldier *noun* member of an army > **soldier on** *verb* to persist doggedly

sole soles soling soled *adjective* **1** one and only **2** not shared; exclusive ▷ *noun* **3** underside of your foot or shoe **4** small edible flatfish ▷ *verb* **5** to put a sole on (a shoe)

solely *adverb* only or alone

solemn *adjective* **1** serious or deeply sincere **2** formal > **solemnity** *noun* > **solemnly** *adverb*

solicit *verb* **1** to ask for or request (money, help or opinion) **2** (of a prostitute) to offer sex for money

solicitor *noun* Brit, Aust, NZ lawyer who gives legal advice to clients and prepares documents and cases

solid *adjective* **1** (of a substance or object) hard or firm **2** not liquid or gas **3** not hollow **4** of the same substance throughout **5** strong or substantial **6** (of a person or firm) sound or reliable **7** whole or without interruption: *I cried for two solid days* ▷ *noun* **8** solid substance or object > **solidly** *adverb*

solidarity *noun* unity and mutual support

solidify solidifies solidifying solidified *verb* (of a liquid) to become solid or firm

soliloquy soliloquies *noun* speech made by a person while alone, especially in a play

solitary *adjective* **1** (of an activity) done alone **2** (of a person or animal) used to being alone **3** single or lonely

solitary confinement *noun* the state of being kept alone, without company, in a prison cell; isolation

solitude *noun* state of being alone

solo solos *noun* **1** music for one performer **2** act performed by one person alone ▷ *adjective* **3** done alone: *my first solo flight* ▷ *adverb* **4** by yourself; alone

soloist *noun* musician or dancer who performs a solo

solstice *noun* either the shortest winter day or the longest summer day

soluble *adjective* **1** (of a substance) able to be dissolved **2** (of a problem) able to be solved

solution *noun* **1** answer to a problem **2** act of solving a problem **3** liquid in which a solid substance has been dissolved

solve solves solving solved *verb* to find the answer to (a problem)

solvent *adjective* **1** having enough money to pay your debts ▷ *noun* **2** liquid capable of dissolving other substances > **solvency** *noun*

Somali Somalis *adjective* **1** belonging or relating to Somalia ▷ *noun* **2** person from Somalia **3** language spoken by Somalis

sombre *adjective* **1** (of a colour or place) dark or gloomy **2** (of a person or atmosphere) serious, sad or gloomy

some *adjective* **1** a number or quantity of **2** unknown or unspecified **3** a considerable number or amount of **4** *informal* remarkable ▷ *pronoun* **5** a number or quantity ▷ *adverb* **6** about or approximately

somebody *pronoun* some person; someone

some day *adverb* at an unknown date in the future

somehow *adverb* in some unspecified way

someone *pronoun* some person; somebody

somersault *noun* **1** forward or backward roll in which the head is placed on the ground and the body is brought over it ▷ *verb* **2** to perform a somersault

something *pronoun* **1** unknown or unspecified thing **2** impressive or important thing

sometime *adverb* **1** at some unspecified time ▷ *adjective* **2** *formal* former

sometimes *adverb* from time to time or now and then; occasionally

somewhat *adverb* to some extent; rather

somewhere *adverb* **1** in, to or at some unspecified or unknown place **2** some time, some number or some quantity: *somewhere between the winter of 1999 and the summer of 2004*

son *noun* male child

sonar *noun* device for calculating the depth of the sea or the position of an underwater object using sound waves

sonata *noun* piece of music, usually in three or more movements, for the piano or another instrument with or without piano

song *noun* **1** music with words that are sung to the music **2** tuneful sound made by certain birds **3** **for a song** very cheaply

songbird *noun* any bird with a musical call

son-in-law sons-in-law *noun*

daughter's husband

sonnet noun poem consisting of 14 lines with a fixed rhyme scheme

soon adverb in a short time

sooner adverb 1 rather 2 in a shorter time or earlier 3 **sooner or later** eventually

soot noun black powder that rises in the smoke from a fire > **sooty** adjective: a black sooty substance

soothe soothes soothing soothed verb 1 to make (someone) calm 2 to relieve (pain etc) > **soothing** adjective: soothing music

soothsayer noun old-fashioned seer or prophet

sop sops sopping sopped noun a concession or something small given to someone to pacify him or her and stop him or her causing trouble > **sop up** verb to soak up or absorb (liquid)

sophisticated adjective 1 (of a person) having refined or cultured tastes or habits 2 (of a machine or device) made using advanced and complicated methods; complex > **sophistication** noun

sophistry sophistries noun clever but invalid argument

sophomore noun US student in second year at college

sopping adjective completely soaked

soppy soppier soppiest adjective informal too sentimental

soprano sopranos noun 1 (singer with) the highest female or boy's voice 2 highest-pitched of a family of instruments

sorbet noun water ice made with fruit

sorcerer noun magician

sorceress sorceresses noun female sorcerer

sorcery noun witchcraft or black magic

sordid adjective 1 dishonest or immoral 2 dirty or squalid

sore sorer sorest; sores adjective 1 painful 2 resentful 3 (of a need) urgent ▷ noun 4 painful place where your skin has become infected > **sorely** adverb greatly: She will be sorely missed > **soreness** noun: Bleeding and soreness can follow

sorghum noun kind of grass grown for grain, hay and syrup

sorrow noun 1 grief or sadness 2 cause of sorrow

sorry sorrier sorriest adjective 1 feeling sadness, sympathy or regret 2 pitiful or wretched

sort noun 1 group sharing certain qualities or characteristics; type 2 **out of sorts** slightly unwell or bad-tempered ▷ verb 3 to arrange into different groups according to kind 4 (also **sort out**) to mend, fix or solve

> When you use sort in its singular form, the adjective before it should also be singular: that sort of car. When you use the plural form sorts, the adjective before it should be plural: those sorts of shop; those sorts of shops

SOS noun signal that you are in danger and need help

so-so adjective informal neither good nor bad; mediocre

soufflé or **souffle** noun light fluffy dish made with beaten egg whites and other ingredients and baked in the oven

sought verb past of **seek**

soul noun 1 spiritual part of a human being believed by many to be immortal 2 essential part or fundamental nature 3 deep and sincere feelings 4 person regarded as typifying some quality: Sonia was the soul of patience **5** person: *There was not a soul there* **6** type of music combining blues, pop and gospel

sound *noun* **1** something heard; noise **2** everything heard **3** impression formed from hearing about someone or something: *I like the sound of your aunt* **4** channel or strait ▷ *verb* **5** to make a sound or cause (something) to make a sound **6** to seem to be as specified: *It sounds great* **7** to pronounce **8** to find the depth of (water etc) **9** to examine (the body, heart etc) by tapping or with a stethoscope **10** to find out the views of ▷ *adjective* **11** in good condition **12** firm or substantial **13** financially reliable **14** showing good judgment **15** ethically correct **16** (of sleep) deep > **soundly** *adverb*: *to sleep soundly*

sound bite *noun* short memorable sentence or phrase extracted from a longer speech, especially by a politician, for use on television or radio

sound effect *noun* sounds created artificially to make a play more realistic, especially a radio play

soundproof *adjective* **1** (of a room) not allowing sound in or out ▷ *verb* **2** to make (something) soundproof

soundtrack *noun* the part of a film that you hear

soup *noun* liquid food made from meat, vegetables, etc and water

sour *adjective* **1** sharp-tasting; acid **2** (of milk) gone bad **3** (of a person's temperament) bad-tempered and unfriendly ▷ *verb* **4** to make (something) sour or to become sour

source *noun* **1** origin or starting point **2** person, book, etc providing information **3** spring where a river or stream begins

┃ Do not confuse the spellings of *source* and *sauce*

sour grapes *plural noun* scornful remark or action that is born of envy

souse souses sousing soused *verb* to drench (something or someone) in liquid

south *noun* **1** direction towards the South Pole, opposite north **2** area lying in or towards the south ▷ *adjective* **3** to or in the south **4** (of a wind) from the south ▷ *adverb* **5** in, to or towards the south

South America *noun* fourth largest continent, having the Pacific Ocean on its west side, the Atlantic on its east side and the Antarctic to the south. South America is joined to North America by the Isthmus of Panama > **South American** *adjective*

south-east *noun, adverb, adjective* halfway between south and east

south-easterly *adjective* **1** to or towards the south-east **2** (of a wind) from the south-east

south-eastern *adjective* in or from the south-east

southerly *adjective* **1** to or towards the south **2** (of wind) from the south

southern *adjective* in or from the south > **southerner** *noun* person from the south of a country or area

Southern Cross *noun* group of stars which can be seen from the southern part of the earth, and which is represented on the national flags of Australia and New Zealand

South Pole *noun* southernmost point of the earth

southward *adjective* **1** towards the south ▷ *adverb* **2** ▷ (also

southwards) towards the south

south-west *noun, adverb, adjective* halfway between south and west

south-westerly *adjective* **1** to or towards the south-west **2** (of a wind) from the south-west

south-western *adjective* in or from the south-west

souvenir *noun* keepsake or memento

sovereign *noun* **1** king, queen or other royal ruler of a country **2** former British gold coin worth one pound ▷ *adjective* **3** (of a state) independent

sovereignty *noun* political power that a country has to govern itself

Soviet *adjective* belonging or relating to the country that used to be the Soviet Union

sow[1] **sows sowing sowed sown** *verb* **1** to scatter or plant (seed) **2** to plant seed in (the ground) **3** to implant or introduce (undesirable feelings or attitudes)

sow[2] *noun* female adult pig

soya *noun* plant whose edible bean (**soya bean**) is used for food and as a source of oil

soya bean *noun* type of edible Asian bean

soy sauce *noun* sauce made from fermented soya beans, used in Chinese and Japanese cookery

spa *noun* resort with a mineral-water spring

space spaces spacing spaced *noun* **1** unlimited expanse in which all objects exist and move **2** interval **3** blank portion **4** unoccupied area **5** the universe beyond the earth's atmosphere ▷ *verb* **6** to place (a series of things) at intervals

spacecraft *noun* vehicle for travel beyond the earth's atmosphere

▪ The plural of *spacecraft* is *spacecraft*

spaceman spacemen *noun* someone who travels in space

spaceship *noun* a spacecraft that carries people through space

space shuttle *noun* vehicle for repeated space flights

spacious *adjective* having or providing a lot of space; roomy

spade *noun* **1** tool for digging **2** playing card of the suit marked with black leaf-shaped symbols

spaghetti *noun* long thin pieces of pasta

span spans spanning spanned *noun* **1** the period of time between two dates or events during which something exists or functions **2** distance between two extreme points (of something) **3** distance from thumb to little finger of the expanded hand ▷ *verb* **4** to last throughout (a period of time) **5** (of bridge) to stretch across (a river or valley)

spangle spangles spangling spangled *noun* **1** small sparkling piece of metal or plastic used to decorate clothing or hair ▷ *verb* **2** to decorate with spangles

Spaniard *noun* someone from Spain

spaniel *noun* type of dog with long ears and silky hair

Spanish *adjective* **1** belonging or relating to Spain ▷ *noun* **2** main language spoken in Spain, also spoken by many people in Central and South America ▷ *plural noun* **3 the Spanish** the people of Spain

spank *verb* to slap (someone) with your hand open on the buttocks or legs

spanner *noun* tool for gripping and turning a nut or bolt

spar spars sparring sparred *verb* **1** to box or fight using light blows for practice **2** to argue (with someone) ▷ *noun* **3** pole that a sail is attached to on a ship or yacht

spare spares sparing spared *adjective* **1** extra **2** in reserve **3** (of time) free ▷ *noun* **4** duplicate kept in case of damage or loss ▷ *verb* **5** to refrain from punishing or harming (someone) **6** to save (someone) from (something unpleasant) **7** to afford to give

sparing *adjective* economical **> sparingly** *adverb*

spark *noun* **1** tiny bright piece of burning material thrown out from a fire **2** fiery particle caused by friction **3** flash of light caused by electricity **4** trace or hint (of a particular quality) ▷ *verb* **5** to give off sparks **> spark off** *verb* to set off or give rise to

sparkle sparkles sparkling sparkled *verb* **1** to glitter with lots of small bright points of light **2** to be lively, intelligent and witty ▷ *noun* **3** sparkling point of light **4** vivacity or wit **> sparkling** *adjective* **1** (of wine or mineral water) slightly fizzy **2** glittering

sparrow *noun* common small bird with brown and grey feathers

sparse sparser sparsest *adjective* thinly scattered or spread **> sparsely** *adverb*: *sparsely populated areas*

spartan *adjective* simple and without luxuries; austere

spasm *noun* **1** involuntary muscular contraction **2** sudden burst of activity or feeling

spasmodic *adjective* occurring for short periods of time or at irregular intervals **> spasmodically** *adverb*

spastic *noun* **1** person with cerebral palsy ▷ *adjective* **2** suffering from cerebral palsy

spat *verb* past of **spit**

spate *noun* large number of things happening within a short period of time

spatial *adjective* of or in space

spats *plural noun* coverings worn by men in the past or as part of a special uniform over their ankles and the front of their shoes

spatter *verb* **1** to scatter or be scattered in drops over (something) ▷ *noun* **2** something spattered in drops

spatula *noun* utensil with a broad flat blade for spreading or stirring

spawn *noun* **1** jelly-like mass containing the eggs of fish or amphibians such as frogs ▷ *verb* **2** (of fish, frogs) to lay eggs **3** to give rise to

spay spays spaying spayed *verb* to remove the ovaries from (a female animal) so that it cannot become pregnant

speak speaks speaking spoke spoken *verb* **1** to say words; talk **2** to give a speech or lecture **3** to know how to talk in (a specified language) **4** to say (something) in words **> speak out** *verb* to publicly state an opinion

speaker *noun* **1** person who speaks, especially at a formal occasion **2** loudspeaker **3** **Speaker** (in Parliament) the official chairperson, whose role is to control proceedings

spear *noun* **1** weapon consisting of a long shaft with a sharp point **2** slender shoot ▷ *verb* **3** to pierce with a spear or other pointed object

spearhead *verb* to lead (an attack or campaign)

spec *noun* **on spec** *informal* as a risk or gamble

special *adjective* **1** distinguished from others of its kind **2** for a specific purpose **3** exceptional **4** particular

specialist *noun* **1** expert in a particular activity or subject ▷ *adjective* **2** having a skill or knowing a lot about a particular subject > **specialism** *noun*

speciality specialities *noun* **1** special interest or skill **2** product specialized in

specialize specializes specializing specialized; also spelt **specialise** *verb* to be a specialist > **specialization** *noun*

specialized or **specialised** *adjective* developed for a particular purpose or trained in a particular area of knowledge

specially *adverb* particularly

species *noun* group of plants or animals that are related closely enough to interbreed naturally ■ The plural of *species* is *species*

specific *adjective* particular > **specifically** *adverb*

specification *noun* detailed description of something to be made or done

specifics *plural noun* particular details

specify specifies specifying specified *verb* to refer to or state specifically

specimen *noun* **1** example or small sample (of something) that gives an idea of what the whole is like **2** sample of urine, blood, etc taken for analysis

speck *noun* small spot or particle

speckled *adjective* covered in small marks or spots

specs *plural noun informal* short for **spectacles**

spectacle *noun* **1** strange, interesting or ridiculous sight **2** impressive public show

spectacles *plural noun* pair of glasses for correcting faulty vision

spectacular *adjective* impressive > **spectacularly** *adverb*

spectate spectates spectating spectated *verb* to watch

spectator *noun* person watching something; onlooker

spectra a plural of **spectrum**

spectre *noun* **1** ghost **2** frightening idea or image

spectrum spectra or **spectrums** *noun* **1** range of colours found in a rainbow and produced when light passes through a prism or a drop of water **2** range (of opinions or emotions) **3** entire range of anything

speculate speculates speculating speculated *verb* **1** to weigh up and make guesses about something **2** to buy property, shares, etc in the hope of selling them at a profit > **speculation** *noun*

speculative *adjective* **1** based on guesses and opinions rather than known facts **2** (of an expression) suggesting that the person concerned is weighing up and making guesses about something

speculator *noun* person who speculates financially

sped *verb* a past of **speed**

speech speeches *noun* **1** ability to speak **2** act or manner of speaking **3** talk given to an audience **4** group of lines spoken by one of the characters in a play **5** language or dialect

speechless *adjective* unable to speak because of great emotion

speed speeds speeding sped or **speeded** *noun* **1** fast movement or travel; swiftness; rapidity **2** rate at which something moves or happens; velocity ▷ *verb* **3** to go quickly **4** to drive faster than the legal limit > **speed up** *verb* to accelerate

speedboat *noun* light fast motorboat

speed dating *noun* dating method in which each participant engages in a timed chat with all the others in turn

speed limit *noun* maximum speed at which vehicles are legally allowed to drive on a particular road

speedometer *noun* instrument in a vehicle that shows how fast it is moving

speedway speedways *noun* **1** track for motorcycle racing **2** *US, Canadian, NZ* track for motor racing

speedy speedier speediest *adjective* rapid > **speedily** *adverb*

spell spells spelling spelt or **spelled** *verb* **1** to provide the letters that form (a word) in the correct order **2** (of letters) to make up (a word) **3** to indicate or suggest: *This method could spell disaster* ▷ *noun* **4** word or sequence of words used to perform magic **5** effect of a spell **6** short period: *a sunny spell* > **spell out** *verb* to explain in detail

spellbound *adjective* so fascinated by something that you cannot think about anything else

spelling *noun* **1** way a word is spelt **2** person's ability to spell

spelt *verb* a past of **spell**

spend spends spending spent *verb* **1** to pay out (money) **2** to use or pass (time) **3** to use up (energy)

spent *adjective* used: *spent matches*

sperm sperms or **sperm** *noun* cell produced in the sex organ of a male which can enter a female's egg and fertilize it

spew *verb* to come out or to send (something) out in a stream > **spew up** *verb informal* to vomit

sphere *noun* **1** perfectly round solid object **2** field of activity or interest > **spherical** *adjective* round

sphinx sphinxes *noun* monster with a lion's body and a human head

spice spices spicing spiced *noun* **1** powder or seeds from a plant added to food to give it flavour **2** something which makes life more exciting ▷ *verb* **3** to flavour with spices > **spice up** *verb* to make (something) more exciting

spicy spicier spiciest *adjective* strongly flavoured with spices

spider *noun* small eight-legged creature which spins a web to catch insects for food

spike spikes spiking spiked *noun* **1** sharp point **2** long pointed metal object or something resembling it **3** **spikes** sports shoes with spikes for greater grip ▷ *verb* **4** to pierce or fasten with a spike **5** to add alcohol to (a drink)

spiky spikier spikiest *adjective* having sharp points

spill spills spilling spilled or **spilt** **1** to allow (something) accidentally to pour out of something **2** to pour from or as if from a container

spillage *noun* the spilling of something, or something that has been spilt

spin spins spinning spun *verb* **1** to turn quickly or to cause (something) to turn quickly round a central point **2** to make thread or yarn by twisting together (fibres) using a spinning machine or spinning wheel **3** (of spiders) to make (a web) **4** *informal* to present information in a way that creates

a favourable impression ▷ *noun*
5 a rapid turning motion around a
central point **6** continuous spiral
descent of an aircraft **7** *informal*
short drive for pleasure **8** *informal*
presentation of information in
a way that creates a favourable
impression > **spin out** *verb* to make
(something) last an unusually long
time; to prolong

spinach *noun* dark green leafy
vegetable

spinal *adjective* relating to your
spine

spin doctor *noun informal* person
who provides a favourable slant to
a news item or policy on behalf of a
politician or a political party

spine *noun* **1** backbone **2** edge of a
book on which the title is printed
3 sharp point on an animal or plant

spinet *noun* small harpsichord

spinifex *noun* coarse spiny
Australian grass

spinning wheel *noun* a wooden
machine for spinning flax or wool

spin-off *noun* unexpected benefit

spinster *noun* woman who has
never married

spiny *adjective* covered with spines

spiral spirals spiralling spiralled
noun **1** something that forms a
continuous curve winding round
and round a central point so that a
circle of increasingly bigger loops
winds out from the middle or else a
tubular shape is formed consisting
of loops above loops **2** steadily
accelerating increase or decrease
▷ *adjective* **3** in the shape of a spiral
▷ *verb* **4** to move in a spiral **5** to
increase or decrease with steady
acceleration

spire *noun* pointed part of at the top
of some church towers

spirit spirits spiriting spirited
noun **1** non-physical part of a
person connected with his or her
deepest thoughts and feelings
2 nonphysical part of a person
believed to live on after death
3 supernatural being; ghost
4 courage and liveliness **5** essential
meaning as opposed to literal
interpretation **6** liquid obtained
by distillation **7 spirits** emotional
state ▷ *verb* **8** (usually followed by
away, off) to carry (something or
someone) away mysteriously

spirited *adjective* lively and
courageous

spirit level *noun* glass tube
containing a bubble in liquid, used
to check whether a surface is level

spiritual *adjective* **1** relating to the
spirit **2** relating to sacred things
▷ *noun* **3** type of religious folk song
originating among Black slaves in
America > **spirituality** *noun*: *People
still want spirituality in their lives*
> **spiritually** *adverb*

spit spits spitting spat *verb* **1** to
eject (saliva or food) from the
mouth **2** to rain slightly ▷ *noun*
3 saliva **4** sharp rod on which meat
is skewered for roasting

spite *noun* **1** deliberate nastiness;
malice **2 in spite of** in defiance of
or regardless of ▷ *verb* **3 to spite** to
annoy or hurt (someone) from spite

spiteful *adjective* deliberately nasty;
malicious

spitting image *noun informal*
person who looks very like another

**splash splashes splashing
splashed** *verb* **1** to scatter liquid
on (something) **2** to scatter
(liquid) in drops **3** (of a liquid) to
be scattered in drops **4** to print (a
story or photograph) prominently
in a newspaper ▷ *noun* **5** splashing
sound **6** small amount (of liquid)

7 contrastive patch (of colour or light) **8** extravagant display **9** small amount of liquid added to a drink ▷ **splash out** verb informal to spend extravagantly

splatter verb **1** to splash ▷ noun **2** splash

splay splays splaying splayed verb to spread out, with ends spreading in different directions

spleen noun organ near your stomach that filters bacteria from the blood

splendid adjective **1** excellent **2** beautiful and impressive > **splendidly** adverb

splendour noun quality of being beautiful and impressive

splint noun long piece of wood or metal used as support for a broken bone

splinter noun **1** thin sharp piece broken off, especially from wood ▷ verb **2** to break into fragments

split splits splitting split verb **1** to break into separate pieces **2** to separate **3** to tear or crack **4** to share (something) ▷ noun **5** crack, tear or division caused by splitting **6 splits** act of sitting with the legs outstretched in opposite directions > **split up** verb to end a relationship or marriage

split second noun extremely short period of time

splitting adjective (of headache) very painful

splutter verb **1** to speak in a confused way because of embarrassment **2** to make hissing or spitting sounds

spoil spoils spoiling spoiled or **spoilt** verb **1** to damage **2** to harm the character of (a child) by giving or pampering him or her too much **3** to treat (someone) **4** to rot or

go bad

spoils plural noun booty

spoilsport noun person who spoils people's fun

spoke verb **1** past tense of **speak** ▷ noun **2** bar joining the hub of a wheel to the rim

spoken verb past participle of **speak**

spokesperson noun person chosen to speak on behalf of a group > **spokesman** noun > **spokeswoman** noun

sponge sponges sponging sponged noun **1** sea animal with a porous absorbent skeleton **2** part of the very light skeleton of a sponge, or something resembling it, used for washing and cleaning **3** type of light cake ▷ verb **4** to wipe (something) with a sponge

sponsor verb **1** to provide financial support for (an event or training) **2** to agree to pay a sum to (a charity fund-raiser) if they successfully complete an activity **3** to put forward and support (a proposal or suggestion) ▷ noun **4** person or organization sponsoring something or someone > **sponsorship** noun

spontaneous adjective **1** not planned or arranged **2** occurring through natural processes without outside influence > **spontaneity** noun ability to act without planning or prior arrangement > **spontaneously** adverb

spoof noun mildly satirical parody

spooky spookier spookiest adjective eerie and frightening

spool noun cylindrical object onto which thread, tape or film can be wound

spoon noun **1** object shaped like a small shallow bowl with a long handle, used for eating, stirring and serving food ▷ *verb* **2** to lift (something) with a spoon

spoonerism *noun* accidental changing over of the initial sounds of a pair of words, such as *half-warmed fish* for *half-formed wish*

spoonful spoonfuls or **spoonsful** *noun* the amount held by a spoon

sporadic *adjective* happening at irregular intervals > **sporadically** *adverb*

spore *noun* minute reproductive body of some plants and bacteria

sporran *noun* pouch worn in front of a kilt

sport *noun* **1** any activity for pleasure, competition or exercise requiring physical effort and skill **2** such activities collectively **3** enjoyment **4** person who reacts cheerfully ▷ *verb* **5** to wear proudly

sporting *adjective* **1** relating to sport **2** behaving in a fair and decent way **3 sporting chance** reasonable chance of success

sports car *noun* fast low-built car, usually open-topped

sports jacket *noun* man's casual jacket

sportsman sportsmen *noun* person who plays sports

sportswoman sportswomen *noun* woman who plays sports

sporty sportier sportiest *adjective* **1** (of car) fast and flashy **2** (of person) good at sports

spot spots spotting spotted *noun* **1** small round coloured area on a surface **2** small lump on your skin, caused by infection or allergy; pimple **3** place or location **4** *informal* small quantity **5** (on a television show) part regularly reserved for a particular performer or type of entertainment **6 on the**

spot a at the place in question **b** immediately ▷ *verb* **7** to notice

spot check *noun* random examination

spotless *adjective* absolutely clean > **spotlessly** *adverb*

spotlight spotlights spotlighting spotlit or **spotlighted** *noun* **1** powerful light which can be directed to light up a small area ▷ *verb* **2** to draw the public's attention to (a situation or problem)

spot-on *adjective informal* absolutely accurate

spotted *adjective* having a pattern of spots

spotter *noun* person whose hobby is watching for things of a particular kind: *a train spotter*

spotty spottier spottiest *adjective* with spots

spouse *noun* husband or wife

spout *verb* **1** to pour out in a stream or jet **2** *informal* to utter (a stream of words) lengthily ▷ *noun* **3** tube with a lip-like end for pouring liquid **4** stream or jet of liquid

sprain *verb* **1** to injure (a joint) by a sudden twist ▷ *noun* **2** such an injury

sprang *verb* past tense of **spring**

sprat *noun* small European sea fish related to the herring

sprawl *verb* **1** to lie or sit with your legs and arms spread out **2** (of a place) to spread out in a straggling manner ▷ *noun* **3** something that has spread untidily over a large area > **sprawling** *adjective*

spray sprays spraying sprayed *noun* **1** fine drops of liquid splashed or forced into the air **2** liquid kept under pressure in a can or other container **3** piece of equipment for spraying liquid **4** branch with buds, leaves, flowers or berries on it ▷ *verb* **5** to scatter in fine drops **6** to cover with a spray

spread spreads spreading spread *verb* **1** to open (something) out or to arrange (something) so that all or most of it can be seen easily **2** to stretch out **3** to put a thin layer of (a substance or coating) on a surface **4** to reach or affect a wider and wider area **5** to distribute (something) evenly ▷ *noun* **6** extent reached or distribution (of something) **7** wide variety **8** *informal* large meal **9** soft food which can be put on bread, biscuits, etc

spread-eagled *adjective* with arms and legs outstretched

spreadsheet *noun* computer program for entering and arranging figures and sums

spree *noun* period of time spent doing something enjoyable to excess: *a shopping spree*

sprig *noun* **1** twig or shoot **2** *Aust, NZ* stud on the sole of a soccer or rugby boot

sprightly sprightlier sprightliest *adjective* lively and active

spring springs springing sprang sprung *noun* **1** season between winter and summer **2** coil of wire which returns to its natural shape after being pressed or pulled **3** place where water comes up through the ground **4** jump **5** elasticity; bounce ▷ *verb* **6** to move suddenly upwards or forwards in a single motion; jump **7** to move suddenly and quickly **8** to result or originate (from) **9** (followed by *on*) to give (a surprising piece of news or a task) to (someone)

springboard *noun* **1** flexible board on which a diver or gymnast jumps

to gain height **2** something that provides a helpful starting point (for an activity or enterprise)

springbok *noun* **1** South African antelope **2** person who has represented South Africa in a sports team

spring-clean *verb* to clean (a house) thoroughly

spring onion *noun* small onion with long green shoots, often eaten raw in salads

sprinkle sprinkles sprinkling sprinkled *verb* to scatter (liquid or powder) in tiny drops or particles over (something)

sprinkling *noun* small quantity or number

sprint *noun* **1** short fast race **2** fast run ▷ *verb* **3** to run a short distance at top speed

sprinter *noun* athlete who runs fast over short distances

sprite *noun* type of fairy; elf

sprout *verb* **1** to produce shoots **2** to begin to grow or develop **3** (followed by *up*) to appear rapidly ▷ *noun* **4** short for **Brussels sprout**

spruce sprucer sprucest; spruces sprucing spruced *noun* **1** kind of fir tree ▷ *adjective* **2** neat and smart ▷ *verb* **3** **spruce up** to make neat and smart

sprung *verb* past participle of **spring**

spun *verb* past of **spin**

spunk *noun informal* **1** *old-fashioned* courage, spirit **2** *Aust, NZ* good-looking person

spur spurs spurring spurred *verb* **1** to urge on, incite (someone) ▷ *noun* **2** encouragement or incentive; stimulus **3** spiked wheel on the heel of a rider's boot used to urge on a horse **4** ridge sticking out from a mountain or hillside

5 on the spur of the moment on impulse

spurious *adjective* not genuine or real

spurn *verb* to refuse to accept; reject

spurt *verb* **1** to gush out in a jet ▷ *noun* **2** sudden gush **3** short sudden burst of activity or speed

sputnik *noun* early Soviet artificial satellite used for space research

sputter *verb, noun* to make hissing and popping sounds; splutter

sputum *noun formal* spittle or phlegm

spy spies spying spied *noun* **1** person employed to obtain secret information **2** person who secretly watches others ▷ *verb* **3** to act as a spy **4** to catch sight of

squabble squabbles squabbling squabbled *verb* **1** to quarrel about something trivial ▷ *noun* **2** a quarrel

squad *noun* small group of people working or training together

squadron *noun* section of one of the armed forces, especially the air force

squalid *adjective* **1** dirty and unpleasant **2** unpleasant, unwholesome and perhaps dishonest; sordid

squall *noun* **1** sudden strong wind ▷ *verb* **2** to cry noisily; yell

squalor *noun* bad or dirty conditions or surroundings

squander *verb* to waste (money or resources)

square squares squaring squared *noun* **1** shape with four equal sides and four right angles **2** flat open area in a town, bordered by buildings or streets **3** product of a number multiplied by itself ▷ *adjective* **4** square in shape **5** in area: 10 *million square feet of office space* **6** in length on

each side: *a towel measuring a foot square* **7** straight or level **8** with all accounts or debts settled ▷ *verb* **9** to multiply (a number) by itself ▷ *adverb* **10** squarely or directly

squarely *adverb* **1** in a direct way **2** in an honest and frank manner

square root *noun* number of which a given number is the square

squash squashes squashing squashed *verb* **1** to crush (something) flat **2** to stop (a difficult or troubling situation), often by force; suppress **3** to push into a confined space **4** to humiliate (someone) with a crushing reply ▷ *noun* **5** sweet fruit drink diluted with water **6** crowd of people in a confined space **7** game played in an enclosed court with a rubber ball and long-handled rackets **8** marrow-like vegetable

squat squats squatting squatted; squatter squattest *verb* **1** to crouch with your knees bent and the weight on your feet **2** to live in unused premises without any legal right to do so ▷ *noun* **3** place where squatters live ▷ *adjective* **4** short and broad

squatter *noun* **1** person who lives in unused premises without permission and without paying rent **2** *Aust, NZ* **a** someone who owns a large amount of land for sheep or cattle farming **b** *History* someone who rented land from the king or queen

squawk *noun* **1** (of a bird) loud harsh cry ▷ *verb* **2** (of a bird) to make a squawking noise

squeak *verb* **1** to give a short high-pitched sound or cry ▷ *noun* **2** short high-pitched cry or sound > **squeaky** *adjective*: *squeaky floorboards*

squeal *verb* **1** to give a long, high-pitched cry or sound **2** *informal* to inform on someone to the police ▷ *noun* **3** long high-pitched cry or sound

squeamish *adjective* easily upset by unpleasant sights or situations

squeeze squeezes squeezing squeezed *verb* **1** to grip or press firmly **2** to crush or press to extract liquid **3** to push into a confined space **4** to get (something out of someone) by force or great effort ▷ *noun* **5** act of squeezing **6** tight fit

squelch squelches squelching squelched *verb* **1** to make a wet sucking sound, as when walking through mud ▷ *noun* **2** wet sucking sound

squib *noun* small firework that hisses before exploding

squid *noun* sea creature with a long soft body and ten tentacles

squiggle *noun* wavy line > **squiggly** *adjective: a squiggly line*

squint *verb* **1** to look at it with your eyes screwed up **2** to have eyes that look in different or slightly different directions ▷ *noun* **3** eye condition in which your eyes look in different or slightly different directions

squire *noun* **1** country gentleman, usually the main landowner in a community **2** *History* knight's apprentice

squirm *verb* **1** to wriggle or writhe **2** to feel embarrassed

squirrel *noun* small furry animal with a bushy tail that lives in trees

squirt *verb* **1** to force (a liquid) out of a narrow opening **2** (of a liquid) to be forced out of a narrow opening ▷ *noun* **3** jet of liquid

Sri Lankan *adjective* **1** belonging or relating to Sri Lanka ▷ *noun* **2** someone from Sri Lanka

stab stabs stabbing stabbed *verb* **1** to push a knife or something pointed into the body of (someone) **2** to jab (at) **3** **stab someone in the back** to behave treacherously towards someone ▷ *noun* **4** act of stabbing **5** sudden unpleasant sensation **6** *informal* attempt

stabilize stabilizes stabilizing stabilized; also spelt **stabilise** *verb* to make or become stable

stable *noun* **1** building in which horses are kept **2** establishment that breeds and trains racehorses **3** establishment that manages or trains several entertainers or athletes ▷ *adjective* **4** firmly fixed or established **5** firm in character **6** *Science* not subject to decay or decomposition > **stability** *noun: a time of political stability*

staccato *adjective* consisting of short abrupt sounds

stack *noun* **1** pile **2** **stacks** large amount ▷ *verb* **3** to pile in a stack

stadium stadiums or **stadia** *noun* sports ground surrounded by rows of tiered seats

staff *noun* **1** people employed in an organization ▷ *verb* **2** to provide the personnel for (an organization)

stag *noun* adult male deer

stage stages staging staged *noun* **1** step or period of development **2** portion of a journey **3** platform in a theatre where actors or entertainers perform **4** **the stage** theatre as a profession ▷ *verb* **5** to put (a play) on stage **6** to organize and carry out (an event)

stagecoach stagecoaches *noun* large horse-drawn vehicle formerly used to carry passengers and mail

stagger *verb* **1** to walk unsteadily **2** to astound (someone) **3** to set (events) apart to avoid them happening at the same time > **staggered** *adjective* > **staggering** *adjective*

stagnant *adjective* (of water or air) stale from not moving

stag night *noun* party for a man who is about to get married, which only men go to

staid *adjective* serious and rather dull

stain *noun* **1** mark that is difficult to remove ▷ *verb* **2** to mark or discolour **3** to colour with a special kind of dye

stained glass *noun* coloured pieces of glass held together with strips of lead

stainless steel *noun* metal made from steel and chromium that does not rust

stair *noun* one of a flight of steps between floors

staircase *noun* flight of stairs with a handrail or banisters

stairway stairways *noun* flight of stairs with a handrail or banisters

stake stakes staking staked *noun* **1** pointed wooden post that can be hammered into the ground as a support or marker **2** money wagered **3** interest, usually financial, held in something **4 at stake** being risked ▷ *verb* **5** to support or mark out with stakes **6** to risk; wager **7 stake a claim to** to claim a right to > **stake out** *verb* *informal* (of police) to keep (a place) under surveillance

stalactite *noun* lime deposit hanging down from the roof of a cave

stalagmite *noun* lime deposit sticking up from the floor of a cave

stale *adjective* **1** (of food or air) not fresh **2** (of a person) lacking energy or ideas through overwork or monotony

stalemate *noun* **1** situation in which neither side in an argument or contest can win; deadlock **2** *Chess* position in which any of a player's moves would put his king in check and which results in a draw

stalk *noun* **1** plant's stem ▷ *verb* **2** to follow or approach stealthily **3** to pursue persistently and, sometimes, attack (a person with whom one is obsessed) **4** to walk in a stiff or haughty manner > **stalker** *noun*

stall *noun* **1** large table for the display and sale of goods **2 stalls** ground-floor seats in a theatre or cinema ▷ *verb* **3** (of a motor vehicle or engine) to stop accidentally **4** to employ delaying tactics

stallion *noun* adult male horse that can be used for breeding

stamen *noun* small delicate stalk inside the head of a flower that produces pollen

stamina *noun* enduring energy and strength

stammer *verb* **1** to speak or say with involuntary pauses or repetition of syllables ▷ *noun* **2** tendency to stammer

stamp *noun* **1** (also **postage stamp**) piece of gummed paper stuck to an envelope or parcel to show that the postage has been paid **2 a** small block with a pattern cut into it, which you press onto an inky pad to print a pattern or mark **b** the mark made by the stamp **3** characteristic feature **4** act of bringing your foot down hard on the ground ▷ *verb* **5** to bring (your foot) down hard on the ground **6** to walk with heavy footsteps **7** to impress (a pattern or mark) on (something) or to mark (something) with (a pattern or mark) **8** to stick a postage stamp on ▷ **stamp out** *verb* to put an end to (something) by force

stampede stampedes stampeding stampeded *noun* **1** sudden rush of frightened animals or of a crowd ▷ *verb* **2** to run or to cause to run in a wild uncontrolled way

stance *noun* **1** attitude **2** manner of standing

stand stands standing stood *verb* **1** to be upright or to rise to an upright position **2** to be situated **3** to place (something) in an upright position **4** to be in a specified state or position **5** to remain unchanged or valid **6** to tolerate or bear **7** to offer oneself as a candidate **8** *informal* to treat (someone) to (something) **9** **stand trial** to be tried in a court of law ▷ *noun* **10** stall for the sale of goods **11** structure for spectators at a sports ground **12** firmly held opinion **13** *US, Aust* witness box **14** rack or piece of furniture on which things may be placed ▷ **stand by** *verb* **1** to support (someone) **2** to remain with or stick to (a decision or promise) **3** to be ready and available (to do something) **4** to look on without taking any action ▷ **stand down** *verb* to resign (from your job or position) ▷ **stand for** *verb* **1** to represent or mean **2** *informal* to tolerate or put up with ▷ **stand in** *verb* (usually followed by *for*) to act as a temporary replacement or substitute (for someone) ▷ **stand out** *verb* to be very noticeable or to be better or more important than other similar things or people ▷ **stand up for** *verb* to support or defend (someone) ▷ **stand up to**

verb **1** to remain undamaged by (rough treatment); withstand **2** to confront or challenge (a bully)

standard *noun* **1** level of quality **2** example against which others are judged or measured **3** moral principle **4** distinctive flag ▷ *adjective* **5** usual, regular or average **6** accepted as correct

standard English *noun* form of English taught in schools, used in textbooks and broadsheet newspapers and spoken and written by most educated people

standardize standardizes standardizing standardized; also spelt **standardise** *verb* to cause to conform to a standard ▷ **standardization** *noun*

standard lamp *noun* lamp attached to an upright pole on a base

stand-by stand-bys *noun* **1** something available for use when you need it: *a useful stand-by* ▷ *adjective* **2** (of a ticket) made available at the last minute if there are any seats left

stand-in *noun* substitute

standing *adjective* **1** permanent or regular ▷ *noun* **2** reputation or status **3** duration: *a friend of 20 years' standing*

standpipe *noun* tap attached to a water main to provide a public water supply in the street when the domestic water supply has been cut off

standpoint *noun* point of view

standstill *noun* complete stop

stank *verb* past tense of **stink**

stanza *noun* verse of a poem

staple staples stapling stapled *noun* **1** small thin piece of wire or metal bent so that the two ends form prongs capable of piercing papers and other materials and fired into place using a stapler ▷ *verb* **2** to fasten with staples ▷ *adjective* **3** (of a food) forming a regular and basic part of someone's everyday diet

stapler *noun* small device used for inserting staples into sheets of paper

star stars starring starred *noun* **1** large ball of burning gas in space that appears as a point of light in the sky at night **2** shape with four, five, six or more points sticking out in a regular pattern **3** asterisk **4** famous actor, sports player or musician **5 stars** astrological forecast; horoscope ▷ *verb* **6** (of an actor or entertainer) to be a star (in a film or show) **7** (of a film or show) to have (someone) as a star ▷ *adjective* **8** leading or famous

starboard *noun* **1** right-hand side of a ship, when facing forward ▷ *adjective* **2** of or on this side

starch starches starching starched *noun* **1** substance used for stiffening fabric such as cotton or linen **2** carbohydrate found in foods such as bread or potatoes ▷ *verb* **3** to stiffen (fabric) with starch

stare stares staring stared *verb* **1** to look or gaze fixedly (at someone or something) ▷ *noun* **2** fixed gaze

starfish starfishes or **starfish** *noun* a flat star-shaped sea creature with five limbs

stark *adjective* **1** harsh, unpleasant and plain **2** absolute ▷ *adverb* **3 stark naked** completely naked

starling *noun* songbird with glossy dark speckled feathers

start *verb* **1** to begin **2** to set (something) in motion or to be set in motion **3** to make a sudden involuntary movement from

fright **4** to establish or set up ▷ *noun* **5** first part of something; beginning **6** place or time of starting **7** advantage or lead in a competitive activity **8** sudden movement made from fright

starter *noun* **1** first course of a meal **2** device for starting a car's engine

startle startles startling startled *verb* to surprise or frighten a little > **startled** *adjective* > **startling** *adjective*

starve starves starving starved *verb* **1** to die or suffer as a result of hunger **2** to prevent (a person or animal) from having any food **3** to deprive (someone) of something needed **4** *informal* to be hungry **5 to be starved of** to suffer through lack of (money, affection, etc) > **starvation** *noun*

stash stashes stashing stashed *informal verb* **1** to store (something) in a secret place ▷ *noun* **2** secret store

state states stating stated *noun* **1** condition of a person or thing **2** country **3** region with its own government **4** the government **5 in a state** *informal* in an excited or agitated condition ▷ *adjective* **6** of or concerning the government **7** (of a ceremony) involving the ruler or leader of the country ▷ *verb* **8** to express in words

state house *noun* NZ publicly-owned house rented to a low-income tenant

stately home *noun* Brit very large old house which belongs or once belonged to an upper-class family

statement *noun* **1** something you say or write when you give facts or information in a formal way **2** printed financial account

state school *noun* school

maintained and funded by the government or a local authority providing free education

statesman statesmen *noun* experienced and respected political leader

static *adjective* **1** never moving or changing: *The temperature remained fairly static* ▷ *noun* **2** electrical charge caused by friction, which builds up in metal objects

station *noun* **1** place where trains stop for passengers **2 bus** or **coach station** place where some buses start their journeys **3** headquarters or local offices of the police or a fire brigade **4** building with special equipment for a particular purpose: *power station* **5** television or radio channel **6** *old-fashioned* position in society **7** *Aust, NZ* large sheep or cattle property ▷ *verb* **8** to send (someone) to a particular place to work or do a particular job

stationary *adjective* not moving

stationery *noun* writing materials such as paper and pens

station wagon *noun US, Aust* car with a rear door and luggage space behind the rear seats

statistic *noun* fact obtained by analysing numerical information > **statistical** *adjective*: *statistical information* > **statistically** *adverb*

statistician *noun* person who compiles and studies statistics

statistics *noun* science of classifying and interpreting numerical information

statue *noun* large sculpture of a human or animal figure

stature *noun* **1** person's height **2** reputation of a person or his or her achievements

status statuses *noun* **1** social position **2** importance given to

something; prestige **3** official classification given to someone or something: *marital status*

status quo *noun* existing state of affairs

statute *noun* written law > **statutory** *adjective* required or authorized by law

staunch stauncher staunchest; *adjective* loyal or firm

stave staves staving staved *noun Music* the five lines that music is written on > **stave off** *verb* to delay or prevent (something)

stay stays staying stayed *verb* **1** to remain in a place or condition **2** to be living temporarily, often as a guest or visitor **3** *Scot, S Afr* to live permanently ▷ *noun* **4** short time spent somewhere

stead *noun* **stand someone in good stead** to be useful to someone

steadfast *adjective* firm and determined > **steadfastly** *adverb*

steady steadier steadiest; steadies steadying steadied *adjective* **1** regular or continuous **2** not shaky or wavering; firm **3** (of a voice or gaze) calm and controlled **4** sensible and dependable ▷ *verb* **5** to make (something, someone or yourself) steady > **steadily** *adverb*

steak *noun* **1** thick slice of meat, especially beef **2** large piece of fish

steal steals stealing stole stolen *verb* **1** to take (something) unlawfully or without permission **2** to move quietly and secretively

stealth *noun* quietness and secrecy

stealthy *adjective* quiet and secret > **stealthily** *adverb*

steam *noun* **1** hot vapour formed when water boils ▷ *adjective* **2** (of engine) operated using steam as a means of power ▷ *verb* **3** to give off steam **4** (of a vehicle) to move by steam power **5** to cook or treat with steam > **steamy** *adjective*

steam engine *noun* engine worked by steam

steamer *noun* **1** ship powered by steam **2** container used to cook food in steam

steed *noun literary* horse

steel *noun* **1** very strong metal containing mainly iron with a small amount of carbon ▷ *verb* **2** to prepare (yourself) for something unpleasant

steel band *noun* a group of people who play music on special metal drums

steely *adjective* **1** having a hard greyish colour **2** determined, hard and strong in nature

steep *adjective* **1** sloping sharply **2** *informal* (of a price) unreasonably high ▷ *verb* **3** to soak (something) thoroughly in liquid > **steeply** *adverb*

steeped *adjective* **steeped in** deeply affected by: *an industry steeped in tradition*

steeple *noun* a tall pointed structure on top of a church tower

steeplechase *noun* **1** horse race with obstacles to jump **2** track race with hurdles and a water jump

steer *verb* **1** to control the direction of (a vehicle or ship) **2** to influence the course or direction of (a person or conversation) ▷ *noun* **3** castrated male ox

stem stems stemming stemmed *noun* **1** long thin central part of a plant **2** long slender part, as of a wineglass **3** part of a word to which endings are added ▷ *verb* **4** to restrict or stop (the flow of something) **5** **stem from** to originate from

stench stenches *noun* foul smell

stencil stencils stencilling stencilled *noun* **1** thin sheet with a cut-out pattern through which ink or paint passes to form the pattern on the surface below **2** pattern made thus ▷ *verb* **3** to make (a pattern) with a stencil

step steps stepping stepped *noun* **1** act of moving and setting down your foot, as when walking **2** distance covered by a step **3** sound made by stepping **4** foot movement in a dance **5** one of a series of actions taken in order to achieve a goal **6** degree in a series or scale **7** raised flat surface, usually one of a series that you can walk up or down **8** **steps** stepladder ▷ *verb* **9** to move and set down the foot, as when walking **10** to walk a short distance > **step down** or **step aside** *verb* to resign from an important position > **step in** *verb* to become involved in something order to help; intervene > **step up** *verb* to increase (the rate of something) by stages

step- *prefix indicating* a relationship created by the remarriage of a parent: *stepmother; stepson*

steppes *plural noun* wide grassy treeless plains in Russia and Ukraine

stepping stone *noun* **1** one of a series of stones for stepping on in crossing a stream **2** means of making progress towards a goal

stereo stereos *adjective* **1** (of a recording or music system) having the sound directed through two speakers ▷ *noun* **2** a piece of equipment that reproduces sound from records, tapes or CDs directing the sound through two speakers

stereotype stereotypes

stereotyping stereotyped
noun **1** fixed image or set of
characteristics that people
consider to represent a particular
type of person or thing ▷ *verb* **2** to
make assumptions about what sort
of person (someone) is and how he
or she will behave, based on beliefs
about group characteristics

sterile *adjective* **1** free from germs
2 unable to produce offspring or
seeds **3** lacking in new ideas and
enthusiasm > **sterility** *noun*

**sterilize sterilizes sterilizing
sterilized**; also spelt **sterilise** *verb*
1 to make (something) completely
clean and free from germs,
usually by boiling or treating with
antiseptic **2** to give (a person or
animal) an operation to make them
unable to have offspring

sterling *noun* **1** British money
system ▷ *adjective* **2** excellent in
quality

stern *adjective* **1** severe, strict ▷ *noun*
2 rear part of a ship > **sternly** *adverb*

steroid *noun* chemical both
occurring naturally in your body
and made artificially as a medicine.
Sometimes sportsmen and
sportswomen illegally take them as
drugs to improve their performance

stethoscope *noun* medical
instrument for listening to sounds
made inside the body

stew *noun* **1** dish of small pieces
of savoury food cooked together
slowly in a liquid ▷ *verb* **2** to cook
(meat, vegetables or fruit) slowly in
a closed pot

steward *noun* **1** person who looks
after passengers on a ship or
aircraft **2** official who helps at a
public event such as a race

stewardess stewardesses *noun*
woman who works on a ship or

plane looking after passengers and
serving meals

stick sticks sticking stuck
noun **1** long thin piece of wood
2 such a piece of wood shaped
for a special purpose: *hockey stick*
3 something like a stick: *stick of
celery* ▷ *verb* **4** to push (a pointed
object) into (something) **5** to
attach (something to something
else) with glue or sticky tape **6** to
become attached (to something)
7 (of a movable part) to become
fixed in position and difficult
to move **8** *informal* to put **9** to
remain for a long time > **stick
by** *verb* to continue to help and
support (someone) > **stick out**
verb **1** to extend or project beyond
something else; protrude **2** to be
very noticeable > **stick to** *verb* to
keep to (something) rather than
changing to something else > **stick
together** *verb* to stay together
and support one another > **stick
up** *verb* to point upwards from a
surface > **stick up for** *verb informal*
to support or defend

sticker *noun* adhesive label or sign

sticking plaster *noun* small piece
of fabric that you stick over a cut or
sore to protect it

stick insect *noun* insect with a
long cylindrical body and long legs,
which looks like a twig

stickler *noun* person who always
insists on a particular quality or
thing: *stickler for detail*

sticky stickier stickiest *adjective*
1 covered with a substance that
can stick to other things **2** (of paper
or tape) with glue on one side so
that you can stick it to a surface
3 *informal* difficult or unpleasant
4 (of weather) warm and humid

stiff *adjective* **1** not easily bent or

moved **2** difficult or severe: *stiff competition for places* **3** unrelaxed or awkward **4** firm in consistency **5** containing a lot of alcohol; strong: *a stiff drink* **6** (of a breeze or wind) blowing strongly ▷ *adverb* **7** *informal* utterly: *bored stiff* > **stiffly** *adverb* > **stiffness** *noun*

stiffen *verb* **1** to become stiff **2** to make (fabric) stiff

stifle stifles stifling stifled *verb* **1** to prevent something from happening or continuing; suppress **2** to suffocate > **stifling** *adjective*: *the stifling heat*

stigma *noun* **1** mark of social disgrace **2** part of a plant that receives pollen

stile *noun* a set of steps allowing people to climb a fence

stiletto stilettos *noun* woman's shoe with a high narrow heel

still *adverb* **1** now as before or in the future as before **2** up to this or that time **3** even or yet: *still more insults* **4** quietly or without movement ▷ *adjective* **5** motionless **6** silent and calm; undisturbed **7** (of a drink) not fizzy ▷ *noun* **8** photograph from a film scene ▷ *verb* **9** to make (something) still > **stillness** *noun*

stillborn *adjective* born dead

still life still lifes *noun* painting of inanimate objects such as fruit or pots

stilt *noun* **1** one of the long upright poles on which some buildings are built, for example on wet land **2** one of a pair of poles with footrests on them for walking on above the ground

stilted *adjective* (of conversation, writing, speech) formal, unnatural and rather awkward

stimulant *noun* drug or other substance that makes your body work faster, increasing your heart rate and making it difficult to sleep

stimulate stimulates stimulating stimulated *verb* **1** to encourage (something) to begin or develop: *to stimulate discussion* **2** to give (someone) new ideas and enthusiasm > **stimulating** *adjective* > **stimulation** *noun*

stimulus stimuli *noun* something that causes a process or event to begin or develop

sting stings stinging stung *verb* **1** (of certain animals or plants) to wound by injecting with poison **2** (of part of your body) to be a source of sharp tingling pain **3** (of a comment or remark) to cause (someone) to feel upset ▷ *noun* **4** sharp pointed organ of certain animals or plants by which poison can be injected

stingy stingier stingiest *adjective* *informal* mean or miserly

stink stinks stinking stank stunk *verb* **1** to give off a strong unpleasant smell ▷ *noun* **2** strong unpleasant smell

stint *noun* **1** period of time spent doing a particular job ▷ *verb* **2** **stint on** to be mean or miserly with

stipulate stipulates stipulating stipulated *verb formal* to specify as a condition of an agreement > **stipulation** *noun*

stir stirs stirring stirred *verb* **1** to mix (a liquid) by moving a spoon etc around in it **2** to move slightly **3** to make (someone) feel strong emotions ▷ *noun* **4** excitement or shock

stirring *adjective* causing excitement, emotion and enthusiasm

stirrup *noun* one of a pair of metal

loops attached to a saddle in which a rider places his or her feet

stitch stitches stitching stitched *verb* **1** to sew or repair by sewing ▷ *noun* **2** one of the loops of thread that can be seen where material or a wound has been sewn **3** loop of yarn formed round a needle or hook in knitting or crochet **4** sharp pain in the side

stoat *noun* small wild animal of the weasel family, with brown fur that turns white in winter

stock *noun* **1** total amount of goods available for sale in a shop **2** supply stored for future use **3** financial shares in, or capital of, a company **4** liquid produced by boiling meat, fish, bones or vegetables **5** farm animals **6** ancestry **7** *History* **stocks** instrument of punishment consisting of a wooden frame with holes into which the hands and feet of the victim were locked ▷ *verb* **8** (of a shop) to keep (goods) for sale **9** to fill (a cupboard or shelf) with goods **10** to supply (a farm) with livestock or (a lake etc) with fish ▷ *adjective* **11** (of phrase) clichéd or hackneyed > **stock up** *verb* (often followed by *with* or *on*) to buy in a supply (of something)

stockade *noun* enclosure or barrier made of stakes

stockbroker *noun* person who buys and sells stocks and shares for customers

stock exchange *noun* institution for the buying and selling of shares

stocking *noun* close-fitting covering for the foot and leg

stockist *noun* dealer who stocks a particular product

stockman stockmen *noun* man who looks after sheep or cattle on a farm

stock market *noun* organization and activity involved in buying and selling stocks and shares

stockpile stockpiles stockpiling stockpiled *verb* **1** to store a large quantity of (something) for future use ▷ *noun* **2** large store of something

stocktaking *noun* counting, checking and valuing of the goods in a shop

stocky stockier stockiest *adjective* (of a person) broad and sturdy

stodgy stodgier stodgiest *adjective* (of food) heavy, solid and filling

stoic *noun* **1** person who suffers hardship without showing his or her feelings ▷ *adjective* **2** (also **stoical**) suffering hardship without showing your feelings > **stoically** *adverb* > **stoicism** *noun*: *He responded to this news with remarkable stoicism*

stoke stokes stoking stoked *verb* to keep (a fire or furnace) burning by moving or adding fuel

stole *verb* **1** past tense of **steal** ▷ *noun* **2** long scarf or shawl

stolen *verb* past participle of **steal**

stolid *adjective* showing little emotion or interest

stomach *noun* **1** organ in your body which digests food **2** front part of your body below the waist; abdomen ▷ *verb* **3** to put up with

stone stones stoning stoned *noun* **1** material of which rocks are made **2** a small piece of rock **3** gem or jewel **4** hard central part of some fruits **5** unit of weight equal to 14 pounds or 6.350 kilograms **6** hard deposit formed in the kidney or bladder ▷ *verb* **7** to throw stones at **8** to remove stones from (a fruit)

stoned *adjective informal* under the

influence of drugs

stony stonier stoniest *adjective*
1 containing stones or like stone
2 unfeeling or hard

stood *verb* past of **stand**

stool *noun* **1** seat with legs but
without arms or a back **2** lump of
excrement or faeces

stoop *verb* **1** to bend (the body)
forward and downward **2** to walk
with your body bent forward and
downward **3** to degrade oneself
▷ *noun* **4** stooping posture

stop stops stopping stopped *verb*
1 to cease from doing (something)
2 to bring to or come to a halt **3** to
prevent or restrain **4** to withhold
5 to block or plug **6** to stay or rest
▷ *noun* **7** stopping or being stopped
8 place where a bus, train or other
vehicle stops **9** full stop **10** **put a
stop to** to prevent (something)
from happening or continuing
11 **come to a stop** to come to
a halt

stopcock *noun* valve to control or
stop the flow of fluid in a pipe

stoppage *noun* mass stopping of
work on account of a disagreement
with an employer

stopper *noun* piece of glass or
cork that fits into the neck of a jar
or bottle

stopwatch stopwatches *noun*
watch which can be stopped
instantly for exact timing of a
sporting event

storage *noun* **1** storing **2** space
for storing

store stores storing stored
noun **1** shop **2** supply kept for
future use **3** storage place, such
as a warehouse **4** **in store** about
to happen **5** **stores** stock of
provisions ▷ *verb* **6** to collect and
keep (things) for future use **7** to put

(furniture etc) in a warehouse for
safekeeping

storeroom *noun* room where
things are kept until they are
needed

storey storeys *noun* floor or level
of a building

stork *noun* very large white and
black wading bird with long red
legs and a long bill

storm *noun* **1** violent weather
with wind, rain or snow and often
thunder and lightning **2** angry or
excited reaction ▷ *verb* **3** (often
followed by *out*) to rush violently
or angrily **4** to shout angrily **5** to
attack or capture (a place) suddenly
> stormy *adjective* **1** characterized
by storms **2** involving violent
emotions

story stories *noun* **1** description of
a series of events told or written for
entertainment **2** plot of a book or
film **3** news report **4** *informal* lie

stout *adjective* **1** fat **2** thick, strong
and sturdy **3** determined, firm and
strong ▷ *noun* **4** strong dark beer
> stoutly *adverb*

stove *noun* apparatus for cooking
or heating

stow *verb* to store or pack **> stow
away** *verb* to hide on a ship or
aircraft in order to travel free

stowaway stowaways *noun*
person who hides on a ship or
aircraft in order to travel free

**straddle straddles straddling
straddled** *verb* **1** to have one leg or
part on each side of (something)
2 to be positioned across and on
two sides of (something), linking
the two parts: *The town straddles
a river*

straight *adjective* **1** not curved or
crooked **2** level or upright **3** honest
or frank **4** (of spirits) undiluted

5 neat and tidy ▷ *adverb* **6** in a straight line **7** immediately **8** in a level or upright position ▷ *noun* **9** straight part, especially of a racetrack

straightaway *adverb* immediately

straighten *verb* **1** to remove any bends or curves from **2** to make (something) neat and tidy **3** to organize and sort out (a confused situation)

straightforward *adjective* **1** (of a task) easy and involving no problems **2** honest or frank

strain *noun* **1** worry and nervous tension **2** force exerted by straining **3** injury from overexertion **4** great demand on strength or resources **5** melody or theme **6** breed or variety ▷ *verb* **7** to cause (something) to be used or tested beyond its limits **8** to injure (yourself or a muscle) by overexertion **9** to make an intense effort **10** to sieve

strained *adjective* **1** not relaxed; tense **2** not natural; forced

strainer *noun* sieve

strait *noun* **1** narrow channel connecting two areas of sea **2** **straits** difficult situation

straitjacket *noun* special strong jacket used to tie the arms of a violent person tightly around their body

strait-laced *adjective* prudish or puritanical

strand *noun* **1** single thread of string, wire, etc **2** element or part **3** *literary* shore

stranded *adjective* stuck somewhere with no means of leaving

strange *adjective* **1** odd or unusual **2** not familiar > **strangely** *adverb* > **strangeness** *noun*

stranger *noun* **1** person you have never met before **2** (followed by *to*) someone who is inexperienced in or unaccustomed to something

strangle strangles strangling strangled *verb* to kill (someone) by squeezing their throat > **strangulation** *noun* strangling

strangled *adjective* (of a sound or cry) unclear and muffled

stranglehold *noun* complete power or control over someone or something

strap straps strapping strapped *noun* **1** strip of flexible material for lifting, fastening or holding something in place ▷ *verb* **2** to fasten (something) with a strap or straps

strapping *adjective* tall, strong and healthy-looking

strata *noun* plural of **stratum**

strategic *adjective* **1** advantageous **2** (of weapons) aimed at an enemy's homeland > **strategically** *adverb*

strategy strategies *noun* **1** overall plan **2** art of planning, especially in war > **strategist** *noun*

stratosphere *noun* atmospheric layer between about 15 and 50 kilometres above the earth

stratum strata *noun* **1** layer, especially of rock **2** social class

straw *noun* **1** dried stalks of grain **2** single stalk of straw **3** long thin tube used to suck up liquid into the mouth **4** **the last straw** the latest in a series of bad events that makes you feel you cannot stand any more

strawberry strawberries *noun* sweet fleshy red fruit with small seeds on the outside

stray strays straying strayed *verb* **1** to wander away **2** (of thoughts or your mind) to move on to other topics **3** to deviate from certain

moral standards ▷ *adjective*
4 having strayed **5** scattered or
random ▷ *noun* **6** stray animal

streak *noun* **1** long band of
contrasting colour or substance
2 quality or characteristic **3** short
stretch (of good or bad luck) ▷ *verb*
4 to mark (something) with streaks
5 to move rapidly **6** *informal* to run
naked in public > **streaky** *adjective*

stream *noun* **1** small river **2** steady
flow of something **3** schoolchildren
grouped together by age and
ability ▷ *verb* **4** to flow steadily **5** to
float in the air **6** to group (pupils)
in streams

streamer *noun* **1** strip of coloured
paper that unrolls when tossed
2 long narrow flag

**streamline streamlines
streamlining streamlined** *verb*
1 to give (a car, plane, etc) a smooth
even shape to offer least resistance
to the flow of air or water **2** to make
(an organization or process) more
efficient by removing parts of it

street *noun* public road, usually
lined with buildings

streetcar *noun* US tram

strength *noun* **1** quality of
being strong **2** quality or ability
considered an advantage **3** how
strong or weak something is **4** total
number of people in a group **5** **on
the strength of** on the basis of

strengthen *verb* **1** to give
(something) more power, influence
or support and make it more likely
to succeed **2** to improve (an object)
or add to its structure so that it
can withstand rough treatment;
reinforce

strenuous *adjective* involving a lot
of effort or energy > **strenuously**
adverb

stress stresses stressing

stressed *noun* **1** worry and nervous
tension **2** emphasis **3** stronger
sound in saying a word or syllable
4 *Physics* force producing strain
▷ *verb* **5** to emphasize **6** to put
stress on (a word or syllable)
> **stressful** *adjective: a stressful time*

**stretch stretches stretching
stretched** *verb* **1** to extend or
be extended **2** to be able to be
stretched **3** to hold out your legs
or arms as far as you can **4** to pull
(something soft or elastic) so that
it becomes longer or bigger **5** to
strain (resources or abilities) to the
utmost ▷ *noun* **6** act of stretching
7 continuous expanse of land or
water **8** period of time

stretcher *noun* frame covered with
canvas, on which an injured person
is carried

strewn *adjective* untidily scattered

stricken *adjective* seriously affected
by disease, grief or pain, etc

strict *adjective* **1** stern or severe
2 sticking closely to specified
rules **3** (of a meaning, sense, etc)
complete or absolute

strictly *adverb* **1** only: *I was in it
strictly for the money* **2** **strictly
speaking** in fact; really

**stride strides striding strode
stridden** *verb* **1** to walk with long
steps ▷ *noun* **2** long step **3** regular
pace **4** **strides** progress

strident *adjective* loud and harsh

strife *noun formal* conflict or
quarrelling

strike strikes striking struck
noun **1** stoppage of work as a
protest **2** military attack: *the
threat of air strikes* ▷ *verb* **3** to hit
4 (of an illness, disaster or enemy)
to attack suddenly **5** to light (a
match) by rubbing the head against
something **6** (of a clock) to indicate

(a time) by sounding a bell **7** (of a thought or idea) to enter the mind of (someone) **8** to discover (gold, oil, etc) **9** to agree (a bargain or deal) **10** to stop work as a protest **11 be struck by** to be impressed by > **strike off** *verb* to remove (someone) from the official register of those allowed to practise in his or her profession > **strike up** *verb* **1** to begin (a conversation or friendship) **2** (of a band or orchestra) to begin to play

striker *noun* **1** striking worker **2** (in soccer) a player whose function is to attack and score goals

striking *adjective* impressive or very noticeable > **strikingly** *adverb*

string strings stringing strung *noun* **1** thin cord used for tying **2** set of objects threaded on a string **3** series of things or events **4** stretched wire or cord on a musical instrument that produces sound when vibrated **5 strings a** restrictions or conditions **b** section of an orchestra consisting of stringed instruments **6 pull strings** to use your influence ▷ *verb* **7** to provide with a string or strings **8** to thread (beads or other objects) on a string > **string along** *verb* to deceive (someone) over a period of time > **string out** *verb* to make (something) last longer than necessary

stringed *adjective* (of a musical instrument) having strings that are plucked or played with a bow

stringent *adjective* (of rules and conditions) strictly controlled or enforced

stringy-bark *noun* any Australian eucalypt that has bark that peels off in long tough strands

strip strips stripping stripped **1** long narrow piece **2** *Brit, Aust, NZ* clothes that a sports team plays in *verb* **3** to take your clothes off **4** to remove the covering from the surface of **5 strip someone of** to take (a title or possession) away from someone **6** to dismantle (an engine)

stripe *noun* **1** long narrow band of contrasting colour or substance **2** narrow band of material worn on a uniform to show someone's rank > **striped** or **stripy** or **stripey** *adjective* with a pattern of stripes

stripper *noun* entertainer who performs a striptease

striptease *noun* entertainment in which a performer undresses to music

strive strives striving strove striven *verb* to make a great effort (to do something)

strode *verb* past tense of **stride**

stroke strokes stroking stroked *verb* **1** to touch or caress (something) lightly with your hand ▷ *noun* **2** light touch or caress with your hand **3** serious medical condition involving a blockage in or a rupture of a blood vessel in your brain **4** blow **5** chime of a clock **6** mark made by a pen or paintbrush **7** style or method of swimming **8 stroke of luck** piece of luck

stroll *verb* **1** to walk in a leisurely manner; amble ▷ *noun* **2** leisurely walk

stroller *noun Aust* pushchair

strong *adjective* **1** having powerful muscles **2** not easily broken **3** great in degree or intensity **4** determined **5** (of argument) supported by evidence **6** having a specified number: *twenty strong* **7** good: *a strong candidate* **8** (of economy, currency or a relationship) stable and successful ▷ *adverb* **9 still going strong** still healthy or doing well after a long time > **strongly** *adverb*

stronghold *noun* **1** place that is held and defended by an army **2** place where an attitude or belief is strongly held

strove *verb* past tense of **strive**

struck *verb* past of **strike**

structure structures structuring structured *noun* **1** something that has been built or constructed; construction **2** the way something is made, built or organized **3** quality of being well planned and organized: *The days have no real structure* ▷ *verb* **4** to arrange (something) into an organized pattern or system > **structural** *adjective* > **structurally** *adverb*

struggle struggles struggling struggled *verb* **1** to try hard (to do something) but with difficulty or in difficult circumstances **2** to move about violently in an attempt to get free **3** to fight (with someone) ▷ *noun* **4** something requiring a lot of effort **5** fight

strum strums strumming strummed *verb* to play (a guitar or banjo) by sweeping the thumb or a plectrum across the strings

strung *verb* past of **string**

strut struts strutting strutted *verb* **1** to walk pompously; swagger ▷ *noun* **2** piece of wood or metal which strengthens or supports part of a building or structure

Stuart *noun* family name of the monarchs who ruled Scotland from 1371 to 1714 and England from 1603 to 1714

stub stubs stubbing stubbed *noun* **1** short piece (of a pencil or cigarette) left after use **2** part of

a cheque or ticket that you keep; counterfoil ▷ *verb* **3** to strike (your toe) painfully against an object > **stub out** *verb* to put out (a cigarette) by pressing the end against a surface

stubble *noun* **1** short stalks of grain left in a field after reaping **2** short growth of hair on the chin of a man who has not shaved recently > **stubbly** *adjective*

stubborn *adjective* **1** refusing to agree or give in; obstinate **2** difficult to deal with > **stubbornly** *adverb* > **stubbornness** *noun*

stuck *verb* **1** past of **stick** ▷ *adjective* **2** fixed or jammed and unable to move **3** unable to get away **4** unable to continue

stuck-up *adjective informal* conceited or snobbish

stud *noun* **1** small piece of metal attached to a surface for decoration **2** disc-like removable fastener for clothes **3** one of several small round objects fixed to the sole of a football boot to give better grip **4** male animal, especially a stallion, kept for breeding **5** (also **stud farm**) place where horses are bred

studded *adjective* decorated with small pieces of metal or precious stones

student *noun* person who studies a subject, especially at university

studied *adjective* (of an action or response) carefully practised or planned

studio studios *noun* **1** workroom of an artist or photographer **2** place containing special equipment where records, films or radio or television programmes are made

studious *adjective* inclined to spend a lot of time studying

studiously *adverb* carefully and deliberately

study studies studying studied *verb* **1** to spend time learning (a subject) **2** to investigate (something) by observation and research **3** to look at (something) carefully ▷ *noun* **4** activity of studying **5** piece of research on a particular subject **6** sketch done as practice or preparation **7** room for studying in

stuff *noun* **1** substance or material **2** collection of unnamed things ▷ *verb* **3** to push (something) somewhere quickly and roughly **4** to fill (something) with a substance or objects **5** to fill (food) with a seasoned mixture **6** to fill (an animal's skin) with material to restore the shape of the live animal

stuffing *noun* **1** seasoned mixture used to stuff poultry or vegetables **2** padding

stuffy stuffier stuffiest *adjective* **1** lacking fresh air; airless **2** very formal and old-fashioned

stumble stumbles stumbling stumbled *verb* **1** to trip and nearly fall **2** to walk in an unsure way **3** to make frequent mistakes in speech > **stumble across** or **on** *verb* to discover (something) accidentally

stump *noun* **1** base of a tree left when the main trunk has been cut away **2** part of a thing left after a larger part has been removed **3** *Cricket* one of the three upright sticks forming the wicket ▷ *verb* **4** to baffle

stun stuns stunning stunned *verb* **1** to shock or overwhelm **2** to knock (a person or animal) unconscious with a blow to the head

stung *verb* past of **sting**

stunk *verb* past participle of **stink**

stunning *adjective* very attractive or impressive

stunt *noun* **1** acrobatic or dangerous action **2** anything spectacular done to gain publicity ▷ *verb* **3** to prevent or impede (the growth or development of something)

stupendous *adjective* very large or impressive > **stupendously** *adverb*

stupid *adjective* **1** lacking intelligence **2** silly or lacking in good judgment > **stupidity** *noun* > **stupidly** *adverb*

sturdy sturdier sturdiest *adjective* strong and firm and unlikely to be damaged or injured > **sturdily** *adverb*

sturgeon *noun* fish from which caviar is obtained

stutter *noun* **1** difficulty in speaking characterized by a tendency to repeat sounds at the beginning of words and a problem completing words ▷ *verb* **2** to hesitate or repeat sounds when speaking

sty sties *noun* pen for pigs; pigsty

stye *noun* infection at the base of an eyelash

style styles styling styled *noun* **1** manner of writing, speaking or doing something **2** shape or design **3** elegance and smartness **4** current fashion ▷ *verb* **5** to shape or design (something)

stylish *adjective* smart, elegant and fashionable; chic; smart > **stylishly** *adverb*

suave *adjective* smooth and sophisticated in manner > **suavely** *adverb*

sub- *prefix meaning* **1** under or beneath: *submarine* **2** subordinate: *sublieutenant* **3** falling short of: *subnormal* **4** forming a subdivision: *subheading*

subconscious *noun* **1** *Psychoanalysis*

part of your mind that can influence you without your being aware of it ▷ *adjective* **2** happening or existing in someone's subconscious and therefore not directly realized or understood by them: *a subconscious fear* > **subconsciously** *adverb*

subcontinent *noun* large land mass that is a distinct part of a continent

subdivide subdivides subdividing subdivided *verb* to divide (a part of something) into smaller parts

subdivision *noun* one of the sections that make up the whole

subdue subdues subduing subdued *verb* **1** to overcome and bring under control **2** to make (a colour, light or emotion) less strong

subdued *adjective* **1** rather quiet and sad **2** not very noticeable or bright

subject *noun* **1** person or thing being discussed, dealt with or studied **2** *Grammar* word or phrase that represents the person or thing performing the action of the verb in a sentence. For example, in the sentence *My cat catches birds*, *my cat* is the subject **3** area of study **4** person living under the rule of a monarch or government ▷ *verb* **5 subject someone to** to cause someone to undergo or experience (something unpleasant) ▷ *adjective* **6 subject to a** affected by; liable to **b** conditional upon

subjective *adjective* based on personal feelings and prejudices rather than on fact and rational thought

subjunctive *Grammar noun* **1** form of the verb sometimes used when expressing doubt supposition or wishes ▷ *adjective* **2** in or of that mood. Compare **indicative**

sublime *adjective* **1** awe-inspiring and uplifting **2** unparalleled; supreme > **sublimely** *adverb*

subliminal *adjective* affecting your mind without your being aware of it

submarine *noun* ship that can travel beneath the surface of the sea

submerge submerges submerging submerged *verb* to go below or to put (something) below the surface of a liquid

submission *noun* **1** state of being submissive and under someone's control **2** act of submitting **3** something submitted for consideration

submissive *adjective* quiet and obedient

submit submits submitting submitted *verb* **1** (often followed by *to*) to surrender yourself or agree (to something) because you are not powerful enough to resist it **2** to send in (an application or proposal) for consideration

subordinate subordinates subordinating subordinated *noun* **1** person under the authority of another ▷ *adjective* **2** of lesser rank or importance ▷ *verb* **3** to treat (something) as less important

subordinate clause *noun* *Grammar* clause which adds details to the main clause of a sentence

subscribe subscribes subscribing subscribed *verb* **1** to pay (a subscription) **2** to give support or approval (to a theory, belief, etc) > **subscriber** *noun*

subscription *noun* sum of money that you pay regularly to belong to an organization or to receive regular copies of a magazine

subsequent *adjective* occurring

or coming into existence after something else: *the December uprising and the subsequent political violence* > **subsequently** *adverb*

subservient *adjective* submissive or servile > **subservience** *noun*

subside subsides subsiding subsided *verb* 1 to become less intense 2 to sink to a lower level

subsidence *noun* act or process of subsiding

subsidiary subsidiaries *noun* 1 company which is part of a larger company ▷ *adjective* 2 of lesser importance

subsidize subsidizes subsidizing subsidized; also spelt **subsidise** *verb* 1 to provide part of the cost of (something) 2 to help (someone) financially > **subsidized** *adjective*

subsidy subsidies *noun* financial aid

subsist *verb* to manage to stay alive > **subsistence** *noun*

substance *noun* 1 solid, powder, liquid or paste 2 essential meaning of something 3 solid or meaningful quality 4 physical composition of something 5 wealth

substantial *adjective* 1 of considerable size or value 2 (of food or a meal) sufficient and nourishing 3 solid or strong

substantially *adverb* generally, essentially or mostly

substitute substitutes substituting substituted *verb* 1 to take the place of (something or someone) or to put (something or someone) in the place of another ▷ *noun* 2 person or thing taking the place of (another) > **substitution** *noun*

subterfuge *noun* the use of tricks or deceitful methods to achieve an objective

subterranean *adjective* underground

subtitle subtitles subtitling subtitled *noun* 1 secondary title of a book 2 **subtitles** printed translation or transcript that appears at the bottom of the screen for some films and television programmes ▷ *verb* 3 to provide (something) with a subtitle or subtitles

subtle subtler subtlest *adjective* 1 very fine, delicate or small in degree 2 using indirect methods to achieve something > **subtlety** *noun* > **subtly** *adverb*

subtract *verb* to take (one number or quantity) from another

subtraction *noun* subtracting of one number from another, or a sum in which you do this

suburb *noun* residential area on the outskirts of a city

suburban *adjective* 1 relating to a suburb or suburbs 2 dull and conventional

suburbia *noun* suburbs and their inhabitants

subversive *adjective* 1 intended to destroy or weaken a political system: *subversive activities* ▷ *noun* 2 person who tries to destroy or weaken a political system > **subversion** *noun*

subvert *verb formal* to cause (something) to weaken or fail

subway subways *noun* 1 passage under a road or railway 2 underground railway

succeed *verb* 1 to achieve the intended result 2 to turn out satisfactorily 3 to come next in order after 4 to take over a position from > **succeeding** *adjective*

success successes *noun* 1 achievement of something

attempted **2** attainment of wealth, fame or position **3** successful person or thing

successful *adjective* having success > **successfully** *adverb*

succession *noun* **1** series of people or things following one another in order **2** act of succeeding someone to an important position **3** right by which someone succeeds to an important position **4 in succession** without a break

successive *adjective* occurring one after the other without a break

successor *noun* person who succeeds someone in a position

succinct *adjective* brief and clear > **succinctly** *adverb*

succour *noun* help in distress

succulent *adjective* juicy and delicious > **succulence** *noun*

succumb *verb* **1** (followed by *to*) to give way (to something overpowering) **2** to die (of an illness)

such *adjective* **1** of the kind specified **2** so, so great or so much: *I have such a terrible sense of guilt* ▷ *pronoun* **3** such things **4 such as** like **5 such and such** something specific but not known or named

suchlike *pronoun* such or similar things: *shampoos, talcs, toothbrushes and suchlike*

suck *verb* **1** to draw (liquid or air) into the mouth **2** to take (something) into your mouth and lick, dissolve or roll it around with your tongue **3** (followed by *in*) to draw (something or someone) in by irresistible force > **suck up to** *verb informal* to do things to please (someone) in order to obtain praise or approval

sucker *noun* **1** *informal* person who is easily fooled or cheated **2** pad,

organ or device which sticks to something using suction

suckle suckles suckling suckled *verb* **1** (of a mother) to feed (a baby) at the breast **2** (of a baby) to feed at its mother's breast

sucrose *noun* chemical name for sugar

suction *noun* **1** force involved when a substance is drawn or sucked from one place to another **2** process by which two surfaces stick together when the air between them is removed

Sudanese *adjective* **1** belonging or relating to the Sudan ▷ *noun* **2** someone from the Sudan

▪ The plural of *Sudanese* is *Sudanese*

sudden *adjective* happening quickly and unexpectedly > **suddenly** *adverb* > **suddenness** *noun*

suds *plural noun* bubbles that form on the surface of soapy water

sue sues suing sued *verb* to start legal proceedings against

suede *noun* thin soft leather with a velvety finish on one side

suffer *verb* **1** to experience pain or misery **2** to deteriorate in condition or quality **3** to undergo or be subjected to (pain or injury) **4** to tolerate > **sufferer** *noun* > **suffer from** *verb* to be affected by (a condition) > **suffering** *noun*

suffice suffices sufficing sufficed *verb formal* to be enough

sufficient *adjective* enough or adequate > **sufficiently** *adverb*

suffix suffixes *noun* letter or letters added to the end of a word to form another word, for example *-ly* and *-ness* in *smartly* and *softness*

suffocate suffocates suffocating suffocated *verb* **1** to be killed or to kill (someone) by deprivation of oxygen **2** to feel uncomfortable from heat and lack of air > **suffocation** noun

suffrage noun right to vote in political elections

suffragette noun (in Britain in the early 20th century) a woman who campaigned militantly for the right to vote

suffused adjective literary **suffused with** flooded with (light or colour)

sugar noun sweet substance used to sweeten food and drinks

suggest verb 1 to propose (an idea, plan) 2 to bring (something) to mind or indicate

suggestion noun 1 thing suggested 2 hint or indication

suggestive adjective 1 suggesting something indecent or sexual in nature 2 **suggestive of** conveying a hint of > **suggestively** adverb

suicidal adjective 1 liable to commit suicide 2 having potentially fatal consequences; very dangerous > **suicidally** adverb

suicide noun 1 killing oneself intentionally 2 person who kills himself or herself intentionally 3 self-inflicted ruin of someone's own prospects or interests

suit noun 1 set of clothes designed to be worn together 2 outfit worn for a specific purpose 3 one of the four sets into which a pack of cards is divided 4 lawsuit ▷ verb 5 to be acceptable to or convenient for 6 (of a colour or piece of clothing) to cause (someone) to look good

suitable adjective appropriate or proper > **suitability** noun: his suitability for the role > **suitably** adverb: suitably qualified

suitcase noun case in which you carry your clothes when you are travelling

suite noun 1 set of connected rooms in a hotel 2 set of matching furniture or bathroom fittings 3 set of musical pieces in the same key

suited adjective right or appropriate for a particular purpose or person: He is well suited to his role

suitor noun old-fashioned man who is courting a woman

sulk verb 1 to be silent and sullen because of resentment or bad temper ▷ noun 2 resentful or sullen mood > **sulky** adjective

sullen adjective silent and unwilling to be sociable in a disagreeable way > **sullenly** adverb

sulphur noun Chemistry pale yellow nonmetallic element which burns with a very unpleasant smell

sultan noun (of certain Muslim countries) ruler or sovereign

sultana noun 1 dried grape 2 wife of a sultan

sultry sultrier sultriest adjective 1 (of weather or climate) hot and humid 2 passionate or sensual

sum sums summing summed noun 1 amount of money 2 problem in arithmetic; calculation 3 total > **sum up** verb 1 to summarize 2 to form a quick opinion of

summarize summarizes summarizing summarized; also spelt **summarise** verb to give a short account of the main points of

summary summaries noun 1 brief account giving the main points of something; précis; résumé ▷ adjective 2 done quickly, without formalities: Summary executions are common > **summarily** adverb

summer noun warmest season of the year, between spring and autumn

summit noun 1 top of a mountain or hill 2 highest point 3 meeting between heads of state or other high officials to discuss particular issues

summon *verb* **1** to order (someone) to come **2** (often followed by *up*) to gather (your courage, strength, etc)

summons summonses summonsing summonsed *noun* **1** official order requiring someone to appear in court **2** an order to go to someone ▷ *verb* **3** to order (someone) to appear in court

sumptuous *adjective* lavish or magnificent

sum total *noun* complete or final total

sun suns sunning sunned *noun* **1** star around which the earth and the other planets of the solar system revolve **2** any star around which planets revolve **3** heat and light from the sun ▷ *verb* **4** to expose (yourself) to the sun's rays

sunbathe sunbathes sunbathing sunbathed *verb* to lie in the sunshine in order to get a suntan

sunburn *noun* painful reddening of the skin caused by overexposure to the sun > **sunburnt** or **sunburned** *adjective*

sundae *noun* ice cream topped with fruit etc

Sunday Sundays *noun* day between Saturday and Monday

Sunday school *noun* special class held on Sundays to teach children about Christianity

sundial *noun* device showing the time by means of a pointer that casts a shadow on a marked dial

sundries *plural noun* several things of various sorts

sundry *adjective* **1** several or various **2 all and sundry** everybody

sunflower *noun* tall plant with large golden flowers

sung *verb* past participle of **sing**

sunglasses *plural noun* spectacles with dark lenses that you wear to protect your eyes from the sun

sunk *verb* past participle of **sink**

sunken *adjective* **1** having sunk to the bottom of the sea, a river or lake **2** constructed below the level of the surrounding area **3** curving inwards: *Her cheeks were sunken*

sunlight *noun* bright light produced when the sun is shining > **sunlit** *adjective*

sunny sunnier sunniest *adjective* full of or exposed to sunlight

sunrise *noun* **1** daily appearance of the sun above the horizon **2** time of this

sunset *noun* **1** daily disappearance of the sun below the horizon **2** time of this

sunshine *noun* light and warmth from the sun

sunstroke *noun* illness caused by spending too much time in hot sunshine

suntan *noun* browning of the skin caused by exposure to the sun > **suntanned** *adjective*

super *adjective informal* very nice or very good; excellent

super- *prefix meaning* **1** above or over: *superimpose* **2** outstanding: *superstar* **3** of greater size or extent: *supermarket*

superb *adjective* excellent, impressive or splendid > **superbly** *adverb*

superbug *noun informal* bacterium resistant to antibiotics

supercilious *adjective* showing arrogant pride or scorn

superego superegos *noun Psychology* part of your mind acts as a conscience

superficial *adjective* **1** not careful or

thorough **2** (of a person) without depth of character; shallow **3** of or on the surface ▷ **superficially** *adverb*

superfluous *adjective formal* unnecessary or no longer needed

superhuman *adjective* beyond normal human ability or experience

superimpose superimposes superimposing superimposed *verb* to place (something) on or over something else

superintendent *noun* **1** senior police officer **2** supervisor

superior *adjective* **1** greater in quality, quantity or merit **2** higher in position or rank **3** believing yourself to be better than others ▷ *noun* **4** person of greater rank or status ▷ **superiority** *noun*

superlative *adjective* **1** of outstanding quality ▷ *noun* **2** *Grammar* the form of an adjective or adverb that indicates the greatest degree of it, *eg quickest, best, easiest*

supermarket *noun* large self-service store selling food and household goods

supernatural *adjective* **1** of or relating to things beyond the laws of nature ▷ *noun* **2 the supernatural** supernatural forces, occurrences and beings collectively

superpower *noun* extremely powerful nation

supersede supersedes superseding superseded *verb* to replace or supplant (something) on account of being more modern

supersonic *adjective* of or travelling at a speed greater than the speed of sound

superstar *noun* very famous entertainer or sports player

superstition *noun* **1** irrational beliefs founded on ignorance or fear **2** idea or practice based on the belief that certain things bring good or bad luck ▷ **superstitious** *adjective*

superstore *noun* large supermarket

supervise supervises supervising supervised *verb* to watch over (an activity) in order to check that it is carried out correctly or safely ▷ **supervision** *noun* ▷ **supervisor** *noun*

supper *noun* light evening meal

supplant *verb* to take the place of (someone or something); oust

supple *adjective* able to bend and move easily

supplement *verb* **1** to add something to (something) in order to improve it **2** to add to ▷ *noun* **3** thing added to complete something or make up for a lack **4** magazine inserted into a newspaper

supplementary *adjective* added to something else to improve it

supplier *noun* firm that provides particular goods

supply supplies supplying supplied *verb* **1** to provide (someone) with something **2** to provide or send (something) ▷ *noun* **3** amount available **4** supplying **5** *Economics* willingness and ability to provide goods and services: *supply and demand* **6 supplies** food or equipment

support *verb* **1** to take an active interest in and hope for the success of (a sports team, political principle, etc) **2** to bear the weight of; hold up **3** to give practical or emotional help to **4** to provide (someone) with money for the necessities of life **5** to help to prove (a theory etc)

▷ *noun* **6** supporting **7** means of support **8** encouragement and help **9** money > **supporter** *noun* person who supports a team, principle, etc

supportive *adjective* (of a person) encouraging and helpful in troubled times

suppose supposes supposing supposed *verb* **1** to presume to be true **2** to consider as a proposal for the sake of discussion **3 be supposed to a** to be expected or required to: *You were supposed to phone me* **b** to be permitted to: *We're not supposed to swim here* > **supposing** or **suppose** *conjunction* what if

supposed *adjective* presumed to be true without proof; alleged > **supposedly** *adverb*

supposition *noun* **1** something supposed **2** supposing

suppress suppresses suppressing suppressed *verb* **1** to put an end to **2** to prevent publication of (information) **3** to restrain (an emotion or response) > **suppression** *noun*

supremacy *noun* **1** supreme power **2** state of being supreme

supreme *adjective* highest in authority, rank or degree > **supremely** *adverb* extremely

surcharge *noun* additional charge

sure surer surest *adjective* **1** free from uncertainty or doubt **2** reliable or accurate **3** inevitable or certain **4 sure of** confident about ▷ *adverb, interjection* **5** *informal* certainly > **surely** *adverb* it must be true that

surf *noun* **1** foam caused by waves breaking on the shore ▷ *verb* **2** to go surfing **3 surf the Internet** to go from website to website reading information > **surfer** *noun*

surface surfaces surfacing

surfaced *noun* **1** outside or top of an object **2** superficial appearance ▷ *verb* **3** to come up from under the water

surfboard *noun* long smooth board used in surfing

surf club *noun Aust* organization of lifesavers in charge of safety on a particular beach, and which often provides leisure facilities

surfeit *noun* excessive amount

surfing *noun* sport of riding towards the shore on a surfboard on the crest of a wave

surge surges surging surged *noun* **1** sudden powerful increase ▷ *verb* **2** to increase suddenly **3** to move forward strongly

surgeon *noun* doctor who performs operations

surgery surgeries *noun* **1** treatment involving cutting open part of the patient's body to treat the affected part **2** place where a doctor, dentist, etc can be consulted **3** occasion when a doctor or dentist is available for consultation **4** *Brit* occasion when an elected politician is available for consultation

surgical *adjective* used in or involving a medical operation > **surgically** *adverb*

surly surlier surliest *adjective* ill-tempered and rude > **surliness** *noun*

surmise surmises surmising surmised *verb, noun* to guess; conjecture

surmount *verb* to overcome (a problem) > **surmountable** *adjective*

surname *noun* family name; last name

surpass surpasses surpassing surpassed *verb formal* to be greater than or superior to

surplice *noun* loose white robe worn by clergymen and choristers

surplus surpluses *noun* amount left over in excess of what is required

surprise surprises surprising surprised *noun* **1** unexpected event **2** amazement and wonder ▷ *verb* **3** to cause (someone) to feel amazement or wonder **4** to come upon, attack or catch (someone) suddenly and unexpectedly > **surprised** *adjective* > **surprising** *adjective*

surreal *adjective* very strange and dreamlike; bizarre

surrealism *noun* movement in art and literature begun in the 1920s that involves putting together images and things that do not normally come together, as in a strange dream > **surrealist** *noun, adjective*

surrender *verb* **1** to stop fighting and give oneself up **2** to give way (to a temptation or influence) **3** to give (something) up to another ▷ *noun* **4** surrendering

surreptitious *adjective* done secretly or stealthily > **surreptitiously** *adverb*

surrogate *adjective* **1** acting as a substitute for someone or something ▷ *noun* **2** substitute

surround *verb* **1** to be or come all around (a person or thing) **2** to encircle or enclose (something or someone) with something ▷ *noun* **3** border or edging

surrounding *adjective* (of area) all around: *the surrounding countryside*

surroundings *plural noun* area or environment around a person, place or thing

surveillance *noun* close observation

survey surveys surveying surveyed *verb* **1** to look at or consider (something or someone) as a whole **2** to inspect (a building) to find out what condition it is in and assess its value **3** to examine and measure (an area), often to make a map **4** to find out the opinions or habits of (a group of people) ▷ *noun* **5** detailed examination of something, often in the form of a report

surveyor *noun* person whose job is to survey buildings or land

survival *noun* managing to go on living or existing in spite of great danger or difficulties

survive survives surviving survived *verb* **1** to continue to live or exist after (a difficult experience) **2** to live on after the death of (another) > **survivor** *noun*

sus- *prefix* another form of **sub-**

susceptible *adjective* (often followed by *to*) liable to be influenced or affected (by) > **susceptibility** *noun*: *a person's susceptibility to illness*

suspect *verb* **1** to believe (someone) to be guilty of something without having any proof: *They suspected her of being a witch* **2** to think (something) to be false or questionable: *He suspected her motives* **3** to believe (something) to be the case: *She suspected he was right* ▷ *noun* **4** person who is suspected ▷ *adjective* **5** not to be trusted

suspend *verb* **1** to hang (something or someone) from a high place **2** to delay or stop (something) **3** to remove (someone) temporarily from a job or team

suspender *noun* **1** strap for holding

up stockings **2 suspenders** US braces

suspense *noun* state of uncertainty while awaiting news, an event, etc

suspension *noun* **1** delaying or stopping of something **2** temporary removal of someone from their job **3** system of springs and shock absorbers supporting the body of a vehicle **4** liquid mixture in which very small bits of a solid material are contained and are not dissolved

suspicion *noun* **1** feeling of not trusting a person or thing **2** belief that something is true or likely to happen without definite proof **3** slight trace

suspicious *adjective* **1** (of a person) feeling suspicion **2** (of a thing or person) causing suspicion **> suspiciously** *adverb*

sustain *verb* **1** to keep up, maintain or prolong **2** to give (someone) the energy, strength and nourishment needed to keep them going **3** to suffer (an injury or loss)

sustainable *adjective* **1** capable of being sustained **2** (of development, resource) capable of being maintained at a steady level without exhausting natural resources or causing ecological damage

sustenance *noun formal* food

svelte *adjective* slim and elegant

swab swabs swabbing swabbed *noun* **1** small piece of cotton wool used to apply medication, clean a wound, etc ▷ *verb* **2** to clean (something) with a mop and a lot of water **3** to clean or take specimens of (a wound) with a swab

swag *noun* **1** *informal* stolen property **2** *Aust, NZ* **a** tramp's bundle of possessions **b swags of** *Aust, NZ informal* lots of

swagger *verb* **1** to walk or behave arrogantly ▷ *noun* **2** *Aust, NZ* **a** bundle of possessions belonging to a tramp **b** arrogant walk or manner

swagman swagmen *noun Aust & NZ history* tramp who carried his belongings in a bundle on his back

swallow *verb* **1** to make (something) go down your throat and into your stomach **2** to make a gulping movement in the throat, as when nervous **3** *informal* to believe (something) gullibly **4** to refrain from showing (a feeling) **5** to engulf or absorb ▷ *noun* **6** small bird with long pointed wings and a forked tail **7** swallowing

swam *verb* past tense of **swim**

swamp *noun* **1** watery area of land; bog ▷ *verb* **2** to cause (something) to fill or be covered with water **3** to overwhelm (something or someone) **> swampy** *adjective*

swan *noun* large usually white water bird with a long graceful neck

swanndri® *noun NZ* weatherproof woollen shirt or jacket; also **swannie**

swap swaps swapping swapped *verb* **1** to exchange (something) for something else ▷ *noun* **2** exchange

swarm *noun* **1** large group of bees or other insects flying together ▷ *verb* **2** (of bees, insects) to fly together in a large group **3** (of people) to go somewhere quickly and at the same time **4** (of a place) to be crowded or overrun

swarthy swarthier swarthiest *adjective* dark-complexioned

swashbuckling *adjective* having the exciting behaviour of pirates, especially those depicted in films

swastika *noun* symbol in the shape of a cross with the arms bent over at right angles. It was the official symbol of the Nazis in Germany, but in India it is a good luck sign

swat swats swatting swatted *verb* to hit (an insect) sharply in order to kill it

swathe swathes swathing swathed *noun* **1** long strip of cloth wrapped around something **2** long strip of land ▷ *verb* **3** to wrap (someone or something) in bandages or layers of cloth

swathed *adjective* **swathed in** wrapped in

sway sways swaying swayed *verb* **1** to swing to and fro or from side to side **2** to waver or to cause (someone) to waver in opinion ▷ *noun* **3** power or influence **4** swaying motion

swear swears swearing swore sworn *verb* **1** to use obscene or blasphemous language **2** to state or promise on oath **3** to state earnestly > **swear by** *verb* to have complete confidence in > **swear in** *verb* to cause (someone new to a position) to take an oath promising to fulfil their duties

swearword *noun* word considered obscene or blasphemous which some people use when they are angry

sweat *noun* **1** salty liquid given off through the pores of the skin when you are hot or afraid ▷ *verb* **2** to have sweat coming through the pores **3** to be anxious

sweater *noun* (woollen) garment for the upper part of the body

sweatshirt *noun* long-sleeved cotton jersey

sweaty sweatier sweatiest *adjective* covered or soaked with sweat

swede *noun* large round root vegetable with yellow flesh and a brownish-purple skin

Swede *noun* someone from Sweden

Swedish *adjective* **1** belonging or relating to Sweden ▷ *noun* **2** main language spoken in Sweden

sweep sweeps sweeping swept *verb* **1** to remove dirt from (a floor) with a broom **2** to move smoothly and quickly **3** to spread rapidly **4** to move majestically **5** to carry (something or someone) away suddenly or forcefully **6** to stretch in a long wide curve ▷ *noun* **7** sweeping **8** sweeping motion **9** wide expanse **10** chimney sweep

sweeping *adjective* **1** (of a curve or movement) long and wide **2** affecting a lot of people to a great extent; wide-ranging **3** (of a statement) based on a general assumption rather than on careful thought; indiscriminate

sweepstake *noun* lottery in which the stakes of the participants make up the prize

sweet *adjective* **1** tasting of or like sugar **2** kind and charming **3** attractive and delightful **4** (of wine) with a high sugar content **5** pleasant and satisfying ▷ *noun* **6 sweets** things such as toffees, chocolates and mints **7** dessert > **sweetly** *adverb* > **sweetness** *noun*

sweet corn *noun* type of maize with sweet yellow kernels, eaten as a vegetable

sweeten *verb* to add sugar or another sweet substance to (food or drink)

sweetener *noun* sweet artificial substance that can be used instead of sugar

sweetheart *noun* **1** form of address for someone you are very fond of **2** boyfriend or girlfriend

sweet pea *noun* climbing plant with bright fragrant flowers

sweet potato sweet potatoes *noun* tropical root vegetable with yellow flesh

sweet tooth *noun* strong liking for sweet foods

swell swells swelling swelled swollen *verb* 1 to becomes larger and rounder 2 to increase in number 3 (of a sound) to become gradually louder ▷ *noun* 4 regular up-and-down movement of waves in the sea ▷ *adjective* 5 US informal excellent or fine

swelling *noun* 1 enlargement of part of the body, caused by injury or infection 2 increase in size

sweltering *adjective* uncomfortably hot

swept *verb* past of **sweep**

swerve swerves swerving swerved *verb* to change direction suddenly to avoid colliding with something

swift *adjective* 1 moving or able to move quickly ▷ *noun* 2 fast-flying bird with narrow crescent-shaped wings > **swiftly** *adverb* > **swiftness** *noun*

swig swigs swigging swigged *verb* 1 to drink (something) in large mouthfuls, usually from a bottle ▷ *noun* 2 large mouthful of drink

swill *verb* 1 to rinse (something) in large amounts of water 2 to drink (something) greedily ▷ *noun* 3 sloppy mixture containing waste food, fed to pigs

swim swims swimming swam swum *verb* 1 to move through water, using your arms and legs to help you 2 to be covered or flooded with liquid 3 to reel: *Her head was swimming* ▷ *noun* 4 act or period of swimming > **swimmer** *noun*

swimming *noun* activity of moving through water using your arms and legs

swimming bath *noun* public swimming pool

swimming costume *noun* clothing worn by a woman when she goes swimming

swimming pool *noun* (building containing) an artificial pond for swimming in

swimming trunks *plural noun* shorts or briefs worn by a man when he goes swimming

swimsuit *noun* swimming costume

swindle swindles swindling swindled *verb* 1 to cheat (someone) out of money or property ▷ *noun* 2 trick in which someone is cheated out of money or property > **swindler** *noun*

swine *noun* 1 pig 2 nasty and unpleasant person

> The plural of *swine* is always *swine* when it refers to pigs. Both *swine* and *swines* are possible when it means people

swing swings swinging swung *verb* 1 to move to and fro from a fixed point 2 to move (something) or to move in a curve 3 (of an opinion or mood) to change sharply 4 *informal* to be hanged ▷ *noun* 5 seat hanging from a frame or a branch, which you can move backwards and forwards when you sit on it 6 sudden or extreme change 7 instance of swinging

swingeing *adjective* punishing or severe

swipe swipes swiping swiped *verb* 1 to strike (at something) with a sweeping blow 2 *informal* to steal 3 to pass (a credit card or debit card) through a machine that electronically reads information

stored in the card ▷ *noun*
4 sweeping blow

swipe card *noun* credit card or debit card that is passed through a machine that electronically reads information stored on the card

swirl *verb* **1** to move quickly in circles ▷ *noun* **2** whirling motion **3** twisting shape

swish swishes swishing swished *verb* **1** to move with a soft whistling or hissing sound ▷ *noun* **2** whistling or hissing sound ▷ *adjective* **3** *informal* fashionable or smart

Swiss *adjective* **1** belonging or relating to Switzerland ▷ *noun* **2** person from Switzerland

▮ The plural of *Swiss* is *Swiss*

switch switches switching switched *noun* **1** small control for an electrical device or machine **2** abrupt change **3** exchange or swap ▷ *verb* **4** to change abruptly (to something) **5** to replace (something) with something else > **switch off** *verb* **1** to turn (a light or machine) off by means of a switch **2** to stop paying attention > **switch on** *verb* to turn (a light or machine) on by means of a switch

switchboard *noun* place in an office where telephone calls are received and connected to the appropriate people

swivel swivels swivelling swivelled *verb* **1** to turn round on a central point ▷ *adjective* **2** (of chair, stool) revolving

swollen *verb* **1** a past participle of **swell** ▷ *adjective* **2** having swelled up; enlarged or puffed up

swoon *verb* **1** to faint ▷ *noun* **2** faint

swoop *verb* to sweep down or pounce suddenly

swop same as **swap**

sword *noun* weapon with a long sharp blade and a short handle

swordfish swordfishes or **swordfish** *noun* large fish with a very long upper jaw

swore *verb* past tense of **swear**

sworn *verb* **1** past participle of **swear** ▷ *adjective* **2** bound by or as if by an oath: *sworn enemies*

swot swots swotting swotted *informal verb* **1** to study or revise hard ▷ *noun* **2** someone who spends too much time studying > **swot up** *verb* to find out as much about a subject as possible in a short time

swum *verb* past participle of **swim**

swung *verb* past of **swing**

sycamore *noun* tree that has large leaves with five points

syllable *noun* part of a word pronounced as a unit

syllabus syllabuses or **syllabi** *noun* list of subjects for a particular course or examination

symbol *noun* shape, design or idea that is used to represent something

symbolic *adjective* having a special meaning that is considered to represent something else

symbolize symbolizes symbolizing symbolized; also spelt **symbolise** *verb* **1** (of shape, design or idea) to be a symbol of **2** to represent (something) with a symbol > **symbolism** *noun* **1** representation of something by symbols **2** movement in art and literature using symbols to express abstract and mystical ideas

symmetrical *adjective* having two halves that are mirror images of each other > **symmetrically** *adverb*

symmetry *noun* state of having two halves that are mirror images of each other

sympathetic *adjective* **1** feeling or showing kindness and understanding to other people **2** likeable or appealing **3** (followed by *to* or *towards*) agreeable or favourably disposed (to something) > **sympathetically** *adverb*

sympathize sympathizes sympathizing sympathized; also spelt **sympathise** *verb* **1** to feel or express understanding and concern **2** to have similar feelings

sympathizer or **sympathiser** *noun* supporter of a particular cause

sympathy sympathies *noun* **1** compassion for someone's pain or distress **2** agreement with someone's feelings or interests

symphony symphonies *noun* composition for orchestra, with several movements

symptom *noun* **1** something wrong with your body that is a sign of an illness **2** sign that something is wrong > **symptomatic** *adjective*: *The price dispute was symptomatic of other problems*

synagogue *noun* place of worship and religious instruction for Jewish people

synchronize synchronizes synchronizing synchronized; also spelt **synchronise** *verb* **1** (of two or more people) to perform (an action) at the same time **2** to set (watches) to show the same time **3** to match (the soundtrack and action of a film) precisely

syncopation *noun Music* stressing of weak beats instead of the usual strong ones

syndicate *noun* group of people or firms undertaking a joint project

syndrome *noun* **1** medical condition characterized by a particular set of symptoms **2** set of characteristics indicating a particular problem

synod *noun* church council

synonym *noun* word with the same meaning as or a similar meaning to another

synonymous *adjective* **1** having the same or a very similar meaning **2** (followed by *with*) closely associated: *the Statue of Liberty is synonymous with New York*

synopsis synopses *noun* summary or outline of a book, play or film

syntax *noun Grammar* way in which words are arranged to form phrases and sentences

synthetic *adjective* **1** (of a substance) made artificially rather than naturally **2** not genuine; insincere

syphon same as **siphon**

Syrian *adjective* **1** belonging or relating to Syria ▷ *noun* **2** someone from Syria

syringe syringes syringing syringed *noun* **1** hollow tube with a part inside that can be raised or pushed down to draw up or squirt down liquid **2** similar device, with a fine hollow needle at one end, for giving injections and taking blood samples ▷ *verb* **3** to clean (part of the body) using a syringe

syrup *noun* **1** solution of sugar in water **2** thick sweet liquid > **syrupy** *adjective*

system *noun* **1** method or set of methods for doing something **2** set of interconnected pieces of equipment **3** *Biology* set of organs that together perform a function: *the immune system* **4** scheme of classification or arrangement

systematic *adjective* following a fixed plan and done in an efficient way > **systematically** *adverb*

tab *noun* small flap or projecting label

tabby tabbies *noun* cat with dark stripes on a lighter background

tabernacle *noun* **1** portable shrine of the Israelites **2** Christian place of worship not called a church **3** Jewish temple

table tables tabling tabled *noun* **1** piece of furniture with a flat top supported by legs **2** arrangement of information in columns ▷ *verb* **3** to submit (a motion) for discussion by a meeting

tablecloth *noun* a cloth used to cover a table

tablespoon *noun* large spoon for serving food

tablet *noun* **1** pill of compressed medicinal substance **2** inscribed slab of stone etc

table tennis *noun* game like tennis played on a table with small bats and a light ball

tabloid *noun* small-sized newspaper with many photographs and a concise, usually sensational style

taboo taboos *noun* **1** social custom that some words, subjects or actions must be avoided because embarrassing or offensive **2** religious custom that forbids people to do something ▷ *adjective* **3** forbidden by a taboo

tacit *adjective* implied but not spoken > **tacitly** *adverb*

taciturn *adjective* habitually not talking very much

tack *noun* **1** short nail with a large head **2** course of action: *in desperation I changed tack* ▷ *verb* **3** to fasten (something to a surface) with tacks **4** to stitch (a piece of fabric) with tacks

tackies or **takkies** *plural noun S Afr informal* tennis shoes or plimsolls

tackle tackles tackling tackled *verb* **1** to deal with (a task) **2** to confront (an opponent) **3** *Sport* to attempt to get the ball from (an opposing player) ▷ *noun* **4** *Sport* act of tackling an opposing player **5** equipment for fishing

tacky tackier tackiest *adjective* **1** slightly sticky **2** *informal* vulgar and tasteless

tact *noun* skill in avoiding giving offence; diplomacy > **tactful** *adjective* careful not to offend people > **tactfully** *adverb* > **tactless** *adjective* > **tactlessly** *adverb*

tactic *noun* **1** method or plan to achieve an end **2 tactics** art of directing military forces in battle > **tactical** *adjective* > **tactically** *adverb*

tactile *adjective* of or having the sense of touch

tadpole *noun* black long-tailed larva of a frog or toad

taffeta *noun* stiff shiny silk or rayon fabric

tag tags tagging tagged *noun* **1** small label made of cloth, paper or plastic **2** children's game where the person being chased becomes the chaser upon being touched ▷ *verb* **3** to attach a tag to > **tag along with** *verb* to accompany (someone), especially if uninvited

tail *noun* **1** part extending beyond the end of the body of an animal, bird, or fish **2** rear or last part or parts of something ▷ *verb* **3** *informal* to follow (someone) secretly > **tail off** *verb* to become gradually less > **tails** *plural noun* **1** *informal* man's coat with a long back split into two below the waist ▷ *adjective, adverb* **2** with the side of a coin uppermost that does not have a head on it

tailback *noun* Brit queue of traffic stretching back from an obstruction

tailor *noun* **1** person who makes men's clothes ▷ *verb* **2** to adapt (something) to suit a purpose

tailor-made *adjective* perfect for a purpose

taint *verb* **1** to spoil (something) with a small amount of decay, contamination or other bad quality ▷ *noun* **2** something that taints

taipan *noun* large poisonous Australian snake

take takes taking took taken *verb* **1** to remove (something) from a place **2** to accompany (someone) somewhere **3** to use (a mode of transport or a road) to go from one place to another **4** to steal **5** to swallow (medicine) **6** to bear (something painful): *We can't take much more of this* **7** to measure (someone's temperature or pulse) **8** to require (time, resources or ability) **9** to accept > **take after** *verb* to look or behave like (a parent etc) > **take down** *verb* to write down (what someone is saying) > **take in** *verb* **1** to understand **2** to deceive or swindle > **take**

off *verb* (of an aircraft) to leave the ground > **take over** *verb* to start controlling > **take to** *verb* to like (someone or something) immediately

takeaway takeaways *noun* shop or restaurant selling meals for eating elsewhere

takeoff *noun* **1** beginning of a flight, when the aircraft leaves the ground **2** humorous imitation of someone

takeover *noun* act of taking control of a company by buying a large number of its shares

takings *plural noun* money received by a shop, theatre or cinema, etc

talc *noun* talcum powder

talcum powder *noun* powder, usually scented, used to dry or perfume the body

tale *noun* story

talent *noun* natural ability; gift > **talented** *adjective*

talisman *noun* object believed to have magic power

talk *verb* **1** to express ideas or feelings by means of speech **2** to gossip **3** to make an informal speech about something ▷ *noun* **4** discussion or gossip **5** speech or lecture > **talkative** *adjective* fond of talking; chatty > **talk down to** *verb* to talk to (someone) as if you are more important or clever than him or her

tall *adjective* **1** higher than average **2** of a specified height: *a wall 2m tall*

tall order *noun* difficult task

tall story tall stories *noun* unlikely and probably untrue tale

tally tallies tallying tallied *verb* **1** (of numbers or statements) to be exactly the same or give the same results or conclusions ▷ *noun* **2** record of a debt or score

Talmud *noun* books containing the

ancient Jewish ceremonies and civil laws

talon *noun* bird's hooked claw

tambourine *noun* percussion instrument like a small drum with jingling metal discs attached

tame tamer tamest; tames taming tamed *adjective* **1** (of animals) brought under human control **2** (of animals) not afraid of people **3** uninteresting and unexciting ▷ *verb* **4** to make (a wild animal) tame

tamper *verb* (followed by *with*) to interfere with (something)

tampon *noun* firm piece of cotton wool inserted into the vagina to absorb the blood during menstruation

tan tans tanning tanned *noun* **1** brown coloration of the skin from exposure to sunlight ▷ *verb* **2** (of skin) to go brown from exposure to sunlight **3** to convert (an animal's hide) into leather ▷ *adjective* **4** yellowish-brown

tandem *noun* bicycle for two riders, one behind the other

tang *noun* strong sharp taste or smell > **tangy** *adjective* having a strong sharp taste or smell

tangata whenua *plural noun* NZ original Polynesian settlers in New Zealand and their descendants

tangent *noun* **1** line that touches a curve without intersecting it **2 go off at a tangent** to move to an unrelated and completely different line of thought or action

tangerine *noun* **1** small orange-like fruit of an Asian citrus tree **2** reddish orange ▷ *adjective* **3** reddish-orange

tangible *adjective* clear or definite enough to be easily seen or felt

tangle tangles tangling tangled *noun* **1** confused mass or situation ▷ *verb* **2** to catch or trap (someone) in wires or ropes so that it is difficult for them to get free

tango tangos *noun* South American dance

taniwha taniwha *noun* NZ mythical Maori monster that lives in water

tank *noun* **1** container for liquids or gases **2** armoured fighting vehicle moving on tracks

tankard *noun* large metal beer mug

tanker *noun* ship or truck for carrying liquid in bulk

tannin *noun* vegetable substance used in tanning

tantalizing or **tantalising** *adjective* excitingly and tormentingly desirable but difficult or impossible to get

tantamount *adjective* **tantamount to** equivalent in effect to

tantrum *noun* childish outburst of temper

Tanzanian *adjective* **1** of Tanzania ▷ *noun* **2** person from Tanzania

tap taps tapping tapped *verb* **1** to hit (something) lightly **2** to fit a device to (a telephone) in order to listen secretly to the calls ▷ *noun* **3** light knock **4** valve to control the flow of liquid from a pipe or cask

tap dancing *noun* style of dancing in which the dancers wear shoes with metal toe caps and heels that click against the floor

tape tapes taping taped *noun* **1** long thin strip of fabric used for binding or fastening **2** strip of sticky plastic used for sticking things together **3** (recording made on) a cassette containing magnetic tape ▷ *verb* **4** to record (sounds or television pictures) using a tape recorder or a video recorder **5** to attach (things) with sticky tape

tape measure *noun* tape marked off in centimetres or inches for measuring

taper *verb* **1** to become narrower towards one end ▷ *noun* **2** long thin candle

tape recorder *noun* device for recording and reproducing sound on magnetic tape

tapestry tapestries *noun* fabric decorated with coloured woven designs

tar *noun* thick, black, sticky substance used in making roads

tarantula *noun* large hairy spider with a poisonous bite

target *noun* **1** something you aim at when firing weapons **2** goal or objective **3** person or thing at which an action or remark is directed: *a target for our hatred*

tariff *noun* **1** tax that a government collects on imported goods **2** list of fixed prices

Tarmac® *noun* mixture of tar, bitumen and crushed stones used for roads etc

tarnish tarnishes tarnishing tarnished *verb* **1** to become stained or less bright **2** to damage or taint

tarot card *noun* card in a special pack used mainly in fortune-telling

tarpaulin *noun* sheet of heavy waterproof fabric

tarragon *noun* herb with narrow green leaves used in cooking

tarry tarries tarrying tarried *verb* *old-fashioned* **1** to linger or delay **2** to stay somewhere briefly

tar-seal *noun* NZ tarred road surface

tart *noun* **1** pie or flan with a sweet filling ▷ *adjective* **2** sour or sharp to taste **3** (of a remark) unpleasant and cruel

tartan *noun* **1** design of straight lines crossing at right angles, especially one associated with a Scottish clan **2** cloth with such a pattern

tartar *noun* hard deposit on the teeth

tarwhine *noun* edible Australian sea fish, especially a sea bream

task *noun* (difficult or unpleasant) piece of work to be done; duty

Tasmanian devil *noun* black-and-white marsupial of Tasmania that eats flesh

tassel *noun* decorative fringed knot of threads

taste tastes tasting tasted *noun* **1** sense by which the flavour of a substance is distinguished in the mouth **2** distinctive flavour **3** small amount tasted **4** brief experience of something **5** liking **6** ability to appreciate what is beautiful or excellent ▷ *verb* **7** to distinguish the taste of (a substance) **8** to take a small amount of (something) into the mouth **9** to have a specific taste: *it tastes like chocolate* > **tasteful** *adjective* having or showing good taste > **tastefully** *adverb* > **tasteless** *adjective* **1** vulgar and unattractive **2** (of a remark or joke) offensive **3** (of food) having very little flavour

taste bud *noun* small organ on the tongue which perceives flavours

tasty tastier tastiest *adjective* pleasantly flavoured

tatters *plural noun* **in tatters** badly torn > **tattered** *adjective* ragged or torn

tattoo tattoos tattooing tattooed *noun* **1** pattern made on the body by pricking the skin and staining it with indelible inks **2** military display or pageant ▷ *verb*

3 to make a pattern on the body of (someone) by pricking the skin and staining it with indelible inks

tatty tattier tattiest *adjective* shabby or worn out

taught *verb* past of **teach**

taunt *verb* **1** to tease (someone) with jeers ▷ *noun* **2** jeering remark

Taurus *noun* second sign of the zodiac, represented by a bull

taut *adjective* drawn tight

tautology *noun* use of words which merely repeat something already stated > **tautological** *adjective*

tavern *noun old-fashioned* pub

tawdry tawdrier tawdriest *adjective* cheap, showy and of poor quality

tawny *adjective* yellowish-brown

tax taxes taxing taxed *noun* **1** amount of money that people have to pay to the government so that it can provide public services ▷ *verb* **2** to levy a tax on (something) **3** to make heavy demands on > **taxation** *noun* levying of taxes

taxi taxis taxiing taxied *noun* **1** (also **taxicab**) car with a driver that may be hired to take people to any specified destination ▷ *verb* **2** (of an aircraft) to run along the ground before taking off or after landing

tea *noun* **1** drink made from infusing the dried leaves of an Asian bush in boiling water **2** cup of this drink **3** leaves used to make this drink **4** *Brit, Aust, NZ* main evening meal **5** *Chiefly Brit* light afternoon meal of tea, cakes, etc **6** drink like tea, made from other plants; infusion

tea bag *noun* small porous bag of tea leaves, placed in boiling water to make tea

teach teaches teaching taught *verb* **1** to tell or show (someone) how to do something **2** to give lessons in (a subject) **3** to cause (someone) to learn or understand > **teacher** *noun* person who teaches, especially in a school > **teaching** *noun*

teak *noun* very hard wood of a large Asian tree

team *noun* **1** group of people forming one side in a game **2** group of people or animals working together > **team up with** *verb* to join (someone) to work together

teamwork *noun* cooperative work by a team

teapot *noun* container with a lid, spout and handle for making and serving tea

tear tears tearing tore torn *noun* **1** (also **teardrop**) drop of fluid appearing in and falling from the eye **2** hole or split ▷ *verb* **3** to rip a hole in (something) **4** to rush somewhere > **tearful** *adjective* weeping or about to weep > **tearfully** *adverb*

tearaway tearaways *noun* wild or unruly person

tease teases teasing teased *verb* **1** to make fun of (someone) in a provoking or playful way ▷ *noun* **2** person who teases

teaspoon *noun* small spoon for stirring tea

teat *noun* **1** nipple of a breast or udder **2** rubber nipple of a feeding bottle

tea tree *noun* tree found in Australia and New Zealand with leaves containing tannin, like tea leaves

tech *noun informal* technical college

technical *adjective* **1** of or specializing in industrial, practical or mechanical arts and applied sciences **2** skilled in technical subjects **3** relating to a particular

field > **technically** *adverb*
according to a strict interpretation
of the rules: *technically illegal*

technical college *noun* college
with courses in subjects like
technology and secretarial skills

technicality technicalities
noun **1** petty point based on
a strict application of rules
2 technicalities detailed methods
used for a process or activity

technician *noun* person skilled in a
particular technical field

technique *noun* **1** method or skill
used for a particular task **2** skill and
ability developed through training
and practice

techno- *prefix meaning* craft or art:
technology

technology technologies
noun **1** application of practical or
mechanical sciences to industry
or commerce **2** area of activity
requiring scientific methods and
knowledge: *computer technology*
> **technological** *adjective*: *an
era of rapid technological change*
> **technologically** *adverb*

teddy teddies *noun* (also **teddy
bear**) soft toy bear

tedious *adjective* causing fatigue
or boredom

tedium *noun* quality of being boring
and lasting for a long time

tee tees teeing teed *noun* **1** small
peg from which a golf ball can be
played at the start of each hole
2 area of a golf course from which
the first stroke of a hole is made
> **tee off** *verb* to make the first
stroke of a hole in golf

teem *verb* **1** (followed by *with*) to
be full of (people or things) **2** to
rain heavily

teenager *noun* person aged
between 13 and 19 > **teenage**

adjective **1** aged between 13 and 19
2 typical of people aged between 13
and 19: *teenage fashion*

teens *plural noun* period of being
a teenager

tee-shirt *noun* same as **T-shirt**

teeter *verb* to wobble or move
unsteadily

teeth *noun* plural of **tooth**

teethe teethes teething teethed
verb (of a baby) to grow his or her
first teeth

teetotal *adjective* drinking no
alcohol > **teetotaller** *noun* person
who never drinks alcohol

tele- *prefix meaning* at or over a
distance: *telecommunications*

telecommunications *noun*
communications using telephone,
radio, television, etc

telegram *noun* formerly, a message
sent by telegraph

telegraph *noun* formerly, a system
for sending messages over a
distance along a cable

telepathy *noun* direct
communication between people's
minds > **telepathic** *adjective*

**telephone telephones
telephoning telephoned** *noun*
1 device for transmitting sound
over a distance along wires ▷ *verb*
2 to call (someone) by telephone

telephone box telephone boxes
noun small shelter in the street
containing a public telephone

telescope telescopes *noun* long
instrument shaped like a tube with
lenses that make distant objects
appear larger and nearer

Teletext® *noun* electronic
system that broadcasts pages of
information onto a television set

**televise televises televising
televised** *verb* to broadcast (an
event) on television

television *noun* **1** system of producing a moving image and accompanying sound on a distant screen **2** device for receiving broadcast signals and converting them into sound and pictures

tell tells telling told *verb* **1** to make (something) known to (someone) in words **2** to order or instruct (someone) to do something **3** to judge correctly (what is happening or what the situation is) **4** (of an unpleasant or tiring experience) to have a serious effect > **teller** *noun* bank cashier > **telling** *adjective* having a marked effect

telltale *noun* **1** person who reveals secrets ▷ *adjective* **2** revealing

telly tellies *noun informal* television

temerity *noun* boldness

temp *noun Brit informal* temporary employee, especially a secretary

temper *noun* **1** outburst of anger **2** calm mental condition: *I lost my temper* **3** frame of mind ▷ *verb* **4** to make (something) less extreme

temperament *noun* person's character or disposition

temperamental *adjective* having changeable moods

temperate *adjective* (of climate) not extreme

temperature *noun* **1** degree of heat or cold **2** *informal* abnormally high body temperature

tempest *noun literary* violent storm

tempestuous *adjective* violent or strongly emotional

template *noun* pattern used to cut out shapes accurately

temple *noun* **1** building for worship **2** region on either side of the forehead

tempo tempos or **tempi** *noun* **1** rate or pace **2** speed of a piece of music

temporary *adjective* lasting only for a short time > **temporarily** *adverb*

tempt *verb* **1** to entice (someone) to do something **2** **be tempted to do something** to want to do something you think might be wrong or harmful

temptation *noun* **1** state of being tempted **2** tempting thing

ten *adjective, noun* the number 10

tenacious *adjective* determined and not giving up easily > **tenaciously** *adverb* > **tenacity** *noun*

tenant *noun* person who rents land or a building > **tenancy** *noun*

tend *verb* **1** to be inclined (to do something) **2** to take care of (someone or something)

tendency tendencies *noun* inclination to act in a certain way

tender *adjective* **1** (of meat) easy to cut or chew **2** (of a person) gentle and affectionate **3** (of a body part) painful and sore **4** **at a tender age** young and inexperienced ▷ *verb* **5** to offer (an apology or your resignation) ▷ *noun* **6** *formal* offer to supply goods or services at a stated cost

tendon *noun* strong tissue attaching a muscle to a bone

tendril *noun* slender stem by which a climbing plant clings

tenement *noun* (especially in Scotland or the US) building divided into several flats

tenet *noun* doctrine or belief

tenner *noun Brit informal* ten-pound note

tennis *noun* game in which players use rackets to hit a ball back and forth over a net

tenor *noun* **1** singer with the second highest male voice **2** general meaning ▷ *adjective* **3** (of a voice or instrument) between alto and baritone

tense tenser tensest; tenses tensing tensed *adjective*
1 emotionally strained; anxious
2 (of a situation or period of time) causing nervousness and worry
3 stretched tight ▷ *verb* **4** to become tense ▷ *noun* **5** *Grammar* form of a verb showing the time of action

tension *noun* **1** emotional strain; anxiety **2** degree of stretching

tent *noun* portable canvas shelter

tentacle *noun* long thin parts of an animal such as an octopus that it uses to feel and hold things

tentative *adjective* cautious or hesitant > **tentatively** *adverb* cautiously or hesitantly

tenterhooks *plural noun* **on tenterhooks** in anxious suspense

tenth *adjective, pronoun* **1** (coming as) number 10 in a series ▷ *noun* **2** one of 10 equal parts

tenuous *adjective* slight or flimsy

tenure *noun* **1** legal right to live in a place or to use land or buildings for a period of time **2** period of the holding of an office or position

tepee *noun* cone-shaped tent, formerly used by Native Americans

tepid *adjective* slightly warm

term *noun* **1** word or expression
2 fixed period **3** period of the year when a school etc is open or a law court holds sessions **4** **terms** conditions of an agreement **5** type of language: *He spoke of her in glowing terms* **6** **come to terms with** to learn to accept (something difficult or unpleasant) ▷ *verb* **7** to give a name to or describe

terminal *adjective* **1** (of an illness) ending in death ▷ *noun* **2** place where people or vehicles begin or end a journey **3** point where current

enters or leaves an electrical device
4 keyboard and VDU having input and output links with a computer > **terminally** *adverb*: *terminally ill*

terminate terminates terminating terminated *verb* to come to an end or bring (something) to an end > **termination** *noun*

terminology terminologies *noun* set of technical terms relating to a subject

terminus terminuses *noun* railway or bus station at the end of a line

termite *noun* white antlike insect that destroys timber

tern *noun* gull-like sea bird with a forked tail and pointed wings

ternary *adjective* consisting of three parts

terrace *noun* **1** row of houses built as one block **2** paved area next to a building

terracotta *noun* brownish-red unglazed pottery

terrain *noun* area of ground, especially with reference to its physical character

terrapin *noun* small turtle-like reptile

terrestrial *adjective* of the earth or land

terrible *adjective* **1** very serious **2** *informal* very bad > **terribly** *adverb* very or very much: *terribly upset*

terrier *noun* a small short-bodied dog

terrific *adjective* **1** great or intense **2** *informal* excellent > **terrifically** *adverb*: *terrifically repressed*

terrify terrifies terrifying terrified *verb* to fill (someone) with fear

territory territories *noun* **1** area under the control of a particular government **2** area inhabited and defended by an animal > **territorial** *adjective* of the ownership of a particular area of land or water: *a territorial dispute*

terror *noun* **1** great fear **2** terrifying person or thing

terrorism *noun* use of violence and intimidation to achieve political ends > **terrorist** *noun, adjective*

terrorize terrorizes terrorizing terrorized; also spelt **terrorise** *verb* to force or oppress (someone) by fear or violence

terse terser tersest *adjective* (of a statement) short and rather unfriendly

tertiary *adjective* **1** third in degree, order, etc **2** (of education) at university or college level

test *verb* **1** to try out (something) to ascertain its worth, capability or endurance **2** to ask (someone) questions to find out how much he or she knows ▷ *noun* **3** deliberate action or experiment to find out whether something works or how well it works **4** set of questions or tasks given to someone to find out what he or she knows > **testing** *adjective* (of a situation or problem) very difficult to deal with

testament *noun Law* will

Testament *noun* one of the two main divisions of the Bible

test case *noun* lawsuit that establishes a precedent

testicle *noun* either of the two male reproductive glands

testify testifies testifying testified *verb* **1** to give evidence under oath **2** **testify to** to be evidence of

testimony testimonies *noun* formal statement, especially in a court of law > **testimonial** *noun* statement saying how good someone or something is

testis testes *noun* testicle

test match test matches *noun* one of a series of international cricket or rugby matches

testosterone *noun* male hormone that produces male characteristics

test tube *noun* narrow round-bottomed glass tube used in scientific experiments

tetanus *noun* painful infectious disease caused by germs getting into wounds

tether *noun* **1** rope or chain for tying an animal to a spot **2** **at the end of your tether** at the limit of your endurance ▷ *verb* **3** to tie (an animal) up with rope

Teutonic *adjective* of or like the (ancient) Germans

text *noun* **1** main written part of a book, rather than the pictures or index **2** any written material **3** novel or play studied for a course **4** text mesage ▷ *verb* **5** to send a text message to > **textual** *adjective*

textbook *noun* book about a particular subject for students to use

textile *noun* fabric or cloth, especially woven

text message *noun* written message sent using a mobile phone

texture *noun* structure, feel or consistency

Thai Thais *adjective* **1** of Thailand ▷ *noun* **2** person from Thailand **3** main language spoken in Thailand

than *conjunction, preposition* used to introduce the second element of a comparison

thank *verb* to express gratitude to

thankful *adjective* grateful > **thankfully** *adverb*: *Thankfully, she was not injured*

thankless *adjective* unrewarding or

unappreciated

thanks *plural noun* **1** words of gratitude **2 thanks to** because of: *We won, thanks to Ian* ▷ *interjection* **3** polite expression of gratitude

thanksgiving *noun* **1** act of thanking God, especially in prayer or in a religious ceremony **2 Thanksgiving** *US*, *Canada* public holiday in the autumn

thank you *interjection* polite expression of gratitude

that those *adjective, pronoun* **1** used to refer to someone or something already mentioned, familiar or at a distance ▷ *conjunction* **2** used to introduce a clause ▷ *pronoun* **3** used to introduce a relative clause

thatch thatches thatching thatched *noun* **1** roofing material of reeds or straw ▷ *verb* **2** to roof (a house) with reeds or straw

thaw *verb* **1** to make or become unfrozen **2** to become more relaxed or friendly ▷ *noun* **3** warmer weather causing snow or ice to melt

the *definite article* used before a noun referring to something known about, already mentioned or about which details are going to be given

theatre *noun* **1** place where plays etc are performed **2** hospital operating room **3** drama and acting in general

theatrical *adjective* **1** involving or performed in the theatre **2** exaggerated or affected > **theatrically** *adverb*

thee *pronoun old-fashioned* objective form of **thou**

theft *noun* act or an instance of stealing

their *adjective* of or associated with them > **theirs** *pronoun* (thing or person) belonging to them

┃ Be careful not to confuse *their*
┃ with *there*

them *pronoun* refers to people or things other than the speaker or those addressed

theme *noun* **1** main idea or subject being discussed **2** tune, especially one played at the beginning and end of a television or radio programme

themselves *pronoun* emphatic and reflexive form of **they** or **them**

then *adverb* **1** at that time **2** that being so

theology *noun* study of religion and religious beliefs > **theologian** *noun* > **theological** *adjective*

theoretical *adjective* **1** based on theory rather than practice or fact **2** not proved to exist or be true > **theoretically** *adverb* in theory

theory theories *noun* **1** set of ideas to explain something **2** idea or opinion **3 in theory** in an ideal or hypothetical situation

therapeutic *adjective* **1** causing you to feel happier and more relaxed **2** *Medicine* (of treatment) designed to treat a disease or improve a person's health

therapy therapies *noun* curing treatment > **therapist** *noun* person skilled in a particular type of therapy

there *adverb* **1** in or to that place ▷ *pronoun* **2** used to say that something exists or does not exist or to draw attention to something: *There are flowers on the table*

┃ Be careful not to confuse
┃ *there* with *their*. A good way to
┃ remember that *there* is connected
┃ to the idea of place is by
┃ remembering the spelling of two
┃ other place words, *here* and *where*

thereby *adverb formal* by that means

therefore *adverb* consequently, that being so

thermal *adjective* 1 of heat 2 (of clothing) retaining heat

thermometer *noun* instrument for measuring temperature

thermostat *noun* device for controlling temperature, *eg* on a central-heating system

thesaurus thesauruses *noun* reference book in which words with similar meanings are grouped together

these *adjective, pronoun* plural of **this**

thesis theses *noun* written work submitted for a university degree

they *pronoun refers to:* 1 people or things other than the speaker or people addressed 2 people in general 3 *informal* he or she

thick *adjective* 1 of great or specified extent from one side to the other 2 measuring a certain amount from one side to the other 3 having a dense consistency 4 *informal* stupid or insensitive

thicken *verb* to become thick or thicker

thicket *noun* dense growth of small trees

thickset *adjective* stocky in build

thief thieves *noun* person who steals

thieving *noun* act of stealing

thigh *noun* upper part of the human leg

thimble *noun* cap protecting the end of the finger when sewing

thin thinner thinnest; thins thinning thinned *adjective* 1 not thick 2 slim or lean 3 (of a liquid) containing a lot of water: *thin soup* ▷ *verb* 4 to make (something such as paint or soup) thinner by adding liquid

thing *noun* 1 an object rather than a plant, animal or human being 2 **things** possessions, clothes, etc

think thinks thinking thought *verb* 1 to consider, judge or believe (something) 2 to make use of the mind 3 to be considerate enough or remember (to do something)

third *adjective, noun* 1 (coming as) number three in a series ▷ *noun* 2 one of three equal parts

Third World *noun* developing countries of Africa, Asia and Latin America

thirst *noun* 1 desire to drink 2 craving or yearning > **thirstily** *adverb* > **thirsty** *adjective*: *Drink when you feel thirsty*

thirteen *adjective, noun* the number 13 > **thirteenth** *adjective, noun*

thirty thirties *adjective, noun* the number 30 > **thirtieth** *adjective, noun*

this *adjective, pronoun* 1 used to refer to a thing or person nearby, just mentioned or about to be mentioned ▷ *adjective* 2 used to refer to the present time: *this morning*

thistle *noun* prickly plant with purple flowers

thong *noun* 1 thin strip of leather etc 2 skimpy article of underwear or beachwear that covers the genitals while leaving the buttocks bare

thorn *noun* prickle on a plant > **thorny** *adjective* 1 covered with thorns 2 (of a subject or question) difficult to discuss or answer

thorough *adjective* 1 complete 2 (of a person) careful or methodical > **thoroughly** *adverb*: *I thoroughly enjoy your programme*

thoroughbred *noun* animal of pure breed

thoroughfare *noun* main road in a town

those *adjective, pronoun* plural of **that**

thou *pronoun old-fashioned* singular form of **you**

though *conjunction* **1** despite the fact that ▷ *adverb* **2** nevertheless

thought *verb* **1** past of **think** ▷ *noun* **2** thinking; reflection **3** concept or idea **4** ideas typical of a time or place > **thoughtful** *adjective* **1** kind and considerate **2** quiet and serious because thinking > **thoughtfully** *adverb* > **thoughtless** *adjective* inconsiderate > **thoughtlessly** *adverb*

thousand *adjective, noun* **1** the number 1000 ▷ *noun* **2** **thousands** large but unspecified number; lots > **thousandth** *adjective, noun*

thrash thrashes thrashing thrashed *verb* **1** to beat (someone), especially with a stick or whip **2** to defeat (someone) completely > **thrash out** *verb* to solve (a problem) by thorough argument

thread *noun* **1** fine strand or yarn **2** idea or theme connecting the different parts of an argument or story **3** spiral ridge on a screw, nut or bolt ▷ *verb* **4** to pass thread, tape or cord through (something) **5** to make (your way) somewhere

threadbare *adjective* (of clothing) old and thin

threat *noun* **1** declaration of intent to harm **2** dangerous person or thing **3** possibility of something unpleasant happening

threaten *verb* **1** to make or be a threat to (someone) **2** to be likely to harm (someone or something)

three *adjective, noun* the number 3

three-dimensional *adjective* having height or depth as well as length and width

threesome *noun* group of three

threshold *noun* **1** bar forming the bottom of a doorway **2** entrance **3** point at which something begins to take effect

threw *verb* past tense of **throw**

thrice *adverb old-fashioned* three times

thrift *noun* wisdom and caution with money > **thrifty** *adjective* inclined to save money and not waste things

thrill *noun* **1** sudden feeling of excitement **2** something causing a sudden feeling of excitement ▷ *verb* **3** to cause (someone) to feel a thrill **4** (followed by to) to feel a thrill because of (something) > **thrilled** *adjective* > **thrilling** *adjective*

thriller *noun* book, film, etc with an atmosphere of mystery or suspense

thrive thrives thriving thrived or **throve thrived** *verb* to be healthy, happy or successful > **thriving** *adjective*

throat *noun* **1** passage from the mouth and nose to the stomach and lungs **2** front of the neck

throb throbs throbbing throbbed *verb* **1** (of a body part) to produce a series of strong beats or dull pains **2** to vibrate with a loud rhythmic noise

throes *plural noun* **1** violent pangs or pains **2** **in the throes of** struggling to cope with (something)

thrombosis thromboses *noun* forming of a clot in a blood vessel or the heart

throne *noun* **1** ceremonial seat of a monarch or bishop **2** position of being king or queen

throng *noun* **1** large crowd ▷ *verb* **2** to go to (a place) in large numbers

**throttle throttles throttling
throttled** *noun* **1** device controlling
the amount of fuel entering
an engine ▷ *verb* **2** to strangle
(someone)

through *preposition* **1** from end to
end or side to side of **2** because of
3 during ▷ *adjective* **4** finished: *I'm
through with this*

throughout *preposition, adverb* in
every part (of)

throve *verb* a past tense of **thrive**

**throw throws throwing threw
thrown** *verb* **1** to hurl (something)
through the air **2** to move (yourself)
suddenly or with force **3** to bring
(someone) into a specified state,
especially suddenly: *It threw them
into a panic* **4 throw a tantrum**
to suddenly begin behaving in an
uncontrolled way **5 throw light
on** to make (something) have light
on it **6 throw yourself into** to
become enthusiastically involved
in (an activity)

throwback *noun* something
that has the characteristics of
something that existed a long time
ago: *a throwback to the fifties*

thrush thrushes *noun* **1** brown
songbird **2** fungal disease of the
mouth or vagina

**thrust thrusts thrusting
thrust** *verb* **1** to push (something)
somewhere forcefully **2** to make
(your way) somewhere by pushing
between people or things ▷ *noun*
3 sudden forceful movement **4** most
important part of an activity, idea
or argument

thud thuds thudding thudded
noun **1** dull heavy sound ▷ *verb* **2** to
make such a sound

thug *noun* violent man, especially
a criminal

thumb *noun* **1** short thick finger set
apart from the others ▷ *verb* **2** to
signal with the thumb for (a lift in
a vehicle)

thump *noun* **1** (sound of) a dull
heavy blow ▷ *verb* **2** to strike
(someone or something) heavily
3 to make a fairly loud, dull sound,
as of something falling **4** (of your
heart) to beat strongly and quickly

thunder *noun* **1** loud noise
accompanying lightning **2** any loud
rumbling noise ▷ *verb* **3** to rumble
with thunder **4** to make a loud
continuous noise

thunderbolt *noun* lightning flash

thunderous *adjective* very loud

Thursday Thursdays *noun* day
between Wednesday and Friday

thus *adverb formal* **1** therefore **2** in
this way

thwart *verb* to foil or frustrate
(someone or his or her plans)

thy *adjective old-fashioned* of or
associated with *thou*

thyme *noun* bushy herb with very
small leaves

thyroid *adjective, noun* (of) a gland
in the neck controlling body growth

tiara *noun* woman's semicircular
jewelled headdress

Tibetan *adjective* **1** of Tibet ▷ *noun*
2 person from Tibet

tic *noun* twitching of a group of
muscles, especially in the face

tick *noun* **1** mark (✓) used to check
off or indicate the correctness of
something **2** recurrent tapping
sound, as of a clock **3** tiny
bloodsucking parasitic animal
▷ *verb* **4** to mark (something) with a
tick **5** (of a clock) to make a ticking
sound > **ticking** *noun*: *the ticking of
the clock* > **tick off** *verb informal* to
reprimand (someone)

ticket *noun* card or paper entitling
the holder to admission, travel, etc

tickle tickles tickling tickled *verb*
1 to touch or stroke (someone) to
produce laughter **2** to please or
amuse (someone)

tidal *adjective* of or relating to tides

tidal wave *noun* very large
destructive wave

tide tides tiding tided *noun* **1** rise
and fall of the sea caused by the
gravitational pull of the sun and
moon **2** current caused by this
3 widespread feeling or tendency
> **tide over** *verb* to help (someone)
through a difficult period of time

tidings *plural noun formal* news

**tidy tidier tidiest; tidies tidying
tidied** *adjective* **1** neat and orderly
2 *Brit, Aust, NZ informal* (of a sum of
money) fairly large ▷ *verb* **3** to put (a
place) in order

tie ties tying tied *verb* **1** to fasten
(one thing to another) with string,
rope, etc **2** to make (a knot or bow)
in (something) **3** to link (one thing
with another) closely **4** (followed by
with) to score the same as (another
competitor) ▷ *noun* **5** long narrow
piece of material worn knotted
round the neck **6** connection or
feeling that links you with a person,
place or organization

tied up *adjective* busy

tier *noun* one of a set of layers or
rows that has other layers or rows
above or below it

tiff *noun* petty quarrel

tiger *noun* large orange-and-black
striped Asian cat

tiger snake *noun* fierce, very
poisonous Australian snake with
dark stripes across its back

tight *adjective* **1** stretched or drawn
taut **2** closely fitting **3** secure or
firm **4** (of a plan or arrangement)
allowing only the minimum time
or money needed to do something
▷ *adverb* **5** held firmly and securely:
He held me tight > **tightly** *adverb*
> **tightness** *noun*

tighten *verb* **1** to stretch or pull (a
rope or chain) until it is straight
2 to make (a rule or system) stricter
or more efficient **3** **tighten your
hold on** to hold (something)
more firmly

tightrope *noun* rope stretched taut
on which acrobats perform

tights *plural noun* one-piece
clinging garment covering the body
from the waist to the feet

tiki tiki or **tikis** *noun NZ* small
carving of an ancestor worn as a
pendant in some Maori cultures

tile tiles tiling tiled *noun* **1** flat
piece of ceramic, plastic, etc used to
cover a roof, floor or wall ▷ *verb* **2** to
cover (a surface) with tiles > **tiled**
adjective covered with tiles

till *conjunction, preposition* **1** until
▷ *verb* **2** to plough (ground) for
raising crops ▷ *noun* **3** drawer for
money, usually in a cash register

tiller *noun* lever to move a rudder
of a boat

tilt *verb* **1** to slant (something) at an
angle ▷ *noun* **2** slope

timber *noun* **1** wood as a building
material **2** wooden beam in
the frame of a house, boat, etc
> **timbered** *adjective*

time times timing timed *noun*
1 past, present and future as a
continuous whole **2** specific point
in time **3** unspecified interval
4 instance or occasion **5** period
with specific features ▷ *verb* **6** to
note the time taken by (an activity
or action) **7** to choose a time for
(something) > **timer** *noun* device
that measures time, especially one
that is part of a machine > **timing**
noun **1** skill in judging the right

moment to do something **2** when an event actually happens

timeless *adjective* not affected by the passing of time or by changes in fashion

timely *adjective* happening at the appropriate time

time-poor *adjective* having little free time

timescale *noun* length of time during which an event takes place

timetable *noun* plan showing the times when something takes place, the departure and arrival times of trains or buses, etc

timid *adjective* **1** easily frightened **2** shy, not bold > **timidity** *noun* > **timidly** *adverb*

timpani *plural noun* set of kettledrums

tin *noun* **1** soft metallic element **2** (airtight) metal container

tinder *noun* dry easily-burning material used to start a fire

tinge *noun* trace: *a tinge of envy* > **tinged** *adjective*: *Her homecoming was tinged with sadness*

tingle tingles tingling tingled *verb, noun* (to feel) a prickling or stinging sensation > **tingling** *noun* **1** prickling or stinging sensation ▷ *adjective* **2** prickling or stinging

tinker *noun* **1** travelling mender of pots and pans ▷ *verb* **2** (followed by *with*) to fiddle with (an engine etc) in an attempt to repair it

tinkle tinkles tinkling tinkled *verb* **1** to ring with a high tinny sound like a small bell ▷ *noun* **2** this sound or action

tinned *adjective* (of food) preserved by being sealed in a tin

tinsel *noun* long threads with strips of shiny paper attached, used as a decoration at Christmas

tint *noun* **1** small amount of a

particular colour **2** weak dye for the hair ▷ *verb* **3** to give a tint to > **tinted** *adjective*

tiny tinier tiniest *adjective* very small

tip tips tipping tipped *noun* **1** narrow or pointed end of anything **2** money given in return for service **3** useful piece of advice or information **4** rubbish dump ▷ *verb* **5** to tilt or overturn (something) **6** to pour (something) somewhere quickly or carelessly > **tipped** *adjective*: *tipped for success*

tipping point *noun* moment or event that marks a decisive change

tipple *noun* alcoholic drink that someone usually drinks

tipsy tipsier tipsiest *adjective* slightly drunk

tiptoe tiptoes tiptoeing tiptoed *verb* to walk quietly with the heels off the ground

tirade *noun* long angry speech

tire tires tiring tired *verb* **1** to reduce the energy of (someone), as by exertion; exhaust (someone) **2** (followed by *of*) to become weary or bored with > **tired** *adjective* exhausted > **tiredness** *noun* > **tiring** *adjective* causing tiredness

tireless *adjective* energetic and determined

tiresome *adjective* boring and irritating

tissue *noun* **1** substance of an animal body or plant **2** piece of thin soft paper used as a handkerchief etc

tit *noun* any of various small songbirds

titanic *adjective* huge or very important

titillate titillates titillating titillated *verb* to excite or stimulate (someone) pleasurably > **titillation** *noun* act of exciting or stimulating

title *noun* **1** name of a book, film, etc **2** name signifying rank or position **3** *Sport* championship ▷ **titled** *adjective* having a high social rank and a title such as *Lord*, *Lady* or *Sir*

titter *verb* to laugh in a nervous or embarrassed way

TNT *noun* trinitrotoluene, a powerful explosive

to *preposition* **1** indicating movement towards, equality or comparison, etc: *walking to school; forty miles to the gallon* **2** used to mark the indirect object or infinitive of a verb ▷ *adverb* **3** to a closed position: *pull the door to*

▌ The preposition *to* is spelt with one *o* and the adverb *too* has two

toad *noun* animal like a large frog

toadstool *noun* poisonous fungus like a mushroom

toast *noun* **1** sliced bread browned by heat **2 drink a toast to** to drink an alcoholic drink in honour of (someone) ▷ *verb* **3** to brown (bread) by heat **4** to warm (oneself) in front of a fire **5** to drink a toast to (someone) ▷ **toaster** *noun* electrical device for toasting bread

tobacco *noun* dried leaves of the tobacco plant, which people smoke in pipes, cigarettes and cigars

tobacconist *noun* person or shop selling tobacco, cigarettes, etc

toboggan *noun* narrow sledge for sliding over snow

today *noun* **1** this day **2** the present age ▷ *adverb* **3** on this day **4** nowadays

toddler *noun* young child beginning to walk ▷ **toddle** *verb* to walk with short unsteady steps

to-do to-dos *noun* Brit, Aust, NZ fuss or commotion

toe *noun* **1** movable part of your foot

resembling a finger **2** part of a shoe or sock covering your toes

toff *noun* Brit informal rich or aristocratic person

toffee *noun* chewy sweet made of boiled sugar

toga *noun* garment worn by citizens of ancient Rome

together *adverb* **1** with each other; jointly **2** at the same time **3** so as to be joined or fixed to each other: *She clasped her hands together* **4** very near to each other ▷ *adjective* **5** *informal* organized ▷ **togetherness** *noun* feeling of closeness and friendship

toil *noun* **1** hard work ▷ *verb* **2** to work hard

toilet *noun* (room with) a bowl connected to a drain for receiving and disposing of urine and faeces

toiletries *plural noun* cosmetics used for cleaning or grooming

token *noun* **1** sign or symbol: *as a token of goodwill* **2** voucher exchangeable for goods of a specified value **3** disc used as money in a slot machine ▷ *adjective* **4** not being treated as important: *a token contribution to your fees*

told *verb* past of **tell**

tolerable *adjective* **1** bearable **2** *informal* quite good

tolerance *noun* **1** acceptance of other people's rights to their own opinions or actions **2** ability to endure something ▷ **tolerant** *adjective*: *tolerant of different beliefs*

tolerate tolerates tolerating tolerated *verb* **1** to allow (something) to exist or happen **2** to endure (something) patiently ▷ **toleration** *noun* act of tolerating something

toll *verb* **1** to ring (a bell) slowly and regularly, especially to announce a death ▷ *noun* **2** charge for the use of a bridge or road **3** total loss or damage from a disaster

tom *noun* male cat

tomahawk *noun* fighting axe of the Native Americans

tomato tomatoes *noun* red fruit used in salads and as a vegetable

tomb *noun* large grave for one or more corpses

tomboy tomboys *noun* girl who acts or dresses like a boy

tome *noun* large heavy book

tomorrow *adverb, noun* **1** (on) the day after today **2** (in) the future

ton *noun* **1** unit of weight equal to 2240 pounds or 1016 kilograms (**long ton**) or, in the US, 2000 pounds or 907 kilograms (**short ton**) **2 tons** *informal* a lot

tone tones toning toned *noun* **1** sound with reference to its pitch, volume, etc **2** quality of a sound or colour **3** style of a piece of writing and the ideas or opinions expressed in it ▷ *verb* **4** to harmonize (with) **5** to give tone to > **tonal** *adjective* involving the quality or pitch of a sound or of music > **tone down** *verb* to make (something) more moderate

tone-deaf *adjective* unable to perceive subtle differences in pitch

tongs *plural noun* large pincers for grasping and lifting

tongue *noun* **1** muscular organ in the mouth, used in speaking and tasting **2** language **3** cooked tongue of an ox **4** flap of leather on a shoe

tonic *noun* **1** medicine that makes you feel stronger, healthier and less tired **2** anything that makes you feel stronger or more cheerful

tonic water *noun* mineral water containing quinine

tonight *adverb, noun* (in or during) the night or evening of this day

tonne *noun* unit of weight equal to 1000 kilograms

tonsil *noun* small gland in the throat

tonsillitis *noun* painful swelling of the tonsils caused by an infection

too *adverb* **1** also, as well **2** to excess

> The adverb *too* has two *o*s and the preposition *to* is spelt with one *o*

tool *noun* **1** implement used by hand **2** object, skill or idea needed for a particular purpose: *a bargaining tool*

toot *verb* (of a car horn) to make a short hooting sound

tooth teeth *noun* **1** bonelike projection in the jaws for biting and chewing **2** toothlike prong or point

toothpaste *noun* paste used to clean the teeth

top tops topping topped *noun* **1** highest point or part **2** lid or cap **3** highest rank **4** garment for the upper part of the body **5** toy that spins on a pointed base ▷ *adjective* **6** at or of the top ▷ *verb* **7** to be at the top of (a poll or chart) **8** to be greater than (a specified amount)

top hat *noun* man's tall cylindrical hat with a brim

topic *noun* subject of a conversation, book, etc > **topical** *adjective* relating to current events

topping *noun* sauce or garnish

topple topples toppling toppled *verb* to become unsteady and fall over

top-secret *adjective* meant to be kept completely secret

topsy-turvy *adjective* in confusion

Torah *noun* Jewish law and teaching

torch torches *noun* **1** small portable battery-powered lamp **2** long stick with burning material wrapped round one end

torment *verb* **1** to cause (someone)

great suffering ▷ *noun* **2** great suffering **3** source of suffering

torn *verb* past participle of **tear** ▷ *adjective* **2** unable to decide between two or more things

tornado tornadoes or **tornados** *noun* violent whirlwind

torpedo torpedoes torpedoing torpedoed *noun* **1** self-propelled underwater missile ▷ *verb* **2** to attack or destroy (a ship) with torpedoes

torrent *noun* **1** rushing stream **2** rapid flow of questions, abuse, etc

torrential *adjective* (of rain) very heavy

torrid *adjective* **1** very hot and dry **2** highly emotional

torso torsos *noun* trunk of the human body

tortoise *noun* slow-moving land reptile with a dome-shaped shell

tortuous *adjective* **1** winding or twisting **2** not straightforward

torture tortures torturing tortured *verb* **1** to cause (someone) severe pain or mental anguish ▷ *noun* **2** severe physical or mental pain **3** torturing > **torturer** *noun*

Tory Tories *noun* member of the Conservative Party in Great Britain or Canada

toss tosses tossing tossed *verb* **1** to throw (something) lightly **2** to throw up (a coin) to decide between alternatives by guessing which side will land uppermost **3** to move (your head) suddenly backwards, esp, when angry **4** to move repeatedly from side to side

tot tots totting totted *noun* **1** small child **2** small amount of strong alcohol such as whisky ▷ *verb* **3** **tot up** to add (numbers) together

total totals totalling totalled *noun* **1** whole, especially a sum of parts ▷ *adjective* **2** complete **3** of or being a total ▷ *verb* **4** to amount to (a certain figure) **5** to add together (a set of numbers or objects) > **totally** *adverb*

totalitarian *adjective* of a dictatorial one-party government > **totalitarianism** *noun* principles of a totalitarian system

tote totes toting toted *verb* to carry (a gun)

totem pole *noun* post carved or painted with symbols and pictures by Native Americans

totter *verb* to move unsteadily

toucan *noun* tropical American bird with a large bill

touch touches touching touched *verb* **1** to come into contact with **2** to tap, feel or stroke **3** to move (someone) emotionally ▷ *noun* **4** sense by which an object's qualities are perceived when they come into contact with part of the body **5** gentle tap, push or caress **6** small amount: *a touch of mustard* **7** detail: *finishing touches* **8** **touch and go** risky or critical

touchdown *noun* landing of an aircraft

touching *adjective* emotionally moving

touchy touchier touchiest *adjective* easily offended

tough *adjective* **1** (of a person) strong and independent and able to put up with hardship **2** (of a substance) difficult to break **3** (of a task, problem or way of life) difficult or full of hardship **4** (of policies or actions) strict and firm > **toughen** *verb* to become stronger or make (something) stronger > **toughness** *noun*

toupee *noun* small wig worn to

cover a bald patch

tour *noun* **1** long journey during which you visit several places **2** short trip round a place such as a city or famous building ▷ *verb* **3** to make a tour of (a place)

tourism *noun* tourist travel as an industry

tourist *noun* person travelling for pleasure

tournament *noun* sporting competition with several stages to decide the overall winner

tourniquet *noun* strip of cloth tied tightly round a limb to stop bleeding

tousled *adjective* (of hair) ruffled and untidy

tout *verb* **1** to seek business in a persistent manner **2** to try to sell (something) ▷ *noun* **3** person who sells tickets for a popular event at inflated prices

tow *verb* **1** (of a vehicle) to drag (another vehicle), especially by means of a rope ▷ *noun* **2** towing **3** **in tow** following closely behind

towards or **toward** *preposition* **1** in the direction of **2** with regard to **3** as a contribution to **4** near to

towel *noun* piece of thick soft cloth for drying yourself

towelling *noun* material used for making towels

tower *noun* tall structure, often forming part of a larger building > **towering** *adjective*: *towering cliffs* > **tower over** *verb* to be much taller than

town *noun* **1** group of buildings larger than a village **2** central part of this

town hall *noun* large building used for council meetings, concerts, etc

township *noun* S Afr urban settlement formerly for Black or Coloured people only

towpath *noun* path beside a canal or river

toxic *adjective* poisonous

toxin *noun* poison of bacterial origin

toy toys toying toyed *noun* something designed to be played with > **toy with** *verb* **1** to consider (an idea) without being very serious about it **2** to play or fiddle with (an object)

toyi-toyi or **toy-toy** *noun* S Afr dance of political protest

trace traces tracing traced *verb* **1** to track down and find **2** to follow the course of **3** to copy (a drawing or a map) exactly by drawing on a thin sheet of transparent paper set on top of the original ▷ *noun* **4** track left by someone or something **5** very small amount

track *noun* **1** rough road or path **2** mark or trail left by the passage of anything **3** railway line **4** course for racing **5** separate section on a record, tape or CD ▷ *verb* **6** to follow the trail or path of (animals or people) > **track down** *verb* to hunt for and find

track event *noun* athletic sport held on a running track

track record *noun* past accomplishments of a person or organization

tracksuit *noun* warm loose-fitting suit worn by athletes etc, especially during training

tract *noun* **1** wide area **2** pamphlet, especially a religious one **3** *Anatomy* system of organs with a particular function: *the digestive tract*

traction *noun* *Medicine* application of a steady pull on an injured limb by weights and pulleys

tractor *noun* motor vehicle with large rear wheels for pulling farm machinery

trade trades trading traded
noun **1** buying, selling or exchange
of goods **2** person's job or craft
▷ verb **3** to buy and sell (goods) **4** to
exchange (things) > **trader** noun
person who trades in goods

trademark noun (legally
registered) name or symbol used by
a firm to distinguish its goods (®)

tradesman tradesmen noun
1 skilled worker **2** shopkeeper

trade union noun society of
workers formed to protect their
interests

tradition noun custom or practice
of long standing; convention
> **traditional** adjective **1** (of
customs or beliefs) having existed
for a long time without changing
2 (of an organization or institution)
using older methods rather than
modern ones > **traditionalist**
noun person who supports the
established customs and beliefs of
his or her society > **traditionally**
adverb

traffic traffics trafficking
trafficked noun **1** vehicles coming
and going on a road **2** illegal trade
in something such as drugs ▷ verb
3 (followed by in) to buy and sell
(drugs or other goods) illegally

traffic lights plural noun set of
coloured lights at a junction to
control the traffic flow

traffic warden noun Brit person
employed to control the movement
and parking of traffic

tragedy tragedies noun **1** shocking
or sad event **2** serious play, film,
etc in which the hero is destroyed
by a personal failing in adverse
circumstances

tragic adjective **1** very sad, often
involving death, suffering or

disaster **2** (of a film, play or book)
sad and serious > **tragically** adverb

trail noun **1** path, track or road
2 tracks left by a person, animal or
object ▷ verb **3** to drag (something)
along the ground **4** to hang down
loosely **5** to move slowly, without
energy or enthusiasm > **trail
off** verb (of a voice) to gradually
become more hesitant until it stops
completely

trailer noun **1** vehicle designed to be
towed by another vehicle **2** extract
from a film or programme used to
advertise it

train verb **1** to instruct in a skill
2 to learn the skills needed to do
a particular job or activity **3** to
prepare for a sports event etc **4** to
aim (a gun etc) **5** to cause (an
animal) to perform or (a plant) to
grow in a particular way ▷ noun
6 line of railway coaches or wagons
drawn by an engine **7** sequence
or series **8** long trailing back
section of a dress **9** line or group of
vehicles or people following behind
something or someone

trainee noun person being trained

trainers plural noun sports shoes

training noun process of training

trait noun characteristic feature

traitor noun person who betrays his
or her country or group

trajectory trajectories noun
curving path followed by an object
moving through the air

tram noun public transport vehicle
powered by an overhead wire and
running on rails laid in the road

tramp verb **1** to walk heavily ▷ noun
2 homeless person who travels on
foot **3** long country walk

trample tramples trampling
trampled verb (followed by on)
1 to tread heavily on and damage

2 to show no consideration for (someone or his or her rights or feelings)

trampoline *noun* tough canvas sheet attached to a frame by springs, used by acrobats, etc

trance *noun* unconscious or dazed state

tranquil *adjective* calm and quiet > **tranquillity** *noun: a haven of peace and tranquillity*

tranquillizer or **tranquilliser** *noun* drug that reduces anxiety or tension

trans- *prefix meaning* across, through or beyond

transaction *noun* business deal that involves buying and selling something

transcend *verb* to go beyond or be superior to (something)

transcribe transcribes transcribing transcribed *verb* to write down (something said)

transcript *noun* written copy of something spoken

transfer transfers transferring transferred *verb* **1** to move (something) from one place to another **2** to move (someone) to a different place or job within the same organization ▷ *noun* **3** movement of something from one place to another **4** design that can be transferred from one surface to another > **transferable** *adjective*

transfixed *adjective* so impressed or frightened by something that you cannot move

transform *verb* to change the shape or character of > **transformation** *noun*

transfusion *noun* injection of blood into the blood vessels of a patient

transient *adjective* lasting only for a short time > **transience** *noun: the transience of the club scene*

transistor *noun* **1** semiconducting device used to amplify electric currents **2** small portable radio using transistors

transit *noun* **1** carrying of goods or people by vehicle from one place to another **2 in transit** travelling or being taken from one place to another: *damaged in transit*

transition *noun* change from one state to another > **transitional** *adjective* (of a period or stage) during which something changes from one form or state to another

transitive *adjective* Grammar (of a verb) requiring a direct object

transitory *adjective* not lasting long

translate translates translating translated *verb* to turn (something) from one language into another > **translation** *noun: an English translation of Faust* > **translator** *noun*

translucent *adjective* letting light pass through, but not transparent

transmission *noun* **1** passing or sending of something to a different place or person **2** broadcasting of television or radio programmes **3** broadcast

transmit transmits transmitting transmitted *verb* **1** to pass (something) from one person or place to another **2** to send out (signals) by radio waves **3** to broadcast (a radio or television programme) > **transmitter** *noun* piece of equipment used to broadcast radio or television programmes

transparency transparencies *noun* **1** transparent quality **2** colour photograph on transparent film that can be viewed by means of a projector

transparent *adjective* **1** able to be seen through, clear **2** easily understood or recognized
> **transparently** *adverb* in a transparent manner

transpire transpires transpiring transpired *verb* **1** *formal* to become known **2** *informal* to happen

> Some people think that it is wrong to use *transpire* to mean 'happen'

transplant *verb* **1** to transfer (an organ or tissue) surgically from one part or body to another **2** to remove and transfer (a plant) to another place ▷ *noun* **3** surgical transplanting **4** thing transplanted

transport *verb* **1** to convey (goods or people) from one place to another **2** to enrapture ▷ *noun* **3** business or system of transporting **4** vehicles used in transport > **transportation** *noun* transporting of people and things from one place to another

transvestite *noun* person who enjoys wearing clothes normally worn by people of the opposite sex

trap traps trapping trapped *noun* **1** device for catching animals **2** plan for tricking or catching someone ▷ *verb* **3** to catch (animals) in a trap **4** to trick (someone) into something > **trapper** *noun* person who traps animals for their fur

trapdoor *noun* door in floor or roof

trapeze *noun* horizontal bar suspended from two ropes, used by circus acrobats

trapezium trapeziums or **trapezia** *noun* four-sided shape with two parallel sides of unequal length

trappings *plural noun* accessories that symbolize an office or position

trash *noun* **1** anything worthless **2** *US, S Afr* rubbish

trauma *noun* emotional shock

traumatic *adjective* very upsetting

travel travels travelling travelled *verb* **1** to go from one place to another, through an area or for a specified distance ▷ *noun* **2** travelling, especially as a tourist
> **traveller** *noun*: *air travellers*
> **travelling** *adjective*: *travelling entertainers* > **travels** *plural noun* journeys to distant places

traveller's cheque *noun* cheque bought at home and then exchanged abroad for foreign currency

traverse traverses traversing traversed *verb* to move over or back and forth over (an area)

travesty travesties *noun* grotesque imitation or mockery

trawl *noun* **1** net dragged at deep levels behind a fishing boat ▷ *verb* **2** to fish with such a net

trawler *noun* trawling boat

tray trays *noun* flat board, usually with a rim, for carrying food or drinks

treachery *noun* wilful betrayal
> **treacherous** *adjective* **1** disloyal or untrustworthy **2** unreliable or dangerous > **treacherously** *adverb*

treacle *noun* thick dark syrup produced when sugar is refined

tread treads treading trod trodden *verb* **1** to set your foot (on something) **2** to crush (something) by walking on it ▷ *noun* **3** way of walking or dancing **4** part of a tyre or shoe that touches the ground

treadmill *noun* **1** cylinder turned by treading on steps projecting from it **2** dreary routine

treason *noun* **1** betrayal of one's sovereign or country **2** treachery

treasure treasures treasuring treasured noun 1 collection of wealth, especially gold or jewels 2 valued person or thing ▷ verb 3 to prize or cherish (something) > **treasured** adjective

treasurer noun official in charge of funds

Treasury noun government department in charge of finance

treat verb 1 to deal with or regard (someone or something) in a certain manner 2 to give medical treatment to (a patient or an illness) 3 to subject (something such as wood or fabric) to a chemical or industrial process 4 to provide (someone) with something as a treat ▷ noun 5 pleasure, entertainment, etc given or paid for by someone else > **treatment** noun 1 medical care 2 way of treating a person or thing

treatise noun formal piece of writing on a particular subject

treaty treaties noun signed contract between states

treble trebles trebling trebled adjective 1 triple ▷ noun 2 (singer with or part for) a soprano voice ▷ verb 3 to increase (something) three times

tree noun large perennial plant with a woody trunk

trek treks trekking trekked noun 1 long difficult journey, especially on foot ▷ verb 2 to make such a journey

trellis trellises noun frame which supports climbing plants

tremble trembles trembling trembled verb 1 to shake or quiver 2 to feel fear or anxiety ▷ noun 3 trembling > **trembling** adjective

tremendous adjective 1 huge 2 informal great in quality or amount > **tremendously** adverb

tremor noun 1 involuntary shaking 2 unsteady quality in the voice, eg when upset 3 minor earthquake

trench trenches noun long narrow ditch, especially one used as a shelter in war

trenchant adjective (of writing or comments) bold and firmly expressed

trend noun general tendency or direction

trendy trendier trendiest adjective informal consciously fashionable

trepidation noun fear or anxiety

trespass trespasses trespassing trespassed verb to go onto another's property without permission > **trespasser** noun

tresses plural noun long flowing hair

trestle noun board fixed on pairs of spreading legs, used as a support

trevally trevallies noun Aust, NZ any of various food and game fishes

tri- prefix meaning three

triad noun 1 group of three 2 chord of three notes consisting of the tonic and the third and fifth above it

trial noun 1 Law investigation of a case before a judge 2 trying or testing

triangle noun 1 geometric figure with three sides 2 triangular percussion instrument > **triangular** adjective having three sides

triathlon noun sports contest in which athletes compete in three different events

tribe noun group of clans or families believed to have a common ancestor > **tribal** adjective of tribes

tribulation noun great distress

tribunal noun board appointed to inquire into a specific matter

tributary tributaries noun stream

or river flowing into a larger one

tribute *noun* **1** sign of respect or admiration **2 a tribute to** positive result of (something): *His success is a tribute to his hard work*

trice *noun* **in a trice** instantly

triceps *noun* muscle at the back of the upper arm

▮ The plural of *triceps* is *triceps*

trick *noun* **1** deceitful or cunning action or plan **2** feat of skill or cunning done in order to entertain ▷ *verb* **3** to cheat or deceive

trickery *noun* deception

trickle trickles trickling trickled *verb* **1** to flow in a thin stream or drops **2** to move gradually ▷ *noun* **3** thin stream of liquid **4** small number or quantity of things or people

tricky trickier trickiest *adjective* difficult to do or deal with

tricycle *noun* three-wheeled cycle

trifle trifles trifling trifled *noun* **1** something that is not very important or valuable **2** dessert of sponge cake, fruit, custard and cream **3 a trifle** a little > **trifle with** *verb* to toy with

trifling *adjective* insignificant

trigger *noun* **1** small lever releasing a catch on a gun or machine **2** action that sets off a course of events ▷ *verb* **3** (usually followed by *off*) to set (an action or process) in motion

trigonometry *noun* branch of mathematics dealing with relations of the sides and angles of triangles

trill *noun* **1** shrill warbling sound made by some birds ▷ *verb* **2** (of a bird) to sing with short high-pitched repeated notes

trillion *noun* **1** one million million; 1,000,000,000,000 **2** formerly, one million million million, 10^{18}

3 trillions large but unspecified number; lots

trilogy trilogies *noun* series of three related books, plays, etc

trim trimmer trimmest; trims trimming trimmed *adjective* **1** neat and smart ▷ *verb* **2** to cut or prune (something) into good shape ▷ *noun* **3** decoration **4** haircut that neatens the existing style > **trimmed** *adjective*: *trimmed with flowers*

trimmings *plural noun* extra parts added to something for decoration

Trimurti *noun Hinduism* three deities Brahma, Vishnu and Siva

Trinity *noun Christianity* union of God the Father, God the Son and God the Holy Spirit in one God

trinket *noun* small or worthless ornament or piece of jewellery

trio trios *noun* **1** group of three musicians who sing or play together **2** piece of music for three performers **3** any group of three

trip trips tripping tripped *noun* **1** journey to a place and back, especially for pleasure ▷ *verb* **2** to stumble or cause (someone) to stumble

tripe *noun* stomach of a cow used as food

triple triples tripling tripled *adjective* **1** having three parts ▷ *verb* **2** to increase (something) three times

triplet *noun* one of three babies born at one birth

tripod *noun* three-legged stand, stool, etc

tripper *noun* tourist

trite triter tritest *adjective* (of a remark or idea) commonplace and unoriginal

triumph *noun* **1** (happiness caused by) victory or success ▷ *verb* **2** to be victorious or successful

triumphal *adjective* celebrating a triumph

triumphant *adjective* feeling or showing triumph

trivia *plural noun* unimportant things

trivial *adjective* to make (something) seem less important or complex than it is

troll *noun* giant or dwarf in Scandinavian folklore

trolley trolleys *noun* **1** small wheeled table for food and drink **2** wheeled cart for moving goods

trombone *noun* brass musical instrument with a sliding tube

troop *noun* **1** large group **2 troops** soldiers ▷ *verb* **3** to move in a crowd

trooper *noun* low-ranking cavalry soldier

trophy trophies *noun* **1** cup, shield, etc given as a prize **2** memento of success

tropic *noun* **1** either of two lines of latitude at 23½°N (**tropic of Cancer**) or 23½°S (**tropic of Capricorn**) **2 the tropics** part of the earth's surface between these lines

tropical *adjective* of or in the tropics

trot trots trotting trotted *verb* **1** (of a horse) to move at a medium pace, lifting the feet in diagonal pairs **2** (of a person) to move at a steady brisk pace ▷ *noun* **3** trotting

trotter *noun* pig's foot

trouble troubles troubling troubled *noun* **1** (cause of) distress or anxiety **2** care or effort **3 in trouble** likely to be punished for doing something wrong ▷ *verb* **4** to cause (someone) to worry **5** to cause inconvenience to or bother > **troubled** *adjective* > **troubling** *adjective* worrying

troublesome *adjective* causing

problems or difficulties

trough *noun* long open container, especially for animals' food or water

trounce trounces trouncing trounced *verb* to defeat (someone) utterly

troupe *noun* group of performers who work together and often travel around together

trousers *plural noun* two-legged outer garment with legs reaching usually to the ankles

trout *noun* game fish related to the salmon
 The plural of *trout* is *trout*

trowel *noun* hand tool with a wide blade for spreading mortar, lifting plants, etc

troy weight or **troy** *noun* system of weights used for gold, silver and jewels

truant *noun* **1** pupil who stays away from school without permission **2 play truant** to stay away from school without permission > **truancy** *noun* staying away from school without permission

truce *noun* temporary agreement to stop fighting

truck *noun* **1** railway goods wagon **2** large vehicle for transporting loads by road > **trucker** *noun* truck driver

truculent *adjective* aggressively defiant > **truculence** *noun* aggressive defiance

trudge trudges trudging trudged *verb* **1** to walk heavily or wearily ▷ *noun* **2** long tiring walk

true truer truest *adjective* **1** in accordance with facts; accurate **2** genuine **3 come true** to actually happen > **truly** *adverb* very

truffle *noun* **1** edible underground fungus **2** sweet flavoured with chocolate

trump *noun* **1** card of the suit outranking the others **2 trumps** suit outranking the others

trumpet *noun* **1** valved brass instrument with a flared tube ▷ *verb* **2** (of an elephant) to cry loudly

truncated *adjective* made shorter

truncheon *noun* club carried by a policeman

trundle trundles trundling trundled *verb* to move (something) heavily on wheels

trunk *noun* **1** main stem of a tree **2** large case or box for clothes etc **3** person's body excluding the head and limbs **4** elephant's long nose

trunks *plural noun* man's swimming shorts

truss trusses trussing trussed *verb* **1** to tie (someone) up ▷ *noun* **2** supporting belt with a pad for holding a hernia in place

trust *verb* **1** to believe in and rely on **2** to consign (something) to someone's care **3** to believe that (someone) will do something successfully or properly ▷ *noun* **4** confidence in the truth, reliability, etc of a person or thing **5** obligation arising from responsibility **6** arrangement in which one person administers property, money, etc on another's behalf **> trusting** *adjective*

trustee trustees *noun* person holding property on another's behalf

trustworthy *adjective* reliable or honest

trusty trustier trustiest *adjective* faithful or reliable

truth *noun* **1** state of being true; reality **2** something true

truthful *adjective* honest **> truthfully** *adverb*

try tries trying tried *verb* **1** to make an effort or attempt (to do something) **2** to test or sample (something) **3** to subject (a person) to a legal process involving the hearing of evidence to decide whether or not they are guilty of a crime ▷ *noun* **4** attempt or effort **5** test of something: *You gave it a try* **6** *Rugby* score gained by touching the ball down over the opponent's goal line

> You can use *try to* in speech and writing: *Try to get here on time for once.* *Try and* is very common in speech, but you should avoid it in written work: *Just try and stop me!*

trying *adjective informal* difficult or annoying

tryst *noun* arrangement to meet

tsar or **czar** *noun History* Russian emperor **> tsarina** or **czarina** *noun History* female tsar or the wife of a tsar

tsetse fly tsetse flies *noun* bloodsucking African fly whose bite transmits disease, especially sleeping sickness

T-shirt *noun* simple short-sleeved cotton shirt with no collar

tuatara *noun* large lizard-like New Zealand reptile

tub *noun* open, usually round container

tuba *noun* valved low-pitched brass instrument

tubby tubbier tubbiest *adjective* (of a person) short and fat

tube *noun* **1** hollow cylinder **2** flexible cylinder with a cap to hold pastes **> tubing** *noun* **1** length of tube **2** system of tubes

tuberculosis *noun* serious infectious disease affecting the lungs

tubular *adjective* of or shaped like a tube

TUC *abbreviation* (in Britain and S Africa) Trades Union Congress

tuck *verb* **1** to push or fold (something) into a small space **2** to push the loose ends of (a piece of fabric) inside or under something to make it tidy ▷ *noun* **3** stitched fold > **tuck away** *verb* **1** to eat (a large amount of food) **2** to locate (something) in a quiet place where few people go

tucker *noun Aust, NZ informal* food

tuckered out *adjective Aust, NZ* exhausted

Tudor *noun* family name of the English monarchs who reigned from 1485 to 1603

Tuesday Tuesdays *noun* day between Monday and Wednesday

tuft *noun* bunch of feathers, grass, hair, etc held or growing together at the base

tug tugs tugging tugged *verb* **1** to pull (something) hard ▷ *noun* **2** hard pull **3** (also **tugboat**) small ship used to tow other vessels

tug of war *noun* contest in which two teams pull against one another on a rope

tuition *noun* instruction, especially received individually or in a small group

tulip *noun* brightly coloured spring flower

tumble tumbles tumbling tumbled *verb* **1** to fall, especially awkwardly or violently ▷ *noun* **2** fall

tumbler *noun* stemless drinking glass

tummy tummies *noun informal* stomach

tumour *noun* abnormal growth in or on the body

tumultuous *adjective* (of an event or welcome) very noisy and excited

tuna *noun* large marine food fish

▰ The plural of *tuna* is *tuna*

tundra *noun* vast treeless Arctic region

tune tunes tuning tuned *noun* **1** (pleasing) sequence of musical notes **2** correct musical pitch: *She sang out of tune* ▷ *verb* **3** to adjust (a musical instrument) so that it is in tune **4** to adjust (a machine) to obtain the desired performance **5** (followed by *to*) to turn or press the controls of a radio or television set to select (a particular station)

tuneful *adjective* having a pleasant and easily remembered tune

tuner *noun* person who tunes pianos

tunic *noun* piece of clothing, often sleeveless and rather shapeless, covering the top part of the body and reaching to the hips, thighs or knees

Tunisian *adjective* **1** of Tunisia ▷ *noun* **2** person from Tunisia

tunnel tunnels tunnelling tunnelled *noun* **1** underground passage ▷ *verb* **2** to make a tunnel

turban *noun* Muslim, Hindu or Sikh man's head covering, made by winding cloth round the head

turbine *noun* machine or generator driven by gas, water, etc turning blades

turbot *noun* large European flat fish that is caught for food

▰ The plural of *turbot* is *turbot*

turbulence *noun* **1** confusion, movement or agitation **2** atmospheric instability causing gusty air currents > **turbulent** *adjective* **1** (of a period of history) involving much uncertainty and possibly violent change **2** (of air or water currents) making sudden changes of direction

tureen *noun* serving dish for soup

turf turves; turfs turfing turfed *noun* 1 short thick even grass > **turf out** *verb informal* to throw (someone) out

turgid *adjective* (of language) pompous

Turk *noun* person from Turkey

turkey turkeys *noun* 1 large bird bred for food 2 meat of this bird

Turkish *adjective* 1 of Turkey ▷ *noun* 2 Turkish language

turmoil *noun* agitation or confusion

turn *verb* 1 to change position or direction 2 to change the position or direction of (something) 3 to move or cause (something) to move round an axis; rotate 4 to direct (your attention or thoughts) to someone or something 5 (usually followed by *into*) to change (something) into (something else) ▷ *noun* 6 turning 7 opportunity to do something as part of an agreed succession 8 change in the way something is happening or being done: *a turn for the worse* 9 **in turn** in sequence one after the other > **turn down** *verb* 1 to reduce the volume or brightness of (a radio or heater) 2 to refuse or reject (a request or an offer) > **turn up** *verb* 1 to arrive or appear 2 to be found 3 to increase the volume or brightness of (a radio or heater)

turncoat *noun* person who deserts one party or cause to join another

turning *noun* road or path leading off a main route

turning point *noun* moment when a decisive change occurs

turnip *noun* root vegetable with orange or white flesh

turnout *noun* number of people appearing at a gathering

turnover *noun* 1 total sales made by a business over a certain period 2 rate at which staff leave and are replaced

turnstile *noun* revolving gate for admitting one person at a time

turpentine *noun* strong-smelling colourless liquid used for cleaning and for thinning paint

turps *noun* turpentine oil

turquoise *adjective* 1 blue-green ▷ *noun* 2 blue-green precious stone

turret *noun* small tower

turtle *noun* sea tortoise

tusk *noun* long pointed tooth of an elephant, walrus, etc

tussle *noun* fight or scuffle

tutor *noun* 1 person teaching individuals or small groups ▷ *verb* 2 to act as a tutor to (someone)

tutorial *noun* period of instruction with a tutor

tutu tutus *noun* short stiff skirt worn by ballerinas

TV TVs *abbreviation* television

twang *noun* 1 sharp ringing sound 2 nasal speech ▷ *verb* 3 to make a twang or cause (something) to make a twang

tweak *verb* 1 to pinch or twist (something) sharply ▷ *noun* 2 tweaking

twee *adjective informal* too sentimental, sweet or pretty

tweed *noun* thick woollen cloth

tweet *noun, verb* (to) chirp

tweezers *plural noun* small pincer-like tool for pulling out hairs or picking up small objects

twelve *adjective, noun* the number 12 > **twelfth** *adjective, noun*

twenty twenties *adjective, noun* the number 20 > **twentieth** *adjective, noun*

twice *adverb* two times

twiddle twiddles twiddling

twiddled *verb* to fiddle or twirl (something) in an idle way

twig *noun* small branch or shoot

twilight *noun* **1** soft dim light just after sunset **2** final stages of something: *the twilight of his career*

twin *noun* **1** one of a pair, especially of two children born at one birth ▷ *adjective* **2** denoting one of two similar things that are close together or happen together

twine twines twining twined *noun* **1** string or cord ▷ *verb* **2** to twist or coil round (something)

twinge *noun* sudden sharp pain or emotional pang

twinkle twinkles twinkling twinkled *verb* **1** to shine brightly but intermittently ▷ *noun* **2** flickering brightness

twirl *verb* to cause (something) to spin or twist round and round

twist *verb* **1** to turn (something) out of the natural position **2** to distort or pervert (something) **3** to wind or twine (something) **4** to injure (a body part) by turning it too sharply or in an unusual direction **5** to change the meaning of or distort (someone's words) slightly ▷ *noun* **6** twisting **7** unexpected development in a plot

twisted *adjective* **1** bent **2** (of person) unpleasantly abnormal

twit *noun informal* foolish person

twitch twitches twitching twitched *verb* **1** to move spasmodically **2** to pull (something) sharply ▷ *noun* **3** little jerky movement

twitter *verb* (of birds) to utter chirping sounds

two *adjective, noun* the number 2

two-edged *adjective* (of a remark) having both a favourable and an unfavourable interpretation

two-faced *adjective* deceitful or hypocritical

twofold *adjective* having two equally important parts or reasons

twosome *noun* two people or things that are usually seen together

two-time two-times two-timing two-timed *verb informal* to deceive (a lover) by having an affair

two-up *noun Aust, NZ* popular gambling game in which two coins are tossed and bets are placed on whether they land heads or tails

tycoon *noun* powerful wealthy businessman

type types typing typed *noun* **1** class or category **2** printed text ▷ *verb* **3** to write (something) with a typewriter or word processor **> typing** *noun*

typewriter *noun* machine that prints a character when the appropriate key is pressed

typhoid *noun* acute infectious feverish disease

typhoon *noun* violent tropical storm

typhus *noun* infectious disease

typical *adjective* true to type; characteristic **> typically** *adverb*

typify typifies typifying typified *verb* to be typical of

typist *noun* person who types

tyrannical *adjective* like a tyrant, oppressive

tyrannosaurus tyrannosauruses *noun* very large meat-eating dinosaur that walked upright on its hind legs

tyranny *noun* tyrannical rule

tyrant *noun* person who treats cruelly and unjustly the people he or she has authority over

tyre *noun* rubber ring, usually inflated, over the rim of a vehicle's wheel to grip the road

ubiquitous *adjective* being or seeming to be everywhere at once

udder *noun* the baglike organ that hangs below a cow's body and produces milk

UFO UFOs *abbreviation* unidentified flying object

Ugandan *adjective* **1** belonging or relating to Uganda ▷ *noun* **2** someone from Uganda

ugly uglier ugliest *adjective* of unpleasant appearance > **ugliness** *noun*

UK *abbreviation* United Kingdom

ulcer *noun* **1** open sore on the surface of the skin which takes a long time to heal **2** something similar inside the body

ulterior *adjective* (of a motive, aim, etc) apart from or beyond what is obvious

ultimate *adjective* **1** final in a series or process **2** highest or supreme ▷ *noun* **3** best or most advanced example of something: *the ultimate in luxury* > **ultimately** *adverb*: *Ultimately, it's your decision*

ultimatum *noun* final warning stating that action will be taken unless certain conditions are met

ultra- *prefix* **1** used to form adjectives describing extreme degrees of a quality; extremely: *ultramodern* **2** used to describe qualities that go beyond a specified extent, range or limit: *ultraviolet*

ultramarine *adjective* vivid, deep blue

ultrasonic *adjective* of or producing sound waves with a higher frequency than the human ear can hear

ultrasound *noun* sound which cannot be heard by the human ear because its frequency is too high

ultraviolet *adjective* **1** (of light) beyond the violet end of the spectrum and invisible to the human eye. It is a form of radiation that causes your skin to darken after being exposed to the sun ▷ *noun* **2** light like this

umbilical cord *noun* long flexible tube of blood vessels that connects an unborn baby with its mother and through which the baby receives nutrients and oxygen

umbrella *noun* device used for protection against rain, consisting of a folding frame covered in material attached to a central rod

umpire umpires umpiring umpired *noun* **1** *Cricket, Tennis* official who makes sure that the game is played according to the rules and who makes a decision if there is a dispute ▷ *verb* **2** to act as umpire in (a game)

umpteen *adjective informal* very many > **umpteenth** *adjective*: *for the umpteenth time*

un- *prefix* **1** *meaning* not: *unidentified* **2** *indicating* reversal of an action: *untie* **3** *indicating* removal from: *unthrone*

unabashed *adjective* not

embarrassed or discouraged by something

unabated *adjective, adverb* without any reduction in intensity or amount

unable *adjective* **unable to** lacking the necessary power, ability or authority to (do something)

unacceptable *adjective* **1** not satisfactory **2** intolerable

unaccompanied *adjective* alone

unaccustomed *adjective* not used (to something)

unadulterated *adjective* with nothing added; pure

unaffected *adjective* **1** not changed in any way by a particular thing **2** genuinely natural; unpretentious

unaided *adverb, adjective* without help

unambiguous *adjective* having only one possible meaning; clear

unanimous *adjective* **1** in complete agreement **2** agreed by all > **unanimity** *noun* > **unanimously** *adverb*

unannounced *adjective* happening unexpectedly and without warning

unarmed *adjective* without weapons

unassuming *adjective* modest or unpretentious

unattached *adjective* neither married nor in a steady relationship

unattended *adjective* left alone or not being cared for

unauthorized or **unauthorised** *adjective* done without official permission

unavoidable *adjective* unable to be prevented or avoided

unaware *adjective* not aware or conscious

unawares *adverb* **1** by surprise: *caught unawares* **2** without knowing

unbalanced *adjective* **1** biased,

one-sided or not organized in such a way that each part receives the right amount of emphasis **2** mentally disturbed **3** unequal

unbearable *adjective* not able to be endured > **unbearably** *adverb*

unbeatable *adjective* unable to be beaten

unbelievable *adjective* **1** hard to believe or imagine **2** very great or surprising > **unbelievably** *adverb*

unborn *adjective* not yet born

unbroken *adjective* continuous or complete

uncanny *adjective* strange and difficult to explain

unceremonious *adjective* **1** relaxed and informal **2** abrupt or rude > **unceremoniously** *adverb*

uncertain *adjective* **1** not knowing what to do **2** doubtful or not known > **uncertainty** *noun*

unchallenged *adjective* accepted without any questions being asked

uncharacteristic *adjective* not typical or usual

uncharitable *adjective* unkind or unfair

uncivil *adjective* rude and impolite

uncivilized or **uncivilised** *adjective* unacceptable, for example by being very cruel or rude

uncle *noun* **1** brother of your father or mother **2** husband of your aunt

unclear *adjective* confusing and not obvious

uncomfortable *adjective* **1** not physically relaxed **2** anxious or uneasy > **uncomfortably** *adverb*

uncommon *adjective* **1** not seen often **2** unusually great > **uncommonly** *adverb*

uncompromising *adjective* not prepared to compromise

unconcerned *adjective* lacking in concern or involvement

unconditional *adjective* without conditions or limitations > **unconditionally** *adverb*

unconscious *adjective* 1 not conscious, as a result of shock, accident or injury 2 unaware 3 (of feeling, attitude) not understood by or in the conscious awareness of the person who has it ▷ *noun* 4 part of the mind containing instincts and ideas that exist without your awareness > **unconsciously** *adverb*

uncontrollable *adjective* not able to be controlled or stopped > **uncontrollably** *adverb*

unconventional *adjective* not behaving in the same way as most other people

unconvinced *adjective* not at all certain that something is true or right

uncouth *adjective* lacking in good manners and refinement

uncover *verb* 1 to find out (something secret or hidden) 2 to remove the cover, top or lid from

undaunted *adjective* not put off or discouraged

undecided *adjective* 1 not having made up your mind 2 (of an issue or problem) not agreed or decided upon

undemanding *adjective* not difficult to do or deal with

undeniable *adjective* unquestionably true > **undeniably** *adverb*

under *preposition* 1 below or beneath 2 subject to or affected by 3 supervised by 4 less than 5 **under way** being carried out; in process

under- *prefix meaning* 1 below: *underground* 2 insufficient or insufficiently: *underrate*

underarm *Sport* 1 *adjective* denoting a style of throwing, bowling or serving in which the hand is swung below shoulder level ▷ *adverb* 2 in an underarm style

undercarriage *noun* 1 the part of an aircraft, including the wheels, that supports it when it is on the ground 2 framework supporting the body of a vehicle

underclass *noun* social group consisting of those who are poorest and whose situation is unlikely to improve

underclothes *plural noun* clothes that you wear under your other clothes and next to your skin

undercoat *noun* coat of paint applied before the final coat

undercover *adjective* done or acting in secret

undercurrent *noun* underlying opinion or emotion that may become stronger

undercut undercuts undercutting undercut *verb* to charge less than (a competitor) to obtain trade

underdeveloped *adjective* (of country) without modern industries and having a low standard of living

underdog *noun* person or team in a weak or underprivileged position

underdone *adjective* not cooked enough

underestimate underestimates underestimating underestimated *verb* to fail to realize how large, great or capable (something or someone) is

underfoot *adverb* under the feet

undergo undergoes undergoing underwent undergone *verb* to experience or have (something)

undergraduate *noun* person studying for a first degree

underground *adjective* 1 below

the surface of the ground **2** secret, unofficial and usually illegal ▷ *noun* **3** railway system in which trains travel in tunnels below ground **4** movement dedicated to overthrowing a government or forces of occupation

undergrowth *noun* small trees and bushes growing beneath taller trees in a wood or forest

underhand *adjective* sly, deceitful and secretive

underlie underlies underlying underlay underlain *verb* to be the foundation, cause or basis of ▷ **underlying** *adjective* fundamental or basic

underline underlines underlining underlined *verb* **1** to draw a line under **2** to emphasize

underling *noun* person of lesser rank; subordinate

undermine undermines undermining undermined *verb* to weaken (something or someone) gradually

underneath *preposition, adverb* **1** below or beneath ▷ *adjective* **2** lower ▷ *noun* **3** lower part or surface

underpants *plural noun* piece of clothing worn by men and boys under their trousers; briefs

underpass underpasses *noun* section of a road that passes under another road or a railway line

underpin underpins underpinning underpinned *verb* to give strength or support to

underprivileged *adjective* lacking the rights and advantages of other members of society

underrate underrates underrating underrated *verb* not to recognize the full worth of ▷ **underrated** *adjective*

understand understands understanding understood *verb* **1** to know or grasp the meaning or nature of **2** to interpret correctly **3** to assume, gather or believe

understandable *adjective* able to be understood; comprehensible ▷ **understandably** *adverb*

understanding *noun* **1** ability to learn, judge or make decisions **2** personal interpretation of a subject **3** mutual agreement, usually an informal or private one ▷ *adjective* **4** kind and sympathetic

understate understates understating understated *verb* **1** to describe or represent (something) in restrained terms **2** to state that (something, such as a number) is less than it is

understatement *noun* a statement that does not say fully how true something is

understudy understudies understudying understudied *noun* **1** actor who studies a part in order to be able to replace the usual actor if necessary ▷ *verb* **2** to act as an understudy for

undertake undertakes undertaking undertook undertaken *verb* to agree to (something) or to do (something)

undertaker *noun* person whose job is to prepare bodies for burial or cremation and arrange funerals

undertaking *noun* **1** task or enterprise **2** agreement to do something

undertone *noun* **1** quiet tone of voice **2** underlying quality or feeling

undervalue undervalues undervaluing undervalued *verb* to rate (something) as less valuable than it really is

underwater *adverb, adjective*

1 beneath the surface of the sea, a river or a lake ▷ adjective **2** designed to work in water

underwear noun clothing that you wear under your other clothes and next to your skin

underwent verb past tense of **undergo**

undesirable adjective not desirable or pleasant, objectionable

undid verb past tense of **undo**

undisputed adjective definite and without any doubt: the undisputed champion

undivided adjective (of attention) complete

undo undoes undoing undid undone verb **1** to open, unwrap or untie **2** to reverse the effects of

undoing noun cause of someone's downfall

undoubted adjective certain or indisputable ▷ **undoubtedly** adverb

undress undresses undressing undressed verb to take off your clothes

undue adjective greater than is reasonable; excessive ▷ **unduly** adverb

undulating adjective formal moving gently up and down

undying adjective never ending; eternal

unearth unearths unearthing unearthed verb to reveal or discover (something) by searching

unearthly adjective **1** strange and unnatural **2** (of time, hour) ridiculous or unreasonable

uneasy adjective worried, anxious or apprehensive ▷ **unease** noun feeling of anxiety ▷ **uneasily** adverb ▷ **uneasiness** noun

unemployed adjective **1** out of work ▷ plural noun **2** people without a job

unemployment noun state of being without a job

unending adjective having lasted for a long time and seeming as if it will never stop

unenviable adjective not to be envied

unequal adjective **1** (of society) not offering the same opportunities and privileges to all people **2** different in size, strength or ability

unerring adjective never mistaken; consistently accurate ▷ **unerringly** adverb

uneven adjective **1** (of surface) not level or smooth **2** not the same or consistent ▷ **unevenly** adverb

uneventful adjective (of a period of time) without any interesting happenings

unexpected adjective surprising; not expected ▷ **unexpectedly** adverb

unfailing adjective continuous or reliable ▷ **unfailingly** adverb

unfair adjective not right, fair or just ▷ **unfairly** adverb ▷ **unfairness** noun

unfaithful adjective having sex with someone other than one's regular partner ▷ **unfaithfulness** noun

unfamiliar adjective **1** (often followed by to) not known (to) **2** (followed by with) not acquainted (with)

unfashionable adjective not popular or no longer common

unfavourable adjective not encouraging or promising, or not providing any advantage

unfeeling adjective without sympathy

unfit adjective **1** in poor physical condition **2** unsuitable

unfold verb **1** to open or spread

(something) out from a folded state **2** (of a situation) to develop and become known

unforeseen *adjective* happening unexpectedly

unforgettable *adjective* impossible to forget; memorable > **unforgettably** *adverb*

unforgivable *adjective* bad or cruel to such an extent that it can never be forgiven or justified > **unforgivably** *adverb*

unfortunate *adjective* **1** unlucky, unsuccessful or unhappy **2** regrettable or unsuitable > **unfortunately** *adverb*

unfounded *adjective* without any truth; groundless

unfriendly *adjective* cold and unpleasant or unwelcoming

ungainly *adjective* moving in an awkward or clumsy way

ungrateful *adjective* not grateful or thankful

unhappy unhappier unhappiest *adjective* **1** sad and depressed **2** not pleased or satisfied **3** unfortunate or wretched > **unhappily** *adverb* > **unhappiness** *noun*

unhealthy *adjective* **1** likely to cause illness **2** not fit or well

unheard-of *adjective* never having happened before and therefore surprising or shocking

unhinged *adjective* mentally ill

unhurried *adjective* slow and relaxed

uni unis *noun informal* short for **university**

uni- *prefix meaning* of, consisting of or having only one: *unicellular*

unicorn *noun* imaginary animal that looks like a white horse with a straight horn growing from its forehead

unidentified *adjective* of which the name or nature is not known

uniform *noun* **1** special set of clothes worn by people at work or school ▷ *adjective* **2** regular and even throughout; unvarying **3** alike or like > **uniformity** *noun* > **uniformly** *adverb*

unify unifies unifying unified *verb* to make (something) one or to become one by joining together different elements > **unification** *noun*: *the unification of Italy*

unilateral *adjective* (of decision, action) made or done by only one person or group > **unilaterally** *adverb*

unimaginable *adjective* impossible to imagine or understand properly

unimportant *adjective* having very little significance or importance

uninhabited *adjective* without anyone living there

uninhibited *adjective* behaving freely and naturally, showing your feelings

unintelligible *adjective formal* impossible to understand

uninterested *adjective* having or showing no interest in someone or something

uninterrupted *adjective* continuing without breaks or interruptions

union *noun* **1** organization of workers that aims to improve the working conditions, pay and benefits of its members **2** uniting or being united

unique *adjective* **1** being the only one of a particular type **2** without equal or like **3** **unique to** belonging or relating only to (a particular person or thing) > **uniquely** *adverb* > **uniqueness** *noun*

unisex *adjective* designed for use by both sexes

unison noun **in unison 1** doing the same thing together at the same time **2** in complete agreement

unit noun **1** single complete thing **2** group or individual regarded as a basic element of a larger whole **3** fixed quantity etc, used as a standard of measurement **4** piece of furniture designed to be fitted with other similar pieces

unite unites uniting united verb **1** to join together to act as a group **2** to cause (people or things) to enter into an association or alliance

United Kingdom noun Great Britain together with Northern Ireland

United Nations noun international organization that tries to encourage peace, cooperation and friendship between countries

unity noun **1** state of being one **2** mutual agreement

universal adjective **1** concerning or relating to everyone in the world or every part of the universe **2** existing everywhere > **universally** adverb

universe noun the whole of space, including all the stars and planets

university universities noun place where students study for degrees

unjust adjective not fair or reasonable > **unjustly** adverb

unjustified adjective (of belief or action) without reason or basis

unkempt adjective untidy and not looked after properly

unkind adjective unpleasant and rather cruel > **unkindly** adverb > **unkindness** noun

unknown adjective **1** not known **2** not famous ▷ noun **3** unknown person, quantity or thing

unlawful adjective not legal

unleaded adjective (of petrol) containing less lead, in order to reduce environmental pollution

unleash unleashes unleashing unleashed verb to release (a powerful or violent force)

unless conjunction except under the circumstances that

unlike adjective **1** dissimilar or different ▷ preposition **2** not like or typical of

unlikely adjective improbable

unlimited adjective (of a supply) not limited or restricted

unload verb to remove (cargo) from (a ship, truck or plane)

unlock verb to turn the key in (a door or container) so that it can be opened

unlucky unluckier unluckiest adjective having or causing bad luck > **unluckily** adverb

unmarked adjective **1** with no marks of damage or injury **2** with no signs or marks of identification

unmentionable adjective too embarrassing or unpleasant to talk about

unmistakable or **unmistakeable** adjective not ambiguous; clear > **unmistakably** or **unmistakeably** adverb

unmitigated adjective **1** not reduced or lessened in severity etc **2** total and complete

unmoved adjective not affected by emotion; indifferent

unnatural adjective **1** strange and frightening because not usual **2** artificial and not typical > **unnaturally** adverb

unnecessary adjective not necessary or required > **unnecessarily** adverb

unnerve unnerves unnerving unnerved verb to cause (someone) to lose courage, confidence or self-control > **unnerving** *adjective*

unobtrusive *adjective* not very noticeable

unoccupied *adjective* without anybody living there

unofficial *adjective* without the approval or permission of a person in authority > **unofficially** *adverb*

unorthodox *adjective* unconventional and not generally accepted

unpack *verb* 1 to remove the contents of (a suitcase, trunk, etc) 2 to take (something) out of a packed container

unpaid *adjective* 1 without pay 2 not yet paid

unpalatable *adjective* very unpleasant and hard to eat or accept

unparalleled *adjective* not equalled; supreme

unpleasant *adjective* not pleasant or agreeable > **unpleasantly** *adverb* > **unpleasantness** *noun*

unpopular *adjective* disliked by most people

unprecedented *adjective formal* that has never happened before or is the best of its kind so far

unpredictable *adjective* having behaviour that is impossible to predict

unprepared *adjective* not ready

unproductive *adjective* not producing anything useful

unprofessional *adjective* at odds with accepted behaviour in a profession > **unprofessionally** *adverb*

unqualified *adjective* 1 lacking the necessary qualifications 2 total or complete

unquestionable *adjective* so obviously true or real that nobody can doubt it > **unquestionably**

adverb

unravel unravels unravelling unravelled *verb* 1 to unwind, disentangle or undo (something) 2 to become unravelled 3 to explain or solve (a mystery)

unreal *adjective* so strange that you find it difficult to believe

unrealistic *adjective* 1 not facing up to reality or the practicalities of a situation 2 not true to life

unreasonable *adjective* unfair and difficult to deal with or justify

unrelated *adjective* not connected

unrelenting *adjective* continuing in a determined way without caring about any hurt that is caused

unreliable *adjective* that cannot be relied upon

unremitting *adjective* continuing without stopping

unrequited *adjective* not returned: *unrequited love*

unrest *noun* anger and dissatisfaction in the people

unrivalled *adjective* better than anything else of its kind

unroll *verb* 1 to open out or unwind (something rolled or coiled) 2 (of something rolled or coiled) to open out or unwind

unruly unrulier unruliest *adjective* difficult to control or organize

unsatisfactory *adjective* not good enough

unsaturated *adjective* (of oil, fat) made mainly from vegetable fats and considered healthier than saturated

unsavoury *adjective* distasteful or objectionable

unscathed *adjective* not harmed or injured

unscrew *verb* to remove (something) by turning it or by removing the screws holding it

unscrupulous *adjective* prepared to act dishonestly; unprincipled

unseemly *adjective* (of behaviour) not suitable for a particular situation and showing a lack of control and good manners

unseen *adjective* not seen

unsettle unsettles unsettling unsettled *verb* to make (someone) restless or worried

unshakable or **unshakeable** *adjective* (of belief, faith, etc) so strong that it cannot be destroyed

unsightly *adjective* unpleasant to look at

unskilled *adjective* (of work) not requiring any special training

unsolicited *adjective* given or happening without being asked for

unsound *adjective* **1** not based on truth or fact **2** unstable

unspeakable *adjective* very unpleasant

unspecified *adjective* not stated specifically

unspoilt or **unspoiled** *adjective* unchanged and still as at a previous time

unspoken *adjective* not talked about

unstable *adjective* **1** likely to change suddenly and create difficulty or danger **2** not firm or fixed properly and likely to wobble or fall

unsteady *adjective* **1** having difficulty in controlling the movement of your legs or hands **2** not held or fixed securely and likely to fall over > **unsteadily** *adverb*

unstuck *adjective* **come unstuck** to becomes separated

unsuccessful *adjective* not having success at something > **unsuccessfully** *adverb*

unsuitable *adjective* not right

or appropriate for a particular purpose > **unsuitably** *adverb*

unsuited *adjective* not appropriate for a particular task or situation

unsung *adjective* not appreciated or praised enough

unsure *adjective* uncertain or doubtful

unsuspecting *adjective* having no idea of what is happening or going to happen

untangle untangles untangling untangled *verb* to undo, removing any twists or knots

untenable *adjective formal* (of theory, argument or position) that cannot be successfully defended

unthinkable *adjective* out of the question; inconceivable

untidy untidier untidiest *adjective* messy and disordered > **untidily** *adverb* > **untidiness** *noun*

untie unties untying untied *verb* to open or free (something that is tied)

until *conjunction* **1** up to the time that ▷ *preposition* **2** in or throughout the period before **3 not until** not before (a time or event)

untimely *adjective* occurring before the expected or normal time

unto *preposition old-fashioned* to

untold *adjective* incalculably great in number or quantity

untouched *adjective* **1** not changed, moved or damaged **2** not eaten

untoward *adjective* unexpected and causing difficulties

untrue *adjective* **1** not true, incorrect or false **2** disloyal or unfaithful

unused *adjective* **1** not yet used **2 unused to** not accustomed to

unusual *adjective* uncommon or extraordinary > **unusually** *adverb*

unveil *verb* to reveal (a statue or painting) officially, by drawing back a curtain

unwanted *adjective* not wanted or desired

unwarranted *adjective formal* not justified or not deserved

unwelcome *adjective* not welcome or wanted

unwell *adjective* not well; ill

unwieldy *adjective* too heavy, large or awkward to be easily handled

unwilling *adjective* not willing or prepared (to do something) > **unwillingly** *adverb*

unwind unwinds unwinding unwound *verb* 1 to relax after a busy or tense time 2 to undo or unravel (something)

unwise *adjective* foolish or not sensible

unwitting *adjective* 1 not intentional 2 not knowing or conscious > **unwittingly** *adverb*

unworthy *adjective formal* not deserving or worthy

unwrap unwraps unwrapping unwrapped *verb* to remove the wrapping from

unwritten *adjective* 1 not printed or in writing 2 operating only through custom

up *adverb, preposition* 1 indicating movement to or position at a higher place ▷ *preposition* 2 along (a road or river) ▷ *adverb* 3 towards or in the north: *I'm flying up to Darwin* 4 **go up** to increase ▷ *adjective* 5 of a high or higher position 6 out of bed

up-and-coming *adjective* likely to be successful

upbringing *noun* education of a person during the formative years

update updates updating updated *verb* to bring (something or someone) up to date

upfront *adjective* 1 open and frank ▷ *adverb, adjective* 2 (of money) paid out at the beginning of a business arrangement

upgrade upgrades upgrading upgraded *verb* 1 to improve (equipment) 2 to promote (a person or job) to a higher rank

upheaval *noun* big change that causes a lot of trouble

uphill *adjective* 1 sloping or leading upwards 2 requiring a great deal of effort ▷ *adverb* 3 up a slope

uphold upholds upholding upheld *verb* to support and maintain (a law or decision) > **upholder** *noun*

upholstery *noun* soft covering on a chair or sofa

upkeep *noun* act, process or cost of keeping something in good repair

upland *adjective* (of area) high or relatively high > **uplands** *plural noun* area of high or relatively high ground

uplifting *adjective* making you feel happy

up-market *adjective* sophisticated and expensive

upon *preposition* 1 on 2 up and on 3 in the course of or immediately after

upper *adjective* 1 higher in physical position, wealth, rank or status ▷ *noun* 2 part of a shoe above the sole

upper class upper classes *noun* highest social class > **upper-class** *adjective*

uppermost *adjective* 1 highest in position, power or importance ▷ *adverb* 2 in or into the highest place or position

upright *adjective* 1 vertical or erect 2 honest or just ▷ *adverb* 3 vertically or in an erect position ▷ *noun* 4 vertical support, such as a post

uprising *noun* rebellion or revolt

uproar *noun* disturbance characterized by loud noise and confusion

uproot *verb* **1** to displace (a person or people) from their native or usual surroundings **2** to pull (a tree or plant) out of the ground together with its roots

upset upsets upsetting upset *adjective* **1** unhappy or distressed ▷ *verb* **2** to sadden, distress or worry (someone) **3** to disturb the normal state or stability of (something) **4** to tip over or spill (something) **5** to make (someone) physically ill ▷ *noun* **6 stomach upset** slight stomach illness > **upsetting** *adjective*

upshot *noun* final result or conclusion

upside down *adjective, adverb* the wrong way up

upstage upstages upstaging upstaged *verb informal* to draw attention away from (someone) by being more attractive or interesting

upstairs *adverb* **1** to or on an upper floor of a building ▷ *noun* **2** upper floor ▷ *adjective* **3** situated on an upper floor

upstart *noun* person who has risen suddenly to a position of power and behaves arrogantly

upstream *adverb, adjective* in or towards the higher part of a stream

upsurge *noun* rapid rise or swell

uptake *noun* **quick** or **slow on the uptake** *informal* quick or slow to understand or learn

uptight *adjective informal* nervously tense, irritable or angry

up-to-date *adjective* **1** modern or fashionable **2** having the latest information

up-to-the-minute *adjective* latest and newest possible

upturn *noun* improvement

upturned *adjective* **1** facing upwards **2** upside down

upward *adjective* **1** towards a higher place, level or condition ▷ *adverb* **2** (also **upwards**) from a lower to a higher place, level or condition

uranium *noun* radioactive silvery-white metallic element, used to produce nuclear energy and weapons

Uranus *noun* seventh planet from the sun in the solar system

urban *adjective* relating to a town or city

urbane *adjective* well-mannered and comfortable in social situations

urchin *noun* mischievous child

Urdu *noun* official language of Pakistan; also spoken by many people in India

urge urges urging urged *noun* **1** strong impulse, inner drive or wish ▷ *verb* **2** to press or try to persuade (someone to do something)

urgent *adjective* requiring speedy action or attention > **urgency** *noun* > **urgently** *adverb*

urinal *noun* bowl or trough fixed to the wall in a men's public toilet for men to urinate in

urinate urinates urinating urinated *verb* to get rid of urine from your body

urine *noun* pale yellow fluid excreted by the kidneys to the bladder and passed as waste from the body > **urinary** *adjective*

urn *noun* **1** vase used as a container for the ashes of the dead **2** large metal container with a tap, used for making and holding tea or coffee

us *pronoun* used by a speaker or writer to refer to himself or herself

and at least one other person;
used as the object of a verb or
preposition

US or **USA** *abbreviation* United
States (of America)

usage *noun* **1** way in which a word
is used in a language **2** degree to
which something is used, or the
way in which it is used

use uses using used *verb* **1** to do
something with (something)
in order to do a job or achieve a
purpose **2** to take advantage of
(someone); exploit **3** to consume
or expend (energy, resources,
etc) **4 used to do something**
previously did or previously had the
habit of doing something: *I used
to live there* ▷ *noun* **5** act of using
something or being used **6** ability
or permission to use something
7 usefulness or advantage
8 purpose for which something is
used > **usable** *adjective* able to be
used > **user** *noun*

used *adjective* **1** second-hand **2 used
to something** accustomed to
something

useful *adjective* helpful > **usefully**
adverb > **usefulness** *noun*

useless *adjective* **1** of no use or
help **2** in vain **3** *informal* very poor
or bad at something; hopeless
> **uselessly** *adverb* > **uselessness**
noun

username *noun Computers* name
entered into a computer for
identification purposes

usher *noun* **1** official who shows
people to their seats, as in a church
▷ *verb* **2** to conduct or escort
(someone) somewhere

usherette *noun* woman who shows
people to their seats in a cinema

USSR *abbreviation* Union of Soviet
Socialist Republics, a country

which was made up of a lot of
smaller countries including Russia,
but which is now broken up

usual *adjective* happening, done or
used most often > **usually** *adverb*
most often or in most cases

usurp *verb* to seize (a position
or power) without authority
> **usurper** *noun*

usury *noun* practice of lending
money at an extremely high rate
of interest

ute *noun Aust, NZ informal* utility
truck

utensil *noun* tool for practical use:
cooking utensils

uterus *noun* womb

utilitarian *adjective* **1** useful rather
than beautiful **2** intended to
produce the greatest benefit for the
greatest number of people

utility utilities *noun* **1** usefulness
2 public service, such as electricity

utility room *noun* room used for
large domestic appliances and
equipment

utility truck *noun Aust, NZ* small
truck with an open body and
low sides

utilize utilizes utilizing utilized;
also spelt **utilise** *verb formal* to
make use of > **utilization** *noun*

utmost *adjective* extreme or
greatest

Utopia *noun* any real or imaginary
society, place or state considered
to be perfect or ideal > **Utopian**
adjective

utter *verb* **1** to express (something)
in sounds or words ▷ *adjective*
2 total or absolute > **utterly** *adverb*

utterance *noun* something uttered

U-turn *noun* **1** turn, made by
a vehicle, in the shape of a U,
resulting in a reversal of direction
2 complete change in policy

V

v. *abbreviation* **1** versus **2** very

vacancy vacancies *noun* **1** unfilled job **2** unoccupied room in a guesthouse

vacant *adjective* **1** (of a toilet, room, position, etc) unoccupied **2** (of expression, look) without interest or understanding > **vacantly** *adverb*

vacate vacates vacating vacated *verb formal* **1** to leave (a place) **2** to give up (a job)

vacation *noun* **1** time when universities and law courts are closed **2** *Chiefly US* holiday

vaccinate vaccinates vaccinating vaccinated *verb* to inject (a person or animal) with a vaccine > **vaccination** *noun*

vaccine *noun* substance designed to cause a mild form of a disease to make a person immune to the disease itself

vacuum *noun* **1** space containing no air, gases or other matter ▷ *verb* **2** to clean (a room, carpet, etc) with a vacuum cleaner

vacuum cleaner *noun* electrical appliance which sucks up dust and dirt from carpets and upholstery

vagina *noun* (in female mammals) passage from the womb to the external genitals

vagrant *noun* person with no settled home; tramp > **vagrancy** *noun*: *You'll get arrested for vagrancy*

vague vaguer vaguest *adjective* **1** not clearly explained **2** unable to be seen or heard clearly **3** absent-minded > **vaguely** *adverb* > **vagueness** *noun*

vain *adjective* **1** excessively proud, especially of your appearance **2** bound to fail; futile ▷ *noun* **3** **in vain** unsuccessfully > **vainly** *adverb*

vale *noun literary* valley

valentine *noun* **1** person to whom you send a romantic card on Saint Valentine's Day, 14th February **2** (also **valentine card**) card sent on Saint Valentine's Day

valet *noun* man's personal male servant

valiant *adjective* brave or courageous > **valiantly** *adverb*

valid *adjective* **1** soundly reasoned **2** officially accepted > **validity** *noun*

validate validates validating validated *verb* to prove (something) to be true

valley *noun* low area between hills, often with a river running through it

valour *noun literary* bravery

valuable *adjective* having great value or worth

valuables *plural noun* valuable personal property

valuation *noun* assessment of how much something is worth

value values valuing valued *noun* **1** importance or usefulness **2** monetary worth **3** **values** moral principles ▷ *verb* **4** to think (something) is important; appreciate **5** to assess the value of

> **valued** *adjective* > **valuer** *noun*

valve *noun* **1** device to control the movement of gas or liquid through a pipe **2** small flap in your heart or in a vein which controls the flow and direction of blood

vampire *noun* (in folklore) corpse that rises at night to drink the blood of the living

van *noun* **1** motor vehicle larger than a car but smaller than a lorry, used for carrying goods **2** railway carriage for goods, luggage or mail

vandal *noun* person who deliberately damages property > **vandalism** *noun* > **vandalize** or **vandalise** *verb*

vane *noun* flat blade on a rotary device such as a weathercock or propeller

vanguard *noun* most advanced group or position in a movement or activity

vanilla *noun* seed pod of a tropical plant, used for flavouring

vanish vanishes vanishing vanished *verb* to disappear

vanity *noun* feeling of excessive pride about your looks or abilities

vanquish vanquishes vanquishing vanquished *verb* *literary* to defeat completely

vapour *noun* **1** moisture suspended in air as steam or mist **2** gaseous form of something that is liquid or solid at room temperature

variable *adjective* **1** not always the same; changeable ▷ *noun* **2** something that can change **3** *Maths* symbol such as x which can represent any value or any one of a set of values > **variability** *noun*

variance *noun* **at variance** at odds or not in agreement (with)

variant *noun* **1** something that differs from a standard or type ▷ *adjective* **2** differing from a standard or type

variation *noun* **1** change from the normal or usual pattern **2** difference in level, amount or quantity

varicose veins *plural noun* knotted and swollen veins, especially in the legs

varied *adjective* of different types, quantities or sizes: *a varied diet*

variety varieties *noun* **1** state of being diverse or various **2** different things of the same kind; assortment **3** particular type **4** light entertainment composed of unrelated acts

various *adjective* **1** several **2** of several kinds > **variously** *adverb*

varnish varnishes varnishing varnished *noun* **1** liquid which when painted onto a surface gives it a hard clear shiny finish ▷ *verb* **2** to apply varnish to

vary varies varying varied *verb* **1** to change **2** to make changes in

vascular *adjective* *Biology* relating to tubes or ducts that carry fluids within animals or plants

vase *noun* ornamental jar, especially for flowers

vasectomy vasectomies *noun* operation to sterilize a man by cutting the tube that carries the sperm

Vaseline® *noun* thick oily skin cream made from petroleum

vast *adjective* extremely large > **vastly** *adverb* > **vastness** *noun*

vat *noun* large container for liquids

VAT *abbreviation* (in Britain) value-added tax: a tax which is added to the costs of making or providing goods and services

vaudeville *noun* *US* variety entertainment of songs and comic turns

vault *noun* **1** secure room for storing valuables **2** underground burial chamber **3** an arched roof, often found in churches ▷ *verb* **4** to jump over (something) by resting your hand(s) on it. > **vaulted** *adjective* having an arched roof

VCR VCRs *abbreviation* video cassette recorder

VDU VDUs *abbreviation* visual display unit: monitor screen attached to a computer or word processor

veal *noun* calf meat

Veda *noun* ancient Hindu sacred text; also these texts as a collection > **Vedic** *adjective*

veer *verb* to change direction suddenly

vegan *noun* person who eats no meat, fish, eggs or dairy products

vegetable *noun* **1** edible roots or leaves such as carrots or cabbage ▷ *adjective* **2** relating to plants or vegetables

vegetarian *noun* **1** person who does not eat meat, poultry or fish ▷ *adjective* **2** suitable for a vegetarian > **vegetarianism** *noun*

vegetation *noun* plant life in a particular area

vehement *adjective* expressing strong feelings > **vehemence** *noun* > **vehemently** *adverb*

vehicle *noun* **1** machine, especially with an engine and wheels, for carrying people or objects **2** something used to achieve a particular purpose or as a means of expression > **vehicular** *adjective*

veil *noun* piece of thin cloth covering the head or face > **veiled** *adjective*

vein *noun* **1** tube that takes blood to the heart **2** line on a leaf or an insect's wing **3** layer of ore or

mineral in rock **4** streak in marble, wood or cheese **5** feature of someone's writing or speech: *a vein of humour* **6** mood or style: *in a lighter vein* > **veined** *adjective*

veld or **veldt** *noun* high grassland in southern Africa

veldskoen or **velskoen** *noun S Afr* tough ankle-length boot

velocity *noun technical* speed at which something is moving in a particular direction

velvet *noun* fabric with a thick soft pile > **velvety** *adjective* soft and smooth

vendetta *noun* long-lasting bitter quarrel which results in people trying to harm each other

vending machine *noun* machine that dispenses goods such as sweets or drinks when you put money in it

vendor *noun* person who sells something

veneer *noun* **1** superficial appearance: *a veneer of sophistication* **2** thin layer of wood etc covering a cheaper material

venerable *adjective* worthy of great respect

venerate venerates venerating venerated *verb formal* to feel great respect for > **veneration** *noun*

venereal disease *noun* disease transmitted sexually

vengeance *noun* **1** act of harming someone because they have harmed you; revenge **2 with a vengeance** very forcefully or strongly

venison *noun* deer meat

venom *noun* **1** poison produced by snakes, scorpions and spiders, etc **2** malice or spite > **venomous** *adjective*

vent *noun* **1** outlet , hole or slit

through which fumes or fluid can escape and fresh air can enter **2 give vent to** to release (a feeling) in an outburst ▷ *verb* **3** to express (a feeling) in an outburst

ventilate ventilates ventilating ventilated *verb* **1** to let fresh air into (a room or building) **2** to discuss (ideas or feelings) openly > **ventilated** *adjective* > **ventilation** *noun*

ventilator *noun* machine that helps people breathe when they cannot breathe naturally, for example if they are very ill

ventriloquist *noun* entertainer who can speak without moving his or her lips, so that the words appear to come from a dummy > **ventriloquism** *noun*

venture ventures venturing ventured *noun* **1** risky undertaking, especially in business ▷ *verb* **2** to go to an unknown and possibly risky place **3** to dare to express (an opinion) **4** to dare (to do something)

venue *noun* place where an event is held

Venus *noun* second planet from the sun in the solar system

veranda or **verandah** *noun* platform with a roof that is attached to an outside wall of a house at ground level

verb *noun* word that expresses the idea of action, happening or being, *eg run, take, become, be*

verbal *adjective* **1** spoken **2** relating to verbs > **verbally** *adverb*

verdict *noun* **1** decision that states whether a prisoner is guilty or not guilty **2** opinion formed after examining the facts

verge verges verging verged *noun* **1** grass border along a road

2 on the verge of having almost reached (a point or condition) > **verge on** *verb* to be near to (a condition)

verify verifies verifying verified *verb* to check the truth or accuracy of > **verifiable** *adjective* > **verification** *noun*

veritable *adjective* rightly called; without exaggeration: *a veritable feast* > **veritably** *adverb*

vermin *plural noun* animals, especially insects and rodents, that spread disease or cause damage

vernacular *noun* most widely spoken language of a particular people or place

verruca *noun* wart, usually on the foot

versatile *adjective* having many skills or uses > **versatility** *noun*

verse *noun* **1** poetry **2** one part of a song, poem or chapter of the Bible

versed *adjective* **versed in** knowledgeable about

version *noun* **1** form of something, such as a piece of writing, with some differences from other forms **2** account of an event from a particular person's point of view

versus *preposition* **1** in opposition to or in contrast with **2** *Sport, Law* against

vertebra vertebrae *noun* one of the bones that form the spine

vertebrate *noun* any animal that has a spine

vertex vertexes or **vertices** *noun* highest point of a triangle or pyramid

vertical *adjective* straight up and down > **vertically** *adverb*

vertigo *noun* dizziness, usually when looking down from a high place

verve *noun* enthusiasm or liveliness

very *adverb* **1** more than usually, extremely ▷ *adjective* **2** absolute or exact: *the very top; the very man*

vessel *noun* **1** ship or large boat **2** *literary* container, especially for liquids **3** *Biology* thin tube along which liquids such as blood or sap move in animals and plants

vest *noun* **1** piece of underwear worn for warmth on the top half of the body **2** *US* waistcoat

vestige *noun formal* small amount or trace

vestry vestries *noun* part of the church building where a priest or minister changes into his or her official clothes

vet vets vetting vetted *noun* **1** medical specialist who treats sick animals; veterinary surgeon **2** *US, Aust, NZ* military veteran ▷ *verb* **3** to check the suitability of

veteran *noun* **1** someone who has served in the armed forces, particularly during a war **2** someone who has been involved in a particular activity for a long time

veterinary *adjective* concerning animal health

veterinary surgeon *noun* medical specialist who treats sick animals

veto vetoes vetoing vetoed *verb* **1** (of person in authority) to say no to ▷ *noun* **2** right of someone in authority to say no to something

vexed *adjective* annoyed, worried or puzzled

VHF *abbreviation* very high frequency: a range of high radio frequencies

via *preposition* by way of

viable *adjective* **1** able to be put into practice **2** *Biology* able to live and grow independently > **viability** *noun*

viaduct *noun* long high bridge that carries a road or railway across a valley

vibrant *adjective* **1** full of life, energy and enthusiasm **2** (of a colour) strong and bright > **vibrancy** *noun* > **vibrantly** *adverb*

vibrate vibrates vibrating vibrated *verb* to move back and forth rapidly by a tiny amount > **vibration** *noun*

vicar *noun* priest in the Church of England

vicarage *noun* house where a vicar lives

vice *noun* **1** serious moral fault in someone's character, such as greed, or a weakness, such as smoking **2** criminal activities connected with prostitution and pornography **3** tool with a pair of jaws for holding an object while working on it

vice- *prefix meaning* deputy or assistant to: *vice-president*

viceregal *adjective* **1** of or concerning a viceroy **2** (in Australia and New Zealand) of or concerning a governor or governor-general

viceroy viceroys *noun* governor of a colony who represents the monarch

vice versa *adverb* the other way round: *Wives criticize their husbands, and vice versa*

vicinity *noun* surrounding area

vicious *adjective* cruel and violent > **viciously** *adverb* > **viciousness** *noun*

vicious circle or **cycle** *noun* situation in which a difficulty leads to a new difficulty, which then causes the original difficulty to occur again

victim *noun* someone who has been harmed or injured by someone or

something

victor *noun* person who has defeated an opponent, especially in war or sport; winner

Victorian *adjective* **1** of or in the reign of Queen Victoria (1837–1901) **2** of or relating to the Australian state of Victoria

victory victories *noun* winning of a battle or contest > **victorious** *adjective*

video videos videoing videoed *noun* **1** short for **video cassette, video cassette recorder, video tape** ▷ *verb* **2** to record (a TV programme, film or event) on video ▷ *adjective* **3** relating to or used in producing sound and pictures

video cassette *noun* cassette containing video tape for playing or recording sound and pictures

video recorder or **video cassette recorder** *noun* tape recorder for recording and playing back TV programmes and films

video tape *noun* magnetic tape used to record sound and pictures

vie vies vying vied *verb* to compete (with someone)

Vietnamese *adjective* **1** belonging or relating to Vietnam ▷ *noun* **2** someone from Vietnam **3** main language spoken in Vietnam

The plural of *Vietnamese* is *Vietnamese*

view *noun* **1** opinion or belief **2** everything that can be seen from a given place **3** picture of this **4** **in view of** taking into consideration **5** **on view** available to be seen by the public; on show ▷ *verb* **6** to think of (something) in a particular way

viewer *noun* person who watches television

viewpoint *noun* **1** opinion or way of thinking about something **2** place from which you get a good view of an area or event

vigil *noun* night-time period of staying awake to look after a sick person, pray, make a protest etc

vigilant *adjective* watchful in case of danger

vigilante *noun* person, especially one of an unofficial group, who takes it upon himself or herself to protect the community and catch and punish criminals

vigorous *adjective* energetic or enthusiastic > **vigorously** *adverb* > **vigour** *noun*

Viking *noun* History seafaring raider and settler from Scandinavia from the 8th to the 11th centuries

vile *adjective* very unpleasant or disgusting

villa *noun* **1** large house with gardens **2** holiday home, usually in the Mediterranean

village *noun* **1** small group of houses and other buildings in a country area **2** rural community > **villager** *noun*

villain *noun* **1** someone who harms others or breaks the law **2** main wicked character in a play > **villainous** *adjective* > **villainy** *noun*

vindicate vindicates vindicating vindicated *verb* to prove (someone) right or to prove (their actions or ideas) to have been justified > **vindication** *noun*

vindictive *adjective* maliciously seeking revenge > **vindictiveness** *noun*

vine *noun* trailing or climbing plant, especially one producing grapes

vinegar *noun* sharp-tasting liquid made from sour wine, beer or cider > **vinegary** *adjective*

vineyard *noun* area of land where grapes are grown

vintage *adjective* **1** (of wine) of a good quality and stored for a number of years to improve **2** best and most typical ▷ *noun* **3** wine from a particular harvest of grapes

vintage car *noun* car built between 1919 and 1930

vinyl *noun* type of plastic, used to make things such as floor coverings and furniture

viola *noun* stringed instrument lower in pitch than a violin

violate violates violating violated *verb* **1** to break (a law or agreement) **2** to disturb (someone's peace or privacy) **3** to treat (a sacred place) disrespectfully > **violation** *noun*

violence *noun* **1** use of physical force, usually intended to cause injury or destruction **2** great force or strength in action, feeling or expression

violent *adjective* **1** (of person) making use of physical force or weapons in a way that may cause injury or death **2** (of event) happening unexpectedly and with great force **3** (of act, feeling, pain, etc) very forceful > **violently** *adverb*

violet *noun* **1** plant with bluish-purple flowers ▷ *adjective, noun* **2** bluish-purple

violin *noun* four-stringed musical instrument played with a bow. > **violinist** *noun*

VIP VIPs *abbreviation* very important person

viper *noun* type of poisonous snake

viral *adjective* of or caused by a virus

virgin *noun* **1** person, especially a woman, who has not had sexual intercourse ▷ *adjective* **2** not yet used or explored; fresh > **virginity** *noun*

Virgin *proper noun* name given to Mary, the mother of Jesus Christ

virginal *adjective* **1** looking young and innocent **2** looking fresh, clean and unused ▷ *noun* **3** keyboard instrument popular in the 16th and 17th centuries

Virgo *noun* sixth sign of the zodiac, represented by a girl

virile *adjective* having the traditional male characteristics of physical strength and a high sex drive > **virility** *noun*

virtual *adjective* **1** having the characteristics of something without being formally recognized as being that thing **2** of or relating to virtual reality > **virtually** *adverb* practically, almost

virtual reality *noun* computer-generated environment that seems real to the user

virtue *noun* **1** moral goodness **2** positive moral quality **3** advantage, merit **4** **by virtue of** *formal* by reason of > **virtuously** *adverb*

virtuoso virtuosos or **virtuosi** *noun* person with impressive skill at something, especially music > **virtuosity** *noun*

virtuous *adjective* morally good

virus viruses *noun* **1** microorganism that can cause disease **2** *Computers* program that alters or damages the information stored in a computer system

visa *noun* permission to enter a country, granted by its government and shown by a stamp on your passport

viscount *noun* British nobleman ranking between an earl and a baron > **viscountess** *noun* **1** woman holding the rank of viscount in her own right **2** wife or widow of a viscount

viscous *adjective* thick and sticky > **viscosity** *noun*

Vishnu *noun* Hindu god; one of the Trimurti

visibility *noun* range or clarity of vision

visible *adjective* **1** able to be seen **2** noticeable or evident > **visibly** *adverb*

vision *noun* **1** ability to see **2** mental image of something **3** foresight **4** unusual experience, in which you see things not seen by others, as a result of a mental disorder, divine inspiration or taking drugs > **visionary** *adjective* **1** showing foresight **2** idealistic but impractical ▷ *noun* **3** visionary person

visit *verb* **1** to go or come to see (someone or something) ▷ *noun* **2** instance of visiting > **visitor** *noun*

visor *noun* transparent part of a helmet that you pull down to protect your eyes or face

visual *adjective* **1** relating to sight **2** designed to be looked at

visualize **visualizes** **visualizing** **visualized**; also spelt **visualise** *verb* to form a mental image of

vital *adjective* **1** essential or very important **2** energetic, exciting and full of life **3** necessary to maintain life > **vitality** *noun* physical or mental energy > **vitally** *adverb*

vitamin *noun* one of a group of substances that you need to stay healthy. They occur naturally in food

vivacious *adjective* full of energy and enthusiasm > **vivacity** *noun*

vivid *adjective* very bright in colour or clear in detail > **vividly** *adverb* > **vividness** *noun*

vivisection *noun* the act of cutting open and experimenting on living animals for medical research > **vivisectionist** *noun*

vixen *noun* female fox

vizor *noun* same as **visor**

vocabulary **vocabularies** *noun* **1** all the words that a person knows in a particular language **2** all the words in a language **3** specialist terms used in a given subject **4** list of words in another language with their translation

vocal *adjective* **1** relating to the voice **2** outspoken > **vocally** *adverb*

vocation *noun* **1** strong wish to do a particular job, especially one which involves serving others **2** occupation that someone feels called to **3** profession or trade

vocational *adjective* (of skills, training) directed towards a particular profession or trade

vociferous *adjective formal* outspoken or strident > **vociferously** *adverb*

vodka *noun* (Russian) spirit distilled from potatoes or grain

vogue *noun* fashion

voice **voices** **voicing** **voiced** *noun* **1** sounds produced by your vocal cords as when speaking, shouting or singing, or the ability to make such sounds ▷ *verb* **2** to express (an opinion or emotion)

void *noun* empty space or feeling

volatile *adjective* **1** liable to sudden change, especially in behaviour **2** evaporating quickly > **volatility** *noun*

volcanic *adjective* (of region) having many volcanoes or created by volcanoes

volcano **volcanoes** *noun* mountain with an opening through which lava, gas and ash are ejected

vole *noun* small mouse-like rodent

volition *noun formal* **of your own volition** from choice rather than because persuaded or forced

volley volleys *noun* **1** simultaneous firing of a lot of shots **2** burst of questions or critical comments **3** *Sport* stroke or kick at a moving ball before it hits the ground

volleyball *noun* team game where a ball is hit with the hands over a high net

volt *noun* unit used to measure the force of an electric current

voltage *noun* force of an electric current measured in volts

volume *noun* **1** amount of space occupied or contained by something **2** amount **3** loudness of sound **4** book or one of a series of books

voluminous *adjective* **1** (of clothes) large and roomy **2** (of writings) extensive

voluntary *adjective* **1** done by choice **2** done without payment > **voluntarily** *adverb*

volunteer *noun* **1** person who offers voluntarily to do something **2** person who voluntarily undertakes military service ▷ *verb* **3** to offer (to do something) **4** to give (information) willingly

voluptuous *adjective* **1** (of a woman) having a plump and sexually exciting figure **2** sensually pleasurable > **voluptuously** *adverb* > **voluptuousness** *noun*

vomit *verb* **1** to be sick or to bring up (the contents your stomach) ▷ *noun* **2** partly digested food and drink that has come back up from someone's stomach

voodoo *noun* form of magic practised in the Caribbean, especially in Haiti

voracious *adjective* **1** craving great quantities of food **2** insatiably eager > **voraciously** *adverb* > **voracity** *noun*

vote votes voting voted *noun* **1** expression of choice made in an election or at a meeting where decisions are taken **2** right to make this choice **3** total number of votes cast **4** collective voting power of a given group: *the Black vote* ▷ *verb* **5** to indicate your choice by writing on a piece of paper or by raising your hand **6** to propose (that something should happen) > **voter** *noun*

vouch vouches vouching vouched *verb* **vouch for 1** to provide evidence for **2** to give your personal assurance about the good behaviour or support of (someone)

voucher *noun* ticket used instead of money to buy specified goods

vow *verb* **1** to promise (something) solemnly ▷ *noun* **2** solemn and binding promise **3** **vows** formal promises made when marrying or entering a religious order

vowel *noun* sound made without your tongue touching the roof of your mouth or your teeth, or one of the letters a, e, i, o, u, which represent such sounds

voyage *noun* long journey by sea or in space > **voyager** *noun*

vulgar *adjective* **1** socially unacceptable or offensive: *vulgar language* **2** showing a lack of good taste or refinement > **vulgarity** *noun* > **vulgarly** *adverb*

vulnerable *adjective* liable to be physically or emotionally hurt > **vulnerability** *noun*

vulture *noun* large bird that lives in hot countries and feeds on the flesh of dead animals

vying *verb* present participle of **vie**

W

wacky wackier wackiest *adjective informal* eccentric or funny

wad *noun* **1** small mass of soft material **2** roll or bundle

wadding *noun* soft material used for padding or stuffing

waddle waddles waddling waddled *verb* **1** to walk with short swaying steps ▷ *noun* **2** swaying walk

waddy waddies *noun Aust* heavy wooden club used by Australian Aborigines

wade wades wading waded *verb* **1** to walk with difficulty through water or mud **2** to proceed with difficulty

wader *noun* **1** long-legged water bird **2 waders** angler's long waterproof boots

wafer *noun* **1** thin crisp biscuit **2** thin disc of special bread used at Communion

waffle waffles waffling waffled *verb* **1** *informal* to speak or write in a vague wordy way ▷ *noun* **2** *informal* vague wordy talk or writing **3** square crisp pancake with a gridlike pattern

waft *verb* to drift or carry gently through the air

wag wags wagging wagged *verb* **1** to move rapidly from side to side ▷ *noun* **2** wagging movement

wage wages waging waged *noun* **1** (*often plural*) payment for work done, especially when paid weekly ▷ *verb* **2** to engage in (war)

wager *noun* **1** bet on the outcome of something ▷ *verb* **2** to bet (money) on the outcome of something

waggle waggles waggling waggled *verb* to move with a rapid shaking or wobbling motion

wagon or **waggon** *noun* **1** four-wheeled vehicle for heavy loads **2** railway freight truck

wagtail *noun* small bird with a long tail that moves up and down

waif *noun* young person who is, or seems, homeless or neglected

wail *verb* **1** to cry out in pain or misery ▷ *noun* **2** long unhappy cry

waist *noun* part of the body between the ribs and hips

waistband *noun* band of material sewn onto the waist of a garment to strengthen it

waistcoat *noun* sleeveless garment that buttons up the front, usually worn over a shirt and under a jacket

wait *verb* **1** to do little or nothing until something happens **2** to be ready (for something) **3** to be delayed **4** to serve food and drink in a restaurant ▷ *noun* **5** act or period of waiting

waiter *noun* man who serves food and drink in a restaurant

waiting list *noun* list of people waiting for medical treatment, etc

waitress waitresses *noun* woman who serves food and drink in a restaurant

waive waives waiving waived *verb* not to enforce (a law, right, etc)

wake wakes waking woke woken verb **1** to rouse (someone) from sleep ▷ noun **2** gathering to mourn someone's death **3** track left by a moving ship **4 in the wake of** following, often as a result > **wake up** verb to stop being asleep or to rouse (someone) from sleep > **wake up to** verb to become aware of

waken verb to wake (someone)

walk verb **1** to move on foot with at least one foot always on the ground **2** to pass through or over (a distance) on foot **3** to accompany (someone) on foot ▷ noun **4** act or instance of walking **5** distance walked **6** manner of walking **7** place or route for walking > **walker** noun

walkabout noun **1** informal walk among the public by royalty or other famous people **2** period when an Australian Aborigine goes off to live and wander in the bush

walkie-talkie noun small portable radio for sending and receiving messages

walking stick noun wooden stick for leaning on while walking

Walkman® noun small portable cassette player with headphones

walk of life walks of life noun social position or profession

walkover noun easy victory in a competition or contest

walkway walkways noun often raised passage or path for walking along

wall noun **1** structure of brick, stone, etc used to enclose, divide or support **2** something having the function or effect of a wall ▷ verb **3** to enclose (someone or something) with a wall or walls

wallaby wallabies noun animal like a small kangaroo

wallaroo wallaroos noun large stocky kangaroo that lives in rocky or mountainous regions of Australia

wallet noun small folding case for paper money, credit cards, etc

wallflower noun garden plant with sweet-smelling flowers

wallop informal verb **1** to hit (someone) hard ▷ noun **2** hard blow

wallow verb **1** (followed by in) to take pleasure (in an unpleasant emotion) **2** to roll (in liquid or mud) ▷ noun **3** act or instance of wallowing

wallpaper noun thick coloured or patterned paper covering the walls of rooms

walnut noun **1** edible nut with a wrinkled shell **2** tree it grows on **3** its wood, used for making furniture

walrus walruses noun large sea animal with long tusks

waltz waltzes waltzing waltzed noun **1** ballroom dance **2** music for this ▷ verb **3** to dance a waltz **4** informal to move in a relaxed confident way

wan wanner wannest adjective pale and sickly-looking

wand noun thin rod, especially one used in performing magic tricks

wander verb **1** to walk about without a definite destination or aim **2** to go astray ▷ noun **3** act or instance of wandering > **wanderer** noun person who wanders

wane wanes waning waned verb **1** to decrease gradually in size or strength **2** (of the moon) to decrease in size ▷ noun **3 on the wane** decreasing in size, strength or power

wangle wangles wangling wangled verb informal to get

(something) by crafty methods

want *verb* **1** to need or long for **2** to desire or wish (to do something) ▷ *noun* **3** act or instance of wanting **4** lack or absence (of something) > **wanted** *adjective* searched for by the police

wanting *adjective* lacking or not good enough: *The department was found wanting*

wanton *adjective* without justification: *wanton destruction*

war wars warring warred *noun* **1** fighting between nations **2** contest or campaign ▷ *adjective* **3** of, like or caused by war ▷ *verb* **4** to fight a war > **warring** *adjective*

waratah *noun* Australian shrub with crimson flowers

warble warbles warbling warbled *verb* to sing in a high voice

warbler *noun* any of various small songbirds

ward *noun* **1** room in a hospital for patients needing a similar kind of care **2** political division of a town **3** child under the care of a guardian or court > **ward off** *verb* to prevent (something) from harming you

-ward or **-wards** *suffix* forming adjectives or adverbs that show the way something is moving or facing: *homeward; westwards*

warden *noun* **1** person in charge of a prison or youth hostel **2** official responsible for the enforcement of laws: *a traffic warden*

warder *noun* prison officer

wardrobe *noun* **1** cupboard for hanging clothes in **2** person's collection of clothes **3** costumes of a theatre company

ware *noun* **1** articles of a specified type or material: *silverware* **2** **wares** goods for sale

warehouse *noun* large building for storing goods before they are sold or distributed

warfare *noun* activity of fighting a war

warhead *noun* explosive front part of a bomb or missile

warlock *noun* man who practises black magic

warm *adjective* **1** moderately hot **2** providing warmth **3** (of a colour) mainly made up of yellow or red **4** affectionate ▷ *verb* **5** to make (someone or something) warm > **warmly** *adverb*: *warmly dressed* > **warm up** *verb* **1** to become warmer or make (something) warmer **2** to do gentle stretching exercises before more strenuous exercise **3** to become more lively or make (someone or something) more lively

warmonger *noun* person who encourages people to start a war

warmth *noun* **1** mild heat **2** friendliness

warm-up *noun* preparation done just before an activity, such as gentle exercising

warn *verb* **1** to make (someone) aware of possible danger or harm **2** to advise (someone) not to do something > **warning** *noun* something said or written to warn people of a problem or danger > **warn off** *verb* to advise (someone) not to become involved

warp *verb* **1** to twist (something) out of shape **2** to damage (someone's mind) ▷ *noun* **3** state of being warped **4** lengthwise threads on a loom

warrant *noun* **1** document giving official authorization to do something ▷ *verb* **2** to make (an action) necessary

warranty warranties *noun*

(document giving) a guarantee

warren *noun* **1** series of burrows in which rabbits live **2** overcrowded building or part of a town

warrigal *Aust noun* **1** dingo **2** wild horse or other wild animal ▷ *adjective* **3** wild

warrior *noun* person who fights in a war

warship *noun* ship designed and equipped for fighting in wars

wart *noun* small hard growth on the skin

wartime *noun* period of time during which a country is at war

wary warier wariest *adjective* watchful or cautious > **warily** *adverb* > **wariness** *noun*

was *verb* first and third person singular past tense of **be**

wash washes washing washed *verb* **1** to clean (oneself, clothes, etc) with water and usually soap **2** to be washable **3** to flow gently **4** *informal* to be believable or acceptable: *That excuse won't wash* ▷ *noun* **5** act or process of washing **6** clothes washed at one time **7** thin coat of paint **8** disturbance in the water after a ship has passed by > **washable** *adjective* > **wash away** *verb* to carry (something) away by moving water > **wash up** *verb* to wash dishes and cutlery after a meal

washbasin *noun* a deep bowl, usually fixed to a wall, with taps for hot and cold water

washer *noun* **1** ring put under a nut or bolt or in a tap as a seal **2** *Aust* cloth for washing yourself

washing *noun* clothes and bedding to be washed

washing machine *noun* machine for washing clothes in

washing-up *noun* washing of

dishes and cutlery after a meal

washout *noun informal* complete failure

wasp *noun* stinging insect with a slender black-and-yellow striped body

waspish *adjective* bad-tempered

wastage *noun* **1** loss by wear or waste **2** reduction in size of a workforce by not replacing people who have left

waste wastes wasting wasted *verb* **1** to use (time, money, etc) carelessly or thoughtlessly **2** to fail to take advantage of (an opportunity) ▷ *noun* **3** act of wasting or state of being wasted; misuse **4** anything wasted **5** rubbish **6** **wastes** desert ▷ *adjective* **7** rejected as worthless or unwanted > **waste away** *verb* to become weak and ill > **waster** or **wastrel** *noun* layabout

wasted *adjective* unnecessary: *a wasted journey*

wasteful *adjective* extravagant

wasteland *noun* land that is not being used, *eg* because it is infertile

wasting *adjective* (of disease) causing gradual and relentless weight loss and loss of strength and vitality

watch watches watching watched *verb* **1** to look at (someone or something) closely **2** to guard or supervise (someone or something) ▷ *noun* **3** small clock for the wrist or pocket **4** period of guarding or supervising **5** sailor's spell of duty > **watch for** *verb* to keep alert for (something) > **watch out** *verb* **1** to be very careful **2** **watch out for** to keep alert for (something)

watchdog *noun* **1** dog kept to guard property **2** person or group guarding against inefficient or illegal conduct in companies

watchful *adjective* careful to notice everything that is happening

watchman watchmen *noun* man employed to guard a building or property

water *noun* **1** clear colourless tasteless liquid that falls as rain and forms rivers etc **2** body of water, such as a sea or lake **3** level of the tide **4** urine: *to pass water* ▷ *verb* **5** to put water on or into **6** (of the eyes) to fill with tears **7** (of the mouth) to fill with saliva > **water down** *verb* **1** to dilute (a drink) **2** to make (something) weaker

water buffalo *noun* large buffalo from the swampy regions of south Asia

water closet *noun* old-fashioned (room containing) a toilet flushed by water

watercolour *noun* **1** paint thinned with water **2** painting done in watercolours

watercress *noun* edible plant growing in clear ponds and streams, whose leaves are eaten in salads

waterfall *noun* place where the waters of a river drop vertically

waterfront *noun* street or piece of land next to an area of water

watering can *noun* container with a handle and a long spout, which you use to water plants

water lily water lilies *noun* water plant with large floating leaves

waterlogged *adjective* (of land) soaked through, with water on the surface

watermark *noun* faint design in a sheet of paper, visible only when held up to the light

watermelon *noun* large melon with green skin and red flesh

water polo *noun* team game played by swimmers with a ball

waterproof *adjective* **1** not letting water through ▷ *noun* **2** waterproof garment ▷ *verb* **3** to make (a garment) waterproof

watershed *noun* important period or event that marks a turning point

watersider *noun Aust, NZ* person employed to load and unload ships

water-skiing *noun* sport of riding over water on skis towed by a speedboat

water table *noun* level below the surface of the ground at which water can be found

watertight *adjective* **1** not letting water through **2** having no loopholes or weak points

waterway waterways *noun* a canal, river, etc that ships or boats can sail along

waterworks *noun* building where the public water supply is stored and cleaned, and from where it is distributed

watery *adjective* (of food or drink) thin like water

watt *noun* unit of electrical power

wattle *noun* Australian acacia tree with spikes of brightly coloured flowers

wave waves waving waved *verb* **1** to move (the hand) from side to side as a greeting or signal **2** to move or flap (something) from side to side ▷ *noun* **3** moving ridge of water on the surface of the sea **4** curve in the hair **5** prolonged spell of something: *the crime wave* **6** gesture of waving **7** vibration carrying energy through a substance

wavelength *noun* distance between the same points of two successive waves of energy

waver *verb* **1** to hesitate or be undecided **2** to be unsteady

wavy wavier waviest *adjective* having waves or regular curves

wax waxes waxing waxed *noun* **1** solid shiny fatty or oily substance used for sealing, making candles, etc **2** sticky yellow substance in the ear ▷ *verb* **3** to coat or polish (something) with wax **4** to increase in size or strength **5** (of the moon) to get gradually larger

waxen *adjective* made of or like wax

waxwork *noun* **1** lifelike wax model of a famous person **2** **waxworks** place exhibiting these

waxy waxier waxiest *adjective* looking or feeling like wax

way ways *noun* **1** manner or method **2** characteristic manner **3** route or direction **4** track or path **5** distance **6** room for movement or activity: *You're in the way* **7** passage or journey

waylay waylays waylaying waylaid *verb* to lie in wait for and attack (someone)

wayside *noun* side of a road

wayward *adjective* difficult to control > **waywardness** *noun*

WC WCs *abbreviation* water closet: toilet

we *pronoun* (used as the subject of a verb) **1** the speaker or writer and one or more others **2** people in general **3** formal word for I used by editors and monarchs

weak *adjective* **1** lacking strength; feeble **2** likely to break **3** unconvincing **4** lacking flavour > **weaken** *verb* to become weak or make (someone or something) weak > **weakly** *adverb* feebly

weakling *noun* feeble person

weakness weaknesses *noun* **1** lack of moral or physical strength

2 great liking (for something)

weal *noun* raised mark left on the skin by a blow

wealth *noun* **1** state of being rich **2** large amount of money and valuables **3** great amount or number

wealthy wealthier wealthiest *adjective* having a large amount of money and valuables

wean *verb* **1** to accustom (a baby or young mammal) to food other than mother's milk **2** to coax (someone) to give up former habits

weapon *noun* **1** object used in fighting **2** anything used to get the better of an opponent > **weaponry** *noun* weapons collectively

wear wears wearing wore worn *verb* **1** to have (clothes or jewellery) on the body **2** to show (a particular expression) on your face **3** to deteriorate by constant use or action **4** to endure constant use (well or badly) ▷ *noun* **5** clothes suitable for a particular time or purpose: *beach wear* **6** damage caused by use > **wear down** *verb* **1** to make (something) flatter and smoother as a result of repeated rubbing **2** to cause (someone) to stop resisting and to fall in with your wishes by repeatedly doing something or asking them to do something > **wearer** *noun*: *contact lens wearers* > **wearing** *adjective* very tiring > **wear off** *verb* to gradually become less intense > **wear on** *verb* (of time) to pass slowly > **wear out** *verb* to become or make (something) worn, weak, damaged and unusable through frequent use

wear and tear *noun* damage caused to something by normal use

weary wearier weariest; wearies wearying wearied *adjective*

1 tired or exhausted **2** tiring ▷ *verb* **3** (followed by *of*) to become weary (of something) > **wearily** *adverb* in a weary manner > **weariness** *noun*

weasel *noun* small animal with a long body and short legs

weather *noun* **1** day-to-day condition of the atmosphere of a place **2** **under the weather** *informal* slightly ill ▷ *verb* **3** to be affected by the weather **4** to come safely through (a difficult time)

weather-beaten *adjective* **1** (of skin) tanned, rough and lined by exposure to the weather **2** worn or damaged by exposure to the weather

weather vane *noun* device on a roof that revolves to show the direction of the wind

weave *verb* **weaves weaving wove woven 1** to make (fabric) by crossing threads on a loom **2** to make up (a story) **3** (*past*: **weaved**) to move from side to side while going forwards > **weaver** *noun* person who weaves cloth

web *noun* **1** net spun by a spider **2** anything intricate or complex: *web of deceit* **3** skin between the toes of a duck, frog, etc **4** **the Web** short for **World Wide Web** > **webbed** *adjective* (of feet) having skin between the toes

webcam *noun* camera that sends images over the Internet

website *noun* group of connected pages on the World Wide Web

wed *verb* **weds wedding wedded** or **wed 1** to marry **2** to unite (things) closely

wedding *noun* act or ceremony of marriage

wedge wedges wedging wedged *noun* **1** piece of something such as wood, metal or rubber with one thin end and one thick end that can be used to wedge something in place ▷ *verb* **2** to fix (something) in place with a wedge **3** to squeeze (something) into a narrow space

wedlock *noun* marriage

Wednesday Wednesdays *noun* day between Tuesday and Thursday

wee weer weest *adjective Brit, Aust, NZ informal* small or short

weed *noun* **1** wild plant growing where undesired **2** *informal* thin feeble person ▷ *verb* **3** to clear (a garden) of weeds > **weed out** *verb* to remove or eliminate (what is unwanted)

week *noun* **1** period of seven days, especially one beginning on a Sunday **2** hours or days of work in a week

weekday weekdays *noun* any day of the week except Saturday or Sunday

weekend *noun* Saturday and Sunday

weekly weeklies *adjective, adverb* **1** happening, done, etc once a week ▷ *noun* **2** newspaper or magazine published once a week

weep weeps weeping wept *verb* **1** to shed tears **2** to ooze liquid

weeping willow *noun* willow tree with long drooping branches

weevil *noun* small beetle that eats grain etc

weft *noun* cross threads in weaving

weigh *verb* **1** to have (a specified weight) **2** to measure the weight of **3** to consider (something) carefully **4** **weigh anchor** to raise a ship's anchor or (of a ship) have its anchor raised > **weigh down** *verb* to stop (someone) moving easily because of added weight > **weigh up** *verb* to assess

weight *noun* **1** heaviness of an

object **2** unit of measurement of weight **3** object of known mass used for weighing **4** heavy object **5** importance or influence ▷ *verb* **6** to add weight to (something)

weighted *adjective* (of a system) organized in such a way that (a particular person or group) will have an advantage

weightless *adjective* having no weight or very little weight, as in space, where there is no gravity **> weightlessness** *noun* state of being weightless

weightlifting *noun* exercise or competitive sport in which participants lift heavy weights **> weightlifter** *noun*

weighty weightier weightiest *adjective* **1** important or serious **2** very heavy

weir *noun* river dam

weird *adjective* **1** strange or bizarre **2** unearthly or eerie

weirdo weirdos *noun informal* peculiar person

welcome welcomes welcoming welcomed *verb* **1** to greet (a guest) with pleasure **2** to receive (something) gladly ▷ *noun* **3** friendly greeting ▷ *adjective* **4** received gladly **5** freely permitted **> welcoming** *adjective*

weld *verb* **1** to join (pieces of metal or plastic) by softening with heat ▷ *noun* **2** welded joint **> welder** *noun* person who welds pieces of metal or plastic

welfare *noun* **1** wellbeing **2** help given to people in need

welfare state *noun* system in which the government takes responsibility for the wellbeing of its citizens

well better best; wells welling welled *adverb* **1** satisfactorily

2 skilfully **3** completely **4** intimately **5** considerably **6** very likely ▷ *adjective* **7** in good health ▷ *interjection* **8** exclamation of surprise, anger, etc ▷ *noun* **9** hole drilled into the earth to reach water, oil or gas ▷ *verb* **10** to flow upwards or outwards

well-advised *adjective* wise

well-balanced *adjective* sensible and without serious emotional problems

wellbeing *noun* state of being well and happy

well-earned *adjective* thoroughly deserved

well-heeled *adjective informal* wealthy

wellies *plural noun Brit, Aust informal* wellingtons

well-informed *adjective* knowing a lot about a subject or subjects

wellingtons *plural noun Brit, Aust* high waterproof rubber boots

well-meaning *adjective* having good intentions

well-off *adjective informal* quite wealthy

well-spoken *adjective* speaking in a clear or polite way

well-to-do *adjective* quite wealthy

well-worn *adjective* **1** (of a word or phrase) boring from overuse **2** so much used as to be shabby

welsh welshes welshing welshed *verb* (followed by *on*) to fail to pay (a debt) or fulfil (an obligation)

Welsh *adjective* **1** of Wales ▷ *noun* **2** language of Wales

Welshman Welshmen *noun* a man from Wales

Welshwoman Welshwomen *noun* a woman from Wales

welt *noun* raised mark on the skin caused by a blow

welter *noun* jumbled mass

wench *wenches noun facetious* young woman

wend *verb literary* to go or travel

went *verb* past tense of **go**

wept *verb* past of **weep**

were *verb* form of the past tense of **be** used after *we*, *you*, *they*, or a plural noun

werewolf *werewolves noun* (in folklore) person who can turn into a wolf

Wesak *noun* Buddhist festival celebrating the Buddha, held in May

west *noun* **1** (direction towards) the part of the horizon where the sun sets **2** region lying in this direction **3 the West** western Europe and the US ▷ *adjective* **4** to or in the west **5** (of a wind) from the west ▷ *adverb* **6** in, to or towards the west > **westerly** *adjective* to or towards the left

western *adjective* **1** of or in the west ▷ *noun* **2** film or story about cowboys in the western US

West Indian *noun* person from the West Indies

westward *adjective* **1** towards the west **2** lying in the west ▷ *adverb* **3** (also **westwards**) towards the west

wet *adjective* **wetter wettest; wets wetting wet** or **wetted 1** covered or soaked with water or another liquid **2** not yet dry **3** rainy **4** *Brit informal* (of a person) feeble or foolish ▷ *noun* **5** moisture or rain **6** *Brit informal* feeble or foolish person **7** *Aust* rainy season ▷ *verb* **8** to make (someone or something) wet > **wetness** *noun*

wet nurse *noun* woman employed to breast-feed another woman's baby

wet suit *noun* close-fitting rubber suit worn by divers etc

whack *verb* **1** to strike (someone or something) with a hard blow ▷ *noun* **2** such a blow **3** *informal* share **4** *informal* attempt

whale *noun* **1** large fish-shaped sea mammal **2 have a whale of a time** *informal* to enjoy yourself very much

whaling *noun* hunting of whales for food and oil > **whaler** *noun* person who hunts whales

wharf *wharves* or **wharfs** *noun* platform at a harbour for loading and unloading ships

what *pronoun* **1** which thing **2** that which **3** request for a statement to be repeated **4 what for?** why? ▷ *interjection* **5** exclamation of anger, surprise, etc ▷ *adverb* **6** in which way, how much: *what do you care?*

whatever *pronoun* **1** everything or anything that **2** no matter what

whatsoever *adverb* at all

wheat *noun* **1** grain used in making flour, bread and pasta **2** plant producing this

wheatmeal *noun* brown flour made from wheat grains

wheedle *wheedles wheedling wheedled verb* (followed by *into*) to coax (someone to do something)

wheel *noun* **1** disc that revolves on an axle, usually fixed under a vehicle to make it move ▷ *verb* **2** to push or pull (something with wheels) **3** to turn round suddenly

wheelbarrow *noun* shallow cart for carrying loads, with a wheel at the front and two handles

wheelchair *noun* chair with wheels for use by people who cannot walk

wheeze *wheezes wheezing wheezed verb* **1** to breathe with a hoarse whistling noise ▷ *noun*

2 wheezing sound **3** *informal* trick or plan ▷ **wheezy** *adjective* making a hoarse whistling noise

whelk *noun* edible snail-like shellfish

whelp *noun* **1** pup or cub ▷ *verb* **2** (of an animal) to give birth

when *adverb* **1** at what time? ▷ *conjunction* **2** at the time that **3** although **4** considering the fact that ▷ *pronoun* **5** at which time

whence *adverb, conjunction old-fashioned* from where

> You should not write *from whence* because *whence* already means 'from where'

whenever *adverb, conjunction* at whatever time

where *adverb* **1** in, at or to what place? ▷ *pronoun* **2** in, at or to which place ▷ *conjunction* **3** in the place at which

whereabouts *noun* **1** present position ▷ *adverb* **2** at what place

whereas *conjunction* but on the other hand

whereby *pronoun* by which

whereupon *conjunction* at which point

wherever *conjunction, adverb* at whatever place

wherewithal *noun* necessary funds, resources, etc

whet whets whetting whetted *verb* **1** to sharpen (a tool) **2** **whet someone's appetite** to increase someone's desire

whether *conjunction* used to introduce an indirect question or a clause expressing doubt or choice

whey *noun* watery liquid that is separated from the curds in sour milk when cheese is made

which *adjective, pronoun* **1** used to request or refer to a choice from different possibilities ▷ *pronoun*

2 used to refer to a thing already mentioned

whichever *adjective, pronoun* **1** any out of several **2** no matter which

whiff *noun* **1** slight smell **2** trace or hint

while whiles whiling whiled *conjunction* **1** at the same time that **2** but ▷ *noun* **3** period of time > **while away** *verb* to pass (time) idly but pleasantly

whilst *conjunction* while

whim *noun* sudden desire; impulse

whimper *verb* **1** to cry in a soft whining way ▷ *noun* **2** soft unhappy cry

whimsical *adjective* unusual and playful

whine whines whining whined *noun* **1** high-pitched unhappy cry **2** annoying complaint ▷ *verb* **3** to make such a sound > **whining** *noun, adjective* making a whining sound

whinge whinges whinging or **whingeing whinged** *Brit, Aust, NZ informal verb* **1** to complain ▷ *noun* **2** complaint

whinny whinnies whinnying whinnied *verb* **1** to neigh softly ▷ *noun* **2** soft neigh

whip whips whipping whipped *noun* **1** cord attached to a handle, used for beating animals or people **2** dessert made from beaten cream or egg whites ▷ *verb* **3** to strike (an animal or a person) with a whip, strap or cane **4** *informal* to pull, remove or move (something) quickly **5** to beat (especially eggs or cream) to a froth **6** to rouse (people) into a particular condition **7** *informal* to steal (something) > **whip up** *verb* to cause and encourage (an emotion) in people: *people who try to whip up hatred* *against minorities*

whip bird *noun* Australian bird whose cry ends with a sound like the crack of a whip

whiplash injury whiplash injuries *noun* neck injury caused by a sudden jerk to the head, as in a car crash

whippet *noun* racing dog like a small greyhound

whirl *verb* **1** to spin or revolve **2** to be dizzy or confused ▷ *noun* **3** whirling movement **4** intense activity **5** confusion or dizziness

whirlpool *noun* strong circular current of water

whirlwind *noun* **1** column of air that spins round and round very fast ▷ *adjective* **2** much quicker than normal

whirr whirrs whirring whirred; also spelt **whir** *noun* **1** continuous soft buzz ▷ *verb* **2** to make a whirr

whisk *verb* **1** to move or remove quickly **2** to beat (especially eggs or cream) to a froth ▷ *noun* **3** egg-beating tool

whisker *noun* **1** any of the long stiff hairs on the face of a cat or other mammal **2 by a whisker** *informal* only just **3 whiskers** hair growing on a man's face

whiskey whiskeys *noun* Irish or American whisky

whisky whiskies *noun* strong alcoholic drink made from grain such as barley

whisper *verb* **1** to speak softly, using the breath but not the throat **2** to rustle ▷ *noun* **3** soft voice **4** *informal* rumour **5** rustling sound

whist *noun* card game in which one pair of players tries to win more tricks than another pair

whistle whistles whistling whistled *verb* **1** to produce a

shrill sound by forcing the breath through pursed lips **2** to signal (something) by a whistle ▷ *noun* **3** whistling sound **4** instrument blown to make a whistling sound

whit *noun* **not a whit** not the slightest amount

white whiter whitest; whites *adjective* **1** of the colour of snow **2** pale **3** light in colour **4** (of coffee) containing milk or cream ▷ *noun* **5** colour of snow **6** clear fluid round the yolk of an egg **7** white part, especially of the eyeball **> whiteness** *noun*

White *noun* member of the race of people with light-coloured skin

white-collar *adjective* (of a worker) working in an office rather than doing manual work

white-hot *adjective* extremely hot

white lie *noun* harmless lie, told to prevent someone's feelings from being hurt

white paper *noun* report by the government, outlining its policy on a particular subject

whitewash whitewashes whitewashing whitewashed *noun* **1** mixture of lime and water used for painting walls white ▷ *verb* **2** to cover (something) with whitewash **3** to conceal or gloss over (unpleasant facts)

whither *adverb* *obsolete* to what place

whiting *noun* edible sea fish

whittle whittles whittling whittled *verb* to cut or carve (wood) with a knife **> whittle down** or **away** *verb* to reduce (something) or wear (it) away gradually

whizz or **whiz whizzes whizzing whizzed** *verb* **1** to make a loud buzzing sound **2** *informal* to move quickly ▷ *noun* **3** loud buzzing sound **4** *informal* person who is skilful at something

whizz kid or **whiz kid** *noun informal* person who is outstandingly able for his or her age

who *pronoun* **1** which person **2** used to refer to a person or people already mentioned

whoa *interjection* command to slow down or stop a horse

whodunnit or **whodunit** *noun informal* detective story, play or film

whoever *pronoun* **1** any person who **2** no matter who

whole *adjective* **1** containing all the elements or parts **2** uninjured or undamaged ▷ *noun* **3** complete thing or system **4 on the whole** in general > **wholeness** *noun* > **wholly** *adverb* completely

wholehearted *adjective* enthusiastic and sincere > **wholeheartedly** *adverb*

wholemeal *adjective* **1** (of flour) made from the whole wheat grain **2** made from wholemeal flour

whole number *noun* number that does not contain a fraction

wholesale *adjective, adverb* **1** buying goods cheaply in large quantities and selling them to shopkeepers **2** on a large scale > **wholesaler** *noun* person who works in the wholesale trade

wholesome *adjective* good for the health or wellbeing

whom *pronoun* object form of **who**: *the girl whom he married*

whoop *verb* **1** to shout or cry in excitement ▷ *noun* **2** shout or cry of excitement

whoopee *interjection informal* cry of joy

whooping cough *noun* infectious disease marked by violent coughing and noisy breathing

whopper *noun informal* **1** anything unusually large **2** huge lie > **whopping** *adjective informal* unusually large

whore *noun offensive* a prostitute, or a woman believed to act like a prostitute

whose *pronoun* of whom or of which

Many people are confused about the difference between *whose* and *who's*. *Whose* is used to show possession in a question or when something is being described: *Whose bag is this? the person whose car is blocking the exit.* *Who's*, with the apostrophe, is a short form of *who is* or *who has: Who's that girl? Who's got my ruler?*

why *adverb* **1** for what reason ▷ *pronoun* **2** because of which

wick *noun* cord through a lamp or candle which carries fuel to the flame

wicked *adjective* **1** morally bad; evil **2** mischievous > **wickedly** *adverb* in a wicked manner > **wickedness** *noun* state of being wicked

wicker *adjective* made of woven cane

wickerwork *noun* material made by weaving twigs, canes or reeds together

wicket *noun* **1** set of three cricket stumps and two bails **2** ground between the two wickets on a cricket pitch

wide wider widest *adjective* **1** large from side to side; broad **2** having a specified width **3** spacious or extensive **4** far from the target **5** opened fully ▷ *adverb* **6** to the full extent **7** over a wide area **8** far from the target > **widely** *adverb* > **widen** *verb* to make (something) wider or to become wider

wide-awake *adjective* completely awake

wide-ranging *adjective* covering a variety of different things or a large area

widespread *adjective* affecting a wide area or a large number of people; common

widow *noun* woman whose husband is dead and who has not remarried

widowed *adjective* whose husband or wife has died

widower *noun* man whose wife is dead and who has not remarried

width *noun* **1** distance from side to side **2** quality of being wide

wield *verb* **1** to hold and use (a weapon) **2** to have and use (power)

wife wives *noun* woman to whom a man is married

wig *noun* artificial head of hair

wiggle wiggles wiggling wiggled *verb* **1** to move jerkily from side to side ▷ *noun* **2** wiggling movement

wigwam *noun* Native American's tent

wild *adjective* **1** (of an animal) not tamed or domesticated **2** (of a plant) not cultivated **3** excited and uncontrolled **4** violent or stormy **5** *informal* furious **6** random ▷ *noun* **7** **the wilds** desolate or uninhabited place > **wildly** *adverb* extremely or intensely state of being wild

wildcat *noun* European wild animal like a large domestic cat

wildebeest *noun* gnu

wilderness wildernesses *noun* uninhabited uncultivated region

wildfire *noun* **spread like wildfire** to spread quickly and uncontrollably

wild-goose chase *noun* search that has little chance of success

wildlife *noun* wild animals and plants collectively

Wild West *noun* western part of the USA when first settled by Europeans

wiles *plural noun* crafty tricks

wilful *adjective* **1** headstrong or obstinate **2** intentional > **wilfully** *adverb* in a wilful manner

will¹ *verb* (often shortened to '*ll*) used as an auxiliary verb to form the future tense, to indicate intention or expectation, and to express invitations and requests: *Tom and I will go shopping later; I will not let you down; Robin will be annoyed; Will you have something to drink?; Will you do me a favour?*

will² *noun* **1** strong determination **2** desire or wish **3** instructions written for disposal of your property after death ▷ *verb* **4** to use your will in an attempt to do (something): *I willed my eyes to open* **5** to wish or desire (something): *if God wills it* **6** to leave (property) to someone in a will: *The farm was willed to her*

willing *adjective* **1** ready or inclined (to do something) **2** keen and obliging > **willingly** *adverb* voluntarily > **willingness** *noun* state of being willing

will-o'-the-wisp *noun* **1** person or thing that is impossible to catch **2** pale light sometimes seen over marshes at night

willow *noun* **1** tree with long thin branches **2** its wood, used for making cricket bats

willowy *adjective* slender and graceful

willpower *noun* ability to control yourself and your actions

willy-nilly *adverb* whether wanted

or not

wilt *verb* to become limp or lose strength

wily wilier wiliest *adjective* crafty or sly

wimp *noun informal* feeble timid person

wimple *noun* garment framing the face, worn by medieval women and now by nuns

win wins winning won *verb* **1** to come first in (a competition, fight, etc) **2** to gain (a prize) in a competition **3** to get (something) by effort ▷ *noun* **4** victory, especially in a game > **win over** *verb* to gain the support or consent of

wince winces wincing winced *verb* **1** to draw back, as if in pain ▷ *noun* **2** act of wincing

winch winches winching winched *noun* **1** machine for lifting or hauling using a cable or chain wound round a drum ▷ *verb* **2** to lift or haul (something) using a winch

wind¹ *noun* **1** current of air **2** hint or suggestion **3** ability to breathe easily **4** gas produced in the stomach, causing discomfort ▷ *verb* **5** to render (someone) short of breath

wind² **winds winding wound** *verb* **1** to coil or wrap (something) round something else **2** to tighten the spring of (a clock or watch) **3** to move in a twisting course > **wind up** *verb* **1** to reach an end or bring (something) to an end **2** to tighten the spring of (a clock or watch) **3** *informal* to annoy or tease

windfall *noun* sum of money received unexpectedly

wind instrument *noun* musical instrument played by blowing

windmill *noun* machine for grinding grain or pumping water, driven by sails turned by the wind

window *noun* **1** opening in a wall, usually with a glass pane or panes, to let in light or air **2** display area behind the window of a shop **3** area on a computer screen that can be manipulated separately from the rest of the display area **4** period of unbooked time in a diary or schedule

window box window boxes *noun* a long narrow container on a windowsill in which plants are grown

window-dressing *noun* arrangement of goods in a shop window

window-shopping *noun* looking at goods in shop windows without intending to buy

windowsill *noun* ledge along the bottom of a window

windpipe *noun* tube linking the throat and the lungs

windscreen *noun* front window of a motor vehicle

windscreen wiper *noun* device that wipes rain etc from a windscreen

windsurfing *noun* sport of riding on water using a surfboard propelled and steered by a sail

windswept *adjective* (of a place) exposed to strong winds

windy windier windiest *adjective* involving a lot of wind: *It was windy and cold*

wine wines wining wined *noun* **1** alcoholic drink made from fermented grapes **2** similar drink made from other fruits ▷ *verb* **3 wine and dine** to entertain (someone) with fine food and drink

wing *noun* **1** one of the limbs or organs of a bird, insect or bat that are used for flying **2** one of the winglike supporting parts of an aircraft **3** side part of a building that sticks out **4** group within a political party **5** part of a car body surrounding the wheels **6** *Sport* (player on) either side of the pitch **7 wings** sides of a stage ▷ *verb* **8** to fly **9** to wound (a bird) slightly in the wing or (a person) slightly in the arm > **winged** *adjective* having wings

winger *noun Sport* player positioned on a wing

wink *verb* **1** to close and open (an eye) quickly as a signal **2** (of a light) to twinkle ▷ *noun* **3** winking **4** smallest amount of sleep

winkle winkles winkling winkled *noun* shellfish with a spiral shell > **winkle out** *verb informal* to get (information) from someone

winner *noun* person who wins a prize, race or competition

winning *adjective* **1** gaining victory **2** charming

winnings *plural noun* money won, especially in gambling

winter *noun* **1** coldest season ▷ *verb* **2** to spend the winter

wintry *adjective* **1** of or like winter **2** cold or unfriendly

wipe wipes wiping wiped *verb* **1** to clean or dry (something) by rubbing **2** to erase (a tape) ▷ *noun* **3** wiping > **wipe out** *verb* to destroy (people or a place) completely

wire wires wiring wired *noun* **1** thin flexible strand of metal **2** length of this used to carry electric current ▷ *verb* **3** to equip (a place) with wires

wireless wirelesses *noun old-fashioned* same as **radio**

wiring *noun* system of wires

wiry wirier wiriest *adjective* **1** lean but strong **2** (of hair) stiff and rough

wisdom *noun* **1** good sense and judgment **2** knowledge collected over time

wisdom tooth wisdom teeth *noun* any of the four large molar teeth that come through usually after the age of twenty

wise wiser wisest *adjective* having wisdom; sensible > **wisely** *adverb*

wisecrack *noun informal* clever, sometimes unkind, remark

wish wishes wishing wished *verb* **1** to want or desire (something) **2** to feel or express a hope about someone's wellbeing, success, etc ▷ *noun* **3** expression of a desire **4** thing desired

wishbone *noun* V-shaped bone above the breastbone of most birds

wishful thinking *noun* hope or wish that is unlikely to come true

wishy-washy *adjective informal* not firm or clear

wisp *noun* **1** light delicate streak **2** twisted bundle or tuft > **wispy** *adjective* (of hair) thin and untidy

wisteria *noun* climbing shrub with blue or purple flowers

wistful *adjective* sadly longing > **wistfully** *adverb* sadly and longingly

wit *noun* **1** ability to use words or ideas in a clever and amusing way **2** person with this ability **3** (*sometimes plural*) practical intelligence

witch witches *noun* **1** person, usually female, who practises (black) magic **2** ugly or wicked woman

witchcraft *noun* use of magic

witch doctor *noun* (in certain societies) a man appearing to cure or cause injury or disease by magic

witchetty grub *noun* large Australian caterpillar, eaten by

Aborigines

witch-hunt *noun* campaign against people with unpopular views

with *preposition* indicating presence alongside, possession, means of performance, characteristic manner, etc: *walking with his dog; a man with two cars; hit with a hammer; playing with skill*

withdraw withdraws withdrawing withdrew withdrawn *verb* to take (something) out or away or to move out or away

withdrawal *noun* **1** taking something away **2** changing or denying a statement **3** taking money from a bank account

withdrawal symptoms *plural noun* unpleasant effects suffered by an addict who has suddenly stopped taking a drug

withdrawn *adjective* unusually shy or quiet

wither *verb* to wilt or dry up

withering *adjective* (of a look or remark) scornful

withers *plural noun* ridge between a horse's shoulder blades

withhold withholds withholding withheld *verb* not to give (something)

within *preposition, adverb* in or inside

without *preposition* not accompanied by, using or having

withstand withstands withstanding withstood *verb* to oppose or resist (something) successfully

witness witnesses witnessing witnessed *noun* **1** person who has seen something happen **2** person giving evidence in court ▷ *verb* **3** to see (an incident) at first hand **4** to sign (a document) to confirm that it is genuine

witter *verb* *Chiefly Brit* to chatter pointlessly or at great length

witticism *noun* witty remark

wittingly *adverb* intentionally

witty wittier wittiest *adjective* clever and amusing > **wittily** *adverb* in a clever and amusing manner

wives *noun* plural of **wife**

wizard *noun* **1** magician **2** person with outstanding skill in a particular field > **wizardry** *noun* something that is very cleverly done

wizened *adjective* wrinkled

woad *noun* blue dye obtained from a plant, used by the ancient Britons as a body dye

wobbegong *noun* Australian shark with brown-and-white skin

wobble wobbles wobbling wobbled *verb* **1** to move unsteadily **2** to tremble or shake ▷ *noun* **3** wobbling movement or sound

wobbly *adjective* unsteady

woe *noun* grief

woeful *adjective* **1** extremely sad **2** of poor quality > **woefully** *adverb*: *woefully inadequate*

wok *noun* bowl-shaped Chinese cooking pan, used for stir-frying

woke *verb* past tense of **wake**

woken *verb* past participle of **wake**

wolf wolves; wolfs wolfing wolfed *noun* **1** wild hunting animal related to the dog **2** **cry wolf** to raise a false alarm ▷ *verb* **3** to eat (food) quickly and greedily

wolf whistle *noun* whistle usually made by a man to show he thinks a woman is attractive

woman women *noun* **1** adult human female **2** women collectively

womanhood *noun* state of being a woman

womb noun hollow organ in female mammals where unborn babies grow

wombat noun small heavily-built burrowing Australian animal

won verb past of **win**

wonder verb 1 to be curious (about something) 2 to be amazed (at something) ▷ noun 3 wonderful thing; marvel 4 emotion caused by an amazing or unusual thing ▷ adjective 5 spectacularly successful: a wonder drug

wonderful adjective 1 very fine 2 magnificent or remarkable > **wonderfully** adverb

wondrous adjective old-fashioned wonderful

wonky wonkier wonkiest adjective Brit, Aust, NZ informal shaky or unsteady

wont adjective 1 accustomed or inclined (to do something) ▷ noun 2 custom

woo woos wooing wooed verb 1 to try to persuade (someone) 2 old-fashioned to try to gain the love of (a woman)

wood noun 1 substance trees are made of, used in carpentry and as fuel 2 area where trees grow

wooded adjective covered with trees

wooden adjective 1 made of wood 2 stiff and without expression

woodland noun forest

woodpecker noun bird that drills holes into trees with its beak to find insects

woodwind adjective, noun (of) a type of wind instrument made of wood, played by being blown into

woodwork noun 1 parts of a house that are made of wood, eg doors and window frames 2 making things out of wood

woodworm woodworm or

woodworms noun insect larva that bores into wood

woody woodier woodiest adjective 1 (of a plant) having a hard tough stem 2 (of an area) covered with trees

woof noun 1 barking noise made by a dog 2 cross threads in weaving

wool noun 1 soft hair of sheep, goats, etc 2 yarn spun from this

woollen adjective made from wool > **woollens** plural noun clothes made from wool

woolly woollies; woollier woolliest adjective 1 of or like wool 2 vague or muddled ▷ noun 3 knitted woollen garment

woolshed noun Aust, NZ large building in which sheep are sheared

woomera noun Aust notched stick used by Australian Aborigines as an aid when throwing a spear

woozy woozier wooziest adjective informal weak, dizzy and confused

word noun 1 single unit of speech or writing 2 brief remark, chat or discussion 3 message 4 promise 5 command ▷ verb 6 to express (something) in words

wording noun choice and arrangement of words

word processor noun machine with a keyboard, microprocessor and VDU for electronic organization and storage of text

wordy wordier wordiest adjective using too many words

wore verb past tense of **wear**

work noun 1 physical or mental effort directed to making or doing something 2 paid employment 3 duty or task 4 something made or done 5 **works a** factory **b** total of a writer's or artist's achievements **c** activities relating to building and construction **d** mechanism of a machine ▷ *adjective* **6** of or for work ▷ *verb* **7** to do work **8** to be employed **9** to operate (something) **10** (of a plan etc) to be successful **11** to cultivate (land) **12** to manipulate, shape or process **13** to cause (someone) to reach a specified condition > **work out** *verb* **1** to find (the solution to a problem) by using your reasoning **2** to happen or progress **3** to do a session of physical exercise > **work up** *verb* **1** to make (yourself) very upset or angry about something **2** to develop **3** **work up to** to progress towards (something) gradually > **worked up** *adjective*

workable *adjective* able to operate successfully; practical

workaholic *noun* person obsessed with work

worker *noun* a person employed in a particular industry or business

workforce *noun* people who work in a particular place

workhouse *noun* (in England, formerly) building where poor people were given food and lodgings in return for work

working class working classes *noun* social class consisting of manual workers > **working-class** *adjective*: *a working-class background*

workings *plural noun* ways in which a machine, system, etc operates

workload *noun* amount of work to be done

workman workmen *noun* a man whose job involves physical skills

workmanship *noun* skill with which an object is made

workmate *noun* fellow worker

workout *noun* session of physical exercise

workshop *noun* room or building with equipment for making or repairing things

worktop *noun* surface in a kitchen, used for food preparation

world *noun* **1** planet earth **2** people in general **3** society of a particular area or period **4** a person's life and experiences ▷ *adjective* **5** of the whole world

worldly worldlier worldliest *adjective* **1** not spiritual **2** wise in the ways of the world

world war *noun* war that involves countries all over the world

world-weary *adjective* no longer finding pleasure in life

worldwide *adjective* throughout the world

World Wide Web *noun* worldwide communication system which people use through computers; the Internet

worm *noun* **1** small thin animal with no bones or legs **2** *Computers* type of virus **3** **worms** illness caused by parasites in the intestines ▷ *verb* **4** to rid (an animal) of worms > **worm out** *verb* to extract (information) from someone craftily

worn *verb* past participle of **wear**

worn-out *adjective* **1** used until too thin or too damaged to be of further use **2** extremely tired

worried *adjective* unhappy and anxious; troubled

worry worries worrying worried *verb* **1** to be anxious or uneasy or to cause (someone) to be anxious or uneasy **2** to annoy or bother (someone) **3** (of a dog) to chase and try to bite (sheep etc) ▷ *noun* **4** (cause of) anxiety or concern > **worrying** *adjective*: *a worrying report about smoking*

worse *adjective, adverb* comparative

of **bad** or **badly**

worsen *verb* to grow worse or make (something) worse

worse off *adjective* having less money or being in a more unpleasant situation than before

worship worships worshipping worshipped *verb* **1** to show religious devotion to (a god) **2** to love and admire (someone) ▷ *noun* **3** act or instance of worshipping **4 Worship** title for a mayor or magistrate > **worshipper** *noun* person who worships

worst *adjective, adverb* **1** superlative of **bad** or **badly** ▷ *noun* **2** worst thing

worth *preposition* **1** having a value of **2** deserving or justifying ▷ *noun* **3** value or price **4** excellence **5** amount to be had for a given sum

worthless *adjective* having no real value or use

worthwhile *adjective* worth the time or effort involved

worthy worthier worthiest; worthies *adjective* **1** deserving admiration or respect ▷ *noun* **2** *informal* notable person

would *verb* (often shortened to *'d*) used as an auxiliary verb to express invitations and requests, to talk about hypothetical situations, to describe habitual past actions and to replace *will* in reported speech: *Would you like some tea?; We'd like two tickets, please; I'd write to him if I were you; I wouldn't have come if I'd known; She would always watch the late news; He said he would call back*

would-be *adjective* wanting to be or claiming to be: *a would-be pop singer*

wound¹ *noun* **1** physical injury, especially a cut **2** injury to the feelings ▷ *verb* **3** to cause a wound to (someone) > **wounded** *adjective*

wound² *verb* past of **wind²**

wove *verb* a past tense of **weave**

woven *verb* a past participle of **weave**

wow *interjection* **1** exclamation of astonishment ▷ *noun* **2** *informal* astonishing person or thing

WPC WPCs *abbreviation* woman police constable

wraith *noun* ghost

wrangle wrangles wrangling wrangled *verb* **1** to argue noisily ▷ *noun* **2** noisy argument

wrap wraps wrapping wrapped *verb* **1** to fold (something) round (a person or thing) so as to cover ▷ *noun* **2** garment wrapped round the shoulders **3** sandwich made by wrapping a filling in a tortilla > **wrap up** *verb* **1** to fold paper round **2** to put warm clothes on **3** *informal* to finish or settle (a matter)

wrapped up *adjective informal* (followed by *in*) giving all your attention (to someone or something)

wrapper *noun* cover for a product

wrapping *noun* material used to wrap

wrath *noun* intense anger

wreak *verb* **wreak havoc** to cause chaos

wreath *noun* twisted ring or band of flowers or leaves used as a memorial or tribute

wreck *verb* **1** to destroy ▷ *noun* **2** remains of something that has been destroyed or badly damaged, especially a vehicle **3** person in very poor condition > **wrecked** *adjective*

wreckage *noun* wrecked remains

wren *noun* small brown songbird

wrench wrenches wrenching wrenched *verb* **1** to twist or pull (something) violently **2** to sprain (a joint) ▷ *noun* **3** violent twist or pull **4** sprain **5** difficult or painful parting **6** adjustable spanner

wrest *verb* to take (something) by force

wrestle wrestles wrestling wrestled *verb* **1** to fight, especially as a sport, by struggling with and trying to throw down (an opponent) **2** to struggle hard (with a problem) > **wrestler** *noun*

wrestling *noun* sport of struggling with and trying to throw down an opponent

wretch wretches *noun* wicked or unfortunate person

wretched *adjective* **1** unhappy or unfortunate **2** worthless > **wretchedly** *adverb* in a wretched manner > **wretchedness** *noun*

wriggle wriggles wriggling wriggled *verb* **1** to move (the body) with a twisting action ▷ *noun* **2** wriggling movement > **wriggle out of** *verb* to manage to avoid (doing something) > **wriggly** *adjective*

wring wrings wringing wrung *verb* **1** to twist, especially to squeeze liquid out of (a wet cloth) **2** to clasp and twist (the hands)

wrinkle wrinkles wrinkling wrinkled *noun* **1** slight crease, especially one in the skin due to age ▷ *verb* **2** to become slightly creased or make (something) slightly creased > **wrinkled** *adjective* > **wrinkly** *adjective*: *wrinkly stockings*

wrist *noun* joint between the hand and the arm

wristwatch wristwatches *noun* watch worn on the wrist

writ *noun* legal document that orders a person to something

write writes writing wrote written *verb* **1** to mark paper etc

with (letters, words or numbers) **2** to set (something) down in words **3** to communicate with someone by (letter) **4** to create (a book, piece of music, etc) > **write down** *verb* to record (something) on a piece of paper > **write up** *verb* to write a full account of (something), often from notes

write-off *noun informal* something damaged beyond repair

writer *noun* **1** author **2** person who has written something specified

write-up *noun* published account of something

writhe writhes writhing writhed *verb* to twist or squirm in or as if in pain

writing *noun* **1** something that has been written **2** person's style of writing **3** piece of written work

written *verb* past participle of **write**

wrong *adjective* **1** incorrect or mistaken **2** immoral or bad **3** not intended or suitable **4** not working properly ▷ *adverb* **5** in a wrong manner ▷ *noun* **6** something immoral or unjust ▷ *verb* **7** to treat (someone) unfairly or unjustly > **wrongly** *adverb*

wrongful *adjective* illegal, unfair or immoral > **wrongfully** *adverb*

wrote *verb* past tense of **write**

wrought *adjective* (of metals) shaped by hammering or beating

wrought iron *noun* pure form of iron formed into decorative shapes

wrung *verb* past of **wring**

wry *adjective* **1** drily humorous **2** (of a facial expression) twisted > **wryly** *adverb* in a wry manner

WWW *abbreviation* World Wide Web

X or **x** *noun* **1** indicating an error, a choice, or a kiss **2** indicating an unknown, unspecified, or variable factor, number, person, or thing

xenophobia *noun* fear or hatred of people from other countries > **xenophobic** *adjective*: *xenophobic attitudes*

Xerox® **Xeroxes** *noun* **1** machine for copying printed material **2** copy made by a Xerox machine

Xmas Xmases *noun informal* Christmas

X-ray X-rays X-raying X-rayed; also spelt **x-ray** *noun* **1** stream of radiation that can pass through some solid materials **2** picture made by sending X-rays through someone's body to examine the inside of it ▷ *verb* **3** to photograph or examine (someone or something) using X-rays

xylem *noun technical* plant tissue that conducts water and minerals from the roots to all other parts. It forms the wood in trees and shrubs

xylophone *noun* musical instrument made of a row of wooden bars of different lengths played with hammers

-y *suffix* used to form nouns: *anarchy*

yabby yabbies *noun* small edible Australian crayfish

yacht *noun* boat with sails or an engine, used for racing or for pleasure trips

yachting *noun* sport or activity of sailing a yacht

yachtsman yachtsmen *noun* man who sails a yacht > **yachtswoman** *noun*

yak *noun* Tibetan ox with long shaggy hair

yakka or **yacker** *noun Aust, NZ informal* work

yam *noun* tropical root vegetable

yank *verb* **1** to pull or jerk (something) suddenly ▷ *noun* **2** sudden pull or jerk

Yankee or **Yank** *noun informal* person from the United States

yap yaps yapping yapped *verb* to bark with a high-pitched sound

yard *noun* **1** unit of length equal to 36 inches or about 91.4 centimetres **2** enclosed area, usually next to a building and often used for a particular purpose: *builder's yard*

yardstick *noun* standard against which to judge other people or things

yarn *noun* **1** thread used for knitting or making cloth **2** *informal* long involved story, often with invented details to make it more interesting or exciting

yashmak *noun* veil worn by some Muslim women over their faces when they are in public

yawn *verb* **1** to open your mouth wide and take in more air than usual, often when tired or bored ▷ *noun* **2** act of yawning

yawning *adjective* (of a gap or opening) very wide

ye *pronoun* **1** *archaic or dialect* you **2** (in language intended to appear old) the

yeah *interjection informal* yes

year *noun* **1** period of twelve months or 365 days (366 days in a leap year), which is the time taken for the earth to travel once around the sun **2** period of twelve consecutive months, not always January to December, on which administration or organization is based: *the current financial year*

yearling *noun* animal between one and two years old

yearly *adjective* **1** happening every year or once a year; annual ▷ *adverb* **2** every year or once a year; annually

yearn *verb* to long (for something or to do something) very much ▷ **yearning** *noun*

yeast *noun* fungus used to make bread rise and to ferment alcoholic drinks

yell *verb* **1** to shout or scream loudly ▷ *noun* **2** loud shout or cry of pain, anger or fear

yellow *noun, adjective* **1** the colour of buttercups, egg yolks or lemons ▷ *adjective* **2** *informal* cowardly ▷ *verb* **3** to become or make

(something) yellow, often with age ▷ **yellowish** *adjective*

yellow box yellow boxes *noun* a large Australian eucalyptus tree

yellow fever *noun* serious infectious tropical disease

Yellow Pages® *plural noun* telephone directory which lists businesses under the headings of the type of service they provide

yelp *verb* **1** to give a sudden, short cry ▷ *noun* **2** sudden, short cry

yen *noun* **1** monetary unit of Japan **2** *informal* longing or desire

▎The plural of *yen* in sense 1 is *yen*

yes *interjection* expresses agreement, acceptance or approval or acknowledges facts

yesterday *adverb* **1** on the day before today **2** in the recent past ▷ *noun* **3** the day before today **4** the recent past

yet *adverb* **1** up until then or now **2** now or until later **3** still **4** used for emphasis: *She'd changed her mind yet again* ▷ *conjunction* **5** nevertheless or still

yeti *noun* large apelike creature said to live in the Himalayas; also **abominable snowman**

yew *noun* evergreen tree with needle-like leaves and red berries

Yiddish *noun* language of German origin spoken by many Jewish people of European origin

yield *verb* **1** to give in **2** to give up control of or surrender (something) **3** to break or give way **4** to produce or bear (a crop or profit) ▷ *noun* **5** amount of food, money or profit produced from a given area of land or from an investment

yippee *interjection* exclamation of happiness or excitement

yob *noun informal* bad-mannered or aggressive youth

yodel yodels yodelling yodelled
verb to sing normal notes with high
quick notes in between

yoga *noun* Hindu method of exercise
and discipline aiming at spiritual,
mental and physical wellbeing

yogurt or **yoghurt** *noun* slightly
sour thick liquid food made from
milk that has had bacteria added to
it, often sweetened and flavoured
with fruit

yoke *noun* **1** wooden bar put across
the necks of two animals to hold
them together, and to which
a plough or other tool may be
attached **2** *literary* oppressive force:
the yoke of the tyrant **3** fitted part of
a garment to which a fuller part
is attached

yokel *noun* person who lives in the
country and is regarded as being
rather stupid and old-fashioned

yolk *noun* yellow part of an egg

Yom Kippur *noun* annual Jewish
religious holiday; Day of Atonement

yonder *adjective, adverb old-fashioned
or dialect* (situated) over there

yore *noun* **of yore** *literary* a long
time ago

Yorkshire pudding *noun* baked
batter made from flour, milk
and eggs and usually eaten with
roast beef

you *pronoun* refers to **1** the person
or people addressed **2** people in
general

young *adjective* **1** in an early stage
of life or growth ▷ *plural noun*
2 young people in general **3** babies
or offspring, especially referring to
young animals

youngster *noun* young person

your *adjective* **1** of, belonging to or
associated with you **2** of, belonging
to or associated with people in
general

yours *pronoun* something belonging
to you

yourself yourselves *pronoun*
1 used as the object of a verb or
pronoun when the person being
spoken to is both doing an action
and being directly affected by it:
Have you hurt yourself?; *Keep a copy for
yourself* **2** used to emphasize *you*: *You
yourself will understand*

youth *noun* **1** time of being young
2 boy or young man **3** young
people as a group > **youthful**
adjective: *youthful enthusiasm*
> **youthfulness** *noun*

youth hostel *noun* place where
young people can stay cheaply
when they are on holiday

yo-yo yo-yos *noun* toy consisting
of a spool attached to a string. You
play by making the yo-yo rise and
fall on the string

Yugoslav *adjective* **1** belonging or
relating to the country that used
to be known as Yugoslavia ▷ *noun*
2 someone who came from the
country that used to be known as
Yugoslavia

Yule *noun old-fashioned* Christmas
(season)

yuppie *noun* young highly-paid
professional person, especially one
who has a materialistic way of life

Z

Zambian *adjective* **1** belonging or relating to Zambia ▷ *noun* **2** someone from Zambia

zany zanier zaniest *adjective* comical in an endearing way

zap zaps zapping zapped *verb* **1** *informal* to kill or destroy **2** to change (TV channels) rapidly by remote control

zeal *noun* great enthusiasm or eagerness > **zealous** *adjective* > **zealously** *adverb*

zealot *noun* fanatic

zebra *noun* black-and-white striped African animal of the horse family

zebra crossing *noun* pedestrian crossing marked by black and white stripes on the road

Zen or **Zen Buddhism** *noun* Japanese form of Buddhism that concentrates on learning through meditation and intuition

zenith *noun literary* height

zero zeros or **zeroes zeroing zeroed** *noun* **1** the number 0 **2** starting point on a scale of measurement **3** lowest point **4** nothing or nil ▷ *adjective* **5** having no measurable quantity or size > **zero in on** *verb* to aim at (a target)

zest *noun* **1** enjoyment or excitement **2** interest, flavour or charm **3** peel of an orange or lemon as flavouring

zigzag zigzags zigzagging zigzagged *noun* **1** a line or course that has a series of sharp turns to the right and left ▷ *verb* **2** to move in a zigzag

Zimbabwean *adjective* **1** belonging or relating to Zimbabwe ▷ *noun* **2** someone from Zimbabwe

zinc *noun* bluish-white metal used in alloys and as a coating

zip zips zipping zipped *noun* **1** (also **zipper**) fastener with two rows of teeth that are closed or opened by a small clip pulled between them ▷ *verb* **2** (also **zip up**) to fasten with a zip

zipper *noun* the same as a **zip**

zodiac *noun* imaginary strip in the sky which contains the planets and stars which astrologers think are important influences on people. It is divided into 12 sections, each with a special name and symbol

zombie *noun* **1** *informal* person who appears to be lifeless, apathetic or unaware **2** (in voodoo) corpse brought back to life by witchcraft

zone *noun* area with particular features or properties

zoo zoos *noun* place where live animals are on view to the public

zoology *noun* study of animals > **zoological** *adjective* > **zoologist** *noun*

zoom *verb* to move or rise very rapidly > **zoom in** *verb* (often followed by *on*) to give a close-up picture (of)

zucchini zucchini or **zucchinis** *noun US, Aust* courgette

Zulu Zulus *noun* **1** member of a group of Black people of southern Africa **2** language of this people